Longman English Grammar

L. G. Alexander

Consultant: R. A. Close, CBE

London and New York

Longman Group UK Limited,
Longman House, Burnt Mill, Harlow,
Essex CM20 2JE, England
and Associated Companies throughout the world.

Distributed in the United States of America by
Longman publishing, New York

First published 1988
Eighth impression 1992

BRITISH LIBRARY CATALOGUING IN PUBLICATION DATA
Alexander L. G.
Longman English Grammar.
1. English language – Text-books for foreign speakers
1. Title
428.2'4 PE 1128

LIBRARY OF CONGRESS CATALOGING IN PUBLICATION DATA
Alexander, L. G.
Longman English Grammar/L. G. Alexander; consultant, R. A. Close.
p. cm.
Includes index.
ISBN 0–582–55892–1
1. English language – Grammar – 1950– 2. English language – Text-books for foreign speakers. 1. Close, R. A. II Title.
PE1112.A43 1988
428.2'4 – dc19 87–22519 CIP.

Set in 8 on $9\frac{1}{2}$ pt Linotron 202 Helvetica
Produced by Longman Group (F. E.) Ltd
Printed in Hong Kong

ISBN 0-582-55892-1

Louis Alexander was born in London in 1932. He was educated at Godalming Grammar School and London University. He taught English in Germany (1954–56) and Greece (1956–65), where he was Head of the English Department of the Protypon Lykeion, Athens. He was adviser to the Deutscher Volkshochschulverband (1968–78) and contributed to the design of two important English examinations in German Adult Education. He was a member of the Council of Europe Committee on Modern Language Teaching (1973–78) and is one of the authors of *The Threshold Level* (1975) and *Waystage* (1977). These modern syllabuses are the basis of many communicative language courses. He is also one of the authors of *English Grammatical Structure* (1975), a basic syllabus for grading structures for teaching/learning purposes. In 1986–88 he was adviser to the University of Cambridge Local Examinations Syndicate for the Cambridge Certificate in English for International Communication.

Louis Alexander is best known as the author of innovative works like *First Things First* (1967), which set new standards in course-design. He has written:

Courses, such as *New Concept English* (1967), *Look, Listen and Learn* (1968–71), *Target* (1972–74), *Mainline* (1973–81), *Follow Me* (1979–80) and *Plain English* (1987–88).

Language Practice Books such as *A First Book in Comprehension* (1964), *Question and Answer* (1967) and *For and Against* (1968).

Readers, such as *Operation Mastermind* (1971), *K's First Case* (1975), *Dangerous Game* (1977) and *Foul Play* (1983).

He created the blueprint for the self-study series in modern languages, *Survive* . . . (1980–83) and has published language courses in the field of computer-assisted language learning.

The *Longman English Grammar* is the culmination of more than thirty years' work in English as a foreign language.

Contents

Acknowledgements

A grammar takes shape over a long period of time, evolving in version after version. An author's ideas must be challenged repeatedly for the work to develop. It is a process which does not end with publication, for, of course, a grammar can never be complete or completed.

I have been privileged to have the many versions of my manuscript read over a period of years by one of the foremost grammarians of our time, R. A. Close. His detailed comments have helped me to shape my ideas and realize my aims. I owe him a debt of gratitude that cannot be measured. I am equally indebted to my editorial and research assistant, Penelope Parfitt, for her invaluable commentaries and for the arduous compilation of lists.

I would also like to thank Philip Tregidgo and Bill Lillie for sharing with me some of their original insights into the workings of English. My particular thanks are due to Michael Palmer whose vigorous and incisive commentary helped me to cut the manuscript down to an acceptable length.

Only a comparison of the successive drafts of this work with the final text could reveal how great is my debt to these commentators – though they certainly will not agree with many of the decisions I have made! I take full responsibility for the book that has finally emerged and lay sole claim to its imperfections.

A grammar taxes the resources of a publisher as much as it strains the abilities of an author. I would like to thank my publishers for their faith and unstinted support while the work was in progress. Specifically, my thanks are due to my publisher, Michael Johnson, for his constructive advice and for the exercise of his formidable managerial skills; to Paul Price-Smith for designing the work with such zest and imagination; to Joy Marshall for her superlative editing and amazingly retentive memory; to Tina Saunders and Joy Cash for photocopying, collating and dispatching recurring mountains of paper; to Ken Moore of the computer department and Clive McKeough of the production department for resolving the innumerable technical problems involved in computer-setting from disks.

Constantly, rather than finally, I depend on the patient support of my wife, Julia, who shared with me not only her own acute linguistic insights, but beyond that, the exhilaration and despair which such work inevitably brings.

L. G. A.

Introduction

Aims and level

Grammatical descriptions of English which are addressed to learners are often oversimplified and inaccurate. This is the inevitable result of lack of time in the classroom and lack of space in course books and practice books. Badly expressed and inaccurate rules, in turn, become enshrined in grammar books directed at teachers and students. The misrepresentation of English grammar gives a false view of the language, perpetuates inaccurate 'rules', and results in errors in communication. It is against this background that the *Longman English Grammar* has been written.

The primary aim of this book is to present a *manageable* coverage of grammar at intermediate and advanced levels, which will serve two purposes:

1 To present information which can be consulted for *reference*.
2 To suggest the range of structures that a student would need to be familiar with receptively and (to a lesser extent) productively to be able to communicate effectively.

In other words, the book aims to be a true pedagogical grammar for everyone concerned with English as a foreign language. It attempts to provide reasonable answers to reasonable questions about the workings of the language and to define what English as a Foreign Language *is* in terms of grammar.

Rationale

Many learners approach the study of English already in possession of a fair knowledge of the grammar of their own languages. They are the product of their own learning traditions, which have often equipped them with a 'grammatical consciousness'. Native-speaking teachers of English gradually acquire the grammatical consciousness of their students through the experience of teaching, so that they, too, learn 'English as a foreign language'. This book assumes the existence of such a consciousness. The grammar has been written, as it were, through the eyes of the user. It has been informed by the common errors made by learners and as a result has been written as precisely as possible for their requirements. This awareness of the learner will be apparent in the way the book has been organized and written, and in the use of technical terms.

Organization

Complex forms of organization, often found in modern grammars, have been avoided. Before they begin the study of English, many students are familiar with the idea of sentence formation and word order and the idea of 'parts of speech': the use of nouns, verbs, prepositions, and so on. And this is the pattern this grammar follows. A glance at the Contents pages will give the user an overview of the way the book has been organized.

The main chapters are followed by an Appendix, which contains useful lists (e.g. of phrasal verbs) that would otherwise clutter the text and make it unreadable. Or they contain detailed notes on e.g. prepositions, dealing with such problems as the similarities and differences between *over* and *above,* which there is not normally room for in a grammar of this size.

Style

Writing about language is difficult because the object of study (language) is also the medium through which it is discussed. There has been a conscious avoidance of passive constructions so that the descriptions of how the English language works are as simple and direct as possible, given the complexity of the subject.

The usual sequence in each section is to present *form* first, followed by *use.* Paradigms, where they occur, are given in full, in traditional style, as this may be the way students have already encountered them in their own languages. These are often followed by notes which focus on particular problems. 'Rules' are descriptive, rather than prescriptive, and are written as simply and accurately as possible.

Technical terms

The book defines common technical terms, such as *noun, verb,* etc. that are probably familiar to the user. While it avoids complex terms, it does introduce (and define) terms which are necessary for an accurate description of what is happening. The index uses the symbol D to refer the user to the point where such terms are defined. An intelligent discussion of English requires the use of terms like *determiner, stative verb, the causative, the zero article,* and so on. If we avoid such terms, descriptions will be unnecessarily wordy, repetitive and/or inaccurate. For example, to speak of 'the omission of the article' in e.g. 'Life is difficult' is a misrepresentation of what happens. We *actively* use the zero article here; we do not 'omit' anything.

Retrieving information

Page headings and numbered subsections indicate at every point what features of the language are being discussed. Users can make their own connexions through the extensive cross-referencing system, or they can find what they want in the detailed index.

Ease of use

Attempting to write a grammar that is up-to-date, accurate and readable is one thing; making a book out of the material is quite another. Through careful presentation and design, we have tried to create a work that will be a pleasure to use. We also hope that it will prove to be a reliable and indispensable companion to anyone interested in the English language.

Pronunciation and spelling table

consonants			vowels		
symbol	key word	other common spellings	symbol	key word	other common spellings
p	**p**en	happy	iː	sh**ee**p	field team key scene amoeba
b	**b**ack	rubber	ɪ	sh**i**p	savage guilt system women
t	**t**ea	butter walked doubt	e	b**e**d	any said bread bury friend
d	**d**ay	ladder called could	æ	b**a**d	plaid laugh (*AmE*) calf (*AmE*)
k	**k**ey	cool soccer lock school cheque	ɑː	f**a**ther	calm heart laugh (*BrE*) bother (*AmE*)
g	**g**et	bigger ghost	ɒ	p**o**t	watch cough (*BrE*) laurel (*BrE*)
tʃ	**ch**eer	match nature question cello	ɔː	c**augh**t	ball board draw four floor cough (*AmE*)
dʒ	**j**ump	age edge soldier gradual	ʊ	p**u**t	wood wolf could
f	**f**at	coffee cough physics half	uː	b**oo**t	move shoe group flew blue rude
v	**v**iew	of navvy	ʌ	c**u**t	some blood does
θ	**th**ing		ɜː	b**ir**d	burn fern worm earn journal
ð	**th**en		ə	cupb**oar**d	the colour actor nation danger asleep
s	**s**oon	city psychology mess scene listen	eɪ	m**a**ke	pray prey steak vein gauge
z	**z**ero	was dazzle example (/gz/)	əʊ	n**o**te	soap soul grow sew toe
ʃ	fi**sh**ing	sure station tension vicious chevron	aɪ	b**i**te	pie buy try guide sigh
ʒ	plea**s**ure	vision rouge	aʊ	n**ow**	spout plough
h	**h**ot	whole	ɔɪ	b**oy**	poison lawyer
m	su**m**	hammer calm bomb	ɪə	h**ere**	beer weir appear fierce
n	su**n**	funny know gnaw	eə	th**ere**	hair bear bare their prayer
ŋ	su**ng**	sink	ʊə	p**oor**	tour sure
l	**l**ed	balloon battle	eɪə	pl**ayer**	
r	**r**ed	marry wriggle rhubarb	əʊə	l**ower**	
j	**y**et	onion use new Europe	aɪə	t**ire**	
w	**w**et	one when queen (/kw/)	aʊə	t**ower**	
x	lo**ch**		ɔɪə	empl**oyer**	

from *Longman Dictionary of Contemporary English*

Symbols and conventions

AmE	American English
BrE	British English
Not * *	likely student error
∅	zero article
( )	optional element
/ /	phonetic transcription
[>]	cross-reference
[> App]	Appendix reference
D	definition of technical terms (used only in the index)
' (as in 'progress)	stress mark

1 The sentence

Sentence word order

1.1 Inflected and uninflected languages

Many modern European languages are **inflected**. Inflected languages usually have the following characteristics:

1 Nouns have endings which change depending on whether they are, for example, the subject or object of a verb.
2 There are complex agreements between articles, adjectives and nouns to emphasize the fact that a noun is, for example, subject or object, masculine or feminine, singular or plural. The more inflected a language is (for example, German or Greek), the more complex its system of endings ('inflexions').
3 Verbs 'conjugate', so that it is immediately obvious from the endings which 'person' (first, second, third) is referred to and whether the 'person' is singular or plural.

English was an inflected language up to the Middle Ages, but the modern language retains very few inflexions. Some survive, like the genitive case in e.g. *lady**'s** handbag* where *lady* requires ***'s*** to show singular possession, or like the third person in the simple present tense (*I work – He/She/It work**s***) where the ***-s*** ending identifies the third person, or in the comparative and superlative forms of many adjectives (*nice, nice**r**, nice**st***). There are only six words in the English language which have different subject and object forms: *I/me, he/him, she/her, we/us, they/them* and *who/whom*. This lack of inflexions in English tempts some people to observe (quite wrongly) that the language has 'hardly any grammar'. It would be more accurate to say that English no longer has a grammar like that of Latin or German, but it has certainly evolved a grammar of its own, as this book testifies.

In inflected languages we do not depend on the word order to understand which noun is the subject of a sentence and which is the object: the endings tell us immediately. In English, the order of words is essential to the meaning of a sentence. We have to distinguish carefully between the subject-group and the verb-group (or **predicate**). The **predicate** is what is said about the subject, i.e. it is all the words in a sentence except the subject:

subject group	verb group (predicate)
The dog	*bit the man.*
The man	*bit the dog.*

As these examples show, a change in word order brings with it a fundamental change in meaning, which would not be the case if the nouns had endings. This means that English is far less flexible in its word order than many inflected languages.

1.2 The sentence: definitions of key terms

No discussion of the sentence is possible without an understanding of the terms **finite verb**, **phrase**, **clause** and **sentence**.

A **finite verb** must normally have:
– a **subject** (which may be 'hidden'): e.g.
__He__ makes. __They__ arrived. __We__ know.
Open the door. (i.e. ***You*** *open the door.*)
– a **tense**: e.g. *He **has finished**. She **will write**. They **succeeded**.*

So, for example, *he writes, she wrote* and *he has written* are finite, but *written*, by itself, is not. *Made* is finite if used in the past tense and if it has a subject (*He made this for me*); but it is not if it is used as a past participle without an auxiliary (*made in Germany*). The infinitive (e.g. *to write*) or the present and past participles (e.g. *writing, written*) can never be finite. Modal verbs [> Chapter 11] are also finite, even though they do not have tense forms like other verbs: e.g. *he must (wait), he may (arrive)* , as are imperatives: e.g. *Stand up!* [> 9.51–56].

A **phrase** is a group of words which can be part of a sentence. A phrase may take the form of:
- a **noun phrase**: e.g. *a tube of toothpaste.*
- a **prepositional** (or **adverbial**) **phrase**: e.g. *over the bridge.*
- a **verb phrase**, e.g. a single verb-form: *built (in stone)*, or a combination of verbs: e.g. *will tell, have done.*
- a **question-word** + **infinitive**: e.g. *what to do, when to go.*

A **clause** is a group of words consisting of a **subject** + **finite verb** (+ **complement** [> 1.9] or **object** [> 1.4, 1.9] if necessary).

A **sentence** which contains one clause is called a **simple sentence**:
Stephen apologized at once. [> 1.7]
Or it may contain more than one clause, in which case it is either a **compound sentence** [> 1.17]:
*Stephen realized his mistake **and** (he) apologized at once.*
or a **complex sentence** [> 1.21]:
When *he realized his mistake, Stephen apologized at once.*

A **sentence** can take any one of four forms:
- a **statement**: *The shops close/don't close at 7 tonight.*
- a **question**: *Do the shops close at 7 tonight?*
- a **command**: *Shut the door!*
- an **exclamation**: *What a slow train this is!*

A sentence is a complete unit of meaning. When we speak, our sentences may be extremely involved or even unfinished, yet we can still convey our meaning through intonation, gesture, facial expression, etc. When we write, these devices are not available, so sentences have to be carefully structured and punctuated. A written sentence must begin with a capital letter and end with a full stop (.), a question mark (?) or an exclamation mark (!).

One-word or abbreviated utterances can also be complete units of meaning, particularly in speech or written dialogue: e.g. *All right!, Good!, Want any help?* . However, these are not real sentences because they do not contain a finite verb.

1.3 Basic word order in an English sentence

Although variations are possible [> 1.6], the basic word order in a sentence that is not a question or a command is usually:

subject group	**verb group (predicate)**				
subject	**verb**	**object**	**adverbials** [usually optional > 7.1]		
			manner	**place**	**time** [> 7.19.1, 7.22]
I	*bought*	*a hat*			*yesterday.*
The children	*ran*			*home.*	
The taxi-driver	*shouted at*	*me*	*angrily.*		
We	*ate*	*our meal*	*in silence.*		
The car	*stopped*		*suddenly.*		
A young girl with long black hair	*walked*		*confidently*	*across the room.*	

1.4 Word order: definitions of key terms

A **subject** is normally a noun, pronoun or noun phrase; it usually goes before the verb. The verb must 'agree' with the subject, so the subject dictates the form of the verb (e.g. *I wait, John waits, I am, you are, I have, the new edition has*). This 'agreement' between subject and verb is often called **concord**. An **object** is normally a noun, pronoun or noun phrase; it usually goes after the verb in the **active**. It can become the subject of a verb in the **passive** [> 12.1–2]:

	subject	**predicate**
active:	*They*	*drove **him** away in a police car.*
passive:	***He***	*was driven away in a police car.*

A sentence does not always require an object. It can just be:
- **subject** + **verb**: *We all laughed.*
- **subject** + **verb** + **adverb**: *We laughed loudly.*

Some verbs do not take an object [> 1.9–10].

1.5 Making the parts of a sentence longer

We can lengthen a subject or object by adding a clause or a phrase:
- lengthening the **subject**:
  The man *ran away.*
  The man who stole the money *ran away.*
- lengthening the **object**:
  *I bought **a raincoat**.*
  *I bought **a raincoat with a warm lining**.*

1.6 Some common variations on the basic word order

We normally avoid separating a subject from its verb and a verb from its object [e.g. with an adverb > 1.3], though there are exceptions even to this basic rule [> 7.16]. However, note these common variations in the basic subject/verb/(object)/(adverbial) order:

- questions [> Chapter 13]:
  Did you take *your car in for a service?*
  When did you take *your car in for a service?*
- reporting verbs in direct speech [> 15.3*n*.4]:
  'You've eaten the lot!' ***cried Frank*** .
- certain conditional sentences [> 14.8, 14.18.3]:
  Should you see him*, please give him my regards.*
- time references requiring special emphasis [> 7.22, 7.24]:
  Last night *we went to the cinema.*
- ***-ly*** adverbs of manner/indefinite time [> 7.16.3, 7.24]:
  The whole building ***suddenly*** *began to shake.*
  Suddenly*, the whole building began to shake.*
- adverbs of indefinite frequency [> 7.40]:
  We ***often*** *played dangerous games when we were children.*
- adverb phrases [> 7.19.2, 7.59.2]:
  Inside the parcel *(there) was a letter.*
- adverb particles (e.g. *back*) and *here, there* [> 7.59.1]:
  Back came *the answer – no!*
  Here/There is *your coat.* ***Here/There it is.***
- negative adverbs [> 7.59.3]:
  Never*, in world history,* ***has there been*** *such a conflict.*
- 'fronting':
  Items in a sentence can be put at the front for special emphasis:
  A fine mess *you've made of this!*

The simple sentence

1.7 The simple sentence

The smallest sentence-unit is the simple sentence. A simple sentence normally has *one* finite verb [but see 1.16]. It has a subject and a predicate:

subject group	verb group (predicate)
I	*'ve eaten.*
One of our aircraft	*is missing.*
The old building opposite our school	*is being pulled down.*

1.8 Five simple sentence patterns

There are five simple sentence patterns. Within each of the five groups there are different sub-patterns. The five patterns differ from each other according to what (if anything) follows the verb:

1 subject + verb:
  My head aches.

2 subject + verb + complement:
Frank is clever/an architect.
3 subject + verb + direct object:
My sister enjoyed the play.
4 subject + verb + indirect object + direct object:
The firm gave Sam a watch.
5 subject + verb + object + complement:
They made Sam redundant/chairman.

The examples listed above are reduced to a bare minimum. To this minimum, we can add adjectives and adverbs:
His old firm gave Sam a beautiful gold watch on his retirement.

1.9 Sentence patterns: definitions of key terms

Any discussion of sentence patterns depends on a clear understanding of the terms **object** [> 1.4] (**direct** or **indirect**), **complement**, **transitive verb** and **intransitive verb**.

A **direct object** refers to the person or thing affected by the action of the verb. It comes immediately after a transitive verb:
Please don't annoy ***me****.*
Veronica threw ***the ball*** *over the wall.*

An **indirect object** usually refers to the person who 'benefits' from the action expressed in the verb: someone you give something *to*, or buy something *for*. It comes immediately after a verb:
Throw ***me*** *the ball.*
Buy ***your father*** *a present.*

A **complement** follows the verb *be* and verbs related to *be*, such as *seem* [> 10.23-26], which cannot be followed by an object. A complement (e.g. adjective, noun, pronoun) completes the sense of an utterance by telling us something about the subject. For example, the words following *is* tell us something about *Frank*:
Frank is ***clever****. Frank is* ***an architect****.*

A **transitive verb** is followed by an object. A simple test is to put *Who(m)?* or *What?* before the the question-form of the verb. If we get an answer, the verb is transitive [> App 1]:

	Wh-	**question-form**	**object**
I met ***Jim*** *this morning.*	*Who(m)*	*did you meet?*	*–* ***Jim****.*
I'm reading ***a book****.*	*What*	*are you reading?*	*–* ***A book****.*

Most transitive verbs can be used in the passive. Some transitive verbs consist of more than one part: e.g. *listen to* [> Apps 28–30, 32–33, 37].

An **intransitive verb** is not followed by an object and can never be used in the passive [> App 1]. Some intransitive verbs consist of more than one part: e.g. *touch down* [> App 36]:
My head ***aches****. The plane* ***touched down****.*

Some verbs, like *enjoy*, can only be used transitively and must always be followed by an object; others, like *ache*, are always intransitive.

Verbs like *open* can be used transitively or intransitively [> App 1.3]:
– verb + object (transitive): *Someone **opened the door**.*
– verb without object (intransitive): *The door **opened**.*

1.10 Pattern 1: subject + verb
My head + aches

Verbs used in this pattern are either always intransitive or verbs which can be transitive or intransitive, here used intransitively.

1.10.1 Intransitive verbs [> App 1.2]
Examples: *ache, appear, arrive, come, cough, disappear, fall, go.*
*Quick! The train**'s arrived**. It**'s arrived** early.*
Some intransitive verbs are often followed by an adverb particle (*come in, get up, run away, sit down,* etc.) or adverbial phrase:
– verb + **particle** [> 7.3.4]: *He came **in**. He sat **down**. He stood **up**.*
– verb + **adverbial phrase** [> 7.3.3]: *A crowd of people came **into the room**.*

1.10.2 Verbs which are sometimes intransitive [> App 1.3]
Many verbs can be used transitively with an object (answering questions like *What did you do?*) and intransitively without an object (answering the question *What happened?*): *break, burn, close, drop, fly, hurt, move, open, ring, shake, shut, understand*:
– with an object: *I **rang the bell**. I **rang it** repeatedly.*
– without an object: *The phone **rang**. It **rang** repeatedly.*
Other examples:
*The fire **burnt** furiously. Your essay **reads** well.*
Sometimes the object is implied:
*William **smokes/eats/drinks** too much.*

1.11 Pattern 2: subject + verb + complement
Frank + is + clever/an architect

The verb in this pattern is always *be* or a verb related to *be*, such as *appear, become, look, seem, sound* and *taste* [> 10.23–26].

1.11.1 Subject + 'be' + complement
The complement may be:
– an **adjective**: *Frank is **clever**.*
– a **noun**: *Frank is **an architect**.*
– an **adjective** + **noun**: *Frank is **a clever architect**.*
– a **pronoun**: *It's **mine**.*
– an **adverb of place or time**: *The meeting is **here/at 2.30**.*
– a **prepositional phrase**: *Alice is **like her father**.*

1.12 Pattern 3: subject + verb + direct object
My sister + answered + the phone

Most verbs in the language can be used in this pattern [> App 1.1]. The direct object may take a variety of forms, some of which are:
– a **noun** [> 2.1]: *We parked **the car** in the car park.*
– a **pronoun** [> 4.1]: *We fetched **her** from the station.*

– a **reflexive pronoun** [> 4.24]: *We enjoyed **ourselves** at the party.*
– an **infinitive** [> 16.13]: *I want **to go home** now.*
– an ***-ing* form** [> 16.42]: *I enjoy **sitting in the sun**.*

1.12.1 Verb + object + 'to' or 'for' + noun or pronoun [> 1.9, 1.13.2–3]
The following verbs can have a direct object followed by *to* + noun or pronoun, or (where the sense permits) *for* + noun or pronoun. They do not take an indirect object: *admit, announce, confess, confide, declare, demonstrate, describe, entrust, explain, introduce, mention, propose, prove, repeat, report, say, state* and *suggest:*

subject	verb	object	(*to* + noun or pronoun)
Martin	*introduced*	*his guests*	*to Jane.*

The noun or pronoun following *to* or *for* cannot be put after the verb, so we cannot say **explain me this** as, for example, we can say *give me this* where the indirect object can immediately follow the verb [> 1.13].
*Gerald **explained the situation to me**.* (Not **explained me**)
*He **explained it to me**.* (Not **explained me**)
***Say it to me**.* (Not **say me**)
*I can't describe this. Would you **describe it for me** please?*
The passive is formed as follows [compare > 1.13.2]:
*The guests **were introduced to Jane**.*
*The situation **was explained to me**.*
To + noun or pronoun normally precedes a *that*-clause or an indirect question when the object is very long:
*Catherine explained **to me what the situation was**.*

1.13 Pattern 4: subject + verb + indirect object + direct object
They** + **gave** + **him** + **a watch

1.13.1 General information about Pattern 4 [compare > 12.3*n*.4]
Verbs like *bring, buy* and *give* can have two objects. The indirect object always follows the verb and usually refers to a person:
*The firm gave **Sam a gold watch**.*
Sam is an indirect object. However, the direct object can come after the verb if we wish to emphasize it. When this is the case, the indirect object is replaced by a prepositional phrase beginning with *to* or *for*:
*The firm gave **a watch with a beautiful inscription on it to Sam**.*
*They bought **a beautiful gold watch for Sam**.*
The indirect object does not have to be a person:
*I gave **the car a wash**.*

If the direct object is a pronoun (very often *it* or *them*) it normally comes immediately after the verb. The indirect object is replaced by a prepositional phrase:
*They gave **it to Sam**. They gave **it to him**.*
However, if both direct and indirect objects are pronouns, some verbs, such as *bring, buy, fetch, give, hand, pass, send, show* and *teach* can be used as follows, particularly in everyday speech:
*Give **me it**. Show **me it**.*
*Give **it me**. Show **it me**.*

Give me it is more common than *Give it me*. The pattern *give it me* does not often occur with verbs other than *give*. The use of the object pronoun *them* (*Give them me*) is very rare.

The verbs in Pattern 4 can fall into three categories:

1.13.2 Pattern 4: Category 1: verbs that can be followed by 'to'

subject +	**verb** +	**indirect object** +	**direct object**
He	*showed*	*me*	*the photo.*
subject +	**verb** +	**direct object** +	***to*** + **noun** or **pronoun**
He	*showed*	*the photo*	*to me.*

In the passive, the subject can be the person to whom something is 'given' or the thing which is 'given', depending on emphasis:

__I__ was shown the photo.

The photo *was shown* ***to me***.

Here is a selection of verbs that can be used in this way: *bring, give, grant, hand, leave* (= bequeath), *lend, offer, owe, pass, pay, play, post, promise, read, recommend, sell, send, serve, show, sing, take, teach, tell, throw* and *write*.

1.13.3 Pattern 4: Category 2: verbs that can be followed by 'for'

subject +	**verb** +	**indirect object** +	**direct object**
He	*bought*	*Jane*	*a present.*
subject +	**verb** +	**direct object** +	***for*** + **noun** or **pronoun**
He	*bought*	*a present*	*for Jane.*

These sentences can be put into the passive in two ways:

Jane *was bought a present.*

A present *was bought* ***for Jane***.

Here is a selection of verbs that can be used in this pattern. Normally only *bring* and *buy* can have a person as a subject in the passive: *bring, build, buy, call, catch, change, choose, cook, cut, do, fetch, find, fix, get, keep, leave, make, order, prepare, reach, reserve, save, sing.*

In Categories 1 and 2, *to* or *for* + noun or pronoun can be used when we wish to emphasize the person who benefits from the action or when the indirect object is longer than the direct object:

Barbara made a beautiful dress ***for her daughter***.

He bought a gift ***for his niece who lives in Australia***.

For can be ambiguous and its meaning depends on context. The emphasis can be on 'the recipient':

Mother cooked a lovely meal for ***me***. (= for my benefit)

or on the person acting on the recipient's behalf:

I*'ll cook the dinner for you.* (= on your behalf/instead of you)

For can be ambiguous when used after most of the verbs listed in 1.13.3; *for* can refer to the person acting on the recipient's behalf when used after most of the verbs in 1.13.2.

1.13.4 Pattern 4: Category 3: verbs that can be used without 'to' or 'for'

subject +	**verb** +	**indirect object** +	**direct object**	
I	*'ll tell*	*you*	*the truth*	*soon.*
subject +	**verb** +	**indirect object only**		
I	*'ll tell*	*you*		*soon.*

The passive can be formed in two ways:
You *will be told the truth soon.*
The truth *will be told to you soon.*
The direct object may often be omitted but is implied after *ask, bet, forgive, grant, owe, pay, promise, show, teach, tell, write:*
I'll write you. I bet you. I grant you. I'll promise you. etc.

1.14 Pattern 5: subject + verb + object + complement
They + appointed + him + chairman

Verbs used in this pattern are often in the passive. Here is a selection of common ones: *appoint, baptize, call, consider, christen, crown, declare, elect, label, make, name, proclaim, pronounce, vote:*
They **appointed him chairman**. **He was appointed chairman**.
They **made Sam redundant**. **Sam was made redundant**.
The complement is usually a noun, though after *call, consider, declare, make, pronounce*, it can be an adjective or a noun:
They **called him foolish/a fool**.

Here are a few verbs that combine with an object + adjectival complement: *drive (me) crazy/mad/wild; get (it) clean/dirty, dry/wet, open/shut; find (it) difficult/easy; hold (it) open/still; keep (it) cool/fresh/shut; leave (it) clean/dirty, open/shut; like (it) hot; make (it) easy/plain/safe; open (it) wide; paint (it) brown/red; prefer (it) fried; pull (it) shut/tight; push (it) open; want (it) raw; wipe (it) clean/dry:*
Loud music **drives me crazy**. **I'm driven crazy** *by loud music.*

1.15 Joining two or more subjects

The subjects of two simple sentences can be joined to make one simple sentence with conjunctions like: *and, but, both...and, either...or, neither...nor* and *not only...but also*. Note the agreement between subject and verb in the following [compare > 5.31]:

The boss **is flying** *to Paris. His secretary* **is flying** *to Paris.*
The boss **and** *his secretary* **are flying** *to Paris.*
Both *the boss* **and** *his secretary* **are flying** *to Paris.*

The boss **is flying** *to Rome. His secretary* **is not flying** *to Rome.*
The boss, **but not** *his secretary,* **is flying** *to Rome.*

The boss **may be flying** *to Berlin. His secretary* **may be flying** *to Berlin.* (One of the two may be flying there.)
Either *the boss* **or** *his secretary* **is flying** *to Berlin.*

The boss **isn't flying** *to York. His secretary* **isn't flying** *to York.*
Neither *the boss* **nor** *his secretary* **is flying** *to York.*

1.16 Joining two or more objects, complements or verbs

The objects of two simple sentences may be joined to make one simple sentence with conjunctions such as *and, both...and*:

I met Jane. I met her husband.
*I met Jane **and** her husband.*
*I met **both** Jane **and** her husband.*

I didn't meet Jane. I didn't meet her husband.
*I didn't meet **either** Jane **or** her husband.*
*I met **neither** Jane **nor** her husband.*

Adjective complements can be joined in the same way:

It was cold. It was wet.
*It was cold **and** wet.*
It wasn't cold. It wasn't wet.
*It wasn't cold **or** wet. It was **neither** cold **nor** wet.*

Two or more finite verbs can be joined to make a simple sentence:

*We **sang** all night. We **danced** all night.*
*We **sang and danced** all night.*

The compound sentence

1.17 The compound sentence

We often need to join ideas. One way we can do this is to link simple sentences to form compound sentences. This linking is achieved by any of the following:

- a **semi-colon**:
  We fished all day; we didn't catch a thing.
- a **semi-colon**, followed by a **connecting adverb** [> App 18]:
  *We fished all day; **however**, we didn't catch a thing.*
- a **co-ordinating conjunction** (e.g. *and, but, so, yet*) often preceded by a comma:
  *We fished all day, **but** (we) didn't catch a thing.*

In a compound sentence, there is no single main clause with subordinate clauses depending on it [> 1.21]: all the clauses are of equal importance and can stand on their own, though of course they follow a logical order as required by the context. We often refer to clauses in a compound sentence as **co-ordinate main clauses**.

1.18 Word order and co-ordinating conjunctions

The word order of the simple sentence is generally retained in the compound sentence:

subject	verb	object	conjunction	subject	verb	complement
Jimmy	*fell off*	*his bike,*	***but***	*(he)*	*was*	*unhurt.*

The co-ordinating conjunctions which can be used to form compound sentences are: *and, and then, but, for, nor, or, so, yet; either...or; neither...nor...; not only...but... (also/as well/too)*. These can be used for the purposes of addition (*and*), contrast (*but, yet*), choice (*or*), reason (*for*), continuation (*and then*) and consequence or result (*so*). However, a single conjunction like *and* can serve a variety of purposes to express:

- **addition**: *We were talking **and** laughing.* (= in addition to)
- **result**: *He fell heavily **and** broke his arm.* (= so)
- **condition**: *Weed the garden **and** I'll pay you £5.* (= If...then)
- **sequence**: *He finished lunch **and** went shopping.* (= then)
- **contrast**: *Tom's 15 **and** still sucks his thumb.* (= despite this)

1.19 Joining sentence patterns to make compound sentences

The five simple sentence patterns [> 1.8] can be joined by means of co-ordinating conjunctions (P1 = Pattern 1, etc.):

subject	**verb**	**manner (P1)**		+	**(subject)**	**verb**	**complement (P2)**
Frank	*worked*	*hard*		*and*	*(he)*	*became*	*an architect.*
subject	**verb**	**object (P3)**		+	**subject**	**verb**	**place (P1)**
I	*'ve got*	*a cold,*		*so*	*I*	*'m going*	*to bed.*
subject	**verb**	**object**	**complement (P5)**	+	**(subject)**	**verb**	**object (P3)**
They	*made*	*him*	*chairman,*	*but*	*(they)*	*didn't increase*	*his salary.*
subject	**verb**	**complement (P2)**		+	**subject**	**verb**	**object object (P4)**
Her birthday	*is*	*next Monday,*		*so*	*I*	*must buy*	*her a present.*

1.20 The use of co-ordinating conjunctions

When the subject is the same in all parts of the sentence, it is usual not to repeat it. We do not usually put a comma in front of *and*, but we generally use one in front of other conjunctions:

1.20.1 Addition/sequence: 'and'; 'both...and'; 'not only...but...(too/as well)'; 'not only...but (also)...'; 'and then'

He washed the car. He polished it.
*He washed the car **and polished** it.*
*He **not only washed** the car, **but polished** it **(too/as well)**.*
*He washed the car **and then polished** it.*

When the subjects are different, they must both be used:

***You** can wait here and **I**'ll get the car.*
***Jim** speaks Spanish, but **his wife** speaks French.*

1.20.2 Contrast: 'but'; 'yet'

He washed the car. He didn't polish it.
*He washed the car, **but didn't polish** it.*
She sold her house. She can't help regretting it.
*She sold her house, **but/yet (she) can't help** regretting it.*

1.20.3 Alternatives: 'either...or...'; 'neither...nor...'

He speaks French. Or perhaps he understands it.
*He **either speaks** French, **or understands** it.* (I'm not sure which)

He doesn't speak French. He doesn't understand it.
*He **neither speaks** French, **nor understands** it.*

1.20.4 Result: 'so'

He couldn't find his pen. He wrote in pencil.
He couldn't find his pen, ***so he wrote*** *in pencil.*
(The subject is usually repeated after *so*.)

1.20.5 Cause: 'for'

We rarely stay in hotels. We can't afford it.
We rarely stay in hotels, ***for we can't*** *afford it.*
For gives the reason for something that has already been stated. Unlike *because* [> 1.48], it cannot begin a sentence. The subject must be repeated after *for*. This use of *for* is more usual in the written language.

1.20.6 Linking simple sentences by commas, etc.

More than two simple sentences can be joined by commas with only one conjunction which is used before the final clause. The use of a comma before *and* is optional here:
I found a bucket, put it in the sink(,) ***and*** *turned the tap on.*
I took off my coat, searched all my pockets, ***but*** *couldn't find my key.*

Sometimes subject and verb can be omitted. In such cases, a sentence is simple, not compound [> 1.15–16]:
The hotel was cheap ***but clean****.*
Does the price include breakfast only, ***or dinner as well****?*
A second question can be avoided by the use of *...or not*:
Does the price include breakfast, ***or not****?* (= or doesn't it?)

The complex sentence: introduction

1.21 The complex sentence

Many sentences, especially in written language, are complex. They can be formed by linking simple sentences together, but the elements in a complex sentence (unlike those of a compound sentence) are not of equal importance. There is always one independent (or 'main') clause and one or more dependent (or 'subordinate') elements. If removed from a sentence, a main clause can often stand on its own.

Complex sentences can be formed in two ways:

1 by joining subordinate clauses to the main clause with conjunctions:
The alarm was raised (main clause) ***as soon as*** *the fire was discovered.* (subordinate clause)
If *you're not good at figures,* (subordinate clause) *it is pointless to apply for a job in a bank.* (main clause)

2 by using infinitive or participle constructions [> 1.57]. These are non-finite and are phrases rather than clauses, but they form part of complex (not simple) sentences because they can be re-expressed as clauses which are subordinate to the main clause:
To get into university *you have to pass a number of examinations.*
(= If you want to get into university...)
Seeing the door open, *the stranger entered the house.*
(= When he saw the door open...)

Many different constructions can be present in a complex sentence:

(a) *Free trade agreements are always threatened* (main clause)
(b) *when individual countries protect their own markets* (subordinate clause dependent on (a))
(c) *by imposing duties on imported goods* (participle construction dependent on (b))
(d) *to encourage their own industries.* (infinitive construction dependent on (c))

The subject of the main clause must be replaced by a pronoun in a subordinate clause if a reference is made to it:

__The racing car__ went out of control before __it__ hit the barrier.

A pronoun can occur in a subordinate clause before the subject is mentioned. This is not possible with co-ordinate clauses:

When __she__ got on the train, __Mrs Tomkins__ realized she had made a dreadful mistake.

Co-ordinate and subordinate clauses can combine in one sentence:

The racing car went out of control __and__ hit the barrier several times __before__ it came to a stop on a grassy bank.

The five simple sentence patterns [> 1.8] can be combined in an endless variety of ways. Subordinate clauses can be classified under three headings:

- **noun clauses**: *He told me __that the match had been cancelled__.*
- **relative** (or **adjectival**) **clauses**: *Holiday resorts __which are very crowded__ are not very pleasant.*
- **adverbial clauses**: ***However hard I try**, I can't remember people's names.*

The complex sentence: noun clauses

1.22 How to identify a noun clause

Compare:

He told me about __the cancellation of the match__.
He told me __that the match had been cancelled__.

Cancellation is a noun; *that the match had been cancelled* is a clause (it has a finite verb). The clause is doing the same work as the noun, so it is called a **noun clause**. Like any noun, a noun clause can be the subject or (far more usually) object of a verb; or the complement of the verb *be* or some of the verbs related to *be*, such as *seem* and *appear*:

I know __that the match will be cancelled__. (object)
***That the match will be cancelled** is now certain.* (subject of *be*)

1.23 Noun clauses derived from statements

Noun clauses derived from statements are usually *that*-clauses (sometimes *what*-clauses), though the conjunction *that* is often omitted. Look at the following statement:

Money doesn't grow on trees.

By putting *that* in front of a statement, we turn it into a subordinate noun clause which can be joined to another clause. As such, it will do the same work as a noun and can be used as follows:

1.23.1 Noun clause as the subject of a verb

Money doesn't grow on trees. This should be obvious.
That money doesn't grow on trees *should be obvious.*

We tend to avoid this construction, preferring to begin with *It*, followed by *be, seem,* etc.:

It is obvious ***(that) money doesn't grow on trees****.*

Such clauses are not objects, but are 'in apposition' to the 'preparatory subject' *it* [> 4.13]. *That* cannot be omitted at the beginning of a sentence, but can be left out after many adjectives [> App 44] and a few nouns such as *(it's) a pity, a shame*.

1.23.2 Noun clause as the object of a verb

That is often omitted before a noun clause which is the object of a verb, especially in informal style:

Everybody knows ***(that) money doesn't grow on trees****.*

After many verbs (e.g. *believe, know, think*) the use of *that* is optional. After some verbs (e.g. *answer, imply*) *that* is generally required. *That* is also usual after 'reporting verbs', such as *assure, inform*, which require an indirect object [> App 45.2]. *That* is usually obligatory in longer sentences, especially when the *that*-clause is separated from the verb:

The dealer told me how much he was prepared to pay for my car and ***that*** *I could have the money without delay.*

A *that*-clause cannot follow a preposition:

He boasted ***about his success****.* = *He boasted* ***that he was successful****.*

However, a preposition is not dropped before a noun clause that begins with a question-word [> 1.24.2]:

He boasted ***about how successful he was****.*

1.23.3 Noun clauses after 'the fact that', etc.

By using expressions like *the fact that* and *the idea that* we can avoid the awkwardness of beginning a sentence with *that*:

The fact that *his proposal makes sense should be recognized.*
The idea that *everyone should be required to vote by law is something I don't agree with.*
His proposal makes sense. This should be recognized.

These expressions can be used after verbs such as *to face*:

We ***must face the fact that*** *we might lose our deposit.*

The fact that also follows prepositions and prepositional phrases [> App 20.3] like *because of, in view of, on account of, owing to, due to, in spite of, despite* and *notwithstanding* (formal):

His love of literature was ***due to the fact that*** *his mother read poetry to him when he was a child.*
In spite of/Despite the fact that *hotel prices have risen sharply, the number of tourists is as great as ever.*

1.23.4 Noun clauses after adjectives describing feelings
Many adjectives describing personal feelings (e.g. *afraid, glad, happy, pleased, sorry*) or certainty (e.g. *certain, sure*) can be followed by *that* (optional) [> App 44]:
I'm afraid ***(that) we've sold out of tickets****.*

1.23.5 Transferred negatives after verbs of thinking and feeling
After verbs like *believe, imagine, suppose, think*, we can transfer the negative from the verb to the *that*-clause without really changing the meaning [compare 'contrasting negatives' > 16.14]. So, for example, these pairs of sentences have almost the same meaning:
I don't believe *she'll arrive before 7.*
I believe ***she won't arrive*** *before 7.*
I don't suppose *you can help us.*
I suppose ***you can't help*** *us.*

1.24 Noun clauses derived from questions

Noun clauses can be derived from Yes/No questions and question-word questions [> Chapter 13].

1.24.1 Noun clauses derived from Yes/No questions [> 15.17–18]
Here is a direct Yes/No question:
Has he signed the contract?

By putting *if* or *whether* in front of it and by changing the word order to subject-predicate, we turn it into a subordinate noun-clause that can be used:

- as a **subject**:
  Whether he has signed the contract (or not) *doesn't matter.*
  (*if* is not possible)
- as a **complement** after ***be***:
  The question is ***whether he has signed the contract****.*
  (*if* is not possible)
- as an **object** after **verbs**, especially in indirect questions [> 15.18*n*.5]:
  I want to know ***whether/if he has signed the contract (or not)****.*
- as an **object** after a **preposition**:
  I'm concerned about ***whether he has signed the contract (or not)****.*
  (*if* is not possible)

Whether is obligatory if the clause begins a sentence; it is obligatory after *be* and after prepositions. Either *whether* or *if* can be used after a verb and after a few adjectives used in the negative, such as *not sure* and *not certain* [> App 44]. If there is doubt about the choice between *whether* and *if* as subordinating conjunctions, it is always safe to use *whether*. Note how *...or not* can be used optionally, particularly with *whether*.

1.24.2 Noun clauses derived from question-word questions [> 15.19–23]
Here is a direct question-word question:
How soon will we know the results?

Question-word questions (beginning with *who(m), what, which, when,*

where, why and *how* plus a change in word order) can function as noun clauses and can be used:
- as a **subject**: ***When he did it*** *is a mystery.*
- after ***be***: *The question is* ***when he did it****.*
- after **reporting verbs**: *I wonder* ***when he did it****.* [> 16.24]
- after **verb + preposition** or **adjective + preposition**:
  It depends on ***when he did it****.*
  I'm interested in ***when he did it****.*

We can use *what* (not *that which*) instead of *the thing(s) that* to introduce a noun clause. *What* may be considered to be a relative pronoun [> 1.27] here:

What matters most *is good health.* (i.e. the thing that matters)

Compare the use of *What* as a question word (when it does not have the meaning 'the thing(s) that') in direct and indirect questions:

What *made him do it? I wonder* ***what*** *made him do it.*

The complex sentence: relative pronouns and relative clauses

1.25 How to identify a relative clause

Compare:

Crowded *holiday resorts are not very pleasant.*
Holiday resorts ***which are crowded*** *are not very pleasant.*

The word *crowded* in the first sentence is an adjective; *which are crowded* is a clause (it has a finite verb: *are*). The clause is doing exactly the same work as the adjective: it is describing the holiday resorts (or 'qualifying' the noun *holiday resorts*). So we can call it an adjectival clause, or (more usually) a relative clause because it 'relates' to the noun, in this case, by means of the word *which*. Relative clauses (like adjectives) can describe persons, things and events.

1.26 The use and omission of commas in relative clauses

There are two kinds of relative clauses in the written language:

1 Relative clauses without commas (sometimes called **defining**, **restrictive**, or **identifying**). They provide essential information about the subject or object:
  What kind of government would be popular?
  – The government which promises to cut taxes.

2 Relative clauses with commas (sometimes called **non-defining**, **non-restrictive** or **non-identifying**). They provide additional information, which can be omitted:
  The government, which promises to cut taxes, will be popular.

The inclusion or omission of commas may seriously affect the meaning of a sentence. Compare:

The government which promises to cut taxes will be popular.
The government, which promises to cut taxes, will be popular.

The first sentence refers to *any* government which may come to power in the future. The second is making a statement about the popularity of the government that is actually in power at the moment. Whatever it does, this government will be popular. Among other things, it promises to cut taxes. Alternative punctuation, such as dashes, would further emphasize the introduction of additional information:

The government – which promises to cut taxes – will be popular.

Or we could use brackets:

The government (which promises to cut taxes) will be popular.

In speech, a break in the intonation pattern indicates these markings, e.g. when reading aloud, or delivering a news bulletin.

Not *all* relative clauses need be rigidly classified as defining or non-defining. The inclusion or omission of commas may be at the writer's discretion when it does not result in a significant change in meaning:

He asked a lot of questions (,) which were none of his business (,) and generally managed to annoy everybody.

1.27 Form of relative pronouns in relative clauses

Relative pronouns as subject:

People:	*He is the man* ***who*** (or ***that***) *lives next door.*
Things:	*This is the photo* ***which*** (or ***that***) *shows my house.*
Possession:	*He is the man* ***whose*** *car was stolen.*

Relative pronouns as object:

People:	*He is the man* (***who/whom/that***) *I met.*
People:	*He is the man* (–) *I gave the money to.*
Things:	*This is the photo* (***which/that***) *I took.*
Things:	*This is the pan* (–) *I boiled the milk in.*
Possession:	*It was an agreement the details* ***of which*** *could not be altered.*

1.28 Relative pronouns relating to people

Relative pronouns which can be used with reference to people are: *who, whom,* and *that* and the possessive *whose*. Don't confuse the relative pronoun *that* with the subordinating conjunction [> 1.23].

1.29 Relative pronoun subject of relative clause: people

Who and *that* can be used in place of noun subjects or subject pronouns (*I, you, he*, etc.) [> 4.3]. When they refer to the subject they cannot normally be omitted. We never use a subject pronoun and a relative pronoun together to refer to the subject: Not **He is the man who he lives next door**. *Who* and *that* remain unchanged whether they refer to masculine, feminine, singular or plural:

masculine:	*He is* ***the man who/that*** *lives next door.*
feminine:	*She is* ***the woman who/that*** *lives next door.*
plural masculine:	*They are* ***the men who/that*** *live next door.*
plural feminine:	*They are* ***the women who/that*** *live next door.*

We can use *that* in place of *who*, but we generally prefer *who* when the reference is to a person or persons as subject of the verb.

1.29.1 Typical defining relative clause with 'who' as subject

Who or *that* is possible in the relative clause:

A doctor examined ***the astronauts. They returned*** *from space today.*
A doctor examined the astronauts ***who returned*** *from space today.*

1.29.2 Typical non-defining relative clause with 'who' as subject

Who must be used in non-defining clauses: *that* is not possible:

The astronauts *are expected to land on the moon shortly.* ***They*** *are reported to be very cheerful.*
The astronauts, ***who are reported to be very cheerful****, are expected to land on the moon shortly.*

1.30 Relative pronouns relating to things and animals

Relative pronouns which can be used with reference to things and animals are *which* and *that* [but compare > 4.8].

1.31 Relative pronoun subject of relative clause: things/animals

Which and *that* can be used in place of noun subjects that refer to things or animals, or in place of the subject pronouns *it* or *they*. When *which/that* refer to the subject, they cannot normally be omitted. We never use a subject pronoun and a relative pronoun together to refer to the subject: Not **The cat which it caught the mouse**. *Which* and *that* remain unchanged whether they refer to the singular or the plural:

singular: *This is* ***the photo which/that*** *shows my house.*
This is ***the cat which/that*** *caught the mouse.*
plural: *These are* ***the photos which/that*** *show my house.*
These are ***the cats which/that*** *caught the mice.*

1.31.1 Typical defining relative clause with 'which' as subject

Which or *that* are possible in the relative clause:

The tiles *fell off the roof.* ***They*** *caused a lot of damage.*
The tiles ***which fell off the roof*** *caused serious damage.*

1.31.2 Typical non-defining relative clause with 'which' as subject

Which must be used in non-defining clauses: *that* is not possible:

The Thames *is now clean enough to swim in.* ***It*** *was polluted for over a hundred years.*
The Thames, ***which is now clean enough to swim in,*** *was polluted for over a hundred years.*

1.32 'Whose' as the subject of a relative clause: people/things

Whose can be used in place of possessive adjectives (*my, your, his, her*, etc.) [> 4.19]. It remains unchanged whether it refers to masculine, feminine, singular or plural:

masculine: *He is* ***the man whose*** *car was stolen.*
feminine: *She is* ***the woman whose*** *car was stolen.*
plural masculine: *They are* ***the men whose*** *cars were stolen.*
plural feminine: *They are* ***the women whose*** *cars were stolen.*

Whose can replace the possessive adjective *its*:

This is the house ***whose*** *windows were broken.*

However, this use of *whose* is often avoided by native speakers who regard *whose* as the genitive of the personal *who*. Instead of this sentence, a careful speaker might say:

This is the house ***where*** *the windows were broken.*

Where the context is formal, *of which* should be used, not *whose*:

It was an agreement the details ***of which*** *could not be altered.*
Or: ... ***of which*** *the details could not be altered.*

1.32.1 Typical defining relative clause with 'whose' as subject

The millionaire *has made a public appeal.* ***His son*** *ran away from home a week ago.*
The millionaire ***whose son ran away from home a week ago*** *has made a public appeal.*

1.32.2 Typical non-defining relative clause with 'whose' as subject

Sally Smiles *has resigned as director.* ***Her cosmetics company*** *has been in the news a great deal recently.*
Sally Smiles, ***whose cosmetics company has been in the news a great deal recently****, has resigned as director.*

1.33 Relative pronoun object of relative clause: people

Who(m) and *that* can be used in place of noun objects that refer to people, or in place of object pronouns (*me, you, him*, etc.) [> 4.3]. When they refer to an object, they are usually omitted, but only in **defining** clauses. When included, *whom* is commonly reduced to *who* in everyday speech. We never use an object pronoun and a relative pronoun together to refer to the object: Not **He is the man (that) I met him**. *Who(m)* and *that* remain unchanged whether they refer to masculine, feminine, singular or plural:

masculine:	*He is* ***the man who(m)/that*** *I met on holiday.*
	He is the man I met on holiday.
feminine:	*She is* ***the woman who(m)/that*** *I met on holiday.*
	She is the woman I met on holiday.
plural masculine:	*They are* ***the men who(m)/that*** *I met on holiday.*
	They are the men I met on holiday.
plural feminine:	*They are* ***the women who(m)/that*** *I met on holiday.*
	They are the women I met on holiday.

1.33.1 Typical defining relative clause with ('who(m)/that') as object

When the reference is to a person or persons as the object of the verb we often use *that*. Alternatively, we omit the relative pronoun to avoid the choice between *who* and *whom*:

That energetic man *works for the EEC. We met* ***him*** *on holiday.*
That energetic man ***(who(m)/that) we met on holiday*** *works for the EEC.*

1.33.2 Typical non-defining relative clause with 'who(m)' as object

Who(m) must be used in non-defining clauses: *that* is not possible:

The author of 'Rebels' *proved to be a well-known journalist. I met* ***him*** *at a party last week.*
The author of 'Rebels', ***who(m) I met at a party last week****, proved to be a well-known journalist.*

1.34 Relative pronoun object of relative clause: things/animals

That and *which*, referring to things and animals, are interchangeable in the object position. However, both are commonly omitted, but only in **defining** clauses. We never use an object pronoun and a relative pronoun together to refer to the object: Not **This is the photo (which) I took it**. *That* and *which* remain unchanged whether they refer to singular or plural:

singular: *This is **the photo that/which** I took.*
This is the photo I took.
*This is **the cat that/which** I photographed.*
This is the cat I photographed.

plural: *These are **the photos that/which** I took.*
These are the photos I took.
*These are **the cats that/which** I photographed.*
These are the cats I photographed.

1.34.1 Typical defining relative clause with 'that' or 'which' as object

***The shed** has begun to rot. We built **it** in the garden last year.*
*The shed **(that/which) we built in the garden last year** has begun to rot.*

1.34.2 Typical non-defining relative clause with 'which' as object

Which must be used in non-defining clauses; *that* is not possible:

***The shed in our garden** has lasted for a long time. My father built **it** many years ago.*
*The shed in our garden, **which my father built many years ago**, has lasted for a long time.*

1.35 Relative pronoun object of a preposition: people

When we wish to refer to a person, only *whom* (not *that*) can be used directly after a preposition. In this position, *whom* cannot be omitted and cannot be reduced to *who* or be replaced by *that*. This use is formal and rare in everyday speech:

*He is the man **to whom** I gave the money.*

The preposition can be moved to the end-position. If this happens, it is usual in speech to reduce *whom* to *who*; it is also possible to replace *who(m)* by *that*:

*She is the woman **whom*** (or ***who***, or ***that***) *I gave the money **to**.*

However, the most usual practice in informal style, when the preposition is in the end-position, is to drop the relative pronoun altogether, but only in **defining** clauses:

*They are the people I gave the money **to**.*
*There's hardly anybody he's afraid **of**.*

1.35.1 Typical defining relative clause with a preposition

***That person** is the manager. I complained **to him**.*
*The person **to whom I complained** is the manager.*
*The person **who(m)/that I complained to** is the manager.*
*The person **I complained to** is the manager.*

1.35.2 Typical non-defining relative clause with a preposition

Who(m) must be used in non-defining clauses: *that* is not possible:

__The hotel manager__ refunded part of our bill. I complained __to him__ about the service.
The hotel manager, __to whom I complained__ (or ***who(m) I complained to***) *about the service, refunded part of our bill.*

1.36 Relative pronoun object of a preposition: things/animals

When we wish to refer to things or animals, only *which* (not *that*) can be used directly after a preposition. When used in this way, *which* cannot be omitted. This use is formal and rare in speech:

This is the pan __in which__ I boiled the milk.

The preposition can be moved to the end-position. If this happens, it is possible to replace *which* by *that*:

This is the pan __that__ (or ***which***) *I boiled the milk __in__.*

However, the relative is usually dropped altogether when the preposition is in the end-position, but only in **defining** clauses:

This is the pan I boiled the milk __in__.
These are the cats I gave the milk __to__.

1.36.1 Typical defining relative clause with a preposition

__The agency__ is bankrupt. We bought our tickets __from it__.
The agency __from which we bought our tickets__ is bankrupt.
The agency __which/that we bought our tickets from__ is bankrupt.
The agency __we bought our tickets from__ is bankrupt.

1.36.2 Typical non-defining relative clause with a preposition

Which must be used in non-defining clauses; *that* is not possible:

__The Acme Travel Agency__ has opened four new branches. Our company has been dealing __with it__ for several years.
The Acme Travel Agency, __with which our company has been dealing__ (or ***which our company has been dealing with***) ***for several years**, has opened four new branches.*

1.37 'Whose' + noun with a preposition

Whose + noun can be used as the object of a preposition. The preposition may come before *whose* or at the end of the clause:

He is the man __from whose house__ the pictures were stolen.
He is the man __whose house__ the pictures were stolen __from__.

1.37.1 Typical defining relative clause using 'whose' with a preposition

In 1980 he caught __a serious illness__. He still suffers __from its effects__.
In 1980 he caught a serious illness __from whose effects he still suffers__ (or ***the effects of which he still suffers from***).

1.37.2 Typical non-defining relative clause using 'whose' with a preposition

__Mr Jason Matthews__ died last night. A valuable Rembrandt was given to the nation __from his collection of pictures__.
Mr Jason Matthews, __from whose collection of pictures a valuable Rembrandt was given to the nation__, died last night.

1.38 Relative clauses of time, place and reason

Defining and non-defining relative clauses of time, place and reason are possible in which *when, where* and *why* are used in place of relative pronouns. They can also replace words like *the time, the place* and *the reason*. Though we can say *the time when, the place where* and *the reason why*, we cannot say **the way how** [> 1.47.1]. Note that *when* follows only 'time' nouns, such as *day, occasion, season*; *where* follows only 'place' nouns, such as *house, place, town, village*; *why* normally follows the noun *reason*.

1.38.1 **Time defining**:

*1979 was **the year (in which)** my son was born.*
*1979 was **(the year) when** my son was born.*

non-defining:

*The summer of 1969, **the year (in which)** men first set foot on the moon, will never be forgotten.*
*The summer of 1969, **(the year) when** men first set foot on the moon, will never be forgotten.*

1.38.2 **Place defining**:

*This is **the place in which** I grew up.*
*This is **the place which** I grew up **in**.*
*This is **the place** I grew up **in**.*
*This is **(the place) where** I grew up.*

non-defining:

***The Tower of London, in which** so many people lost their lives, is now a tourist attraction.*
***The Tower of London, (the place) where** so many people lost their lives, is now a tourist attraction.*

1.38.3 **Reason defining**:

*That's **the reason (for which)** he dislikes me.*
*That's **(the reason) why** he dislikes me.*

non-defining:

***My success in business, (the reason) for which** he dislikes me, has been due to hard work.*
***My success in business, the reason why** he dislikes me, has been due to hard work.* (*The reason* cannot be omitted before *why*.)

1.38.4 **('That') in place of 'when', 'where', 'why'**

That is possible (but optional) in place of *when, where* and *why* but only in defining clauses:

*I still remember the summer **(that)** we had the big drought.* (*(That)* can be replaced by *when* or *during which*.)
*I don't know any place **(that)** you can get a better exchange rate.* (*(That)* can be replaced by *where* or *at which*.)
*That wasn't the reason **(that)** he lied to you.* (*(That)* can be replaced by *why* or *for which*.)

For relatives after *it* [> 4.14].

1.39 Relative clauses abbreviated by 'apposition'

We can place two noun phrases side-by-side, separating the phrases by commas, so that the second adds information to the first. We can then say that the noun phrases are 'in apposition' [> 3.30]. This is more common in journalism than in speech. A relative clause can sometimes be replaced by a noun phrase in this way:

My neighbour Mr Watkins *never misses the opportunity to tell me the latest news.* (defining, without commas)
Mr Watkins, a neighbour of mine, *never misses the opportunity to tell me the latest news.* (non-defining, with commas)
(= Mr Watkins, who is a neighbour of mine, ...)

1.40 'That' after 'all', etc. and superlatives

That (Not **which**) is normally used after words like *all, any, anything, everything, a few* and *the only one* when they do not refer to people. Clauses of this kind are always defining:

All that *remains for me to do is to say goodbye.*
Everything that *can be done has been done.*
I'll do ***anything (that)*** *I can.*

Who is used after *all, any* and *a few* when they refer to people:

God bless this ship and ***all who*** *sail in her.* [> 5.24]

That is also common after superlatives. It is optional when it refers to the object [> 6.28.1]:

It's ***the silliest argument (that)*** *I've ever heard.*

but not optional when it refers to the subject:

Bach's the greatest composer ***that's*** (or ***who's***) *ever lived.*

1.41 'Of' + relative referring to number/quantity

Of can be used before *whom* and *which* in non-defining clauses to refer to number or quantity after numbers and words like the following: *a few, several, some, any, many, much (of which), the majority, most; all, none; either/neither; the largest/the smallest; the oldest/the youngest; a number, half, a quarter:*

Both players, ***neither of whom*** *reached the final, played well.*
The treasure, ***some of which*** *has been recovered, has been sent to the British Museum.*

1.42 'Which' in place of a clause

Which can be used to refer to a whole clause, not just one word. In such cases, it can be replaced by *and this* or *and that*:

She married Joe, ***which*** (= and this/that) *surprised everyone.*

Which, in the sense of *this* or *that*, can also be used in expressions such as *in which case, at which point, on which occasion*, which can refer back to a complete clause:

I may have to work late, ***in which case*** *I'll telephone.*
The speaker paused to examine his notes, ***at which point*** *a loud crash was heard.*

Which, in the sense of *this* or *that*, can replace a whole sentence and, in informal style, can even begin a sentence:

He was fined £500. ***Which*** *we all thought served him right.*

1.43 Reference in relative clauses

A relative clause follows the person or thing it refers to as closely as possible to avoid ambiguity. Compare:

*I cut out **the advertisement which you wanted** in yesterday's paper.* (an unambiguous reference to the *advertisement*)
*I cut out **the advertisement** in yesterday's **paper which you wanted**.* (*which* could refer either to the *advertisement* or the *paper*)

A sentence can contain more than one relative:

*It's the only building **(which)** I've ever seen **which** is made entirely of glass.* (The first *which* would normally be omitted.)

The complex sentence: adverbial clauses

1.44 How to identify an adverbial clause

Compare:

***I try hard, but** I can never remember people's names.*
***However hard I try**, I can never remember people's names.*

Hard is an adverb; *however hard I try* is an adverbial (or adverb) clause: it is telling us something about (or 'modifying') *can never remember*. Adverbs can often be identified by asking and answering the questions *When?, Where?, How?, Why?*, etc. [> 7.2] and adverbial clauses can be identified in the same way:

time: *Tell him **as soon as he arrives**.* (***When?***)
place: *You can sit **where you like**.* (***Where?***)
manner: *He spoke **as if he meant business**.* (***How?***)
reason: *He went to bed **because he felt ill**.* (***Why?***)

1.45 Adverbial clauses of time

1.45.1 Conjunctions in adverbial clauses of time

These clauses broadly answer the question *When?* and can be introduced by the following conjunctions: *when, after, as, as long as, as soon as, before, by the time (that), directly, during the time (that), immediately, the moment (that), now (that), once, since, until/till, whenever*, and *while*. We generally use a comma when the adverbial clause comes first:

*You didn't look very well **when you got up this morning**.*
***After she got married**, Madeleine changed completely.*
*I pulled a muscle **as I was lifting a heavy suitcase**.*
*You can keep these records **as long as you like**.* [compare *as long as* in conditional sentences > 14.21]
***Once you've seen one penguin**, you've seen them all.*
*He hasn't stopped complaining **since he got back from his holidays**.* [compare *since* in clauses of reason > 1.48]
*We always have to wait **till/until the last customer has left**.*

1.45.2 Tenses in adverbial clauses of time: 'no future after temporals'

When the time clause refers to the future, we normally use the simple present after *after, as soon as, before, by the time, directly, immediately, the moment, till, until* and *when* where we might expect a simple future; or we use the present perfect where we might expect the future perfect. These two tenses are often interchangeable after temporal conjunctions:

The Owens will move to a new flat ***when their baby is born*** (or ***has been born***).

The present perfect is often used after *once* and *now that*:

Once (= when) ***we have decorated the house****, we can move in.*
Now that we have decorated the house*,* (action completed) *we can move in.*

1.45.3 'Will' after 'when'

Though we do not normally use the future in time clauses, *will* can be used after *when* in noun clauses [> 1.24.2]:

The hotel receptionist wants to know ***when we will be checking out tomorrow morning****.*

When meaning 'and then' can be followed by present or future:

I shall be on holiday till the end of September, ***when I return*** (or ***when I shall return***) *to London.*

1.46 Adverbial clauses of place

These clauses answer the question *Where?* and can be introduced by the conjunctions *where, wherever, anywhere* and *everywhere*. Adverbial clauses of place normally come *after* the main clause:

You can't camp ***where/wherever/anywhere you like*** *these days.*

Anywhere, everywhere and *wherever* (but not usually *where*) can begin a sentence, depending on the emphasis we wish to make:

Everywhere Jenny goes *she's mistaken for Princess Diana.*

Where generally refers to a definite but unspecified place [> 1.38]:

The church was built ***where there had once been a Roman temple****.*

Wherever, anywhere and *everywhere* suggest 'any place':

With a special train ticket you can travel ***wherever/anywhere/everywhere you like*** *in Europe for just over £100.*

1.47 Adverbial clauses of manner

1.47.1 'As' [> App 25.25] **and 'in the way (that)'**

These clauses answer the question *How?* and can be introduced by the conjunction *as*. Adverbial clauses of manner normally come after the main clause:

Type this again ***as I showed you a moment ago****.* (i.e. in the way I showed you)
This fish isn't cooked ***as I like it****.* (i.e. in the way I like it)

How and *the way* can be used colloquially in place of *as*:

This steak is cooked just ***how/the way*** *I like it.*

Clauses of manner can also express comparison when they are introduced by expressions like *(in) the way, (in) the way that, the way in which, (in) the same way, (in) the same way as:*

She's behaving ***(in) the same way her elder sister used to****.*

1.47.2 'As if' and 'as though' after 'be', 'seem', etc.

Adverbial clauses of manner can also be introduced by the conjunctions *as if* and *as though* after the verbs *be, act, appear, behave, feel, look, seem, smell, sound, taste:*

*I **feel as if/as though** I'm floating on air.*

Note also constructions with *It*:

***It sounds as if/as though** the situation will get worse.*

***It feels as if/as though** it's going to rain.* (i.e. I feel that this is going to happen)

As if/as though can be used after any verbs describing behaviour:

***Lillian was trembling as if/as though** she had seen a ghost.*

***She acted as if** she were mad.* [> 11.75.1*n*.2]

1.48 Adverbial clauses of reason

1.48.1 Conjunctions in adverbial clauses of reason

These clauses broadly answer the question *Why?* and can be introduced by the following conjunctions: *because, as, seeing (that)* and *since*:

***As/Because/Since there was very little support**, the strike was not successful.* [compare *since* in time clauses > 1.45.1]

*I'm afraid we don't stock refills for pens like yours **because there's little demand for them**.*

1.48.2 The relative position of clauses of reason and main clauses

As a general rule, whatever we want to emphasize (reason or main clause) comes at the end.

We often begin sentences with *as* or *since* because the reasons they refer to may be known to the person spoken to and therefore do not need to be emphasized:

***As/Since you can't type the letter yourself**, you'll have to ask Susan to do it for you.*

Because generally follows the main clause to emphasize a reason which is probably not known to the person spoken to [see *for* > 1.20.5]:

*Jim's trying to find a place of his own **because he wants to feel independent**.*

Because can always be used in place of *as, since* and *for* to give a reason or reasons, but these conjunctions cannot always be used in place of *because*.

1.49 Adverbial clauses of condition [> Chapter 14]

These clauses can be introduced by conjunctions such as *assuming (that), if, on condition (that), provided (that), providing (that), so/as long as* and *unless*.

1.50 Adverbial clauses of concession

Adverbial clauses of concession introduce an element of contrast into a sentence and are sometimes called **contrast clauses**. They are introduced by the following conjunctions: *although, considering (that), though, even though, even if; much as ..., while, whereas, however*

much/badly/good, etc., *no matter how*, etc., *no matter how much*, etc.
Even though is probably more usual than *though/although* in speech:

Although/Though/Even though I felt sorry for him, *I was secretly pleased that he was having difficulties.*
We intend to go to India, ***even if air fares go up again*** *between now and the summer.*
Much as I'd like to help, *there isn't a lot I can do.*
While I disapprove of what you say, *I would defend to the death your right to say it.*

However combines with numerous adjectives and adverbs:

However far it is, *I intend to drive there tonight.*

No matter can combine with question words (*who, when, where*, etc.) to introduce clauses of concession:

No matter where you go, *you can't escape from yourself.*

Compounds with *-ever* can introduce clauses of concession in the same way as *No matter*:

Whatever I say, *I seem to say the wrong thing.* (No matter what ...)

We can use *may* in formal style in place of the present after all conjunctions introducing clauses of concession:

However brilliant you are/may be, *you can't know everything.*
Whatever you think/may think, *I'm going ahead with my plans.*

As and *though* to mean 'regardless of the degree to which' can be used after some adjectives, adverbs and verbs to introduce clauses of concession in formal style:

Unlikely as it sounds/may sound, *what I'm telling you is true.* (i.e Though it sounds/may sound unlikely ...)
Beautiful though the necklace was, *we thought it was over-priced so we didn't buy it.* (i.e. Though the necklace was beautiful ...)
Try as he might, *he couldn't solve the problem.* (i.e. Though he tried he couldn't ...)

1.51 Adverbial clauses of purpose

1.51.1 Conjunctions in adverbial clauses of purpose

These clauses answer the questions *What for?* and *For what purpose?* and can be introduced by the following conjunctions: *so that, in order that, in case, lest* and *for fear (that)*.

So as to and *in order to* also convey the idea of purpose, but they are variations on the *to*-infinitive, not conjunctions. They do not introduce a group of words containing a finite verb [> 1.21*n*.2]. Constructions with *to, so as to* and *in order to* are much simpler than those with *that* and are generally preferred [> 16.12.1].

1.51.2 Sequence of verb forms in adverbial clauses of purpose

When the verb in the main clause is in the present, present perfect or future, *so that* and *in order that* can be followed by *may, can* or *will* *So that* is more common than *in order that*:

I've arrived early ***so that/in order that I may/can/will get*** *a good view of the procession.*

So that and *in order that* may also be followed by the present:
Let us spend a few moments in silence ***so that/in order that we remember*** *those who died to preserve our freedom.*

When the verb in the main clause is in the simple past, the past progressive, or the past perfect, *so that* and *in order that* are followed by *should, could, might* or *would*:
I arrived early ***so that/in order that I should/could/might/would get*** *a good view of the procession.*

Note the negative after *so that* and *in order that*:
I arrived early ***so that/in order that I might not miss*** *anything.*
(*Should not* and *would not* would be possible, but not *could not*)
Infinitive constructions with *not to, so as not to* and *in order not to* are more natural [> 16.12.1]:
I arrived early ***so as not to miss*** *anything.*
They must have worn gloves ***in order not to leave*** *any fingerprints.*

1.51.3 'In case', 'lest' and 'for fear'

Should, might or the present must be used after *in case* when there is a future reference:
We've installed an extinguisher next to the cooker ***in case there is ever (there should/might ever be)*** *a fire.*
I'm taking a raincoat with me ***in case I need it****.*
Should is optional after (the relatively rare) *lest*:
We have a memorial service every year ***lest we (should) forget*** *our debt to those who died in battle.* (i.e. so that/in order that we might not forget...)
The subjunctive [> 11.75.1*n*.2] could also be used after *lest*:
I avoided mentioning the subject ***lest he be offended****.*
I asked them to ring first ***lest we were out****.*

For fear is usually followed by *might*, but the same idea can be expressed more easily with *in case* + past:
I bought the car at once ***for fear (that) he might change*** *his mind.*
I bought the car at once ***in case he changed*** *his mind.*

1.52 Adverbial clauses of result

1.52.1 Conjunctions and sequence of verb forms in clauses of result

These clauses describe **consequences**. They can be introduced by *that* after *so* + adjective to answer, e.g. *How (quick)...?*:
His reactions are ***so quick (that) no one can match him****.*
and by *that* after *so* + adverb to answer, e.g. *How (quickly)...?*:
He reacts ***so quickly (that) no one can match him****.*
They can also be introduced by *that* after *such (a)* + noun (or adjective + noun) to answer questions like *What's (he) like?*:
He is ***such a*** *marvellous joker* ***(that) you can't help laughing****.*
They are ***such*** *wonderful players* ***(that) no one can beat them****.*
When *that* is omitted informally, a comma is sometimes used:
His reactions are so quick(,) no one can match him.
Such + obligatory *that* can be used in formal English as follows:
His reactions are ***such that no one can match him****.*

Result clauses with and without *that* can also be used after *so* + *much, many, few, little*, etc.:

There was ***so much*** *to lose* ***(that) we couldn't take any risks****.*

They can also be used after *such a lot of* :

There was ***such a lot of*** *rain* ***(that) we couldn't go out****.*

So and *such* (heavily stressed in speech) can be used without *that*, so a *that*-clause may be strongly implied:

He was ***so*** *angry!* (i.e. that there were consequences)
The children made ***such*** *a mess!* (i.e. that there were consequences)

In colloquial English *that* is sometimes heard in place of *so*:

It was ***that*** *cold, (that) I could hardly get to sleep.*
The roads were ***that*** *icy!* (i.e. that there were consequences)

1.52.2 Clauses of purpose compared with clauses of result

In a purpose clause we can always replace *so that* by *in order that*, which we cannot do in a result clause:

We arrived early ***so that*** (or ***in order that***) ***we could/should/ might/would get*** *good seats.* (i.e. we arrived early for that purpose)
We arrived early, ***so (that) we got*** *good seats.* (i.e. we got good seats as a result of arriving early)
Or: *We arrived* ***so early that we got*** *good seats.*

A further difference is that a result clause always follows the main clause, whereas a purpose clause can precede the main clause:

So that I shouldn't worry*, he phoned me on arrival.*

In the spoken language there are differences in intonation between *so that* (purpose) and *so that* (result).

1.53 Adverbial clauses of comparison [compare > 4.7.3, 6.27.1]

These clauses often answer *How?* followed by or implying *in relation to* or *compared with (How quick is he in relation to/compared with...?)*. They involve the use of *as* + adjective + *as (as quick as), as* + adverb + *as (as quickly as), not so/as...as, -er than, more...than, less...than, the...the*. When continuing with the same verb in the same tense, we can omit the second verb, so the clause of comparison is implied:

He is as quick in answering ***as his sister (is)****.*
He answers as quickly ***as his sister (does)****.*
He is not so/as quick in answering ***as his sister (is)****.*
His sister is quicker ***than he (is)****.*
He moves more slowly ***than his sister (does)****.*
The more *you practise* ***the better you get****.*

There are instances when we can drop both subject and verb:

When I spoke to him on the phone this morning, he was more agreeable ***than*** *(he was)* ***last night****.*

Adverbial clauses of comparison can involve the use of *as* (or *so*) *much* + noun + *as* and *as many* + noun + *as*. Words like *half, nearly* and *nothing like* will often combine with *as* or *so*:

He didn't sell ***half as/so*** *many videos* ***as he thought he would****.*

Words like *just, twice/ten times* will combine only with *as*:

You've made ***just as*** (Not **so**) *many mistakes* ***as I have****.*

1.54 Limiting clauses

A main clause can be qualified or limited by clauses introduced by *in that*, *in so far as* and *inasmuch as*:

The demonstration was fairly peaceful ***in that/in so far as there were only one or two clashes with the police****.*

Inasmuch as can be used like *in so far as* but is formal and rare.

1.55 Abbreviated adverbial clauses

Most kinds of clauses can be abbreviated by deleting the subject and the verb *be* after the conjunction:

time: ***While*** *(she was)* ***at college****, Delia wrote a novel.*
place: ***Where*** *(it is)* ***necessary****, improvements will be made.*
manner: *He acted* ***as if*** *(he was)* ***certain*** *of success.*
condition: ***If*** *(it is)* ***possible****, please let me know by this evening.*
concession: ***Though*** *(he was)* ***exhausted****, he went to bed very late.*

Clauses of reason cannot be abbreviated in this way. However, they can often be replaced by participle constructions. Such constructions also have the effect of shortening clauses [> 1.58].

The complex sentence: participle constructions

1.56 Form of participles [compare > 16.41]

	present	**perfect**	**past**
active:	*finding*	*having found*	–
passive:	*being found*	*having been found*	*found*

1.57 Joining sentences with participles

Simple sentences can be combined into one sentence that contains a main clause + a participle or an infinitive construction [> 1.58, 16.12.1]. Participle constructions are generally more typical of formal style than of informal, though they can easily occur in both:

simple sentences: *He walked out of the room. He slammed the door behind him.*
compound sentence: *He* ***walked out*** *of the room* ***and slammed*** *the door behind him.*
participle construction: *He* ***walked out*** *of the room,* ***slamming*** *the door behind him.*

simple sentences: *You want to order a vehicle. You have to pay a deposit.*
complex sentence: ***If you want*** *to order a vehicle,* ***you have to pay*** *a deposit.*
infinitive construction: ***To order*** *a vehicle,* ***you have to pay*** *a deposit.*
participle construction: ***When ordering*** *a vehicle,* ***you have to pay*** *a deposit.*

Participle constructions can come before or after the main clause, depending on the emphasis we wish to make:

__Making sure__ I had the right number, I phoned again.
Or: *I phoned again, __making sure__ I had the right number.*

More than one participle construction is possible in a sentence:

After __looking up__ their number in the phone book and __making sure__ I had got it right, I phoned again.

1.58 Present participles in place of clauses

1.58.1 Participle constructions in place of co-ordinate clauses

The co-ordinating conjunction *and* must be dropped:

She lay awake all night __and recalled__ the events of the day.
She lay awake all night, __recalling__ the events of the day.

1.58.2 Present participle constructions in place of clauses of time

Present participles can be used after the time conjunctions *after, before, since, when* and *while*. They cannot be used after the conjunctions *as, as soon as, directly, until*, etc.:

__Since I phoned you__ this morning, I have changed my plans.
__Since phoning you__ this morning, I have changed my plans.
We cannot use this construction when *since* = *because* [> 1.48].

On and *in* can be used to mean 'when' and 'while':

__On finding__ the front door open, I became suspicious.
(i.e. When/At the moment when I found...)
__In/While trying__ to open the can, I cut my hand.
(i.e. During the time when I was trying...)

1.58.3 Present participle constructions in place of clauses of reason

__As I was__ anxious to please him, I bought him a nice present.
__Being__ anxious to please him, I bought him a nice present.

1.58.4 Present participle constructions in place of conditionals

The present participle can be used after *if* and *unless*:

__If you are travelling__ north, you must change at Leeds.
__If travelling__ north, you must change at Leeds.
__Unless you pay__ by credit card, please pay in cash.
__Unless paying__ by credit card, please pay in cash.

1.58.5 Present participles in place of clauses of concession

The present participle can be used after the conjunctions *although, even though, though* and *while*:

__While he admitted__ that he had received the stolen jewellery, he denied having taken part in the robbery.
__While admitting__ that he had received the stolen jewellery, he denied having taken part in the robbery.

1.58.6 Present participle constructions in place of relative clauses

The present participle can be used in place of defining [> 1.26] clauses in the simple present or present progressive after relative pronouns:

__The train which is arriving__ at Platform 8 is the 17.50 from Crewe.
__The train arriving__ at Platform 8 is the 17.50 from Crewe.

1.59 Perfect participle constructions

Perfect participle constructions can be used in place of clauses in the present perfect and past perfect and the simple past. The action described in the perfect participle construction has always taken place before the action described in the main clause.

active: ***We have invited him*** *here to speak, so we'd better go to his lecture.*
Having invited him *here to speak, we'd better go to his lecture.*

passive: ***I have been made*** *redundant, so I'm going abroad.*
Having been made *redundant, I'm going abroad.*

1.60 Participle constructions with 'being' and 'having been'

The present participle form of *be* (*being*) can be used in place of the finite forms *is/are/was/were*; the perfect participle form (*having been*) can be used in place of the finite forms *have been* and *had been*. These participle constructions are rare in everyday speech and only likely to occur in formal writing:

He is so ill *he can't go back to work yet.*
Being so ill*, he can't go back to work yet.*
He was so ill *he couldn't go back to work for a month.*
Being so ill*, he couldn't go back to work for a month.*
He has (or ***had***) ***been ill*** *for a very long time, so he needs/needed more time to recover before he can/could go back to work.*
Having been ill *for a very long time, he needs/needed more time to recover before he can/could go back to work.*

These forms occur in passive constructions [> 12.2].

Participle constructions with *it* and *there* occur in formal style:

It being a bank holiday*, all the shops were shut.* (i.e. As it was...)
There being no further business*, I declare the meeting closed.*
(As there is no further business, I declare the meeting closed.)

Participle constructions are common after *with/without* [> App 25.36]:

The crowds cheered. The royal party drove to the palace.
With the crowds cheering*, the royal party drove to the palace.*
They debated for hours. No decision was taken.
They debated for hours ***without a decision being taken****.*

1.61 Avoiding ambiguity with present participle constructions

The participle must relate to the subject of both verbs:

Reading my newspaper, I *heard the doorbell ring.*
(= *I* was reading my newspaper and *I* heard the doorbell ring.)

Now compare: **Reading my newspaper, the doorbell rang**.

This sentence suggests that the doorbell is the subject and *it* was reading my newspaper. *Reading* is here called an 'unrelated participle' and the sentence is unacceptable. However, this rule does not apply to a number of fixed phrases using 'unrelated participles', e.g. *broadly/generally/strictly speaking, considering..., judging, supposing..., taking everything into account:*

__Strictly speaking, you__ ought to sign the visitors' book before entering the club. (*you* are not *strictly speaking*)
__Judging from past performances, he__ is not likely to do very well in his exams. (*he* is not *judging*)

When the participle construction follows the object, it must be related to the object, and then the sentence is acceptable:
I found __him lying on the floor__. (= He was lying on the floor.)

1.62 Past participle constructions in place of clauses

Past participle constructions are more likely to occur in formal and literary style than in conversation:

1.62.1 Past participle constructions in place of the passive

The past participle can be used *without* any conjunction in front of it, in place of the passive:
__When it was viewed from a distance__, the island of Nepenthe looked like a cloud.
__Viewed from a distance__, the island of Nepenthe looked like a cloud.

1.62.2 Past participle constructions in place of adverbial clauses

The past participle can also be used *with* a conjunction in front of it to replace a passive:
__Although it was built__ before the war, the engine is still in perfect order.
__Although built__ before the war, the engine is still in perfect order.
__If you are accepted__ for this post, you will be informed by May 1st.
__If accepted__ for this post, you will be informed by May 1st.
__Unless it is changed__, this law will make life difficult for farmers.
__Unless changed__, this law will make life difficult for farmers

After, before, since, on and *in* cannot be followed directly by a past participle: they require *being* + past participle:
__After/When we were informed__ the flight would be delayed, we made other arrangements.
__After/On being informed__ the flight would be delayed, we made other arrangements.

1.62.3 Past participle constructions in place of relative clauses.

Past participle constructions can be used in place of defining clauses [> 1.26] deleting *which* + *be*:
__The system which is used__ in this school is very successful.
__The system used__ in this school is very successful.

1.63 Avoiding ambiguity with past participle constructions

Same subject, therefore acceptable [compare > 1.61]:
__Seated in the presidential car, the President__ waved to the crowd.
Unrelated, therefore unacceptable:
Seated in the presidential car, the crowd waved to the President.
Past participle related to the object:
We preferred __the house painted white__.
(Not **Painted white, we preferred ...**)

2 Nouns

One-word nouns

2.1 What a noun is and what it does

A noun tells us what someone or something is called. For example, a noun can be the name of a person (*John*); a job title (*doctor*); the name of a thing (*radio*); the name of a place (*London*); the name of a quality (*courage*); or the name of an action (*laughter/laughing*). Nouns are the names we give to people, things, places, etc. in order to identify them. Many nouns are used after a determiner, e.g. *a, the, this* [> 3.1] and often combine with other words to form a **noun phrase**: e.g. *the man, the man next door, that tall building, the old broom in the cupboard*. Nouns and noun phrases answer the questions *Who?* or *What?* and may be:

- the subject of a verb [> 1.4]:
  Our agent in Cairo *sent a telex this morning.*
- the direct object of a verb [> 1.9]:
  Frank sent ***an urgent telex*** *from Cairo this morning.*
- the indirect object of a verb [> 1.9]:
  Frank sent ***his boss*** *a telex.*
- the object of a preposition [> 8.1]:
  I read about it in ***the paper***.
- the complement of *be* or a related verb like *seem* [> 1.9]:
  Jane Forbes is ***our guest***.
- used 'in apposition' [> 1.39, 3.30]:
  Laura Myers, a BBC reporter*, asked for an interview.*
- used when we speak directly to somebody:
  Caroline*, shut that window, will you please?*

2.2 Noun endings

Some words function only as nouns (*desk*); others function as nouns or verbs (*work*), while others function as nouns or adjectives (*cold*): we cannot identify such words as nouns from their **endings** or **suffixes**. However, many nouns which are related to verbs or adjectives have characteristic endings. For example, *-er*, added to a verb like *play*, gives us the noun *player*; *-ity*, added to the adjective *active*, gives us the noun *activity*. There are no easy rules to tell us which endings to use to make nouns. A dictionary can provide this kind of information, but [> App 2].

2.3 Noun/verb contrasts

Some words can be either nouns or verbs. We can often tell the difference from the way they are stressed and pronounced.

2.3.1 Nouns and verbs distinguished by stress

e.g. *discount, entrance, export, import, object* [> App 3.1].
When the stress is on the first syllable, the word is a noun; when the stress is on the second syllable, it is a verb.
The meanings are generally related:
noun: *We have finished Book 1. We have made good '**progress**.*
verb: *We are now ready to **pro'gress** to Book 2.*
but can be different:
noun: *My son's '**conduct** at school hasn't been very good.*
verb: *Mahler used to **con'duct** the Vienna Philharmonic.*

2.3.2 Nouns distinguished by pronunciation: /s/ /z/ ; /f/ /v/ ; /θ/ /ð/

When the ending is pronounced with no 'voice', it is a noun; when it is pronounced 'hard', it is a verb. Sometimes this difference is reflected in the spelling:
/s/ and /z/: *abuse/abuse, advice/advise, house/house, use/use*
/f/ and /v/: *belief/believe, proof/prove, shelf/shelve*
/θ/ and /ð/: *cloth/clothe, teeth/teethe*
Exceptions: /s/ only in *practice* (noun)/ *practise* (verb) and *licence* (noun)/ *license* (verb).
And note words like *associate, graduate* and *estimate* where the pronunciation of the noun is different from that of the verb:
*I'm not a university **graduate*** /'grædʊət/ *yet.*
*I hope to **graduate*** /'grædjʊeɪt/ *next summer.*

2.3.3 Nouns and verbs with the same spelling and pronunciation

e.g. *answer, change, dream, end, hope, offer, trouble* [> App 3.2].

Compound nouns

2.4 Compound nouns

Many nouns in English are formed from two parts (*classroom*) or, less commonly, three or more (*son-in-law, stick-in-the-mud*). Sometimes compounds are spelt with a hyphen, sometimes not [> 2.11]. They are usually pronounced with the stress on the first syllable, but there are exceptions noted below.

2.5 Single-word compound nouns

There are many words which we no longer think of as compounds at all, even though they are clearly made up of two words:
e.g. *a 'cupboard, a 'raincoat, a 'saucepan, the 'seaside, a 'typewriter.*

2.6 Nouns formed with adjective + noun

e.g. *a 'greenhouse, a 'heavyweight, 'longhand, a 'redhead.*
Note the difference in meaning when these words are rearranged as adjective + noun:
a 'heavyweight (= a boxer).
a 'heavy 'weight (= a weight that is heavy).

2.7 Nouns formed with gerund + noun

e.g. *'drinking water, a 'frying pan, a 'walking stick.* [> 2.11*n*.3]
The meaning is 'something which is used for doing something': e.g. *a frying pan* (hyphen optional, = a pan that is used for frying).

Compare other *-ing* + noun combinations which are not compound nouns and where the *-ing* form is a participle used as an adjective. These combinations are not 'fixed', are not spelt with a hyphen, and are stressed in both parts: *'boiling 'water* (= water that is boiling). [> 6.2, 6.3.1, 6.14, 16.38, 16.39.3]

2.8 Nouns formed with noun + gerund

e.g. *'horse-riding, 'sight-seeing, 'sunbathing.* [> 2.11*n*.3]
Here the meaning is 'the action of...': *horse-riding* (= the action of riding a horse).

2.9 Nouns formed with adverb particles

These compound nouns are combinations of verbs and adverb particles: e.g. *'breakdown, 'income, 'make-up* [> Apps 31, 35].

2.10 Nouns formed with noun + noun

When two nouns are used together to form a compound noun, the first noun (**noun modifier**) usually functions like an adjective and is nearly always in the singular. This is the largest category of compound nouns and it can be considered under several headings:

2.10.1 Compound nouns in place of phrases with 'of'

e.g. *a 'car key, a 'chair leg, a 'door knob, a 'typewriter key.*

When we want to say that one (non-living) thing is part of another, we can use *of: the key of the car* [> 2.47]. However, this can sound rather emphatic, so we often use a compound noun instead (e.g. *a car key*) for things which are closely associated.

2.10.2 Compound nouns which refer to place

The first word refers to a place and the second word to something that is in that place. Both words are closely associated and are stressed but not hyphenated:
e.g. *the 'bank 'safe, a 'personal com'puter, a 'kitchen 'sink.*

Also note place names: *'London 'Airport, 'Moscow 'Stadium*, etc.

2.10.3 Compound nouns which refer to streets and roads

Where the word *street* occurs, the stress is on the first syllable: e.g. *'Baker Street*, *'Oxford Street*. Where the word *road* occurs, both parts are stressed: e.g. *'Canterbury 'Road, the 'Oxford 'road.* Compound place names are not hyphenated.

2.10.4 Compound nouns which tell us about purpose [compare > 2.7]

e.g. *a 'bookcase, a 'can-opener, a 'meeting point, a 'sheep dog.*

The second word suggests a use relating to the first (hyphen normally optional). *A can-opener* is 'a device for opening cans'.

2.10.5 Compound nouns which tell us about materials and substances

e.g. *a 'cotton 'blouse, a 'gold 'watch, a 'plastic 'raincoat.*
The first word refers to a substance or material; the second to something made of that substance or material [> 6.13].

2.10.6 Compound nouns which 'classify types'

e.g. *a 'horror film, a 'headlamp, a 'seat belt.*
The first word answers the question *What kind of...?*. These combinations can be extended to people and the things they do, as in: *a 'bookseller, a 'factory worker, a 'taxi-driver.*

Note the difference between *an 'English teacher* (i.e. one who teaches English) and *an English 'teacher* (i.e. one who is English). Other compounds refer to pieces of apparatus and what operates them, as in: *a 'gas boiler, a 'pressure cooker, a 'vacuum cleaner.*

Note the many combinations with *shop: a 'flower shop, a 'shoe shop*, etc. For combinations like *'butcher's (shop)* [> 2.51, 3.20.4].

2.10.7 Compound nouns which refer to 'containers'

e.g. *a 'biscuit tin, a 'coffee-cup, a 'teapot, a 'sugar bowl.*
The second item is designed to contain the first [> 2.18.2].

2.10.8 Compound nouns which relate to time

A number of combinations relate specifically to the time at which an activity takes place or to its duration: e.g. *'afternoon 'tea, 'morning 'coffee, the 'Sunday 'lunch, a 'two-hour 'walk*. Also note other nouns relating to time: *an 'evening 'dress, a 'night 'nurse.*

2.10.9 Compound nouns formed with 'self', 'man', 'woman' and 'person'

self- (stress on some part of the second word):
e.g. *self-'consciousness, self-con'trol, self-den'ial, self-res'pect.*
man/woman (stress on first word):
e.g. *an 'airman, a 'fireman, a 'gentleman/woman, a 'man-eater, a 'man-hour, a 'horseman/woman, a 'policeman/woman, a 'workman.*
Some people replace *man* by *person* in a few nouns when the reference is to either sex: *a chairperson, a salesperson* [> 2.40.4].

2.10.10 Proper nouns with two or more parts

e.g. *a 'Ford 'car, an 'IBM com'puter, 'Longman 'Books, 'Shell 'Oil, a 'North Sea 'oil rig, a/the 'Tate 'Gallery Exhi'bition.*

2.11 A note on hyphens

There are no precise rules, so the following are brief guidelines:

1 When two short nouns are joined together, they form one word without a hyphen (*a teacup*). We do not join two short nouns if this leads to problems of recognition: *bus stop* (Not **busstop**).
2 Hyphens are often used for verb + particle combinations (*make-up*) [> Apps 31, 35] and *self-* combinations (*self-respect*).
3 When a compound is accepted as a single word (e.g. it has an entry in a dictionary) the tendency is to write it as one word (*sunbathing*). In other cases, the use of the hyphen is at the discretion of the writer (*writing paper* or *writing-paper*), but the tendency is to avoid hyphens where possible.

Countable and uncountable nouns

2.12 Types of nouns

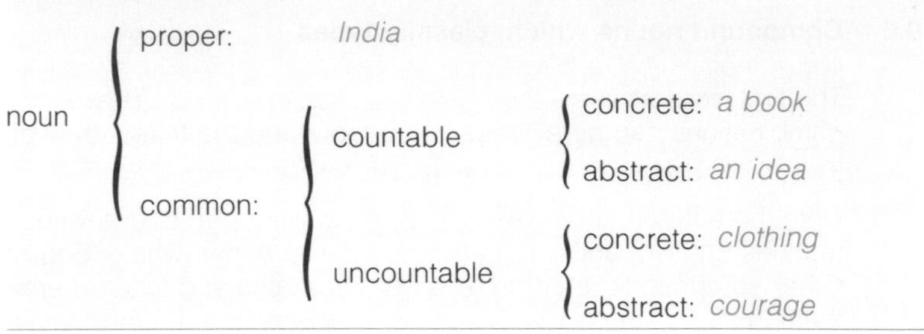

2.13 Proper nouns and common nouns

All nouns fall into one of two classes. They may be either **proper nouns** or **common nouns**.

2.13.1 Proper nouns

A proper noun (sometimes called a 'proper name') is used for a particular person, place, thing or idea which is, or is imagined to be, unique. It is generally spelt with a capital letter. Articles are not normally used in front of proper nouns, but [> 3.9.4, 3.31]. Proper nouns include, for example:

Personal names (with or without titles):	*Andrew, Andrew Smith, Mr Andrew Smith, President Kennedy.*
Forms of address:	*Mum, Dad, Auntie, Uncle Fred.*
Geographical names:	*Asia, Berkshire, India, Wisconsin.*
Place names:	*Madison Avenue, Regent Street.*
Months, days of the week, festivals and seasons [> Apps 24, 48]:	e.g. *April, Monday, Easter, Christmas.* Seasons are usually spelt with a small letter but sometimes with a capital: *spring* or *Spring*

For other names [> 3.22, 3.27, 3.31].

First names commonly used in other languages often have their English equivalents (e.g. *Charles* for Carlos, Karl, etc.) Well-known foreign place names are normally anglicized: e.g. *Cologne* for Köln, *Prague* for Praha, *Rome* for Roma, *Vienna* for Wien.

2.13.2 Common nouns

Any noun that is not the name of a particular person, place, thing or idea is a common noun. We can use *a/an, the* or the zero article in front of common nouns [> Chapter 3].

2.14 How to identify countable and uncountable nouns

All common nouns fall into one of two sub-classes: they may be either **countable nouns** (sometimes known as **unit** or **count** nouns) or **uncountable nouns** (sometimes known as **mass** or **non-count** nouns). The distinction between countable and uncountable nouns is fundamental in English, for only by distinguishing between the two can we understand when to use singular or plural forms and when to use the indefinite, definite and zero articles: *a/an, the* and *Ø* [> 3.2–3], or the appropriate quantifier: *a few, much, many*, etc. [> 3.1, 5.1].

Unfortunately, we cannot always rely on common sense (using the idea of counting as a guide) to tell us when a noun is countable or uncountable. For example, the noun *information* is uncountable in English, but its equivalent in another language may refer to an item or items of information and will therefore be countable [> 2.17].

Experience is uncountable, but we can refer to *an experience* to mean an event which contributes to *experience*:

*They want someone with **experience** for this job.*
*I had **a strange experience** the other day.*

Many nouns which are normally uncountable can be used as countables in certain contexts [> 2.16.3]. This suggests that strict classifications of nouns as countable or uncountable are in many cases unreliable. It would be better to think in terms of countable and uncountable *uses* of nouns. For detailed information about individual nouns, consult a good dictionary.

2.14.1 Countable nouns

If a noun is countable:

- we can use *a/an* in front of it: ***a*** *book*, ***an*** *envelope.*
- it has a plural and can be used in the question *How many?*:
  How many *stamps/envelopes? – Four stamps/envelopes.*
- we can use numbers: ***one*** *stamp*, ***two*** *stamps.*

2.14.2 Uncountable nouns

If a noun is uncountable:

- we do not normally use *a/an* in front of it: ***Sugar*** *is expensive.*
- it does not normally have a plural and it can be used in the question *How much?*: ***How much*** *meat/oil? – A lot of meat/A little oil.*
- we cannot normally use a number (*one, two*) in front of it.

2.15 Concrete and abstract nouns

Many **countable nouns** are **concrete** (having an individual physical existence), for example:

Persons, animals, plants:	*a girl, a horse, a geranium.*
Objects:	*a bottle, a desk, a typewriter.*
Groups:	*an army, a crowd, a herd.*
Units of measurement:	*a franc, a kilo, a litre, a metre.*
Parts of a mass:	*a bit, a packet, a piece, a slice.*

Concrete uncountable nouns (sometimes having physical but not 'individual' existence) include words like:

Materials, liquids, gases:	*cotton, milk, air.*
'Grains' and 'powder':	*barley, rice, dust, flour.*
Activities:	*camping, drinking, eating, sailing.*
Languages:	*Arabic, Italian, Japanese, Turkish.*

A few countable nouns are **abstract**: e.g. *a hope, an idea, a nuisance, a remark, a situation*. A number of abstract nouns can be used *only* as countables: e.g. *a denial, a proposal, a scheme, a statement.* Many uncountable nouns are abstract: e.g. *anger, equality, honesty.*

2.16 Nouns which can be either countable or uncountable

Some nouns may be countable or uncountable depending on their use.

2.16.1 Nouns we can think of as 'single items' or 'substances'

e.g. *a chicken/chicken, an egg/egg, a ribbon/ribbon.*

When we use these as **countables**, we refer to them as **single items**; when we use them as **uncountables**, we refer to them as **substances**.

countable (a single item)	**uncountable** (substance/material)
*He ate **a whole chicken**!*	*Would you like **some chicken**?*
*I had **a boiled egg** for breakfast.*	*There's **egg** on your face.*
*I tied it up with **a ribbon**.*	*I bought **a metre of ribbon**.*

2.16.2 Nouns which refer to objects or material

e.g. *a glass/glass, an ice/ice, an iron/iron, a paper/paper.*

When we use such nouns as **countables**, we refer to e.g. a thing which is made of the material or which we think of as being made of the material; when we use them as **uncountables**, we refer only to the material.

countable ('thing')	**uncountable** ('material')
*I broke **a glass** this morning.*	***Glass** is made from sand.*
*Would you like **an ice**?*	***Ice** floats.*
*I've got **a new iron**.*	*Steel is an alloy of **iron**.*
*What do the **papers** say?*	***Paper** is made from wood.*

2.16.3 Normally uncountable nouns used as countables

Many nouns which are normally uncountable can be used as countables if we refer to particular varieties. When this occurs, the noun is often preceded by an adjective (*a nice wine*) or there is some kind of specification (*a wine of high quality*):

*This region produces **an excellent wine**.* (i.e. a kind of wine which ...)
*Kalamata produces some of the best olive oil in the world; it's **an oil** of very high quality.* (i.e. a kind of oil which...)
*The North Sea produces **a light oil** which is highly prized in the oil industry.*

Normally uncountable nouns used exceptionally as countables can also occur in the plural:

*This region produces **some awful wines** as well as good ones.*
*I go out in **all weathers**.*

Note also many words for drinks, which are uncountable when we think of them as substances:

***Beer/coffee/tea** is expensive these days.*

However, we can sometimes use *a/an* to mean e.g. *a glass of*, etc. [> 2.18] or numbers in front of these words, or we can make them plural, for example when we are ordering in a restaurant:

__A__ (or __One__) __beer__, please. __Two teas__ and __four coffees__, please.

2.16.4 Nouns which can refer to something specific or general

e.g. *an education/education, a light/light, a noise/noise.*

As **countables**, these nouns refer to something specific (*He has had __a good education__. I need __a light__ by my bed*). As **uncountables**, the reference is general (*Standards of __education__ are falling. __Light__ travels faster than __sound__*).

countable ('specific')	**uncountable** ('general')
__A good education__ is expensive.	*__Education__ should be free.*
Try not to make __a noise__.	*__Noise__ is a kind of pollution.*

Some countable nouns like this can be plural (*a light/lights, a noise/noises*). Other nouns (*education, knowledge*) cannot be plural; as countables they often have some kind of qualification (*a classical education, a good knowledge of English*).

2.16.5 Nouns ending in '-ing'

e.g. *a drawing/drawing, a painting/painting, a reading/reading.*

-ing forms are generally uncountable [> 16.39.1], but a few can refer to a specific thing or event.

countable ('specific')	**uncountable** ('general')
Are these __drawings__ by Goya?	*I'm no good at __drawing__.*
He has __a painting__ by Hockney.	*__Painting__ is my hobby.*
She gave __a reading__ of her poems.	*__Reading__ is taught early.*

A few *-ing* forms (*a thrashing, a wedding*) are only countable.

2.16.6 Selected uncountable nouns and their countable equivalents

Some uncountables cannot be used as countables to refer to a single item or example. A quite different word must be used:

uncountable	**equivalent countable**
bread	*a loaf*
clothing	*a garment*
laughter	*a laugh*
luggage	*a case, a bag*
poetry	*a poem*
money	*a coin, a note*
work [but > 2.31, 2.33]	*a job*

Nouns for *animals* are countable; nouns for *meat* are uncountable: *a cow/beef, a deer/venison, a pig/pork, a sheep/mutton.*

2.17 Nouns not normally countable in English

A number of nouns which are countable in other languages (and are therefore used in the singular and plural in those languages) are usually uncountable in English (and therefore not normally used with *a/an* or in the plural). A few common examples are: *baggage, furniture, information, macaroni, machinery, spaghetti* [> App 4]:

We bought (some) ***new furniture*** *for our living room recently.*
I'd like ***some information*** *please.*

2.18 Partitives: nouns which refer to part of a whole

We can refer to a single item (*a loaf of bread*), a part of a whole (*a slice of bread*) or a collection of items (*a packet of biscuits*) by means of **partitives**. Partitives are useful when we want to refer to specific pieces of an **uncountable** substance, or to a limited number of **countable** items. They can be singular (*a piece of paper; a box of matches*) or plural (*two pieces of paper; two boxes of matches*) and are followed by *of* when used before a noun. The most useful are:

2.18.1 General partitives

Words such as *piece* and (less formal) *bit* can be used with a large number of uncountables (concrete or abstract):

singular: *a piece of/bit of chalk/cloth/information/meat/plastic.*
plural: *pieces of/bits of chalk/cloth/information/meat/plastic.*

2.18.2 Specific partitives

Here is a brief summary, but [> App 5] for more examples:

Single items or amounts:

a ball of string; a bar of chocolate; a cube of ice;
a lump of sugar; a sheet of paper; a slice of bread.

A few of these can be re-expressed as compounds:
e.g. *a sugar lump, ice cubes.*

'Containers' used as partitives:

a bag of flour; a box of matches; a cup of coffee; a jar of jam;
a packet of biscuits; a pot of tea; a tube of toothpaste.

Most of these can be re-expressed as compounds: e.g. *a jam-jar, a matchbox, a teapot*, to describe the container itself. Thus *a teapot* describes the container (which may be full or empty), while *a pot of tea* describes a pot with tea in it [> 2.10.7].

Small quantities:	*a drop of water; a pinch of salt.*
Measures:	*a kilo of sugar; a metre of cloth.*
'a game of':	*a game of football.*
Abstract concepts:	*a period of calm; a spell of work.*
Types and species:	*a make of car; a sort of cake.*
'a pair of':	*a pair of gloves; a pair of jeans.* [> App 5.8]

2.19 Collective nouns followed by 'of'

These describe groups (or 'collections') of people or things:

People:	*an army of soldiers; a board of directors.*
Animals, birds, insects:	*a flock of birds/sheep; a swarm of bees.*
Plants and fruit:	*a bunch of flowers; a crop of apples.*
Things:	*a set of cutlery; a suit of clothes.*

For more examples [> App 6]. For other collective nouns [> 2.28].

Number (singular and plural)

2.20 Singular and plural forms of nouns

regular spelling		**singular**	**plural**	
-s after most nouns:		*cat*	*cats*	
		tub	*tubs*	
-es after nouns ending in	*-o*:	*potato*	*potatoes*	[> 2.25]
	-s:	*class*	*classes*	
	-x:	*box*	*boxes*	
	-ch:	*watch*	*watches*	
	-sh:	*bush*	*bushes*	
consonant + *-y* becomes	*-ies*:	*country*	*countries*	
Note that vowel +,*-y* adds *-s*:	*-ay*:	*day*	*days*	
	-ey:	*key*	*keys*	
	-oy:	*boy*	*boys*	
	-uy:	*guy*	*guys*	
Proper nouns ending in *-y* add *-s* in the plural:				
		Fry	*the Frys*	[> 2.36]
		Kennedy	*the Kennedys*	
irregular spelling				
Some endings in *-f*/*-fe* take	*-ves*:	*wife*	*wives*	[> 2.23]
Internal vowel change:		*man*	*men*	[> 2.26]
Nouns with plurals in	*-en*:	*ox*	*oxen*	[> 2.26]
No change:		*sheep*	*sheep*	[> 2.27]
Foreign plurals, e.g		*analysis*	*analyses*	[> 2.34]

2.21 Pronunciation of nouns with regular plurals

The rules for pronunciation are the same as those for the 3rd person simple present of regular verbs [> 9.7].

/s/ after	/f/:	*chiefs, coughs, proofs* [> 2.23]
	/k/:	*cakes, forks, knocks*
	/p/:	*drops, taps, tapes*
	/t/:	*pets, pockets, skirts*
	/θ/:	*depths, months, myths* [> 2.22]
/z/ after	/b/:	*tubs, tubes, verbs*
	/d/:	*friends, hands, roads*
	/g/:	*bags, dogs, legs*
	/l/:	*bells, tables, walls*
	/m/:	*arms, dreams, names*
	/n/:	*lessons, pens, spoons*
	/ŋ/:	*songs, stings, tongues*
	vowel + /r/:	*chairs, doors, workers*
	vowel sounds:	*eyes, ways, windows*

Note that *e* is not pronounced in the categories above when the plural ends in *-es*: e.g. *cakes, clothes, stones, tapes, tubes.*

Nouns ending in the following take an extra syllable pronounced /ɪz/:

/z/:	*mazes, noises, noses*	/ʃ/:	*bushes, crashes, dishes*
/dʒ/:	*bridges, oranges, pages*	/tʃ/:	*matches, patches, speeches*
/s/:	*buses, classes, masses*	/ks/:	*axes, boxes, taxes*

2.22 Nouns with regular spelling/irregular pronunciation

The ending of the following nouns is pronounced /z/ in the plural: *baths, mouths, oaths, paths, truths, wreaths, youths.*
The plural of *house (houses)* is pronounced /hauzɪz/.

2.23 Nouns with irregular pronunciation and spelling

The following thirteen nouns with spellings ending in *-f* or *-fe* (pronounced /f/) in the singular, are all spelt with *-ves* in the plural (pronounced /vz/): *calf/calves, elf/elves, half/halves, knife/knives, leaf/leaves, life/lives, loaf/loaves, self/selves, sheaf/sheaves, shelf/shelves, thief/thieves, wife/wives, wolf/wolves.*

The following nouns have regular and irregular plural pronunciation and spellings:
dwarf/dwarfs or *dwarves, hoof/hoofs* or *hooves, scarf/scarfs* or *scarves, wharf/wharfs* or *wharves*.

But note the following nouns which have regular spelling, but both regular and irregular pronunciation in the plural (/fs/ or /vs/): *handkerchief/handkerchiefs, roof/roofs.*

2.24 Nouns with plurals ending in -'s

There are a few instances where *'s* is commonly used to form a plural:
– after letters: *Watch your p's and q's.*

After the following, the plural is normally formed with the addition of *s*, but *'s* also occurs:
– years: *the l890s* or *1890's, the 1980s* or *1980's.*
– abbreviations: *VIPs* or *VIP's (Very Important Persons), MPs* or *MP's (Members of Parliament)*. Note the final *s* is a small letter.

2.25 The plural of nouns ending in -o

Many commonly used nouns (*echo, hero, potato, tomato*) ending in *-o* are spelt *-oes* in the plural. The following are spelt with *-oes* or *-os*: *buffalo, cargo, commando, grotto, halo, mosquito, tornado, volcano.* All these endings are pronounced /əʊz/.

The following have plurals spelt with *-os*:
– nouns ending in vowel + *-o* or *double o*: *bamboos, folios, kangaroos, oratorios, radios, studios, videos, zoos.*
– abbreviations: *kilos* (for *kilograms*); *photos* (for *photographs*).
– Italian musical terms: e.g. *concertos, pianos, solos, sopranos.*
– proper nouns: *Eskimos, Filipinos.*

2.26 Irregular spelling: internal vowel change

The following nouns form their plurals by changing the internal vowel(s) (this is a survival from old English): *foot/feet, goose/geese, louse/lice, man/men, mouse/mice, tooth/teeth, woman/women.* Compound nouns formed with *-man* or *-woman* as a suffix form their

plurals with *-men* or *-women*: *policeman/policemen, policewoman/policewomen.* Both *-man* and *-men* in such compounds (but not *-woman/women*) are often pronounced /mən/.
Other survivals from the past are a few nouns which form their plurals with *-en*: *brother/brethren, child/children, ox/oxen. Brethren* is used in religious contexts; otherwise *brothers* is the normal plural of *brother.*

Penny can have a regular plural *pennies* when we are referring to separate coins (*ten pennies*) or a collective plural, *pence*, when we are referring to a total amount (*tenpence*).

2.27 Nouns with the same singular and plural forms

Some nouns do not change in form. These include:
- names of certain animals, birds and fish: *deer, grouse, mackerel, plaice, salmon, sheep, trout.*
  *This **sheep is** from Australia. These **sheep are** from Australia.*
- *craft* and *aircraft/hovercraft/spacecraft*:
  *The **craft was** sunk. All the **craft were** sunk.*
  (But compare: ***Arts and crafts are** part of the curriculum.*)
- certain nouns describing nationalities: e.g. *a Chinese, a Swiss, a Vietnamese* [> App 49].
  *He **is a Vietnamese**. **The Vietnamese are** noted for their cookery.*

Note that some names of fish, etc. can form a regular plural:
  Herrings were (or ***Herring were***) *once very plentiful.*
Fish is the normal plural of *fish* (singular), but *fishes* can also be used, especially to refer to species of fish.
  *My goldfish **has** died.* (one) *My goldfish **have** died.* (more than one)
  *You'll see many kinds of **fish(es)** in the fish market.*

2.28 Collective noun + singular or plural verb

2.28.1 Collective nouns which have plural forms

Some collective nouns such as *audience, class, club, committee, company, congregation, council, crew, crowd, family, gang, government, group, jury, mob, staff, team* and *union* can be used with singular or plural verbs. They are singular and can combine with the relative pronouns *which/that* and be replaced by *it* when we think of them in an impersonal fashion, i.e. as a whole group:
  *The present **government, which hasn't** been in power long, **is trying** to control inflation. **It isn't having** much success.*
They are plural and can combine with *who* and be replaced by *they* or *them* when we think of them in a more personal way, i.e. as the individuals that make up the group:
  *The **government, who are looking** for a quick victory, **are calling** for a general election soon. **They expect** to be re-elected. A lot of people are giving **them** their support.*
These collective nouns can also have regular plural forms:
  ***Governments** in all countries **are trying** to control inflation.*
For plural nouns in a collective sense (e.g. *the workers*) [> 3.19.4].
Some proper nouns (e.g. football teams) can be used as collectives:
  ***Arsenal is/are** playing away on Saturday.*

2.28.2 Collective nouns which do not have plural forms

The following collective nouns have no regular plural but can be followed by a singular or plural verb: *the aristocracy, the gentry, the proletariat, the majority, the minority, the public, the youth of today:*

Give the public what ***it wants/they want****.*

Offspring has no plural form but can be followed by a singular verb to refer to one or a plural verb to refer to more than one:

Her ***offspring is*** *like her in every respect.* (one child)
Her ***offspring are*** *like her in every respect.* (more than one child)

The youth of today (= all young people) should not be confused with *a/the youth* (= a/the young man), which has a regular plural *youths*:

The youth of today is/are *better off than we used to be.*
The witness said he saw ***a youth/five youths*** *outside the shop.*

Youth (= a time of life) is used with singular verbs:

Youth is *the time for action;* ***age is*** *the time for repose.*

2.29 Collective noun + plural verb

The following collective nouns must be followed by a plural verb; they do not have plural forms: *cattle, the clergy, the military, people, the police, swine, vermin:*

Some people are *never satisfied.*
The police/the military have *surrounded the building.*

People should not be confused with *a/the people*, meaning 'nation' or 'tribe', which is countable:

The British are ***a sea-faring people****.*
The English-speaking ***peoples*** *share a common language.*

For *the* + adjective + plural verb (e.g. *the blind*) [> 6.12.2].

2.30 Nouns with a plural form + singular verb

The following nouns, though plural in form, are always followed by a verb in the singular:

- the noun *news*, as in: ***The news*** *on TV* ***is*** *always depressing.*
- games, such as *billiards, bowls, darts, dominoes:*
  Billiards is *becoming more and more popular.*
- names of cities such as *Athens, Brussels, Naples:*
  Athens has *grown rapidly in the past decade.*

2.31 Nouns with a plural form + singular or plural verb

The following nouns ending in *-ics* take a singular verb: *athletics, gymnastics, linguistics, mathematics* and *physics*:

Mathematics is *a compulsory subject at school.*

However, some words ending in *-ics*, such as *acoustics, economics, ethics, phonetics* and *statistics* take a singular or plural verb. When the reference is to an academic subject (e.g. *acoustics* = the scientific study of sound) then the verb must be singular:

Acoustics is *a branch of physics.*

When the reference is specific, (e.g. *acoustics* = sound quality) then the verb must be plural:

The acoustics in the Festival Hall are *extremely good.*

Plural-form nouns describing illnesses [> 3.15] have a singular verb:
German measles is a dangerous disease for pregnant women.
However, a plural verb is sometimes possible:
***Mumps are** (or **is**) fairly rare in adults.*

Some plural-form nouns can be regarded as a single unit (+ verb in the singular) or collective (+ verb in the plural). Examples are: *barracks, bellows, crossroads, gallows, gasworks, headquarters, kennels, series, species* and *works* (= factory).
- single unit: ***This species** of rose **is** very rare.*
- more than one: ***There are thousands of species** of butterflies.*

The word *means* (= a way to an end) is followed by a singular or plural verb, depending on the word used before it:
***All means have** been used to get him to change his mind.*
***One means is** still to be tried.*

2.32 Nouns with a plural form + plural verb

Nouns with a plural form only (+ plural verb) are:
- nouns which can combine with *a pair of* [> App 5.8]:
  ***My trousers are** torn.*
  Used with *a pair of*, these words must have a singular verb:
  ***A pair of glasses costs** quite a lot these days.*
  We cannot normally use numbers in front of these words, but we can say *two*, etc. *pairs of*:
  ***Two pairs of your trousers are** still at the cleaner's.*
  Some of these nouns can have a singular form when used in compounds: e.g. *pyjama top, trouser leg:*
  *Where did I put my **pyjama top**?*
- a few words which occur only in the plural and are followed by a plural verb. Some of these are: *Antipodes, belongings, brains* (= intellect), *clothes, congratulations, earnings, goods, greens* (= green vegetables), *lodgings, looks* (= good looks), *means* (= money or material possessions), *oats, odds* (in betting), *outskirts, particulars, quarters* (= accommodation), *remains, riches, stairs, suds, surroundings, thanks, tropics:*
  *All my **belongings are** in this bag.*

2.33 Nouns with different singular and plural meanings

Some nouns have different meanings in the singular and plural. Typical examples: *air/airs, ash/ashes, content/contents, custom/customs, damage/damages, drawer/drawers, fund/funds, glass/glasses, look/looks, manner/manners, minute/minutes, pain/pains, scale/scales, saving/savings, spectacle/spectacles, step/steps, work/works.* Sometimes the meanings are far apart (*air/airs*), sometimes they are quite close (*fund/funds*).
***One small step** for man; one giant leap for mankind.*
*You can only reach that cupboard with **a pair of steps**.*

Of course, the countable nouns in the above list have their own plurals: *dirty looks, five minutes, sharp pains, two steps,* etc.

2.34 Nouns with foreign plurals

There is a natural tendency to make all nouns conform to the regular rules for the pronunciation and spelling of English plurals. The more commonly a noun is used, the more likely this is to happen. Some native English speakers avoid foreign plurals in everyday speech and use them only in scientific and technical contexts.

2.34.1 Nouns of foreign origin with anglicized plurals, e.g.

album/albums, apparatus/apparatuses, genius/geniuses.

2.34.2 Nouns with both foreign and anglicized plurals, e.g.

-us: *cactus/cacti/cactuses;* ***-a:*** *antenna/antennae/antennas;*
-ex/ix: *index/indices/indexes, appendix/appendices/appendixes;*
-um: *medium/media/mediums;* ***-on:*** *automaton/automata/automatons;*
-eu/-eau: *adieu/adieux/adieus, plateau/plateaus/plateaux* (/z/).

Alternative plurals can have different meanings: e.g. *antennae* is a biological term; *antennas* can describe e.g. radio aerials.

2.34.3 Nouns with foreign plurals only, e.g.

-us: *alumnus/alumni;* ***-a:*** *alumna/alumnae;* ***-um:*** *stratum/strata;*
-is: *analysis/analyses;* ***-on:*** *criterion/criteria.*

Media + singular or plural verb is used to refer to the press, TV, etc.; *data* is used with a singular or plural verb; *agenda* is a foreign plural used in the singular in English with a regular plural, *agendas*.

2.35 Compound nouns and their plurals

2.35.1 Plural mainly in the last element

The tendency is to:

- put a plural ending (*-s, -es*, etc.) on the second noun in noun + noun combinations: *boy**friends**, flower **shops**, match**boxes***, etc. and in gerund + noun combinations: *frying **pans***.
- put a plural ending on the noun: *on**lookers**, **lookers**-on, **passers**-by.*
- put a plural ending on the last word when no noun is present: *break**downs**, forget-me-**nots**, grown-**ups**, lay-**offs***, etc.

2.35.2 Plural in the first element in some compounds

*attorney general/**attorneys** general, court-martial/**courts**-martial, man-of-war/**men**-of-war, mother-in-law/**mothers**-in-law* (but ***in-laws*** in general references: *Our **in-laws** are staying with us*); *notary public/**notaries** public, spoonful/**spoonsful*** (or ***spoonfuls***).

2.35.3 Plural in the first and last element

When the first element is *man* or *woman*, then both elements change: *man student/**men** student**s**; woman student/**women** student**s***, but note compounds with *lady*: *lady friend/lady **friends***.
Other compounds with *man* and *woman* form their plurals only in the second word: *man-**eaters**, man**holes**, woman-**haters***, etc. [> 2.10.9].

2.36 The plural of proper nouns

Plural surnames occur when we refer to families:
\+ *-s*: ***The Atkinsons/The Frys*** *are coming to dinner.*
\+ *-es*: *They're forever trying to keep up with **the Joneses**.*

Other examples with proper nouns are:

*There are **three Janes** and **two Harrys** in our family.*
*We've had **two very cold Januarys** in a row.* [not *-ies* > 2.20]

We do not add *-(e)s* to the spelling where this would suggest a false pronunciation: *three King Louis, the Dumas, father and son.*

2.37 Numbers and their plurals [> App 47]

2.37.1 Dozen(s), hundred(s), etc.

The word *dozen* and numbers do not add *-s* when they are used in front of plural nouns: *two dozen eggs, three hundred men, ten thousand pounds*, etc. They add *-s* before *of* (i.e. when the number is not specified):

***Hundreds of people** are going to the demonstration.*
***Thousands of pounds** have been spent on the new hospital.*
*I said it was a secret but she's told **dozens of people**.*

2.37.2 'A whole amount'

When the reference is to 'a whole amount' a plural subject is followed by a singular verb, with reference to:

Duration: ***Three weeks is** a long time to wait for an answer.*
Money: ***Two hundred pounds is** a lot to spend on a dress.*
Distance: ***Forty miles is** a long way to walk in a day.*

2.38 Two nouns joined by 'and'

Nouns that commonly go together such as *bacon and eggs, bread and butter, cheese and wine, fish and chips, lemon and oil, tripe and onions, sausage(s) and mash* are used with verbs in the singular when we think of them as a single unit. Noun combinations of this kind have a fixed order of words:

***Fish and chips is** a popular meal in Britain.*

If we think of the items as 'separate', we use a plural verb:

***Fish and chips make** a good meal.*

Gender

2.39 General information about gender

people:	*man, actor:*	*he*
	woman, actress:	*she*
	guest, student, teacher:	*he* or *she*
animals:	*bull, cow:*	*it*
things:	*chair, table:*	*it*

In many European languages the names of things, such as *book, chair, radio, table* have **gender**: that is they are classified grammatically as masculine, feminine or neuter, although very often gender doesn't relate to sex. Grammatical gender barely concerns nouns in English. It mainly concerns personal pronouns, where a distinction is drawn between e.g. *he, she* and *it*; possessive adjectives, *his, her* and *its* [> 4.1]; and relative pronouns, where a distinction is drawn between *who* and *which* [> 1.27]. The determiners [> 3.1] we use do not vary according to gender in front of nouns. We can refer to ***a*** *man,* ***a*** *woman,* ***a*** *box,* ***the*** *man,* ***the*** *woman,* ***the*** *box;* ***many*** *men,* ***many*** *women,* ***many*** *boxes.*

2.40 Identifying masculine and feminine through nouns

A few nouns are automatically replaced by masculine or feminine pronouns, or by *it*. Some of these are as follows:

2.40.1 Contrasting nouns describing people (replaceable by e.g. 'he/she')

bachelor/spinster, boy/girl, brother/sister, father/mother, gentleman/lady, grandfather/grandmother, grandson/granddaughter, husband/wife, king/queen, man/woman, monk/nun, Mr/Mrs, nephew/niece, sir/madam, son/daughter, uncle/aunt.

2.40.2 Contrasting nouns describing animals (normally replaceable by 'it')

bull/cow, cock (or *rooster*)*/hen, dog/bitch, gander/goose, pig/sow, ram/ewe, stallion/mare.*

2.40.3 '-ess' endings and other forms indicating sex/gender

A common way of indicating sex or gender is to change the ending of the masculine noun with the suffix *-ess:*
actor/actress, god/goddess, heir/heiress, host/hostess, prince/princess, steward/stewardess, waiter/waitress.
This distinction is becoming rarer so that words like *author, instructor* and *manager* are now commonly used for both sexes. Some words, such as *poetess*, are falling into disuse because they are considered disparaging by both sexes. In a few cases, *-ess* endings are used for female animals, e.g. *leopard/leopardess, lion/lioness, tiger/tigress.* Or *he-/she-* (stressed) is used as a prefix in e.g. *he-goat/she-goat*, or *wolf/she-wolf.*

Similar references can be made with other endings, etc. as well:
bridegroom/bride, hero/heroine, lad/lass, landlord/landlady, male/female, masseur/masseuse, usher/usherette, widower/widow.

2.40.4 Identifying masculine and feminine by 'man', 'woman', etc.

Certain nouns ending in *-man* refer to males: e.g. *dustman, policeman, postman, salesman.* Others, ending in *-woman*, refer to women: e.g. *policewoman, postwoman, saleswoman.* A few, such as *chairman*, can be used for men and women [> 2.10.9].

We tend to assume that words like *model* and *nurse* refer to women and words like *judge* and *wrestler* refer to men. If this is not the case and we wish to make a point of it, we can refer to a *male model* or a *male nurse*, or to a *woman judge* or a *woman wrestler.*

2.41 Identifying masculine or feminine through pronouns

With many nouns we don't know whether the person referred to is male or female until we hear the pronoun:

My accountant *says* ***he*** *is moving his office.*
My doctor *says* ***she*** *is pleased with my progress.*

This applies to nouns such as: *adult, artist, comrade, cook, cousin, darling, dear, doctor, enemy, foreigner, friend, guest, journalist, lawyer, librarian, musician, neighbour, orphan, owner, parent, passenger, person, pupil, relation, relative, scientist, singer, speaker, spouse, stranger, student, teacher, tourist, traveller, visitor, writer.*
Sometimes we can emphasize this choice by using both pronouns:
*If **a student** wants more information, **he** or **she** should apply in writing.*
However, this is becoming less acceptable. The tendency is to avoid this kind of construction by using plurals [compare > 4.40]:
***Students** who want more information should apply in writing.*

The genitive

2.42 Form of the genitive

Add *'s* to singular personal nouns:	*child*	+	*'s : child's*
Add *'s* to singular personal nouns ending in *-s*:	*actress*	+	*'s : actress's*
Add *'s* to the plural of irregular personal nouns:	*children*	+	*'s : children's*
Add *'* to the plural of personal nouns ending in *-s*:	*girls*	+	*' : girls'*
Add *'s* to some names ending in *-s*:	*James*	+	*'s : James's*

2.43 The survival of the genitive in modern English

The only 'case-form' for nouns that exists in English is the **genitive** (e.g. *man'***s**), sometimes called **the possessive case** or **the possessive form**. The *-es* genitive ending of some classes of nouns in old English has survived in the modern language as *'s* (apostrophe *s*) for some nouns in the singular and *s'* (*s* apostrophe) for some nouns in the plural, but with limited uses.

2.44 When we add 's and s'

We normally use *'s* and *s'* only for people and some living creatures [> 2.48]. The possessive appears before the noun it refers to. However, it can be used without a noun as well [> 2.51]:
*I'll go in **Frank's car** and you can go in **Alan's**.*
The simplest rule to remember is: 'add *'s* to any personal noun unless it is in the form of a plural ending in *-s* – in which case, just add an apostrophe *(')*'. In practice, this means:

2.44.1 Singular and plural common nouns and names not ending in -s

- add *'s* to singular nouns and to names not ending in *-s*:
  a child's dream; the dog's kennel; Frank's new job.
  If two names are joined by *and*, add *'s* to the second:
  John and Mary's bank balance; Scott and Amundsen's race.
- add *'s* to singular nouns ending in *-s*:
  an actress's career; a waitress's job.
- add *'s* to irregular plural nouns:
  children's games; the men's club; sheep's wool.
- add an apostrophe *(')* after the *s* of regular plurals:
  boys' school; girls' school; Cheltenham Ladies' College.

2.44.2 's with compound nouns

With compound nouns the *'s* comes after the last word:

My ***sister-in-law's*** *father is a pilot.*

The rule also applies to titles, as in: *Henry the Eighth's marriages; the Secretary of State's visit.*

Two genitives are also possible, as in:

My ***brother's neighbour's*** *sister is a nurse.*

2.44.3 The use of the apostrophe after names ending in -s

We add *'s* to names ending in *-s*: *Charles's address; Doris's party.* However, we can sometimes use *'* or *'s*: *St James'* (or *St James's*) *Park; Mr Jones'* (or *Jones's*) *car; St Thomas'* (or *St Thomas's*) *Hospital*. No matter how we write the genitive in such cases, we normally pronounce it as /ɪz/. With some (especially famous) names ending in *-s* we normally add an apostrophe after the *-s* (pronounced /s/ or /ɪz/: *Keats' works; Yeats' poetry.*

We can show possession in the plural forms of names ending in *-s* by adding an apostrophe at the end: *the Joneses' houses*, etc.

With ancient Greek names we add an apostrophe after the *-s*, but there is no change in pronunciation, *Archimedes'* being pronounced the same as *Archimedes: Archimedes' Principle.*

Initials can be followed by *'s* when the reference is singular: *an MP's salary* (= a Member of Parliament's salary), or *s'* when the reference is plural: *MPs' salaries* [> 2.24].

2.45 The pronunciation of 's and s'

The pronunciation of *'s* and *s'* depends on the sound that precedes them and follows the same rules as for plural nouns [> 2.21]: e.g.

/s/: *Geoff's hat; Jack's job; a month's salary; Pat's handbag*
/z/: *Ben's opinion; Bill's place; Bob's house; the workers' club*
/ɪz/: *an actress's career; the boss's office; Mrs Page's jam*

2.46 The use of 's/s' for purposes other than possession

While the genitive is generally associated with possession (usually answering the question *Whose ...?*), apostrophe *s* serves other purposes as well, for example:

Regular use:	*Father's chair* (= the one he usually sits on)
Relationship:	*Angela's son* (i.e. Angela has a son)
+ *favourite*:	*Fish and chips is John's favourite dish.*
Actions:	*Scott's journey* (i.e. the journey Scott made)
Purpose:	*A girls' school* (= a school for girls)
Characteristics:	*John's stammer* (i.e. John has a stammer)
Others:	*Building oil rigs is a man's work.* (= suitable for)
	Mozart is a composer's composer. (= appreciated by)

2.47 The use of 's and s' compared with the use of 'of'

The *'s* construction is not possible in e.g. *the key of the door* or *the leg of the table* because we do not normally use *'s* with non-living things [> 2.10.1, 2.44]. When *-s* indicates ownership, every *'s* construction can have an *of* equivalent, but not every *of*-construction can have an *'s* equivalent. So:

a man's voice can be expressed as *the voice of a man*
Keats' poetry can be expressed as *the poetry of Keats*

And instead of *the leg of the table*, we can say *the table-leg*

2.48 The use of 's and s' with living things

We may use *'s* or *s'* after:

Personal names: *Gus's Restaurant; Jones's car.*
Personal nouns: *the doctor's surgery; man's future.*
Indefinite pronouns: *anyone's guess; someone's responsibility.*
Collective nouns: *the army's advance; the committee's decision.*
'Higher animals': *the horse's stable; the horses' stables.*
Some 'lower animals': *an ant's nest; a bee's sting.*

When we refer to material which is produced or made by a living animal, *'s* is generally required (stress on first word): *a 'bird's nest, 'cow's milk, 'lamb's wool*, etc. Where the source of a material is an animal that has been slaughtered, *'s* is not generally used (varied stress): *'beef 'broth, 'cowhide, a 'ham sandwich, 'sheepskin*, etc.

2.49 The use of 's and s' with non-living things

We may use *'s/s'* or the *of*-construction with the following:

Geographical reference: *America's policy; Hong Kong's future.*
Institutional reference: *the European Economic Community's exports.*

's or *s'* are normally used with the following:

Place noun + superlative: *New York's tallest skyscraper.*
Churches and cathedrals: *St Paul's Church; St Stephen's Cathedral.*
Time references: *a day's work; an hour's delay; a month's salary; today's TV; a year's absence; a week or two's time; two days' journey.*
'Money's worth': *twenty dollars' worth of gasoline.*
Fixed expressions: *(keep someone) at arm's length; (be) at death's door; the earth's surface; for goodness' sake; (to) one's heart's content; journey's end; the ship's company.*

An *'s* is sometimes used with reference to cars, planes and ships: *the car's exhaust, the plane's engines, the ship's propeller.*

We can only learn from experience when to use *'s* with non-living things. When in doubt, it is best to use the *of*-construction.

2.50 The use of the 'of-construction' to connect two nouns

We normally use the *of*-construction (not *'s/s'*) when referring to:

Things (where a compound noun [> 2.10.1] is not available): *the book of the film; the shade of a tree.*
Parts of things: *the bottom/top/side/inside of the box.*
Abstract reference: *the cost of living; the price of success.*

The *of*-construction can be used to suggest *be/behave/look like* in e.g. *an angel of a child; that fool of a ticket-inspector*. We also use this construction when the noun in the *of*-phrase is modified by an additional phrase or clause:

Can't you look at ***the book of the boy behind you****?*
This was given to me by ***the colleague of a friend of mine****.*

The *of*-construction can be used with plural nouns to avoid ambiguity. *The advice of the specialists* may be preferable to *the specialists' advice* (more than one specialist), which could be confused with *the specialist's advice* (only one specialist).

A noun + *of* can sometimes be used in place of an infinitive:

It's forbidden ***to remove books*** *from this reference library.*
The removal of books *from this reference library is forbidden.*

2.51 Omission of the noun after 's and s'

The *'s/s'* construction can be used on its own when we refer to:

– a noun that is implied:
We need a ladder. We can borrow ***our neighbour's****.*
– where someone lives:
I'm staying ***at my aunt's****. I'm a guest* ***at the Watsons'****.*
– shops and businesses: e.g. *the butcher's, the hairdresser's:*
Would you mind going to ***the chemist's*** *for me?*
– medical practitioners: e.g. *the dentist's, the doctor's:*
I've got an appointment ***at the dentist's*** *at 11.15.*

When we refer to well-known stores (e.g. *Macys, Harrods*), an apostrophe before the *s* is optional, but is usually omitted:

You can't go to London without visiting ***Harrods/Harrod's****.*

When we refer to well-known restaurants by the name of the owner or founder (e.g. *Langan's, Scott's*) *'s* is included.
Churches and colleges (often named after saints) are frequently referred to in the same way, always with *'s*:

They were married in ***St Bartholomew's****.*

2.52 The double genitive

The *'s* construction can be used after the *of*-construction in: e.g. *a friend of my father's; a play of Shakespeare's* (= one of my father's friends; one of Shakespeare's plays). This can happen because we usually put only one determiner in front of a noun [> 3.4], so, for example, we would not use *this* and *my* together in front of e.g. *son*. Instead, we have to say *this son of mine*. And note other possessive pronouns: *a friend of yours; a cousin of hers*, etc. We can use *a, this, that, these, those, some, any, no*, etc. in front of the noun, but not *the*:

Isn't Frank Byers ***a friend of yours****?*

He's a friend of mine is more common than *He is my friend*, which implies he is my special or only friend. *He's no friend of mine* can mean 'I don't know him' or 'He's my enemy'.
The use of demonstratives [> 4.32–36] often suggests criticism:

That silly uncle of yours *has told me the same joke five times.*

3 Articles

General information about 'a/an', 'the' and the zero article

3.1 Determiners: what they are and what they do

We use a number of words in front of common nouns (or adjective + common noun) which we call **determiners** because they affect (or 'determine') the meaning of the noun. Determiners make it clear, for example, which particular thing(s) we are referring to or how much of a substance we are talking about. Singular countable nouns must normally have a determiner in front of them. There are two classes:

1 Words which help us to **classify** or **identify**:

- **indefinite article**: *I bought **a** new shirt yesterday.*
(but it's not necessary to say which)
- **definite article**: ***The** shirt I am wearing is new.*
(i.e. I am telling you which)
- **demonstratives** [> 4.32]: *I bought **this/that** shirt yesterday.*
(i.e. the one I am showing you)
- **possessives** [> 4.19]: *Do you like **my** new shirt?*
(i.e. the one that belongs to me)

2 Words which enable us to indicate **quantity**:

- **numbers** [> App 47]: *I bought **two** new shirts yesterday.*
(i.e. that's how many I bought)
- **quantifiers** [> 5.1]: *I did**n't** buy **many** new shirts yesterday.*
(i.e. not a great number)
*There was**n't much** material in the shop.*
(i.e. not a great quantity)

Proper nouns [> 2.13] do not generally require identification, but for place names, etc. [> 3.22, 3.31]:

__John__ is flying to __Helsinki__ on __Tuesday.__

3.2 Indefinite ('a/an'), definite ('the'), or zero (Ø)?

In most European languages there are rules about when to use (or not to use) indefinite and definite articles. These rules generally depend on the gender of the noun and on whether it is singular or plural. In English, gender does not affect our choice [> 2.39], but whether a word is singular or plural may do so.

We often use no article at all in English. This non-use of the article is so important that we give it a name, **the zero article** [> 3.24]. The problems of choice can be summarized as follows:

- whether to use *a/an* or *the*.
- whether to use *a/an* or nothing (*zero*).
- whether to use *the* or nothing (*zero*).

In addition we have to decide:
- whether to use *zero* or *some*.
- whether to use *the* or *some*.

Because articles don't have gender or special plural forms in English, their use seems easy to learners at first. However, choice is complicated by three factors:
- whether a noun is countable or uncountable.
- whether we are making general statements.
- whether we are referring to something the listener or reader can positively identify or not.

3.3 'A/an', 'the' or zero before countables and uncountables

The distinction between countable and uncountable nouns [> 2.14] must be clearly understood because it affects our choice of article. The rules for the use of *a/an, the* and *zero* + countable or uncountable can be summarized as follows:

a/an is used only in front of a singular countable:		*a hat*
the can be used in front of	a singular countable:	*the hat*
	a plural countable:	*the hats*
	an uncountable:	*the water*
zero: we often use no article in front of	a plural countable:	*hats*
	an uncountable:	*water*

Putting it in another way, we can use:

a/an or *the* +	singular countable:	*a hat – the hat*
the or *zero* +	plural countable:	*the hats – hats*
the or *zero* +	uncountable:	*the water – water*

Examples of **a singular countable** preceded by:

a: *The man who lives next door is* ***a doctor****.*
an: *My sister is* ***an architect****.*
the: ***The architect*** *who designed this block won a prize.*

Examples of **a plural countable** preceded by:

zero: *The people who work next door* ***are architects****.*
the: ***The architects*** *who designed this block won a prize.*

Examples of **an uncountable** preceded by:

zero: ***Sugar*** *is bad for you.*
the: ***The sugar*** *you bought yesterday has got damp.*

3.4 Word order and determiners

We usually put only one determiner in front of a noun or noun phrase; and the determiner is nearly always the first word in a noun phrase: e.g. *a new pen*. We can never use two of the following before a noun: *a, the, this, that, these, those, my, your, his, her, Susan's,* etc.
So, for example, we can say:

the pen or *my pen*

but we cannot use *the* and *my* together in front of a noun or noun phrase. Some words (called **pre-determiners**) can come before articles and other determiners: for example *both* and *all* [> 5.18].

The indefinite article: 'a/an'

3.5 Form and use of 'a/an', zero article and 'some'

a/an and *zero* for classification/identification [> 3.9]

singular	**plural**	**singular**	**plural**
a book	*books*	*It's a book.*	*They're books.*
an egg	*eggs*	*It's an egg.*	*They're eggs.*

a/an and *some* referring to quantity [> 3.10]

a book	*some books*	*I've got a book.*	*I've got some books.*
an egg	*some eggs*	*I've got an egg.*	*I've got some eggs.*

3.6 How we refer to singular and plural

To **classify** or **identify** something, we can say:
It's ***a book****.* (*a/an* + singular noun)
The plural of this is:
They're ***books****.* (*zero* + plural noun)

To refer to **quantity**, we can say:
I've got ***a book****.* (*a/an* + singular noun)
In the plural, when the exact number is not important, we can use quantifiers like *some, a few, a lot of* [> 5.2]. *Some/any* [> 5.10] are the commonest of these and can be said to be the plural of *a/an* when we are referring to unspecified number:
I've got ***some books****.* (*some* + plural noun)

3.7 The pronunciation of 'a' and 'an'

A (pronounced /ə/ in fluent speech) is used before consonant sounds (not just consonant letters); *an* /ən/ is used before vowel sounds (not just words beginning with the vowel letters, *a, e, i, o, u*). This can be seen when we use *a* or *an* with the alphabet (e.g. *This is* ***a U****. This is* ***an H****.*):

(This is) a B, C, D, G, J, K, P, Q, T, U, V, W, Y, Z.
(This is) an A, E, F, H, I, L, M, N, O, R, S, X.

Compare: *a fire* but *an F* — *a noise* but *an N*
a house but *an H* — *a radio* but *an R*
a liar but *an L* — *a sound* but *an S*
a man but *an M* — *a xylophone* but *an X*

an umbrella but *a uniform*
an unusual case but *a union*
a year, a university, a European, but *an eye, an ear*

a hall but *an hour* (*h* not pronounced,
a hot dinner but *an honour* see below)

A few words beginning with *h* may be preceded by *a* or *an* at the discretion of the speaker: e.g. *a hotel, a historian* or *an hotel, an historian.* If such words are used with *an*, then *h* is not pronounced or is pronounced softly. *H* is not pronounced at all in a few words: e.g. *an heir, an honest man, an honour, an hour.*

Some common abbreviations (depending on their first letter) are preceded by *a*: *a B.A.* (a Bachelor of Arts), or by *an*: *an I.Q.* (an Intelligence Quotient).

The pronunciation /eɪ/ instead of /ə/ for *a* is often used when we are speaking with special emphasis, with or without a pause:

He still refers to his record-player as 'a /eɪ/ gramophone'.

Many native speakers disapprove of the strong pronunciation of *a*, commonly heard in the language of e.g. broadcasters, because it sounds unnatural.

3.8 Basic uses of 'a/an'

There is no difference in meaning between *a* and *an*. When using *a/an* we must always bear in mind two basic facts:

1 *A/an* has an indefinite meaning, (i.e. the person, animal or thing referred to may be not known to the listener or reader, so *a/an* has the sense of *any* or *I can't/won't tell you which*, or *it doesn't matter which*).

2 *A/an* can combine only with a singular countable noun.

These two facts underlie all uses of *a/an*. Some of the most important of these uses are discussed in the sections that follow.

3.9 Classification: 'a/an' to mean 'an example of that class'

3.9.1 Classification: general statements and descriptive labels

When we say *a rose is a flower*, we mean that *a rose* is an example of a class of items we call *flowers*; *a daffodil* is another example; *a daisy* is another example, and so on. We use *a/an* in this way when we wish to **classify** people, animals or things. We can classify them in two ways:

1 By means of **general statements**:

***An architect** is a person who designs buildings.*
***A clever politician** never promises too much.*

2 By means of **labels** (*a/an* + noun after the verb *be*):

*Andrew Bright is **an architect**.*

3.9.2 Classification by means of general statements

General statements with *a/an* often take the form of **definitions**:

***A cat** is a domestic animal.*

Definitions of this kind are possible because we can easily think of one cat at a time. If we make general statements with *cats*, we are referring to the whole species, not one example, but the meaning is the same [> 3.19.1, 3.26.1]:

***Cats** are domestic animals.*

Many uncountable nouns can be used after *a/an* when we are referring to 'an example of that class' [> 2.16.3]:

*This is **a very good coffee**. Is it Brazilian?*

3.9.3 Classification by means of descriptive labels [compare > 3.19.1]

We often wish to classify people in terms of the work they do, where they come from, etc. In English (unlike many other European languages) we need to use *a/an* when we are, as it were, attaching labels to people with regard to: e.g.

Origins: *He's **a Frenchman/an American**.* [> App 49]
Occupation: *She's **a doctor**./He's **an electrician**.*
Religion: *She's **a Catholic**./He's **an Anglican**.*
Politics: *He's **a Socialist/a Republican**.*

The plurals would be: *They're Frenchmen/doctors*, etc. Adjectival equivalents (where they exist) can be used in place of nouns for all the above examples except occupation:

*He's **European/French/Catholic/Socialist**.* But:
*What does he do? – He's **a taxi-driver**.*

We need *a/an* with any kind of 'labelling': e.g.
- with nouns: *You're **an angel/a saint/a wonder**.*
- with adjective + noun: *You're **a good girl/a real angel**.*

Things, animals, etc. can also be classified with *a/an*:
Objects: *It's **a (kind of/sort of/type of) bottle-opener**.*
Insects: *It's **a (kind of/sort of/type of) beetle**.*
Plants: *It's **a (kind of/sort of/type of) rose**.*

A kind of, etc. is more specific when used with reference to things, etc. than when it is used for people:

*I'm **a kind of (sort of/type of) engineer**.*
(= That's the nearest I can come to describing my job.)
*It's **a kind of (sort of/type of) beetle**.*
(= It's a member of a particular class of beetle.)

3.9.4 The uses of 'a/an' to classify people, etc. [> 2.13.1]

A/an can be used freely to refer to 'an example of that class'. We can use *He's/It's a* + name for 'tangible examples': *He's a Forsyte; It's a Picasso; It's a Dickens novel.* Other examples are: *a Brecht play; a Laura Ashley dress; a Shakespeare sonnet; a Smith and Wesson revolver; a Titian; a Wren church.* [compare > 3.27.4]

3.9.5 The use of 'a/an' to refer to 'a certain person'

A/an can be used before titles (*Mr, Mrs, Miss*, etc.) with the sense of 'a certain person whom I don't know':

***A Mr Wingate** phoned and left a message for you.*
***A Mrs Tadley** is waiting to see you.*

The phrase *a certain*, to refer to people whose identity is not yet known, is common in fables and folk stories:

*Many years ago **a certain merchant** arrived in Baghdad.*

3.10 Quantity: the use of 'a/an' to mean 'only one'

3.10.1 The use of 'a/an' with reference to quantity

The most common use of *a/an* is in the sense of 'only one' when we are not specifying any particular person or thing:

*I'd like **an apple**.* (i.e. only one; it doesn't matter which)

When we express this in the plural, we use *some* or *any* [> 5.10]:

*I'd like **some apples**./I don't want **any apples**.* [compare > 3.28.8]

For *a/an* + uncountable to refer to 'only one' [> 2.16.3, 3.9.2].

3.10.2 The use of 'a/an' when something is mentioned for the first time

A/an is used before a countable noun mentioned for the first time: the speaker assumes the listener does not know what is referred to:

I looked up and saw ***a plane***. (Mentioned for the first time – you don't know which plane I mean.) ***The plane*** *flew low over the trees.* (You now know exactly which plane I mean and the plane is, in that sense, identified.) [> 3.20.1]

This rule governing the choice between definite and indefinite article is common in European languages.

3.11 The difference between 'a/an' and 'one'

One and *a/an* cannot normally be used interchangeably. We use *one* when we are counting (*one apple*, as opposed to two or three):

It was ***one coffee*** *we ordered, not* ***two***.

But we could not use *one* to mean 'any one' (not specified):

A knife *is no good. You need* ***a screwdriver*** *to do the job properly.*

One is often used with *day, morning*, etc. in story-telling:

One day, *many years later, I found out what had really happened.*

A/an and *one* can be used interchangeably when we refer to:

Whole numbers:	*a* (or *one*) *hundred, thousand, million* [> App 47]
Fractions:	*a* (or *one*) *quarter, third, half*, etc.
Money:	*a* (or *one*) *pound/dollar*, etc. We say '*One pound 50*'
Weight/measure:	*a* (or *one*) *pound/kilo, foot/metre*, etc.

A/an and *one* are interchangeable in some expressions (*with a/one blow*), but not in others (*a few*). For *one* as a pronoun [> 4.9–11].

3.12 The use of 'a/an' with reference to measurement

A/an is used when we refer to one unit of measurement in terms of another. If we want to emphasize 'each', we use *per* instead of *a/an*:

Price in relation to weight:	*80p* ***a/per*** *kilo.*
Distance in relation to speed:	*40 km* ***an/per*** *hour.*
Distance/fuel consumption:	*30 miles* ***a/per*** *gallon.*
Frequency/time:	*twice* ***a/per*** *day.*

3.13 The use of 'a/an' after 'what' and 'such'

A/an is used with countable nouns after *What* in exclamations:

What a *surprise!* ***What an*** *interesting story!*

A/an is used after *such* when we wish to emphasize degree [> 7.51.1]:

That child is ***such a*** *pest! My boss is* ***such an*** *idiot!*

What a lot...! (Not **How much/many...!**) is used for exclamations:

What a lot of *flowers!* ***What a lot of*** *trouble!*

3.14 The use of 'a/an' with pairs of nouns

Many nouns are 'paired', that is they are considered to accompany each other naturally, and *a/an* is used before the first noun of a pair: *a cup and saucer, a hat and coat, a knife and fork:*

It's cold outside. Take ***a hat and coat*** *with you.*

If two words are used which are not considered to be a 'natural pair', the indefinite article must be used before each noun:

When you go on holiday, take ***a raincoat and a camera****.*

3.15 The use of 'a/an', etc. with reference to illnesses/conditions

The use of the indefinite and zero articles with illnesses can be defined in four categories:

1 Expressions where the use of the indefinite article is compulsory: e.g *a cold, a headache, a sore throat, a weak heart, a broken leg:*
I've got ***a headache/a cold****.*

2 Expressions where the use of the indefinite article is optional: e.g. *catch (a) cold, have (a) backache/stomach-ache/toothache, (an) earache:*
I've had ***(a) toothache*** *all night.*

3 With illnesses which are plural in form (e.g. *measles, mumps, shingles*) no article is used [compare > 2.31]:
My children are in bed with ***mumps****.*

4 With illnesses which are defined as 'uncountable' (e.g. *flu, gout, hepatitis*, etc.) no article is used:
I was in bed with ***flu*** *for ten days.*

The will also combine with e.g. *flu, measles* and *mumps*:
He's got ***the flu/the measles/the mumps****.*

The definite article: 'the'

3.16 Form of 'the'

The never varies in form whether it refers to people or things, singular or plural:

singular:

the man:	*He's*	*the man*	*I was telling you about.*
the woman:	*She's*	*the woman*	*I was telling you about.*
the book:	*That's*	*the book*	*I was telling you about.*

plural:

the men:	*They're the men*	*I was telling you about.*
the women:	*They're the women*	*I was telling you about.*
the books:	*They're the books*	*I was telling you about.*

3.17 The pronunciation of 'the'

The is pronounced /ðə/ before consonant sounds: *the day, the key, the house, the way.*

The is pronounced /ðiː/ before vowel sounds (i.e. words normally preceded by *an*): *the end, the hour, the inside, the outside, the ear, the eye, the umbrella.*

When we wish to draw attention to the noun that follows, we use the pronunciation /ðiː/ = 'the one and only' or 'the main one':

Do you mean ***the*** *Richard Burton, the actor?*
If you get into difficulties, Monica is ***the*** *person to ask.*
Mykonos has become ***the*** *place for holidays in the Aegean.*

Some common abbreviations are preceded by *the*, pronounced /ðə/: *the BBC* (the British Broadcasting Corporation) or /ðiː/ *the EEC* (the European Economic Community). Compare *B.A.* [> 3.7]: we tend to use full stops with titles, but not with institutions, etc.

3.18 Basic uses of 'the'

When using *the*, we must always bear in mind two basic facts:

1 *The* normally has a definite reference (i.e. the person or thing referred to is assumed to be known to the speaker or reader).

2 *The* can combine with singular countable, plural countable, and uncountable nouns (which are always singular).

These two facts underlie all uses of *the*. Some of the most important of these uses are discussed in the sections that follow.

3.19 The use of 'the' for classifying

3.19.1 Three ways of making general statements: 'the', zero, 'a/an'

1 With *the* + singular:

***The cobra** is dangerous.* (a certain class of snakes as distinct from other classes, such as *the grass snake*)

2 With *zero* + plural:

***Cobras** are dangerous.* (the whole class: all the creatures with the characteristics of snakes called *cobras*)

3 With *a/an* + singular:

***A cobra** is a very poisonous snake.* (*a cobra* as an example of a class of reptile known as *snake*)

3.19.2 The group as a whole: 'the' + nationality adjective [> App 49]

Some nationality adjectives, particularly those ending in *-ch, -sh* and *-ese* are used after *the* when we wish to refer to 'the group as a whole': e.g. *The British* = The British people in general.

However, we cannot say **many British** or **those two British**, etc. Plural nationality nouns can be used with *the* or the *zero article* to refer to the group as a whole: *the Americans* or *Americans*; or with numbers or quantifiers like *some* and *many* to refer to individuals: *two Americans, some Americans:*

***The British** and **the Americans** have been allies for a long time.*

***The Japanese** admire the traditions of **the Chinese**.*

For the use of *the* + adjective (*the young, the old,* etc.) [> 6.12.2].

3.19.3 The group as a whole: 'the' + plural names [compare > 3.22]

The + plural name can refer to 'the group as a whole':

Families: ***The Price sisters** have opened a boutique.*
'Races': ***The Europeans** are a long way from political unity.*
Politics: ***The Liberals** want electoral reform.*

Titles beginning with *the* are given to particular groups to emphasize their identity: e.g. *the Beatles, the Jesuits.*

3.19.4 Specified groups: 'the' + collective noun or plural countable

We can make general statements about specified groups with *the* + collective nouns, such as *the police, the public* [> 2.28.2, 2.29]:

*This new increase in fares won't please **the public**.*

Many plural countables can be used in a collective sense in the same way when particular groups are picked out from the rest of the human community: e.g. *the bosses, the unions* [compare > 2.28.1]:

*Getting **the unions** and **the bosses** to agree isn't easy.*

3.20 The use of 'the' for specifying

When we use *the*, the listener or reader can already identify what we are referring to, therefore *the* shows that the noun has been specified by the context/situation or grammatically. For example:

3.20.1 Specifying by means of back-reference [compare > 3.10.2]
Something that has been mentioned is referred to again:

*Singleton is **a quiet village** near Chichester. **The village** has a population of a few hundred people.*

3.20.2 Specifying by means of 'the' + noun + 'of' [compare > 3.26.2]
The topics referred to (e.g. *freedom, life*) are specified:

***The freedom of the individual** is worth fighting for.*
***The life of Napoleon** was very stormy.*

3.20.3 Specifying by means of clauses and phrases
We can specify a person, thing, etc. grammatically by means of *the ...* + clause or *the ...* + phrase:

***The Smith you're looking for** no longer lives here.*
***The letters on the shelf** are for you.*

3.20.4 Specifying within a limited context
The can be used in contexts which are limited enough for the listener or reader to identify who or what is referred to.
Reference can be made to:

- people: *Who's at the door? – It's **the postman**.*
- places [> Apps 21-23]:

*Where's Jenny? – She's gone to **the butcher's**.*
*– She's at **the supermarket**/in **the garden**.*

Most references of this kind refer to a single identifiable place. However, in big towns and cities, it is a matter of linguistic convention to say *He's gone to the cinema/the doctor's*, etc. without referring to any specific one. This convention extends to locations like *the country, the mountains, the seaside*. Locations which are 'one of a kind' always require *the*: e.g. *the earth, the sea, the sky, the sun, the moon, the solar system, the galaxy, the universe* [compare > 3.22, 3.31].

- things: *Pass me **the salt**, please.*
- parts of a whole. When we know what is being referred to ('the whole') we can use *the* to name its parts. Assuming the listener or reader knows that we are talking about: e.g.
  - a human being, we can refer to *the body, the brain, the head, the heart, the lungs, the mind, the stomach, the veins.*
  - a room, we can refer to *the ceiling, the door, the floor.*
  - an object, we can refer to *the back/the front, the centre, the inside/the outside, the top/the bottom.*
  - a town, we can refer to *the shops, the street.*
  - an appliance, we can refer to *the on/off switch.*

3.21 The use of 'the' in time expressions [> App 48]

3.21.1 The use of 'the' in time sequences

e.g. *the beginning, the middle, the end; the first/last; the next; the following day; the present, the past, the future:*

*In **the past**, people had fewer expectations.*

3.21.2 The use of 'the' with parts of the day [compare > 8.13]

e.g. *in the morning, in the afternoon, in the evening*, etc.:

*We spent **the day** at home. In **the evening**, we went out.*

Note that though many time references require *the*, many do not: e.g. *next week, on Tuesday, last year.*

3.21.3 The use of 'the' with the seasons [> App 24]

(The) spring/summer/autumn/winter. The is optional:

*We get a good crop of apples in **(the) autumn**.*

3.21.4 The use of 'the' in dates [> App 47.4]

Ordinal numbers usually require *the* when they are spoken, but not when they are written.
Compare:

*I'll see you on **May 24th**.* (spoken as *May the 24th*)
(e.g. on a letter): *24(th) May* (spoken as *the 24th of May*)

3.21.5 The use of 'the' in fixed time expressions

all the while, at the moment, for the time being, in the end, etc.:

*I'm afraid Mr Jay can't speak to you **at the moment**.*

3.22 The use of 'the' with unique items other than place names

We often use *the* with 'unique items' (i.e. where there is only one of a kind). A few examples [> 3.31 for place names]:

Institutions and organizations: *the Boy Scouts, the United Nations.*
Compare items with *zero*: *Congress, Parliament.*
Historical events, etc.: *the French Revolution, the Victorian age.*
Ships: *the Canberra, the Discovery, the Titanic.*
Documents and official titles: *the Great Charter, the Queen.*
Political parties: *the Conservative Party, the Labour Party.*
Public bodies: *the Army, the Government, the Police.*
The press (*The* is part of the title): *The Economist, The New Yorker, The Spectator, The Times.*
Note: *the press, the radio, the television.*
Compare: *What's on (the) television? What's on TV?*
Items with *zero*: *Life, Newsweek, Punch, Time.*
Titles (books, films, etc.: *The* is part of the title): *The Odyssey, The Graduate.* Items with *zero*: *Exiles, Jaws.*
Beliefs: *the angels, the Furies, the gods, the saints.*
Compare *God, Muhammed*, etc. (proper nouns) [> 2.13, 3.27].
Climate, etc.: *the climate, the temperature, the weather.*
Species: *the dinosaurs, the human race, the reptiles.*
(Compare: *Man developed earlier than people think.*)

3.23 Other references with 'the'

Examples of items with *the*:
- with superlatives [> 6.28]: *It's* ***the worst play I've ever seen***.
- with musical instruments: *Tom plays* ***the piano/the flute/the violin***.
  The is often omitted in references to jazz and rock:
  This is a 1979 recording with Ellison ***on bass guitar***.
- fixed phrases with *the...the* [> 6.27.3]: *the sooner the better.*
- fixed expressions: *do the shopping, make the beds.*

The zero article

3.24 The zero article: summary of 'form' and use

plural countables:	*Ø**Girls** do better than Ø **boys** at school.*
	*Some people want Ø **chips** with everything.*
uncountables (always singular):	*Ø**Butter** makes you fat.*
	*Ø **Honesty** is the best policy.*
proper nouns:	*Ø **John** lives in Ø**London**.*

The use of nouns on their own without an article is so fundamental in English that we should not regard this merely as 'the omission of the article', i.e. as something negative. We should think of the non-use of the article as something positive and give it a name: **the zero article**, which is usually given the symbol Ø.

Abbreviations with *zero*, often **acronyms** (i.e. words made from the first letters of other words), include:

Organizations: *NATO* (North Atlantic Treaty Organization).
Chemical symbols: *H_2O* (water).
Acronyms which form 'real words': *BASIC* (Beginners' All-purpose Symbolic Instruction Code); *radar* (Radio Detection And Ranging).

3.25 Basic uses of the zero article

We use the zero article before three types of nouns:
1 Plural countable nouns: e.g. *beans*.
2 Uncountable nouns (always singular): e.g. *water*.
3 Proper nouns [> 2.13]: e.g. *John*.

The can occur in front of plural countables and (singular) uncountables in normal use to refer to specific items [> 3.20]:

The pens *I gave you were free samples.*
The water *we drank last night had a lot of chlorine in it.*

The can even occur in front of names [> 3.20.3]:

The Chicago *of the 1920s was a terrifying place.*
Compare: ***Chicago*** *is a well-run city today.*

For *a/an* + uncountable [> 2.16.3].

Articles are frequently not used in general statements in English where they would be required in other European languages. Examples are given in the sections that follow.

3.26 The class as a whole: zero article + countable/uncountable

A few examples of general statements are [compare > 3.19.1]:

3.26.1 Zero article + plural countable nouns

People: ***Women*** *are fighting for their rights.*
Places: ***Museums*** *are closed on Mondays.*
Food: ***Beans*** *contain a lot of fibre.*
Occupations: ***Doctors*** *always support each other.*
Nationalities: ***Italians*** *make delicious ice-cream.* [> 3.19.2]
Animals: ***Cats*** *do not like cold weather.*
Insects: ***Ants*** *are found in all parts of the world.*
Plants: ***Trees*** *don't grow in the Antarctic.*
Products: ***Watches*** *have become very accurate.*

These can be modified by adjectives and other phrases: e.g. *women all over the world, local museums, broad beans, quartz watches.*

3.26.2 Zero article + uncountable nouns (always singular)

Food: *Refined foods like* ***sugar*** *should be avoided.*
Drink: ***Water*** *must be pure if it is to be drunk.*
Substances: ***Oil*** *is essential for the manufacture of* ***plastic****.*
Collections: ***Money*** *makes the world go round.*
Colours: ***Red*** *is my favourite colour.*
Activities (*-ing*): ***Smoking*** *is bad for the health.*
Other activities: ***Business*** *has been improving steadily this year.*
Sports, games: ***Football*** *is played all over the world.*
Abstract: ***Life*** *is short;* ***art*** *is long.*
Politics: ***Capitalism*** *is a by-product of free enterprise.*
Philosophy: ***Determinism*** *denies the existence of free will.*
Languages: ***English*** *is a world language.*

These can be modified by adjectives and other phrases:
e.g. *purified water, oil from the North Sea, heavy smoking.*

3.27 Unique items: zero article + proper nouns

3.27.1 Zero article + names of people

First names: ***Elizabeth*** *was my mother's name.*
Surnames: *These tools are made by* ***Jackson and Son****.*
Full names: ***Elizabeth Brown*** *works for this company.*
Initials: ***J. Somers*** *is the pseudonym of a famous author.*

Names can be modified by adjectives: *young Elizabeth, old Frank Robinson, Frank Robinson Jr* (= Junior, AmE), *Tiny Tim.*

3.27.2 Zero article + titles

Mr, Mrs, Miss, Ms, Dr (full stops may be used optionally after the abbreviations *Mr, Mrs* and *Dr*).
Mr and *Mrs* are always followed by a surname or first name + surname (not just a first name!):

Mr and Mrs Jackson *are here to see you.*

Mr and *Mrs* cannot normally be used on their own as a form of address. *Miss* is also followed by a surname (*Miss Jackson*) but is used as a form of address by schoolchildren (*Please Miss!*).
It is sometimes heard as a form of address by adults, though this is

not universally acceptable: *Can I help you, Miss? Ms* /**məz**/, a recent innovation, is rarely heard in speech, but is common nowadays in the written language to apply to both married and unmarried women.
Dr is usually followed by a surname and is abbreviated in writing (*This is Dr Brown*), but can also be used on its own as a form of address (written in full):

*It's my liver, **Doctor**.*

Some other titles that can be used with surnames or on their own are: *Captain, Colonel, Major, Professor*:

*May I introduce you to **Captain/Colonel/Major Rogers**?*
*Yes, **Captain/Colonel/Major**!*

Headmaster and *Matron* are not used with a name after them: *Thank you, Headmaster; Yes, Matron.*
Madam and *Sir* are often used in BrE as a form of address (e.g. by shop-assistants in *Can I help you, Madam/Sir?*). *Sir* is common in AmE when we are speaking to strangers. In formal letter-writing we use *Dear Sir* and *Dear Madam* as salutations to address people whose names we do not know.

Given titles (e.g. *Sir* + first name + surname or *Lord* + surname) are peculiar to BrE: *Lord Mowbray, Queen Elizabeth, Sir* (unstressed) *John Falstaff* (*Sir John*, but not **Sir Falstaff**). And note also: *Chancellor Adenauer, Pope John, President Lincoln*, etc.

The only titles applied to relations which can be used with names or on their own as forms of address are *uncle* and *aunt* (or *auntie*):

*Here comes **Uncle Charlie/Aunt Alice**.* (Note: first names only.)
*Thank you, **Uncle/Aunt/Auntie**.*

Some other titles that are used on their own as forms of address are: *Mother, Mum* (BrE), *Mom* (AmE), *Mummy* (BrE), *Mommy* (AmE), *Father, Dad* (BrE), *Pop* (AmE), *Pa, Daddy, Granddad, Grandpa, Grandma, Baby*. Words like *cousin, sister, brother* are no longer used as forms of address with reference to relations. *Mother* and *Sister* can be used for nuns and *Brother* for monks. *Sister* can sometimes be used for nurses, like *Nurse*. *Mother* + surname occurs as a nickname (*Mother Reilly*) and *Father* is used as a form of address for Roman Catholic priests (*Father O'Brien*). People often refer to (but do not usually address) grandparents as *Grandpa Jenkins* or *Grandma Jenkins* to distinguish them from another set of grandparents with a different surname.

Adjectives can be used in front of many titles: *kind Aunt Lucy, old Mrs Reilly, mad Uncle Bill*. In some contexts, the adjective can be capitalized so that it is part of the name: *Old Mrs Reilly*. No article is required in familiar reference (*Good old/Poor old George*), but other adjectives need the definite article (*the illustrious Dr Schweitzer, the notorious Mr Hyde*). *The* is optional and often omitted when the title is a complement:

*Wilson became **(the) President** of the USA.*

The is omitted when *as* is used or implied:

*Wilson was elected **President** of the USA.*

3.27.3 Zero article for days, months, seasons and holidays [> Apps 24, 48]

__Mondays__ are always difficult. __Monday__ is always a difficult day.
__June__ is my favourite month. __Spring__ is a lovely season.
__Christmas__ is the time for family reunions.

For *next, last* [> 3.21.2, 8.12]; for *all* [> 5.22.2].

3.27.4 Zero article for artists and their work [compare > 3.9.4]

The names of artists can represent their work as a whole:
e.g. *Brahms, Keats, Leonardo, Lorca, Rembrandt:*

__Bach__ gives me a lot of pleasure. (i.e. Bach's music)
__Chaucer__ is very entertaining. (i.e. Chaucer's writing)

Adjectival combinations: *early Beethoven, late Schubert*, etc.

3.27.5 Zero article for academic subjects and related topics

Art, Biology, Chemistry, Geography, History, Physics, etc.:

According to Henry Ford, '__History__ is bunk'.
__English__ is a difficult language to learn well.

Adjectival combinations: e.g. *Renaissance Art, American History.*

3.28 Other combinations with the zero article

3.28.1 Zero article for times of the day and night [> 8.11–13, App 48]

Combinations are common with *at, by, after* and *before*: *at dawn/daybreak, at sunrise/sunset/noon/midnight/dusk/night, by day/night, before morning, at/by/before/after 4 o'clock:*

We got up __at dawn__ to climb to the summit.

3.28.2 Zero article for meals

breakfast, lunch, tea, dinner, supper:

__Dinner__ is served. Michael's __at lunch__. Let's have __breakfast__.

The zero article is used after *have* [> App 42.1.1], but note the use of *the* where a meal is specified [> 3.20]:

__The breakfast__ I ordered still hasn't arrived.

and the use of *a* when classifying:

That was __a very nice dinner__.

3.28.3 Zero article for nouns like 'school', 'hospital', etc.

The following nouns are used with the zero article when we refer to their 'primary purpose', that is the activity associated with them: e.g. *He's in bed* (for the purpose of sleeping): *bed, church, class, college, court, hospital, market, prison, school, sea, town, university, work.* [> 10.9.7, 10.13.4 for *home.*] They frequently combine with *be in/at, have been/gone to* [> Apps 21–23]:

He was sent __to prison__ for four years.
The children went __to school__ early this morning.

But note the use of *the* when the item, etc. is specified:

Your bag is under __the bed__. There's a meeting at __the school__ at 6.

Words such as *cathedral, factory, mosque, office*, etc. are always used with *a* or *the*.

3.28.4 Zero article for transport

by air, by bicycle, by bike, by boat, by bus, by car, by coach, by land, by plane, by sea, by ship, by train, by tube, on foot:

We travelled all over Europe __by bus__.

By + noun is used in fixed expressions of this kind, but not where the means of transport is specified:

I came here ***on the local bus****. You won't go far* ***on that old bike****.*

3.28.5 Zero article in fixed phrases

e.g. *arm in arm, come to light, face to face, from top to bottom, hand in hand, keep in mind, make friends, make fun of.*

3.28.6 Zero article for 'pairs' joined by 'and' [compare > 2.38, 3.14, 6.12.2]

e.g. *day and night, father and son, husband and wife, light and dark, young and old, pen and ink, sun and moon:*

This business has been run by ***father and son*** *for 20 years.*

3.28.7 Zero article after 'what' and 'such' [> 3.13]

The noun is stressed after *What*; *such* is stressed before the noun:

– + plural countable:

What fools *they are!*

We had ***such problems*** *getting through Customs!*

– + (singular) uncountable:

What freedom *young people enjoy nowadays!*

Young people enjoy ***such freedom*** *nowadays!*

3.28.8 Zero article for unspecified quantity [> 3.6, 5.3, 5.10]

Sometimes we do not use *some* or *any* to refer to indefinite number or amount:

I have ***presents*** *for the children. I have* ***news*** *for you.*

Are there ***presents*** *for me too? Is there* ***news*** *for me too?*

3.29 Deliberate omission of 'a/an' and 'the'

There are many instances in everyday life when we deliberately omit both definite and indefinite articles to save space, time and money. For example:

Newspaper headlines: *HOTEL FIRE DISASTER*

Nouns in apposition: The use of the zero article is very common in journalism: e.g. *Film star Britt Ekland...; War hero Douglas Bader...; Miracle heart-swap man Keith Castle...* (no commas)

'Small ads': *1st fl flt in mod blk close West End, dble recep* (= A first floor flat in a modern block close to the West End with a double reception room...)

Notes: *Causes of 2nd World War: massive re-armament, invasion Czechoslovakia,* etc. (= The causes of the Second World War: massive re-armament, the invasion of Czechoslovakia, etc.)

(Shopping) lists: *Cleaner's: collect skirt*
Supermarket: meat, eggs, sugar, melon

Instructions: *Cut along dotted line* (= Cut along the dotted line.)

Notices: *Lift out of order* (= The lift is out of order.)

Labels: Beside e.g. a picture of a bicycle, an arrow pointing to the 'frame', with the label *FRAME* (for *the frame*)

Some dictionary definitions: *filling: material used to fill cavity in tooth* (= filling: a material used to fill a cavity in a tooth.)

3.30 'A/an', 'the', zero article + nouns in apposition

When two nouns or noun phrases are used in apposition [> 1.39], the use of the indefinite, definite and zero articles before the second noun or noun phrase sometimes affects the meaning:

D.H. Lawrence, ***an author*** *from Nottingham, wrote a book called 'Sons and Lovers'.* (This implies that the reader may not have heard of D.H. Lawrence.)

D.H. Lawrence, ***the author*** *of 'Sons and Lovers', died in 1930.* (This implies that many people have heard of D.H. Lawrence, or, if not, of 'Sons and Lovers'.)

D.H. Lawrence, ***author*** *of 'Sons and Lovers', died in 1930.* (This implies that everyone has heard of D.H. Lawrence.)

3.31 Zero article or 'the' with place names

Most place names are used with *zero*, but there is some variation. In particular, *the* is used when a countable noun like one of the following appears in the title: *bay, canal, channel, gulf, kingdom, ocean, republic, river, sea, strait, union. The* is often omitted on maps.

	zero	**the**
Continents:	*Africa, Asia, Europe*	–
Geographical areas:	*Central Asia, Inner London, Lower Egypt, Outer Mongolia, Upper Austria*	*the Arctic, the Balkans, the Equator, the Middle East, the North Pole, the West*
Historical references:	*Ancient Greece, Medieval Europe, pre-war/post-war Germany, Roman Britain*	*the Dark Ages, the Renaissance, the Stone Age*
Lakes:	*Lake Constance, Lake Erie, Lake Geneva*	–
Oceans/seas/rivers:	–	*the Pacific (Ocean), the Caspian (Sea), the Nile* (or *the River Nile*), *the Mississippi* (or *the Mississippi River*), *the Suez Canal*
Mountains:	*Everest, Mont Blanc*	*the Jungfrau, the Matterhorn*
Mountain ranges:	–	*the Alps, the Himalayas*
Islands:	*Christmas Island, Delos, Easter Island*	*the Isle of Capri, the Isle of Man*
Groups of islands:	–	*the Azores, the Bahamas*
Deserts:	–	*the Gobi (Desert), the Kalahari (Desert), the Sahara (Desert)*

	zero	**the**
Countries:	Most countries: *Finland, Germany, Turkey*, etc.	Unions and associations: *the ARE (the Arab Republic of Egypt), the UK (the United Kingdom), the USA (the United States of America), the USSR (the Union of Soviet Socialist Republics)* A few countries: *the Argentine* (or *Argentina*), *the Netherlands, the Philippines, (the) Sudan, (the) Yemen*
States/counties:	Most states/counties: *Bavaria, Ohio, Surrey*	*the Vatican*
Cities:	Most cities: *Denver, London, Lyons*	*the City (of London), The Hague*
Universities:	*Cambridge University*	*the University of Cambridge*
Streets, etc.:	Most streets: *London Road, Madison Avenue, Oxford Street, Piccadilly Circus*	*the High Street, the Strand, The Drive.* Note: *the London road* (= the road that leads to London)
Parks:	*Central Park, Hyde Park*	–
Addresses:	*49 Albert Place, 3 West Street, 2 Gordon Square*	*25 The Drive, 74 The Crescent*
Buildings:	*Buckingham Palace, Westminster Abbey*	*the British Museum, the Library of Congress*
Other locations:	*The* is sometimes part of the title, sometimes not:	
Bridges	*London Bridge*	*The Golden Gate Bridge*
Cinemas	–	*The Gaumont* *The Odeon*
Hospitals	*Guy's (Hospital)*	*The London Hospital*
Hotels	*Brown's Hotel*	*The Hilton (Hotel)*
'Places'	*Death Valley* *Heaven, Hades*	*The Everglades* *The Underworld*
Pubs	–	*The White Horse*
Restaurants	*Leoni's (Restaurant)*	*The Café Royal*
Shops	*Selfridges* *Marks and Spencers*	*The Scotch House*
Stations	*Victoria (Station)* *Waterloo (Station)*	–
Theatres	*Her Majesty's (Theatre)* *Sadler's Wells (Theatre)*	*The Phoenix (Theatre)* *The Coliseum (Theatre)*

4 Pronouns

General information about pronouns, possessives and determiners

4.1 Form of personal/reflexive pronouns and possessives

	personal pronouns: subject	object	possessives: adjectives	pronouns	reflexive pronouns:
singular:	*I*	*me*	*my*	*mine*	*myself*
	you	*you*	*your*	*yours*	*yourself*
	he	*him*	*his*	*his*	*himself*
	she	*her*	*her*	*hers*	*herself*
	it	*it*	*its*	–	*itself*
	one	*one*	*(one's)*	–	*oneself*
plural:	*we*	*us*	*our*	*ours*	*ourselves*
	you	*you*	*your*	*yours*	*yourselves*
	they	*them*	*their*	*theirs*	*themselves*

- demonstrative adjectives and pronouns: *this/that/these/those* [> 4.32].
- indefinite pronouns: *some, any* and their compounds [> 4.37].
- relative pronouns: *who, whom, that, which* [> 1.27].
- possessive adjectives (*my*, etc. [> 4.19]) function as **determiners** rather than pronouns, but they are treated together with possessive pronouns (*mine*, etc.) because they are related in form and meaning.

4.2 The difference between pronouns and determiners

4.2.1 Pronouns

A pronoun is a word that can be used in place of a noun or a noun phrase, as the word itself tells us: pro-noun. We do not normally put a noun after a pronoun except in special combinations such as *you students, she-bear*, etc. We use pronouns like *he, she, it* and *they* when we already know who or what is referred to. This saves us from having to repeat the name or the noun whenever we need to refer to it:

__John__ arrived late last night. __He__ had had a tiring journey.
I wrote to __Kay__ and told __her__ what had happened.

However, we normally use *I/me, you* and *we/us* for direct reference to ourselves or the person(s) addressed and not in place of nouns.

4.2.2 Determiners [> 3.1] compared with pronouns

Determiners are always followed by a noun. Words such as *some* [> 5.10] and *this* [> 4.32] followed by a noun function as determiners. When they stand on their own, they function as pronouns:

I want __some milk__.	(*some* + noun, functioning as **determiner**)
I want __some__.	(*some* on its own, functioning as **pronoun**)
I want __this book__.	(*this* + noun, functioning as **determiner**)
I want __this__.	(*this* on its own, functioning as **pronoun**)

Personal pronouns

4.3 Form of personal pronouns

subject [> 1.4]:	*I*	*you*	*he*	*she*	*it*	*one*	*we*	*you*	*they*
object [> 1.9]:	*me*	*you*	*him*	*her*	*it*	*one*	*us*	*you*	*them*

4.4 Notes on the form of personal pronouns

1 Though these words are called **personal pronouns**, they do not refer only to people. For example:

Your breakfast is ready. It is on the table.

We call them 'personal pronouns' because they refer to grammatical 'persons' (1st, 2nd, 3rd) and can be grouped like this:

1st person: *I, we*
2nd person: *you*
3rd person: *he, she, it, one, they*

2 Most European languages have two forms of *you*, an informal one for family, close friends, children, etc. and a formal one for strangers, superiors, etc. In English, we do not make this distinction: the one word, *you*, is used for everybody. There aren't different singular and plural forms of *you* (except for *yourself, yourselves*).

3 Note that the singular subject pronouns *he, she* and *it* have the same plural form: *they*; and the singular object pronouns *him, her* and *it* have the same plural form: *them*.

4 The choice of pronoun depends on the noun that is being replaced [> 2.39–40, 4.2.1]. Pronouns (except for *you*) agree with the nouns they replace in **number** (showing us whether they are referring to singular or plural). Some agree in **gender** (showing us whether they are referring to masculine, feminine or neuter):

John is here. He (replacing *John*) *can't stay long.*
The windows are dirty. I must wash them (replacing *windows*).
If you see Joanna please give her (replacing *Joanna*) *this message.*

5 We do not normally use a noun and a pronoun together:

My friend invited me to dinner. (Not **My friend, he...**)
I parked my car outside. (Not **My car, I parked it...**)

4.5 Subject pronouns

Subject pronouns nearly always come before a verb in statements. They are used when the person or thing referred to can be identified by both speaker and hearer:

John didn't find us in so he left a message.

In English, the subject of a sentence *must be expressed*. If it is not directly expressed, its presence is strongly implied [> 4.5.8]. This can be contrasted with some other European languages, where the use of subject pronouns can be optional.

4.5.1 The first person singular: 'I'

The speaker or writer uses *I* when referring to himself or herself. This is the only personal pronoun which is always spelt with a capital letter.

Note that *I* is written as a capital letter whether it's at the beginning of a sentence or not:

__I__ think, therefore __I__ am. John told me __I__ needn't wait.

In polite usage it is usual to avoid mentioning yourself first:

***Jane and I** have already eaten.* (in preference to *I and Jane*)

4.5.2 The second person singular and plural: 'you'

We use this when we address another person, or two or more people:

*Are **you** ready, **Jill**?* Or: *Are **you** (both/all) ready?*

For *you* in the sense of 'anyone in general' [> 4.9].

4.5.3 The third person singular masculine: 'he' [compare > 4.8]

He stands for a male person who has already been mentioned:

*Don't expect **David** to accept your invitation. **He**'s far too busy.*

He is used in certain proverbial expressions to mean 'anyone':

***He** who hesitates is lost.*

4.5.4 The third person singular feminine: 'she' [compare > 4.8]

She stands for a female person who has already been mentioned:

*Ask **Jennifer** if **she**'ll be home in time for dinner.*

4.5.5 The third person singular neuter: 'it' [compare > 4.8]

It can refer to a thing, a quality, an event, a place, etc.:

*That **vase** is valuable. **It**'s more than 200 years old.*
***Loyalty** must be earned. **It** can't be bought.*
*I love **swimming**. **It** keeps me fit.*
*Last night **I ran out of petrol**. **It** really taught me a lesson.*
*You should visit **Bath**. **It**'s not far from Bristol.*

We can use *it* to identify people:

*There's a knock at the door. Who is **it**? – **It**'s the postman.*
*Who's that? – **It**'s our new next-door neighbour, Mrs Smith.*

Compare this request for information (not identification):

*Who's Mrs Smith? – **She**'s our new next-door neighbour.*

We also use *it* when we don't know the sex of a baby or child:

***It**'s a lovely baby. Is **it** a boy or a girl?*

We refer to an animal as *it* when the sex is not known or not worth identifying:

*I'm fed up with that dog of yours. **It** never stops barking.*

4.5.6 The first person plural: 'we' (two or more people)

We can include the listener or not:

*Let's go, shall **we**?* (including the listener)
***We**'re staying here. What about **you**?* (not including the listener)

We is often used to mean 'anyone/everyone', e.g. in newspapers:

***We** should applaud the government's efforts to create more jobs.*

We is used in the same way in general statements:

***We** all fear the unknown.*

4.5.7 The third person plural: 'they' (two or more people, things, etc.)

They can stand for persons, animals or things already mentioned:

***John and Susan** phoned. **They**'re coming round this evening.*
*Look at those **cows**! **They** never stop eating.*
***Our curtains** look dirty. **They** need a good wash.*

They can be used in general statements to mean 'people':
__They__ say (or ***People** say*) *oil prices will be going up soon.*
They is also commonly used to refer to 'the authorities':
***They**'re putting up oil prices again soon.*
They is also used to mean 'someone else, not me':
*If you ask at Reception, **they** will tell you where it is.*
For *they* in place of *anyone*, etc. [> 4.40].
For the use of *we, you* and *they* with *both* and *all* [> 5.19–20].

4.5.8 Omission of subject in abbreviated statements

In everyday speech, we sometimes omit subject pronouns:
Found this in the garden. Know who it belongs to?
(= *I* found this in the garden. *Do you* know who it belongs to?)

4.6 Object pronouns

Object pronouns replace nouns in object positions. They can be:
- direct objects [> 1.9]: *Have you met **Marilyn**? I've never met **her**.*
- indirect objects [> 1.9]: *If you see Jim, give **him** my regards.*
- objects of prepositions [> 8.1]: *I really feel sorry **for them**.*

In polite usage it is usual to avoid mentioning yourself first:
*They were met by **John and me**.* (in preference to *me and John*)
We often use *both* and *all* with *you* to avoid ambiguity (since *you* can refer to *both* or *all*) [> 5.19–20]:
*Good luck to **you both/all**.*

Us is often used very informally in place of *me*, particularly after the imperatives of verbs like *give* and *pass*:
*Give **us** a hand with this trunk, will you?*
In everyday speech, it is normal for unstressed *him, her* and *them* to be pronounced *'im, 'er* and *'em*:
*Give **'im** the money. Give **'er** a kiss. Give **'em** all you've got.*

4.7 Subject or object pronoun?

Here are a few exceptions to the rules for using subject and object pronouns outlined in 4.5 and 4.6:

4.7.1 Object pronouns after 'be'

Object pronouns are normally used in preference to subject pronouns after *be* in everyday speech:
*Who is it? – It's **me/him/her/us/them**.*

4.7.2 Object pronouns (especially 'me') as subjects [> 13.29.3, 13.42*n*.2]

Subject pronouns (*I, she*, etc.) are not normally used by themselves or in short answers with *not*. Object pronouns are used instead:
*Who wants a ride on my bike? – **Me**!/**Not me**!*
An object pronoun can also occur as the subject of a particular kind of exclamatory question for stress or emphasis:
*You can tell him. – **Me** tell him? Not likely!*
Me occurs very informally in 'cleft sentences' [> 4.14]:
*Don't blame Harry. **It was me who** opened the letter.*
where careful usage would require:
***It was I who**...* (Or: *I was the one who...*)

4.7.3 Object or subject pronouns after comparatives with 'as' and 'than'

Object pronouns are commonly used in statements like the following when *as* and *than* function as prepositions:

*She's as old **as me/as him**. You're taller **than me/than her**.*

However, subject pronouns are used if *as* or *than* function as conjunctions, i.e. when they are followed by a clause [> 1.53, 6.27.1]:

*She's as old **as I am/he is**. You're taller **than I am/she is**.*

4.7.4 Object pronouns in exclamations

Object pronouns often occur in exclamations like the following:

*He's got to repay the money. – Poor **him**!* (= Isn't he unlucky!)
*She's been promoted. – Lucky **her**!* (= Isn't she lucky!)

4.8 Gender in relation to animals, things and countries

Animals are usually referred to with *it* as if they were things [> 4.5.5]. We only use *he, she, who*, etc. when there is a reason for doing so. For example, animals may be 'personalized' as pets, as farm animals, or in folk tales, and referred to as male or female:

*What kind of dog is **Spot**? – **He**'s a mongrel.*

Other 'lower animals' and insects are only referred to as *he, she*, etc. when we describe their biological roles:

*The **cuckoo** lays **her** eggs in other birds' nests.*

or, sometimes, when we regard their activities with interest:

*Look at that **frog**! Look at the way **he** jumps!*

Ships, cars, motorbikes and other machines are sometimes referred to as if they were feminine when the reference is affectionate:

***My car**'s not fast, but **she** does 50 miles to the gallon.*

Countries can also be 'personified' as feminine: e.g.

*In 1941 **America** assumed **her** role as a world power.*

'One'

4.9 General statements with 'one' and 'you'

One, used as an indefinite pronoun meaning 'everyone/anyone' [> 4.37], is sometimes used (formally) in general statements:

*World trade is improving, but **one** cannot expect miracles.*

In everyday speech, the informal *you* is preferred:

*Can **you** buy refrigerators in Lapland?* (= Can *anyone* ...?)

One may be used to replace *I*, but this tends to sound pompous:

***One** likes to have **one's** breakfast in bed now and again.*

One can be linked with *one's*, just as *you* can be linked with *your*. However, constructions with *one, one's* and *oneself* are often awkward because of the repetition of *one*:

***One** should do **one's** best at all times.*
(For: ***You** should do **your** best at all times.*)
***One** shouldn't be too hard on **oneself**.*
(For: ***You** shouldn't be too hard on **yourself**.*)

In AmE *one's/oneself* can be replaced by *his/her, himself/herself*:

***One** should give **himself/herself** a holiday from time to time.*

For the use of the passive in place of *one* [> 12.4.3].

4.10 'One' as a 'prop word' after a determiner [compare > 4.16, 5.30]

One and *ones* are frequently used as substitution words after a determiner (*that one*, etc). *One(s)* is sometimes called a **prop word** because it 'supports' the meaning of the noun it replaces. *One* is used to replace a countable noun in the singular and *ones* to replace a plural countable. *One* and *ones* can refer to people or things and we use them when we wish to avoid repeating a noun:

Things: *Have you seen **this dictionary**?* (singular countable)
*– Is that **the one** that was published recently?*
People: *Have you met **our German neighbours**?* (plural countable)
*– Are they **the ones** who moved here recently?*

We cannot use *one* when referring to an uncountable noun:
*Don't use powdered **milk**. Use this fresh (**milk**).* (Not **one**)

One and *ones* as prop words are most commonly used when we are identifying people and things, particularly after *Which?*, *this/that*, and adjectives [compare > 6.6]. *One* and *ones* are optional after *Which?*, after *this/that* and after superlatives. *Ones* can be used after *these/those*, though it is usually avoided:
Which (one) *would you like?* – ***This (one)*** *or* ***that (one)****?*
Which (ones) *would you like?* – ***These (ones)*** *or* ***those (ones)****?*
Which (one/ones) *do you want?* – ***The cheapest (one/ones)****.*

We normally use *one/ones* after the positive form of adjectives:
Which (one/ones) *do you want?* – ***The large one/ones****.*
After colour adjectives, *one* and *ones* may be omitted in answers:
Which (one/ones) *do you want?* – *I'll have* ***the red (one/ones)****.*

In statements, requests, etc. *one* and *ones* must be used after *this/that/these/those* + adjective:
*I'll try on a few of these shirts. Please pass me **that white one**.*

One and *ones* can be used in specific references after the definite article (*the one/the ones*), demonstratives (*this one*) or with defining phrases (*the one/ones with pink ribbons*) to identify or to indicate the location of people and things:
Which woman *do you mean?* – ***The one in the green dress****.*
Which boys *rang the doorbell?* – ***The ones in the street****.*
Which shirt(s) *do you want?* – ***The one(s) in the window****.*

4.11 Reference to two: 'the one...the other'

We can refer to two people or things (or to two groups) through the following combinations: *(the) one... the other; the first... the second*; or more formally, *the former...the latter:*
You shouldn't get Botticelli and Boccherini mixed up.

(The) one		***the other***	
The first	*is a painter and*	***the second***	*is a composer.*
The former		***the latter***	

The former and *the latter* can have a plural verb:
*Beans and peas are good value. **The former/The latter** are cheap.*

'It'

4.12 'It' as an 'empty subject'

We often use *it* in sentences referring to time, the weather, temperature or distance. When used in this way, *it* is sometimes called an **empty subject** because it carries no real information. It is present because every English sentence has to contain a subject and a verb [> 4.5]:

Time:	***It**'s 8 o'clock. **It**'s Tuesday. **It**'s May 25th.*
It's time... [> 11.43]:	***It's time** (for us) to leave.*
Weather:	***It**'s hot. **It**'s raining. **It** rains a lot here.*
Temperature:	***It**'s 37° centigrade/Celsius.*
Distance:	***It**'s 20 miles to/from London.*
The tides:	***It**'s high tide at 11.44.*
Environment:	***It**'s noisy/smoky in here.*
Present situation:	*Isn't **it** awful! Isn't **it** a shame!*
With *since*:	***It**'s three years **since** we last met.*
With *says*:	***It says** here there was a big fire in Hove.*
With *take* [> 16.21]:	***It takes** (us) half an hour to get to work.*

And note many expressions with *it*, e.g. ***it** doesn't matter; **it**'s no use*, (*it* as subject); *I've had **it**; That does **it**!* (*it* as object).

4.13 'It' as a 'preparatory subject'

Sometimes sentences beginning with *it* continue with an infinitive, a gerund or a noun clause [> 1.23.1, 16.27.2, 16.47]. It is possible to begin such sentences with an infinitive or gerund, but we generally prefer *it*:

***It**'s pleasant to lie in the sun.*	(***To lie in the sun** is pleasant.*)
***It**'s pleasant lying in the sun.*	(***Lying in the sun** is pleasant.*)
***It**'s a shame that Tom isn't here.*	(***That Tom isn't here** is a shame.*)
***It** doesn't matter when we arrive.*	(***When we arrive** doesn't matter.*)

The true subject in the above sentences with *it* is the infinitive, gerund or noun clause and *it* is preparatory to the subject.

It as a preparatory subject often combines with:

adjectives: e.g. *difficult, easy, important, vital* [> App 44]:
***It's easy** (for me) to make mistakes.*

nouns: e.g. *fun, a pity, a pleasure, a shame* [> 1.23.1, 16.34]:
***It's a pleasure** (for us) to be here.*

verbs: e.g. *appear, happen, look, seem* [> 1.47.2, 10.25]:
***It appears** that he forgot to sign the letter.*
***It** now **looks certain** that the fire was caused by a cigarette end.*

4.14 The use of 'it' in 'cleft sentences'

We can begin sentences with *It is* or *It was* + subject + *that* or *who(m)*, if we wish to emphasize the word or phrase that follows. Sentences formed in this way are called **cleft sentences** because a simple sentence is split up (cleft) into two clauses using the *it*-construction:

Freda phoned Jack last night. (simple sentence, no emphasis)
It was Freda who *phoned Jack last night.* (and not Rita)
It was Jack who(m) *Freda phoned last night.* (and not Richard)
It was last night that *Freda phoned.* (and not this morning)

4.15 'It' as a 'preparatory object' [compare > 1.14]

It + adjective can be used after verbs like *find* [> 16.22] to prepare us for the infinitive or the *that*-clause that follows:

+ infinitive: *Tim **finds** **it difficult** **to concentrate**.*
+ *that*-clause: *Jan **thinks** **it funny** **that I've taken up yoga**.*

It can also be used after verbs like *enjoy, hate, like, love:*
*I don't **like it** when you shout at me.*

4.16 Specific 'it/they', etc. and non-specific 'one/some', etc.

4.16.1 Obligatory subjects: 'it', 'they', 'one', 'some' (for things)

It and *they* are used as subjects if the reference is specific:

specific: *Did **the letter** I've been expecting come?*
*– Yes, **it** came this morning.* (*the* + singular noun = *it*)
*Did **the letters** I've been expecting come?*
*– Yes, **they** came this morning.* (*the* + plural noun = *they*)

One and *some*, functioning on their own as pronouns, can be used as subjects if the reference is non-specific:

non-specific: *Did **a letter** come for me?*
*– Yes, **one** came/**some** came for you this morning.*
(*a/an* + singular noun = *one*)
*Did **any letters** come for me?*
*– Yes, **some** came/**one** came for you this morning.*
(*any/some* + plural noun = *some* in a positive answer or *none* in a negative answer)

4.16.2 Obligatory objects: 'it', 'them', 'one', 'some', 'any' (for things)

An object is obligatory after transitive verbs, such as *enjoy* or *make*, and verbs which are being used transitively, such as *play* [> App 1]. *It, them* or a noun must be used as objects when the reference is specific [> 4.16.1]:

*What do you think of **this cake**?*
*– I like **it**/I don't like **it**.* (Not **I like/don't like**)
*What do you think of **these cakes**?*
*– I like **them**/I don't like **them**.* (Not **I like/don't like**)

One must be used as an object when it stands for *a/an* + countable noun (i.e. the reference is non-specific) [> 4.16.1]:

*Have **a biscuit**. – I've had **one**/I don't want **one** thank you.*
*Would you like **a drink**? – I'd love **one** thank you.*

Some and *any* [> 5.10] must be used as objects when there is a non-specific reference to uncountable nouns and plural countables:

*Have you got **any sugar**? Can you lend me **some** please?*
*– Sorry, I haven't got **any** (to spare).*
*Have you got **any drawing-pins**? Can I borrow **some** please?*
*– I'm afraid I haven't got **any** (to spare).*

4.17 'So', not 'it' with certain verbs [compare > 1.23.5]

After verbs such as *believe, expect, fear, guess* (especially AmE: *I guess so*), *hope, imagine, presume, say, suppose, tell someone, think* (also after *I'm afraid* and *It seems/appears*), it is usual to follow with *so* (never *it*) in affirmative responses, so that we do not repeat a whole clause:

Is it true that Geoff has had a heart attack?
*– I am afraid **so**/I believe **so**/I think **so**. It seems **so***

In negative responses, *not* can be used directly after *be afraid, believe, expect, fear, guess* (especially AmE: *I guess not*), *hope, imagine, presume, suppose, think* (and *It seems/appears*):

Has Anne got into university?
*– I am afraid **not**/I believe **not**/I think **not**. It seems **not**.*

Alternative responses using *not...so* are possible with *believe, expect, imagine, say, suppose* and *think*:

*I **don't** believe **so**/...imagine **so**/...suppose **so**/...think **so**.*

So can also precede the subject in short responses:
– with verbs like *believe, gather, hear, notice, see, understand:*
The stock market share-index has risen sharply.
*– **So** I believe/gather/hear/notice/see/understand.*
– with verbs like *say, tell, seem, appear:*
***So** you said. **So** he told me. **So** it seems. **So** it appears.*
– before or after *(I) should/would* + verbs like *expect, hope, say, think* (implying 'this is what ought to happen'):
***So** I should* (or *would*) *hope!* Or: *I should* (or *would*) *hope **so**!*

4.18 'So' or 'it' after certain verbs

So and *it* are normally interchangeable after *do*, when *do* substitutes for another verb which has already been used and when it reflects an action that has been deliberately performed:

*Please lay the table. – I've just done **so**./I've just done **it**.*

After verbs like *guess, know, remember, it* can be used or omitted:

*Jack and Jill were secretly married. – Yes, **I know**. **I had guessed**.*
(= I know *it*. I had guessed *it*.)

Possessive adjectives/possessive pronouns

4.19 Form of possessive adjectives and possessive pronouns

adjectives:	*my*	*your*	*his*	*her*	*its*	*(one's)*	*our*	*your*	*their*
pronouns:	*mine*	*yours*	*his*	*hers*	–	–	*ours*	*yours*	*theirs*

4.20 Notes on form (possessive adjectives/pronouns)

1 With the exception of *one's*, the apostrophe *s* (*'s*) is unacceptable with possessive adjectives and pronouns. We should not confuse *its* (possessive) with *it's* = *it is* [> 10.6] or *it has* [> 10.29].

2 There are no familiar/non-familiar forms for the second person singular and plural [> 4.4*n*.2]: *your* and *yours* are used in all cases.
3 *One's* can be used as an impersonal possessive adjective, but not as a pronoun: ***One's first duty** is to **one's family**.* [> 4.9]

4.21 Possessive adjectives and possessive pronouns compared

Possessive adjectives and pronouns show possession, i.e. that someone or something belongs to somebody. They answer the question *Whose?* The possessive adjectives *my, your*, etc. are determiners [> 3.1, 4.2.2] and must always be used in front of a noun. Their form is regulated by the possessor, not by the thing possessed.
His refers to possession by a male: *John's daughter* (= *his daughter*).
Her refers to possession by a female: *Jane's son* (= *her son*).
Its refers to possession by an animal or thing: *the cat's milk* (= *its milk*); *the jacket of this book* (= *its jacket*).
My, your and *their* refer to possession by males or females:

*'**My** house is there,' **Sally** said./**John** said.*
*'Here is **your** tea, **Sally/John**,' mother said.*
*The **boys'** coats are here and **their** caps are there.*
*The **girls'** coats are here and **their** berets are there.*

Their can also refer to possession by animals or things, as in:

***Dogs** should have **their** own kennels outside the house.*
***Cars with their engines** at the back are very noisy.*

The possessive pronouns *mine, yours*, etc. are never used in front of nouns and are stressed in speech. They refer equally to persons and things, singular or plural. *Its* is never used as a pronoun.

*These are my children. These children are **mine**.*
*These are my things. These things are **mine**.*
*I can't find my pen. Can you lend me **yours**?*

Possessive pronouns can come at the beginning of a sentence:

*This is my cup. **Yours** is the one that's chipped.*
*My father/My mother is a lawyer. – **Mine** is a doctor.*

For *'s/s'* possession without a noun [> 2.44, 2.51].

Noun + *of it* can sometimes be used in place of *its* + noun [compare > 2.50]:

*How much is that book? I've forgotten **the price of it/its price**.*

For the use of *of* + possessive pronoun [> 2.52].

4.22 The use of 'my own'

Extra emphasis can be given to the idea of possession by the addition of *own* to all possessive adjectives (not pronouns). The resulting combinations can function as possessive adjectives (*my own room*) or possessive pronouns (*it is my own*). Instead of *(my) own* + noun we often use *a/an* + noun *of (my) own*:

*I'd love to have **my own room/a room of my own**.*
*Our cat has **its own corner/a corner of its own** in this room.*

Further emphasis can be given with *very*:

*I'd love to have **my very own room/a room of my very own**.*

We can say *one's own room* or *a room of one's own*, but we do not use *one* as a prop word [> 4.10] after *(my) own*:

Don't use my comb. Use ***your own****.* (Not **your own one**)

4.23 The use of 'the' in place of possessive adjectives

The is never used with possessive adjectives and pronouns:

This is ***my*** *car. This car is* ***mine****.* (no *the*) [> 3.4]

However, sometimes *the* is used where we might expect a possessive adjective, e.g. with parts of the body after prepositions:

He punched me ***in the face****. A bee stung her* ***on the nose****.*

This use can be extended to hair and clothes (i.e. things which are 'attached' to the body):

Miss Pringle pulled Clarinda ***by the hair/by the sleeve****.*

Possessive adjectives (not **the**) must be used in most other cases:

She shook ***her*** *head/cleaned* ***her*** *teeth. I've hurt* ***my*** *finger.*

In informal contexts, *the* can be used instead of (usually) *my/your/our children, family, kids*, as in:

How's ***the family****? Where are* ***the children****?*

But e.g. *Meet the wife* is familiar but not universally acceptable.

Reflexive pronouns

4.24 Form of reflexive pronouns

singular:	*myself*	*yourself*	*himself, herself, itself, oneself*
plural:	*ourselves*	*yourselves*	*themselves*

Reflexive pronouns are really compounds formed from possessive adjectives + *-self*: e.g. *myself, yourself*; or from object pronouns + *-self*: e.g. *himself*.

4.25 Obligatory use of reflexive pronouns after certain verbs

There are only a very few verbs in English which must always be followed by a reflexive pronoun: e.g. *absent, avail, pride:*

The soldier ***absented himself*** *without leave for three weeks.*

Other verbs are very commonly followed by reflexives: e.g. *amuse, blame, cut, dry, enjoy, hurt, introduce:*

I ***cut myself*** *shaving this morning.*

We really ***enjoyed ourselves*** *at the funfair.*

Of course, these verbs can be followed by ordinary objects:

I've cut ***my lip****. We enjoyed* ***the funfair****.*

The important thing to remember is that verbs of this kind are never followed by object pronouns (*me, him, her*, etc.) when the subject and object refer to the same person:

I've cut ***myself****.* (Not **me**)

Note that these verbs are all transitive [> 1.9]. This means they must have an object and this is commonly a reflexive pronoun. The one exception is the intransitive verb *behave*, which can be followed (but need not be) by a reflexive pronoun:

Please ***behave (yourself)****! The children* ***behaved (themselves)****.*

4.26 Optional use of reflexive pronouns after certain verbs

Other verbs which can point the action back to the subject (e.g. *dress, hide, shave, wash*) can be intransitive, so we don't need reflexive pronouns, though it would not be 'wrong' to use them. When these verbs are intransitive, it is assumed that the subject is doing the action to himself:

*I must **dress/wash**.* (as opposed to *dress/wash myself*)

We often use (and stress) reflexive pronouns after such verbs when referring to children, the very old, invalids, etc. to indicate that an action is performed with conscious effort:

*Polly's nearly learnt how to **dress herself** now.*

4.27 Verbs which are not normally reflexive

Verbs such as *get up, sit down, stand up, wake up* and combinations with *get* (*get cold/hot/tired, dressed, married*), often reflexive in other European languages, are not normally so in English:

*I **got up** with difficulty.*

Reflexives would be used for special emphasis only:

*Will you **get yourself dressed**? We're late.*

4.28 Reflexive pronouns as objects of ordinary verbs

Reflexive pronouns can be used after many ordinary verbs if we wish to point back to the subject:

*I got such a shock when I **saw myself** in the mirror.*

Reflexives can be used as indirect objects:

*The boss **gave himself** a rise.* (= gave a rise to himself)

Note there are a number of short conversational expressions with reflexive pronouns: e.g. *Help yourself!, Make yourself at home!, Don't upset yourself!*; and also a few fixed expressions: e.g. *hear (yourself) speak, make (yourself) heard:*

*I couldn't **make myself heard** above the noise.*

There is a difference in meaning between *themselves* and *each other* after verbs such as *accuse, blame, help, look at* [compare > 5.28]:

*The two bank clerks **blamed themselves** for the mistake.*
(= They both took the blame.)
*The two bank clerks **blamed each other** for the mistake.*
(= The one blamed the other.)

4.29 Reflexive pronouns as objects of prepositions

Reflexive pronouns can occur after prepositions which often follow verbs, nouns or adjectives [> Apps 27–29]:

***Look after yourself**!*
*Lucy's looking very **pleased with herself**.*

or in combination with adverb particles: the reflexive comes between the verb and the particle [> 8.28]:

*We gave **ourselves** up.*
*We pulled **ourselves** out (of the water).*

Myself is sometimes used (unnecessarily) instead of *me* or *I*:
*They sent invitations to Geoff and **myself**.* (*me* is preferable)
*Kate and **myself** think...* (*Kate and I...* is preferable)
Reflexives also occur in a few idiomatic expressions, such as:
***Strictly between ourselves**, do you think she's sane?*
***In itself**, his illness is nothing to worry about.*

In all other cases we use object pronouns after prepositions when the reference is to place or after *with*:
*I haven't got any money **on me**.* (Not **myself**)
*There was a bus **in front of us**.* (Not **ourselves**)
*Did you bring any money **with you**?*

By + reflexive means 'unaided' or 'alone':
*Susie made this doll's dress all **by herself**.* (= unaided)
*He lives **by himself**.* (= alone)
Reflexives can be used for emphasis after e.g. *but* and *than*:
*You can blame no one **but yourself**.* (= except yourself)
*Harry would like to marry a girl younger **than himself**.*
After some prepositions we can use either form of pronoun:
*I think this new magazine is aimed at people **like us/ourselves**.*
*Who's prepared to work overtime **besides me/myself**?*

4.30 Reflexive pronouns used for emphasis

Reflexive pronouns can be used freely (but optionally) after nouns and pronouns for emphasis to mean 'that person/thing and only that person/thing' (*I myself; you yourself; Tom himself,* etc.):
***You yourself** heard the explosion quite clearly.*
***The engine itself** is all right, but the lights are badly damaged.*
The reflexive can also come at the end of a sentence or clause:
***You** heard the explosion **yourself**.*
and particularly where there is a comparison or contrast:
***Tom's** all right **himself**, but his wife is badly hurt.*
When used for special emphasis, reflexives are stressed in speech, especially when there is a possibility of ambiguity:
*Mr Bates rang the **'boss** him'**self**.* (and not the boss's secretary)

Reflexive pronouns are used in (often rude) rejoinders, such as:
*Can you fetch my bags, please? – Fetch them **yourself**!*
And note the special use of *Do it yourself* (often abbreviated to D.I.Y.) to refer to decorating, repairs, etc. we do ourselves (e.g. to save money) instead of employing others:
*I read about it in a **Do It Yourself** magazine.*

4.31 Reflexive pronouns after 'be' and verbs related to 'be'

After *be* and related verbs such as *feel, look, seem*, reflexives can be used to describe feelings, emotions and states:
*I don't know what's the matter with me. I'**m not myself** today.*
Occasionally, we use a possessive adjective + adjective + *self* (noun):
*Meg **doesn't look her usual cheerful self** today.*
*Frank **didn't sound his happy self** on the phone this morning.*

Demonstrative adjectives and pronouns

4.32 Form of demonstrative adjectives and pronouns

'Near' references matching *here*:

singular:	*this*	*boy*	*girl*	*tree*	*book*	*money*
plural:	*these*	*boys*	*girls*	*trees*	*books*	–

'Distant' references matching *there*:

singular:	*that*	*boy*	*girl*	*tree*	*book*	*money*
plural:	*those*	*boys*	*girls*	*trees*	*books*	–

4.33 'This/that' and 'these/those': nearness and distance

'Nearness' may be physical. *This* and *these* may refer to something you are actually holding or that is close to you, or that you consider to be close to you, or to something that is present in a situation. We can associate *this* and *these* with *here*:

The picture I am referring to is ***this one here****.*
The photographs I meant are ***these here****.*

This and *these* can refer to nearness in time (*now*):

Go and tell him now, ***this instant****!*

'Distance' may be physical. *That* and *those* can refer to something that is not close to you, or that you do not consider to be close to you. We can associate *that* and *those* with *there*:

The picture I am referring to is ***that one there****.*
The photographs I meant are ***those there****.*

That and *those* can refer to distance in time (*then*):

Operations were difficult in the 18th century. In ***those days*** *there were no anaesthetics.*

4.34 Demonstrative adjectives/pronouns compared

Demonstratives can be adjectives: that is, they can be determiners [> 3.1] and go before a noun or *one/ones* [> 4.10]; or they can be pronouns used in place of a noun or noun phrase [> 4.2.1]:

adjective + noun: *I don't like* ***this coat****.*
adjective + *one*: *I don't like* ***this one****.*
pronoun: *I don't like* ***this****.*

Demonstratives used as pronouns normally refer to things, not people:

I found ***this wallet****. I found* ***this****.* (pronoun)
I know ***this girl****.* (*this* cannot stand on its own here)

Demonstrative pronouns after *What?* refer to things:

What's ***this/that****? What are* ***these/those****?*

This and *that* as pronouns after *Who?* refer to people:

Who's ***this****? Who's* ***that****?*

These and *those* referring to people are followed by a (plural) noun. Compare *What are* ***these/those****?* (i.e. things) with:

Who are ***these/those people/men/women/children****?*

But *those*, closely followed by *who*, can be used on its own:

Those *(of you)* ***who*** *wish to go now may do so quietly.*

4.35 Common uses of 'this/that' and 'these/those'

This/that/these/those used as adjectives or as pronouns have many different uses. For examples [> App 7].

4.36 Subject pronouns replacing demonstratives

Demonstratives are replaced by *it* or *they* in short responses when the thing or things referred to have been identified [compare > 13.19*n*.7]:

*Is **this/that yours**? Yes, **it** is.* (Not **Yes, this/that is**)
*Are **these/those** yours? Yes, **they** are.* (Not **Yes, these/those are**)

He/she can replace *this/that* when the reference is to people:

***This/That** is Mrs/Mr Jones. **She**'s/**He**'s in charge here.*

Indefinite pronouns

4.37 Form of indefinite pronouns

Compounds of *some, any, no* and *every*:

some-	*any-*	*no-*	*every-*
someone	*anyone*	*no one*	*everyone*
somebody	*anybody*	*nobody*	*everybody*
something	*anything*	*nothing*	*everything*

4.38 Notes on the form of indefinite pronouns

1 There is no noticeable difference in meaning and use between *-one* forms and *-body* forms. They refer to male(s) and female(s).
2 These compounds (except *no one*) are normally written as one word.
3 These compounds (except those formed with *-thing*) have a genitive form [> 2.48]: *Grammar isn't **everyone's idea** of fun.*
4 Compare compound adverbs which are formed with *-where*: *somewhere, anywhere, nowhere* and *everywhere* [> 7.18].

4.39 Uses of 'some/any/no/every' compounds

Some/any/no/every compounds (except *-where* compounds) function as pronouns. They are called indefinite because we do not always know who or what we are referring to. These compounds follow the rules given for the use of *some, any* and *no* [> 5.10–11].

Briefly, *some* compounds are used in:

– the affirmative: ***I met someone** you know last night.*
– questions expecting 'yes': ***Was there something** you wanted?*
– offers and requests: ***Would you like something** to drink?*

Any compounds are used:

– in negative statements: ***There isn't anyone** who can help you.*
– in questions when we are doubtful about the answer: ***Is there anyone** here who's a doctor?*
– with *hardly*, etc: *I've had **hardly anything** to eat today.*

No compounds are used when the verb is affirmative [> 13.9]:

***There's no one** here at the moment.*
(= There isn't anyone...)

4.40 Personal pronoun reference with indefinite pronouns

The main problem (also for native speakers) is to know which personal pronouns to use to 'replace' the indefinite pronouns referring to people (*someone/anyone/no one/everyone*). This is because English has no singular personal pronouns for both male and female. If we want to use personal pronouns (in place of the gaps) in a sentence like:

***Everyone** knows what...has to do, doesn't...?*

the traditional rule is to use masculine pronouns, unless the context is definitely female (e.g. a girls' school):

***Everyone** knows what **he** has to do, doesn't **he**?*

However, in practice, the plural pronouns, *they, them*, etc. (which refer to both sexes) are used instead without a plural meaning:

***Everyone** knows what **they** have to do, don't **they**?*

This has the advantage of avoiding clumsy combinations like *he or she* and does not annoy mixed groups of people. However, it is not considered acceptable by some native speakers [compare > 2.41, 5.31].

4.41 Indefinite pronouns + adjectives and/or the infinitive

Indefinite pronouns can combine with:

– positive adjectives:	*This is **something special**.*
	*This isn't **anything important**.*
– comparative adjectives:	*I'd like **something cheaper**.*
– the infinitive:	*Haven't you got **anything to do**?*
– *for (me)* + infinitive:	*Is there **anything for me to sit on**?*

(Note that adjectives come after indefinite pronouns.)

4.42 Indefinite pronouns + 'else'

Like question-words (*What, Who*, etc. [> 13.31*n*.8]), indefinite pronouns readily combine with *else* (*everyone else, someone else, anything else*, etc.); *else* can mean 'additional/more' or 'different':

– 'more': *We need one more helper. Can you find **anyone else**?*
– 'different': *Take this back and exchange it for **something else**.*

Anything (else) and *nothing (else)* can be followed by *but*:

***Nothing (else) but** a major disaster will get us to realize that we can't go on destroying the rain forests of the world.*

Else than is also heard, but this is usually replaced by *other than*, especially with reference to people:

***Someone other than** your brother should be appointed manager.*

Indefinite pronouns referring to people can combine with *else's*:

*This isn't mine. It's **someone else's**. It's **someone else's coat**.*

5 Quantity

General introduction to quantity

5.1 Quantifiers: what they are and what they do

Quantifiers are words or phrases like *few, little, plenty (of)*, which often modify nouns and show how many things or how much of something we are talking about. Some quantifiers combine with countable nouns; some with uncountable and some with both kinds [> 2.14].

1 Quantifiers combining with countable nouns answer *How many?*:
__How many eggs__ are there in the fridge? – There are __a few__.

2 Quantifiers combining with uncountable nouns answer *How much?*:
__How much milk__ is there in the fridge? – There is __a little__.

3 Quantifiers combining with uncountable or with countable answer *How many?* or *How much?*:
__How many eggs__ are there in the fridge? – There are __plenty__.
__How much milk__ is there in the fridge? – There is __plenty__.

Quantifiers can function as **determiners** [> 3.1] or (with the exception of *every* and *no*) as **pronouns** [> 4.2.2]; some of them can function as **adverbs**: *I don't like coffee __very much__.* [> 7.41]

5.2 Quantifier + noun combinations

Quantifiers combine with different types of nouns:

1 **Quantifier + plural countable noun**: ***not many books***
any number more than *one* (*2, 3*, etc.), *both, a couple of, dozens/hundreds of, (a) few, fewer, the fewest, a/the majority of, (not) many, a minority of, a number of, several:*
We have __fewer students__ specializing in maths than in English.

2 **Quantifier + uncountable noun**: ***not much sugar***
a (small) amount of, a bit of, a drop of (liquid), a great/good deal of, (a) little, less [but > 5.16], *the least, (not) much:*
I'd like __a bit of bread__ with this cheese.

3 **Quantifier + plural countable noun**: ***a lot of books***
or **+ (singular) uncountable noun**: ***a lot of sugar***
some (of the), any (of the), all (the), hardly any, enough, half of the/half the, a lot of, lots of, more, most, most of the, no, none of the, the other, part of the, plenty of, the rest of the:
There aren't __any cars__ on the road at the moment.
There isn't __any traffic__ on the road at the moment.

4 **Quantifier + singular countable noun**: ***each book***
all (of) the, another, any (of the), each, either, every, half (of) the, most of the, neither, no, none of the, one, the only, the other, some (of the), the whole (of the):
It's __each/every man__ for himself in this business.

5.3 Degrees of indefinite quantity

References to quantity can be **definite**: that is, we can say exactly how many or how much:

*We need **six** eggs and **half a kilo** of butter.*

However, most quantifiers are **indefinite**: that is, they do not tell us exactly how many or how much.

Some, any [> 5.10] and *zero* [> 3.24, 3.28.8] refer to indefinite number or amount:

Are there	***(any)***	***apples***	*in the bag?*
There are	***(some)***	***apples***	*in the bag.* (We are not told how many.)
Is there	***(any)***	***milk***	*in the fridge?*
There is	***(some)***	***milk***	*in the fridge.* (We are not told how much.)

No + noun indicates a complete absence of the thing mentioned:

*There are **no apples**. There is **no milk**.*

Most quantity words give us more information than *some* and *any*, telling us the comparative degree of the number or amount: e.g.

plural countable nouns	uncountable nouns
Approximately ***how many***:	Approximately ***how much***:
*There are **too many** eggs.*	*There is **too much** milk.*
***plenty of** eggs.*	***plenty of** milk.*
***a lot of/lots of** eggs.*	***a lot of/lots of** milk.*
***(not) enough** eggs.*	***(not) enough** milk.*
***a few** eggs.*	***a little** milk.*
***very few** eggs.*	***very little** milk.*
***not many** eggs.*	***not much** milk.*
***hardly any** eggs.*	***hardly any** milk.*
***no** eggs.*	***no** milk.*

5.4 Distributives: whole amounts and separate items

Words like *all, both, each, every, either* and *neither* are sometimes called **distributives**. They refer to whole amounts (*all/both the children, all/both the books, all the cheese*); or to separate items (*each child, either of the books*) [> 5.18–31].

5.5 The use of 'of' after quantifiers

Some quantity phrases used as determiners always take *of*:

*We've had **a lot of answers**.* (*a lot of answers* = determiner + noun)

But when they are used as pronouns, *of* is dropped:

*We've had **a lot**.* (*a lot* as a pronoun)

5.5.1 General references with quantifiers

Quantifiers which always take *of* before nouns/pronouns include:

a couple of
dozens of/hundreds of
the majority/a minority of
a number of } *people/books* (plural countable)

a large/small amount of } *cheese* (uncountable)
a bit of

a lot of
lots of } *books/cheese* (plural countable or uncountable)
plenty of

These references are general, i.e. we are not saying which particular people, etc.
Other quantifiers (*any, (a) few, more, most, some*, etc.) go directly before the noun (no *of*) in general references:

There are ***hardly any eggs/a few eggs*** *in the fridge.*
There is ***some butter/no butter*** *in the dish.*

5.5.2 Specific references with quantifiers

If we need to be specific (i.e. point to particular items) we can follow a quantifier with *of* + a determiner (*the, this, my*) [> 3.1].

Have ***some of this/a little of my wine****.* (e.g. the wine in this bottle)
I'll lend you ***some of these/a few of my books****.* (specified books)

In the same way we can make specific references with quantifiers which are always followed by *of* [> 5.5.1] by using determiners after them. Compare:

A lot of students *missed my lecture yesterday.* (general reference)
A lot of the students *who missed my lecture yesterday want to borrow my notes.* (specific reference)

Note the following quantifiers which are always specific and which must therefore be followed by *of* + determiner:

None of the/this milk *can be used.*
Part of/The rest of this food *will be for supper.*
Put ***the rest of those biscuits*** *in the tin.*

Note the omission and use of *of* in:

How much is left? – ***None*** *(of it).* ***Part of*** *it.* ***The rest of*** *it.*
How many are left? – ***None*** *(of them).* ***Part of/The rest of*** *them.*

5.6 The use of 'more' and 'less' after quantifiers

5.6.1 Quantifier + 'more'

More can be used after these quantifiers with plural countable nouns: *some/any, a couple, dozens/hundreds, a few, hardly any, a lot, lots, many, no,* numbers; *plenty, several,* weights, measures.
More can be used after these quantifiers with uncountable nouns: *some/any, a bit, a good/great deal, hardly any, a little, a lot, lots, much, no, plenty,* weights.

Quantifier + *more* combinations can be used as follows:

– directly in front of nouns: *I'd like* ***some more chips/milk****.*
– before *of* + determiner: *Do you want* ***some more of these chips****?*
– as pronouns: *I don't want* ***any more*** *thank you.*

5.6.2 Quantifier + 'less' [see also > 5.16.1]

Less can be used after these quantifiers with uncountable nouns: *any, a bit, a good/great deal, a little, a lot, lots, much*, as follows:

– directly in front of nouns: *Much less soup please.*
– before *of* + determiner: *I'd like **much less of that soup**.*
– as pronouns: *I want **much less** please.*

5.7 The use of '...left' and '...over' after quantifiers

Left (= not consumed or remaining) and *over* (= more than is wanted) combine with many quantifiers whether they are used as determiners or pronouns:

*Are there **any sweets left**? – I haven't got **any left**, I'm afraid.*
*We prepared too much food for the party and we had **a lot over**.*
*I thought we mightn't have enough pies, but there's **one over**.*

5.8 The use of 'not' before quantifiers

Not (Not **no**) can be used directly in front of: e.g. *all, another (one), enough, every, a few, half, the least, a little, many, more, much, one, the only one*, as follows [compare > 5.13, 13.13]:

– to begin statements:
__Not much__ is happening in our office at the moment.
– to emphasize the opposite in front of e.g. *a few* and *a little*:
*She's had **not a few proposals** of marriage in her time.* (= a lot)
– in short negative answers:
*How much did they offer you? – **Not enough**!*
– (in a few cases) to express surprise:
*I bought a new hat. – **Not another one**!*

Particular quantifiers and their uses

5.9 Numbers [> App 47]

Exact indications of quantity can be conveyed by means of numbers.

5.9.1 Cardinal numbers [compare > 2.37.1, 3.11]

Cardinal numbers can be used as quantifiers (*two apples*) or pronouns (*I bought two*). The number *one* will combine with any noun used as a singular countable noun:

*We've got **one micro** and **two electric typewriters** in our office.*

All other numbers combine with plural countable nouns:

*__Two cabbages__, **three pounds of tomatoes** and **twelve oranges**.*

Note also ordinals followed by cardinals (*the first three, the second two*, etc.) and: *the next/last two*, etc.:

__The first three runners__ won medals.

5.9.2 Counting

A number of adverbial expressions can be used to describe quantities and groups: e.g. *one at a time; one by one; two by two; by the dozen; by the hundred; in tens; in five hundreds*:

*How would you like your money? – **In fives** please.*

5.9.3 Fractions [> App 47.3.2]

We can say: e.g. $\frac{1}{2}$ (*a/one half*), $\frac{1}{4}$ (*a/one quarter*, or *one fourth*, AmE) and $\frac{1}{3}$ (*a/one third*). Otherwise, we make use of cardinal and ordinal numbers when referring to a fraction on its own: *9⁄16* (*nine sixteenths*), or to a whole number + fraction: *2⅔* (*two and two thirds*):

*2¼ (**Two and a quarter**) plus 3½ (**three and a half**) equals 5¾ (**five and three quarters**).*

We use *a* (Not **one**) with fractions for weights and measures [> 3.11]:

*I bought **half a pound of tea** and **a quarter of a pound of coffee**.*

This could also be expressed as: *a half pound of tea, a quarter pound of coffee.*

5.9.4 Decimals [> App 47.3.3]

Fractions expressed as decimals are referred to as follows: *0.5* (*nought point five* or *point five*); *2.05* (*two point nought five* or *two point oh five*); *2.5* (*two point five*):

*The front tyre pressure should be 1.8 (**one point eight**) and the rear pressure 1.9 (**one point nine**).*

5.9.5 Multiplying and dividing quantity

The following can be used to refer to quantity: *double (the quantity* or *amount*); *twice as much* (or *twice the quantity* or *amount*); *half as much* (or *half the quantity* or *amount*), etc.:

*We need **double/twice/three times** the quantity/amount.*

5.9.6 Approximate number and quantity

Numbers can be modified by: e.g. *about, almost, exactly, fewer than, at least, less than, more than, nearly, over, under:*

*There were **over seventy people** at the party.* (= more than)
*You can't vote if you're **under eighteen**.* (= less than)

5.10 The use of 'some' and 'any'

Some and *any* are the most frequently used quantity words in the language. They never answer *How many?* and *How much?*:

How many do you want? – e.g. ***Just a few***. (Not **some**)
How much do you want? – e.g. ***Just a little***. (Not **some**)

We generally use *some* and *any* when it is not important to state exactly how great or how small the quantity is. They often function as if they were the plural of *a/an* [> 3.6, 4.16]:

*There are **some letters** for you.*	(unspecified number)
*How many (letters are there)? – **Seven**.*	(number specified)
*There's **some bread** in the bread-bin.*	(unspecified amount)
*How much (bread is there)? – **Half a loaf**.*	(amount specified)

It is sometimes possible to omit *some* or *any* [> 3.28.8, 5.3]:

*My wife bought me **medicine** and **pastilles** for my cough.*

Some (= indefinite quantity or amount) is normally used
– in the affirmative:
*There are **some eggs** in the fridge.* (i.e. an unstated number)
*There is **some milk** in the fridge.* (i.e. an unstated quantity)
– in questions when we expect (or hope to get) the answer 'Yes':
*Have you got **some paper-clips** in that box?* (i.e. I know or I think you've got some and expect you to say 'Yes'.)
– in offers, requests, invitations and suggestions when we expect the answer 'Yes' or expect implied agreement.

The following are in the form of questions, though we are not seeking information [> 11.35–36]:
*Would you like **some** (more) **coffee**?* (expecting 'Yes')
*May I have **some** (more) **coffee**?* (expecting 'Yes')
– to mean 'certain, but not all':
***Some people** believe anything they read in the papers.*
Not...some can be used in certain contexts to mean 'not all':
*I did**n't** understand **some** of the lectures/**some** of the information.*

Some, + countable or uncountable noun, is normally unstressed in fluent speech and is pronounced /səm/:
*There are **some** /səm/ letters for you.*
As a pronoun, *some* is pronounced /sʌm/ but not usually stressed:
*Would you like any sugar? – I've had **some** /sʌm/ thank you.*
Some, meaning 'certain but not all' (see note above), is usually stressed and is pronounced /sʌm/. It can be stressed at the beginning of a statement to emphasize a contrast:
***'Some** /sʌm/ **people** have no manners.*
It can be stressed to refer to an unspecified person/thing:
***'Some** /sʌm/ **boy** left his shirt in the cloakroom.* [> 5.12.1]

Any (= indefinite quantity or amount) is normally used
– in negative statements containing *not* or *n't*:
*We have**n't** got **any shirts** in your size.*
*There is**n't any milk** in the fridge.*
– in questions when we are not sure about the answer or expect 'No':
*Have you got **any paper-clips** in the box?* (i.e. I don't know if you've got any and wouldn't be surprised if you said 'No'.)
– in sentences containing a negative word other than *not*, such as *hardly, never, seldom* or *without*, or when there is any suggestion of doubt, e.g. with *if* or *whether* [implied negatives, > 13.8]:
*There's **hardly any petrol** in the tank.*
*We got to Paris **without any problems**.*
*I don't know **if/whether there's any news** from Harry.*
– with *at all* and (more formally) *whatever* for special emphasis:
*I have**n't** got **any idea at all/whatever** about what happened.*

5.11 The use of 'not...any', 'no' and 'none'

5.11.1 'Not...any' and 'no'

An alternative way of forming a negative is with *no* [compare > 13.9]:

not...any: *There **aren't any buses** after midnight.*
no: *There **are no buses** after midnight.*

A clause can contain only *one* negative word, so that *not* and e.g. *no* or *never* cannot be used together [> 7.39, 13.10]:
*I could get **no information**.* (Not **I couldn't**)
When used in preference to *not...any*, *no* is slightly more formal and makes a negative idea more emphatic. Negatives with *not...any* are used in normal conversation, but we must always use *no* (Never **not any**) if we wish to begin a sentence with a negative:
***No department stores** open on Sundays.*

No can combine with a singular noun:
*There's **no letter** for you.* (= There isn't a letter for you.)
*I'm **no expert**, but I think this painting is a fake.*
No at the beginning of a statement strongly emphasizes a negative idea [compare > 13.9].

5.11.2 **'No' and 'none'** [compare 'none of', > 5.5.2]
No meaning *not...any* is a determiner and can only be used before a noun; *none* stands on its own as a pronoun:
*There is**n't any bread**.* *There's **no bread**.* *There's **none**.*
*There are**n't any sweets**.* *There are **no sweets**.* *There are **none**.*
Like *no*, *none* is more emphatic than *not...any*. When *no* or *none* are used, *not* cannot be used as well [> 7.39, 13.10]:
*I could**n't** get **any information** about flights to the USA.*
*I could get **no information** about flights to the USA.*
*Do you have any new diaries? – We've got **none** at the moment.*

5.12 Special uses of 'some', 'any' and 'no'

5.12.1 'Some'

Apart from its common use as a quantifier, *some* can be used to refer to an unspecified person or thing, etc. When used in this way it is generally stressed [> 5.10] and can mean:

– 'several': *I haven't seen Tom for **some years**.*
– 'approximately': *There were **some 400 demonstrators**.*
– 'extraordinary': *That's **some radio** you've bought!* (informal)
– 'an unknown': *There must be **some book** which could help.*
– 'no kind of': *That's **some consolation**, I must say!* (ironic)

With abstract nouns *some* can be used to mean 'an amount of':
*We've given **some thought** to your idea and find it interesting.*

5.12.2 'Any'

Apart from its common use as a quantifier, *any* can be used to refer to an unspecified person or thing and can occur in affirmative statements. When used in this way it is stressed and can mean:

– 'usual': *This isn't just **any cake**.* (it's special)
– 'the minimum/maximum': *He'll need **any help** he can get.*
– 'I don't care which': *Give me a plate. **Any plate/one** will do.*

5.12.3 'Any' and 'no' + adjective or adverb

Any and *no*, used as adverbs to mean 'at all', will combine with adjectives and adverbs in the comparative:
*Is he **any better** this morning? – No, he's **no better**.*
Any and *no*, used as adverbs, combine with a few positive adjectives, e.g. *good (any good)* and *different (any different)*:
*Is that book **any good**? – It's **no good** at all.*

5.13 Common uses of 'much' and 'many' [also > 6.24, 7.4]

We normally use *much* (+ uncountable) and *many* (+ plural countable):
– in negative statements:
*I **haven't much time**. There **aren't many pandas** in China.*

– in questions: (For questions with *How much/many?* [> 13.40.1])
__Is there much milk__ in that carton? __Have you had many inquiries__?
In everyday speech we usually avoid using *much* and *many* in affirmative statements. We use other quantifiers, especially *a lot of* [> 5.14]. *Much* and *many* occur in formal affirmative statements:
__Much__ has been done to improve conditions of work.
__Many teachers__ dislike marking piles of exercise books.

Combinations like *as much as* and *as many as* are used in the affirmative or negative:
You can/can't have __as much as (as many as)__ you like.
When *much* and *many* are modified by *much* and *far* (*much/far too much, far too many*) they tend to be used in the affirmative:
Your son gets __much/far too much pocket money__.
There are __far too many accidents__ at this junction.
Many in time expressions occurs in the affirmative or negative:
I have lived here/haven't lived here __(for) many years__.

Not much and *not many* commonly occur in short answers:
Have you brought much luggage? – No, __not much__.
Have you written many letters? – No, __not many__.
Not much and *not many* can be subjects or part of the subject:
__Not much__ is really known about dinosaurs.
__Not many people__ know about Delia's past.

Much occurs in a number of expressions (e.g. *there's not much point in ...; it's a bit much; he's not much of a ...*):
__There's not much point in__ telling the same story again.

Not so much occurs in comparisons:
It's __not so much__ a bedroom, __more__ a studio.
Dennis __is not so much__ a nuisance __as__ a menace.
It's __not so much that__ he dislikes his parents, __as that/but that__ he wants to set up on his own.

Many (like *few* [> 5.15.1]) can be modified by *the, my, your*, etc.:
One of __the many__ people he knows can help him to get a job.

5.14 'A lot of' compared with similar quantifiers

Much and *many* do not normally occur in the affirmative in everyday speech [> 5.13]. Instead, we use *a lot of* and (informally) *lots of*:
I've got __a lot of/lots of time__. I've got __a lot of/lots of books__.
A lot of, lots of and *plenty of* (+ plural countable or singular uncountable) are normally used in the affirmative. They also occur in questions, especially when we expect the answer 'Yes':
I met __a lot of/lots of interesting people__ on holiday.
Don't worry. We've got __plenty of time__ before the train leaves.
Were there __a lot of/lots of questions__ after the lecture?
A lot of and *lots of* occur in the negative as well, especially when we are emphasizing a negative or denying, but the use of *plenty of* in negative statements is less common:
I have__n't__ got __a lot of patience__ with hypochondriacs!

A lot of (not *lots of* or *plenty of*) can be modified by *quite/rather*
*Jimmy's caused **quite a lot of trouble** at his new school.*
*The new law has affected **rather a lot of people**.*

Plenty of, a lot of and *lots of* can be used with singular or plural verbs depending on the noun that follows them:
*There **has been a lot of/lots of/plenty of gossip** about her.*
(uncountable noun, so singular verb)
*There **have been a lot of/lots of/plenty of inquiries**.*
(plural countable, so plural verb)

Several can only be used with plural countables in the affirmative:
*We've already had **several offers** for our flat.*
It can also combine with *dozen, hundred, thousand, million*, etc.:
***Several hundred people** took part in the demonstration.*

A lot of/lots of are often considered unsuitable in formal style. Instead, we use *much/many* [> 5.13] or other quantifiers, such as:
- *a great deal of* or *a great amount of* + uncountable noun:
***A great deal of/A great amount of money** is spent on research.*
- *a large number of* or *a great number of* + plural countable noun:
***A large number of/A great number of our students** are American.*

Some native speakers use *amount of* with countable nouns as well:
***A large/great amount of our investments** are in property.*

5.15 '(A) few' and '(a) little'

5.15.1 'Few' and 'a few'

Few and *a few* are used with plural countables.
Few is negative, suggesting 'hardly any at all', and is often used after *very*:
*Mona has had **very few opportunities** to practise her English.*
In everyday speech we prefer *not...many* or *hardly any*:
*Mona has**n't had many opportunities** to practise her English.*
*Mona has had **hardly any opportunities** to practise her English.*
Few can also convey the idea of 'not as many as were expected':
*A lot of guests were expected, but **few** came.*

A few is positive, suggesting 'some, a (small) number':
*The police would like to ask him **a few questions**.*
A few can mean 'a very small number', or even 'quite a lot'. The size of the number depends on the speaker's viewpoint:
*I don't know how much he's got, but it must be **a few million**.*
A few can be used to mean 'more than none, more than expected':
*Have we run out of sardines? – No, there are **a few tins** left.*

A few can also combine with other words: e.g.

just:	*How many do you want? **Just a few** please.* (i.e. a limited number, not many)
only:	*There are **only a few** seats left.* (i.e. very few, hardly any)
quite:	*How many do you want? **Quite a few** please.* (i.e. quite a lot)

a good:	*We had **a good few** letters this morning.* (i.e. quite a lot)
dozen, 100, 1000:	*The film director employed **a few hundred** people as extras.* (i.e. several hundred)
the, my, etc:	***The few** people who saw the film enjoyed it.*
	***Her few** possessions were sold after her death.* (i.e. the small number of)

5.15.2 'Little' and 'a little'

Little and *a little* are used with (singular) uncountables.
Little (like *few*) is negative, suggesting 'hardly any at all' and is often used after *very*:

*He has **very little hope** of winning this race.*

In everyday speech we prefer *not...much* or *hardly any*:

*He has**n't much hope** of winning this race.*
*He has **hardly any hope** of winning this race.*

Little can also convey the idea of 'not as much as was expected':

*We climbed all day but made **little progress**.*

Little occurs in idiomatic 'negative' phrases such as *little point, little sense, little use*, etc.:

*There's **little point** in trying to mend it.*

A little and, in very informal contexts, *a bit (of)* are positive, suggesting 'some, a (small) quantity':

*I'd like **a little*** (or ***a bit of***) ***time** to think about it please.*

The size of the amount depends on the viewpoint of the speaker:

*Mrs Laccy left **a little money** in her will – about $1,000,000!*

A little can also mean 'more than none, more than expected':

*Have we got any flour? – Yes, there's **a little** in the packet.*

A little can combine with other words: e.g.

just:	*How much do you want? – **Just a little** please.* (i.e. a limited quantity, not much)
only:	*There's **only a little** soup left.* (i.e. very little, hardly any)

Few and *little* can be modified by e.g. *extremely, relatively:*

*There are **relatively few jobs** for astronauts.*

A few and *a little* can modify other quantifiers, as in *a few more*, and *a little less* [compare > 6.27.5, 7.45–46].

5.16 'Fewer/the fewest' and 'less/the least'

These are the comparative and superlative forms of *few* and *little*. In theory, *fewer/the fewest* should be used only with plural countables (*fewer/the fewest videos*) and *less/the least* only with uncountables (*less/the least oil*):

***Fewer videos** were sold this year than last.*
***Less oil** was produced this year than last.*

In practice, however, the informal use by native speakers of *less* and *the least* with plural countables or collective words like *people* is commonly heard (*less people, less newspapers*, etc.) but is not generally approved:

***Less and less people** can afford to go abroad for their holidays.*
*Political programmes on TV attract **the least viewers**.*

Less (not *fewer*) is used before *than* for prices and periods of time:
It costs ***less than £5****. I'll see you in* ***less than three weeks****.*

5.16.1 The modification of 'fewer' and 'less'

Fewer is modified by *even, far, many, a good deal/many* and *a lot*:
There are ***far fewer/a lot fewer*** *accidents in modern factories.*
Less is commonly modified by *even, far, a good deal, a little, a lot, many* (*many less* – see 5.16) and *much*:
I've got ***much/a lot/far less*** *free time than I used to have.*

5.17 'Enough'

Enough, meaning 'adequate in quantity or number', can be used in front of plural countable nouns and (singular) uncountable nouns in all kinds of utterances: statements, questions or negatives:
Have we got ***enough books*** *to read while we are on holiday?*
Have we got ***enough food*** *in the house to last the next few days?*
Compare the use of *enough*, meaning 'of an adequate degree', after adjectives and adverbs [> 7.47–48]:
Is there ***enough hot water*** *for me to take a bath?* (quantity)
Is the ***water hot enough*** *for me to take a bath?* (degree)

Enough of will combine with a singular countable:
Your education is ***enough of a problem*** *for me.*

Enough can be modified by *about, almost, hardly, less than, more than, nearly, not, not nearly, quite, not quite* and *scarcely*:
There is ***hardly enough cake****./There are* ***hardly enough biscuits****.*
In special contexts, *little* and *few* can modify *enough*:
I can't lend you any money. I have ***little enough*** *as it is.*
I can't give you any stamps. I have ***few enough*** *as it is.*
(i.e. less than enough money/fewer than enough stamps)

Enough (= sufficient) is associated with *plenty* (= more than enough), especially in questions and answers:
Have you got ***enough cream*** *on your strawberries?*
– Yes, I've got ***plenty*** *thank you.*

Distributives

5.18 'Both', 'all' and 'half' + nouns [> 5.4]

5.18.1 'Both', 'all' and 'half' + plural countable nouns – examples and notes

Both *books are expensive.*	***All*** *books are expensive.*	–
Both *the/my/these books are expensive.*	***All*** *the/my/these books are expensive.*	***Half*** *the/my/these eggs are bad.*
Both of *the/my/these books are expensive.*	***All of*** *the/my/these books are expensive.*	***Half of*** *the/my/these eggs are bad.*

1 *Both, all* and *half* can be used equally with:
– people: *both (the) women/all (the) women/half the women.*
– things: *both (the) forks/all (the) forks/half the forks.*

2 *Both* refers to *two* people, things, etc. only:
e.g. *both books/both the books/both of the books* (interchangeable). The reference is to specific items (e.g. *the books on this subject*). *Both* means 'not only one, but also the other' and refers to two things together. By comparison, *the two* (*the two things are different*) refers to the two considered separately.

3 *Half* + plural countable refers to 'more than two':
e.g. *half the eggs/half of the eggs* (interchangeable).
Half (of) cannot be used without a determiner (*the, this, my*, etc.) before plural countables [compare > 5.18.3*n*.1].

4 *All* refers to 'the whole number of' people, things, etc.:
e.g. *all the books/all of the books* (interchangeable).
With *the*, the reference is to specific items: (e.g. *the books on this subject*). However, *all books* is general, referring to e.g. *all (the) books in the world*. It is not interchangeable with *all the books/all of the books*.

5 *All* with or without *the*, however, refers to specific items when it is followed by a number before a plural countable:
All (the) thirty passengers *on the boat were saved.*

5.18.2 'All' and 'half' + uncountable nouns – examples and note

All *bread gets stale quickly.*	–
All *the bread was stale.*	***Half*** *the bread was stale.*
All of *the bread was stale.*	***Half of*** *the bread was stale.*

The first statement with *all* is general; the second and third are interchangeable and refer to a specific amount of bread. The two statements with *half* are interchangeable and refer to a specific amount of bread. The word *both* cannot be used with uncountable nouns because it refers to *two* units.

5.18.3 'All' and 'half' + singular countable nouns – examples and notes

All *the country was against it.*	***Half*** *the country was against it.*
All of *the country was against it.*	***Half of*** *the country was against it.*

1 When we are referring to a specific thing, we must use *the* or *of the* after *all* and *half* [compare *the whole*, > 5.22]. However, *all* and *half* can be used directly in front of many proper nouns:
All London/Half New York *was buzzing with gossip.*

2 *Half a* can be followed by singular countables as in *half a loaf, half a minute, half an orange*, etc. to refer to one thing divided into halves.

5.19 'Both' and 'all': word order with verbs

5.19.1 'Both' and 'all' after auxiliary verbs

Both and *all* as pronouns are normally used *after* auxiliary verbs (*be, have* [> 10.1] and modal auxiliaries like *can, could* [> 11.1]):

The girls ***are both*** *ready.*
(= Both girls/Both the girls/Both of the girls are ready.)

*The girls **are both** waiting.*
(= Both girls/Both the girls/Both of the girls are waiting.)
*The girls **have all** left.*
(= All the girls/All of the girls have left.)
*The girls **can/must**, etc. **all** go home now.*
(= All the girls/All of the girls can/must go home now.)

Both/all come *before* auxiliary and modal verbs in short answers:

Are you ready?	–	*Yes, we **both are**.*	*Yes, we **all are**.*
Have you finished?	–	*Yes, we **both have**.*	*Yes, we **all have**.*
Do you like it?	–	*Yes, we **both do**.*	*Yes, we **all do**.*
Can you see it?	–	*Yes, we **both can**.*	*Yes, we **all can**.*

5.19.2 'Both' and 'all' before full verbs

Both and *all* as pronouns must be used *before* full verbs:
*The girls **both left** early.*
(= Both girls/Both the girls/Both of the girls left early.)
*The girls **all left** early.*
(= All the girls/All of the girls left early.)
And note *both/all* before *have* as a full verb [> 10.27, 10.32]:
*We **all have** our books. We **both had** a haircut.*

5.20 'Both', 'all' and 'half': word order with pronouns

5.20.1 'Both' and 'all': pronoun subject

Both and *all* must be followed by *of* before pronouns like *us, them*:
***Both of us/them** left early.* (= We/They both left early.)
***All of us/them** left early.* (= We/They all left early.)
***All of it** went bad.* (= It all went bad.)

5.20.2 'Both' and 'all': pronoun object with verbs and prepositions

*I love **both/all of you**.* or *I love **you both/all**.*
*He gave some to **both/all of us**.* or *He gave some to **us both/all**.*
*You've eaten **all of it**.* or *You've eaten **it all**.*

5.20.3 'Half' as a distributive and as an adverb

***Half (of) the bottles** are empty.*
(i.e. half of them are not empty)
However, there is a different meaning when *half* is an adverb:
*The bottles are **half empty**.*
(i.e. no bottle is completely empty)

5.21 The 'negative' of 'all' and 'both'

We can use *not all* to mean 'some but not all':
***Not all** the girls left early.* (= Only some of them left early.)
Compare the above with the following negative:
***All** the girls **didn't leave** early.*
This negative statement is ambiguous because it can mean 'some of them left early' or 'none of them left early'.
To avoid ambiguity we should use *none of* to make the negative of *all* and *neither of* to make the negative of *both:*
***All** the girls left early.* → ***None of** the girls left early.*
***Both** the girls left early.* → ***Neither of** the girls left early.*

5.22 'All (the)' compared with '(the) whole'

5.22.1 'All the' and 'the whole' with nouns

We usually prefer *the whole* to *all the* with singular concrete nouns. *The whole* is not normally used with plurals and uncountables:

He ate ***the whole loaf*** (= all the loaf) *by himself.*

All and *the whole* combine with a number of (often abstract) nouns. For example, we can use *all* or *the whole* in: *all my business/my whole business, all my life/my whole life, all the time/the whole time*, etc., but normally only *all* in: e.g. *all my hair, all the money*; and normally only *the whole* in: e.g. *the whole situation, the whole story, the whole truth. Whole* can follow *a*, as in *a whole collection, a whole loaf, a whole week/hour.*

5.22.2 Time references with 'all' and 'the whole'

All combines with words like *(the) day, (the) night, (the) week, (the) year, (the) summer* (but not with *hour* or *century*) in time references (*all of the* is possible, but less common):

I waited ***all (the) week*** *for him to answer.*

The whole is stronger than *all* in time references and can also be used with *hour* and *century*:

I waited ***the whole week*** *for him to answer.*

Of the is possible after *the whole*, but is usually absent. *The whole* followed by *of the* functions as a noun and is more common in references not concerned with time: e.g. *the whole (of the) book, the whole (of the) building.*

5.22.3 'All' and 'whole' + plural countable nouns

All and *whole* + plural countable have different meanings in: e.g.

All forests *in North Africa were destroyed during Roman times.*
(= every single one of them)

Whole forests *in North Africa were destroyed during Roman times.*
(= entire areas of forest)

5.23 'All' compared with 'every'

All refers to a collection of things seen as one, or to an amount:

I've read ***all these books***. (= this whole collection)
She's used ***all the butter***. (= the whole amount)

Every emphasizes single units within a group and is used only with singular countables:

I've read ***every book*** *in the library.* (= every single one)

All can be used before a noun or on its own [> 5.18, 5.24]; *every* can never stand on its own (*every day, every man*, etc.).

Every is often found in time references: *every day, every week*, etc. and can be followed by ordinal and cardinal numbers and *other*: *every third day, every six weeks, every other day*, etc.:

I work ***every other day****: Monday, Wednesday and Friday.*

All and *every* are not normally interchangeable in time references:

Monica spent ***all day*** *with us.* (= one whole day)
Monica spent ***every day*** *with us while she was here on holiday.*
(all the days of her holiday, thought of separately)

5.24 'All' compared with 'everyone/everybody/anyone/anybody'

All, meaning 'everybody', is uncommon in modern English:
Everyone/Everybody *wanted Marilyn's autograph.* (Not **All**)
In older English, *all* (= everybody) can occur:
All *but Emily had guessed the truth.*

All can occur in formal contexts to mean 'all the people', but it generally needs to be qualified by e.g. a relative clause [> 1.40]:
All (those) who wish to apply *must do so in writing.*
All could be replaced by *anyone/anybody* :
Anyone/Anybody who wishes to apply *must do so in writing.*
Anyone/anybody is the equivalent of *whoever* here and is preferable to *everyone/everybody*. *All*, used on its own to mean 'all the people', occurs in a few fixed expressions:
A good time was had ***by all****. The law applies equally* ***to all****.*

5.25 'All' compared with 'everything'

All and *everything* + singular verb can be used interchangeably, though *all* is more formal and usually requires qualification:
All/Everything *I have belongs to you.*
All, used to mean 'everything', occurs in a few fixed phrases:
Winner takes ***all****.*
All, but not *everything*, can be used to mean 'the only thing':
All *he wants is more pay for less work.*

5.26 'Every' compared with 'each'

5.26.1 'Every' and 'each' with reference to 'more than two'

Every and *each* refer to particular people or things. They can point to more than two. *Each* is more individual and suggests 'one by one' or 'separately'. We use it to refer to a definite and usually limited number:
Each child in the school *was questioned.*
Every child is less individual and is used in much the same way as *all children* [> 5.18.1] to refer to a large indefinite number:
Every child *enjoys Christmas.* (= All children enjoy Christmas.)
This difference is not always important and the two words are often used interchangeably, as in:
Every/Each time *I wash the car it rains.*
Each cannot be modified; *every* can be modified by *almost, nearly*, and *practically* and can be followed by *single*:
Almost every *building was damaged in the earthquake.*
I answer ***every single*** *letter I receive.*
We can use *not* in front of *every*, but not in front of *each*:
Not every *house on the island has electricity.*
Every, but not *each*, can be used in front of a few uncountables such as *assistance, encouragement*, etc. though this is unusual:
My parents gave me ***every encouragement*** *when I was a child.*

5.26.2 'Each' referring to both members of a pair

Each, but not *every*, can refer to both the members of a pair:
As they had ***both*** *worked so hard, they* ***each*** *received a bonus.*

Both usually means 'two items considered together'; *each* considers two things separately:

I spoke to ***both of the twins*** *this morning.* (i.e. together)

I spoke to ***each of the twins*** *this morning.* (i.e. separately)

5.26.3 'Each': word order

Each, but not *every*, has word order variations similar to *all/both* [> 5.19–20]. *Each*, combining with a plural subject, takes a plural verb:

They ***have each taken*** *their own share.* (after an auxiliary)

They ***each have*** *their own share.* (before a full verb)

Each takes a singular verb when it begins a subject-phrase:

Each of us is *responsible for his/our actions.* [> 4.40]

Each can also occur at the end of a statement:

Give the delivery-men $5 ***each***.

5.27 'Another' compared with '(the) other(s)'

Another can have two meanings:

- 'additional'/'similar': *Do you need* ***another*** *cup? – No, I have enough.*
- 'different': *Give me* ***another*** *cup. This one's cracked.*

Another and *others* are indefinite; *the* (or *my, your*, etc.) *other* and *the others* are definite. *Another*, as a determiner, always goes with a singular noun unless it is followed by a cardinal number or by *few*:

I need ***another three driving lessons*** *before my test.*

I need ***another few days*** *before I can make up my mind.*

The other can be followed by a singular or plural noun:

This seat is free; ***the other seat is*** *taken.*

These seats are free; ***the other seats are*** *taken.*

Another is followed by a singular noun; *other* by a plural noun:

There must be ***another way*** *of solving the problem; that can't be the only way. There must be* ***other ways*** *of solving the problem.*

The other + *one* or a noun refers to a specific alternative:

I don't like this shirt. Can I try ***the other one*** *please?*

Compare: *Can I try* ***another (one)****?* (= any other one, non-specific)

The others, the other and *others* (like *another*) can stand on their own as pronouns to refer to specific alternatives:

I'll take these shirts but leave ***the other(s)***.

The other(s) is often used in contrast to *one*:

One *has buttons and* ***the other*** *hasn't.*

Others is often used in contrast to *some*:

Some *people enjoy exercise,* ***others*** *don't.*

Other can also mean 'additional' in: e.g.

Jane and some ***other girls*** *went shopping.*

The other (day) can mean 'a few (days) ago' in time references:

Karen phoned ***the other day*** *to apologize for her behaviour.*

This is not to be confused with *the next*, meaning 'the following':

Karen phoned ***the next day*** *to apologize for her behaviour.*

or with *another* to mean 'a different':

We aren't free tomorrow. Can we arrange ***another day****?*

5.28 'Each other' and 'one another' [compare > 4.28]

Sometimes a distinction is drawn between *each other* (used to refer to two people) and *one another* (used to refer to more than two). In everyday speech, both phrases are normally interchangeable:

*Karen and Dave are deeply in love with **each other/one another**.*

Both phrases can be used with an *'s*:

*Those two are always copying **each other's/one another's** homework.*

5.29 'Either' compared with 'neither'

Either and *neither* refer to two people, things, etc. (singular nouns) only. *Either* means 'one or the other' and *neither* means 'not one and not the other'. Constructions with *neither* are generally more emphatic than those with *not...either*:

Do you want an appointment at 9 or at 10?
*– **Either time** is difficult. **Neither time** is convenient.*

5.29.1 'Either' and 'neither' + 'of'

When followed by *of*, *either* and *neither* refer to each of two items:

*Which pot shall I use? – **Either (of them)**. It doesn't matter which.*
*Which pot shall I use? – **Neither (of them)**. Use this frying pan.*

5.29.2 'Either + or'; 'neither + nor' [> 1.15, 5.31]

*You can have **either** this one **or** that one.*
***Neither** this house **nor** the house next door has central heating.*

5.29.3 'Either' and 'both' compared

Either refers to two things considered separately. Compare:

*You can't have **either of them**.* (= you can't have one or the other)
*You can't have **both of them**.* (= you can have only one of them)

5.30 The use of 'one (of)' after distributives [compare > 4.10]

We may use *one of* after *another, any, each, either, every* and *neither* before nouns or pronouns. *One* is optional, except in the case of *every*:

***Each guidebook** in the series has been carefully written.*
***Every guidebook** in the series has been carefully written.*
***Each of these guidebooks** has been carefully written.*
***Each one of these guidebooks** has been carefully written.*
***Every one of these guidebooks** has been carefully written.*

We can use *single* after *every* for special emphasis:

***Every single apple** in the bag was bad.*
***Every single one of the apples** in the bag was bad.*

If we wish to use *another, each* and *either* as pronouns, we can use them with or without *one*:

*I didn't like the red skirt, so I asked to see **another (one)**.*
*Look at these names. **Each (one)** should have a tick beside it.*

Neither is generally used without *one*:

*I've tested both those TVs. **Neither** works very well.*

Every and *the only* cannot stand on their own as pronouns: they must always be followed by a noun or *one* (also *ones* after *the only*):

We need some more eggs. You ate ***every one*** *last night.*
You can't borrow my pen. It's ***the only one*** *I've got.*
These keys are ***the only ones*** *I've got.*

5.31 Singular and plural verbs with quantifiers [compare > 4.40]

Sometimes the reference is clearly singular or plural and a singular or plural verb is needed:

Most of us have *experienced sorrow in our lives.*
Most of our steel is *imported.*

But after *neither* (= not either) and *none* (= not one), when the reference is plural, we can use a plural verb in everyday speech, or a singular verb when we wish to sound 'correct' or formal:

Neither of us is/are *happy about the situation.*
None of my friends has/have *been invited to the party.*

In the above examples, *us* and *friends* attract plural verbs.
With *either...or* and *neither...nor* the verb generally agrees with the nearest noun [> 1.15, 5.29.2]:

Neither my brother nor ***my sister is*** *red-haired.*
Neither my brother nor ***my sisters are*** *red-haired.*
Neither my brothers nor ***my sister is/are*** *red-haired.*
Neither James nor ***I am*** *interested.*
Neither my brother nor ***my sister is/are*** *interested.*

6 Adjectives

Formation of adjectives

6.1 What an adjective is and what it does

An adjective describes the person, thing, etc. which a noun refers to. We use adjectives to say what a person, etc. is like or seems like. For example, adjectives can give us information about:

Quality:	*a **beautiful** dress; a **nice** day.*
Size:	*a **big** car; a **small** coin; a **tall** man.*
Age:	*a **new** handbag; a **young** man.*
Temperature:	*a **cool** evening; a **hot** day.*
Shape:	*a **round** table; a **square** box.*
Colour:	***blue** eyes, **grey** hair; a **white** horse.*
Origin:	*a **Japanese** camera; a **Swiss** watch.*

An adjective can also describe the idea(s) contained in a whole group of words, as in:

*Professor Roberts' lecture on magnetism was **fascinating**.*
*To maintain that we can survive a nuclear war is **absurd**.*

Many adjectives can answer the question *What...like?* and, depending on context, can give general or precise information:

What's Tom like (to look at)?	*– He's **dark/short/tall**.*
What's Pam like (as a person)?	*– She's **clever/kind/witty**.*
What's the car like?	*– It's **new/old/red/rusty**.*
What's the car like to drive?	*– It's **difficult/fast/slow**.*

6.2 The suffixes and prefixes of one-word adjectives

Some words function only as adjectives (*tall*). Others function as adjectives or nouns (*cold*). Many adjectives which are related to verbs or nouns have a characteristic ending (or **suffix**). For example, *-able* added to a verb like *enjoy* gives us the adjective *enjoyable*; *-ful* added to a noun like *truth* gives us the adjective *truthful*. For further examples [> App 8.1].

Present participle *-ing* forms often function as adjectives (*running water* [> 2.7, 16.38, 16.39.3]). Many of these *-ing* forms have *-ed* adjectival past participle equivalents (*interesting/interested*) [> 6.15]. Some irregular past participles function as adjectives (*broken*) [> 6.14].

Prefixes added to adjectives generally have a negative effect. For example, *dis-* added to *agreeable* gives us *disagreeable*; *un-* added to *interesting* gives us *uninteresting*. For further examples [> App 8.2]. Not every 'positive' adjective can be turned into a negative one by the addition of a prefix. Sometimes we have to use *not* (*not taxable*). Similarly, not every 'negative' adjective (especially those formed with past participles) has a positive equivalent (*discontinued, mistaken*).

6.3 The formation of compound adjectives

Compound adjectives are often written with hyphens [> 2.11]. Some of the commonest types are:

6.3.1 Compound adjectives formed with participles, etc.

- compounds formed with past participles: e.g. *a* ***candle-lit*** *table; a* ***horse-drawn*** *cart; a* ***self-employed*** *author; a* ***tree-lined*** *avenue.*
- compounds formed with present participles: e.g. *a* ***long-playing*** *record; a* ***long-suffering*** *parent; a* ***time-consuming*** *job.*
- *-ed* words that look like participles although they are formed from nouns: e.g. *cross-eyed, flat-chested, hard-hearted, open-minded, quick-witted, slow-footed.*

6.3.2 Compound adjectives of measurement, etc.

Cardinal numbers combine with nouns (usually singular) to form compound adjectives relating to time, measurement, etc.: e.g.

Age:	*a* ***three-year-old*** *building; a* ***twenty-year-old*** *man.*
Area/volume;	*a* ***three-acre*** *plot; a* ***two-litre*** *car.*
Duration:	*a* ***four-hour*** *meeting; a* ***two-day*** *conference.*
Length/depth:	*a* ***twelve-inch*** *ruler; a* ***six-foot*** *hole.*
Price:	*a* ***$50*** *dress; a* ***£90,000*** *house.*
Time/distance:	*a* ***ten-minute*** *walk; a* ***three-hour*** *journey.*
Weight:	*a* ***ten-stone*** *man; a* ***five-kilo*** *bag of flour.*

Ordinal numbers can be used in compounds: e.g. *a* ***first-rate*** *film; a* ***second-hand*** *car; a* ***third-floor*** *flat; a* ***nineteenth-century*** *novel.*

6.3.3 Compound adjectives formed with prefixes and suffixes

Compounds can be formed from a variety of prefixes and suffixes: e.g. *class-conscious, tax-free, loose-fitting, waterproof, fire-resistant, car-sick, tight-lipped, vacuum-sealed, airtight.*
Many compounds can be formed with *well* and *badly*: *-behaved, -built, -done, -paid*, etc. Similarly, *ill* and *poorly* combine with some past participles: *-advised, -educated, -informed, -paid*, etc.

Types of adjectives and their uses

6.4 Form and use of adjectives

An adjective never varies in form no matter whether it refers to people or things, etc. in the singular or plural:

singular:			
a tall man:	*Bob is tall.*	*He is tall.*	*He is a tall man.*
a tall woman:	*Maggie is tall.*	*She is tall.*	*She is a tall woman.*
a tall horse:	*That horse is tall.*	*It is tall.*	*It is a tall horse.*
a tall tree:	*That tree is tall.*	*It is tall.*	*It is a tall tree.*
plural:			
tall men:	*Bob and Jim are tall.*	*They are tall.*	*They are tall men.*
tall women:	*Mary and Ann are tall.*	*They are tall.*	*They are tall women.*
tall people:	*Bob and Ann are tall.*	*They are tall.*	*They are tall people.*
tall horses:	*Those horses are tall.*	*They are tall.*	*They are tall horses.*
tall trees:	*Those trees are tall.*	*They are tall.*	*They are tall trees.*

6.5 Gradable and non-gradable adjectives

Adjectives can be divided into two classes: a large class of words which can be graded (gradable adjectives) and a small class that cannot be graded (non-gradable adjectives).

An adjective is **gradable** when:

- we can imagine degrees in the quality referred to and so can use it with words like *very, too*, and *enough*:
  very good, too good, less good, not good enough, etc. [> 7.50].
- we can form a comparative and superlative from it [> 6.22, 6.24–25]:
  (big), bigger, biggest; (good), better, best, etc.

An adjective is **non-gradable** when:

- we cannot modify it (i.e. we cannot use it with *very, too*, etc.)
- we cannot make a comparative or superlative from it: e.g.
  daily, dead, medical, unique, etc. [> 7.42].

6.6 Some problems for the learner in the use of adjectives

Learners may experience interference from their own language in relation to the following characteristics of adjectives in English:

- they do not vary in form to 'agree' with nouns [> 6.4]:
  *a **tall** man/woman/tree, **tall** men/women/trees.*
- they generally precede nouns when used attributively [> 6.7]:
  *a **cool** drink, a **long** day, a **pretty** dress.*
- when used attributively, they nearly always combine with a noun or with *one/ones* [> 4.10]. So we must use a noun in expressions like *You poor thing! You lucky girl!* [compare > 4.7.4].
  a young man, a one-eyed man [compare > 6.12.2].
- the verbs *be, seem*, etc. combine with adjectives like *afraid, cold, hot, hungry, lucky, right, sleepy, thirsty, unlucky, wrong*, where in some European languages such words are used as nouns after *have*, or an idea can be expressed by a verb. So, in English, depending on context, *She is cold* may relate to temperature (i.e. *not warm*) or attitude (i.e. *not friendly*). Nor do adjectives like *cold, hot*, etc. combine with *make* to refer to the weather:
  It (i.e. the weather) ***is** cold/hot/windy.*
- for adjectives and adverbs often confused (*fast*, etc.) [> App 14].

6.7 Attributive and predicative adjectives

The terms **attributive** and **predicative** refer to the position of an adjective in a phrase or sentence. We say that an adjective is attributive or is used attributively when it comes before a noun (and is therefore part of the **noun phrase** [> 2.1]):

*an **old** ticket, a **young** shop-assistant, he is an **old** man.*

We say that an adjective is predicative or that it is used predicatively when it comes directly after *be, seem*, etc. It can be used on its own as the **complement** [> 1.9, 1.11.1, 6.17]:

*This ticket **is old**. Your mother **seems angry**.*

For predicative adjectives after verbs other than *be, seem*, etc: *turn yellow* [> 10.26.1]. Most adjectives can be used either attributively or predicatively. A few can be used in one way and not in the other.

A few adjectives such as *old, late* and *heavy* can take on a different meaning when used attributively. Compare:

*Agatha Withers is very **old** now.* (i.e. in years – predicative)
*He's an **old** friend.* (i.e. I've known him a long time – attributive)
*Your suitcase is very **heavy**.* (i.e. in weight – predicative)
*Paterson is a **heavy** smoker.* (i.e. he smokes a lot – attributive)
*You're **late** again.* (i.e. not on time – predicative)
*My **late** uncle was a miner.* (i.e. he's dead now – attributive)

Adjectives used attributively in this way tend to combine with a limited selection of nouns: e.g. *a heavy drinker/sleeper*, but not e.g. *worker*. There are other restrictions as well: e.g. *old* (*an old friend*), *heavy* (*a heavy smoker*) and *late* (*my late uncle*) cannot be used predicatively in these senses. However, *old* (in years) and *heavy* (weight) can be used attributively or predicatively. *Late* (not on time) is used attributively in limited contexts:

***Late** arrivals will not be allowed to enter the auditorium.*

For problems connected with adjectives which can be confused with adverbs, e.g. *fast, hard/hardly, late/lately* [> Apps 14, 15].

6.8 Adjectives used predicatively

6.8.1 Predicative adjectives describing health

The following are used predicatively [> 6.7] in connexion with health: *faint, ill, poorly, unwell* and *well*:

*What's the matter with him? – He**'s ill/unwell**. He **feels faint**.*
*How are you? – I**'m** very **well** thank you. I**'m fine** thanks.*

Fine relating to health is predicative; used attributively it means 'excellent' (e.g. *She's a fine woman.*).
The adjectives *sick* and *healthy* can be used in the attributive position where *ill* and *well* normally cannot:

*What's the matter with Mr Court? – He's **a sick man**.*
*Biggles **was** very **ill**, but he's now **a healthy man**.*

(But note that 'He's an *ill man*' is increasingly heard.)

Well, to mean 'in good health', is an adjective and should not be confused with *well*, the adverbial counterpart of *good* [> 6.17, 7.5*n*.4]. *Faint* can be used attributively when not referring to health in e.g. *a faint chance; a faint hope; a faint sound*, as can *ill* in fixed phrases such as: *an ill omen; an ill wind.*

6.8.2 Predicative adjectives beginning with 'a-'

Adjectives like the following are used only predicatively: *afloat, afraid, alight, alike, alive, alone, ashamed, asleep, awake:*

*The children **were asleep** at 7, but now they**'re awake**.*

We can express similar ideas with attributive adjectives:

*The vessel **is afloat**...*	→	*The **floating vessel**...*
*The children **are afraid**...*	→	*The **frightened children**...*
*The buildings **are alight**...*	→	*The **burning buildings**...*
*Everything that **is alive**...*	→	*All **living things**...*
*That lobster **is alive**...*	→	*It's a **live lobster**...*
*The children **are asleep**...*	→	*The **sleeping children**...*
*When I **am awake**...*	→	*In my **waking hours**...*

Attributive adjectives can only replace predicative ones in suitable contexts. For example, *living* cannot replace *alive* in:

*All the hostages on the plane **are alive** and **well**.*

(Not **all the living hostages** in this context)

Shameful is not the attributive counterpart of *ashamed*:

*It was a **shameful act**.* (describing the act)

*He ought to **be ashamed**.* (describing the person)

Similarly, *lonely* is not the exact equivalent of *alone*:

*You can be **alone** without being **lonely**.*

Alone (predicative) means 'without others'; *lonely* (attributive: *a lonely woman*, or predicative: *she is lonely*) generally means 'feeling sad because you are on your own'.

Some of these adjectives are modified in special ways and not by *very*: *safely afloat, all alight, all alone, fast/sound asleep, fully/wide awake* [compare > 6.9, 7.51]. However, the following can be modified by *very much*: *afraid, awake, alive, alone* and *ashamed*; *afraid* and *ashamed* can also be modified directly by *very* [compare > 7.51]:

*Is that lobster alive? – Yes, be careful! It's **very much alive**!*

*I behaved badly yesterday and still feel **very ashamed** of myself.*

6.8.3 Predicative adjectives describing feelings, reactions, etc.

Some adjectives describing feelings, etc., (*content, glad, pleased, sorry, upset*) and a few others, e.g. *far* and *near* (except in e.g. *the Far East/the Near East*) are normally used only predicatively:

*I **am** very **glad** to meet you.* [> 16.26]

*Your hotel **is** quite **near** here. It **isn't far** from here.*

We can express the same ideas with attributive adjectives:

*She is **a happy** (or **contented**) **woman**.* (= She is glad/content.)

6.8.4 Predicative adjectives followed by prepositions [> App 27]

Many adjectives used predicatively may be followed by prepositions:

***A capable person** is one who manages well.* (attributive)

*He **is capable of** managing well.* (adjective + preposition: predicative)

6.9 Adjectives used attributively to mean 'complete', etc.

A few adjectives can behave like adverbs of degree or intensifiers [> 7.41, 7.50], more or less in the sense of 'complete', and can be used only in the attributive position, e.g. *mere, out and out, sheer, utter:*

*Ken can't be promoted. He's **a mere boy/an out and out rogue**.*

*What you say is **sheer/utter nonsense**.*

(*Very* itself is used as an adjective in fixed expressions like *the very end; the very limit; the very thing I want/need.*)

Other adjectives which can have the sense of *very* when used attributively are: *close* (*a close friend*); *complete/perfect/total* (*a complete, perfect, total fool*); *pure* (*pure nonsense*); and *strong* (*a strong supporter*). Most of these can be attributive or predicative in their normal meanings:

***Pure** drinking **water** is best. This water **is pure**.*

Some *-ing* adjectives can qualify other adjectives. They have an intensifying effect equivalent to *very* in (often) fixed phrases like *boiling hot; freezing cold; hopping mad; soaking wet.*

Adjectives which restrict the reference of the noun are always attributive: *certain* (*a woman of a certain age*); *chief* (*my chief complaint*); *main* (*my main concern*); *only* (*the only explanation*); *particular* (*my particular aim*); *principal* (*the principal reason*); *sole* (*my sole interest*) and *very* itself (*the very man I wanted to see*). These adjectives cannot be used predicatively, except for *certain* and *particular*, which then change in meaning:

*You should be **certain** of your facts before you rush into print.*
*Some people aren't very **particular** about the food they eat.*

6.10 Adjectives after nouns in official titles, etc.

The adjective follows the noun in a number of 'titles': e.g. *Attorney General, Governor General, Heir Apparent, Poet Laureate, Postmaster General, President Elect* (or *elect*), *Sergeant Major.*
And note: *Asia Minor*, and a number of fixed phrases, such as *body politic, Goodness gracious!, hope eternal, penny dreadful, sum total, time immemorial.*

6.11 Adjectives which can come before or after nouns

6.11.1 Adjectives before or after nouns with no change in meaning

A limited number of adjectives, mostly ending in *-able* and *-ible*, can come before or after nouns, usually with no change of meaning. Some of these are: *available, eligible, imaginable, taxable:*

*I doubt whether we can complete our contract in the **time available**/in the **available time**.*

6.11.2 Adjectives before or after nouns with a change in meaning

A few adjectives change in meaning depending on whether they are used before or after a noun. Some of these are: *concerned, elect, involved, present, proper, responsible:*

*The **concerned*** (= worried) ***doctor** rang for an ambulance.*
*The **doctor concerned*** (= responsible) *is on holiday.*
*This **elect*** (= specially chosen) ***body** meets once a year.*
*The **president elect*** (= who has been elected) *takes over in May.*
*It was a very **involved*** (= complicated) ***explanation**.*
*The **boy involved*** (= connected with this) *has left.*
Present employees (= those currently employed) *number 3,000.*
Employees present (= those here now) *should vote on the issue.*
*It was a **proper*** (= correct) ***question**.*
*The **question proper*** (= itself) *has not been answered.*
*Janet is a **responsible girl**.* (= She has a sense of duty.)
*The **girl responsible*** (= who can be blamed) *was expelled.*

6.12 Adjectives which can be used as if they were nouns

6.12.1 Adjectives used as nouns

A few adjectives can be used as if they were nouns (e.g. after *a/an*) and can sometimes have a plural. The listener mentally supplies the 'missing' noun:

*I've got my **medical** on Thursday.* (= medical examination)
*Don't be such **a silly**!* (= a silly fool)
*There's something the matter with **the electrics** in my car.* (= the electrical system)

Other words which are both adjectives and nouns are: e.g. *a black/blacks; a red/reds; a white/whites.*

6.12.2 'The' + adjective: e.g. 'the young' [> App 9]

Adjectives like the following are used after *the*, never after *a/an*, to represent a group as a whole: e.g. *the blind; the deaf; the living/the dead; the rich/the poor; the young/the old; the unemployed.* So *the deaf* means 'a group of people who are all deaf':

*Andrew was sent to a special school for **the deaf**.*

These adjectives are followed by a plural verb:

*You can always judge a society by the way **the old are** cared for.*

We can never use these adjectives on their own to refer to a single individual (Not **he is a young** **they are youngs**). If we wish to refer to single individuals, we must use an adjective + noun [> 6.6]:

*He's **a young man** with a lot of ambition. They are young men . . .*

Some of these adjectives may be modified: e.g. *the extremely poor; the idle rich; the super-rich; the young at heart.*

Sometimes after e.g. *both*, *the* can be dropped [> 3.28.6]:

***Both young and old** enjoyed themselves at the party.*

The reference can be general or abstract in: e.g. *the supernatural; the unexpected; the unheard of; the unknown.* So *the unknown* means 'that thing or those things which are not known':

*Scott's march to the South Pole was a journey into **the unknown**.*

These are followed by a singular verb:

***The unknown is** always something to be feared.*

For *the former...the latter* [> 4.11].

For nationality adjectives used without nouns [> 3.19.2, App 49].

6.13 Nouns that behave like adjectives

Names of materials, substances, etc. (*leather, nylon, plastic*) [> 2.10.5, 6.20.1] resemble adjectives. So do some nouns indicating use or purpose, e.g. *kitchen chairs*. Examples of such nouns are:

*It's a **cotton** dress.* (= it's cotton/made of cotton)
*It's a **summer** dress.* (= a dress to be worn in summer)

Words like *cotton* or *summer* behave like adjectives in this one way: they do not have comparative or superlative forms; they cannot be modified by *very*, etc. They remain essentially nouns, often modifying a second noun [> 2.10]. Most of these noun modifiers can be used without change. But note *wooden* and *woollen*:

*It's a **wooden** spoon./It's made of **wood**.*
*It's a **woollen** dress./It's made of **wool**.*

Here *wooden* and *woollen* are adjectives, not nouns. Some other names for materials have adjectival forms: *gold, golden; lead, leaden; silk, silken, silky; stone, stony*; but the adjectival form generally has a metaphorical meaning ('like...'): So, for example, *a gold watch* is a 'watch made of gold', but a *golden sunset* is a sunset which is 'like gold'. Compare *a silvery voice; leaden steps; silky* (or *silken*) *hair; (a) stony silence.*

6.14 Present and past participles used as adjectives

Most present participles can be used as adjectives: e.g. *breaking glass, frightening stories* [> 2.7, 6.2, 6.3.1, 16.38, 16.39.3].
Many past participles of verbs can be used as adjectives: e.g. *a broken window* (= a window which has been broken); *a frozen lake* (= a lake which is frozen); *a locked door* (= a door which is locked), etc. Regular past participles follow the normal pronunciation rules [> 9.14.1]. However, note that some adjectives ending in *-ed* are not past participles, and here the ending is normally pronounced /ɪd/, as in: *an aged parent; a crooked path; a learned professor; a naked man; a ragged urchin; a wicked witch.*

6.15 Adjectival participles ending in '-ed' and '-ing' [> App 10]

Common pairs of *-ed/-ing* adjectives are: *amazed/amazing; annoyed/annoying; bored/boring; excited/exciting; interested/interesting; pleased/pleasing; tired/tiring.* Similar pairs: *delighted/delightful; impressed/impressive; upset/upsetting.*
Adjectives ending in *-ed* often combine with personal subjects and those ending in *-ing* often combine with impersonal ones [> 16.32.1]:

*This story excites **me**. → **I** am excit**ed** by it. → **It** is excit**ing**.*

Most *-ing* adjectives can also be applied to people. Compare:

***Gloria** was quite **enchanting** to be with.*
(i.e. That was the effect she had on other people.)
***Gloria** was quite **enchanted**.*
(i.e. That was the effect someone or something had on her.)

A few *-ed* adjectives can be applied to things:

***The old tin mine** was quite **exhausted**.* (= used up)

6.16 Adjectives used in measurements

Words such as *deep, long, wide*, etc. can function as adjectives or adverbs after the question word *How* [> 13.40.2]:

***How deep** is that pool?* (adjective)
***How deep** did you dive?* (adverb)

In responses to such questions, the adjective (or adverb) follows the noun. It can sometimes be omitted:

*It's five **metres (deep)**./I went five **metres deep**.*

And compare:

*How old are you? – I'm **five years old**.* or *I'm **five**.*
*How old is your car? – It's **five years old**.* (Not **It's five.**)

Measurement nouns are plural when they are followed by adjectives or adverbs (*six metres high*); they are singular when they precede the noun (*a six metre wall*) [> 6.3.2]. But note this exception:

*Jim is **six foot/feet tall**.* (singular or plural)
*He's **a six-foot man**.* (singular only)

6.17 Adjectives as complements after e.g. verbs of perception

We use adjectives, not adverbs, after verbs of perception, particularly those relating to the senses, such as *look, taste* [> 9.3, 10.23–25, App 38] e.g. *appear strange; feel rough; look good; look well; seem impossible; smell sweet; sound nice; taste bad:*

*That pie **looks good**, but it **tastes awful**.*
*A day in the country **sounds nice**, but think of the traffic!*
*Scratch my back there please. Ah! That **feels better**.*

The words used after these verbs are adjectives because they are describing the subject of the verb, not modifying the verb itself. They function as adjectival complements [> 1.9, 1.11]. Compare:

*You **look well**.* (*Well* = 'in good health' is an adjective.)
*You **play well**.* (*Well* is an adverb modifying *play*.)

Adjectives can be used as complements of the subject after other verbs in expressions such as: *break loose; die/marry young; keep/sit still; live close to; remain open; ring true/false:*

*Many famous poets **have died young**.*
*It's impossible for young children to **sit still**.*
*The murder was not solved and the case **remains open**.*

Adjectives are often used as complements after verbs such as *lie* or *stand*, particularly in descriptive writing [> 7.59.2]:

*The crowd **stood** (or **was**) **silent** at the end of the ceremony.*

6.18 Adverbs that can function as adjectives

A few adverbs and adverb particles [> 7.3.4] can function as attributive adjectives, especially in fixed phrases: e.g. *the above statement; an away match; the down train/the up train; the downstairs lavatory/the upstairs bathroom; a home win; the inside cover; inside information; an outside line; the then chairman.*

6.19 Adjectives easily confused

Many common adjectives are easily confused. For details [> App 11].

6.20 Adjectives: word order

When we use more than one adjective to describe a noun, we have to take care with the word order. Hard-and-fast rules cannot be given, since much depends on the emphasis a speaker wishes to make. A general guide is as follows:

adjectives: usual order					**noun**
quality	**size/age/shape**	**colour**	**origin**	**past participle**	
beautiful	*old*	*brown*	*French*	*handmade*	*cupboard*
					kitchen cupboard
					teak cupboard

Note that general qualities go before particular qualities. The more particular the quality, the closer the adjective is to the noun. Let's begin with the noun and work backwards:

6.20.1 The noun

A noun may be [> 2.10, 6.13]:
- one-word: *a cupboard.*
- two-word: *a kitchen cupboard, a teak cupboard.*
- three-word: *a teak kitchen cupboard.*

Where there are three words, **material** (*teak*) precedes **purpose** or **use** (*kitchen*): *a cotton shirt, a summer shirt, a cotton summer shirt.*
Compound nouns are never separated by adjectives.

6.20.2 Adjectival past participle

This is usually closest to the noun:

*a **handmade** teak cupboard; a **handmade** kitchen cupboard;*
*a **handmade** teak kitchen cupboard.*

6.20.3 Origin

A nationality word indicating **origin** [> App 49] or an adjective referring to a historical period (e.g. *Victorian*) usually precedes an adjectival past participle:

*a **Chinese** handmade shirt; a **Chinese** handmade cotton shirt.*

This is not invariable: *handmade Chinese shirt* is also possible.
If a present participle adjective is used (i.e. the *-ing* form), then it precedes origin:

***quick-selling** Chinese handmade shirts.*

6.20.4 Size/age/shape/temperature/flavour, etc.

Size generally precedes **age** and **shape**, etc.:

*a **large** old table; a **large** round tablc; a **large** old round table;*
*a **huge** ice-cold strawberry milkshake.*

6.20.5 Quality (i.e. subjective assessment)

Adjectives expressing our general opinion of the **quality** of people or things come first: e.g. *beautiful, big, clean, dirty, nice:*

*a **beautiful** tall building; a **cheap** Indian restaurant.*

If there is more than one 'general quality' adjective, then the most general usually comes first:

*a **beautiful spacious** airy room.*

6.20.6 Modification with '(great) big' and 'little'

The adjectives *big* or *great big* generally precede **quality** adjectives, while *little* generally comes after:

***great big** boots; a **(great) big tall** policeman;*
*a **nice little** restaurant; a **friendly little** waiter.*

6.21 The use of commas and 'and' to separate adjectives

6.21.1 Separating adjectives used attributively [> 6.7]

When we have two or more adjectives in front of a noun we only need commas to separate those which are equally important (i.e. where the order of the first two could easily be reversed):

*a **beautiful, bright** clean room.*

That is, we put a comma after the **quality** adjective. We never use a comma after the adjective that comes immediately before the noun:

*The hotel porter led me to a **beautiful**, bright clean room.*
*Joy is engaged to a **daring**, very attractive young Air Force pilot.*

In journalism, writers frequently try to give condensed descriptions by stringing adjectives together, as in: e.g.

Ageing, recently-widowed popular dramatist, Milton Fairbanks, announced recently that 'Athletes' was to be his last play.

Some fixed pairs of adjectives are often linked by *and*: *old and musty wine; a long and winding road; hard and fast rules*. Pairs of colour adjectives are often hyphenated: *a blue-and-white flag*.

6.21.2 Separating adjectives used predicatively [> 6.7]

If there are two adjectives, we separate them with *and*:

My shoes are old and worn.

If there are more than two adjectives, we may separate them by commas, except for the last two which are separated by *and*:

My shoes are dirty, wet, old and worn.

We do not usually put a comma after the adjective in front of *and* [compare > 1.20].

The comparison of adjectives

6.22 Shorter adjectives: form of regular comparison

Only **gradable** [> 6.5] adjectives compare. Most common adjectives are short words (usually of one syllable and not more than two syllables). They form their comparatives and superlatives as shown.

	adjective	comparative	superlative
1	*clean*	*cleaner*	*cleanest*
2	*big*	*bigger*	*biggest*
3	*nice*	*nicer*	*nicest*
4	*tidy*	*tidier*	*tidiest*
5	*narrow* [> 6.26*n*.1]	*narrower*	*narrowest*

6.23 Notes on the comparison of shorter adjectives

6.23.1 Spelling of comparative and superlative forms

1 Most one-syllable adjectives form their comparatives and superlatives like *clean*: *-er* and *-est* are added to their basic forms. Other examples like *clean* are: *cold, cool, great, hard, high, low, neat, new, short, small, thick, weak*.

2 Many one-syllable adjectives end with a single consonant after a single vowel-letter. This consonant doubles in the comparative and superlative, as in the case of *big*. Other examples like *big* are: *fat, fatter, fattest; sad, sadder, saddest; thin, thinner, thinnest; wet, wetter, wettest*. Compare adjectives like *full, small, tall*, etc. which end with a double consonant and form their comparatives and superlatives like *clean*: *tall, taller, tallest*.

3 Many one-syllable adjectives end in *-e*, like *nice*. These add *-r* and *-st* to the basic form, pronounced e.g. /naɪsə, naɪsəst/. Other examples like *nice* are: *fine, large, late, safe, strange*. And note *free/freer*.

4 Some adjectives, like *tidy*, end in *-y* with a consonant letter before it. These adjectives are usually two-syllable. In the comparative and

superlative *-y* is replaced by *i* (*tidy, tidier, tidiest*). Other examples like *tidy* are: *busy, dirty, dry, early, easy, empty, funny, heavy, ready, sleepy*. (But note *shy, shyer, shyest*.) A few adjectives have a vowel before a *-y* ending, like *gay, grey, fey*, and these simply take the endings *-er* and *-est*.

5 Some other two-syllable adjectives can form their comparatives and superlatives regularly. Other examples like *narrow* are: *clever, common, gentle, simple* [> 6.26*n*.1].

6.23.2 Pronunciation of comparative and superlative forms

In comparatives and superlatives containing the letters *ng*, /g/ is pronounced after /ŋ/: e.g. *younger, longer, strongest*. In other words containing *ng*, /g/ is not pronounced: e.g. *singer* /'sɪŋə/.

6.24 Some irregular comparative and superlative forms

adjective	**comparative**	**superlative**
good	*better*	*best*
bad	*worse*	*worst*
far	*farther*	*farthest* [> 7.5*n*.4]
	further	*furthest*
old	*older*	*oldest* [> App 12.3–4]
	elder	*eldest*
quantifier [> 5.13]	**comparative**	**superlative**
much / *many*	*more*	*most*
little	*less*	*least*

6.25 Longer adjectives: form of regular comparison

Most longer adjectives (i.e. of two or more syllables) combine with the quantifiers *more/less* to form their comparatives and *most/least* to form their superlatives. *Less* can be used with one-syllable adjectives (*less big*) but *more, most* and *least* are not normally used in this way. *More* is occasionally used with one-syllable adjectives (e.g. *It's more true to say that British English is influenced by American, rather than the other way round.*) *More/less* can never be used in front of a comparative (e.g. *happier*); nor can *most/least* be used in front of a superlative (e.g. *happiest*).

	adjective	**comparative**	**superlative**
1	*pleasant*	*pleasanter*	*pleasantest*
		more pleasant	*most pleasant*
		less pleasant	*least pleasant*
2	*careful*	*more careful*	*most careful*
		less careful	*least careful*
	expensive	*more expensive*	*most expensive*
		less expensive	*least expensive*
3	*bored/boring*	*more bored/boring*	*most bored/boring*
		less bored/boring	*least bored/boring*

6.26 Notes on the comparison of longer adjectives

1 Some two-syllable adjectives can form their comparatives and superlatives either with *-er* and *-est* or with *more/less* and *most/least*

Other examples like *pleasant* are: *clever, common, gentle, handsome, happy, narrow, quiet, shallow, simple, stupid, tired* [> 6.23.1*n*.5]. The opposites of such words, when formed with the prefix *un-*, can also form their comparatives and superlatives in two ways: e.g. *uncommon, unhappy, unpleasant: unhappier* or *more unhappy, unhappiest* or *most unhappy*. Where there is uncertainty, it is safest to use *more* and *most* with two-syllable adjectives.

2 The comparatives and superlatives of other two-syllable adjectives must always be with *more/less* and *most/least*. These include all adjectives ending in *-ful* or *-less* (*careful, careless, useful, useless*).

Other examples of adjectives which form comparisons in this way are: *(un)certain, (in)correct, (in)famous, foolish, (in)frequent, modern, (ab)normal*. Adjectives with more than two syllables compare with *more/most* and *less/least: beautiful, (un)comfortable, dangerous, expensive, (un)important, (un)natural, (un)necessary*.

This applies to most compound adjectives as well, such as: *quick-witted, waterproof*. But note compounds with *good, well* and *bad: good-looking* → *better-looking*, (or *more good-looking); well-built* → *better-built* (but *more well-built* is sometimes heard); *bad-tempered* → *worse-tempered* (or *more bad-tempered*).

3 Adjectives ending in *-ed* and *-ing* such as *amused/amusing, annoyed/annoying* [> 6.15] require *more/less* and *most/least* to form their comparatives and superlatives.

4 Note the form *lesser* which, though formed from *less*, is not a true comparative because it cannot be followed by *than*. *Lesser* means *not so great* in fixed phrases such as: *to a lesser degree/extent; the lesser of two evils*.

6.27 The use of the comparative form of adjectives

We use the comparative when we are comparing one person or thing, etc. with another. Comparison may be between:

– single items:	***Jane** is taller than **Alice**.*
– a single item and a group:	***Jane** is taller than **other girls**.*
– two groups:	***The girls in class 3** are taller than **the girls in class 1**.*

6.27.1 The use of 'than' in the comparative

A comparative can stand on its own if the reference is clear:

*The grey coat is **longer**.*

This implies that the hearer understands that the grey coat is being compared with another coat or something similar. If two things of exactly the same kind are being compared, we can use *the* before a comparative in formal style:

*Which is **(the) longer**?* (of the two coats)

*The grey coat is **(the) longer**.* (of the two coats)

However, if we need to mention each item, then we must use *than* after the comparative. When *than* is followed by a noun or pronoun, it functions as if it were a preposition [> 4.7.3]; when it is followed by a clause [> 1.53], it functions as if it were a conjunction, but note the ambiguity of:

I know him better than ***you***. This could mean:

I ***know him better than*** *you know him.* (*than* is a conjunction)

I know him better ***than (I know) you***. (*than* could be a preposition)

We can avoid ambiguity by using e.g. *... than you do.*

Examples with comparative + *than*:

My room is ***better/cleaner/worse than*** *the one next door.*

Driving is certainly ***less tiring than*** *walking.*

A scheduled flight is ***more expensive than*** *a charter flight.*

It's ***pleasanter/more pleasant*** *today* ***than*** *it was yesterday.*

I feel ***less tired*** *today* ***than*** *I felt yesterday.*

Comparison with *than* + adjective also occurs in fixed phrases, such as *(taller) than average*; *(more/less expensive) than usual.*

6.27.2 Comparatives with '-er and -er'

Two comparatives (adjectives or adverbs), joined by *and*, can convey the idea of general increase or decrease:

Debbie is growing fast. She's getting ***taller and taller***.

Computers are becoming ***more and more*** *complicated.*

Holiday flights are getting ***less and less*** *expensive.*

More and more and *less and less* do not normally combine with one-syllable adjectives.

6.27.3 'the' + comparative + 'the'

This construction can be used with adjectives or adverbs to show cause and effect: when one change is made, another follows:

The more *money you make,* ***the more*** *you spend.*

The more expensive *petrol becomes,* ***the less*** *people drive.*

6.27.4 'More' and 'most' in comparisons of relative quantity

More is used with countables and uncountables [> 5.2*n*.3]:

More food *is wasted than is eaten in this canteen.*

More also combines with numbers [> 5.6.1]:

How many more stamps *do you want? –* ***Four more*** *please.*

Most can mean 'the largest number of', 'the greatest amount of':

Most doctors *don't smoke.* ***Most wine*** *is imported.* (Not **the most**)

Compare *the most* in the superlative:

Which country in the world produces ***the most wine***?

6.27.5 Modification of comparatives [> 7.41–46]

We can use intensifiers and adverbs of degree like *very, too* and *quite* to modify adjectives: *very tall, too cold, quite hot*, etc. However, we cannot use these intensifiers with the comparative. We must use *a bit* (informal), *(very) much, far, even, hardly any, a lot, lots, a little, no, rather, somewhat* (formal), etc.:

It's ***much/far/a lot/a little colder*** *today than it was yesterday.*

Houses are ***much/far/a lot more expensive*** *these days.*

There have been ***many more/many fewer*** *burglaries this year.*

Even and *all the* can often be used interchangeably for emphasis in front of *more*, especially with *-ed/-ing* adjectival participles:

This term his behaviour has become ***even more annoying***.

When I told her the news, she became ***all the more depressed***.

6.28 The use of the superlative form of adjectives

We use the superlative when we are comparing one person or thing with more than one other in the same group. The definite article *the* is used before a superlative in a phrase or sentence:

*This is **the cleanest/tidiest** room in the house.*
*This is **the best/worst** room in the hotel.*
*Who is **the tallest**: John, Mary or Sue? – Sue is **the tallest**.*
*First class is **the most expensive** way to travel.*

Informally, we sometimes use the superlative instead of a comparative when we are comparing two people or things:

*Who's **the most reliable**, Frank or Alan?*

Similarly, *the* is sometimes dropped, especially after *Which?* :

*Which is **best**? The red one or the green one?*

and when the superlative is in front of a *to*-infinitive:

*I think it's **safest to overtake** now.*

6.28.1 The use of a qualifying phrase or a relative

A qualifying phrase is not necessary after a superlative if the reference is clear:

*John is **the tallest**.*

This implies that the hearer understands that John is being compared with two or more people in the same group. If the comparison is not clear, then we must use a qualifying phrase after the superlative. Phrases of this kind usually begin with *in* or (less frequently) *of* :

*John is easily the tallest boy **in our class**.*
*Yesterday was the hottest day **of the year**.*

Other fixed prepositional phrases are possible:

*It's the oldest trick **on earth/under the sun**.*

Alternatively, we can use a relative clause [> 1.40] after a superlative. This is often accompanied by a present perfect with *... ever heard, met, read, seen*, etc. [> 9.25.1]:

*'War and Peace' is the longest book (that) **I have ever read**.*
*Penfold is the most conceited man (that/whom) **I have ever met**.*

6.28.2 Modification of superlatives

Superlatives can be modified by adverbs of degree like *almost, altogether, by far, far, much, nearly, practically, quite, the very:*

*This is **quite/(by) far the most expensive** bicycle in the shop.*
*This is **much the worst** stretch of motorway in the country.*

Note the position of *very* after *the* [> 7.51.1]:

*I want to give my children **the very best** education I can afford.*

6.29 Comparatives and superlatives confused and misused

Many common comparatives are easily confused [> App 12].

6.30 Comparison, similarity and contrast

6.30.1 'as...as' to indicate the same degree

As...as can combine with one-syllable and longer adjectives to show that two people, things, etc. are similar:

*Jane is **as tall as/as intelligent as** Peter.*

A number of everyday expressions with *as* + adjective + *as* are commonly in use [> App 13]: e.g. *as clear as crystal; as cold as ice; as good as gold; as light as a feather; as old as the hills; as white as snow.* The first *as* is often dropped:

*How has Jimmy behaved himself? – He's been **(as) good as gold**.*

Some of these expressions can occur as compound adjectives: e.g. *grass-green* (for 'as green as grass' = colour or 'inexperienced'). Like *than* [> 6.27.1], *as* can function as a preposition [> 4.7.3] or as a conjunction [> 1.53]. For differences between *like* and *as* [> App 25.25].

6.30.2 'not as...as'; 'not so...as' to indicate lower degree

We can use either *as* or *so* after *not* to compare two people, things, etc.:

*Soames is **not as/not so** suitable for the job **as** me/as I am.*

But note: *He's **not so** suitable in my view.* This use of *so* is informal and can replace *very*. *Not such a/an* (+ adjective) + noun is also possible:

*He's **not such a** hard worker **as** his brother.*

6.30.3 'More than', 'less than' and 'worse than' + adjective

More than, less than and *worse than* can be used in front of a number of adjectives in the following way:

*I was **more than pleased** with my pay rise. I was over the moon!*
*This foot-pump is **worse than useless**.*
(i.e. to a degree which *pleased* and *useless* cannot convey)

6.30.4 'The same as'; 'different from'

Note that *as* follows *the same*:

*He's angry because my marks are **the same as** his.*
(Not **the same like** or **the same with**)

Compare the use of *with* after *the same* in: e.g.

*Butterflies come from caterpillars. It's **the same with** moths.*
(i.e. moths do the same thing)

The same (with singular or plural) can also be used without *as*:

*This cup's cracked. What's that one like? – It**'s the same**.*
*Those two dresses **are the same**.* (plural)

Different is normally followed by *from*, especially in BrE:

*We have the same make of car, but yours is **different from** mine.*
*I know we look alike, but we're quite **different from** each other.*

To and *than* (especially in AmE) are also heard after *different*. However, *than* cannot replace *from* in uncomplicated comparisons:

*Roses are **different from/different to** violets.*

Than is commonly used after *different* to introduce a clause:

*We're doing something quite **different** for our holiday this year **than (what) we did last year/from what we did last year**.*

6.30.5 Degrees of similarity

Degrees of similarity can be expressed by means of *almost, exactly, just, nearly* + *as* + adjective [> 7.41]:

*Jeffrey is **nearly as** tall as his father now.*

or + *like* + noun: *Sandra is **just like** her mother.*

Almost, exactly, just, nearly and *(not) quite* will combine with *the same*:

*Those two boys are **exactly the same**.*

Completely, entirely and *quite* will combine with *different*:

*Those two boys are **completely different**.*

7 Adverbs

General information about adverbs

7.1 What an adverb is and what it does

The word **adverb** (ad-verb) suggests the idea of adding to the meaning of a verb. This is what many adverbs do. They can tell us something about the action in a sentence by **modifying** a verb, i.e. by telling us how, when, where, etc. something happens or is done:

*Paganini played the violin **beautifully**.* (How did he play?)

However, adverbs can also modify:

- adjectives: ***very** good; **awfully** hungry.*
- other adverbs: ***very** soon; **awfully** quickly.*
- prepositional phrases: *You're **entirely** in the wrong.*
- complete sentences: ***Strangely enough**, I won first prize.*
- nouns: *The man **over there** is a doctor.*

Adverbs can be single words (*slowly*) or phrases (*in the garden*) and the term **adverbial** is often used to describe both types.

Adverbs are not always essential to the structure of a sentence, but they often affect the meaning. Compare:

Doris has left.	*Doris has **just** left.*
I have finished work.	*I have **nearly** finished work.*

Sometimes adverbs are essential to complete a sentence:

1 after some intransitive verbs such as *lie, live, sit*, etc.:
*Lie **down**.* [> 8.29] *Sit **over there**. I live **in Rome**.*

2 after some transitive verbs (e.g. *lay, place, put*) + object:
*He put his car **in the garage**.*

For the general position of adverbs in a sentence [> 1.3].

7.2 Kinds of adverbs

Many adverbs can be thought of as answering questions, such as *How?* [**manner**, > 7.7]; *Where?* [**place**, > 7.17]; *When?* [**time**, > 7.20]; *How often?* [**frequency**, > 7.37]; *To what extent?* [**degree**, > 7.41]. Others 'strengthen' adjectives, other adverbs or verbs [**intensifiers**, > 7.50]; focus attention [**focus**, > 7.54]; reveal our attitudes, or help us to present information in a coherent fashion [**viewpoint adverbs and connectives**, > 7.57–58].

7.3 How to identify an adverb

7.3.1 One-word adverbs ending in '-ly'

A great many adverbs, particularly those of manner, are formed from adjectives by the addition of *-ly*: e.g. *patient, patiently*. Some adverbs of frequency are also formed in this way: e.g. *usual, usually*, as are a few adverbs of degree: e.g. *near, nearly*. Many viewpoint adverbs end in *-ly*: e.g. *fortunately*.

7.3.2 One-word adverbs not ending in '-ly'

Many adverbs cannot be identified by their endings. These include adverbs of manner which have the same form as adjectives, e.g. *fast* [> App 14]; adverbs of place (*there*); of time (*then*); of frequency (*often*); viewpoint adverbs (*perhaps*) and connectives (*however*).

7.3.3 Adverbial phrases

Adverbial phrases of manner, place and time are often formed with a preposition + noun: *in a hurry, in the garden, at the station.*
Other examples of adverbial phrases: *again and again* (frequency); *hardly at all* (degree); *very much indeed* (intensifying); *as a matter of fact* (viewpoint); *in that case* (connective).

7.3.4 Adverb particles

Certain words, such as *in, off, up*, function either as prepositions or as adverb particles [> 8.4]. When such words are followed by an object, they function as prepositions; when there is no object, they are adverb particles:

preposition: *The children are* ***in the house****.*
adverb: *The children have just gone* ***in****.*

The comparison of adverbs

7.4 Form of comparison of adverbs

Only **gradable** adverbs [compare > 6.5] can have comparative and superlative forms. Comparison is not possible with adverbs such as *daily, extremely, only, really, then, there, uniquely*, because they are not gradable. Gradable adverbs form comparatives and superlatives as follows:

	adverb	**comparative**	**superlative**
1 Same form as adjective:	*fast*	*faster*	*fastest*
2 *-ly* adverbs of manner:	*easily*	*more easily*	*most easily*
3 Some adverbs of frequency:	*rarely*	*more rarely*	*most rarely*
4 Exceptions:	*badly*	*worse*	*worst*
	far	{ *farther*	*farthest*
		{ *further*	*furthest*
	late	*later*	*last*
	little	*less*	*least*
	much	*more*	*most*
	well	*better*	*best*

7.5 Notes on the comparison of adverbs [compare 6.22–26]

1 Many adverbs like *early, fast*, etc. [> App 14] form their comparatives and superlatives in the same way as shorter adjectives (e.g. *earlier, earliest*).

2 As most adverbs of manner have two or more syllables, they form their comparatives and superlatives with *more/less* and *most/least*. Other examples: *more/less/most/least briefly, clearly, quickly.*

3 Some adverbs of frequency form their comparative and superlative with *more/less, most/least* (e.g. *more seldom, most seldom*); *often* has two comparative forms: *more often* and (less common) *oftener*.

4 Compare *latest/last*: both words can be adjectives:
I bought the ***latest*** (i.e. most recent) *edition of today's paper.*
I bought the ***last*** (i.e. final) *edition of today's paper.*
But normally only *last* is used as an adverb:
That was a difficult question, so I answered it ***last***.
or before the main verb:
It ***last*** *rained eight months ago.* (= The last time it rained was ...)

Both *farther* and *further* can be used to refer to distance:
I drove ten miles ***farther/further*** *than necessary.*
Further, but not *farther*, can be used to mean 'in addition':
We learnt, ***further***, *that he wasn't a qualified doctor.*

Note the irregular adverb *well* (related to the adjective *good*) which means 'in a pleasing or satisfactory way':
Jane Somers writes ***well***. [compare *bad/badly* and > 6.8.1, 6.17]

7.6 How we make comparisons using adverbs

Adverbial comparisons can be made with the following [compare > 6.27–30]:

as...as:	*Sylvia sings* ***as sweetly as*** *her sister.*
not as/so...as:	*I can****'t*** *swim* ***as well as*** *you (can).*
	*She can****'t*** *jump (quite)* ***so high as*** *Billy (can).*
...than:	*The rain cleared* ***more quickly than*** *I expected.*
the...the:	***The faster*** *I type,* ***the more*** *mistakes I make.*
...and...:	*It rained* ***more and more heavily***.
comparative:	*Dave drives* ***faster than*** *anyone I know.*
superlative:	*I work* ***fastest*** *when I'm under pressure.*
	Tim tries ***the hardest of all*** *the boys in his class.*

We often use the comparative + *than ever, than anyone, than anything* in: e.g.
Magnus concentrated ***harder than ever/than anyone***.

This is preferable to the superlative in: e.g.
Magnus concentrated ***the hardest***.

Adverbs of manner

7.7 Spelling and form of adverbs ending in '-ly'

	adjective	**adverb**
1 Add *-ly* to an adjective:	*bad*	*badly*
	careful	*carefully*
2 *-y* becomes *-ily*: consonant + *y*:	*happy*	*happily*
Compare: vowel + *y*:	(*day* – noun)	*daily*
3 Delete *-e* and add *-ly* for endings in *-le*:	*noble*	*nobly*
4 Adjectives ending in *-ic* take *-ally*:	*fantastic*	*fantastically*

7.8 Notes on the spelling and form of '-ly' adverbs

1 Most adverbs of manner are formed by adding *-ly* to adjectives: e.g. *mad/madly, plain/plainly, sudden/suddenly*. This applies to adjectives ending in *-l* so that the *l* is doubled: *beautiful/beautifully, musical/musically*. But note: *full/fully*.
2 *-y* after a consonant becomes *-ily*: e.g. *busy/busily, funny/funnily*. Sometimes two formations are possible: e.g. *dry/drily/dryly*, but in e.g. *sly/slyly*, *-yly* is the acceptable form.
3 Delete *-e* and add *-(l)y* if an adjective ends in *-le:* e.g. *able/ably, nimble/nimbly, possible/possibly, whole/wholly*. Other adjectives ending in *-e* retain the *-e* when adding *-ly*: *extreme/extremely, tame/tamely*. Exceptions: *due/duly* and *true/truly*.
4 Adjectives ending in *-ic* take *-ally*: e.g. *basic/basically, systematic/systematically*. Common exception: *public/publicly*.

Some *-ly* adverbs (relating to manner/frequency) have the same form as adjectives: e.g. *daily, weekly, monthly, quarterly, yearly:*

*I receive **quarterly** bills. I pay my bills **quarterly**.*

Early can be used as an adjective or an adverb, but unlike e.g. *week/weekly* is not formed from another word:

*I hope to catch an **early** train. I want to arrive **early**.*

7.9 Suffixes other than '-ly' used to form adverbs of manner

A few other suffixes can be added to adjectives (and to some nouns and adverbs) to form adverbs of manner (or in some cases direction): *(Indian)-**fashion**; (American)-**style**; back**wards**, for**wards**, north**wards**, up**wards**; cross**ways**, length**ways**, side**ways**; clock**wise**, length**wise**.* The suffix *-wise* is often used to make new adverbs meaning 'relating to (the noun)'. *money**wise**, tax**wise** (How do you manage **taxwise**?)*

7.10 Adverbs of manner with dynamic and stative verbs [> 9.3]

Most adverbs of manner naturally refer to action verbs (*laugh loudly, perform badly, drive carefully*, etc.). A smaller number of adverbs can also refer to stative verbs (e.g. *understand perfectly, know well*):

*I **hear** very **badly**.*

7.11 Prepositional phrases used adverbially

When there is no *-ly* adverb for what we want to say, we have to use an adverbial phrase beginning with a preposition to refer to 'means' or 'method':

*I came here **by bus**. She answered me **in a loud whisper**.*

Sometimes we can choose between a phrase and an *-ly* adverb:

*He left **in a hurry/hurriedly**.* [> App 26]

7.12 '-ly' adjectives and equivalent adverbial forms

Here is a selection of adjectives which end in *-ly*:
brotherly/sisterly, cowardly, elderly, friendly/unfriendly, heavenly, likely/unlikely, lively, lovely, manly/womanly, motherly/fatherly, sickly,

silly and *ugly*. We use most of these adjectives to describe people's qualities. We cannot use them as adverbs, so we form phrases with *way*, *manner* or *fashion*:

adjective: *Susan is a **friendly** girl.*
adverb: *She always greets me **in a friendly way/manner/fashion**.*

7.13 Adjectives/adverbs: same form, same meaning [> Apps 14, 15.1]

Some words can be used as adjectives or as adverbs of manner without adding *-ly*: *fast, hard*, etc.:

*A **fast*** (adjective) *train is one that goes **fast**.* (adverb)
*I work **hard*** (adverb) *because I enjoy **hard*** (adjective) *work.*

7.14 Adverbs with two forms [> App 15]

Some adverbs have two forms which may have:

- the same meaning: e.g. *cheap:* *I bought this car **cheap/cheaply**.*
- different meanings: e.g. *hard:* *I work **hard** and play **hard**.*
  *I did **hardly** any work today.*

7.15 Adverbs differing in meaning from corresponding adjectives

Some adverbs differ in meaning from their corresponding adjectives: e.g. *express/expressly, ready/readily:*

*If it's urgent, you should send it by **express** mail.* (fast)
*You were told **expressly** to be here by 7.* (clearly/deliberately)

Some adverbs, such as *coldly, coolly, hotly* and *warmly*, can refer to feelings and behaviour and can be used with verbs such as *act, behave, react, speak*. Compare adjective/adverb uses in: e.g.

*It's **cold** today.*	*The whole queue stared at me **coldly**.*
*It's a **warm/cool** day.*	*Emily greeted me **warmly/coolly**.*
*It's a **hot** day.*	*Edward **hotly** denied the accusation.*

7.16 Position of adverbs of manner

7.16.1 Adverbs of manner: after the object or after the verb

The most usual position of adverbs of manner is after the object or after the verb [> 1.3]: e.g.

- after the object: *Sue watched the monkeys **curiously**.*
  *Look at this photo **carefully**.*
- after the verb: *It snowed **heavily** last January.*
- after an adverb particle: *He took the picture down **carefully**.*

The important thing is not to put the adverb between the verb and its object. (Not **He speaks well English**). But even this is possible if the object is very long:

*We could see **very clearly** a strange light ahead of us.*

7.16.2 Adverbs of manner: between subject and verb

One-word adverbs of manner can sometimes go between the subject and the verb. (This rarely applies to adverbial phrases.) If we wish to emphasize the subject of the verb, we can say:

*Gillian **angrily** slammed the door behind her.*
(i.e. Gillian was angry when she slammed the door.)

However, *well* and *badly*, when used to evaluate an action, can only go at the end of a sentence or clause:

*Mr Gradgrind pays his staff **very well/badly**.* [compare > 7.10]

With some adverbs of manner, such as *bravely, cleverly, cruelly, foolishly, generously, kindly, secretly, simply*, a change of position results in a difference in emphasis. Compare the following:

*He **foolishly** locked himself out.*
(= It was foolish (of him) to . . .) [> 16.27.2]
*He behaved **foolishly** at the party.* (= in a foolish manner)

With others, such as *badly, naturally*, a change of position results in a change in meaning and function:

*You **typed** this letter **very badly**.*	(adverb of manner)
*We **badly need** a new typewriter.*	(intensifier, > 7.53.1)
*You should always **speak naturally**.*	(adverb of manner)
***Naturally**, I'll accept the invitation.*	(viewpoint adverb, > 7.57)

7.16.3 Adverbs of manner: beginning a sentence

In narrative writing (but not normally in speech) sentences can begin with adverbs of manner, such as *gently, quietly, slowly, suddenly*. We do this for dramatic effect, or to create suspense. Such adverbs are followed by a comma:

*O'Connor held his breath and stood quite still. **Quietly**, he moved forwards to get a better view.*

Adverbs of place

7.17 The meaning of 'place'

The idea of **place** covers:
– location: *Larry **is in Jamaica**.*
– direction (*to, away from*): *Larry **flew to Jamaica**.*

A distinction can be drawn between location and direction:
1 **Location** adverbials answer the question *Where?* and go with 'position verbs' such as *be, live, stay, work*. They can begin a sentence: ***In Jamaica** Larry stayed at the Grand Hotel.*
2 **Direction** adverbials answer the questions *Where to?* and *Where from?*. They often go with 'movement verbs' like *go* and cannot usually begin a sentence: *Larry went by plane **to Jamaica**.*

7.18 How to identify adverbs of place

Adverbs of place may be:
– words like: *abroad, ahead, anywhere/everywhere/nowhere/somewhere, ashore, away/back, backwards/forwards, here/there, left/right, north/south, upstairs/downstairs.*
– words like the following, which can also function as prepositions [> 8.4.1]: *above, behind, below, beneath, underneath.*
– two words combining to emphasize place, such as: *down below, down/up there, far ahead, far away, over here, over there.*

Prepositional phrases often function as adverbials of place: e.g. *at my mother's; from New York; in hospital; on the left* [> 7.3.3, 7.30].

7.19 Position of adverbs of place

Adverbs of place never go between subject and verb.

7.19.1 Adverbs of place: after manner but before time

When there is more than one kind of adverb in a sentence, the usual position of adverbs of place is after manner, but before time (following a verb or verb + object [> 1.3]):

	manner	**place**	**time**
Barbara read	*quietly*	*in the library*	*all afternoon.*

However, adverbs of direction can often come after movement verbs (*come, drive, go*) and before other adverbials:

I went to London (direction) *by train* (manner) *next day* (time).

If there is more than one adverb of place, then 'smaller places' are mentioned before 'bigger places' in ascending order:

She lives | in a small house | in a village | outside Reading | in Berkshire, | England.

7.19.2 Adverbs of place: beginning a sentence

If we wish to emphasize location (e.g. for contrast), we may begin with an adverb of location, especially in descriptive writing:

***Indoors** it was nice and warm. **Outside** it was snowing heavily.*

To avoid ambiguity, the initial position is usual when there is more than one adverbial of place:

***On many large farms**, farm workers live **in tied cottages**.*

For inversion after initial place adverbials [> 7.59.1–2].

Adverbs of time

7.20 How to identify adverbs of time

Adverbs and adverbial phrases of time can refer to **definite time** [> 7.21], answering questions like *When (exactly)?*:

*I'll see you **tomorrow/on Monday**.*

They refer to **duration** [> 7.30], answering *Since when?/For how long?*:

*I haven't seen her **since Monday/for a year**.*

Other adverbials refer to **indefinite time** [> 7.23], i.e. they do not answer time questions precisely:

*He doesn't live here **now/any more**.*

Some time adverbs can also act as nouns:

***Tomorrow** is Tuesday, isn't it?*

7.21 Adverbs of definite time

Adverbs of definite time answer the question *When?* and are generally used with past tenses, or refer to the future:

*I started my job **last Monday**. I'll ring **tomorrow**.*

Two main categories can be defined:

1 'Points of time' such as *today, tomorrow, yesterday* [> App 48]. These can be modified by the words *early, earlier, late* and *later*: e.g. *earlier today; late/later this year.*

2 Prepositional phrases which function as adverbials of time [> 8.11–14]. They often begin with *at, in* or *on* : e.g. *at five o'clock* [> App 47.5]; *at Christmas; in July; on November 20th.*
Some of these can be modified: *early in July; punctually at 5.*

7.22 Position of adverbs of definite time

The most usual position is at the very end of a sentence [> 1.3]:
We checked in at the hotel ***on Monday/yesterday*** , etc.
Definite time references can also be made at the beginning [> App 48]:
This morning *I had a telephone call from Sheila.*

If there is more than one time reference, we usually progress from the particular to the general, i.e. time + day + date + year:
Gilbert was born ***at 11.58 on Monday November 18th 1986****.*

7.23 Adverbs of indefinite time

Some common adverbs of indefinite time are: *afterwards, already* [> 7.26, 7.28], *another day, another time, at last, at once, early, eventually, formerly, immediately, just* [> 7.29], *late, lately* (= recently), *now, nowadays, once, one day, presently, recently, some day, soon, still* [> 7.25], *subsequently, suddenly, then, these days, ultimately* and *yet* [> 7.27–28].

7.24 Position of adverbs of indefinite time

The following usually come at the end of a sentence, although they can also come before the verb and (usually to focus interest or for contrast) at the beginning of a sentence: *afterwards, eventually, formerly, immediately, lately, once, presently, recently, soon, subsequently, suddenly, then, ultimately:*
I went to Berlin ***recently****. I* ***recently*** *went to Berlin.*
Recently*, I went to Berlin. It was very interesting...*
When the verb is *be*, these adverbs usually come after it:
I was ***recently*** *in Berlin.*

Early and *late* come at the end of a sentence or clause:
We arrived at the airport too ***early/late*** *for our flight.*

Another day/time, one day (referring to past or future), *some day* (referring to future), can come at the beginning or the end:
Some day *I'll tell you. I'll tell you* ***some day****.*

Some adverbs of indefinite time can be modified with *only* (*only just, only recently*) or with *very* (*very early, very recently*).

7.25 Position and use of 'still'

Still, referring to time, emphasizes continuity. It is mainly used in questions and affirmatives, often with progressive tenses [> 9.20.1]. Its position is the same as for adverbs of indefinite frequency [> 7.40]:
Mrs Mason is ***still*** *in hospital.*
I'm ***still*** *waiting for my new passport.*
Tom ***still*** *works for the British Council.*

For special emphasis, it can come before an auxiliary [> 7.40.6]:
*Martha **still 'is** in hospital, you know.*
Used after the subject in negative sentences, *still* can express dissatisfaction or surprise:
*I **still** haven't heard from her.*
(Compare *I haven't heard from her **yet***, which is neutral.)

7.26 Position and use of 'already'

Already is not normally used in negative sentences. Its position is the same as for adverbs of indefinite frequency [> 7.40], though it can also come at the end:
*This machine is **already** out of date. It is out of date **already**.*
*I've **already** seen the report. I've seen it **already**.*
*Tom **already** knows the truth. He knows it **already**.*

For special emphasis it can come before an auxiliary [> 7.40.6]:
*You'd better lock up. – I **already 'have** (locked up).*
In the end position, *already* can emphasize 'sooner than expected':
*Don't tell me you've eaten it **already**!*

7.27 Position and use of 'yet'

Yet generally comes at the end in questions and negatives:
*Have the new petrol prices come into force **yet**?*
*Haven't the new petrol prices come into force **yet**?*
*The new petrol prices haven't come into force **yet**.*
In negatives, *yet* can come before the main verb:
*The new petrol prices haven't **yet** come into force.*
Yet is often used after *not* in short negative answers:
*Has the concert finished? - No, **not yet**.*
Before an infinitive, *yet* has almost the same meaning as *still*:
*Who'll be appointed? - It's **yet/still** to be decided.*

7.28 'Yet' and 'already' compared

Both these adverbs are commonly used with perfect tenses [> 9.26.2], though in AmE they commonly occur with the past:
*Have you seen 'Tosca' **yet**? – I've **already** seen it.* (BrE)
*Did you see 'Tosca' **yet**? – I **already** saw it.* (AmE)
We use *yet* in questions when we want information:
*Have you received your invitation **yet**?* (i.e. I don't know.)
We sometimes use *already* when we want confirmation:
*Have you **already** received your invitation?* (i.e. Please confirm.)

7.29 Position and use of 'just'

Just (referring to time) has the same position as for adverbs of indefinite frequency [> 7.40] and is used:
– with perfect tenses to mean 'during a very short period before now or before then' [> 9.26.2, 9.29.1]:
*I've **just** finished reading the paper. Would you like it?*
*I saw Mrs Mason yesterday. She had **just** come out of hospital.*

– with the past, especially in AmE, to mean 'a very short time ago':
*I **just** saw Selina. She was going to the theatre.*
– to refer to the immediate future, with progressive tenses or *will*:
*Wait. I'm **just** coming. I'll **just** put my coat on.*
Just has other meanings, e.g. 'that and nothing else':
*How do I work this? – You **just** turn on that switch.*

7.30 Adverbials of duration

Duration (periods of time) can be expressed by adverbs (e.g. *ago, all (day) long, (not) any more, (not) any longer, no longer, no more*), and by prepositional phrases functioning as adverbials (beginning with e.g. *by, during, for, from...to/till, since, throughout*).

7.31 'Since' and 'ago' [> 9.25.2, 9.29.1, 9.33.1, 10.13.5, 9.18]

Since combines with points of time to answer the question *Since when?* It is often associated with the present perfect to mark the beginning of a period lasting till *now*, or with the past perfect to mark the beginning of a period lasting till *then*:
*I haven't seen Tim **since January/since last holidays**.*
*I met John last week. I hadn't seen him **since 1984**.*
Since can be used as an adverb on its own:
*I saw your mother last January, but I haven't seen her **since**.*

Period of time + *ago* (answering *How long ago?* or *When?*) marks the start of a period going back from now:
*I started working at Lawson's **seven months ago**.*
Note that *since* is placed before the point in time it refers to; *ago* is placed after the period it refers to.

7.32 'For' [> App 25.20]

For (+ period of time, answering *How long?*) marks the duration of a period of time in the past or in the future, or up to the present:
*The Kenways lived here **for five years**.* (They no longer live here.)
*The Kenways have lived here **for five years**.* (They are still here.)
For combines with e.g. *ages, hours, days, weeks, months, years*, etc. to emphasize or exaggerate duration:
*I haven't seen Patricia **for months**. How is she?*

In affirmative sentences with a 'continuity verb' like *be, live, work* [> 9.33.1] *for* is often omitted when the verb is present perfect or past:
Patricia has been (or *has lived, has worked*) *here **(for) a year**.*
Sometimes *for* can be omitted in future reference:
I'll be (or *stay, work*) *in New York **(for) six months**.*
For cannot be omitted in negative sentences or when it comes at the beginning of a sentence or clause:
*I haven't seen him **for six years. For six years**, he lived abroad.*

7.33 'From...to/till/until'

From...to/till/until refer to a defined period:
*The tourist season runs **from** June **to/till** October.*

From can be omitted informally with *till* but not usually with *to*:
I'm at my office ***(from)*** *nine* ***till*** *five.* (*...***from** *nine* **to** *five*)
We worked on the project ***(from)*** *March* ***till*** *June.*

7.34 'By', 'till/until' and 'not...till/until'

Till (or *until*) and *by* mean 'any time before and not later than'. When we use 'continuity verbs' [> 9.33.1] which indicate *a period of time* (e.g. *stay, wait*) we can only use *till/until* (Not **by**):
I'll ***stay*** *here* ***till/until*** *Monday.*
I ***won't stay*** *here* ***till/until*** *Monday.*
Will you ***stay*** *here* ***till/until*** *Monday?*

When we use verbs which indicate *a point of time* (e.g. *finish, leave*), we can only use *till/until* in the negative:
I ***won't leave till/until*** *Monday.* (= on Monday, not before)

We can only use *by* with point of time verbs, so we can say:
I'll have left by *Monday.* (= any time before and not later than)
I ***won't have left by*** *Monday.* (= I'll still be here on Monday)

7.35 'During', 'in' and 'throughout'

During, always followed by a noun, can refer to a whole period:
It was very hot ***during the summer.***
or to points during the course of a period:
He's phoned ***four times during the last half hour.***
In (= within a period) can replace *during* in the above examples.
Vagueness can be emphasized by the use of *some time* + *during*:
I posted it ***some time during*** (Not **in**) ***the week.***
During cannot be replaced by *in* when we refer to an event or activity rather than to a period of time:
I didn't learn much ***during my teacher-training.***

Throughout can replace *in* or *during* if we wish to emphasize 'from the beginning to the end of a whole period':
There were thunderstorms ***throughout July.***
During or *throughout* (Not **in**) can combine with e.g. *the whole, the entire* to emphasize that something happened over a period:
During the whole/the entire winter *she never saw a soul.*

7.36 'All (day) long', '(not) any more'

All ... long emphasizes duration and is commonly used with words like *day* and *night*. *Long* gives extra emphasis and is optional:
It rained ***all night (long).***

Not...any more, not...any longer and *no longer* are used to show that an action with duration has stopped or must stop. They come at the end of a sentence or clause:
*Hurry up! I ca****n't*** *wait* ***any longer/any more.***
No longer can come before a full verb or at the end of a sentence, though the end position is sometimes slightly more formal:
I'm sorry, Professor Carrington ***no longer*** *lives here.*

Adverbs of frequency

7.37 How to identify adverbs of frequency

These adverbs fall into two categories: **definite frequency** and **indefinite frequency**. Both kinds of adverbs answer *How often?*

7.38 Adverbs of definite frequency and their position

These include words and phrases like the following:
- *once, twice; three/several times* (*a day/week/month/year*, etc.).
- *hourly/daily/weekly/fortnightly/monthly/yearly/annually.*
- *every* + e.g. *day/week/month/year;* + *morning/afternoon/evening/night*; and in combinations like *every other day, every 3 years, every few days, every third* (etc.) *day.*
- *on* + *Mondays, Fridays, weekdays*, etc.

These adverbials usually come at the end of a sentence:

There's a collection from this letter box ***twice daily***.

Some of them can also begin a sentence, just like adverbs of time. This may be necessary to avoid ambiguity:

Once a month *we visit our daughter who's at Leeds University.*

avoids the ambiguity of:

We visit our daughter who's at Leeds University ***once a month***.

The *-ly* adverbs (*hourly, daily*, etc.) are not normally used to begin sentences.

7.39 Adverbs of indefinite frequency

These adverbs give general answers to *How often?*. Here are some of the most common, arranged on a 'scale of frequency':
- *always* (i.e. 'all of the time').
- *almost always, nearly always.*
- *generally, normally, regularly, usually.*
- *frequently, often.*
- *sometimes, occasionally.*
- *almost never, hardly ever, rarely, scarcely ever, seldom.*
- *not...ever, never* (i.e. 'none of the time').

Negative frequency adverbs (*almost never*, etc. above) cannot be used with *not* [> 13.10]:

I ***hardly ever see*** *Brian these days.* (Not **I don't hardly ever**)

The following can be intensified with *very*: *frequently, occasionally, often, rarely, regularly* and *seldom*. But note that *very occasionally* means 'not very often':

We only have dinner parties ***very occasionally*** *these days.*

The following can be modified by *fairly* and *quite*: *frequently, often* and *regularly.*

Other adverbials that suggest indefinite frequency are: *again and again; at times; every so often; (every) now and again; from time to time; (every) now and then*; and ordinary *-ly* adverbs such as *constantly, continually, continuously, repeatedly.*

Not ... any more, not ... any longer, etc. refer both to duration and frequency, indicating activities that used to occur frequently, but have now stopped [> 7.36].

7.40 Position of adverbs of indefinite frequency

7.40.1 Adverbs of frequency: affirmatives/questions: mid-position

The normal position of most adverbs of indefinite frequency is 'after an auxiliary or before a full verb'. This means:

- after *be* when it is the only verb in a sentence [but > 7.40.6]:
  I ***was never*** *very good at maths.*
- after the first auxiliary verb when there is more than one verb:
  You ***can always contact me*** *on 032 5642.*
- before the main verb when there is only one verb:
  Gerald ***often made*** *unwise decisions.*

These adverbs usually come before *used to, have to* and *ought to*:

We ***never used to*** *import so many goods.*

They can also come before a *to*-infinitive, though this is formal:

You ***ought always to check*** *your facts when you write essays.*

In questions, these adverbs usually come after the subject:

Do you usually have *cream in your coffee?*

7.40.2 Adverbs of frequency: negative sentences: mid-position

Not must come before *always* and it commonly comes before *generally, normally, often, regularly* and *usually*:

*Public transport is****n't always*** *very reliable.*
*We do****n't usually*** *get up before nine on Sundays.*

The following is also possible with slightly different emphasis:

We ***usually*** *do****n't*** *get up before 9 on Sundays.*

Not must come after *sometimes* and *frequently*:

Debbie is ***sometimes not*** *responsible for what she does.*

Some frequency adverbials such as *almost always, nearly always* and *occasionally* are not used in the negative.

7.40.3 Adverbs of frequency: end position

'Affirmative adverbs' can be used at the end of a sentence:

I get paid on Fridays ***usually****.*

We can use *often* at the end in questions and negatives:

Do you come here ***often****? I don't come here* ***often****.*

Always may occur at the end, but in the sense of 'for ever':

I'll love you ***always****.*

The 'negative adverbs' *rarely* and *seldom* can sometimes occur at the end, especially when modified by *only* or *very*:

Nowadays, we drive down to the coast ***only rarely****.*

7.40.4 Adverbs of frequency: beginning a sentence

Where special emphasis or contrast is required, the following can begin a sentence: *frequently, generally, normally, occasionally, ordinarily, sometimes* and *usually*:

Sometimes *we get a lot of rain in August.*

Often is generally preceded by *quite* or *very* when it is used for emphasis at the beginning of a sentence:

Quite/Very often *the phone rings when I'm in the bath.*

Always and *never* can be used at the beginning in imperatives:
__Always__ pay your debts. __Never__ borrow money. [> 9.52*n*.6]
When negative adverbs (*never, seldom*, etc.) are used to begin sentences, they affect the word order that follows [> 7.59.3].

7.40.5 Adverbs of frequency: 'ever' and 'never'

Ever, meaning 'at any time', is used in questions:
Have you __ever__ thought of applying for a job abroad?
We can use *ever* after *any-* and *no-* indefinite pronouns [> 4.37]:
Does __anyone ever__ visit them? __Nothing ever__ bothers Howard.
Ever can occur in affirmative *if*-sentences:
__If__ you __ever__ need any help, you know where to find me.
and after *hardly, scarcely* and *barely* [> 7.39].
Never is used in negative sentences and frequently replaces *not* when we wish to strengthen a negative [> 13.8]. Compare:
I __don't smoke__. I __never smoke__.
The negative *not...ever* may be used in preference to *never* for extra emphasis in e.g. promises, warnings, etc.:
I promise you, he wo__n't ever__ trouble you again!

7.40.6 Adverbs of frequency before auxiliaries

Adverbs of indefinite frequency can be used before auxiliaries (*be, have, do, can, must*, etc.) when we want to place special emphasis on the verb, which is usually heavily stressed in speech:
It's just like Philip. He __always 'is__ late when we have an important meeting. You __never 'can__ rely on him.

We often use this word order in short responses, especially to agree with or contradict something that has just been said:
Philip is late again. – *Yes, he __always 'is__.*
Note this use when *do, does* and *did* replace a full verb:
Your son never helps you. – *No, he __never 'does__.*
or: *But he __always 'does__!*
A response of this kind can be part of a single statement:
Joan promised to keep her room tidy, but she __never did__.
The same kind of emphasis can be made with more than one verb:
George __never should have joined__ the army.

Adverbs of degree

7.41 How to identify adverbs of degree

Adverbs of degree broadly answer the question *'To what extent?'* Some of the most common are: *almost, altogether, barely, a bit, enough, fairly, hardly, nearly, quite, rather, somewhat, too.* Most of these go before the words they modify: e.g.
– adjectives: *__quite good__.*
– adverbs: *__quite quickly__.*
– verbs: *I __quite like__ it.*
– nouns (in a few instances): *__quite an experience__.*
However, not all adverbs of degree can form all these combinations. Adverbs of degree change the meaning of a sentence, often by

weakening the effect of the word they modify. In speech, the information they provide can vary according to stress:

The film was ***quite good****.* (rising tone: = I enjoyed it on the whole)
The film was ***quite good****.* (falling tone: = I didn't particularly enjoy it)

For adverbs of degree which will combine with the comparative and superlative of adjectives and adverbs [> 6.27.5, 6.28.2].

Some quantifiers, such as *a little, a lot, much*, etc. can be used as adverbs of degree [> 7.45–46]. Compare:

I don't like coffee ***very much****.* (degree)
I don't drink ***much*** *coffee.* (quantity)

Fractions and percentages also function as adverbs to show degree:

Business is so bad that the department stores are ***half*** *empty.*
We have a ***60%*** *chance of winning the next election.*

Some adverbs of degree (*almost, nearly*, etc.) do not pose problems in usage; others (*fairly, rather*, etc.) are more complicated. Details follow.

7.42 'Quite'

The meaning of *quite* depends on the kind of word it modifies. With adjectives and adverbs which are gradable [> 6.5] *quite* means 'less than the highest degree', or it can mean 'better than expected'. This use of *quite* (= less than, etc.) is not very common in AmE.

The lecture was ***quite good****. He lectured* ***quite well****.* (= less than)

However, with ungradable words (*dead, perfect(ly), unique(ly)*) and 'strong' gradable words (*amazing(ly), astounding(ly)*), *quite* means 'absolutely' or 'completely':

The news is ***quite amazing****. She plays* ***quite amazingly****.*

Not quite, roughly meaning 'not completely', is normally used with ungradable words only (*not quite dead, not quite perfect*, etc.):

Your answer is ***not quite right****.*

Quite is not used with the comparative but can modify a few verbs:

I ***quite enjoy*** *mountain holidays.* (i.e. to a certain extent)
I ***quite forgot*** *to post your letter.* (i.e. completely)

And note: *He's* ***quite better****.* (= He has completely recovered.)

Quite is often used in BrE in understatements. Thus, if a speaker says, *He's* ***quite clever***, he might mean, 'He's very intelligent'. Where a slightly different emphasis is required, *quite* can be replaced by *not at all* + a negative word: *He's* ***not at all*** *stupid.* [compare > 5.8]

7.42.1 'Quite a/an', 'quite some' and 'quite the'

Quite a/an + countable noun suggests 'noteworthy':

Madeleine is ***quite an expert*** *on Roman coins.*

Quite some + uncountable noun suggests 'considerable':

It's ***quite some time*** *since we wrote to each other.*

Quite a/an (or *a quite*) + adjective + noun is positive in its effect:

It is ***quite an interesting*** *film/****a quite interesting*** *film.*

Quite the (= e.g. 'certainly') can combine with:

– superlatives: *It's* ***quite the worst*** *play I have ever seen.*
– nouns: *Wide lapels are* ***quite the fashion*** *this spring.*

7.43 'Fairly'

Fairly suggests 'less than the highest degree' and often combines with adjectives/adverbs that suggest a good state of affairs (e.g. *good, nice, well*). It is less 'complimentary' than *quite*:

*The lecture was **fairly good**. He lectured **fairly well**.*

Fairly does not combine with comparatives. Compared with *quite* and *rather*, it combines with verbs in restricted contexts:

*You **fairly drive me mad** with your nagging.* (= very nearly)

A fairly combines with adjective + noun:

*He's **a fairly good speaker**.* (less complimentary than *quite a/an*)

7.44 'Rather'

Rather can be stronger than *quite* and *fairly* and suggests 'inclined to be'. It can combine with adjectives which suggest a good state of affairs or a bad one:

– inclined to be **good**: *good, nice, clever, well.*
– inclined to be **bad**: *bad, nasty, stupid, ill.*

Rather combines with:

– adjectives: *This jacket's getting **rather old**.*
– adverbs: *I did **rather badly** in the competition.*
– some verbs: *I **rather like** raw fish.*
– comparatives: *Clive earns **rather more** than his father.*

Rather tends to combine with 'negative' adjectives:

*Frank is clever but **rather lazy**.*

With 'positive' adjectives, *rather* often suggests 'surprisingly':

*Your results are **rather good** – better than I expected.*

In BrE *rather*, like *quite* [> 7.42], is used in understatements:

*Professor Boffin was **rather pleased** when he won the Nobel Prize.*

7.44.1 'Rather a/an' and 'a rather'

Rather a/an combines with a noun:

*Old Fortescue's **rather a bore**.* (= he's inclined to be a bore)

Rather a/an or *a rather* can precede adjective + noun:

*It's **rather a** sad story.* = *It's **a rather** sad story.*

7.45 'Much', 'far' and 'a lot'

Normally, *much* and *far* combine with comparative/superlative forms [> 6.27.5, 6.28.2]: *much bigger, far better, far the best*; and *a lot* combines with comparatives: *a lot more expensive*.

Much can be used like *very* [> 7.51] and *any* [> 5.12.3] with a few positive (i.e. not comparative or superlative) forms such as *good* and *different*. It is normally used with a negative:

*I don't think this battery is **much good/much different**.*

A lot and *far* combine with *different*, but not with *good*:

*This edition is **a lot/far different** from the earlier one.*

Not much and *a lot* combine with verbs like *like* and *enjoy*:

*I do**n't much like** fish. I do**n't** like fish **(very) much/a lot**.*

Far combines with verbs like *prefer* and *would rather* [>11.44]:

*I **far prefer** swimming to cycling.*

7.46 'A (little) bit', 'a little', 'somewhat'

A bit (or *a little bit*), *a little* and *somewhat* combine with:
- adjectives: *It's **a bit/a little/somewhat expensive**.*
- adverbs: *He arrived **a bit/a little/somewhat late**.*
- comparatives: *You're **a bit/a little/somewhat taller** than Alice.*
- verbs: *I've turned up the oven **a bit/a little/somewhat**.*

Not a bit (like *not in the least, not in the slightest*) is often used for extra emphasis as a negative intensifier [compare > 5.8]:
*She was**n't** even **a bit upset** when she heard the news.*

7.47 'Enough' and 'fairly' [compare > 5.17]

Enough and *fairly* should not be confused. *Enough*, as an adverb, follows an adjective or adverb and suggests 'for some purpose':
*The water in the pool **is fairly warm**.*
*The water in the pool is **warm enough** (to swim in).* [> 16.32.2]

7.48 'Too', 'very' and 'enough'

Too goes before adjectives and adverbs. It conveys the idea of 'excess', 'more than is necessary', and should not be confused with the intensifier *very*, which does not suggest excess [> 7.51]. *Too* and *enough* point to a result:
*I arrived at the station **too late**.* (I missed the train.)
*I didn't arrive at the station **early enough**.* (I missed the train.)
*I didn't arrive at the station **too late**.* (I caught the train.)
*I arrived at the station **early enough**.* (I caught the train.)

Too can be modified by *a bit, far, a little, a lot, much* and *rather* (*far too much work; a bit too difficult*, etc.).
For *too* and *enough* with adjective + infinitive [> 16.32].

7.49 'Hardly', 'barely' and 'scarcely'

These adverbs are similar in meaning. They can be used in front of:
- adjectives: *This soup is **hardly/barely/scarcely warm** (enough).*
- adverbs: *She plays **hardly/barely/scarcely well** enough.*

Hardly and *scarcely* can be used with verbs:
*It might stop raining, but I **hardly/scarcely think** it likely.*
Barely combines with a smaller range of verbs:
*Jimmy **barely knows** his multiplication tables yet.*

Hardly, barely and *scarcely* are negative words and do not combine with *not* or *never*. They combine with *ever* [> 7.39] and *any* [> 5.10]:
*I've got so little time, I **hardly ever read** newspapers.*
*There's **hardly any** cheerful news in the papers.*

Hardly/barely/scarcely ever can be replaced by *almost never*:
*I **almost never** visit London these days.* (= I hardly ever...)
Nearly will not combine with *never*; we must use *almost never*.

We can say *not nearly*, but we cannot say **not almost**:
*There are **not nearly** enough members present to hold a meeting.*

Intensifiers

7.50 How to identify intensifiers

Intensifiers are adverbs which are used with gradable [> 6.5] adjectives and adverbs (***very*** *slow/****very*** *slowly*) and, in some cases, verbs (*I* ***entirely*** *agree*). While an adverb of degree normally weakens or limits the meaning of the word it modifies, an intensifier normally strengthens (or 'intensifies') the meaning:

Your work is ***good****.*
Your work is ***very good****.* (intensifier: meaning strengthened)
Your work is ***quite good****.* (adverb of degree: meaning weakened)

7.51 'Very', etc. [compare > 6.9]

Very is the most common intensifier. We use it before:
- adjectives: *Martha has been* ***very ill****.*
- adjective + noun: *Boris is not* ***a very nice person****.*
- adverbs: *The wheels of bureaucracy turn* ***very slowly****.*

Very on its own cannot go before comparatives, but *very* + *much* can: *very much better/faster*. Nor can it go before many predicative adjectives like *alone* [> 6.8.2] except with *much*:

Since her husband's death, Mrs Kay has been ***very much alone****.*

Combinations with *not* (*not very good, not very well*) are often used in preference to positive forms (*bad, ill*) because they are sometimes more polite (*Your work is* ***not very good***).

Very can be used before gradable adjectival present participles (*very interesting*) and adjectival past participles (mostly ending in *-ed*, e.g. *very interested* [> App 10] and a few others, e.g. *very mistaken*). When past participles are used to form verb tenses, they can sometimes be preceded by *much* or *very much*:

These developments ***have very much interested*** *us.* (Not **very**)

7.51.1 'Very', '(very) much', 'so', 'such a/an'

Much, with or without *very* or *so*, can be used in mid-position:

Byron is ***very much/so much/much*** *admired in Greece.*

Very much and *so much* (but never *much* on its own) can also go in the end position:

I enjoyed *your party* ***very much/so much****.*

We can use *the* (or e.g. *my*) *very* before a superlative (*the very best*) but we must use *very much* or *so much* before a comparative (*so much better*) [> 6.27.5]. *The very* can also combine with a few nouns (*the very beginning*) [> 6.9]. *Very* can be replaced by *most* before some adjectives describing personal feelings, attitudes (*most obliged, most concerned*, etc.).

Such a/an + (adjective) + noun can be used in place of *so* + adjective:

It was ***such a nice party****!/The party was* ***so nice****!*

Compare *so...a/an* in:

It was ***so important an occasion****, we couldn't miss it.*

So + adjective can replace *very*, informally, e.g. in exclamations:
*This new cheese is **so good**!* [> App 7.18]
For extra emphasis, *very* may be repeated:
*This new cheese is **very very good**.* (also: *so very very good*)

7.51.2 'Jolly', 'pretty' and 'dead' in place of 'very'

Jolly and the weaker *pretty* can be used in (informal) BrE in place of *very* before adjectives or adverbs:
*She's a **jolly good** player. The traffic is moving **pretty slowly**.*
Pretty can also combine with *well* to mean 'nearly':
*The film was **pretty well** over by the time we got to the cinema.*
Dead is used, usually informally, with a limited selection of adjectives (not adverbs): *dead certain, dead drunk, dead level, dead quiet, dead right, dead straight, dead tired, dead wrong:*
*You're **dead right**! The war in Europe did end on May 7, 1945.*

7.51.3 'Indeed' and 'not (...) at all'

Very (but not *so*) can be intensified by *indeed* in affirmative sentences:
*That's **very good indeed**. I enjoyed it **very much indeed**.*
At all (with or without *very much*) can be used in negatives:
*Mike does**n't** enjoy classical music (**very much**) **at all**.*

7.52 -ly intensifiers used in place of 'very'

A few *-ly* adverbs such as *extremely, particularly, really* and (informally) *awfully, frightfully*, and *terribly* are commonly used for extra emphasis in place of *very* with:

- adjectives: *Miss Hargreaves is **extremely helpful**.*
- adverbs: *Dawson works **really slowly**.*
- past participles: *I'm **terribly confused** by all this information.*
- *-ing*-form adjectives: *The information is **terribly confusing**.*
- adjective + noun: *Dawson is a **particularly good worker**.*

Some *-ly* adverbs will combine with verbs:
*I **really appreciate** all you've done for me.*

7.53 -ly intensifiers that retain their basic meaning

Many *-ly* adverbs which can act as intensifiers retain their basic meaning: e.g. *absolutely, completely, definitely, entirely, greatly, perfectly, seriously* [> App 16]. Each of these will combine with some words and not with others. For example, *greatly* will combine with verbs, but not with adjectives (except a few ending in *-ed*) or adverbs:
*Many people **greatly admire** English gardens.*

Many *-ly* adverbs commonly combine with past participles (*completely mistaken, horribly injured, perfectly planned*, etc.).
In the passive *-ly* adverbs can come before or after past participles:
*He was **unexpectedly delayed/delayed unexpectedly**.*

7.53.1 Limited combinations with -ly adverbs

Some *-ly* adverbs, such as *badly, deeply, lightly, sharply, strikingly, utterly*, combine with relatively small sets of words: e.g. *badly needed, deeply suspicious, highly respected*. More combinations are possible with adverbs like *deeply* and *utterly* than with e.g. *sharply*.

Focus adverbs

7.54 The use of adverbs when 'focusing'

Adverbs such as *even, just, merely, only, really* and *simply* can precede the word they qualify to focus attention on it. Others, like *too* and *as well*, focus our attention by adding information.

7.55 The position of 'even' and 'only'

The position of some adverbs such as *even* and *only* is particularly flexible, conveying slightly different meanings according to where they are placed. A few examples are:

***Even** Tom knows that 2 and 2 make 4.* (i.e. although he's stupid)
*Tom **even** knows that 2 and 2 make 4.* (i.e. of the many things he knows)
***Only** Tom knows the answer.* (i.e. nobody else does)
*Tom knows **only** half of it.* (i.e. nothing else)
*Tom **only** met Helen.* (i.e. no one else)

The pre-verb position of *even* and *only* often leads to ambiguity. In the written language we can avoid ambiguity by putting these words before the words they qualify. In the spoken language, this is not necessary (and rarely happens). We rely on stress and intonation:

*I **only** asked Jim to lend me his **'ladder**.* (i.e. not anything else)

7.55.1 Other uses of 'only' [compare > 16.12.2]

Only + *too*, in the sense of 'extremely':

*I'm **only too** glad to be of help.*

Only before a verb in explanations and excuses:

*I don't know why you're so angry. I **only** left the door open.*

7.56 'Too', 'as well', 'not...either' and 'also'

Too and *as well* usually go in the end position in the affirmative:

*I like John and I like his wife, **too/as well**.*

In negative sentences these words are replaced by *either*:

*I do**n't** like John and I do**n't** like his wife, **either**.*

Also, used as a replacement for *too* and *as well*, is more common in writing than in speech. It comes:

- after auxiliaries:
  *Sue is an engineer. She **is also** a mother.*
- after the first verb when there is more than one:
  *I've written the letters. I **should also have posted** them.*
- before the main verb:
  *I play squash and I **also play** tennis.*

Note in the above example that *also* generally refers to the verb that follows it (i.e. tennis is not the only game I play). Compare *I, **too**, play tennis* which refers to the subject (= My friend plays tennis and I play tennis, *too/as well*). The use of *too*, directly after the subject, is formal and the end position is generally preferred, especially in informal speech. Like *too* and *as well*, *also* is not used in negative sentences and must be replaced by *not...either* [compare > 13.28–29].

Viewpoint adverbs and connectives

7.57 Expressing a viewpoint [> App 17]

Many adverbs and adverbial phrases tell us something about a speaker's (or writer's) attitude to what he is saying or to the person he is talking to (or writing to or for). We call these 'viewpoint' or 'sentence' adverbs because they qualify what is being said (or written), but do not affect its grammatical structure. For example, a speaker or writer may use adverbs such as *clearly* or *evidently* to tell us he is drawing conclusions; *frankly* or *honestly* to impress us with his sincerity; *generally* or *normally* to make generalizations; *briefly* or *in short* to suggest he will not be tedious or go into details. Viewpoint adverbs may come at the very beginning of a sentence, and are followed by a brief pause in speech or a comma in writing. They then modify the sentence or sentences that follow:

__Frankly__, I am not satisfied with your work.

Some viewpoint adverbs may also come in mid-position:

He smiled nastily. He __evidently__ knew something I didn't.

Hopefully is an adverb of manner in:

To travel __hopefully__ is better than to arrive.

Nowadays, *hopefully* is often used as a viewpoint adverb, though not all native speakers approve of this use:

Hopefully, (= I hope) *I'll see you sometime tomorrow.*
Hopefully, (= it is hoped) *they'll arrive at an agreement.*

7.58 Connecting words and phrases [> App 18]

Numerous adverbs introduce additions to, modifications or summaries of what has already been said. They are essential when we wish to present information in a coherent fashion in speech or writing. For example, a speaker or writer may use adverbs such as *however* or *on the contrary* to draw a contrast; *at the same time* or *meanwhile* to tell us about something else that was happening at the same time; *as a result* or *consequently* to draw our attention to results; *furthermore* or *moreover* to add information.

Connectives may come at the beginning, followed by a pause in speech or a comma in writing:

The police were sure Griffiths was lying. They had found his fingerprints everywhere. __Furthermore__, they knew for a fact that he hadn't been at his mother's at the time of the crime.

Some connectives may also come in mid-position and are then separated from the rest of the sentence by commas:

Penrose gambled heavily and, __as a result__, lost a lot of money.

Inversion after adverbs

7.59 Inversion after adverbs

Sometimes the normal subject-verb order in a sentence is reversed if a sentence begins with an adverb. This can happen as follows:

7.59.1 Inversion after adverbs of place like 'here', 'there'

After *here* and *there* and after adverb particles such as *back, down, off, up*, etc. the noun subject comes *after* the verb. This is common with verbs of motion, such as *come* and *go*:

*Here **comes a taxi**! There **goes the last train**!* (Note the progressive is not used here.)
*Down **came the rain** and up **went the umbrellas**.*

This kind of inversion is common after *be* when we are offering things or identifying location (often with a plural subject) [> 10.18]:

*Here's **a cup of tea** for you.* (offer)
*Here's **your letters**.* (offering or indicating)
'There's (stressed) ***Johnny Smith***. (identifying location)

Inversion does not occur if the subject is a pronoun:

*Here **it comes**. There **she goes**. Up **it went**.*
*Here **you are**.* (offer) *There **she is**.* (identifying location)

7.59.2 Inversion after adverbials of place [compare > 6.17]

After adverbials of place with verbs of position (e.g. *lie, live, sit, stand*) or motion (e.g. *come, go, rise*), the noun subject can follow the verb. This happens mainly in descriptive writing:

*At the top of the hill **stood the tiny chapel**.*
*In the fields of poppies **lay the dying soldiers**.*

This inversion also occurs in the passive with other verbs:

*In the distance **could be seen the purple mountains**.*

Inversion does not occur if the subject is a pronoun:

*At the top of the hill **it stood out against the sky**.*

7.59.3 Inversion after negative adverbs, etc.

Certain adverbs, when used at the beginning of a sentence, must be followed by auxiliary verbs (*be, do, have, can, must*, etc.) + subject + the rest of the sentence. This kind of inversion, which may be used for particular emphasis, is typical of formal rhetoric and formal writing. It occurs after the following:

– negative or near-negative adverbs (often of time or frequency, such as *never, rarely, seldom*); or adverbs having a negative effect, e.g. *little, on no account* [> App 19]:

*Never/Seldom **has there been so much protest** against the Bomb.*
*Little **does he realize** how important this meeting is.*
*On no account **must you accept** any money if he offers it.*

The word order is, of course, normal when these adverbs do not begin a sentence:

***There has never/seldom been** so much protest against the Bomb.*
***He little realizes** how important this meeting is.*

– combinations with *only* (e.g. *only after, only then*):

*The pilot reassured the passengers. Only then **did I realize** how dangerous the situation had been.*

– *so* + adjective (+ *that*) and *such* (+ *that*):

*So sudden **was the attack** (that) we had no time to escape.*
*Such **was his strength** that he could bend iron bars.*

For normal word order with *so* and *such* [> 1.52.1].

8 Prepositions, adverb particles and phrasal verbs

General information about prepositions and adverb particles

8.1 What a preposition is and what it does

We normally use prepositions in front of nouns or noun phrases, pronouns or gerunds to express a relationship between one person, thing, event, etc. and another:

preposition + **noun**: *I gave the book **to Charlie**.*
preposition + **pronoun**: *I gave it **to him**.*
preposition + **gerund**: *Charlie devotes his time **to reading**.*

Some relationships expressed by prepositions are:
Space: *We ran **across** the field.*
Time: *The plane landed **at** 4.25 precisely.*
Cause: *Travel is cheap for us **because of** the strength of the dollar.*
Means: *You unlock the door **by** turning the key to the right.*

Prepositions always have an object. Even when a preposition is separated from its object, for example in questions [> 8.22, 13.31*n*.4, 13.33] or relatives [> 1.35–38], the relationship is always there:

*__Who(m)__ were you talking **to** just now on the phone?* (= To whom ...)
*__The chair__ I was sitting **on** was very shaky.* (= The chair on which ...)

8.2 Form and stress of prepositions

Prepositions may take the form of:
– single words: *at, from, in, to, into*, etc.
– two or more words: *according to, apart from, because of*, etc.
One-syllable prepositions are normally unstressed in speech:

There's 'someone at the 'door. (No stress on *at*.)

Prepositions of two or more syllables are normally stressed on one of the syllables: *'opposite the 'bank; be'hind the 'wall*, etc.
For examples of common prepositions [> App 20].

8.3 Pronouns after prepositions

English nouns do not have 'case' [> 1.1], so they do not change in form when they are e.g. the object of a verb or a preposition:

*There's a chair **behind/by/in front of/near the door**.*

But the object form of pronouns must be used after prepositions:

*The car stopped **behind/in front of/near me/him/her/us/them**.*
***Between you and me**, there's no truth in the report.*

Some native speakers mistakenly use *I* instead of *me* after prepositions, especially when there are two pronouns separated by *and* (Not **between you and I**).

8.4 When is a word a preposition, adverb or conjunction?

A preposition 'governs' an object, so it is always related to a noun, a noun phrase, pronoun or gerund; an adverb particle does not 'govern' an object, so it is more closely related to a verb [> 7.3.4].

8.4.1 Words that can be used as prepositions or adverb particles

Some words function both as prepositions and as adverb particles. When they are followed by an object, they function as **prepositions**:

*We drove **round the city**.* (*round* + object = preposition)

When no object is stated, these words function as **adverb particles** (even if an object is implied):

*We drove **round**.* (no object = adverb particle)

Unlike prepositions, adverb particles are stressed in speech.

The most common of the words that can be used as prepositions or as adverb particles are: *about, above, across, after, along, around, before, behind, below, beneath, beyond, by, down, in, inside, near, off, on, opposite, outside, over, past, round, through, under, underneath, up, without.*

8.4.2 Words that are used as prepositions, but not as particles

The following words are used only as prepositions (that is, they take an object): *against, at, beside, despite, during, except, for, from, into, of, onto, per, since, till/until, to, toward(s), upon, via, with* and prepositions ending in *-ing* such as *excepting, regarding* [> App 20.2]. A few phrasal verbs [> 8.23] are formed with verb + *to* as an adverb particle: e.g. *come to, pull to.*

8.4.3 Words that are used as adverb particles, but not as prepositions

The following words are used only as particles (that is, they do not take an object): *away, back, backward(s), downward(s), forward(s), out* [except informally > App 25.31] and *upward(s)*:

*The children rang the bell and ran **away**.*

8.4.4 Words that can be used as prepositions or conjunctions

Some words can be used as prepositions (when followed by an object) or as conjunctions (when followed by a clause): e.g. *after, as, before, since, till, until* [> 1.44–53]:

*I haven't seen him **since this morning**.* (preposition)
*I haven't seen him **since he left** this morning.* (conjunction)

When used as conjunctions, *as well as, but, except* and *than* can be followed by a bare infinitive [> 16.1]:

*I've done everything you wanted **except*** (or ***but***) ***make** the beds.*

8.5 Some problems for the learner in the use of prepositions

English uses more prepositions than most other European languages, partly because 'case' [> 1.1] is no longer expressed by noun endings. This may cause problems of choice because:

- many English prepositions have nearly the same meaning: e.g. *beside, by, near, next to*; or: *above, on top of, over.*
- a single preposition in the student's mother tongue may do the work of several English prepositions. So, for example, there may be one

preposition to cover the meanings of *by, from*, and *of*, or *at, in, on* and *to*, particularly after 'movement verbs' [> 8.7].
- some prepositions (e.g. *at*) perform different functions. For example, they express relationships in time (*at six o'clock*), space (*at the bank*) and other relationships as well.

Movement and position

8.6 Position in space seen from different viewpoints

When referring to space (i.e. a very wide area), we have a choice of preposition, depending on the meaning we wish to express. For example, we can say:

in/at/to/from/under/over/across London.

A speaker's personal viewpoint of a place may affect his choice of preposition. If a speaker says:

*I live **in London**.*

he feels 'enclosed' by London.

But if a speaker says:

*We stopped **at London** on the way to New York.*

he sees London as a point on a route.

We use *at* to imply that the location has a special purpose: it may be a stopping place, a meeting place, an eating place, a work place, etc. seen externally.

We can consider position in space in relation to:

- a **point** (i.e. a place or e.g. event):
  at the cinema; at a party; to/from London
  *We stood **at the door** and waited.* (i.e. at that point)
- a **line** (i.e. a place we think of in terms of length):
  across/along/on a border/river/road
  *There's a letter box **across the road**.* (i.e. across that line)
- a **surface** (i.e. a place we think of as a flat area):
  across/off/on a table/floor/wall/ceiling
  *I stared at a fly **on the wall**.* (i.e. on that surface)
- **area** or **volume**: (i.e. a place which can 'enclose'):
  in/into/out of/outside/within a room/ship/car/factory/forest
  *We all sat **in the car**.* (i.e. in that area)

A single place (e.g. *river*) can be viewed from different angles:

*We went **to the river**.*	(a point)
*Greenwich is **down the river**.*	(a line)
*The paper boat floated **on the river**.*	(a surface)
*We swam **in the river**.*	(an area or volume)

8.7 Prepositions reflecting movement or lack of movement

A preposition takes on the idea of movement (*fly under*) or lack of movement (*stop under*) from the verb in the sentence. Some prepositions combine either with 'movement verbs' (e.g. *bring, drive, fly, get, go, move, pull, run, take, walk*) or with 'position verbs' (e.g. *be, live, keep, meet, stay, stop, work*).

movement			position (lack of movement)		
We **drove** **flew** **ran**	*above* *across* *along* *behind* *beside* *between* *near*, etc.	+ object.	*We* **were** **live** **work**	*above* *across* *along* *behind* *beside* *between* *near*, etc.	+ object.

Some prepositions, such as *into, onto, out of, to*, etc., normally combine only with 'movement verbs':

A bird ***flew into my bedroom*** *this morning.*

I ***drove out of the car park****.*

Other prepositions, such as *at, in, on*, etc. normally combine only with 'position verbs':

The bird ***perched on the curtain rail****.*

I ***waited in the hotel lobby****.*

Verbs which describe 'movement with an end': e.g. *lay, place, sit, stand* do not combine with prepositions like *into, onto* or *to*:

She ***laid*** *the letter* ***on*** *the table.*

She ***sat*** *the baby* ***on*** *the table.*

We can often use the verb *be* with prepositions that normally combine with 'movement verbs' to convey the idea of 'having reached a destination' (real or metaphorical):

At last we were ***into/out of the forest/over the river****.*

At last we were ***out of/over our difficulties****.*

8.8 Adverb particles reflecting movement or lack of movement

The same contrast between movement and lack of movement can also be expressed by verb + adverb particle:

movement: *We went* *away/back/inside/outside/up/down.*
position: *We stayed* *away/back/inside/outside/up/down.*

Compare:

Where's Jim? – I don't know. He ***went out****.* (movement)
*Where's Jim? – I don't know. He****'s out****.* (position)

8.9 Prepositions reflecting direction and destination

The difference between direction and destination can often be expressed by contrasting prepositions. The choice depends on whether we are referring to a point, a surface or an area [> 8.6].

8.9.1 'To/from a point' compared with 'at a point' [> 8.6]

To and *from* a point (indicating direction) may contrast with *at* a point (indicating destination or position after movement):

direction to or from		destination after movement	
Jim has gone ***to*** *(has come* ***from****)*	*The Grand Hotel* *school* *London Airport* *my brother's*	*and now he's* ***at***	*The Grand Hotel.* *school.* *London Airport.* *my brother's.*

To and *at* combine with a variety of nouns [> App 21].

8.9.2 'To/from a point' compared with 'in an area' [> 8.6]

To and *from* a point (indicating direction) may contrast with *in* an area (indicating destination or position after movement):

direction to or from		destination after movement	
*Jim has gone **to***	*the country* / *Paris* / *bed*	*and now he's **in***	*the country.* / *Paris.* / *bed.*

To and *in* combine with a variety of nouns [> App 22].

8.9.3 'To/from a point' compared with 'at a point/in an area' [> App 23]

With certain nouns, the destination after movement may be *at* or *in* depending on whether the location is seen as a point or an area.

direction to or from		destination after movement		
*Jim has gone **to***	*the restaurant* / *the hotel* / *the bank*	*and now he's*	***in*** / ***at***	*the restaurant.* / *the hotel.* / *the bank.*

At cannot replace *in* for words that represent very wide areas: e.g. *in the sky, in the universe, in the world*. Note that the use of *at* or *in* after the verb *arrive* depends on which preposition the noun is normally used with (arrive *at a party*, arrive *in the country*). Sometimes either preposition is possible depending on whether we regard the location as a point or an area [> 8.6]: *arrive **at** Brighton* or *arrive **in** Brighton*.

8.9.4 'On(to) a line or surface', 'off a line or surface'

On(to) (direction) and *on* (destination or location) can be used to indicate 'being supported by' a line or surface:

direction on(to)	destination after movement
*I put the pen **on(to)** the table*	*and now it is **on** the table.*

Onto is spelt as one word or two: *on to*. *On* (without *to*) can sometimes indicate direction, often with a change of level:

*I put the pen **on** the table.*

However, *onto* is sometimes preferable to *on* with movement verbs like *climb, lift, jump* [> 8.7] to avoid ambiguity:

*Mr Temple **jumped onto** the stage.* (i.e. from somewhere else)
*Mr Temple **jumped on** the stage.* (which could mean 'jumped up and down on it', or 'jumped once to test its strength')

On (indicating destination or location) can also contrast with *to* (indicating direction) with reference to levels:

*He's gone **to** the fourth floor and now he's **on** the fourth floor.*

Off (= 'not on', indicating separation from a line or surface) combines with movement verbs or position verbs:

*I took the plate **off** the table and now it is **off** the table.*

8.9.5 'In(to) and in an area or volume'

Into always reflects movement and is never used for destination or position. *In* usually reflects position, but with some movement verbs like *drop, fall* and *put* it can also reflect movement:

direction in(to)	destination after movement
*I have put the coin **in(to)** my pocket*	*and now it is **in** my pocket.*

However, with other movement verbs, such as *run* and *walk*, *in* does not reflect movement from one place to another:

*We walked **into the park**.* (= we were outside it and entered it)
*We walked **in the park**.* (= we were already inside it and walked within the area)

Inside can replace *in* when we refer to e.g. rooms, buildings:

*I'll meet you **inside/in** the restaurant.*

8.9.6 'Out of an area or volume'

Out of can reflect direction and destination:

direction out of	**destination after movement**
*We ran **out of** the building*	*and then we were **out of** the building.*

Outside can replace *out of* when we refer to e.g. rooms, buildings:

*We were **outside** the building.*

But *outside* and *out of* are not always interchangeable [> App 25.31].

Within, to mean 'inside', can occur in a few limited and formal contexts:

*Everyone **within** the London area was affected by the bus strike.*

Without, to mean 'outside', is now archaic.

8.9.7 'Get' + preposition/particle reflecting movement

Get, followed by a preposition or particle, often suggests 'movement with difficulty' [compare > 12.13.1]:

*We **got into** the house through the window.* (i.e. with difficulty)
*How did the cat **get out** (of the box)?* (i.e. it must have been difficult)

Time

8.10 General remarks about prepositions of time

The prepositions *at, on* and *in* refer not only to place, but also to time. We can refer to approximate time with *approximately, about, around, round* or *round about*:

*The accident happened **at approximately** 5.30.*
*The accident happened **(at) about/around** 5.30.*

For other prepositions of time such as *during, for, from, since, till*, functioning in adverbial phrases [> 7.30–35], and also [> App 25].

8.11 Time phrases with 'at'

Exact time:	*at 10 o'clock; at 14 hundred hours.* [> App 47.5]
Meal times:	*at lunch time; at tea time; at dinner time.*
Other points of time:	*at dawn; at noon; at midnight; at night.*
Festivals:	*at Christmas; at Easter; at Christmas-time.*
Age:	*at the age of 27; at 14.*
+ *time*:	*at this time; at that time.*

At is often omitted in questions with *What time ...?* and in short answers to such questions:

***What time** do you arrive? – **Nine o'clock** in the morning.*

The full question and answer is formal:

***At what time** do you arrive? – **At nine o'clock** in the morning.*

8.12 Time phrases with 'on'

Days of the week: *on Monday; on Fridays.* [> App 24.1]
Parts of the day: *on Monday morning; on Friday evening.*
Dates: *on June 1st; on 21st March.* [> App 47.4.2]
Day + date: *on Monday, June 1st.*
Particular occasions: *on that day; on that evening.*
Anniversaries, etc.: *on your birthday; on your wedding day.*
Festivals: *on Christmas Day; on New Year's Day.*

In everyday speech *on* is often omitted:

*I'll see you **Friday**. See you **June 21st**.*

Prepositions (and the definite article) must be omitted when we use *last, next* and *this, that* [compare > App 48]:

*I saw him **last/this April**. I'll see you **next/this Friday**.*

8.13 Time phrases with 'in' (= some time during [compare > 7.35])

Parts of the day: *in the evening; in the morning.*
Months: *in March; in September.* [> App 24.2]
Years: *in 1900; in 1984; in 1998.* [> App 47.4.1]
Seasons: *in (the) spring; in (the) winter.* [> App 24.2]
Centuries: *in the 19th century, in the 20th century.*
Festivals: *in Ramadan; in Easter week.*
Periods of time: *in that time; in that age; in the holidays.*

8.14 'In' and 'within' to refer to stated periods of time

In and, more formally, *within*, sometimes mean 'before the end of' a stated period of time, which may be present, past or future:

*I always eat my breakfast **in ten minutes**.*
*I finished the examination **in (within) an hour and a half**.*

When we refer to the future in phrases like *in ten days* (or *in ten days' time*), we mean 'at the end of a period starting from now'; *-s* apostrophe or apostrophe *-s* + *time* is optional [compare > 2.49]:

*The material will be ready **in ten days/in ten days' time**.*

However, when we mean 'within a period of time, not starting from now', we cannot use *-s* apostrophe + *time*. Compare:

*Sanderson will run a mile **in four minutes**.*
(That's how long it will take him to do it.)
*Sanderson will run a mile **in four minutes' time**.*
(That's when he'll start running.)

Particular uses of prepositions and particles

8.15 Particular prepositions, particles and contrasts

Many prepositions/particles have special uses. For details [> App 25].

8.16 Pairs of prepositions and particles

Prepositions and particles can be repeated for extra emphasis:

*We went **round and round** (the town) looking for the hotel.*

Some prepositions function as contrasting pairs:

Please don't keep running ***up and down*** *(the stairs).*

Or the second word adds something to the meaning of the first:

Martha was ill for a long time, but she's ***up and about*** *now.*

8.17 Prepositional phrases

A large number of fixed prepositional phrases are in common use: e.g. *by right, in debt, on time, out of breath*, etc. Some of these phrases have metaphorical or idiomatic uses which extend their time/place associations: e.g. *above average, beneath contempt, beyond belief*. Many phrases follow the pattern preposition + noun + preposition: e.g. *in danger of, on account of* [> Apps 20.3, 26].

8.18 Combinations of particles and prepositions

Prepositions often follow particles, e.g. *across/along/back/down/off/on* + *to, for*, etc. [also > 8.30.2]:

I'm just ***off for*** *a swim. I'm going* ***down to*** *the beach.*

Prepositions sometimes combine directly with each other, as in:

That's the boy ***from over*** *the road.*

Come out ***from under*** *there, will you?*

8.19 Adjectives + prepositions

Many adjectives used predicatively [> 6.7, 6.8.4] are followed by particular prepositions: *absent from, certain of*, etc.

Simon's often ***absent from*** *school because of illness.*

Sometimes a single adjective can be followed by different prepositions: e.g. *embarrassed about, embarrassed at, embarrassed by* [> App 27].

8.20 Nouns + prepositions

Nouns usually take the same prepositions as the adjectives or verbs they relate to [> Apps 27–29].

adjective	**noun**
embarrassed about/at/by	*embarrassment about/at*
keen on	*keenness on*
successful in	*success in*
verb	**noun**
emerge from	*emergence from*
object to	*objection to*

This correlation does not always apply: e.g. *be proud of/take pride in*. Or a noun takes a preposition and the verb does not:

I fear something	*My fear* ***of*** *something*
I influence somebody	*My influence* ***on*** *somebody*

8.21 Modification of prepositions and adverb particles

Prepositions and adverb particles can be modified by adverbs: *directly above our heads; quite out of his mind; right off the main road; well over $200*. In particular, *all*, to mean 'entirely', can combine with numerous prepositions and particles, such as *about, along, down, during, round, through*:

*Our baby went on crying **all through** the night.*

Straight (= immediately) is frequently used with movement and *right* (= in the exact location) is commonly associated with destination:

*He went **straight** to bed/into my office/up to his room.*
*He lives **right** at the end of the street/across the square.*

8.22 Word order in relation to prepositions

Single-word prepositions except e.g. *but, during, except* and *since* [> App 20] can be separated from the words they refer to in:

Wh-questions:	***Where** did you buy that jacket **from**?* [> 13.31*n*.4]
Relative clauses:	***The painting** you're looking **at** has been sold.* [> 1.35–38]
Wh-clauses:	***What he asked me about** is something I can't discuss.* (Separation is obligatory here.)
Indirect speech:	*Tell me **where** you bought that **(from)**.* (optional)
Exclamations:	***What a lot of trouble** he put me **to**!*
Passives:	*Our house **was broken into** last night.* (The end-position is obligatory in the passive.)
Infinitives:	*I need someone **to talk to**.* [> 16.36]

Nowadays not many native speakers believe that it is 'bad style' to end a sentence with a preposition, though the choice of position does depend to some extent on style and balance.

Verb + preposition/particle: non-phrasal and phrasal

8.23 General information about phrasal verbs

One of the most common characteristics of the English verb is that it can combine with prepositions and adverb particles [> 7.3.4]. Broadly speaking, we call these combinations **phrasal verbs**. Though grammarians differ about the exact definition of a phrasal verb, we may use the term to describe any commonly-used combination of verb + preposition or verb + adverb particle.

Essential combinations

Sometimes this combination is essential to the use of the verb. So, for example, the verb *listen* (which can occur on its own in e.g. *Listen!*) must be followed by *to* when it has an object:

*We spent the afternoon **listening to** records.*

Non-essential combinations

Sometimes the combination is not essential but reinforces the meaning of a verb. So, for example, the verb *drink*, in *Drink your milk!* can be reinforced by *up* to suggest 'finish drinking it' or 'drink it all':

***Drink up** your milk!* Or: ***Drink** your milk **up**!* [> 8.28]

Idiomatic combinations

Sometimes the primary meaning of a verb is completely changed when it combines with a preposition or particle: a new verb is formed, which may have a totally different idiomatic meaning, or even several meanings. For example, there are numerous combinations with *make*: *make for* (*a place*) (= go towards), *make off* (= run away), *make up* (= invent), etc. See examples in 8.23.2.

8.23.1 The use of phrasal verbs in English

There is a strong tendency (especially in informal, idiomatic English) to use phrasal verbs instead of their one-word equivalents. It would be very unusual, for instance, to say *Enter!* instead of *Come in!* in response to a knock at the door. Similarly, *blow up* might be preferred to *explode*, *give in* to *surrender*, etc. Moreover, new combinations (or new meanings for existing ones) are constantly evolving:

Share prices ***bottomed out*** (= reached their lowest level) *in 1974.*
The book ***took off*** (= became successful) *as soon as it appeared.*

8.23.2 How common phrasal verbs are formed

The most common phrasal verbs are formed from the shortest and simplest verbs in the language: e.g. *be, break, bring, come, do, fall, find, get, give, go, help, let, make, put, send, stand, take, tear, throw, turn*, which combine with words that often indicate position or direction, such as *along, down, in, off, on, out, over, under, up*. Not only can a single verb like *put* combine with a large number of prepositions or particles to form new verbs (*put off, put out, put up with*, etc.) but even a single combination can have different meanings:

Put out *your cigarettes.* (= extinguish)
I felt quite ***put out****.* (= annoyed)
We ***put out*** *a request for volunteers.* (= issued)
They're ***putting*** *the programme* ***out*** *tomorrow.* (= broadcasting)
This stuff will ***put*** *you* ***out*** *in no time.* (= make you unconscious)
Martha's ***put out*** *her hip again.* (= dislocated)

8.24 Some problems in the use of verb + preposition/particle

Apart from the obvious problem that the use of phrasal verbs is extremely common and a standard feature of good idiomatic English, interference with the learner's own language may arise from:

1 Verbs which may be followed by an infinitive in the learner's language, but which in English can be followed by a preposition or particle + object, but never by an infinitive: e.g. *dream of, insist on, succeed in, think of* [> 8.27]:
Your father ***insists on coming*** *with us.* [> 16.51, 16.54]

2 Verbs which are followed by *to* as a preposition, not as an infinitive. There are relatively few of these [> 16.56]:
I ***look forward to seeing*** *you soon.*

3 Verbs which are followed by different prepositions from the ones used in the learner's language: e.g. *believe in, consist of, depend on, laugh at, live on, rely on, smell of, taste of:*
Everybody ***laughed at*** *my proposal to ban smoking on trains.*

4 Verbs which take a preposition in English, but may not need one in the learner's language: e.g. *ask for, listen to, look at, look for, wait for:*
You should ***ask for*** *the bill.*

5 Verbs which may be followed by a preposition in the learner's language, but not normally in English: e.g. *approach, discuss, enter, lack, marry, obey, remember, resemble:*
We all turned and looked at Mildred when she ***entered the room****.*

8.25 Non-phrasal verbs compared with phrasal verbs

What is a phrasal verb? Very often a verb is followed by a prepositional or adverbial phrase [> 7.3.3, 7.18, 7.30]:
Let's eat ***in the garden/on the terrace/under that tree****.*
In the above examples, *in* and *on* do not have a 'special relationship' with *eat*: they are in 'free association' so that *eat in* and *eat on* are not phrasal verbs here. Most verbs (especially verbs of movement) can occur in free association with prepositions and particles, but these combinations are not always phrasal verbs. For example: *climb, come, go, walk*, etc. will combine freely with *down, from, in, up*, etc.:
I ***go to*** *the bank on Fridays.* (verb + preposition, non-phrasal)
You can ***come out*** *now.* (verb + particle, non-phrasal)
In examples of this kind, the verbs before the prepositions or particles are replaceable:
He ***hurried/ran/walked/went up*** *(the hill).*
Furthermore, in such examples, a verb + preposition or particle is used in its literal sense. The meaning of the verb is a combination of the two words used: e.g. *come* + *out* (i.e. it is the same as the meaning of its separate parts). However, a verb may have an obvious literal meaning in one context and a highly idiomatic one in another:
We'd better not ***step on that carpet****.* (literal)
We'd better ***step on it****.* (i.e. hurry up: idiomatic phrasal verb)
The combination of verb + preposition or particle can be described as **phrasal** when the two (or three) parts are in common association (not 'free association') and yield a particular meaning which may either be obvious (e.g. *I* ***took off*** *my jacket*) or idiomatic (*the plane* ***took off*** = rose into the air). However, the dividing-line between non-phrasal and phrasal verbs is not always easy to draw.

8.26 Four types of verb + preposition/particle

We can distinguish four types of combinations with different characteristics:
Type 1: verb + preposition (transitive): e.g. *get over (an illness)*
Type 2: verb + particle (transitive): e.g. *bring up (the children)*
Type 3: verb + particle (intransitive): e.g. *come about* (= happen)
Type 4: verb + particle + preposition (transitive): e.g. *run out of (matches)*

8.27 Type 1: Verb + preposition (transitive)

8.27.1 General characteristics of Type 1 verbs [compare > 12.3*n*.7]

a Verbs of this type are followed by a preposition [> 8.4] which takes an object (they are transitive [> 1.9]):
I'm looking for ***my glasses****.* (noun object)
I'm looking for ***them****.* (pronoun object)

b We cannot put the preposition after the object:
Look at this picture. (Never **Look this picture at**)
However, separation of the preposition from the verb is sometimes possible in relative clauses and questions (and see note e below):
*The picture **at** which you are **looking** was bought at an auction.*
***At** which picture are you **looking**?*
c Verb + preposition can come at the end of a sentence or clause:
*She's got more work than she can **cope with**.*
*There's so much to **look at** when you visit the National Gallery.*
d Some combinations can go into the passive [> Apps 28, 30]:
*Every problem that came up **was dealt with** efficiently.*
e An adverb may come after the object:
*Look at **this drawing carefully**.*
or, for emphasis, immediately before or after the verb [> 7.16]:
*Look **carefully** at this drawing.*
f Monosyllabic prepositions are not usually stressed:
*This cake **consists of** a few common ingredients.*

Three sub-groups can be identified:

8.27.2 Verb + preposition: non-idiomatic meanings
e.g. *approve of, associate with, believe in, emerge from, fight against, hope for, listen to*, etc. [> App 28].

The verbs are used in their normal sense. The problem is to remember which preposition(s) are associated with them. Sometimes different prepositions are possible: e.g. *consist of, consist in*, where the meaning of the verb remains broadly unchanged:
*Cement **consists of** sand and lime.* (i.e. what the subject (*cement*) is made of)
*Happiness **consists in** having a cheerful outlook.* (i.e. *consists* defines the subject, *happiness*)

8.27.3 Verb + object + preposition: non-idiomatic meanings
e.g. *remind someone of, tell someone about, thank someone for:*
***Tell us about** your travels in China, grandpa.*
Most of these verbs can be used in the passive [> App 29].

8.27.4 Verb + preposition: idiomatic meanings
The parts of such verbs cannot be so easily related to their literal meanings. Relatively few of these verbs can go into the passive, and the preposition can hardly ever be separated from the verb. (See 8.27.1 note b above.)
e.g. *come over* (= affect), *get over* (= recover), *go for* (= attack), *run into* (= meet by accident) [> App 30]:
*I can't explain why I did it. I don't know what **came over** me.*
*Has Martha **got over** her illness yet?*
*Our dog **went for** the postman this morning.*

8.28 Type 2: Verb + particle (transitive)

8.28.1 General characteristics of Type 2 verbs [compare > 12.3*n*.7]
a These verbs are followed by particles or words that can be used as prepositions or particles [> 8.4]. A word following a verb may in

some cases function as a preposition in one context and as a particle in another:

*Come **up** the stairs.* (preposition)

*Come **up**.* (particle)

b These verbs are transitive: *Drink up **your milk**!*
though some of them can be used intransitively: *Drink up!*

c The particle can be separated from its verb and can go immediately after the noun or noun-phrase object [> 8.28.2]:
*Please **turn** every light in the house **off**.*
With long objects, we avoid separating the particle from the verb:
*She **turned off** all the lights which had been left on.*

d All transitive verbs can be used in the passive:
*All the lights in the house **have been turned off**.*

e When the particle comes at the end of the sentence, it is stressed:
*He **took off** his 'coat. He **took** his coat **'off**.*

f Often a verb + particle can be transitive with one meaning:
*We have to **turn our essays in/turn in our essays** by Friday.*
and intransitive, therefore Type 3 [> 8.29] with another meaning:
*I feel sleepy, so I think I'll **turn in**.* (= go to bed)

g Nouns can be formed from many verbs of this type: e.g.
a breakdown, a knockout, a follow-up, a setback [> App 31].

8.28.2 Type 2 verbs: word order

When there is a noun object, the particle can go:

- before the object: *She gave **away all her possessions**.*
- or after the object: *She gave **all her possessions away**.*

Even though we may put an object after e.g. *away* as in the first example above, *away* is a particle, not a preposition. A particle is more closely related to the verb and does not 'govern' the object as a preposition does [> 8.4]. It is mobile to the extent that it can be used before or after the object.

If the object is a pronoun, it always comes before the particle:
*She gave **them away**. She let **me/him/her/it/us/them out**.*
In some cases, the particle comes only after the object [> App 32]:
*We can **allow the children out** till 9.*

Three sub-groups can be identified:

8.28.3 Non-phrasal verbs with obvious meanings ('free association')

Verbs in this group can be used with their literal meanings [> 8.25]:
*You'd better **pull in** that fishing line.*
*You'd better **pull** that fishing line **in**.*

8.28.4 Particles that strengthen or extend the effect of the verb

e.g. *call out, eat up, stick on, write down*. The verbs in this group retain their literal meanings [> App 32]. In some cases, the particle can be omitted altogether:
***Write** their names.*
or it can have a strengthening effect on the verb:
***Write down** their names./**Write** their names **down**.*

In other cases, the particle can extend the meaning of a verb:
***Give out** these leaflets.* (i.e. distribute)

The difference between 'literal (non-idiomatic) meanings' and 'extended meanings' is often hard to draw.

8.28.5 Type 2 verbs with idiomatic meanings

This is a very large category [> App 33] in which the verb + particle have little or no relation to their literal meanings: for example, *make up* can mean 'invent', as in *make up a story*; *take off* can mean 'imitate', as in *take off the Prime Minister*. Verb combinations, therefore, can have many different meanings, depending on the particles used. Here are just a few examples of the combinations possible with *bring*:

*bring **up** the children* (= train/educate)
*bring **off** a deal* (= complete successfully)
*bring **on** an attack of asthma* (= cause)
*bring somebody **round** to our point of view* (= persuade)
*bring someone **round*** (= revive)
*bring **down** the house* (= receive enthusiastic applause)

There is also a large category of fixed expressions with nouns. These remain invariable at all times: e.g. *make up your mind* (where *mind* cannot be replaced by another word); *push the boat out* (= take risks), etc. Such expressions are too numerous to list and can only be found in good dictionaries. [but > App 34]

8.29 Type 3: Verb + particle (intransitive)

8.29.1 General characteristics of Type 3 verbs

a The verbs in this category are intransitive, that is they cannot be followed by an object:
*Hazel **is out**. We **set off** early.* etc.
b Passive constructions are not possible.
c The same combination of verb + particle can sometimes belong to Type 2 (with an object: *We broke down the fence*) and Type 3 (without an object: *The car broke down*). [compare > 8.28.1f]
d Nouns can be formed from verbs of this type: e.g. *a climb-down, a dropout, an outbreak, an onlooker* [> App 35].

Two sub-groups can be identified:

8.29.2 Non-phrasal verbs with obvious meanings ('free association')

Verbs in this group can be used with their literal meanings [> 8.25]. Combinations with *be* are common, but occur with many other verbs, often in the imperative: e.g. *hurry along, go away, sit down, keep on, drive over* ([> App 32] for particle meanings). The 'strengthening effect' noted in 8.28.4 can apply to some of these verbs too, as in *hurry up, move out*, etc.

8.29.3 Type 3 verbs with idiomatic meanings

The verbs in this category [> App 36] often have little or no relation to their literal meanings: e.g. *break down* (collapse), *die away* (become quiet), *pull up* (stop when driving a car), *turn up* (appear unexpectedly):

*Mrs Sims **broke down** completely when she heard the news.*
*The echoes **died away** in the distance.*
*The bus **pulled up** sharply at the traffic lights.*
*Harry **turned up** after the party when everyone had left.*

8.30 Type 4: Verb + particle + preposition (transitive)

8.30.1 General characteristics of Type 4 verbs [compare > 12.3*n*.7]

a These are three-part verbs (e.g. *put up with*). They are transitive because they end with prepositions and must therefore be followed by an object:

I don't know how you ***put up with these conditions****.*

Some of these verbs take a personal object: *take someone up on something* (pursue a suggestion someone has made):

May I ***take you up on*** *your offer to put me up for the night?*

b Some verbs can go into the passive and others cannot:

All the old regulations ***were done away with****.* (passive)

I find it difficult to ***keep up with*** *you.* (no passive)

c Two-part nouns can be formed from some three-part verbs: e.g. someone who *stands in for* someone is *a stand-in.*

Two sub-groups can be identified:

8.30.2 Non-phrasal verbs with obvious meanings ('free association')

Three-part combinations, which can be used with their literal meanings, are common [> 8.18]: e.g. *come down from, drive on to, hurry over to, run along to, stay away from, walk up to*, etc.:

After stopping briefly in Reading, we ***drove on to*** *Oxford.*

8.30.3 Type 4 verbs with idiomatic meanings

The verbs in this category [> App 37] often have little or no relation to their literal meanings: e.g. *put up with* (tolerate), *run out of* (use up). Unlike the 'free association verbs' noted above, there is no choice in the preposition that can be used after the particle: each verb conveys a single, indivisible meaning:

I'm not prepared to ***put up with*** *these conditions any longer.*

We're always ***running out of*** *matches in our house.*

9 Verbs, verb tenses, imperatives

General information about verbs and tenses

9.1 What a verb is and what it does

A verb is a word (*run*) or a phrase (*run out of*) which expresses the existence of a state (*love, seem*) or the doing of an action (*take, play*). Two facts are basic:

1 Verbs are used to express distinctions in time (past, present, future) through **tense** (often with adverbials of time or frequency).

2 Auxiliary verbs [> 10.1] are used with full verbs to give other information about actions and states. For example *be* may be used with the present participle of a full verb to say that an action was going on ('in progress') at a particular time (*I was swimming*); *have* may be used with the past participle of a full verb to say that an action is completed (*I have finished*).

9.2 Verb tenses: simple and progressive

Some grammarians believe that tense must always be shown by the actual form of the verb, and in many languages present, past and future are indicated by changes in the verb forms. On this reckoning, English really has just two tenses, the present and the past, since these are the only two cases where the form of the basic verb varies: *love, write* (present); *loved, wrote* (past).

However, it is usual (and convenient) to refer to all combinations of *be* + present participle and *have* + past participle as tenses. The same goes for *will* + bare infinitive [> 16.3] to refer to the future (*It will be fine tomorrow*). But we must remember that tense in English is often only loosely related to time.

Tenses have two forms, **simple** and **progressive** (sometimes called 'continuous'). The progressive contains *be* + present participle:

	simple	**progressive**	
present:	*I work.*	*I am*	*working.*
past:	*I worked.*	*I was*	*working.*
present perfect:	*I have worked.*	*I have been*	*working.*
past perfect:	*I had worked.*	*I had been*	*working.*
future:	*I will work.*	*I will be*	*working.*
future perfect:	*I will have worked.*	*I will have been*	*working.*

Simple forms and progressive combinations can also occur with:

conditionals [> Chapter 14]:	*I would work.*	*I would be*	*working.*
modals [> Chapter 11]:	*I may work.*	*I may be*	*working.*

Both simple and progressive forms usually give a general idea of when an action takes place. But the progressive forms also tell us that

an activity is (or was, or will be, etc.) in progress, or thought of as being in progress.
This activity may be in progress at the moment of speaking:
*What **are** you **doing**? – **I'm making** a cake.*
or not in progress at the moment of speaking:
*I'**m learning** to type.* (i.e. but not at the moment of speaking)
Or the activity may be temporary or changeable:
*Fred **was wearing** a blue shirt yesterday.*
Or the activity may be uncompleted:
*Vera **has been trying** to learn Chinese for years.*
Our decision about which tense to use depends on the context and the impression we wish to convey.

9.3 Stative and dynamic verbs

Some verbs are not generally used in progressive forms. They are called **stative** because they refer to **states** (e.g. experiences, conditions) rather than to actions. In a sentence like:
*She **loves/loved** her baby more than anything in the world.*
loves (or *loved*) describes a state over which the mother has no control: it is an involuntary feeling. We could not use the progressive forms (*is/was loving*) here.

Dynamic verbs, on the other hand, usually refer to **actions** which are deliberate or voluntary (*I'm making a cake*) or they refer to changing situations (*He's growing old*), that is, to activities, etc., which have a beginning and an end. Dynamic verbs can be used in progressive as well as simple forms. Compare the following:

	progressive forms	**simple forms**
1	Dynamic verbs with progressive and simple forms:	
	I'm looking at you.	*I often look at you.*
	I'm listening to music.	*I often listen to music.*
2	Verbs which are nearly always stative (simple forms only):	
	–	*I see you.*
	–	*I hear music.* [> 11.13]
3	Verbs that have dynamic or stative uses:	
	deliberate actions	**states**
	I'm weighing myself.	*I weigh 65 kilos.*
	I'm tasting the soup.	*It tastes salty.*
	I'm feeling the radiator.	*It feels hot.*

Stative verbs usually occur in the simple form in all tenses. We can think of 'states' in categories like [> App 38]:

1 Feelings: *like, love*, etc.
2 Thinking/believing: *think, understand*, etc.
3 Wants and preferences: *prefer, want*, etc.
4 Perception and the senses: *hear, see*, etc.
5 Being/seeming/having/owning: *appear, seem, belong, own*, etc.

Sometimes verbs describing physical sensations can be used in simple or progressive forms with hardly any change of meaning:
*Ooh! It **hurts**!* = *Ooh! It'**s hurting**.*

Can/can't and *could/couldn't* often combine with verbs of perception to refer to a particular moment in the present or the past where a progressive form would be impossible [> 11.13]:

*I **can smell** gas.* = *I **smell** gas.*

9.4 Time references with adverbs [> App 48]

Some adverbs like *yesterday* and *tomorrow* refer to past or future:

*I **saw** Jim **yesterday**. **I'll be seeing** Isabel **tomorrow**.*

Other adverbs, such as *already, always, ever, often, never, now, still* can be used with a variety of tenses, though they may often be associated with particular ones. For example, *always* is often associated with the simple present or past for habits:

*We **always have** breakfast at 7.30.*
*Roland **always took** me **out** to dinner on my birthday.*

But it can be used with other tenses as well:

*I **shall always remember** this holiday.* (future)
*Natasha **has always been** generous.* (present perfect)
*Mr Biggs said he **had always travelled** first class.* (past perfect)

The sequence of tenses

9.5 The sequence of tenses

In extended speech or writing we usually select a governing tense which affects all other tense forms. The problem of the 'sequence of tenses' is not confined to indirect speech [> 15.5]. Our choice of tense may be influenced by the following factors:

9.5.1 Consistency in the use of tenses

If we start a narrative or description from the point of view of **now**, we usually maintain 'now' as our viewpoint. This results in the following combinations:

– present (simple/progressive) accords with present perfect/future:

*Our postman usually **delivers** our mail at 7 every morning.*
***It's** nearly lunch-time and the mail still **hasn't arrived**. I **suppose** the mail **will come** soon. Perhaps our postman **is** ill.*

If we start a narrative or description from the point of view of **then**, we usually maintain 'then' as our viewpoint. This results in the following combinations:

– past (simple/progressive) accords with past perfect:

*When I **lived** in London the postman usually **delivered** our mail at 7 every morning. Usually no one in our household **had got up** when the mail **arrived**.*

9.5.2 The proximity rule

A present tense in the main clause (for example, in a reporting verb) normally attracts a present tense in the subordinate clause:

***He tells me he's** a good tennis-player.*

A past tense normally attracts another past:

***He told me he was** a good tennis-player.*

In the second example only a more complete context would tell us whether *he was a good tennis-player* refers to the past (i.e. 'when he was a young man') or to present time. A speaker or writer can ignore the 'proximity rule' and use a present tense after a past, or a past after a present in order to be more precise:

He told me he is a good tennis-player. (i.e. he still is)
He tells me he used to be a good tennis-player.

However, combinations such as *you say you are* or *you told me you were* tend to form themselves automatically. That is why we can refer to the idea of 'sequence of tenses' in which present usually combines with present, and past usually combines with past.

9.5.3 Particular tense sequences

Refer to the following for particular tense sequences:
Indirect speech [> Chapter 15].
Conditional sentences [> Chapter 14].
Temporal clauses [> 1.45.2].
After *wish*, etc. [> 11.41–43]; *I'd rather* [> 11.45].
Clauses of purpose [> 1.51].

The simple present tense

9.6 Form of the simple present tense

We add *-s* or *-es* to the base form of the verb in the third person singular.

I	*work*	
You	*work*	
He	*works*	
She	*works*	*in an office.*
It	*works*	
We	*work*	
You	*work*	
They	*work*	

9.7 The third person singular: pronunciation and spelling

9.7.1 Pronunciation of the 3rd person singular [compare > 2.21]

/s/ after /f/, /p/, /k/, /t/: *laughs, puffs, drops, kicks, lets*

Verbs ending in /z/, /dʒ/, /s/, /ʃ/, /tʃ/, and /ks/ take an extra syllable in the third person which is pronounced /ɪz/: *loses, manages, passes, pushes, stitches, mixes.*

Other verbs are pronounced with a /z/ in the third person: after /b/ *robs*; after /d/ *adds*; after /g/ *digs*; after /l/ *fills*; after /m/ *dreams*; after /n/ *runs*; after /ŋ/ *rings*; after vowel + *w* or *r*: *draws*; *stirs*; after /v/ *loves*; after vowels *sees, pays*. *Says* is normally pronounced /sez/ and *does* is pronounced /dʌz/.

9.7.2 Spelling of the 3rd person singular [compare > 2.20]

Most verbs add *-s*: *work/works, drive/drives, play/plays, run/runs*
Verbs normally add *-es* when they end in *-o*: *do/does*; *-s*: *miss/misses*; *-x*: *mix/mixes*; *-ch*: *catch/catches*; *-sh*: *push/pushes*

When there is a consonant before *-y*, change to *-ies*: *cry/cries*, but compare: *buy/buys, say/says, obey/obeys.*

9.8 Uses of the simple present tense

9.8.1 Permanent truths

We use the simple present for statements that are always true:

*Summer **follows** spring. Gases **expand** when heated.*

9.8.2 'The present period'

We use the simple present to refer to events, actions or situations which are true in the present period of time and which, for all we know, may continue indefinitely. What we are saying, in effect, is 'this is the situation as it stands at present':

*My father **works** in a bank. My sister **wears** glasses.*

9.8.3 Habitual actions

The simple present can be used with or without an adverb of time to describe habitual actions, things that happen repeatedly:

*I **get up** at 7. John **smokes** a lot.*

We can be more precise about habitual actions by using the simple present with adverbs of indefinite frequency (*always, never*, etc. [> 7.39]) or with adverbial phrases such as *every day* [> 7.38]:

*I **sometimes stay up** till midnight.*
*She **visits** her parents **every day**.*

We commonly use the simple present to ask and answer questions which begin with *How often?*:

***How often do you go** to the dentist? – I **go every six months**.*

Questions relating to habit can be asked with *ever* and answered with e.g. *never* and sometimes *not...ever* [> 7.40.5]:

***Do you ever eat** meat? – No, I **never eat** meat.*

9.8.4 Future reference

This use is often related to timetables and programmes or to events in the calendar:

***The exhibition opens on January 1st** and **closes on January 31st**.*
***The concert begins at 7.30** and **ends at 9.30**.*
***We leave tomorrow at 11.15** and **arrive at 17.50**.*
***Wednesday, May 24th marks** our 25th wedding anniversary.*

For the use of the simple present after *when*, etc. [> 1.45.2].

9.8.5 Observations and declarations

We commonly use the simple present with stative and other verbs to make observations and declarations in the course of conversation: e.g.

***I hope/assume/suppose/promise** everything will be all right.*
***I bet** you were nervous just before your driving test.*
***It says** here that the police expect more trouble in the city.*
***I declare** this exhibition open.*
***I see/hear** there are roadworks in the street again.*
***I love** you. **I hate** him.*
***We live** in difficult times. – **I agree**.*

The present progressive tense

9.9 Form of the present progressive tense

The progressive is formed with the present of *be* + the *-ing* form. See under *be* for details about form [> 10.6].

I	*am*		*I'm*	
You	*are*		*You're*	
He	*is*	*waiting.*	*He's*	*waiting.*
She	*is*	*writing.*	*She's*	*writing.*
It	*is*	*running.*	*It's*	*running.*
We	*are*	*beginning.*	*We're*	*beginning.*
You	*are*	*lying.*	*You're*	*lying.*
They	*are*		*They're*	

9.10 Spelling: how to add '-ing' to a verb

wait/waiting

We can add *-ing* to most verbs without changing the spelling of their base forms. Other examples: *beat/beating, carry/carrying, catch/catching, drink/drinking, enjoy/enjoying, hurry/hurrying.*

write/writing

If a verb ends in *-e*, omit the *-e* and add *-ing*. Other examples: *come/coming, have/having, make/making, ride/riding, use/using.* This rule does not apply to verbs ending in double *e: agree/agreeing, see/seeing*; or to *age/ageing* and *singe/singeing.*

run/running

A verb that is spelt with a single vowel followed by a single consonant doubles its final consonant. Other examples: *hit/hitting, let/letting, put/putting, run/running, sit/sitting.*
Compare: e.g. *beat/beating* which is not spelt with a single vowel and which therefore does not double its final consonant.

begin/beginning

With two-syllable verbs, the final consonant is normally doubled when the last syllable is stressed. Other examples: *for'get/forgetting, pre'fer/preferring, up'set/upsetting*. Compare: *'benefit/benefiting, 'differ/differing* and *'profit/profiting* which are stressed on their first syllables and do not double their final consonants. Note *'label/labelling, 'quarrel/quarrelling, 'signal/signalling* and *'travel/travelling* (BrE) which are exceptions to this rule. Compare: *labeling, quarreling, signaling, traveling* (AmE) [compare > 9.14.2].
-ic at the end of a verb changes to *-ick* when we add *-ing*: *panic/panicking, picnic/picnicking, traffic/trafficking.*

lie/lying

Other examples: *die/dying, tie/tying.*

9.11 Uses of the present progressive tense

9.11.1 Actions in progress at the moment of speaking

We use the present progressive to describe actions or events which are in progress at the moment of speaking. To emphasize this, we often use adverbials like *now, at the moment, just*, etc.:

*Someone**'s knocking** at the door. Can you answer it?*
*What **are you doing**? – **I'm just tying up** my shoe-laces.*
*He**'s working at the moment**, so he can't come to the telephone.*

Actions in progress are seen as uncompleted:
*He**'s talking** to his girlfriend on the phone.*
We can emphasize the idea of duration with *still* [> 7.25]:
*He**'s still talking** to his girlfriend on the phone.*

9.11.2 Temporary situations

The present progressive can be used to describe actions and situations which may not have been happening long, or which are thought of as being in progress for a limited period:

*What**'s** your daughter **doing** these days?*
*– She**'s studying** English at Durham University.*

Such situations may not be happening at the moment of speaking:
*Don't take that ladder away. Your father**'s using** it.* (i.e. but perhaps not at the moment)
*She's at her best when she**'s making** big decisions.*

Temporary events may be in progress at the moment of speaking:
*The river **is flowing** very fast after last night's rain.*

We also use the present progressive to describe current trends:
*People **are becoming** less tolerant of smoking these days.*

9.11.3 Planned actions: future reference

We use the present progressive [and *be going to* > 9.46.3] to refer to activities and events planned for the future. We generally need an adverbial unless the meaning is clear from the context:
*We**'re spending next winter** in Australia.*

This use of the present progressive is also commonly associated with future arrival and departure and occurs with verbs like *arrive, come, go, leave*, etc. to describe travel arrangements:
*He**'s arriving tomorrow morning** on the 13.27 train.*
The adverbial and the context prevent confusion with the present progressive to describe an action which is in progress at the time of speaking:
*Look! The train**'s leaving**.* (i.e. it's actually moving)

9.11.4 Repeated actions

The adverbs *always* (in the sense of 'frequently'), *constantly, continually, forever, perpetually* and *repeatedly* can be used with progressive forms to describe continually-repeated actions:
*She**'s always helping** people.*
Some stative verbs can have progressive forms with *always*, etc.:
***I'm always hearing** strange stories about him.* [> 9.3]

Sometimes there can be implied complaint in this use of the progressive when it refers to something that happens *too* often:
*Our burglar alarm **is forever going off** for no reason.*

9.12 The present tenses in typical contexts

9.12.1 The simple present and present progressive in commentary

The simple present and the present progressive are often used in commentaries on events taking place at the moment, particularly on radio and television. In such cases, the simple present is used to describe rapid actions completed at the moment of speaking and the progressive is used to describe longer-lasting actions:

MacFee passes to Franklyn. Franklyn makes a quick pass to Booth. Booth is away with the ball, but he's losing his advantage.

9.12.2 The simple present and present progressive in narration

When we are telling a story or describing things that have happened to us, we often use present tenses (even though the events are in the past) in order to sound more interesting and dramatic. The progressive is used for 'background' and the simple tense for the main events:

I'm driving along this country road and I'm completely lost. Then I see this old fellow. He's leaning against a gate. I stop the car and ask him the way. He thinks a bit, then says, 'Well, if I were you, I wouldn't start from here.'

9.12.3 The simple present in demonstrations and instructions

This use of the simple present is an alternative to the imperative [> 9.51]. It illustrates step-by-step instructions:

First (you) boil some water. Then (you) warm the teapot. Then (you) add three teaspoons of tea. Next, (you) pour on boiling water...

9.12.4 The simple present in synopses (e.g. reviews of books, films, etc.)

Kate Fox's novel is an historical romance set in London in the 1880's. The action takes place over a period of 30 years...

9.12.5 The simple present and present progressive in newspaper headlines and e.g. photographic captions

The simple present is generally used to refer to past events:

FREAK SNOW STOPS TRAFFIC
DISARMAMENT TALKS BEGIN IN VIENNA

The abbreviated progressive refers to the future. The infinitive can also be used for this purpose [> 9.48.1]:

CABINET MINISTER RESIGNING SOON (or: *TO RESIGN SOON*)

The simple past tense

9.13 Form of the simple past tense with regular verbs

The form is the same for all persons [> App 39].

	pronunciation		**spelling**
I / You / He / She / It / We / You / They	*played*	/d/	*arrive/arrived*
	arrived	/d/	*wait/waited*
	worked	/t/	*stop/stopped*
	dreamed/dreamt	/driːmd/ or /dremt/	*occur/occurred*
	posted	/ɪd/	*cry/cried*

9.14 The regular past: pronunciation and spelling [> App 39]

9.14.1 Pronunciation of the regular past

Verbs in the regular past always end with a *-d* in their spelling, but the pronunciation of the past ending is not always the same:

play/played /d/
The most common spelling characteristic of the regular past is that *-ed* is added to the base form of the verb: *opened, knocked, stayed,* etc. Except in the cases noted below, this *-ed* is not pronounced as if it were an extra syllable, so *opened* is pronounced: /əʊpənd/, *knocked*: /nɒkt/, *stayed*: /steɪd/, etc.

arrive/arrived /d/
Verbs which end in the following sounds have their past endings pronounced /d/: /b/ *rubbed*; /g/ *tugged*; /dʒ/ *managed*; /l/ *filled*; /m/ *dimmed*; /n/ *listened*; vowel + /r/ *stirred*; /v/ *loved*; /z/ *seized*. The *-ed* ending is not pronounced as an extra syllable.

work/worked /t/
Verbs which end in the following sounds have their past endings pronounced /t/: /k/ *packed*; /s/ *passed*; /tʃ/ *watched*; /ʃ/ *washed*; /f/ *laughed*; /p/ *tipped*. The *-ed* ending is not pronounced as an extra syllable.

dream/dreamed /d/ or ***dreamt*** /t/
A few verbs function as both regular and irregular and may have their past forms spelt *-ed* or *-t* pronounced /d/ or /t/: e.g. *burn, dream, lean, learn, smell, spell, spill, spoil* [> App 40].

post/posted /ɪd/
Verbs which end in the sounds /t/ or /d/ have their past endings pronounced /ɪd/: *posted, added*. The *-ed* ending is pronounced as an extra syllable added to the base form of the verb.

9.14.2 Spelling of the regular past

The regular past always ends in *-d*:

arrive/arrived
Verbs ending in *-e* add *-d*: e.g. *phone/phoned, smile/smiled*. This rule applies equally to *agree, die, lie*, etc.

wait/waited
Verbs not ending in *-e* add *-ed*: e.g. *ask/asked, clean/cleaned, follow/followed, video/videoed*.

stop/stopped
Verbs spelt with a single vowel letter followed by a single consonant letter double the consonant: *beg/begged, rub/rubbed*.

occur/occurred
In two-syllable verbs the final consonant is doubled when the last syllable contains a single vowel letter followed by a single consonant letter and is stressed: *pre'fer/preferred, re'fer/referred*. Compare: *'benefit/benefited, 'differ/differed* and *'profit/profited* which are stressed on their first syllables and which therefore do not double their

final consonants. In AmE *labeled, quarreled, signaled* and *traveled* follow the rule. In BrE *labelled, quarrelled, signalled* and *travelled* are exceptions to the rule [compare > 9.10].

cry/cried [compare > 2.20]
When there is a consonant before *-y*, the *y* changes to *i* before we add *-ed*: e.g. *carry/carried, deny/denied, fry/fried, try/tried.* Compare: *delay/delayed, obey/obeyed, play/played*, etc. which have a vowel before *-y* and therefore simply add *-ed* in the past.

9.15 Form of the simple past tense with irregular verbs

The form is the same for all persons [> App 40].

I / *You* / *He* / *She* / *It* / *We* / *You* / *They*	*shut* / *sat on*	*the suitcase.*

9.16 Notes on the past form of irregular verbs

Unlike regular verbs, irregular verbs (about 150 in all) do not have past forms which can be predicted:

shut/shut
A small number of verbs have the same form in the present as in the past: e.g. *cut/cut, hit/hit, put/put.* It is important to remember, particularly with such verbs, that the third person singular does not change in the past: e.g. *he shut* (past); *he shuts* (present).

sit/sat
The past form of most irregular verbs is different from the present: *bring/brought, catch/caught, keep/kept, leave/left, lose/lost.*

9.17 Uses of the simple past tense

9.17.1 Completed actions

We normally use the simple past tense to talk about events, actions or situations which occurred in the past and are now finished. They may have happened recently:

Sam ***phoned a moment ago****.*

or in the distant past:

The Goths ***invaded Rome in A.D. 410****.*

A time reference must be given:

I ***had*** *a word with Julian* ***this morning****.*

or must be understood from the context:

I ***saw*** *Fred in town.* (i.e. when I was there this morning)
I ***never met*** *my grandfather.* (i.e. he is dead)

When we use the simple past, we are usually concerned with *when* an action occurred, not with its duration (*how long* it lasted).

9.17.2 Past habit

Like *used to* [> 11.60], the simple past can be used to describe past habits [compare present habit > 9.8.3]:

*I **smoked forty cigarettes a day** till I gave up.*

9.17.3 The immediate past

We can sometimes use the simple past without a time reference to describe something that happened a very short time ago:

Jimmy punched me in the stomach.
Did the telephone ring?
Who left the door open? (Who's left the door open? [> 9.26.1]).

9.17.4 Polite inquiries, etc.

The simple past does not always refer to past time. It can also be used for polite inquiries (particularly asking for favours), often with verbs like *hope, think* or *wonder*. Compare:

***I wonder** if you could give me a lift.*
***I wondered** if you could give me a lift.* (more tentative/polite)

For the use of 'the unreal past' in conditional sentences [> 14.12].

9.18 Adverbials with the simple past tense

The association of the past tense with adverbials that tell us *when* something happened is very important. Adverbials used with the past tense must refer to past (not present) time. This means that adverbials which link with the present (*before now, so far, till now, yet*) are not used with past tenses.

Some adverbials like *yesterday, last summer* [> App 48] and combinations with *ago* are used only with past tenses:

*I **saw** Jane **yesterday/last summer**.*

Ago [> 7.31], meaning 'back from now', can combine with a variety of expressions to refer to the past: e.g. *two years ago; six months ago; ten minutes ago; a long time ago:*

*I **met** Robert Parr **many years ago** in Czechoslovakia.*

The past is often used with *when* to ask and answer questions:

***When did you learn** about it? – **When I saw it** in the papers.*

When often points to a definite contrast with the present:

*I **played** football every day **when I was a boy**.*

Other adverbials can be used with past tenses when they refer to past time, but can be used with other tenses as well [> 9.4]:

adverbs:	*I **always** liked Gloria.*
	*I **often** saw her in Rome.*
	*Did you **ever** meet Sonia?*
	*I **never** met Sonia.*
adverbial/prepositional phrases:	*We left **at 4 o'clock/on Tuesday**.*
	*We had our holiday **in July**.*
adverbial clauses:	*I waited **till he arrived**.*
	*I met him **when I was at college**.*
***as** + **adverb** + **as**:*	*I saw him **as recently as** last week.*

The past progressive tense

9.19 Form of the past progressive tense

The past progressive is formed with the past of *be* + the *-ing* form. See under *be* [> 10.8] for details about form.

I	*was*	
You	*were*	
He	*was*	
She	*was*	*waiting.* [For spelling, > 9.10]
It	*was*	
We	*were*	
You	*were*	
They	*were*	

9.20 Uses of the past progressive tense

9.20.1 Actions in progress in the past

We use the past progressive to describe past situations or actions that were in progress at some time in the past:

*I **was living abroad in 1987**, so I missed the general election.*

Often we don't know whether the action was completed or not:

*Philippa **was working** on her essay last night.*

Adverbials beginning with *all* [> 5.22.2, 7.36] emphasize continuity:

*It was raining **all night/all yesterday/all the afternoon**.*

In the same way, *still* can emphasize duration [> 7.25]:

***Jim was talking to his girlfriend** on the phone when I came in **and was still talking** to her when I went out an hour later.*

9.20.2 Actions which began before something else happened

The past progressive and the simple past are often used together in a sentence. The past progressive describes a situation or action in progress in the past, and the simple past describes a shorter action or event. The action or situation in progress is often introduced by conjunctions like *when* and *as, just as, while:*

***Just as I was leaving** the house, the phone rang.*

*Jane met Frank Sinatra **when she was living** in Hollywood.*

Or the shorter action can be introduced by *when:*

*We were having supper **when the phone rang**.*

We can often use the simple past to describe the action in progress, but the progressive puts more emphasis on the duration of the action, as in the second of these two examples:

***While I fumbled** for some money, my friend paid the fares.*

***While I was fumbling** for some money, my friend paid the fares.*

9.20.3 Parallel actions

We can emphasize the fact that two or more actions were in progress at the same time by using e.g. *while* or *at the time (that):*

***While I was working** in the garden, **my wife was cooking dinner**.*

9.20.4 Repeated actions [compare > 9.11.4]

This use is similar to that of the present progressive:

*When he worked here, Roger **was always making** mistakes.*

9.20.5 Polite inquiries [compare > 9.17.4]
This use is even more polite and tentative than the simple past:
__I was wondering__ if you could give me a lift.

9.21 Past tenses in typical contexts

The simple past combines with other past tenses, such as the past progressive and the past perfect, when we are talking or writing about the past. Note that the past progressive is used for scene-setting. Past tenses of various kinds are common in story-telling, biography, autobiography, reports, eye-witness accounts, etc.:

On March 14th at 10.15 a.m. I was waiting for a bus at the bus stop on the corner of Dover Road and West Street when a black Mercedes parked at the stop. Before the driver (had) managed to get out of his car, a number 14 bus appeared...

It was evening. The sun was setting. A gentle wind was blowing through the trees. In the distance I noticed a Land Rover moving across the dusty plain. It stopped and two men jumped out of it.

It was just before the Second World War. Tom was only 20 at the time and was living with his mother. He was working in a bank and travelling to London every day. One morning, he received a mysterious letter. It was addressed to 'Mr Thomas Parker'.

The simple present perfect tense

9.22 Form of the simple present perfect tense

The present perfect is formed with the present of *have* [> 10.27] + the past participle (the third part of a verb). For regular verbs [> App 39] the past participle has the same form as the simple past tense: e.g. *arrive, arrived,* ***have arrived***. For irregular verbs [> App 40] the simple past and the past participle can be formed in a variety of ways: e.g. *drink, drank,* ***have drunk***.

I	*have*	*(I've)*			
You	*have*	*(You've)*	*arrived*	/d/	(regular)
He	*has*	*(He's)*	*finished*	/t/	(regular)
She	*has*	*(She's)*	*started*	/ɪd/	(regular)
It	*has*	*(It's)*	*shut*		(irregular)
We	*have*	*(We've)*	*lost*		(irregular)
You	*have*	*(You've)*	*drunk*		(irregular)
They	*have*	*(They've)*			

9.23 Present time and past time

Students speaking other European languages sometimes misuse the present perfect tense in English because of interference from their mother tongue. The present perfect is often wrongly seen as an alternative to the past, so that a student might think that *I've had lunch* and *I had lunch* are interchangeable. It is also confused with the present, so that an idea like *I've been here since February* is wrongly expressed in the present with *I am*.

The present perfect always suggests a relationship between present time and past time. So *I've had lunch* (probably) implies that I did so very recently. However, if I say *I had lunch*, I also have to say or imply *when*: e.g. *I had lunch an hour ago*. Similarly, *I've been here since February* shows a connexion between past and present, whereas *I am here* can only relate to the present and cannot be followed by a phrase like *since February*.

In the present perfect tense, the time reference is sometimes **undefined**; often we are interested in **present results**, or in the way something that happened in the past affects the present situation. The present perfect can therefore be seen as a present tense which looks backwards into the past (just as the past perfect [> 9.29] is a past tense which looks backwards into an earlier past). Compare the simple past tense, where the time reference is **defined** because we are interested in past time or **past results**. The following pairs of sentences illustrate this difference between present time and past time:

***I haven't seen him** this morning.* (i.e. up to the present time: it is still morning)
***I didn't see him** this morning.* (i.e. the morning has now passed)

***Have you ever flown** in Concorde?* (i.e. up to the present time)
***When did you fly** in Concorde?* (i.e. when, precisely, in the past)

9.24 Uses of the simple present perfect tense [compare > 10.13]

The present perfect is used in two ways in English:

1 To describe actions beginning in the past and **continuing up to the present moment** (and possibly into the future).
2 To refer to actions occurring or not occurring **at an unspecified time in the past** with some kind of connexion to the present.

These two uses are discussed in detail in the sections below.

9.25 Actions, etc. continuing into the present

9.25.1 The present perfect + adverbials that suggest 'up to the present'

We do not use the present perfect with adverbs relating to past time (*ago, yesterday*, etc.) [> 9.18, App 48]. Adverbial phrases like the following are used with the present perfect because they clearly connect the past with the present moment: *before (now), It's the first time..., so far, so far this morning, up till now, up to the present.* Adverbs like *ever* (in questions), and *not...ever* or *never* (in statements) are commonly (but not exclusively) used with the present perfect:

*I**'ve planted** fourteen rose-bushes **so far this morning**.*
*She**'s never eaten** a mango before. **Have you ever eaten** a mango?*
*It's the most interesting book I**'ve ever read**.* [compare > 6.28.1]
*Olga **hasn't appeared** on TV **before now**.*

9.25.2 The present perfect with 'since' and 'for' [> 7.31–32, 10.13.5]

We often use *since* and *for* with the present perfect to refer to periods of time up to the present. *Since* (+ point of time) can be:

– a conjunction: *Tom **hasn't been** home **since he was a boy**.*

– an adverb: *I saw Fiona in May and I* ***haven't seen her since****.*
– a preposition: ***I've lived*** *here* ***since 1980****.*

Since, as a conjunction, can be followed by the simple past or present perfect:

I retired in 1980 and came to live here. I've lived here ***since I retired****.* (i.e. the point when I retired: 1980)
I have lived here for several years now and I've made many new friends ***since I have lived here****.* (i.e. up to now)

For + period of time often occurs with the present perfect but can be used with any tense. Compare:

I've lived here for five years*.* (and I still live here)
I ***lived here for five years****.* (I don't live here now)
I ***am here for six weeks****.* (that's how long I'm going to stay)

9.26 Actions, etc. occurring at an unspecified time

9.26.1 The present perfect without a time adverbial

We often use the present perfect without a time adverbial, especially in conversation. We do not always need one, for often we are concerned with the consequences *now* of something which took place *then*, whether 'then' was very recently or a long time ago. If further details are required (e.g. precise answers to questions like *When?*, *Where?*) we must generally use the simple past:

Have you passed *your driving test?* (Depending on context, this can mean 'at any time up to now' or 'after the test you've just taken'.)
– Yes, I ***passed*** *when I was 17.* (simple past: exact time reference)
Jason Villiers ***has been arrested****.* (Depending on context, this can imply 'today' or 'recently' or 'at last'.) *He* ***was seen*** *by a Customs Officer who* ***alerted*** *the police.* (simple past with details)

However, adverbs like *just*, used with the present perfect, can provide more information about actions in 'unspecified time'. Details follow.

9.26.2 The present perfect for recent actions

The following adverbs can refer to actions, etc. in recent time:

– *just* [> 7.29]: ***I've just tidied up*** *the kitchen.*
– *recently*, etc: ***He's recently arrived*** *from New York.*
– *already* in questions and affirmative statements [> 7.26, 7.28]:
Have you typed *my letter* ***already****? – Yes,* ***I've already typed*** *it.*
– *yet*, in questions, for events we are expecting to hear about:
Have you passed *your driving test* ***yet****?* [> 7.27–28]
or in negatives, for things we haven't done, but expect to do:
I haven't passed *my driving test* ***yet****.*
– *still* [> 7.25], *at last, finally*:
I still haven't passed *my driving test.* (despite my efforts)
I have passed *my driving test* ***at last****.* (after all my efforts)

9.26.3 The present perfect for repeated and habitual actions

This use is associated with frequency adverbs (*often, frequently*) and expressions like *three/four/several times* [> 7.38–39]:

I've watched him *on TV* ***several times****.* (i.e. and I expect to again)
I've often wondered *why I get such a poor reception on my radio.*
She's attended *classes* ***regularly****.* ***She's always worked*** *hard.*

9.27 The simple present perfect tense in typical contexts

The present perfect is never used in past narrative (e.g. stories told in the past, history books). Apart from its common use in conversation, it is most often used in broadcast news, newspapers, letters and any kind of language-use which has connexion with the present. Examples:

9.27.1 Broadcast reports, newspaper reports

Interest rates rose again today and the price of gold has fallen by $10 an ounce. Industrial leaders have complained that high interest rates will make borrowing expensive for industry.

9.27.2 Implied in newspaper headlines

VILLAGES DESTROYED IN EARTHQUAKE (= have been destroyed)

9.27.3 Letters, postcards, etc.

We've just arrived in Hong Kong, and though we haven't had time to see much yet, we're sure we're going to enjoy ourselves.

The simple past perfect tense

9.28 Form of the simple past perfect tense

The past perfect is formed with *had* + the past participle. See under *have* [> 10.28] for details about form.

I	*had*	*(I'd)*	
You	*had*	*(You'd)*	*arrived*
He	*had*	*(He'd)*	*finished*
She	*had*	*(She'd)*	*started* [> 9.22]
It	*had*	*(It'd)*	*shut*
We	*had*	*(We'd)*	*lost*
You	*had*	*(You'd)*	*drunk*
They	*had*	*(They'd)*	

9.29 Uses of the past perfect tense

It is sometimes supposed that we use the past perfect simply to describe 'events that happened a long time ago'. This is not the case. We use the simple past for this purpose [> 9.17.1]:

Anthony and Cleopatra ***died in 30 B.C.***

9.29.1 The past perfect referring to an earlier past

The main use of the past perfect is to show which of two events happened first. Here are two past events:

The patient ***died****. The doctor* ***arrived****.*

We can combine these two sentences in different ways to show their relationship in the past:

The patient ***died when*** *the doctor* ***arrived****.* (i.e. the patient died at the time or just after the doctor arrived)

The patient ***had died when*** *the doctor* ***arrived****.* (i.e. the patient was already dead when the doctor arrived)

The event that happened first need not be mentioned first:

The doctor ***arrived*** *quickly, but the patient* ***had already died****.*

Some typical conjunctions used before a past perfect to refer to 'an earlier past' are: *when* and *after, as soon as, by the time that.* They often imply a cause-and-effect relationship:

*We **cleared up as soon as** our guests **had left**.*

Adverbs often associated with the present perfect [> 9.25–26]: *already, ever, for* (+ period of time), *just, never, never...before, since* (+ point of time) are often used with the past perfect to emphasize the sequence of events:

*When I rang, Jim **had already left**.*
*The boys **loved** the zoo. They **had never seen** wild animals **before**.*

9.29.2 The past perfect as the past equivalent of the present perfect

The past perfect sometimes functions simply as the past form of the present perfect:

*Juliet is excited because she **has never been** to a dance **before**.*
*Juliet was excited because she **had never been** to a dance **before**.*

This is particularly the case in indirect speech [> 15.13*n*.3].

Used in this way, the past perfect can emphasize completion:

*I began collecting stamps in February and **by November I had collected** more than 2000.*

Yet can be used with the past perfect, but we often prefer expressions like *until then* or *by that time*. Compare:

*He **hasn't finished yet**.*
*He **hadn't finished by yesterday evening**.*

9.29.3 The past perfect for unfulfilled hopes and wishes

We can use the past perfect (or the past simple or progressive) with verbs like *expect, hope, mean, suppose, think, want*, to describe things we hoped or wished to do but didn't [> 11.42.3]:

*I **had hoped** to send him a telegram to congratulate him on his marriage, but I didn't manage it.*

9.30 Obligatory and non-obligatory uses of the past perfect

We do not always need to use the past perfect to describe which event came first. Sometimes this is perfectly clear, as in:

*After I **finished**, I **went** home.*

The sequence is often clear in relative clauses [> 1.27] as well:

*I **wore** the necklace (which) my grandmother **(had) left** me.*

We normally use the simple past for events that occur in sequence:

*I **got out** of the taxi, **paid** the fare, **tipped** the driver and **dashed** into the station.*
*'I **came**, I **saw**, I **conquered**,' Julius Caesar declared.*

But there are instances when we need to be very precise in our use of past or past perfect, particularly with *when*:

***When** I **arrived**, Anne **left**.* (i.e. at that moment)
***When** I **arrived**, Anne **had left**.* (i.e. before I got there)

In the first sentence, I saw Anne, however briefly. In the second, I didn't see her at all. See also indirect speech [> 15.12].

We normally use the past perfect with conjunctions like *no sooner...than* or *hardly/scarcely/barely...when:*

Mrs Winthrop ***had no sooner left*** *the room* ***than*** *they began to gossip about her.*

Mr Jenkins ***had hardly/scarcely/barely begun*** *his speech* ***when*** *he was interrupted.*

9.31 Simple past and simple past perfect in typical contexts

The past perfect combines with other past tenses (simple past, past progressive, past perfect progressive) when we are talking or writing about the past. It is used in story-telling, biography, autobiography, reports, eye-witness accounts, etc. and is especially useful for establishing the sequence of events:

When we returned from our holidays, we found our house in a mess. What had happened while we had been away? A burglar had broken into the house and had stolen a lot of our things. (Now that the time of the burglary has been established relative to our return, the story can continue in the simple past). *The burglar got in through the kitchen window. He had no difficulty in forcing it open. Then he went into the living-room...*

Note the reference to an earlier past in the following narrative:

Silas Badley inherited several old cottages in our village. He wanted to pull them down and build new houses which he could sell for high prices. He wrote to Mr Harrison, now blind and nearly eighty, asking him to leave his cottage within a month. Old Mr Harrison was very distressed. (The situation has been established through the use of the simple past. What follows now is a reference to an earlier past through the use of the simple past perfect.) *He had been born in the cottage and stayed there all his life. His children had grown up there; his wife had died there and now he lived there all alone.*

The present perfect progressive and past perfect progressive tenses

9.32 Form of the present/past perfect progressive tenses

The present perfect progressive is formed with *have been* + the *-ing* form. The past perfect progressive is formed with *had been* + the *-ing* form. See under *be* [> 10.12] for details about form.

present perfect progressive				**past perfect progressive**			
I	*have*	*(I've)*		*I*	*had*	*(I'd)*	
You	*have*	*(You've)*		*You*	*had*	*(You'd)*	
He	*has*	*(He's)*		*He*	*had*	*(He'd)*	
She	*has*	*(She's)*	*been waiting.*	*She*	*had*	*(She'd)*	*been waiting.*
It	*has*	*(It's)*		*It*	*had*	*(It'd)*	[For spelling, > 9.10]
We	*have*	*(We've)*		*We*	*had*	*(We'd)*	
You	*have*	*(You've)*		*You*	*had*	*(You'd)*	
They	*have*	*(They've)*		*They*	*had*	*(They'd)*	

9.33 Uses of the present/past perfect progressive tenses

9.33.1 Actions in progress throughout a period

We use the present perfect progressive when we wish to emphasize that an activity has been in progress throughout a period, often with consequences *now*. Depending on context, this activity may or may not still be in progress at the present time. This use often occurs with *all* + time references: e.g. *all day* [compare > 9.20.1]:

*She is very tired. She**'s been typing** letters **all day**.* (Depending on context, she is still typing or has recently stopped.)

The past perfect progressive, in the same way, is used for activities in progress during an earlier past, often with consequences *then*:

*She was very tired. She **had been typing** letters **all day**.* (Depending on context, she was still typing or had recently stopped.)

Some verbs like *learn, lie, live, rain, sit, sleep, stand, study, wait, work* naturally suggest *continuity* and often occur with perfect progressives with *since* or *for* [> 7.31–32, 9.25.2] and also in questions beginning with *How long...?* [> 10.13.5]:

***I've been working** for Exxon **for 15 years**.* (Depending on context, I am still *now*, or I may have recently changed jobs or retired.)

*When I first met Ann, she **had been working** for Exxon **for 15 years**.* (Depending on context, Ann was still working for Exxon *then* or she had recently changed jobs or retired.)

With 'continuity verbs', simple and progressive forms are often interchangeable, so in the above examples 'I've worked' and 'she had worked' could be used. The only difference is that the progressive puts more emphasis on continuity.

9.33.2 The present/past perfect progressive for repeated actions

The perfect progressive forms are often used to show that an action is (or was) frequently repeated:

*Jim **has been phoning** Jenny every night for the past week.*

*Jenny was annoyed. Jim **had been phoning** her every night for a whole week.*

9.33.3 The present/past perfect progressive for drawing conclusions

We use the progressive (seldom the simple) forms to show that we have come to a conclusion based on direct or indirect evidence:

*Your eyes are red. You**'ve been crying**.*

*Her eyes were red. It was obvious she **had been crying**.*

The present perfect progressive often occurs in complaints:

*This room stinks. Someone**'s been smoking** in here.*

9.34 The present/past perfect simple and progressive compared

The difference between an activity still in progress and one that has definitely been completed is marked by context and by the verbs we use. The simple and progressive forms are *not* interchangeable here:

a ***I've been painting this room**.*

***I've painted this room**.*

In the first example, the activity is uncompleted. In the second example, the job is definitely finished.

b *When I got home, I found that* ***Jill had been painting her room.***
When I got home, I found that ***Jill had painted her room.***
In the first example, the activity was uncompleted *then*. In the second example, the job was definitely finished *then*.

The simple future tense

9.35 Form of the simple future tense

The simple future is formed with *will* [but > 9.36] and the base form of the verb.

affirmative		short form	negative		short forms				
I	*will*	*I'll*	*I*	*will not*	*I'll*	*not*	*I*	*won't*	
You	*will*	*You'll*	*You*	*will not*	*You'll*	*not*	*You*	*won't*	
He	*will*	*He'll*	*He*	*will not*	*He'll*	*not*	*He*	*won't*	
She	*will*	*She'll*	*She*	*will not*	*She'll*	*not*	*She*	*won't*	*stay.*
It	*will*	*It'll*	*It*	*will not*	*It'll*	*not*	*It*	*won't*	
We	*will*	*We'll*	*We*	*will not*	*We'll*	*not*	*We*	*won't*	
You	*will*	*You'll*	*You*	*will not*	*You'll*	*not*	*You*	*won't*	
They	*will*	*They'll*	*They*	*will not*	*They'll*	*not*	*They*	*won't*	

9.36 Notes on the form of the simple future tense

1 *Shall* and *will*
Will is used with all persons, but *shall* can be used as an alternative with *I* and *we* in pure future reference [> 9.37.1].
Shall is usually avoided with *you and I*:
You and I will work *in the same office.*

2 Contractions
Shall weakens to /ʃəl/ in speech, but does not contract to *'ll* in writing. *Will* contracts to *'ll* in writing and in fluent, rapid speech after vowels (*I'll, we'll, you'll*, etc.) but *'ll* can also occur after consonants. So we might find *'ll* used: e.g.
- after names: ***Tom'll*** *be here soon.*
- after common nouns: *The* ***concert'll*** *start in a minute.*
- after question-words: ***When'll*** *they arrive?*

3 Negatives
Will not contracts to *'ll not* or *won't; shall not* contracts to *shan't*:
I/We won't or ***shan't*** *go.* (***I/We will not*** or ***shall not*** *go.*)
In AmE *shan't* is rare and *shall* with a future reference is unusual.

4 Future tense
When we use *will/shall* for simple prediction, they combine with verbs to form tenses in the ordinary way [> 9.2, 11.7]:
simple future: *I will see*
future progressive: *I will be seeing*
future perfect: *I will have seen*
future perfect progressive: *I will have been seeing*

9.37 Uses of the 'will/shall' future

9.37.1 'Will/shall' for prediction briefly compared with other uses

Will and *shall* can be used to predict events, for example, to say what we think will happen, or to invite prediction:

*Tottenham **will win** on Saturday.*
*It **will rain** tomorrow. **Will** house prices **rise** again next year?*
*I don't know if I **shall see** you next week.*

This is sometimes called 'the pure future', and it should be distinguished from many other uses of *will* and *shall*: e.g.

***I'll buy you** a bicycle for your birthday.* [promise, > 11.73]
(Note that *will* is not used to mean 'want to')
***Will you hold** the door open for me please?* [request, > 11.38]
***Shall I get** your coat for you?* [offer, > 11.39]
***Shall we go** for a swim tomorrow?* [suggestion, > 11.40]
*Just wait – **you'll regret** this!* [threat, > 11.23, 11.73]

Though all the above examples point to future time, they are not 'predicting'; they are 'coloured' by notions of willingness, etc. *Will/shall* have so many uses as modal verbs [> Chapter 11] that some grammarians insist that English does not have a pure future tense [also > 9.2].

9.37.2 'Will' in formal style for scheduled events

Will is used in preference to *be going to* [> 9.44] when a formal style is required, particularly in the written language:

*The wedding **will take place** at St Andrew's on June 27th. The reception **will be** at the Anchor Hotel.*

9.37.3 'Will/shall' to express hopes, expectations, etc.

The future is often used after verbs and verb phrases like *assume, be afraid, be sure, believe, doubt, expect, hope, suppose, think:*

***I hope she'll get** the job she's applied for.*

The present with a future reference is possible after *hope*:

***I hope she gets** the job she's applied for.* [compare > 11.42.1]

Lack of certainty, etc. can be conveyed by using *will* with adverbs like *perhaps, possibly, probably, surely:*

*Ask him again. **Perhaps** he'**ll change** his mind.*

9.38 Time adverbials with the 'will/shall' future tense

Some adverbials like *tomorrow* [> App 48] are used exclusively with future reference; others like *at 4 o'clock, before Friday*, etc. are used with other tenses as well as the future:

*I'**ll meet** you **at 4 o'clock**.*

Now and *just* can also have a future reference [> 7.29]:

*This shop **will now be open** on June 23rd.* (a change of date)
*I'm nearly ready. I'**ll just put** my coat **on**.*

For *in* + period of time [> 8.14] and *by, not...until* [> 7.34].

9.39 Other ways of expressing the future

We can express the future in other ways, apart from *will/shall*:

be going to:	*I'**m going to see** him tomorrow.* [> 9.44]
be to:	*I'**m to see** him tomorrow.* [> 9.47]
present progressive:	*I'**m seeing** him tomorrow.* [> 9.11.3]
simple present:	*I **see** him tomorrow.* [> 9.8.4]

These ways of expressing the future are concerned less with simple prediction and more with intentions, plans, arrangements, etc.

The future progressive tense

9.40 Form of the future progressive tense

The future progressive is formed with *will/shall* + *be* + the *-ing* form:

I	*will/shall*	*(I'll)*	*be*	*expecting you/me.*
You	*will*	*(You'll)*	*be*	
He	*will*	*(He'll)*	*be*	
She	*will*	*(She'll)*	*be*	
It	*will*	*(It'll)*	*be*	
We	*will/shall*	*(We'll)*	*be*	
You	*will*	*(You'll)*	*be*	
They	*will*	*(They'll)*	*be*	

[For spelling, > 9.10]

9.41 Uses of the future progressive tense

9.41.1 Actions in progress in the future

The most common use of the progressive form is to describe actions which will be in progress in the immediate or distant future:

Hurry up! The guests ***will be arriving*** *at any minute!*
A space vehicle ***will be circling*** *Jupiter in five years' time.*

It is often used for visualizing a future activity already planned:

By this time tomorrow, ***I'll be lying*** *on the beach.*

9.41.2 The 'softening effect' of the future progressive

Sometimes the future progressive is used to describe simple futurity, but with a 'softening effect' that takes away the element of deliberate intention often implied by *will*:

I'll work *on this tomorrow.* (intention, possibly a promise)
I'll be working *on this tomorrow.* (futurity)

In some contexts, the future progressive sounds more polite than *will*, especially in questions when we do not wish to appear to be pressing for a definite answer:

When ***will you finish*** *these letters?* (e.g. boss to assistant)
When ***will you be seeing*** *Mr White?* (e.g. assistant to boss)

Sometimes there really is a difference in meaning:

Mary ***won't pay*** *this bill.* (she refuses to)
Mary ***won't be paying*** *this bill.* (futurity)
Will you join *us for dinner?* (invitation)
Will you be joining *us for dinner?* (futurity)
Won't you come *with us?* (invitation)
Won't you be coming *with us?* (futurity)

9.41.3 Arrangements and plans [compare > 9.11.3]

The future progressive can be used like the present progressive to refer to planned events, particularly in connexion with travel:

*We****'ll be spending*** *the winter in Australia.* (= we are spending)
Professor Craig ***will be giving*** *a lecture on Etruscan pottery tomorrow evening.* (= is giving)

The future perfect simple and future perfect progressive tenses

9.42 Form of the future perfect simple and progressive tenses

The future perfect simple is formed with *will have* + the past participle. The future perfect progressive is formed with *will have been* + the *-ing* form.

future perfect simple				**future perfect progressive**		
I	*will/shall*	*have*		*will/shall*	*have been*	
You	*will*	*have*		*will*	*have been*	
He	*will*	*have*		*will*	*have been*	
She	*will*	*have*	*received it*	*will*	*have been*	*living here for 20 years*
It	*will*	*have*	*by then.*	*will*	*have been*	*by the end of the year.*
We	*will/shall*	*have*		*will/shall*	*have been*	
You	*will*	*have*		*will*	*have been*	
They	*will*	*have*		*will*	*have been*	

9.43 Uses of the future perfect simple and progressive tenses

9.43.1 'The past as seen from the future'

We often use the future perfect to show that an action will already be completed by a certain time in the future:

*I **will have retired by** the year 2020.*

(That is, before or in the year 2020, my retirement will already be in the past.)

This tense is often used with *by* and *not...till/until* + time [> 7.34] and with verbs which point to completion: *build, complete, finish*, etc. We also often use the future perfect after verbs like *believe, expect, hope, suppose:*

***I expect you will have changed** your mind by tomorrow.*

9.43.2 The continuation of a state up to the time mentioned

What is in progress now can be considered from a point in the future:

***By this time next week**, I **will have been working** for this company for 24 years.*

*We **will have been married** a year on June 25th.*

The 'going to'-future

9.44 Form of the 'going to'-future

The *going to*-future is formed with *am/is/are going to* + the base form of the verb.

I	*am*	
You	*are*	
He	*is*	
She	*is*	*going to arrive tomorrow.*
It	*is*	
We	*are*	
You	*are*	
They	*are*	

9.45 The pronunciation of 'going to'

There can be a difference in pronunciation between *be going to* (which has no connexion with the ordinary verb *go*) and the progressive form of the verb *go*.
In: ***'I'm going to** have a wonderful time' going to* is often pronounced /gənə/ in everyday speech.
In: ***'I'm going to** Chicago' going to* can only be pronounced /gəʊɪŋ tuː/ or /gəʊɪntə/.

9.46 Uses of the 'going to'-future

9.46.1 The 'going to'-future for prediction

The *going to*-future is often used, like *will*, to predict the future. It is common in speech, especially when we are referring to the immediate future. The speaker sees signs of something that is about to happen:

*Oh, look! **It's going to rain!** Look out! **She's going to faint!***

This use of *going to* includes the present, whereas *It will rain* is purely about the future. Alternatively, the speaker may have prior knowledge of something which will happen in the near future:

***They're going to be married** soon.* (Her brother told me.)

A future time reference may be added with such predictions:

***It's going to rain** tonight. **They're going to be married** next May.*

We usually prefer *will* to the *going to*-future in formal writing and when there is a need for constant reference to the future as in, for example, weather forecasts.

9.46.2 The 'going to'-future for intentions, plans, etc.

When there is any suggestion of intentions and plans, we tend to use the *going t*o-future rather than *will* in informal style:

***I'm going to practise** the piano for two hours this evening.* (i.e. That's my intention: what I have planned/arranged to do.)

However, we generally prefer *will* to *going to* when we decide to do something at the moment of speaking:

*We're really lost. **I'll stop and ask** someone the way.*

Intention can be emphasized with adverbs like *now* and *just* which are generally associated with present time [compare > 7.29]:

***I'm now going to show you** how to make spaghetti sauce.*
***I'm just going to change**. I'll be back in five minutes.*

The use of *be going to* to refer to the remote future is less common and generally requires a time reference:

*She says **she's going to be a jockey when she grows up**.*

If we want to be precise about intentions and plans, we use verbs like *intend to, plan to, propose to*, rather than *going to*:

***They're going to build** a new motorway to the west.* (vague)
***They propose to build** a new motorway to the west.* (more precise)

9.46.3 The 'going to'-future in place of the present progressive

The *going to*-future may be used where we would equally expect to have the present progressive [> 9.11.3] with a future reference:

***I'm having dinner** with Janet tomorrow evening.*
***I'm going to have dinner** with Janet tomorrow evening.*

However, we cannot use the present progressive to make predictions, so it would not be possible in a sentence like this:

It's going to snow tonight.

Though *be going to* can combine with *go* and *come*, the present progressive is preferred with these verbs for reasons of style. We tend to avoid *going* next to *go* or *come* (e.g. *going to go/going to come*):

I'm going/coming home *early this evening.*

9.46.4 The 'going to'-future after 'if'

We do not normally use *will* after *if* to make predictions [> 14.24.2], but we can use *be going to* to express an intention:

If you're going to join us*, we'll wait for you.*

Be going to can often be used in the main clause as well:

If you invite Jack, ***there's going to be*** *trouble.*

Other ways of expressing the future

9.47 Forms of future substitutes

I am/You are, etc.	*to*	*see Mr Jones tomorrow.*
I am/You are, etc.	*due to*	*leave at 7.30.*
I am/You are, etc.	*about to*	*get a big surprise.*
I am/You are, etc.	*on the point of*	*leaving.*
I am/You are, etc.	–	*leaving immediately.* [> 9.11.3]
I/You, etc.	–	*leave at 7 tomorrow.* [> 9.8.4]

9.48 Uses of future substitutes

9.48.1 The use of 'am/is/are to'

Be to is used to refer to the future when the actions are subject to human control. Thus statements such as *I'm going to faint* or *It's going to rain* cannot be expressed with *be to*, which has restricted uses: e.g.

Formal arrangements/public duties:

OPEC representatives ***are to meet*** *in Geneva next Tuesday.* Compare:
OPEC REPRESENTATIVES ***TO MEET*** *IN GENEVA* [> 9.12.5]

Formal appointments/instructions:

active: *You****'re to deliver*** *these flowers before 10.*
passive: *Three tablets* ***to be taken*** *twice a day.*

Prohibitions/public notices:

*You****'re not to tell him*** *anything about our plans.* (= you mustn't)
POISON: ***NOT TO BE TAKEN****!*

9.48.2 The use of 'be about to', 'be on the point of'

These constructions are used to refer to the immediate future:

Look! The race ***is about to start****.*

On the point of conveys even greater immediacy:

*Look! They****'re on the point of starting****!*

The use of *just* with *about to* and *be on the point of* increases the sense of immediacy, as it does with the present progressive:

*They**'re just starting**!*

9.48.3 **The use of 'be due to'**

This is often used in connexion with timetables and itineraries:

The BA 561 ***is due to arrive*** *from Athens at 13.15.*
The BA 561 ***is not due*** *till 13.15.*

The future-in-the past

9.49 The future-in-the-past [compare *be supposed to* > 12.8*n*. 3]

The future-in-the-past can be expressed by *was going to, was about to, was to, was to have* + past participle, *was on the point of, was due to* and (in more limited contexts) *would*. These forms can refer to events which were planned to take place and which did take place:

I couldn't go to Tom's party as I ***was about to go*** *into hospital.*

or refer to an outcome that could not be foreseen:

Little did they know they ***were to be reunited ten years later****.*

However, the future-in-the-past can also be used to describe events which were interrupted (*just...when*) [compare > 9.20.2]:

We ***were just going to leave when*** *Jean fell and hurt her ankle.*

or to describe events which were hindered or prevented (*...but*):

I ***was to see/was going to see/was to have seen*** *Mr Kay tomorrow,* ***but*** *the appointment has been cancelled.*

Note the possible ambiguity of:

I ***was going to see*** *Mr Kay.* (the meeting did or did not take place)

compared with:

I ***was to have seen*** *Mr Kay.* (I did not see him)

9.50 Future-in-the-past: typical contexts

The future-in-the-past is often used in narrative to describe 'events that were destined to happen':

Einstein was still a young man. His discoveries had not yet been published, but they ***were to change*** *our whole view of the universe.*

Would can also express future-in-the-past in such contexts:

We had already reached 9,000 feet. Soon we ***would reach*** *the top.*

The imperative

9.51 Form of the imperative

The imperative form is the same as the bare infinitive [> 16.1]:

Affirmative form (base form of the verb):	*Wait!*
Negative short form (*Don't* + base form):	*Don't wait!*
Emphatic form (*Do* + base form):	*Do wait a moment!*
Addressing someone (e.g. pronoun + base form):	*You wait here!*
Imperative + question tag:	*Wait here, will you?*
Imperatives joined by *and*:	*Go and play outside.*

9.52 Some common uses of the imperative [compare > 10.5]

We use the imperative for direct orders and suggestions and also for a variety of other purposes. Stress and intonation, gesture, facial expression, and, above all, situation and context, indicate whether the use of this form is friendly, abrupt, angry, impatient, persuasive, etc. The negative form is usually expressed by *Don't*. The full form (*Do not*) is used mainly in public notices. Here are some common uses:

1 Direct commands, requests, suggestions:
Follow me. Shut the door *(please).* ***Don't worry!***

2 Warnings:
Look out! *There's a bus!* ***Don't panic!***

3 Directions:
Take the 2nd turning *on the left and then* ***turn right****.*

4 Instructions:
Use a moderate oven and bake *for 20 minutes.*

5 Prohibitions (in e.g. public notices):
Keep off the grass! Do not feed the animals!

6 Advice (especially after *always* and *never* [> 7.40.4]):
Always answer *when you're spoken to!* ***Never speak*** *to strangers!*

7 Invitations:
Come and have *dinner with us soon.*

8 Offers:
Help yourself. Have a biscuit.

9 Expressing rudeness:
Shut up! Push off!

For uses of *let* as an imperative [> 16.4.1].

9.53 Uses of the imperative with 'do'

We use *do* (always stressed) before the imperative when we particularly wish to emphasize what we are saying: e.g.

- when we wish to be polite:
Do have *another cup of coffee.*
- or when we wish to express impatience:
Do stop *talking!*
- or when we wish to persuade:
Do help me *with this maths problem.*

In reponse to requests for permission, offers, etc. *do* and *don't* can be used in place of a full imperative:
May/Shall I switch the light off? – ***Yes, do. No, don't.***

9.54 The use of the imperative to address particular people

The imperative, e.g. *Wait here!*, might be addressed to one person or several people: *you* is implied. However, we can get the attention of the person or people spoken to in the following ways. (For 1st person plural imperative with *let's* [> 16.4.1]):

1 *You* + imperative:
You wait *here for a moment.*
Intonation and stress are important. If, in the above example, *you* is unstressed, the sentence means 'this is where you wait'. If it is

stressed, it means 'this is what I want you to do'. When *you* is stressed, it might also convey anger, hostility or rudeness:
'You mind *your own business!*
'You try teaching *40 noisy children five days a week!*
Don't (not *you*) is stressed in the negative:
'Don't you speak *to me like that!*

2 *You* + name(s) or name(s) + *you*:
You wait *here,* ***Jim****, and* ***Mary****,* ***you*** *wait there.*

3 Imperative + name or name + imperative:
Drink up *your milk,* ***Sally****!* ***Sally****,* ***drink up*** *your milk!*

4 Imperative + reflexive [> 4.25]:
Enjoy yourself. Behave yourself.

5 We can use words like *everybody, someone* with the imperative when we are talking to groups of people [> 4.37]:
Everyone keep *quiet!* ***Keep*** *still* ***everybody****!*
Nobody say *a word!* ***Somebody answer*** *the phone please.*
Any compounds are used after negative commands:
Don't say *a word* ***anybody****!* ***Don't anybody say*** *a word!*

9.55 The imperative with question tags [> 13.17–22]

Tags like *will you?, won't you?, can you?, can't you?, could you?* and *would you?* can often be used after an imperative for a variety of purposes: e.g.

- to express annoyance/impatience with *will/won't/can't you?* (rising tone):
  Stop *fiddling with that TV,* ***will you/won't you/can't you****?*
- to make a request (*can you?* for neutral requests; *could/would you?* for more polite ones); or to sound less abrupt:
  Post *this letter for me* ***can you****?/****could you****?/****would you****?*
- to offer polite encouragement or to make friendly offers and suggestions (*will you?* and *won't you?*):
  Come in, will you/won't you? Take *a seat,* ***will you/won't you****?*
- to obtain the co-operation of others with *Don't...will you?*:
  Don't tell *anyone I told you,* ***will you****?*

  And note *why don't you?* as a tag in: e.g.
  Go off for the weekend, ***why don't you****?*

9.56 Double imperatives joined by 'and' [compare > 16.12.2]

Some imperatives can be followed by *and* and another imperative where we might expect a *to*-infinitive:
Go and buy *yourself a new pair of shoes.* (Not **Go to buy**)
Come and see *this goldfish.* (Not **Come to see**)
Come and play *a game of bridge with us.* (Not **Come to play**)
Wait and see. (Not **Wait to see**)
Try and see *my point of view.* (Note *Try to* is also possible.)

In AmE *go* is sometimes followed directly by a bare infinitive:
Go fetch *some water.* (= Go and fetch)
A *to*-infinitive can follow an imperative to express purpose:
Eat to live*; do not* ***live to eat****.* [> 16.12.1]

10 Be, Have, Do

'Be', 'have' and 'do' as auxiliary verbs

10.1 'Be', 'have', 'do': full verbs and auxiliary verbs

Be is a full verb when it combines with adjectives and nouns [> 10.9]; *have* is a full verb when it is used to mean 'possess', etc. [> 10.27, 10.32]; *do* is a full verb when it is used to mean 'perform an activity', etc. [> 10.40]. The three verbs are auxiliary (or 'helping') verbs when they combine with other verbs to 'help' them complete their grammatical functions (see below).

10.2 Uses of 'be' as an auxiliary verb

1 *Be*, on its own or in combination with *have*, is used for progressive tense forms [> 9.1–2]: e.g.
*I **am**/He **is**/We **are working**.* (present progressive)
*I **have been working**.* (present perfect progressive)
2 *Be* combines with the past participle to form passives: e.g.
*It **was taken**.* [> 12.2*ns*.1–2]; *It can't **be done**.* [> 12.2*n*.2]

10.3 Uses of 'have' as an auxiliary verb

1 *Have* + past participle forms simple perfect tenses: e.g.
*I **have**/He **has eaten**. I **had eaten**.* [> 9.1–2]
2 *Have* + *been* + present participle forms perfect progressive: e.g.
*I **have**/I **had been eating**.* [> 9.2]
3 *Have* + *been* + past participle forms passives: e.g.
*It **has been eaten**.* [> 12.2*n*.1]
*She must **have been delayed**.* [> 12.2*n*.2]

Questions/negatives with *be* and *have* as auxiliary verbs follow the same pattern as those for *be* as a full verb [> Chapter 13]. *Have* can function as an auxiliary and full verb in the same sentence [> 10.34–36].

10.4 Uses of 'do' as an auxiliary verb

1 The most important use of *do* as an auxiliary verb is that it combines with the base form of verbs to make questions and negatives in the simple present and simple past tenses, and is used in place of a verb in short answers and question tags [> Chapter 13]. Note that *do* can function both as a auxiliary verb and as a full verb in the same sentence [> 10.41–42].
Do (auxiliary verb) *you* **do** (full verb) *your shopping once a week?*
2 *Do* is also used for emphasis [compare > 9.53]:
***Do** sit down. I **did** turn the gas off.*
*Drive carefully! – I **do** drive carefully.*
3 *Do* is used in place of a verb in: e.g.
*I like ice-cream and Ann **does**, too.* [> 4.18, 10.44.2, 11.31, 13.28]

'Be' as a full verb

10.5 Uses of 'be' in the imperative [compare > 9.51]

The imperative of *be* is restricted to the following combinations:

10.5.1 'Be' + noun

Many combinations of *be* (affirmative) + noun are idiomatic:

Be a man!
Be an angel *and fetch me my slippers please.*
Go on! Have another slice! ***Be a devil!***

Don't be + noun is much more common and very often refers to (foolish) behaviour. The negative response is *I'm not!*:

Don't be an ass/a clown/a fool/an idiot/an imbecile! etc.

And note combinations of *be* + adjective + noun:

Be a good girl *at school.* ***Don't be a silly idiot!***

Be can have the sense of 'become' especially in advertisements:

Be a better cook! Be the envy *of your friends!*

The negative *don't be* (= don't become) is often used for advice. Agreement is expressed with *I won't (be).*:

Don't be a racing driver! *It's so dangerous.*

Be is also used to mean 'pretend to be', especially after *you*:

(You) be the fairy godmother *and I'll* ***be Cinderella****.*
Be a monster*, granddad!*

And note:

Now ***be yourself*** *again!*

10.5.2 'Be' + adjective

Only adjectives referring to passing behaviour can be used after *be/don't be*, e.g. *careful/careless, patient/impatient, quiet, silly* [> App 41]. (*Be/Don't be* will not usually combine with adjectives describing states, e.g. *hungry/thirsty, pretty*):

Be quiet! (negative response: *I won't!*)
Don't be so impatient! (negative response: *I'm not!*)

10.5.3 'Be' + past participle

Be combines with a few past participles: e.g. *Be prepared!, (Please) be seated!, Be warned!* Compare: *Get washed!* [> 12.6].

10.5.4 'Do' + 'be' in place of the imperative and the present tense

The imperative:

Be careful*, or you'll break that vase!*

can be re-phrased with *if* in the following way:

If you don't be careful*, you'll break that vase.*

This is less common than [> 14.4]:

If you're not careful*, you'll break that vase.*

We can use *be* like any other imperative where the sense allows:

- after *do* [> 9.53]: ***Do be careful*** *with that vase!*
- after *you* [> 9.54]: ***You be quiet!***
- with tags [> 9.55]: ***Be quiet*** *for a moment,* ***will you****?*

10.6 The simple present form of 'be'

affirmative				short form		negative short forms				
		I	*am*		*I'm*	*I'm*	*not*			
		You	*are*		*You're*	*You're*	*not* =	*You*	*aren't*	
Tom	*is*	= *He*	*is*	*Tom's*	= *He's*	*He's*	*not* =	*He*	*isn't*	
Ann	*is*	= *She*	*is*	*Ann's*	= *She's*	*She's*	*not* =	*She*	*isn't*	
My ticket	*is*	= *It*	*is*	*My ticket's*	= *It's*	*It's*	*not* =	*It*	*isn't*	*old.*
Tom and I	*are*	= *We*	*are*		*We're*	*We're*	*not* =	*We*	*aren't*	
Ann and you	*are*	= *You*	*are*		*You're*	*You're*	*not* =	*You*	*aren't*	
Tom and Ann	*are*	= *They*	*are*		*They're*	*They're*	*not* =	*They*	*aren't*	

10.7 Notes on the present form of 'be'

1 Short forms never occur at the end of a sentence:
*I don't know where **they are**.*

2 There are two negative short forms (e.g *You aren't* and *You're not*) and there is no difference in their use. The short negative forms can stand on their own (*I'm not/They aren't*). The affirmative short forms (*I'm*, etc.) cannot stand on their own. Only the full affirmative forms can do this:
*Are you ready? – Yes, **I am**. No, **I'm not**.*

3 Note the formation of negative questions and negative question tags [> 13.14, 13.18] with *I*. The (rare) full form is *Am I not...?*, but this contracts to *Aren't I...?* (Not **Amn't I...?**):
– negative question: ***Am I not** late?* → ***Aren't I** late?*
– negative *Wh*-question: ***Why am I not** invited?* → ***Why aren't I** invited?*
– negative question tag: ***I'm** late, **am I not**?* → ***I'm** late, **aren't I**?*
Aren't I is only possible in negative questions/negative question tags and is never used in negative statements in standard English:
***I am not** late* → ***I'm not** late.* (the only possible contraction)
There are no variations with other persons: e.g.
***He isn't** late. **Isn't he** late? He's late, **isn't he**?*

4 The non-standard form *ain't*, in place of *am not, is not* and *are not* [also > 10.30*n*.8], is frequently heard in all persons and is avoided by educated speakers (except perhaps in joking):
Ain't you late? *He ain't late.*
I ain't late. *They ain't late.*

10.8 The simple past form of 'be'

affirmative			negative				negative short form		
I	*was*		*I*	*was*	*not*		*I*	*wasn't*	
You	*were*		*You*	*were*	*not*		*You*	*weren't*	
He	*was*		*He*	*was*	*not*		*He*	*wasn't*	
She	*was*		*She*	*was*	*not*		*She*	*wasn't*	
It	*was*	*late.*	*It*	*was*	*not*	*late.*	*It*	*wasn't*	*late.*
We	*were*		*We*	*were*	*not*		*We*	*weren't*	
You	*were*		*You*	*were*	*not*		*You*	*weren't*	
They	*were*		*They*	*were*	*not*		*They*	*weren't*	

10.9 Uses of 'be' in the simple present and simple past

We use the present and past of *be* when we are identifying people and things or giving information about them, and when we are talking about existence with *There...* [> 10.17]. For verbs related in meaning to *be*, such as *seem, look, appear* [> 10.23].

10.9.1 'Be' + names/nouns/pronouns: identification/information

Her name ***is/was Helen****. This* ***is Tom****. That* ***was Harry****.*
*Who****'s that****? – It****'s me****. Who* ***was that****? – It* ***was Jane****.*
Which one ***is Mary****? – That****'s her*** *on the left.*
The capital of England ***is London****. In the past it* ***was Winchester****.*
She ***is/was a doctor****. They* ***are/were doctors****.*
He ***is/was an American****. They* ***are/were Americans****.*

10.9.2 'Be' + adjective

He ***is hungry****. They* ***are hungry****.*	(state)
He ***was angry****. They* ***were naughty****.*	(mood, behaviour)
She ***was tall****. Her eyes* ***are green****.*	(description, colour)
She ***is French****. They* ***are French****.*	(nationality)
It ***was fine/wet/cold/windy****.*	(weather)

10.9.3 'Be' + adjective(s) + noun

He ***is an interesting man****. They* ***are interesting men****.*
It ***is a blue jacket****. They* ***are blue jackets****.*

10.9.4 'Be': time references, price, age, etc.

It ***is Monday/July 23/1992****. It* ***is £5.50****. Tom* ***is 14****.*

10.9.5 'Be' + possessives

*It****'s*** *mine/****Tom's****. They* ***are mine/Tom's****.*

10.9.6 'Be' + adverbs and prepositional phrases [> 7.3.3]

She ***is here/there****. They* ***are upstairs****.*
The play ***is next Wednesday****.* (future reference)
He ***is in the kitchen****. They* ***are at the door****.*

10.9.7 'Be' + adverb particle and 'home' [compare > 8.29.2, 10.13.4]

Be combines with adverb particles (*away, in, out*, etc. [> 8.4]);
Is *Tim* ***in****? No, he****'s out****. He****'s back*** *in an hour.*
Be combines with *home* (*at* is optional):
Where ***was*** *Tim?* ***Was*** *he* ***home****?/****Was*** *he* ***at home****?*

Compare:	*Tim****'s home*** *now.*	(= he has arrived at his home)
	*Tim****'s at home*** *now.*	(= he may not have left home at all)

10.9.8 'Be' in the present and past replacing 'have/had'

In informal English, the present and past of *be* can replace *have/had* [present and past perfect, > 9.22, 9.28] with verbs like *do, finish, go*:
*I****'m done*** *with all that nonsense.* (= I have done, i.e. finished)
I left my keys just there and next moment they ***were*** (had) ***gone****.*
*Have you finished with the paper? – I****'m*** (have) *nearly* ***finished****.*

10.9.9 'Empty subject' + 'be' [> 4.12]

It's *foggy.* ***It's*** *20 miles to London.*

10.9.10 'Be' + infinitive [> 9.47–48, 16.16]

My aim ***is to start up*** *my own company.*

10.10 Form of the present and past progressive of 'be'

present progressive					**past progressive**			
I	*am*	*(I'm)*	*being*		*I*	*was*	*being*	
You	*are*	*(You're)*	*being*		*You*	*were*	*being*	
He	*is*	*(He's)*	*being*		*He*	*was*	*being*	
She	*is*	*(She's)*	*being*	*silly.*	*She*	*was*	*being*	*silly.*
(It	*is*	*(It's)*	*being)*		*(It*	*was*	*being)*	
We	*are*	*(We're)*	*being*		*We*	*were*	*being*	
You	*are*	*(You're)*	*being*		*You*	*were*	*being*	
They	*are*	*(They're)*	*being*		*They*	*were*	*being*	

The forms *He's* ***being*** *silly* and *He's* ***been*** *silly* [> 10.12] should not be confused.

10.11 The use of 'be' + 'being' to describe temporary behaviour

The progressive forms normally occur only with the present and the past forms of *be*. They are used with a few adjectives and nouns [> App 41] (or adjective and noun combinations). The progressive is possible with adjectives such as *naughty, silly*, referring to passing behaviour, but is not possible with adjectives describing states (*hungry, thirsty*, etc.) With some combinations there is a strong implication that the behaviour is deliberate. Compare temporary and usual behaviour in the following:

Your brother ***is being very annoying*** *this evening.*
He ***isn't usually so annoying****.*
Your brother ***was being a (silly) fool*** *yesterday.*
He ***isn't usually such a (silly) fool****.*

10.12 Form of the present perfect and past perfect of 'be'

present perfect					**past perfect**				
full form		**short form**			**full form**		**short form**		
I	*have been*	*I've*	*been*		*I*	*had been*	*I'd*	*been*	
You	*have been*	*You've*	*been*		*You*	*had been*	*You'd*	*been*	
He	*has been*	*He's*	*been*		*He*	*had been*	*He'd*	*been*	
She	*has been*	*She's*	*been*	*ill.*	*She*	*had been*	*She'd*	*been*	*ill.*
(It	*has been)*	*(It's*	*been)*		*(It*	*had been)*	–		
We	*have been*	*We've*	*been*		*We*	*had been*	*We'd*	*been*	
You	*have been*	*You've*	*been*		*You*	*had been*	*You'd*	*been*	
They	*have been*	*They've*	*been*		*They*	*had been*	*They'd*	*been*	

The forms *He's* ***been*** *silly* and *He's* ***being*** *silly* [> 10.10] should not be confused.

10.13 Uses of 'have been' and 'had been' [compare > 9.24]

In many of the uses described below, other languages require the present or past of *be* where English requires *has been* or *had been*.

10.13.1 'Have been/had been' + adjective: behaviour and states

Have been and *had been* will combine not only with adjectives describing temporary behaviour (*annoying*, etc., [> 10.11]), but also with those describing states and moods continuing up till now or till then. *Have been* is common in conversation and *had been* in reported speech and written narrative:

Behaviour: *She's been very* ***quiet****.* *I said she had been very* ***quiet****.*
States: *I've never been so* ***tired****.* *I said I'd never been so* ***tired****.*
Moods: *He's been very* ***gloomy****.* *I said he'd been very* ***gloomy****.*

Some participles used as adjectives combine with *have/had been*:
My uncle ***has been retired*** *for more than two years.*
Their dog ***has been missing*** *for three days.*
And notice especially:
*She****'s been gone*** (= away) *for half an hour.*

10.13.2 'Have been/had been' + adjective: weather, etc.
Have been and *had been* also combine with adjectives describing the weather (i.e. states):
*It****'s been*** *very* ***cold*** *lately. I said it* ***had been*** *very* ***cold****.*

In certain contexts other adjectives (e.g. numbers) are possible:
You're speaking as if ***you'd never been 15 years old*** *in your life.*

10.13.3 'Have been/had been' + noun: professions, behaviour
Have been and *had been* will combine with noun (or with adjective + noun) to ask about or describe professions:
Have you ever been a teacher*?*
I've been a teacher*, but now I'm a computer salesman.*
How long ***have you been a computer salesman****?*

Nouns referring to behaviour will also combine with *have been*:
What a good girl you are! ***You've been an angel!***

All the above examples can be transferred to the past perfect:
He told me ***he had been a waiter*** *before he became a taxi-driver.*

10.13.4 'Have been/had been' and 'have gone/had gone'
Have been (generally + *to* or *in* [> Apps 21–23]) has the sense of 'visit a place and come back'. *Have gone* (followed by *to* and never by *in*) has the sense of 'be at a place or on the way to a place':
So there you are! Where ***have you been****?*
– ***I've been to*** *a party/****in*** *the canteen.* (= and come back)
Where's Pam? – ***She's gone to*** *a party/****to*** *Paris/****to*** *the canteen.*
(= She's on her way there, or she's there now.)

Have been and *have gone* will combine with adverb particles like *out, away*, and with *home* (not preceded by *to* [>10.9.7]):
Where ***have you been****? –* ***I've been out/away/home.***
(i.e. I'm here now)
Where ***has Tim gone****? –* ***He's gone out/away/home.***
(i.e. he's not here now)

We can use *from* before *home* in: e.g.
He's come ***from home****.* (i.e. 'home' is where he started out from.)
Compare: *He's come* ***home****.* (= He has arrived at his home.)
Have been/had been combine with other adverbials as well:
He's been a long time*.* (i.e. He hasn't come back yet.)

Have been and *have gone* are interchangeable only when they have the sense of 'experience'. This can occur when they are used with *ever* or *never* and followed by:
- a gerund: ***Have you ever been/gone skiing*** *in the Alps?*
- *for* + noun: ***I've never been/gone for a swim*** *at night.*
- *on* + noun: ***Have you ever been/gone on holiday*** *in winter?*

10.13.5 'Have been/had been' with 'since' and 'for' [compare > 9.25.2]

With *How long...?, since..., for..., have been* can be used in the sense *have lived/worked/waited* or *have been living/working/waiting:*

How long have you been *in London?* (i.e. lived/been living)
– ***I've been*** *here* ***since*** *January/****for*** *six months.*
How long have you been *with IBM?* (i.e. worked/been working)
– ***I've been*** *with them* ***since*** *November/****for*** *three months.*
How long have you been *in this waiting-room?* (waited/been waiting)
– ***I've been*** *here* ***since*** *3 o'clock/****for*** *half an hour.*

The past perfect replaces the present perfect in reported speech:
She told me she had been *with IBM for three months.*

10.14 Form of the future and future perfect of 'be'

future [compare > 9.35]		**future perfect** [compare > 9.42]		
full form	**short form**	**full form**	**short form**	
I will/shall be	*I'll be*	*I will/shall*	*I'll have been*	
You will be	*You'll be*	*You will*	*You'll have been*	
He will be	*He'll be*	*He will*	*He'll have been*	
She will be	*She'll be*	*She will*	*She'll have been*	*late.*
It will be	*It'll be*	*It will*	*It'll have been*	
We will/shall be	*We'll be*	*We will/shall*	*We'll have been*	
You will be	*You'll be*	*You will*	*You'll have been*	
They will be	*They'll be*	*They will*	*They'll have been*	

10.15 The future of 'be' as a full verb

Will be combines with many of the nouns and adjectives possible after the simple present/past of *be* for normal *will*-future uses:
It ***will be sunny*** *tomorrow.* ***I'll be*** *here by 7.* [> 9.35–37]
Will be can be used for deduction: *That* ***will be*** *Helen.* [> 11.33]

10.16 The future perfect of 'be' as a full verb

Will have been combines with the same nouns and adjectives possible after *have been* for normal uses in the future perfect [> 9.43]:
How long ***will you have been a teacher****?*
By the end of next week, I ***will have been a teacher*** *for 25 years.*
Will have been can be used to mean 'lived, worked, waited':
How long ***will you have been with IBM****?*
By the end of January, I ***will have been with IBM*** *for six months.*
Will have been can also be used for deduction [> 11.33]:
That ***will have been Roland****. He said he'd be back at 7.*

'There' + 'be'

10.17 Some forms of 'there' + 'be' [For 'there' + modals > 11.76]

the simple present
There is a man at the door.
There are two men at the door.

the present perfect
There has been an accident.
There have been a lot of enquiries.

the simple future
There will be a letter for you tomorrow.

the simple past
There was someone to see you.
There were some people to see you.

the past perfect
He said there had been an accident/ a lot of enquiries.

the future perfect
There will have been a definite result before Friday.

tag questions [> 13.17–22]
There is a big match on TV tonight, isn't there?
There has been some awful weather lately, hasn't there?

common contractions

There is	=	*There's:*	*There's a man at the door.*
There has	=	*There's:*	*There's been an accident.*
There have	=	*There've:*	*There've been a lot of accidents round here.*
There had	=	*There'd:*	*He told me there'd been an accident near here.*
There would	=	*There'd:*	*There'd be fewer accidents if drivers took care.*
There will	=	*There'll:*	*There'll be a good harvest this year.*

10.18 Notes on the form and pronunciation of 'there' + 'be'

1 The singular form *There's* is often used informally in place of *There are* to refer to the plural:
There's lots of cars *on the roads these days.*
There's a man and a dog *in our garden.*

2 When we are talking about existence, *There is/There's* and *There are* are unstressed and pronounced /ðeərɪz, ðəz/ and /ðeərɑː/. Compare the stressed form to show we have just seen something:
Look! '***There's*** /ðeəz/ *the new Fiat.* [also > 7.59.1]

10.19 When we use 'there' + 'be' combinations

We use *there* + *be* combinations when we are talking or asking about the existence of people, things, etc. It is more idiomatic and 'natural' to say 'There's a man at the door' than to say 'A man is at the door'. The construction with *there* allows important new information to come at the end of the sentence for emphasis. We use *there*:

– when it is a 'natural choice':
There's been an accident. (= An accident has occurred.)
Is there a hotel *near here?* – ***There's one*** *on the corner.*

– to announce or report events, arrangements, facts, etc.:
There'll be a reception *for the President at the Grand Hotel.*
There's been a wedding *at the local church.*

– for scene-setting in story-telling:
There hadn't been any rain *for months. The earth was bare and dry.* ***There wasn't a blade of grass*** *growing anywhere.*

10.20 'There is', etc. compared with e.g. 'it is'

Once existence has been established with *there*, we must use personal pronouns + *be* (or other verbs) to give more details:

***There's** a bus coming, but **it's** full.*
***There's** a man at the door. **It's** the postman.* [> 3.20.4]
***There's** a man at the door. **He wants** to speak to you.* [> 4.5.5]
***There are** some children at the door. **They want** to see Jimmy.*
***There's** a van stopping outside. **It's** someone delivering something.*
[compare > 1.60, 11.76.3–4, 16.52]
***There's to be** a concert at the Albert Hall tonight. **It's to be** broadcast live.* (*There/It is to be* = There/It is going to be)

10.21 'There is', etc. + determiner

There is, etc. can combine with: e.g.

– *a* and *an* [> 3.10]:
***There's a letter** for you from Gerald.* (Not **It has**)
***There'll be an exhibition** of Hockney paintings in December.*
– the zero article [> 3.28.8]:
***There are wasps** in the jam.*
– *some, any* and *no* [> 5.10–11]:
***There are some changes** in the printed programme.*
***Are there any lemons** in the fridge?* (Not * *It has* *)
***There are no volunteers** for a job like this!*
– *some, any* and *no* compounds [> 4.37]:
***Is there anyone** here who can read Arabic?*
*I'm starving and **there's nothing** in the fridge.*
– numbers and quantity words [> 5.3]:
***There are seventeen** people coming to dinner!*
***There aren't many** Sanskrit scholars in the world.*
***There'll be thousands of** football fans in London this weekend.*
– definite determiners (*the, this, that, my*, etc. [>3.1]).
The use of *the*, etc. after *there is* is relatively rare:
*What can we carry this shopping in? – **There's the/this/my briefcase.** Will that be all right?*

10.22 'There' + verbs other than 'be'

There can be used with a few verbs besides *be* (usually in the affirmative and in formal style). These verbs must be regarded as variations of *be* in that they describe a state: e.g. *exist, live* (*there lived* is common in fairy stories) *lie, remain*:

***There remains** one matter still to be discussed.*
*It is highly probable that **there exist** any number of systems resembling our own solar system.*

There combines with verbs related to *be*, such as *appear* [> 10.25]:
***There appears/seems** to be little enthusiasm for your idea.*
There combines with a few other verbs, such as *arrive, come, enter, follow, rise*. Such combinations have restricted uses:
***There will follow** an interval of five minutes.*

Verbs related in meaning to 'be'

10.23 Verbs related in meaning to 'be': selected forms

		verbs related to 'be'
present of 'be':	*He is quite rich.*	*He appears/seems (to be) quite rich.*
	It is quite dark.	*It appears/seems (to be) quite dark.*
past of 'be':	*He was quite rich.*	*He appeared/seemed (to be) quite rich.*
	It was quite dark.	*It appeared/seemed (to be) quite dark.*
present progressive:	*He is working hard.*	*He appears/seems to be working hard.*
	It's working.	*It appears/seems to be working.*
past progressive:	*He was working hard.*	*He appeared/seemed to be working hard.*
	It was working.	*It appeared/seemed to be working.*
present perfect:	*He has been hurt.*	*He appears/seems to have been hurt.*
	It has been broken.	*It appears/seems to have been broken.*

10.24 Expressing uncertainty with verbs related to 'be'

We can express certainty about states with *be*:
***He is** ill.*
We can express less certainty about states with modals [> 11.27–28]:
***He may/might/could be** ill.*
or through the use of verbs related to *be*:
***He seems (to be)** ill.*

Some common verbs related in meaning and function to *be* are: *appear, feel, look, seem, smell, sound* and *taste* [> 9.3, App 38.5]; *chance, happen* and *prove* can also be used in certain patterns.

10.25 Some possible constructions with verbs related to 'be'

We cannot normally omit *to be* after *appear* and *seem* except in the simple present and simple past:
***He appears/seems (to be)** ill. **He seems (to be)** a fool.*
***It seems/seemed (to be)** a real bargain.*
To be is usually included before predicative adjectives beginning with *a-* [> 6.8.2]:
*The children **appear/seem to be asleep**.*
*The children **seemed to be awake** when I went into their room.*

We can use other infinitives after *appear, happen, prove* and *seem*:
***You seem to know** a lot about steam engines.*
***Juan happens to own** a castle in Toledo.*

We cannot use *to be* after *feel, look, smell, sound* or *taste*:
***He feels/looks** hot. **You smell** nice.*
***Gillian sounded** very confident when she spoke to me.*
*I like your new jacket. **It looks** comfortable.*
***It feels** cold in here. **It smells** funny in here.*

Feel, look, seem, smell, sound and *taste* can be followed by *like* + noun or adjective + noun:
***This looks/tastes/smells/feels like** an orange.* (obligatory *like*)
***Jennifer seems/sounds/looks (like)** the right person for the job.*

To + object pronoun is commonly used after an adjective:
He seems/appears/looks tired ***to me****.* (Not **seems to me**)
This material feels quite rough ***to me****.* (Not **feels to me**)
Or *to* + object pronoun can come immediately before an infinitive:
He seems ***to me*** *to be rather impatient.*

We can use *that* after *it* + *appear, chance, happen* and *seem*:
It seemed (that) *no one knew where the village was.*
For the use of *as if* after verbs [> 1.47.2].

There will combine with *appear, chance, happen, prove* and *seem* + *to be* and *to have been*:
There seems to be *a mistake in these figures.*
There appears to have been *an accident.*

10.26 Process verbs related to 'be' and 'become'

10.26.1 Process verb + adjective complement [> 1.9, 1.11]

Process verbs (e.g. *become, come, fall, go, get, grow, run, turn, wear*) + adjective complement describe a change of state. Unlike *appear, seem*, etc. they can be used in the progressive to emphasize the idea that change is actively in progress:
It ***was*** *gradually* ***growing dark****.*
As she waited to be served, she ***became very impatient****.*
Old Mr Parsons ***gets tired*** *very easily since his operation.*
The milk in this jug ***has gone bad****.*
The leaves ***are turning yellow*** *early this year.*
My shoelaces ***have come undone****.*
The River Wey ***ran dry*** *during the recent drought.*
My pyjamas ***are wearing*** *rather* ***thin****.*

The most common process verbs are *get, become* and *grow*.
Get is used informally with a variety of adjectives: *get annoyed, get bored, get depressed, get ill, get tired, get wet* [compare > 12.6].
Used to is common after *get* (and to a lesser extent after *become*) to describe the acquisition of a habit. In such cases, *used to* functions as an adjective and can be replaced by *accustomed to* [> 16.56]:
I hated jogging at first, but I eventually ***got used to*** *it.*

Process verbs are often used in fixed phrases: e.g. *come right, come true, fall ill, go mad, run wild, turn nasty, wear thin.*

10.26.2 Process verb + noun complement

Nouns are not so common after process verbs, but note that:
– *become* + noun can describe a change of state or occupation:
The ugly frog ***became a handsome prince****.*
Jim ***became a pilot/a Buddhist/a CND supporter****.*
– *make* + noun can be used to suggest a change of state:
I'm sure Cynthia ***will make a good nurse*** *one day.*
This piece of wood ***will make a very good shelf****.*

10.26.3 Process verb + infinitive

Come, get and *grow* can be followed directly by a *to*-infinitive:
We didn't trust Max at first, but we soon ***grew to like*** *him.*

'Have' as a full verb = 'possess'; 'have got' = 'possess'

10.27 The present form of 'have' as a full verb

affirmative full form					**short form**	**negative short form** [> 10.30*n*.2]		
			I	*have*	*I've*	*I*	*haven't*	
			You	*have*	*You've*	*You*	*haven't*	
Tom	*has*	=	*He*	*has*	–	*He*	*hasn't*	
Mary	*has*	=	*She*	*has*	–	*She*	*hasn't*	*a chance.*
My car	*has*	=	*It*	*has*	–	*It*	*hasn't*	
Tom and I	*have*	=	*We*	*have*	*We've*	*We*	*haven't*	
Tom and you	*have*	=	*You*	*have*	*You've*	*You*	*haven't*	
Tom and Mary	*have*	=	*They*	*have*	*They've*	*They*	*haven't*	

10.28 The past form of 'have' as a full verb

affirmative full form					**short form**	**negative short form** [>10.30*n*.5]		
			I	*had*	*I'd*	*I*	*hadn't*	
			You	*had*	*You'd*	*You*	*hadn't*	
Tom	*had*	=	*He*	*had*	*He'd*	*He*	*hadn't*	
Mary	*had*	=	*She*	*had*	*She'd*	*She*	*hadn't*	*a chance.*
My car	*had*	=	*It*	*had*	–	*It*	*hadn't*	
Tom and I	*had*	=	*We*	*had*	*We'd*	*We*	*hadn't*	
Tom and you	*had*	=	*You*	*had*	*You'd*	*You*	*hadn't*	
Tom and Mary	*had*	=	*They*	*had*	*They'd*	*They*	*hadn't*	

10.29 The present form of 'have got'

affirmative full form				**short form**			**negative short forms**			
	I	*have*	*got*		*I've*	*got*	*I*	*haven't*	*(I've not)*	*got*
	You	*have*	*got*		*You've*	*got*	*You*	*haven't*	*(You've not)*	*got*
Tom	= *He*	*has*	*got*	*Tom's*	= *He's*	*got*	*He*	*hasn't*	*(He's not)*	*got*
Mary	= *She*	*has*	*got*	*Mary's*	= *She's*	*got*	*She*	*hasn't*	*(She's not)*	*got*
My car	= *It*	*has*	*got*	*My car's*	= *It's*	*got*	*It*	*hasn't*	*(It's not)*	*got*
Tom and I	= *We*	*have*	*got*		*We've*	*got*	*We*	*haven't*	*(We've not)*	*got*
Mary and you	= *You*	*have*	*got*		*You've*	*got*	*You*	*haven't*	*(You've not)*	*got*
Tom and Mary	= *They*	*have*	*got*		*They've*	*got*	*They*	*haven't*	*(They've not)*	*got*

10.30 Notes on the forms of 'have' and 'have got' = 'possess'

Have and *have got* (= possess) are often interchangeable, but there are differences between British and American usage.

1 *Have got* is basically a perfect form. Compare the following:

a) *get* (= obtain)

A *Go and* ***get*** *the tickets. What* ***have you got****?*

B ***I've got*** *the tickets.* (= I have obtained them.)

b) *have got* (= possess)

A ***Have you got*** *the tickets?*

B *Yes,* ***I've got*** *the tickets.* (= I possess them.)

In BrE, *have got* can be used as the perfect form of *get* to mean 'have obtained', as in a) above. This meaning is emphasized in the

AmE form *have gotten*, which always means 'have obtained'. However, in BrE (more rarely in AmE) *have got* can also mean 'possess' – as in b) above, so that e.g. *I have the tickets* and *I've got the tickets* are equivalents. Indeed, in spoken, idiomatic BrE, *I've got*, etc. is more common than *I have*, etc.

2 In BrE, questions and negatives with *have* = 'possess' can be formed in the same way as for *be*:
Are you *ready?* ***Have you*** *a pen?* (= Have you got...?)
Aren't you *ready?* ***Haven't you*** *a pen?* (= Haven't you got...?)
You aren't *ready.* ***You haven't*** *a pen.* (= You haven't got...)
There is an alternative negative form for *have got*: *I've not got*, etc., but this is less common than *I haven't got*. *Have* on its own (without *got*) can also form questions and negatives with *do, does* and *did*. This is usual in AmE and is becoming more common in BrE to the extent that *You hadn't a/an ...* and *Had/Hadn't you a/an...?* are becoming rare:
You don't have *a pen.* ***You didn't have*** *a pen.*
Do you have *a pen?* ***Did you have*** *a pen?*

3 *Have* (= possess) is a stative verb [> 9.3]. It cannot be used in the progressive, though it can be used in all simple tenses:

present:	*I* ***have*** *a Ford.*
past:	*He* ***had*** *a Ford last year.*
present perfect:	*I* ***have had*** *this car for three years.*
past perfect:	*He told me he* ***had had*** *a Ford for several years.*
future:	*I* ***will have*** *a new car soon.*
future perfect:	*By May I* ***will have had*** (= possessed) *this car five years.*
with modals:	e.g. *I* ***can have*** *a Ford as a company car.*

Have (= possess) is not normally used in the passive. The imperative (never with *got*) is rare: *Have patience!*

4 *Have got* (= possess) is normally used only for present reference:
*I****'ve got*** *a Ford.*
The affirmative *had got* is sometimes possible in the past, but *had* on its own is generally preferred:
The bride looked lovely. Her dress ***had (got)*** *a fine lace train.*
We can never use *had got* for certain states:
He ***had*** (Not **had got**) ***long hair*** *when he was a teenager.*
Had got is generally used in its original sense of 'had obtained':
When I saw him he ***had just got*** *a new car.*
Will have got is only used in the sense of 'will have obtained':
By May I ***will have got*** (= will have obtained) *a new car.*
Have got in the passive is impossible.

5 *Hadn't got* is usually possible as an alternative to *didn't have*:
I ***didn't have (hadn't got)*** *an appointment, so I made one for 4 p.m.*
I felt cold. I ***didn't have (hadn't got)*** *a coat.*
Hadn't on its own (always contracted) is possible (*I hadn't an appointment, I hadn't a coat*) but not very usual.
In past questions, the usual form is *Did you have...?*:
Did you have *an appointment? When* ***did you have*** *one?*

Had you...? sounds old-fashioned and formal. *Had you got...?* can be used in Yes/No questions, but sounds awkward in *Wh*-questions, so is usually avoided:
***Had you got** an appointment?* (but not usually *When had you got?*)
Have got is preferable to *have* in *Which* subject-questions:
***Which** (pen) **have you got**?* (or ***do you have**?*), but not usually *Which (pen) have you?*

6 Some forms of *have* (= possess) are rare or not encountered at all:
- the short form of the affirmative, especially in the third person (*he's/she's*). The full form is used: *He/She has a pen.*
- the uncontracted negative. The contracted form is normal: *I haven't* (or *hadn't*) *a pen.*
- some question-forms, except when formed with *do*, etc. (note 5).

7 Compare:
*My bag**'s** old. It**'s** old.* (= My bag *is* old/It *is* old)
*My bag**'s** got a hole in it. It**'s** got a hole in it.*
(= My bag *has* got a hole in it/It *has* got a hole in it)

8 The non-standard form *ain't got* is commonly heard in place of *haven't got* and *hasn't got* [compare > 10.7*n*.4]:
I ain't got my bag. She ain't got her bag.
Similarly, *have* and *has* are often omitted before *got*:
I got my car outside. (for *I have got*)

10.31 When we use 'have' and 'have got' = 'possess'

In all the examples below, *have* can be replaced by *have got* in the present and sometimes in the past. Short forms with *got* (*I've got*) are much more common than full forms (*I have got*), especially in speech.

1 In the sense of 'own' or 'possess' [> App 38.5]:
*I **have (got) a new briefcase**.*

2 In the sense of 'be able to provide':
Do you have/Have you (got) any ink? (= Can you let me have some?)

Do you have/Have you (got) any fresh eggs? (= Can you let me have some?)

3 *Have (got)* + number (of things)/quantity of a substance:
*I **have (got) fourteen pencils**. I **have (got) a lot of milk**.*

4 Possession of physical characteristics [> App 25.37]:
Have and *have got* combine with nouns like: *a beard, blue eyes, long hair, a scar, a slim figure*, to describe appearance:
*You should see our baby. He **has (got) big brown eyes**.*
*Our dog **has (got) long ears**.*
*This plant **has (got) lovely russet leaves**.*
*Our house **has (got) five rooms**.*

5 Possession of mental and emotional qualities [> App 42.1.10]:
Have and *have got* combine with nouns like: *faith, a good mind, patience, a quick temper*, to describe character:
*She **has (got) nice manners**, but she **has (got) a quick temper**.*

6 Family relationships:
I ***have (got) two sisters****.*

7 Contacts with other people:
I ***have (got) a good dentist****.* (i.e. whom I can recommend to you)

8 In the sense of 'wear' [> App 25.37]:
That's ***a nice dress you have/you've got****.*
In this sense, *have* often combines with *on*: *have something on, have got something on:*
That's ***a nice dress you have on/you've got on****.*
I can't answer the door. I ***have (got) nothing on****.*

9 Illnesses [> App 42.1.7]:
Have and *have got* combine with nouns describing pains and illnesses. For the use of *a/an* with such nouns [> 3.15]:
I ***have (got) a cold/a bad headache****.*
The baby ***has (got) measles****.*

10 Arrangements [> App 42.1.4]:
Have and *have got* combine with nouns like: *an appointment, a conference, a date, an interview, a meeting, time*, etc.:
I ***have (got) an appointment*** *with my dentist tomorrow morning.*
Sally ***has (got) an interview*** *for a job today.*

11 Opinions [> App 42.1.10]:
Have and *have got* combine with nouns like: *an idea, influence, an objection, an opinion, a point of view, a proposal, a suggestion:*
I ***have (got) an idea****!*
Have you (got) any objection *to this proposal?*

12 In the sense of 'there is':
You ***have (got) a stain*** *on your tie.* (= There is a stain on your tie.)
You ***have (got) sand*** *in your hair.* (= There is sand in your hair.)

'Have' as a full verb meaning something other than 'possess'

10.32 Forms of 'have' meaning something other than 'possess'

imperative:	*Have a cup of coffee!*
simple present:	*I always have milk in my tea.*
present progressive:	*We're having a nice time.*
simple past:	*We had a lovely holiday last summer.*
past progressive:	*I was having a bath when the phone rang.*
present perfect:	*Poor Jim has just had an accident.*
present perfect progressive:	*The children have been having a lot of fun.*
past perfect:	*I woke up because I had had a bad dream.*
past perfect progressive:	*I woke up – I had been having a bad dream.*
simple future:	*I'll have a haircut tomorrow.*
future progressive:	*If anyone phones, I'll be having a bath.*
future perfect:	*You'll have had an answer by tomorrow.*
future perfect progressive:	*She will have been having treatment all her life.*
with modal verbs:	e.g. *You could have a cup of tea if you like.*

10.33 The forms 'have' (= possess) and 'have' (other meanings)

1 *Have*, in the sense of 'eat, enjoy, experience, drink, take', etc., is a dynamic verb [> 9.3] so it is concerned with actions (e.g. *have a walk*), not states like *have* in the sense of 'possess' (e.g. *I have (got) a car*). Because of this, it can be used in the progressive form of all the tenses. Compare:

I have (= I've got) ***a drink**, thanks.*
(i.e. it's in my hand: stative)
***I'm having a drink**.*
(= I'm drinking: dynamic)
***I have a drink** every evening before dinner.*
(= I drink: dynamic)

Have got can *never* replace *have* used as a dynamic verb.

2 *Have* in the sense of 'take', etc. is used like any other English verb. This means that:

– questions and negatives in the simple present and simple past must be formed with *do, does* and *did*:

***Do you have** milk in your tea?* ***I don't have** milk in my tea.*
***Did you have** a nice holiday?* ***I didn't have** a nice holiday.*

Compare *have* meaning 'possess':

***Have you (got) any** milk in your tea?* (= Is there any?)
***I haven't (got) any** milk in my tea.* (= There isn't any.)

– it occurs freely in all active tenses as the context permits, but passive forms are rare: e.g. *a good time was had by all.*

– the passive infinitive sometimes occurs in: e.g.
*I tried to buy some extra copies of this morning's newspaper, but there were none **to be had**.* (i.e. they were not available)

3 There are no contracted forms of *have* (= 'take', etc.) as a full verb in the simple present and simple past:

***I have** a cold shower every morning.* (Not **I've...**)

Compare *have*, meaning 'possess':

***I have/I've/I've got** a new shower in my bathroom.*

4 The present and past perfect tenses of *have* involve the use of *have* as both auxiliary verb and main verb. For this reason, the present perfect and past perfect forms are given in full below.

10.34 Form of the simple present perfect of 'have' = 'take'

affirmative		short form		negative short forms				
I	*have had*	*I've*	*had*	*I've*	*not had*	= *I*	*haven't had*	
You	*have had*	*You've*	*had*	*You've*	*not had*	= *You*	*haven't had*	
He	*has had*	*He's*	*had*	*He's*	*not had*	= *He*	*hasn't had*	
She	*has had*	*She's*	*had*	*She's*	*not had*	= *She*	*hasn't had*	*lunch.*
It	*has had*	*It's*	*had*	*It's*	*not had*	= *It*	*hasn't had*	
We	*have had*	*We've*	*had*	*We've*	*not had*	= *We*	*haven't had*	
You	*have had*	*You've*	*had*	*You've*	*not had*	= *You*	*haven't had*	
They	*have had*	*They've*	*had*	*They've*	*not had*	= *They*	*haven't had*	

10.35 Form of the simple past perfect of 'have' = 'take'

affirmative			short form		negative short forms					
I	*had*	*had*	*I'd*	*had*	*I'd*	*not had*	= *I*	*hadn't*	*had*	
You	*had*	*had*	*You'd*	*had*	*You'd*	*not had*	= *You*	*hadn't*	*had*	
He	*had*	*had*	*He'd*	*had*	*He'd*	*not had*	= *He*	*hadn't*	*had*	
She	*had*	*had*	*She'd*	*had*	*She'd*	*not had*	= *She*	*hadn't*	*had*	*lunch.*
It	*had*	*had*	*It'd*	*had*	*It'd*	*not had*	= *It*	*hadn't*	*had*	
We	*had*	*had*	*We'd*	*had*	*We'd*	*not had*	= *We*	*hadn't*	*had*	
You	*had*	*had*	*You'd*	*had*	*You'd*	*not had*	= *You*	*hadn't*	*had*	
They	*had*	*had*	*They'd*	*had*	*They'd*	*not had*	= *They*	*hadn't*	*had*	

10.36 Notes on the forms 'have had' and 'had had'

1 These forms are, of course, quite regular: *I have had my lunch* and *I had had my lunch* work in the same way as *I have eaten my lunch* and *I had eaten my lunch.*
Here are a few more examples of *have* as a full verb in the present perfect and past perfect:
***Have you ever had** lunch at Maxim's?*
*That boy looks as if he**'s never had** a haircut.*
*I **had never had** a ride on an elephant before I went to India.*

2 In general, the negative forms *I haven't had, I hadn't had*, etc. are more common than *I've not had* and *I'd not had.*

3 The following forms should not be confused:
*He**'s** ill.* (= He *is* ill.) and *He**'s** had lunch.* (= He *has* had lunch.)
*He**'d** had lunch.* (= He *had* had lunch.) and
*He said he**'d** have lunch now.* (= he *would* have lunch now)

10.37 Common 'have' + noun combinations

Have combines with a great many nouns. In this respect, it is similar to other phrases with such verbs as *give* (e.g. in *give a thought*) and *take* (in e.g. *take an exam*). For verb phrases of this kind and for examples with *have* [> App 42]:
*Let's **have lunch**. I'd like to **have a sandwich** please.*

10.38 'Have' + noun in place of other verbs

The verbs *to sleep, to swim*, etc. can be expressed with *have* + noun in the sense of 'perform that activity': e.g.

to dance – *to have a dance: I **had two dances** with Molly.*
to fight – *to have a fight: Those twins are always **having fights**.*
to look – *to have a look: Just **have a look** at this.*
to rest – *to have a rest: I want to **have a rest** this afternoon.*
to ride – *to have a ride: Can I **have a ride** in your car?*
to talk – *to have a talk: Jim and I **have** just **had a** long **talk**.*
to swim – *to have a swim: Come and **have a swim** with us.*
to wash – *to have a wash: I must **have a wash** before lunch.*

Have commonly replaces verbs like the following:
receive: ***I had** a letter from Jim this morning.*
permit: ***I won't have** that kind of behaviour in my house.*

10.39 The use of 'have' in the imperative

One of the most common uses of *have* (= 'take', etc.) is in the imperative. It is often used after *do* [> 9.53] for emphasis and/or encouragement (*Do have...*). Common instances are:

Offers:	***Do have*** *some oysters!* ***Don't have*** *tomato soup!*
Suggestions:	***Have*** *a bath and a rest and you'll feel better.*
Encouragement:	***Have a go! Have a try! Have a shot*** *at it!*
Good wishes:	***Have fun! Have a good time! Have a good day!*** (fixed expressions)

There are no direct references to appetite, digestion, etc. (like *Bon appetit!* in French or *Guten Appetit!* in German), but expressions with *have* can be coined to suit particular occasions:

Have *a really good meal!* ***Have*** *a lovely party!*
Have *a really restful holiday!*
Have *a really interesting debate!* etc.

'Do' as a full verb

10.40 Forms of 'do' as a full verb

imperative:	*Do your homework!*
simple present:	*I do the shopping every morning.*
present progressive:	*I'm doing this crossword puzzle.*
simple past:	*He did a lot of work this morning.*
past progressive:	*We were doing sums all yesterday evening.*
present perfect:	*We've just done the washing-up.*
present perfect progressive:	*I've been doing this exercise all day.*
past perfect:	*We went home after we had done our work.*
past perfect progressive:	*We had been doing business with each other for years before we quarrelled.*
simple future:	*I'll do the housework tomorrow morning.*
future progressive:	*I'll be doing jobs about the house tomorrow.*
future perfect:	*If you finish this job as well, you will have done far more than I expected.*
future perfect progressive:	*By this time next year, we will have been doing business with each other for 20 years.*
with modal verbs:	e.g. *Would you do me a favour please?*

10.41 The present form of 'do' as a full verb

affirmative			**negative full form**			**negative short form**		
I	*do*	*the work.*	*I*	*do*	*not*	*I*	*don't*	*do the work.*
You	*do*		*You*	*do*	*not*	*You*	*don't*	
He	*does*		*He*	*does*	*not*	*He*	*doesn't*	
She	*does*		*She*	*does*	*not*	*She*	*doesn't*	
It	*does*		*It*	*does*	*not*	*It*	*doesn't*	
We	*do*		*We*	*do*	*not*	*We*	*don't*	
You	*do*		*You*	*do*	*not*	*You*	*don't*	
They	*do*		*They*	*do*	*not*	*They*	*don't*	

10.42 The past form of 'do' as a full verb

affirmative		negative full form		negative short form	
I did		*I did not*		*I didn't*	
You did		*You did not*		*You didn't*	
He did		*He did not*		*He didn't*	
She did	*the work.*	*She did not*		*She didn't*	*do the work.*
It did		*It did not*		*It didn't*	
We did		*We did not*		*We didn't*	
You did		*You did not*		*You didn't*	
They did		*They did not*		*They didn't*	

10.43 The present perfect form of 'do' as a full verb

affirmative	negative full form	negative short form	
I have done	*I have not done*	*I haven't (I've not) done*	
You have done	*You have not done*	*You haven't (You've not) done*	
He has done	*He has not done*	*He hasn't (He's not) done*	
She has done	*She has not done*	*She hasn't (She's not) done*	*it.*
It has done	*It has not done*	*It hasn't (It's not) done*	
We have done	*We have not done*	*We haven't (We've not) done*	
You have done	*You have not done*	*You haven't (You've not) done*	
They have done	*They have not done*	*They haven't (They've not) done*	

10.44 Uses of 'do' as a full verb

10.44.1 'Do' = 'perform an activity or task'

Do often has the sense of 'work at' or 'be engaged in something'. 'Doing something' can be deliberate or accidental. We can use verbs other than *do* to answer questions like *What are you doing?*:

*What **are you doing**?*
*– **I'm reading**.* (i.e. that's what I'm doing)
*What **did you do** this morning?*
*– **I wrote some letters**.* (i.e. that's what I did)
*What **have you done**?*
*– **I've broken** this vase.* (i.e. that's what I've done)

We often use *do* in this sense with *some/any/no* compounds:
*Haven't you got **anything to do**? I've got **nothing to do**.*

We can use *do* to refer to an unnamed task and then we can refer to named tasks by means of other verbs:
*I **did** a lot of **work** around the house today. I **took down** the curtains and **washed** them and I **cleaned** the windows.*

10.44.2 The use of 'do' to avoid repeating a previous verb

We can use *do* to avoid repeating a previous verb [> 4.18]:
*Antonia **works** 16 hours a day. I don't know how she **does** it.*
***Take** the dog for a walk. – **I've already done it/done so**.*

We can avoid repeating the verb in short answers, such as:
Shall I take** the dog for a walk? – **Yes, do./No, don't. [> 9.53]
(i.e. take/don't take the dog for a walk)

10.44.3 'Do' = 'be in the wrong place'

Used in this sense, *do* often conveys disapproval, e.g.

– of present results of past actions:
What are those clothes ***doing*** *on the floor?*
(i.e. they shouldn't be there)

– of people:
What are those boys ***doing*** *in our garden?*
(i.e we disapprove of their presence, not their actions)

10.44.4 'Do' before gerunds

We can use *do* + gerund to refer to named tasks:

I've ***done the shopping/the ironing/the washing up****.*
We ***did*** *all* ***our shopping*** *yesterday.*
I ***do a lot of swimming****.* (in preference to 'I swim a lot.')
I stayed at home last night and ***did some reading****.*

10.45 'Do' and 'make' compared

Make conveys the sense of 'create'; *do* (often suggesting 'be engaged in an activity') is a more general term:

What ***are you doing****?* – ***I'm making*** *a cake.*
What ***are you making****?* – *A cake.*

Both *do* and *make* can be used in a variety of fixed combinations [> App 43]. Here is a brief selection:

do + *one's best; business with someone; damage to something; one's duty; an experiment; someone a favour; good*, etc.
make + *an accusation against (someone); an agreement with (someone); an appointment; an arrangement; a bed*, etc.

Sometimes both *make* and *do* are possible:

I'll make/I'll do the beds *this morning, if you like.*

10.46 'Do' in fixed expressions

Do occurs in numerous fixed expressions, such as:

What ***does*** *he* ***do****?* (i.e. What work does he do for a living?)
How ***do you do****?* [> 13.40.6]
*That****'ll do****!* (e.g. That will be enough.)
How many miles ***does it do*** *to the gallon?* (*do* in the sense of 'go')
This simply ***won't do****.* (i.e. It's unacceptable.)
How ***did*** *you* ***do****?* (i.e. How did you manage?)
I could ***do with*** *a drink.* (i.e. I would like a drink.)
It's got ***nothing to do with*** *me.* (i.e. It doesn't concern me.)
I can ***do without*** *a car.* (i.e. manage without a car)
I ***was done****!* (i.e. I was cheated.)
Shall I ***do*** *your room* ***out****?* (i.e. clean it)
You ***did*** *me* ***out of*** *my share.* (i.e. cheated me)

11 Modal auxiliaries and related verbs

General characteristics of modal verbs

11.1 Which verbs are modal auxiliaries and what do they do?

Verbs like *can* and *may* are called **modal auxiliaries**, though we often refer to them simply as **modal verbs** or **modals**. We frequently use modals when we are concerned with our relationship with someone else. We may, for example, ask for permission to do something; grant permission to someone; give or receive advice; make or respond to requests and offers, etc. We can express different levels of politeness both by the forms we choose and the way we say things. The bluntest command (*You must see a doctor*), with a certain kind of stress, might be more kindly and persuasive than the most complicated utterance (*I think it might possibly be advisable for you to see a doctor*).

Modals sharing the same grammatical characteristics [> 11.5–6] are:
can – *could*
may – *might*
will – *would*
shall – *should*
must – –
ought to – –

Verbs which share *some* of the grammatical characteristics of modals are: *need* [> 11.49], *dare* [> 11.65], *used to* [> 11.58].
By comparison, *need to* and *dare to* are full verbs.

Modals have two major functions which can be defined as **primary** and **secondary**.

11.2 Primary function of modal verbs

In their primary function, modal verbs closely reflect the meanings often given first in most dictionaries, so that:

- *can/could* relate mainly to **ability**: *I **can lift** 25 kg/I **can type**.*
- *may/might* relate mainly to **permission**: *You **may leave** early.*
- *will/would* relate mainly to **prediction** [> 9.35]: *It **will rain** soon.*
- *shall* after *I/We* [> 9.36n.1] relates mainly to **prediction**: *Can we find our way home? – I'm sure **we shall**.*
- *should/ought to* relate mainly to **escapable obligation** or **duty**: *You **should do*** (or ***ought to do***) *as you're told.*
- *must* relates mainly to **inescapable obligation**: *You **must be** quiet.*
- *needn't* relates to **absence of obligation**: *You **needn't wait**.*

11.3 Secondary function of modal verbs

In their secondary function, nine of the modal auxiliaries (not *shall*) can be used to express the degree of certainty/uncertainty a speaker feels about a possibility. They can be arranged on a scale from the greatest uncertainty (*might*) to the greatest certainty (*must*). The order of modals between *might* and *must* is not fixed absolutely. It varies according to situation. For example, one arrangement might be:

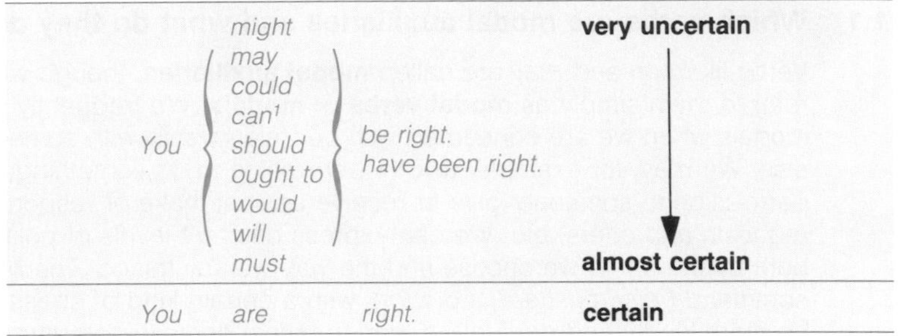

[1]*Can* requires qualification to be used in this way [> 11.29*ns*.2, 4]:
*He **can hardly be** right.*
***Do you think he can be** right?*
***I don't think he can be** right.*

11.4 Primary and secondary functions of 'must' compared

This example of *must* shows that it is 'defective' [> 11.6.1]:

1 In its primary function it requires another full verb (*have to*) to make up its 'missing parts'. (In the same way *can*, for example, in its primary function requires the full verb *be able to* to make up its missing parts.)
2 In its secondary function *must* (like the other modals listed in 11.1) has only two basic forms: a form which relates to the present and a form which relates to the perfect or past [> 11.8.4].

	primary (inescapable obligation)	**secondary (certainty)**
infinitive:	*to have to leave*	–
***-ing* form**:	*having to leave*	–
present:	*They **must leave**.*	*They **must be** right.*
future:	*They **must leave tomorrow**.*	–
perfect:	*They have had to leave.*	
past:	*They had to leave.*	*They **must have been** right.*
past perfect:	*They had had to leave*	
future perfect:	*They will have had to leave.*	–
'conditional':	*They would have had to leave.*	–

11.5 Some ways in which modals resemble 'be', 'have', 'do'

Structurally, modal auxiliaries resemble the auxiliaries *be, have* and *do* in some ways and differ completely from them in others. Some of the most important similarities are noted in this section and some differences are explained in 11.6.

11.5.1 The negative [> 13.1–2]

The negative is formed (as it is for *be, have* and *do*) by the addition of *not* after the modal. In informal spoken English *not* is often reduced to the unemphatic *n't*:

be	*(is) not*	*(is)n't*	[> 10.6, 10.8]
have	*(have) not*	*(have)n't*	[> 10.27–28]
do	*(do) not*	*(do)n't*	[> 10.41–42]
can	*cannot*	*can't*	
could	*could not*	*couldn't*	
may	*may not*	*mayn't*	
might	*might not*	*mightn't*	
will	*will not*	*won't*	[> 9.35]
would	*would not*	*wouldn't*	
shall	*shall not*	*shan't*	[> 9.36*n*.3]
should	*should not*	*shouldn't*	
must	*must not*	*mustn't*	
ought to	*ought not to*	*oughtn't to*	
need	*need not*	*needn't*	
dare	*dare not*	*daren't*	

The full form *cannot* is written as one word.
Mayn't is rare, but does occur. For *used not* and *usedn't* [> 11.59*n*.2].

11.5.2 Questions [> 13.1–3, 13.30, 13.41]

Yes/No questions are formed as for *be, have* and *do*. We begin with the modal, followed by the subject and then the predicate:

__May we__ leave early?

In **question-word questions**, the question-word precedes the modal:

__When may we__ leave?

With Yes/No questions, the modal used in the answer is normally the same as the one used in the question [> 11.31, 13.6*n*.1]:

__Can__ you come and see me tomorrow? – Yes, I __can__./No, I __can't__.

Modals also behave like *be, have* and *do* in **tag questions** [> 13.17]:

You __can__ do it, __can't__ you?

11.5.3 Negative questions [> 13.14]

As with *be, have* and *do*, the full form of negative questions with modals requires *not* after the subject (***Can you not** help me?*). This is formal and rare. Contracted forms are normally used:

***Can't you** help me?* [compare > 13.16]

Shouldn't (you)...? is usually preferred to *Oughtn't (you) to...?* perhaps because the latter is more difficult to pronounce.
Negative questions with *Used?* on the above patterns are rare [> 11.59].

11.6 Some ways in which modals differ from 'be', 'have', 'do'

11.6.1 'Defective verbs'

Modals are sometimes called **defective verbs** because they lack forms ordinary full verbs have [> 11.4]. For example:

1 Modals cannot be used as infinitives (compare *to be, to have, to do*). If ever we need an infinitive, we have to use another verb:
*If you want to apply for this job, you have **to be able to** type at least 60 words a minute.* (Not *to* before *can* or *can* alone)

2 We do not use a *to*-infinitive after modals (compare *be to, have to*). Only the bare infinitive [> 16.3] can be used after modals (except *ought*, which is always followed by *to*):
*You **must/mustn't phone** him this evening.* (Not **to phone**)
3 Modals have no *-ing* form (compare *being, having, doing*). Instead of *-ing*, we have to use another verb or verb-phrase:
*I **couldn't go**/I **wasn't able to go** home by bus, so I took a taxi.* (= Not being able to go...)
4 Modals have no *-(e)s* in the 3rd person singular (compare *is, has, does*):
*The boss **can see** you now.* (No *-s* on the end of *can*)
5 Each modal has a basic meaning of its own. By comparison, as auxiliaries, *be/have/do* have only a grammatical function [> 10.1].

11.6.2 Contracted forms

Unlike *be* and *have* (but not *do*), modals in the affirmative do not have contracted forms, except for *will* and *would* [*I'll, I'd* > 9.35, 14.17*n*.3]. In speech, *can, could* and *shall* are 'contracted' by means of unemphatic pronunciation:

I, (etc.) *can* /kən/, *I*, (etc.) *could* /kəd/, *I/We shall* /ʃəl/

11.6.3 One modal at a time

Only *one* modal can be used in a single verb phrase:

*We **may call** the doctor.*
*We **must call** the doctor.* } but not *may* and *must* together.

If we wish to combine the two ideas in the above sentences, we have to find a suitable paraphrase:

*It **may be necessary** (for us) **to call** a doctor.*

By comparison, we can use e.g. *be* and *have* together:

*It **has been** necessary to call a doctor.*

11.7 Form of modal auxiliaries compared with future tenses

Each of the modals fits into the four patterns for future tense forms:

I will see	simple future [> 9.35]
I will be seeing	future progressive [> 9.40]
I will have seen	future perfect simple [> 9.42]
I will have been seeing	future perfect progressive [> 9.42]

	active	**passive**
modal + (bare infinitive):	*I may see*	*I may be seen*
modal + *be* + present participle:	*I may be seeing*	– [but > 12.3*n*.6]
modal + *have* + past participle:	*I may have seen*	*I may have been seen*
modal + *have been* + present participle:	*I may have been seeing*	–

11.8 Forms and uses of modals compared with verb tenses

The labels we use to describe the verb tenses (e.g. **present, progressive, past, perfect**) cannot easily be applied to modals.

11.8.1 'Present'

All modals can refer to the immediate present or the future, therefore 'present' is not always a reliable label:

*I **can/may** (etc.) phone **now**. I **can/may** (etc.) phone **tomorrow**.*

11.8.2 'Progressive'

There is no progressive form for modals. But we can put the verb that follows a modal into the progressive form:

*Meg **is phoning** her fiancé.* (present progressive)
*Meg may be **phoning** her fiancé.* (modal + *be* + verb-*ing*)
*Meg may have been **phoning** her fiancé.* (modal + *have been* + *-ing*)

It is the *phoning* that is or was in progress, not 'may'.

11.8.3 'Past'

Would, could, might and *should* can be said to be past in **form**, but this usually has little to do with their **use** and **meaning**. They can be called 'past' when used in indirect speech [> 15.13*n*.6]:

*He **says** you **can/will/may** leave early.* (present)
*He **said** you **could/would/might** leave early.* (past)

Might can have a past reference in historical narrative:

*In the 14th century a peasant **might** have the right to graze pigs on common land.*

However, *might* usually expresses more uncertainty than *may*:

*I **might** see you tomorrow.*

is less certain than:

*I **may** see you tomorrow.*

Could sometimes expresses ability in the past [> 11.12.1]:

*He **could*** (or ***was able to***) *swim five miles when he was a boy.*

but *could* is not possible in:

*I **managed to/was able to** finish the job yesterday.* [> 11.12.3]

However, *couldn't* and *wasn't able to* are usually interchangeable:

*I **couldn't/wasn't able to** finish the job yesterday.*

The other main use of *could*, as a more polite alternative to *can* in requests, has nothing to do with time:

***Could** you help me please?*

Would expresses the past in [> 11.61]:

*When we **were** young we **would** spend our holidays in Brighton.*

Otherwise, *would* and *should* have special uses [e.g. > 11.74–75].

Must can express past time only in indirect speech [> 15.13*n*.6]; otherwise it has to be replaced by *have to*, etc. [> 11.4]:

*He told us **we must wait*** (or ***we had to wait***) *until we were called.*
*She asked her boss if **she must work*** (or ***had to work***) *overtime.*

11.8.4 'Perfect' and 'past'

Forms with modal + *have* + past participle or with modal + *have been* + progressive are not necessarily the equivalent of the present perfect. The modal refers to the present, while *have* + past participle refers to the past. So, depending on context,

You must have seen him can mean:

I assume (now) *you have seen him.* (i.e. before now; equivalent to the present perfect)
I assume (now) *you saw him.* (i.e. then; equivalent to the past)
I assume (now) *you had seen him.* (i.e. before then; equivalent to the past perfect)

11.9 Modal + verb and modal + 'be/have been' + progressive

Two observations need to be made here:

1 Modal + *be/have been* + progressive is not always possible in the primary function. For example:
*He **can't leave** yet.* (= it's not possible for him to leave yet)
is quite different from the secondary function:
*He **can't be leaving** yet.* (= I don't think he is)
But compare the primary and secondary functions of *must* in:
primary: *You **must be working** when the inspector comes in.* (i.e. it is necessary (for you) to be working.)
secondary: *You **must be joking**!* (i.e. I'm almost certain you are joking.)

2 Occasionally, in the primary function, a modal + *be* + progressive has a 'softening effect' similar to the use of the future progressive [> 9.41.2]. So:
*We **must/may/should** (etc.) **be leaving** soon.*
is more polite and tentative than:
*We **must/may/should** (etc.) **leave** soon.*

Uses of modals, etc. to express ability

11.10 Form of modals and related verbs expressing ability

can/could:
Can/could express ability, which may be natural or learned:

present reference:	*I/You/He* (etc.) *can/can't hear music.*
past or **perfect reference**:	*I/You/He* (etc.) *could/couldn't play chess.*
	I/You/He (etc.) *could have/couldn't have danced all night.*
future reference:	None. We use *will be able to* [but compare > 11.19, 11.26].

Verbs and verb phrases related in meaning to *can* (ability):

be (un)able to:	*I am (not) able/I am unable to attend the meeting.*
be (in)capable of:	*He is (not) capable/He is incapable of doing the job.*
manage to:	*We managed/didn't manage to persuade him to accept.*
succeed in:	*They'll succeed/won't succeed in getting what they want.*

11.11 'Can' = ability: the present

11.11.1 'Can' + verb (natural ability)

Natural ability can be expressed as follows:
***Can you run** 1500 metres in 5 minutes?*
(= Are you able to run? Are you capable of running?)
*I **can/cannot/can't run** 1500 metres in 5 minutes.*

Can and *am/is/are able to* are generally interchangeable to describe natural ability, though *able to* is less common:
*Billy is only 9 months old and he **can already stand up**.*
*Billy is only 9 months old and he **is already able to stand up**.*
However, *am/is/are able to* would be unusual when we are commenting on something that is happening at the time of speaking:
*Look! I **can stand on my hands**!*

11.11.2 'Can' + verb (learned ability or 'know-how')

Learned ability can be expressed as follows:

Can you drive a car?
(= Do you know how to? Have you learnt how to?)
I can/cannot/can't drive a car.

Verbs such as *drive, play, speak, understand* indicate skills or learned abilities. *Can*, and to a lesser extent, *am/is/are able to*, often combine with such verbs and may generally be used in the same way as the simple present tense:

I can/can't play chess. (= I play/don't play chess.)

11.12 'Could/couldn't' = ability: the past

11.12.1 Past ability (natural and learned) expressed with 'could'

Could, couldn't or *was/were (not) able to* can describe natural and learned ability in the past, not related to any specific event:

Jim could/couldn't run very fast when he was a boy.
Barbara could/couldn't sing very well when she was younger.
Jim was able to/was unable to run fast when he was a boy.

We also often use *used to be able to* to describe past abilities:

I used to be able to hold my breath for one minute under water.

Could and *was* (or *would be*) *able to* occur after reporting verbs:

He said he could see me next week.

For 'unreal past' *could* (= was/were able to) after *if* [> 14.10–12, 14.14].

11.12.2 The past: 'could' + verb: achievement after effort

Could and *was/were able to* can be interchangeable when we refer to the acquisition of a skill after effort:

I tried again and found I could swim/was able to swim.

11.12.3 Specific achievement in the past

Could cannot normally be used when we are describing the successful completion of a specific action; *was/were able to, managed to* or *succeeded in* + *-ing* must be used instead:

In the end they { *were able to rescue* / *managed to rescue* / *succeeded in rescuing* } *the cat on the roof.*

If an action was not successfully completed, we may use *couldn't*;

They tried for hours, but they couldn't rescue the cat.
(or *weren't able to, didn't manage to*, etc.)

Could can be used when we are *asking* about a specific action (as opposed to describing it):

Could they rescue the cat on the roof? (= did they manage to?)
– No, they couldn't. It was too difficult.

However, an affirmative response requires an alternative to *could*:

– Yes, they managed to. (Not **could**)

11.13 'Can/could' + verbs of perception [> App 38.4]

Verbs of perception [> 9.3], like *see, hear, smell*, rarely occur in the progressive. *Can*, and to a lesser extent, *am/is/are able to*, combine with such verbs to indicate that we can see, hear, etc. something happening at the moment of speaking. In such cases *can* has a grammatical function equivalent to the simple present in statements and to *do/does* in questions and negatives:

*I **can smell** something burning.* (= I smell something burning.)
*I **can't see** anyone.* (= I don't see anyone.)

Could can be used in place of the simple past in the same way:

*I listened carefully, but **couldn't hear** anything.*
(= I listened carefully, but didn't hear anything.)

Can/could can be used with verbs suggesting 'understanding':

*I **can/can't understand** why he decided to retire at 50.*
*I **could/couldn't understand** why he had decided to retire at 50.*

Can't/couldn't cannot be replaced by the simple present or simple past when conveying the idea 'beyond (my) control' (impossible):

*I **can't (couldn't) imagine** what it would be like to live in a hot climate.* (Not **I don't/I didn't imagine**)

11.14 'Could' and 'would be able to'

We can use *could* as an 'unreal past' [> 14.10, 14.14] in the sense of 'would be able to'. When we do this, an *if*-clause is sometimes implied:

*I'm sure you **could get into** university (if you applied).*

Could + never has the sense of 'would never be able to':

*I **could never put up with** such inefficiency if I were running an office.* (i.e. I would never be able to)

Could is often used to express surprise, anger, etc. in the present:

*I **could eat my hat**! I **could slap** your face!*

11.15 'Could have' and 'would have been able to'

We do not use *can/can't have* + past participle to express ability or capacity. We use them for possibility or conjecture (*He can't have told you anything I don't already know*) [> 11.32].
However, in conditional sentences and implied conditionals we may use *could have* + past participle (in place of *would have been able to*) to refer to ability or capacity that was not used owing to personal failure or lack of opportunity [> 14.19]:

***If it hadn't been for** the freezing wind and blinding snow, the rescue party **could have reached** the injured man before nightfall.*

For *could have* (= had been able to) in conditions [> 14.16–17].

11.16 Ability in tenses other than present and past

If we need to express ability in other tense combinations (e.g. the future or the present perfect), then the appropriate forms of *be able to, manage to* or *succeed in* must be used:

*I'**ll be able to pass** my driving test after I've had a few lessons.*
*I've been trying to contact him, but I **haven't managed to**.*

Can, referring to ability, skill, or perception, is usable in clauses after *if* and *when* [> 14.4] to refer to the future:

***If** you **can pass** (or **are able to pass**) your driving test at the first attempt, I'll be very surprised.*

11.17 Expressing ability with 'can' and 'could' in the passive

Passive constructions with *can* and *could*, indicating ability, are possible where the sense allows:

This car ***can only be driven*** *by a midget.*
The lecture ***couldn't be understood*** *by anyone present.*
The injured men ***could have been reached*** *if heavy equipment had been available during the rescue operation.*

11.18 'Can/could' = capability/possibility

Can + *be* + adjective or noun has the effect of 'is sometimes' or 'is often' and refers to capability or possibility. It can be replaced by *be capable of* + *-ing*, but not by *am/is/are able to*:

It ***can be quite cold*** *in Cairo in January.*
(= It is sometimes – or often – quite cold.)
He ***can be very naughty.*** (or 'a very naughty boy') [> 10.11]

(When used for people, the effect is generally negative, even when the adjective is favourable: *She can look quite attractive when she wants to* – which implies she doesn't usually look attractive.)

Could has the same effect in the past:

It ***could be quite cold*** *in Cairo in January when I lived there.*
(= It was sometimes – or often – quite cold.)
He ***could be very naughty*** *when he was a little boy.*

Could can also have a future reference in this kind of context:

It ***could be quite cold when you get to Cairo****.*

Uses of modals, etc. to express permission and prohibition

11.19 Form of modals and related verbs: permission/prohibition

can/could/may/might [compare > 11.34, 11.36–38]:

Can I stay out late? *Could I stay out late?*	*You* (etc.) *can/can't/mustn't stay out late.*
May I stay out late? *Might I stay out late?*	*You* (etc.) *may/may not/mayn't/mustn't stay out late.*

can/could (= be free to)
present or **future reference**:

I can see him now/tomorrow.
I could see him now/tomorrow.

Verbs and verb phrases related in meaning to *can/could/may/might/mustn't*:

(not) be allowed to:	*You're (not) allowed to stay out late.*
(not) be permitted to:	*You're (not) permitted to stay out late.*
be forbidden to:	*You're forbidden to stay out late.*
be prohibited:	*Smoking is (strictly) prohibited.*
be not to:	*You're not to smoke.*
negative imperative:	*Don't smoke!*

11.20 Asking for permission/responding: 'can/could/may/might'

Requests for permission can be graded on a 'hesitancy scale', ranging from a blunt request to an extremely hesitant one. Requests for permission can refer to the present or future. The basic forms are:

Can
Could } ***I borrow*** *your umbrella (please)?*
May
Might

1 *Can* is the commonest and most informal:
Can I borrow *your umbrella (please)?*
A few (old-fashioned) native speakers still hold that *can* is the equivalent of *am/is/are able to* and therefore *may* must be used instead. The idea of e.g. asking for a favour is less strong in *can* than in *could/may/might*.

2 *Could* is more 'hesitant' and polite than *can*. We often use it when we are not sure permission will be granted:
Could I borrow *your umbrella (please)?*

3 *May* is more formal, polite and 'respectful' than *can* and *could*:
May I borrow *your umbrella (please)?*

4 *Might* is the most hesitant, polite and 'respectful' and is rather less common than the other three:
Might I borrow *your umbrella (please)?*

In practice, *can, could* and *may* are often interchangeable in 'neutral' requests.

Common responses with modals are: e.g.
– affirmative: *Of course you can/may.* (Not **could**/**might**)
– negative: *No, you can't/may not.* (Not **could not**/**might not**)

Numerous non-modal responses are possible ranging from the polite *Of course* (affirmative), *I'm afraid not, I'd rather you didn't* (negative), to blunt refusal like *Certainly not*. A polite refusal is usually accompanied by some kind of explanation (*I'm afraid you can't because...*).

Permission to ask an indiscreet question may be requested with the formulas *if I may ask* and (more tentative) *if I might ask*:
How much did you pay for this house ***if I may/might ask****?*

11.21 Asking for permission with 'can't' and 'couldn't'

Can't and *couldn't* are often used in place of *can* and *could* when we are pressing for an affirmative answer [> 13.6]:

Can't
Couldn't } ***I stay out*** *till midnight (please)?*

May I not...? is old-fashioned.
Mayn't I...? is unlikely.
Might I not...? is rare, but all these forms occur in formal style.

11.22 Very polite requests: 'can/could/may/might'

There are numerous variations on straightforward request forms to express degrees of politeness. *Possibly* is commonly added to make requests more polite. Requests may be hesitant:

Can/Could I *(possibly)*
Do you think I could/might } *use your phone?*
I wonder if I could/might

Or they may be over-cautious or obsequious:
Might I (possibly) be allowed to...*?*

11.23 Granting and refusing permission

Permission can be granted or refused as follows:

You { ***can (not)*** / ***may (not)*** } *watch TV for as long as you like.* (Not **could**) (Not **might**)

You may/may not carries the authority of the speaker and is the equivalent of 'I (personally) give you permission'. *You can/cannot* is more general and does not necessarily imply personal permission. Permission issuing from some other authority can be granted or withheld more emphatically with *be allowed to, be permitted to*, and *be forbidden to*, as follows:

You can/cannot or *You're allowed to/not allowed to*
You can/cannot or *You're permitted to/not permitted to* } *smoke here.*
You mustn't or *You're forbidden to*

Granting/refusing permission is not confined to 1st and 2nd persons:

Johnny/Frankie { ***can/can't*** / ***may/may not/mustn't*** } *stay up late.*

This can be extended to:
- rule-making e.g. for games: *Each player* ***may choose*** *five cards.*
- other contexts: *Candidates* ***may not attempt*** *more than three questions.*

Permission may also be given by a speaker with *shall* in the 2nd and 3rd persons (formal and literary):
You shall do *as you please.* (i.e. You have my permission to.)
He shall do *as he pleases.* (i.e. He has my permission to.)

Permission may also be denied with *shan't* in BrE only [> 9.36*n*.3]:
If you don't behave yourself, ***you shan't*** *go out/be allowed out.*
If he doesn't behave himself, ***he shan't*** *go out/be allowed out.*

Numerous alternative forms are available to express anything from mild refusal (*I'd rather you didn't if you don't mind*) to strong prohibition (*I forbid you to...*). Formal and strong statements with non-modal forms are often found in public notices [compare > 12.9.1]:
Thank you ***for not smoking****.* (i.e. please don't)
Passengers ***are requested to remain seated*** *till the aircraft stops.*
Trespassing ***is strictly forbidden****.*

11.24 Permission/prohibition in other tenses

The gaps in the 'defective' verbs *may* and *must* [> 11.4, 11.6.1] can be filled with the verb phrases *be allowed to* and the more formal *be permitted to*. Examples of other tenses:

present perfect: *Mrs James is in hospital and **hasn't been allowed to** have any visitors.*

past: *We **were allowed to** stay up till 11 last night.*

Could can only express past 'permission in general' [compare > 11.12.1]:

*When we were children we **could watch*** (or ***were allowed to watch***) *TV whenever we wanted to.*

11.25 Conditional sentences with 'could' and 'could have'

Could may imply 'would be allowed to':

*I **could** have an extra week's holiday if I asked for it.*

Could have + past participle can be used in place of *would have been allowed to* to show that permission was given but not used:

*You **could have** had an extra week's holiday. You asked for it.*
I said you could have it, but you didn't take it. [compare > 11.15]

11.26 'Can/could' = 'am/is/are free to': present or future

'Being free to' is often linked to the idea of 'having permission'. *Can*, in the sense of 'am/is/are free to', can be used to refer to the present or the future:

*I **can see** him **now**.* (= I am free to)
*I **can see** him **tomorrow**.* (= I am/will be free to)

Could expresses exactly the same idea, but is less definite:

*I **could see** him **now**.* (= I am free to)
*I **could see** him **tomorrow**.* (= I am/will be free to)

Compare *can/could* (= ability) which cannot be used to refer to the future [> 11.10, 11.16].

Uses of modals, etc. to express certainty and possibility

11.27 Certainty, possibility and deduction

If we are certain of our facts, we can make statements with *be* or any full verb [compare > 10.24]:

*Jane **is*** (or ***works***) *at home.* (a certain fact)

If we are referring to possibility, we can use combinations of *may*, *might* or *could* + verb:

*Jane **may/might/could be*** (or ***work***) *at home.* (a possibility)

We may draw a distinction between the expression of possibility in this way (which allows for speculation and guessing) and deduction based on evidence. Deduction [> 11.32], often expressed with *must be* and *can't be*, suggests near-certainty:

*Jane's light is on. She **must be** at home. She **can't be** out.*

11.28 Forms of tenses (certainty) versus modals (possibility)

certain (expressed by verb tenses)	**possible/less than certain** (expressed by *may*, *might* and *could*)
He is at home.	*He may/might/could be at home (now).*
He will be at home tomorrow.	*He may/might/could be at home tomorrow.*
He was at home yesterday.	*He may/might/could have been at home yesterday.*
He leaves at 9.	*He may/might/could leave at 9.*
He will leave tomorrow.	*He may/might/could leave tomorrow.*
He has left.	*He may/might/could have left.*
He left last night.	*He may/might/could have left last night.*
He will have left by 9.	*He may/might/could have left by 9.*
He is working today.	*He may/might/could be working today.*
He will be working today.	*He may/might/could be working today.*
He was working today.	*He may/might/could have been working today.*
He has been working all day.	*He may/might/could have been working all day.*
He will have been working all day.	*He may/might/could have been working all day.*

11.29 Notes on modal forms expressing possibility

1 *Should be* and *ought to be* to express possibility
In addition to the above examples, we can also express possibility with *should be* and *ought to be*:
John ***should be/ought to be*** *at home.*
John ***should be working/ought to be working****.*
John ***should have left/ought to have left*** *by tomorrow.* etc.
However, because *should* and *ought to* also express obligation [> 11.46] they can be ambiguous, so are not used as much as *may/might/could* to express possibility. For example, *He should have arrived* (*ought to have arrived*) *yesterday* could mean 'I think he probably has arrived' or 'He failed in his duty to arrive yesterday'.

2 Questions about possibility
When we are asking about possibility, we may use *Might...?, Could ...?* and sometimes *Can...?* and (rarely) *May...?*. (We do not normally use *should* and *ought to* in affirmative questions about possibility because of the risk of confusion with obligation):
Might/Could/Can *this be true?*
†***Might/Could*** *he know the answer?*
Might/Could/Can *he still be working?* (or *be still working*)
†***Might/Could*** *he be leaving soon?*
Might/Could/Can *he have been waiting long?*
†***Might/Could*** *he have left by tomorrow?*

†*Can* is not always possible in questions like these, probably because of the risk of confusion with *can* = ability [> 11.10]. However, in questions like *Can this be true?*, *can* often indicates disbelief. *Can* is possible in some indirect questions:
I wonder where he ***can have left*** *the key?*

3 Negative questions about possibility
Negative questions about possibility can be asked with *Mightn't* and *Couldn't*. *May not* (Not **Mayn't**) can sometimes be used, as can *Shouldn't* and *Oughtn't to*:
***Mightn't** he be at home now?* etc.
***Couldn't** he know the answer?* etc.

4 Negative possibility
Negative possibility is expressed with *may not, mightn't, can't* and *couldn't*, but not usually with *shouldn't* and *oughtn't to*:
*He **may not be*** (or ***have been***) *here.* etc.
*He **may not be*** (or ***have been***) ***working** late.* etc.
Can't + *be* often suggests disbelief:
*What you're saying **can't be** true! I can hardly believe it!*
Can may be used in negative indirect questions:
*I **don't think** he **can have left** home yet.*
or in semi-negatives: *He **can hardly be** at home yet. It's only 6.*

11.30 Modals on a scale of certainty

Degrees of certainty can be expressed on a scale:
*He **is** at home.* (= it's a certain fact: non-modal *be*)
*He **could be** at home.* (= doubtful possibility)
*He **should be** at home.* (= doubtful possibility)
*He **ought to be** at home.* (= doubtful possibility)
*He **may be** at home.* (= it's possible, but uncertain)
*He **might be** at home.* (= less certain than *may*)

*He **isn't** at home.* (= it's a certain fact)
*He **can't be** at home.* (= it's nearly certain)
*He **couldn't be** at home.* (= more 'tentative' than *can't*)
*He **may not be** at home.* (= possible, but uncertain)
*He **mightn't be** at home.* (= less certain than *may not*)
(See 11.29*ns*.1, 3 for *shouldn't* and *oughtn't to*)
(See under deduction [> 11.32], for *must be, can't be*, etc.)

In speech, the element of doubt is increased with heavy stress:
*He '**could** be at home* (i.e. but I very much doubt it).
Particular stress is also used in exclamations:
*It '**can't** be true! You '**can't** 'mean it! You '**must** be mistaken!*

11.31 Certain and uncertain responses to questions

Yes/No answers to questions can reflect varying degrees of certainty felt by the speaker. For example, a 'certain' question may elicit an 'uncertain' answer:

Does he like ice-cream?	(direct question)
– Yes, he does. No, he doesn't.	('certain' response)
– He might (do). He may (do). He could (do).	(possibility)
– He mightn't. He may not.	(uncertainty)

Similarly, an 'uncertain' question may elicit a 'certain' answer:

Can he still be working?	(disbelief)
Mightn't he be working?	(possibility)
– Yes, he is. No, he isn't.	('certain' response)

– *He might (be). He may (be).* (possibility)
– *He may not be. I don't think he can be.* (possibility)
– *He can't be. He couldn't be.* (disbelief)

Of course, any other answer, not necessarily involving the use of a modal verb, may be available, depending on circumstances:
– *I don't know. I'm not sure. I don't think so.* etc.

Be and *have been* are normally used in answers to questions with *be*:
***Is** he ill? – He may **be**.*
***Was** he ill? – He may **have been**.*

Do often replaces other verbs:
***Will you catch** an early train? – I may **do**.*
***Has he received** my message? – He **could have/could have done**.*

Uses of modals to express deduction

11.32 Examples of modal forms for deduction

must and ***can't***

present reference:

Certainty expressed by verb tenses:

He is here.	*He lives here.*	*He is leaving.*
He isn't here.	*He doesn't live here.*	*He isn't leaving.*

Deduction expressed by *must be* and *can't be*:

He must be here.	*He must live here.*	*He must be leaving.*
He can't be here.	*He can't live here.*	*He can't be leaving.*

perfect and **past reference**:

Certainty expressed by verb tenses:

He was here.	*He has left/He left early.*	*He has been/was working late.*

Deduction expressed by *must have been* and *can't/couldn't have been*:

He must have been here.	*He must have left early.*	*He must have been working late.*
He can't have been here.	*He can't have left early.*	*He can't have been working late.*
He couldn't have been here.	*He couldn't have left early.*	*He couldn't have been working late.*

11.33 Expressing deduction with 'must be' and 'can't be', etc.

The distinction between possibility (often based on speculation) and deduction (based on evidence) has already been drawn [> 11.27]. The strongest and commonest forms to express deduction are *must* and *can't*. For teaching and learning purposes, it is necessary to establish the following clearly:

1 *can't be* (Not **mustn't be**) is the negative of *must be*.
2 *can't have been* (Not **mustn't have been**) is the negative of *must have been*.

Have to/have got to be (affirmative) can express deduction in AmE:
*This **has to be/has got to be** the most stupid film I have ever seen.*

Compare deduction [secondary use of modals > 11.3–4, 11.9] in:

*He **can't be** thirsty.* *He **must be** hungry.*
*He **can't have been** thirsty.* *He **must have been** hungry.*

with inescapable obligation [primary use of modals > 11.2, 11.4, 11.9] in:

*He **mustn't be** careless.* *He **must be** careful.*
*He **didn't have to be** at the dentist's.* *He **had to be** at the doctor's.*

We also use *may/might/could* and *should/ought to* for making deductions (as well as for expressing possibility); and, when we are almost certain of our evidence, we may use *will* and *won't*:

*That **will be** Roland. I can hear him at the door.*
*That **will have been** Roland. He said he'd be back at 7.*
*That **won't be** Roland. I'm not expecting him yet.*
*That **won't have been** Roland. I'm not expecting him till 7.*

Again [> 11.31], it is possible to give varying responses to a question:

Is Roland in his room?
*– Yes, **he is**. No, **he isn't**.* (certainty)
*– Yes, **he must be**. I heard him come in.* (deduction)
*– No, **he won't be**. He had to go out.* (near-certainty)
*– No, **he can't be**. There's no light in his room.* (deduction)

Uses of modals for offers, requests, suggestions

11.34 General information about offers, requests and suggestions

Modal verbs are used extensively for 'language acts' or **functions** such as offering, asking for things, expressing preferences. Fine shades of meaning are conveyed not only by the words themselves, but particularly by stress, intonation, and gesture. (Note that we can also make suggestions, etc. with non-modal forms, e.g. *Have a drink, Let's go to the zoo*). In this section, offers, requests, etc. are considered from six points of view under two headings:

11.34.1 Things and substances

1 Offering things and substances + appropriate responses.
2 Requests for things and substances + appropriate responses.

11.34.2 Actions

3 Making suggestions, inviting actions + appropriate responses.
4 Requesting others to do things for you + appropriate responses.
5 Offering to do things for others + appropriate responses.
6 Suggestions that include the speaker.

11.35 Things and substances: offers with modals

11.35.1 Typical offers inviting Yes/No responses

Can/Could I offer you }
Will/Won't you have } *a sandwich/some coffee?*
Would/Wouldn't you like }

11.35.2 Typical responses

There are many non-modal forms (*Yes please, No thank you*, etc.) and a few modal ones:

Yes, I'd like one/some please. Yes, I'd love one/some please.

However, we don't usually repeat the modal when we refuse an offer. A reply like *No, I won't* in answer to *Will you have...?* could sound rude [> 11.74.1].

11.35.3 Typical offers with 'What'

What will you have? What would you like to have?
What would you prefer? What would you rather have?

11.36 Things and substances: requests with modals

11.36.1 Typical requests inviting Yes/No responses [> 11.19–20, 13.6]

Can/Could/May/Might I have a sandwich/some coffee (please)?

11.36.2 Typical responses

Of course you can/may. (Not **could/might** [compare > 11.23])
No, you can't/may not (I'm afraid).

(These answers with modals would be likely where e.g. a parent is addressing a child. Adult responses would be e.g. *Certainly* or *I'm afraid there isn't any*, etc.)

11.37 Actions: suggestions/invitations with modals

11.37.1 Typical suggestions inviting Yes/No responses

Will you/Won't you } *come for a walk (with me)?*
Would you/Wouldn't you like to }

11.37.2 Typical responses

(Yes,) I'd like to. I'd love to.
(No,) I'd prefer not to, thank you.

Note that *to* must follow *like, love*, etc. [> 16.17]. Negative responses like *No, I won't* are not appropriate [> 11.74.1].

11.37.3 Typical inquiry with 'What' to invite suggestions

What would you like to do?

11.38 Actions: using modals to ask someone to do something

11.38.1 Typical requests inviting Yes/No responses [> 11.19–20]

Will you...?, Would you...? in these requests refer to willingness. *Can you...?, Could you...?* refer to ability.

Will you (please) }
Can/Could you (please) } *open the window (for me)?*
Would you (please) }
Would you like to }
Would you mind opening the window (for me)?

Will/Would you sounds even more polite with the addition of *kindly*, and *can/could* with the addition of *possibly* [compare > 11.22]:

Will/Would you kindly...? Can/Could you possibly...?

We cannot use *May you...?* in requests for help.

11.38.2 Typical responses

Yes, of course (I will). No, I'm afraid I can't (at the moment).

11.39 Actions: using modals to offer to do things for others

11.39.1 Typical offers to do things [> 11.19–20]

Offers beginning *Shall I...?, Shall we...?* are very common:

Can I/Could I/Shall I open the window (for you)?
Would you like me to open the window (for you)?
That's the phone. I'll get it for you, (shall I)?
What shall/can I do for you?

And note very polite offers with *may* in: e.g.

May I take your coat?

11.39.2 Typical responses

The usual responses are *Yes please, No thank you*, or tag responses like *Can/Could/Would you? – that's very kind*, but not *Yes, you can/No, you can't*, which could sound rude.

11.40 Actions: suggestions that include the speaker

11.40.1 Typical suggestions inviting Yes/No responses

Shall we go for a swim? We can/could/might go for a swim.

11.40.2 Typical responses

Yes, let's, (shall we)? [compare > 16.4.1]
No, I'd rather we didn't./No, I'd rather not.

11.40.3 Typical inquiries with 'What'

What shall/can/could we do this afternoon?

Expressing wishes with 'wish', 'if only', etc.

11.41 The expression of wishes

The verb *wish* can be followed by *to* and can be used like *want to* in formal style to express an immediate desire:

I wish to (or ***want to***) ***apply*** *for a visa.*

In addition, we can express hypothetical wishes and desires with:

- the verb *wish*: often for something that might happen.
- the phrase *if only*: often to express longing or regret.
- the phrases *it's (high) time* and *it's about time* to express future wishes and impatience that a course of action is overdue.

After *wish, if only, it's (high) time, it's about time*, we use:

- the **past** tense to refer to **present** time.
- the **past perfect** tense to refer to **past** time.
- *would* and *could* to make general wishes or refer to the future.

In other words, we 'go one tense back' [compare > 15.13*n*.3].

Though *wish* and *if only* are often used interchangeably, *if only* expresses more strongly the idea that the situation wished for does not exist, whereas *wish* is used for something that might happen. Details follow.

11.42 The verb 'wish' and the phrase 'if only'

11.42.1 Present reference: 'wish/if only' with 'be' + complement

After *wish* and *if only* we may use:
– the simple past of *be*:
I wish/If only Tessa was *here now.*
– the subjunctive [> 11.75.1] of *be*, i.e. *were* after all persons.
This is formal and has the effect of making a wish more doubtful:
I wish/If only Tessa were *here now.*
Wish and *if only* can also be followed by the past progressive:
I wish/If only the sun was (or ***were***) ***shining*** *at this moment.*
Compare *hope* + simple present or future for an immediate 'wish':
I hope he is *on time.* ***I hope he won't be*** *late.* (Not **I wish**) [> 9.37.3]

11.42.2 Present reference: 'wish/if only' + verbs other than 'be'

I wish/If only I knew *the answer to your question.*
I wish/If only I didn't have to *work for a living.*
If only (but not *wish*) will also combine with the simple present:
If only he gets *this job, it will make a great deal of difference.*
Here, *if only* functions like *if* in Type 1 conditionals [> 14.4] and that is why the present (which has a future reference) can be used.

11.42.3 Past reference with 'wish' and 'if only'

– *be* + complement: ***I wish/If only I had been*** *here yesterday.*
– verbs other than *be*: ***I wish/If only you had let me know*** *earlier.*
I wish/If only we had been travelling *yesterday when the weather was fine.*

In sentences like the above, *if only* particularly expresses regret:
If only I had been *here yesterday. The accident would never have happened.*
Compare:
I wish I had been *here yesterday. You all seem to have had such a good time.* (a simple wish, not the expression of regret)

11.42.4 'Would' and 'could' after 'wish' and 'if only'

I wish you would/wouldn't often functions like a polite imperative.
Because the wish can easily be fulfilled, *if only* is less likely:
I wish you would *be quiet.*
I wish you wouldn't *make so much noise.*

We must use *could* and not *would* after *I* and *We*:
I wish I could *be you.*
If only we could *be together.*
I wish I could *swim.* ***I wish I could have been*** *with you.*

Would expresses willingness; *could* expresses ability:
I wish he would come *tomorrow.* (i.e. I don't know if he wants to)
I wish he could come *tomorrow.* (i.e. I'm sure he can't)
I wish Tessa could have come *to my party.* (i.e. she wasn't able to)

Wishes expressed with *would* at the beginning of a sentence have either become obsolete (*Would that it were true!*) or have become fossilized idioms (*Would to God I knew! Would to God I had known!*)

11.42.5 The position of 'only' after 'if'

Only can be separated from *if* and can be placed:

- after *be*: *If he **was/were only** here now!*
- before the past participle: *If I had **only known**!*
- after the modal: *If you **would only** try harder!*

Though the separation of *only* from *if* is common in exclamations (as above), it is also possible in longer sentences:

*If more people were **only** prepared to be as generous as you are, many children's lives would be saved.* (***If only** more people...*)

11.42.6 The use of 'wish' and 'if only' in short responses

Short responses can be made with *wish* and *if only*:

It would be nice if Tessa was/were/could be here now!
*– **I wish/If only she was!/she were!/she could be!***
*You should have come with us. – **I wish/If only I had!***
*I can help you with that box. – **I wish/If only you would!***

11.43 'It's (high) time' and 'It's about time'

These expressions are used with the past tense or the subjunctive [> 11.42.1, 11.75.1] to refer to the present and future:

***It's (high) time** he **was** (or **were**) **taught** a lesson.*
***It's about time** he **learnt** to look after himself.*
(= the time has come)

Could (but not *would*) is sometimes possible:

***Isn't it about time** our baby **could walk**?*

Negatives are not used after *it's (high) time* and *it's about time*.
Short responses are possible with these expressions:

I still haven't thanked Aunt Lucy for her present.
*– **It's time you did.*** (you're taking too long over it)

Compare the use of *it's time* in:

*We've enjoyed the evening, but **it's time (for us) to go**.*
(i.e. the time has now arrived for us to go)
*We've enjoyed the evening, but **it's time we went**.*
(i.e. we should probably have left before this)

Expressing preferences with 'would rather' and 'would sooner'

11.44 'Would rather/sooner' to express preference

Would + *rather/sooner* + bare infinitive [> 16.5] expresses our personal preference, or enables us to talk about someone else's. This can refer to present time:

***I'd rather/sooner be** a miner than a bank clerk.*
***He'd rather (not) go** by car.*

or to past time:

*If I'd lived in 1400, **I'd rather have been** a knight than a monk.*
*If she'd had the chance, **she'd rather have lived** 100 years ago.*

In negative responses, we can omit the infinitive:

*Are you coming with us? – **I'd rather not**.*

*Would you rather have been a knight? – **I'd rather not (have been)**.*

Would rather/sooner can be modified by *far* and *(very) much*:

***I'd far** (or **much**) **rather** be happy than rich.*

***I'd far** (or **much**) **sooner** be young than old.*

11.45 'Would rather/sooner' + clause

Would rather and *would sooner* can introduce a clause with its own subject (different from the subject of *would rather/sooner*). We use this construction when we want to say what we would prefer someone or something else to do or to be:

*I'd rather/sooner **he/Jack** (etc.) left on an earlier train.*

Note the use of past tenses after *I'd rather* + clause:

– the past with present or future reference:

***I'd rather you were** happy (or **weren't** unhappy).*

***I'd rather she sat** (or **didn't sit**) next to me.*

– the past perfect with past reference:

***I'd rather you had been/hadn't been** present.*

***I'd rather he had told/hadn't told** me about it.*

When expressing negative preferences (to refer to the present or future), we can use *didn't* to avoid repeating the main verb:

*You always go without me and **I'd rather you didn't**.*

We can use *hadn't* in the same way to refer to the past:

*Katie **went** by car and **I'd rather she hadn't**.*

Short responses to express preferences are possible as follows:

present and future: *Frank wants to buy a motorbike. – **I'd rather he didn't**.*

past: *I've told everyone about it. – **I'd rather you hadn't**.*

Advisability, duty/obligation and necessity

11.46 Examples of forms expressing advisability, etc.

present advisability	**past advisability not acted upon**
I should stop smoking. *I ought to stop smoking.* *I'd better stop smoking* (I still smoke.)	*I should have stopped smoking.* *I ought to have stopped smoking.* (I was advised to stop but ignored the advice.)
present inescapable obligation	**past inescapable obligation**
I must stop smoking. (I am obliged to stop smoking and I shall: it is my duty.)	*I had to stop smoking.* (I was obliged to stop smoking and I did: it was my duty.)

For *should* and *ought to* in indirect speech [> 15.13*n*.6].
For the ambiguity of *should have* and *ought to have* [> 11.29*n*.1].
For the uses of *must* and *had to* in indirect speech [15.13*n*.6].

11.47 Advisability → necessity: 'a scale of choice'

We can use modals and other verbs to express advisability on a scale which reflects a degree of choice. This scale may vary according to the subjective point of view of the speaker.

advisability	*should*:	generally means 'in my opinion, it is advisable to' or 'it is (your) duty'.
↓	*ought to*:	can be slightly stronger than *should* in that it is sometimes used to refer to regulations or duties imposed from the outside: *You ought to vote* (= it is your public duty). *Should* is more likely than *ought to* in questions and negatives.
	had better:	is stronger than *should* and *ought to*. It is used to recommend future action on a particular occasion, not in general. It carries a hint of threat, warning or urgency: *You'd better see a doctor*.
	am/is/are to:	can be used for instructions [compare > 9.48.1]: *You're to report for duty at 7.*
	need (to):	(= it is necessary to).
	have to:	is an alternative to *must* and fills the gaps in that defective verb [> 11.4].
	have got to:	like *have to*, but more informal.
necessity	*must*:	like *have to* and *have got to*, suggests inescapable obligation. In the speaker's opinion there is no choice at all.

11.48 'Must', 'have to' and 'have got to'

As far as meaning is concerned, these three forms are largely interchangeable. However, there are differences between them. When used in the first person, *have to* and *have got to* (often pronounced / hævtə/ and /həv'gɒtə/ in everyday speech) can refer to an external authority and might be preferable to *must* in: e.g.

We have to/We've got to *send these VAT forms back before the end of the month.* (i.e. we are required to do so by law)

On the other hand, *must* can express a speaker's authority over himself and might be preferable to *have to/have got to* in:

I/We *really* ***must*** *do something about the weeds in this garden.* (i.e. but I don't have to account to anybody if I don't)

In other persons (*you*, etc.) *must* conveys more strongly than *have to* the idea of inescapable obligation or urgency in: e.g.

You must *phone home at once. It's urgent.*

Have to and *have got to* are interchangeable for single actions:

I have to/have got to *check the oil level in the car.*

However they are not always interchangeable when we refer to habitual actions. The following are possible:

I have to/I have got to *leave home every morning at 7.30.*

But when one-word adverbs of frequency (*always, sometimes*, etc.) are used *have to* is always preferable to *have got to*:

***I often have to** get up at 5. **Do you ever have to** get up at 5?*

Must (not *have to* or *have got to*) is used in public notices or documents expressing commands:

*Cyclists **must** dismount. Candidates **must** choose five questions.*

We generally prefer *Must you...?* to *Do you have to...?/Have you got to...?* to mean 'Can't you stop yourself...?'

***Must you always** interrupt me when I'm speaking?*

Must is also used in pressing invitations, such as:

***You really must** come and see us some time.*

and in emphatic advice, such as:

***You really must** take a holiday this year.*

Even when heavily stressed, these uses of *must* do not mean or imply 'inescapable obligation'.

11.49 'Need' as a modal

Need has only some of the characteristics of modal verbs [> 11.1] in that it occurs in questions, *Need you go?*, and negatives, *You needn't go* [> 11.52–53]. In Yes/No questions, a negative answer is often expected:

***Need you leave** so soon?* (= surely not/I hope not)

Yes/No questions with *Need?* can be answered with *must* or *needn't*:

***Need I type** this letter again? – Yes, **you must**./No, **you needn't**.*

Need + *have* + past participle behaves in the same way:

***Need you have told him** about my plans?*
***You needn't have told him** about my plans.*

Yes/No questions with *Need...have...?* can be answered:

*Yes, **I had to**.* (no choice) *No, **I needn't have**.* (I had a choice)

Need as a modal verb also occurs in combination with negative-type adverbs like *hardly, never, seldom, rarely* and *scarcely* to make what are effectively negative statements:

***She need never know** what you have just told me.*
***I need hardly tell you** how badly I feel about her departure.*
***All you need do** is to take a taxi from the airport.* (i.e. you need to do nothing except take a taxi)

Need can also occur in clauses with a negative main clause:

***I don't think you need** leave yet.*

Need as a modal is mostly used in the negative (*I needn't go* [> 11.53]) to express lack of necessity. Otherwise we generally use the full verb *need to* (used like any regular verb):

***I need to/I needed to** go to the dentist this morning.*
***I don't need to/I didn't need to** go to the dentist.*
***When will you next need to** go to the dentist?*
***Why did you need to** go to the dentist?* etc.

11.50 Advisability/necessity: the present and future

Should, ought to, etc. refer to present time (except in indirect speech [> 15.13*n*.6]). With the addition of adverbials such as *this afternoon, tomorrow*, etc., they refer to future time.

I	***should ought to had better have to have got to must***	***be leave be leaving***	*at the office (before 9 tomorrow). (before 9 tomorrow). (before 9 tomorrow).*

Will/shall will combine with *have to* and *need to* (full verb) for explicit future reference:

I'll	***need to have to***	***be leave be leaving***	*at the office before 9 (tomorrow). London before 9 (tomorrow). London before 9 (tomorrow).*

11.51 Advisability/necessity: the perfect and past

Reference to the past can be made in the following ways:

I	***should have ought to have***	***been left been leaving***	*at the office before 9. London before 9. London before 9.*
I	***had to***	***be leave be leaving***	*at the office before 9. London before 9. London before 9.*

Should have and *ought to have* could be followed (here) by *but I wasn't/I didn't* to suggest that whatever was advisable or necessary did not happen:

I should have left *London before 9,* ***but I didn't****.*

Had to suggests that the action was performed in the past because this was necessary. It could be followed by *and I was/did*:

I had to leave *London before 9* ***and I did****.*

The form *had got to* also exists, but it is not always suitable; *had to* is generally preferred.

When other tenses are required, appropriate forms of *have to* must be used to fill the gaps of the defective modal *must* [> 11.4]:

I have had to remind *him several times to return my book.*
Because of the bus strike ***I've been having to walk*** *to work every day.*
The reason for our late arrival was that ***we had had to wait*** *for hours while they checked the plane before take-off.*
If he had asked me, ***I would have had to tell him*** *the truth.*

Lack of necessity, inadvisability, prohibition

11.52 Examples of modal forms to express inadvisability, etc.

present lack of necessity *You needn't go there.* Or: *You don't need to go there.* *You don't have to go there.* *You haven't got to go there.*	**past lack of necessity** *You needn't have gone there.* (= you went there unnecessarily) *You didn't have to go there.* Or: *You didn't need to go there.* (= there was no necessity to go there, whether you did go or not)
present inadvisability *You shouldn't start smoking.* *You ought not to start smoking.*	**past inadvisability, not acted upon** *You shouldn't have started smoking.* *You oughtn't to have started smoking.* (but e.g. you ignored this advice)
present prohibition *You can't park here.* *You mustn't park here.*	**failure to observe a prohibition** *You shouldn't have parked there.* *You ought not to have parked there.*

For *should(n't)* and *ought(n't) to* in indirect speech [> 15.13*n*.6].
Shouldn't have and *oughtn't to have* are not ambiguous in the way that *should have* and *ought to have* can sometimes be ambiguous [compare > 11.29*n*.1].
For the use of *must(n't)* in indirect speech [> 15.13*n*.6].
Have to can replace *must* in the present [> 11.48, 11.50], but *don't/didn't have to* cannot replace *mustn't* in the present and past [> 11.55, 11.57.1].

11.53 Lack of necessity: 'needn't/don't have to/haven't got to'

Lack of necessity can be expressed by *needn't, don't have to* and the more informal *haven't got to* (where *got* is often stressed):

*You **needn't*** }
*You **don't have to*** } ***work** such long hours.*
*You **haven't got to*** }

(i.e. you can work fewer hours, if you choose to)

The above forms can be used to express the subjective point of view of the speaker that the listener has a choice or has permission not to do something. Note that *(You) haven't to* is a regional BrE variation of *(You) don't have to*

11.54 Inadvisability → prohibition: 'a scale of choice'

We can use modals and other verbs to express inadvisability → prohibition on a scale which reflects a degree of choice. This scale may vary according to the subjective view of the speaker. This is particularly the case when we are addressing others directly with *you*, or when we are referring to others with *he, she*, and *they*. At one end of the scale (see next page) the advice (however strong) can be ignored. At the other end of the scale, the prohibition is total and, in the speaker's opinion, there is no choice at all.

inadvisability	*shouldn't*:	generally means 'in my opinion, it is inadvisable to/it is (your) duty not to'.
↓	*oughtn't to*:	can be slightly stronger than *shouldn't*. It is sometimes used to refer to regulations and duties imposed from the outside. *You oughtn't to park so near the crossing* suggests 'it's your public duty not to do this'.
	had better not:	is stronger than *shouldn't* and *oughtn't to.* It is used to recommend future action on a particular occasion, not in general. It carries a hint of threat, warning, or urgency: *You'd better not overtake here!*
	am/is/are not to:	can be used for instructions [> 9.48.1].
	can't:	is nearly as strong as *mustn't* to suggest something is prohibited: *You can't park here.*
prohibition	*mustn't*:	conveys absolute prohibition. In the opinion of the speaker, there is no choice at all. This opinion may be subjective or may be supported by some outside authority, as in *You mustn't turn left.* (e.g. there's a road sign forbidding it).

11.55 'Mustn't', 'needn't', 'don't have to', 'haven't got to'

Though *must*, *have to* and *have got to* are generally interchangeable in the affirmative [> 11.48], *don't have to* and *haven't got to* can never replace *mustn't* to convey prohibition. Like *needn't* they convey lack of necessity [> 11.56.1].

Mustn't conveys the strongest possible opinion of the speaker:

You really ***mustn't say*** *things like that in front of your mother.*
Julian ***mustn't hitchhike*** *to Turkey on his own.*

Prohibition reflecting external authority (in e.g. public notices, documents) is often expressed as *must not* (in full):

Life belts ***must not*** *be removed.*
Candidates ***must not*** *attempt more than four questions.*

Haven't got to should be avoided with adverbs of frequency (*always*, *sometimes*, etc.) for reasons of style. So:

I { ***needn't always*** / ***don't always have to*** } ***be*** *at the office by 9.*

is usually preferred to: *I haven't always got to be...*

11.56 Lack of necessity, etc.: present/future

11.56.1 Lack of necessity: 'needn't', 'don't have to', 'haven't got to'

Reference to present or future time can be made as follows. These forms are normally interchangeable [compare > 11.57.1]:

I	**needn't** / **don't have to**	**be**	*at the office (until 9 tomorrow).*
		leave	*until 9 (tomorrow).*
		be leaving	*until 9 (tomorrow).*

(*Haven't got to* is not generally used with progressive forms.)

Won't (and *shan't* in BrE [> 9.36*n*.3]) will combine with *have to* and *need to* (full verb) for explicit reference to the future:

I won't need to/have to be *at the office before 9 tomorrow.*

11.56.2 **Inadvisability/prohibition: 'shouldn't/oughtn't to/mustn't', etc.**

You ***shouldn't/oughtn't to/can't/mustn't be*** *late for meetings.* ('present/habitual')

You ***shouldn't/oughtn't to/had better not/can't/mustn't be*** *late tomorrow.* (future)

Shouldn't, oughtn't to, had better not, can't and *mustn't* are used to refer to the future, although they do not have future forms. Possible alternatives are:

Shouldn't/oughtn't to/had better not can be replaced by:

It won't be advisable *(for her) to play games for the next month.*

Can't and *mustn't* can be replaced by:

We ***won't be allowed*** *to park here for long.*

You ***will be forbidden*** *to enter the courtroom before 9.30.*

Traffic in this street ***will be prohibited*** *by law.*

11.57 Lack of necessity/inadvisability/prohibition: perfect/past

11.57.1 **Lack of necessity: 'needn't have', 'didn't have to', 'didn't need to'**

These forms mean roughly the same thing in: e.g.

I needn't have gone *to the office yesterday.*

I didn't 'have to (or ***I didn't 'need to***) ***go*** *to the office yesterday.*

(*have* and *need* are stressed)

(= I went there, but it was unnecessary)

When *have* and *need* are unstressed, they mean something different from *needn't have*:

I didn't have to/I didn't need to go *to the office yesterday.*

(= I knew it was unnecessary and I didn't go)

Because modals are defective [> 11.4, 11.6.1] appropriate alternatives must be used in some tenses:

It wouldn't have been necessary *to change at Leeds if we had caught the earlier train.*

I haven't had to cancel *my appointment after all.*

If he had asked me, ***I would have had to tell*** *him the truth.*

11.57.2 **Inadvisability: 'shouldn't have' and 'oughtn't to have'**

Both these forms suggest criticism of an action:

You ***shouldn't have*** / ***oughtn't to have*** ***paid*** *the plumber in advance.*

or failure to observe a prohibition:

You ***shouldn't have*** / ***oughtn't to have*** ***stopped*** *on the motorway.*

Uses of modals to express habit

11.58 Modal forms expressing habit

will:	*He will always complain if he gets the opportunity.*
would:	*When we were students we would often stay up all night.*
used to:	*Jackie used to make all her own dresses.*
	Fred never used to be so bad-tempered.

11.59 Notes on the form of 'used to'

1 *Used to* occurs only in the simple past form.

2 Questions and negatives with *used to* may be formed without the auxiliary *do*:

***Used he to** live in Manchester? **You usedn't (used not) to** smoke.*

These forms are relatively rare. *Usedn't* /ju:sənt/ is probably avoided because it is difficult to say and spell. *Did* and *didn't* are more commonly used to form questions and negatives. In such instances, *use* is often treated as an infinitive in writing:

***Did he use to** live in Manchester? **You didn't use to** smoke.*

In spoken English, we cannot tell whether a speaker is saying *Did he use to* or *Did he used to*, since what we hear is /ju:st/ not /ju:zd/ as in *used* (= made use of). The forms *did (he) use to* and *(he) didn't use to* are logical on grounds of grammatical *form* (compare *didn't do*, Not **didn't did**/**didn't done**). We can avoid the problem of the negative by using *never* [compare > 7.40.1]:

*Fred **never used to** be so difficult.*

3 Question tags [> 13.17–18] and short responses are formed with *didn't*, rather than *usedn't*:

*He **used to** live in Manchester, **didn't he**?*

Note these short answers, etc. [compare > 13.5]:

*Did you use to smoke? – Yes, **I did**.* or *Yes, **I used to**.*
*– No, **I didn't**.* or *No, **I didn't use to**.*
(*No, I used not to* is rare.)

*He **used to** live in Manchester and so **did** I.* (Not **used**)

11.60 Past habit: 'used to' and the simple past

Used to refers only to the past. If we wish to refer to *present* habit, we must use the simple present tense (Not **I use to**) [> 9.6–8]. We rely on *used to* to refer to habits that we no longer have, so there is a contrast between past and present. This contrast is often emphasized with expressions like *but now...*, *but not...any more/any longer* which combine with the simple present:

***I used to** smoke, **but I don't any more/any longer**.*
***I never used to** eat a large breakfast, **but I do now**.*

However, *used to* can refer simply to discontinued habit without implying a contrast with the present. For *be used to* [> 10.26.1, 16.56]. If we wish to use the simple past to refer to past habit, we always need a time reference. Compare:

I ***collected*** *stamps* ***when I was a child****.* (simple past + time reference)
I ***used to collect*** *stamps (when I was a child).* (time reference not necessary with *used to*, but may be included)

Used to is not possible with *since* [> 7.31] and *for* [> 7.32]:
I ***lived*** *in the country* ***for three years****.* (Not **used to live**)

For the past progressive referring to repeated actions [> 9.20.4].

11.61 Past habit: 'used to', 'would' and the simple past

We can refer to past habit in the following ways:
When I worked on a farm, I ***always used to get up*** *at 5 a.m.*
When I worked on a farm, I ***would always get up*** *at 5 a.m.*
When I worked on a farm, I ***always got up*** *at 5 a.m.*

Would can be used in place of *used to*, but, like the simple past, it always requires a time reference. We often use it to talk about regular activities, particularly in narrative, or when we are reminiscing. *Would* is never used at the beginning of a story: the scene must first be set with the simple past or *used to*. In familiar narrative, *would* can be reduced to *'d*:
When I was a boy we always spent (or *used to spend*) *our holidays on a farm. We'd get up at 5 and we'd help milk the cows. Then we'd return to the farm kitchen, where we would eat a huge breakfast.*

11.62 'Used to' to describe past states, etc.

Used to (not *would*) combines with *be, have* (possession) and other stative verbs [> 9.3] to describe past states:
I ***used to be*** *a waiter, but now I'm a taxi-driver.* (past state)
I ***used to have*** *a beard, but I've shaved it off.* (past possession)

If we use past tenses instead of *used to*, we need a time reference:
I ***was*** *a waiter* ***years ago****, but now I'm a taxi-driver.*

11.63 'Will/would' to describe characteristic habit/behaviour

Will can sometimes be used in place of the simple present and *would* in place of the simple past to refer to a person's characteristic habits or behaviour. *Will* and *would* are unstressed when used in this way:
In fine weather, he ***will often sit*** *in the sun for hours.*
As he grew older, he ***would often talk*** *about his war experiences.*

And note common fixed phrases with *will*:
Boys will be boys*.* ***Accidents will happen****.*

Will and *would* (usually with heavy stress) are often used accusingly to criticize a person's characteristic behaviour:
Harriet ***will keep leaving*** *her things all over the floor.*
That's just typical of Harry. He ***would*** *say a thing like that!*

Sometimes *will* used in this way implies insistence, or wilful refusal to follow advice. Note that although *will* is not normally used after *if* [> 14.4–6, 14.24.2], it can be in this sense:
If you 'will (stressed) ***go*** *to bed so late, no wonder you're tired.*

11.64 'Will' and 'would' to describe natural tendency

Like the simple present tense [> 9.6–8] *will* (with a 3rd person subject) can refer to general truths or to the qualities of things; *would* can sometimes refer to the past:

*Water **will boil** at 100°C. It **won't boil** at under 100°C.*
*I planted a vine last year but it **wouldn't grow** because it didn't get enough sun.*

In the same way *will* and *would* can suggest 'has the capacity to'. *Would* is more tentative than *will*:

*That container **will/won't** hold a gallon.* (definite statement)
*That container **would/wouldn't** hold a gallon.* ('tentative')

'Dare' as a modal verb and as a full verb

11.65 Forms of 'dare' as a modal verb and as a full verb

Like *need dare* can work as a modal verb or as a full verb with little or no difference in meaning.

present reference	**past reference**
modal verb:	**modal verb**:
dare/daren't/don't dare + go	*dared/dared not/didn't dare + go*
full regular verb:	**full regular verb**:
dare/don't dare + to go	*dared/didn't dare + to go*

11.66 Notes on the forms of 'dare'

Dare as a modal is not nearly as common as *need* and *used to* as modals. Its function is generally filled by verb phrases like *(not) be afraid to* or *(not) have the courage to* [> 11.67].

Like modal *need* [> 11.49], modal *dare* occurs in questions and negatives and is rare in the affirmative, unless a negative is expressed or implied:

***Dare you do** it? – I **daren't do** it.*
*I **hardly dare tell** him what happened.* (implied negative)

Questions/negatives are more commonly formed with *do/does/did*:

***Do** you **dare tell** him? – I **don't dare tell** him.*
***Did** you **dare tell** him? – I **didn't dare tell** him.*

Such forms are anomalous because *dare* is like a full verb in taking *do*, but like an auxiliary in taking a bare infinitive.

To can be used after *dare* in the examples with *do/don't* and *did/didn't*, making it a full verb, but not changing its meaning:

***Do** you **dare to tell** him? – I **don't dare to tell** him.* etc.

Both *dare not* and *dared not* can be used to refer to the past, though this is more formal:

*Mother **dare(d) not tell** father she'd given away his old jacket.*

Dare cannot combine with *be* + progressive, but it can combine with *have* + past participle, though this is not very common:

*I didn't like their new house, though **I daren't have said so**.*

11.67 The use of 'dare' to express courage or lack of courage

Daren't is used in the present (to refer to present or future time) and can be replaced by *am/is/are afraid to*:

I'd like to ask for the day off, but ***I daren't****.* (= I'm afraid to)

Don't dare to (regular verb) is acceptable in the present:

I'd like to ask for the day off, but ***I don't dare (to)****.*

Didn't dare to is used in the past:

I wanted to ask for the day off, but ***I didn't dare (to)****.*

Dare can also be used in the affirmative, but this is less common:

Sally is the only person in our class who ***dares (to)*** *answer Miss Thompson back.*

11.68 'Dare' for 'challenging'

Dare as a full transitive verb is used especially by children when challenging each other to do something dangerous:

I dare you to *jump off that wall.*
I didn't want to do it, but ***he dared me (to)****.*

11.69 'Dare' for expressing outrage

Dare, as a modal, is often used to reprimand and express outrage or strong disapproval. It is especially common after *How*:

How dare you! How dare she *suggest such a thing!*
Don't you dare speak *to me like that again!*
You dare raise *your voice!* [imperative, > 9.54]
I'm going to smash this vase! – ***Just you dare!***

Dared can be used after *How* in: e.g.

How dared he *tell everybody I was looking for a new job!*

11.70 The use of 'daresay'

The verbs *dare* and *say* can combine into a single verb, *daresay*, (sometimes spelt as two separate words, *dare say*) which can be used in the first person singular and plural (present tense only) to mean *I suppose* or *it's possible*:

I daresay *you'll phone me if you're going to be late tonight.*

Or in the sense of 'accept what you say':

This is supposed to be a cheap restaurant. It says so in this guidebook. – ***I daresay*** *it does, but look at these prices!*

Other uses of modal auxiliaries

11.71 'May' in formulas for expressing wishes

May occurs in fixed phrases like:

May God be *with you!* ***May you live*** *to be a hundred!*

May can also be used in the sense of 'We hope very much that...':

May there never be *a nuclear war!*

11.72 'May/might'

11.72.1 'May/might (just) as well'

May as well and *might as well* can be used interchangeably to express the idea 'it makes no difference':

*It's not very far, so **we may/might as well go** on foot.*

May as well and *might as well* can differ as follows:

Shall we walk or take a bus?
*– **We may/might as well walk**.* (i.e. it makes no difference)
What a slow bus this is!
*– Yes, we **might*** (Not **may**) ***just as well walk**.* (i.e. we'd get there more quickly)

11.72.2 'May/might/could well' = 'it is extremely likely'

May well, might well and *could well* can be used interchangeably:

***He may/might/could well find** that the course is too difficult.*

11.72.3 'May/might' in the sense of 'I grant you...'

This construction is often used in discussion and argument:

*Your typewriter **may/might be** a wonderful machine, but it's still old-fashioned compared with a word-processor.*

11.72.4 'Might/could (at least)' in nagging complaints/reproach

***You might (at least) clean** the bathtub after you've used it!*

(I) might have + past participle of verbs like *guess, know* and *suspect* can reinforce complaint:

***I might have guessed** he'd fail to read the instructions.*

11.72.5 'Might' in requests

Might can replace the imperative [> 9.52] in:

*While you're out **you might*** (no stress) ***post** this letter for me.*

11.73 'Shall'

Apart from its main uses with *I/we* to refer to the future [> 9.36], and to make offers/suggestions [> 11.39–40], *shall* can be used with other persons (*you, he, they*, etc.) in e.g. the following ways [compare > 11.23]:

***You shall pay** for this.*	(threat)
You shall (stressed) ***have a car** for your birthday.*	(promise)
They shall not pass!	(determination)
*When he comes in nobody **shall say** a word.* [> 9.54*n*.5]	(order)

11.74 'Won't/wouldn't' and 'would/wouldn't'

11.74.1 'Won't' and 'wouldn't' for 'refusal'

Won't and *wouldn't* are commonly used to express refusal in the present and the past:

*Drink your milk, Jimmy! – **I won't**.* (Also, BrE: ***I shan't!***)
*I offered Jimmy some milk, but **he wouldn't drink it**.*

'Refusal' (or resistance to effort) can be extended to things:

***The car won't start. The car wouldn't start** this morning.*

11.74.2 'Would' and 'wouldn't' in place of the simple present tense

We often use *would* and *wouldn't* in place of the simple present tense and sometimes in place of *will/won't*, when we want to sound less definite (*I would think that...*, etc):

*That **seems** the best solution to me.* (definite)
*That **would seem** the best solution to me.* (less definite)
*Friday evening **is not*** (or ***won't be***) *very convenient.* (definite)
*Friday evening **wouldn't be** very convenient.* (less definite)

11.75 'Should'

11.75.1 Noun clauses with 'should'

There are two classes here:

1 Many verbs, particularly reporting verbs: *say*, etc. [> App 45] can be followed by *(that)...should* or *(that)...ought to* referring to obligation, advice, etc.:
*He said **(that) I should*** (or ***ought to***) *see a doctor.*

2 After verbs referring to proposals, suggestions, requests and orders (e.g. *propose, suggest*), we may follow with *(that)...should* (not *ought to*), the simple present, or the subjunctive [> App 45.3]. The subjunctive (rare in English) refers to what could or should happen in hypothetical situations.

In the present, the base form of the verb remains the same in all persons: *If I/you/he* (etc.) *be*; *It is important that you/he* (etc.) *go.*

The past subjunctive of *be* is *were*: *If I/you/he* (etc.) *were*; *I wish I/he* (etc.) *were.*

11.75.2 'That... should' after 'suggest', etc.

– **future reference**: affirmative/negative after (*that*):
That...should can be used after such verbs as *ask, propose, recommend* and *suggest*; alternatively, the present or subjunctive can be used in BrE or the subjunctive in AmE. *That* is generally dropped in informal style:

*I suggest (that) **he should/shouldn't apply** for the job.* (*should*)
*I suggest (that) **he applies/doesn't apply** for the job.* (present)
*I suggest (that) **he apply/not apply** for the job.* (subjunctive)

– **past reference**: affirmative/negative after (*that*):
In past reported suggestions, the *(that)...should* construction and the subjunctive can be replaced by a past tense:

*I suggested (that) **they should/shouldn't drive** along the coast.*
*I suggested (that) **they drive/not drive** along the coast.*
*I suggested (that) **they drove/didn't drive** along the coast.*

11.75.3 'That...should' after certain adjectives

Adjectives referring to desirability or urgency, such as *essential* and *urgent*, can be used in the same way [> App 44]:

*It is vital (that) we **should be** present.* (*should*)
*It is vital (that) we **are** present.* (present)
*It is vital (that) we **be** present.* (subjunctive)

The reference may also be to the past:
*It was important (that) he **should apply/apply/applied** for the job.*

11.75.4 'That...should' after 'I'm surprised', etc.

That...should can be used after phrases with adjectives and nouns expressing feelings and emotions: e.g. *I'm annoyed, I'm surprised, It's funny, It's a pity:*

__I'm surprised that he should feel__ like that.

If we wish to be more emphatic, we may use the simple present:

__I'm surprised that he feels__ like that.

Shouldn't is possible but often avoided (because of its ambiguity) in such cases and the negative present or past are preferred:

present reference: *I'm surprised that __he doesn't feel__ any remorse.*
past reference: *I'm surprised that __he didn't feel__ any remorse.*

The past or *should have* can be used in: e.g.

I was surprised that __he made/should have made__ the same mistake.

11.76 'There' + modal auxiliaries

Parallel structures to *there is/there are*, etc. [> 10.17] can be formed with modal auxiliaries in various combinations. Here are some examples:

11.76.1 'There' + modal + 'be'

__There could be__ no doubt about it.
__There won't be__ an election in June.
__There must be__ a mistake.

11.76.2 'There' + modal + 'have been' + complement

__There can't have been__ any doubt about it.
__There might have been__ a strike.
__There oughtn't to have been__ any difficulty about it.

11.76.3 'There' + modal + 'be' + complement + verb'-ing'

__There can't be anyone waiting__ outside.
__There__ never __used to be anyone living__ next door.
__There could be something blocking__ the pipe.

11.76.4 'There' + modal + 'have been' + complement + verb'-ing'

__There might have been someone waiting__ outside.
__There must have been something blocking__ the pipe.
__There could have been someone crossing__ the road.

11.76.5 'There' + modal: question forms

All the usual question forms are possible: e.g.

Yes/No questions: *__Could there__ have been any doubt?*
__Might there__ have been someone waiting?
negative questions: *__Wouldn't there__ have been a strike?*
__Couldn't there__ have been an accident?
question-word questions: *__When might there__ be an answer?*
__Why couldn't there__ have been a mistake?

12 The passive and the causative

The passive: general information about form

12.1 Active voice and passive voice

Active voice and passive voice refer to the form of a verb. In the active, the subject of the verb is the person or thing doing the action:

*John **cooked** the food last night.*

Other typical active verb forms: *eats, made, will take.*

In the passive, the action is done to the subject:

*The food **was cooked** last night.*

Other typical passive verb forms: *is eaten, was made, will be taken.*

The passive occurs very commonly in English: it is not merely an alternative to the active, but has its own distinctive uses.

12.2 Form of the passive

Passives can be formed in the following ways:

1 A tense of *be* [> 10.6–14] + past participle:

active: *He cooks/has cooked/will cook the food.*
He is/was cooking the food.

passive: *The food is/has been/will be + cooked.*
The food is/was being + cooked.

2 Modal [> 11.1] + *be/have been* + past participle:

active: *He may cook/may have cooked the food.*

passive: *The food may be/have been + cooked.*

3 Infinitive [> 16.2]: *to be/to have been* + past participle:

active: *He is/was to cook the food.*

passive: *The food is to be/was to have been + cooked.*

4 *-ing* form [> 16.41]: *being/having been* + past participle:

active: *Cooking/Having cooked...*

passive: *Being/Having been + cooked...*

12.3 Notes on the form of the passive

1 Formation: regular and irregular past participles

We form the passive with a form of *be* and a past participle. The past participle does not necessarily refer to past time. For regular and irregular past participles [> Apps 39, 40]. (The past participle is used to form perfect active tenses, e.g. *He has left* [> 9.22], as well as all passives). Rules applying to the use of tenses in the active [> 9.2] apply in the passive. For example, an action in progress *now* requires the present progressive in: e.g.

*Your steak **is being grilled** and will be ready in a minute.*

2 Transitive and intransitive verbs

The passive occurs only with verbs used transitively, that is, verbs

that can be followed by an object [> 1.9]:
active: *Someone* ***found this wallet*** *in the street.*
passive: ***This wallet was found*** *in the street.*
Many verbs can be used transitively or intransitively:
The door ***opened***. (perhaps by itself)
The door ***was opened***. (perhaps by someone)

3 Personal and impersonal subjects
The passive can refer to things (*a letter was written*, etc.) or people:
active: *The company* ***has sent Smithers*** *to California for a year.*
passive: ***Smithers has been sent*** *to California for a year.*

4 Direct and indirect objects [> 1.9, 1.13]
Verbs like *bring* and *give*, which can have two objects, e.g. *Tom gave me* (indirect) *a pen* (direct), can have two passive forms:
I was given *a pen by Tom.* (indirect object becomes subject)
A pen was given *(to) me by Tom.* (direct object becomes subject)
Because we are often more interested in people (or animals) than things, personal subjects tend to be more common than impersonal ones. Thus, ***I was given*** *this pen* is more likely to occur than ***This pen was given*** *to me*. In sentences like the second example, *to* (or *for*) can be omitted before a personal pronoun (*This pen* ***was given me***) but not usually otherwise: *This pen* ***was given to my father***.

5 Stative verbs [> 9.3, App 38]
Many stative verbs cannot be used in the passive, even when they are transitive: *I* ***love beans*** *on toast.* (active voice only)
Verbs like *measure*, which can be stative or dynamic, can only be passive in their dynamic sense:
stative: *This desk* ***measures*** *125 x 60 cms.*
dynamic: *This desk* ***has been measured***.

6 Progressive forms
Only present and past progressive forms are common:
He ***is being interviewed*** *now. He* ***was being interviewed*** *at 10.*
However, modals with progressive passive sometimes occur:
I know Mark was going to have an interview some time this afternoon. ***He may be being interviewed*** *at this very moment.*

7 Phrasal verbs [> 8.23–30]
Transitive constructions with the pattern verb + adverb particle (*A gust of wind* ***blew*** *the tent* ***down***) can be used in the passive:
Our tent ***was blown down*** *(by a gust of wind).*
For possible passives with verb + preposition [> Apps 28–30]:
The newsagent's ***has been broken into***.
Only a few verbs of the type verb + particle + preposition (*We* ***have done away with*** *the old rules*) can be used in the passive:
The old rules ***have been done away with***.

8 The *-ing* form and the *to*-infinitive [> 16.13, 16.42, 16.58–59]
Passive constructions are common after verbs followed by the *-ing* form, such as *enjoy, like* and *remember*:
Most people ***don't like being criticized***.
and after verbs followed by a *to*-infinitive:
He ***hates to be criticized***.

We can use the passive (*-ing* form only) after conjunctions such as *on* and *after* [> 1.62.2, 8.4.4]:
On/After being informed *that her mother was seriously ill, she hurried back to England.* (i.e. When she was informed...)

9 Active verbs with a passive meaning
A few active verbs sometimes have a passive meaning: *This surface* ***cleans*** *easily* really means 'It can be/It is cleaned easily':
These clothes ***wash*** *well. This wine* ***is selling*** *quickly.*
*What****'s showing*** *at the cinema this week?*
Her novel ***is reprinting*** *already.*

10 Verbs generally used in the passive
A small number of verbs are used more frequently in the passive than in the active: e.g. *be born, be married, be obliged:*
I'm not obliged *to work overtime if I don't want to.*

11 Adverbs of manner in passive sentences [> 7.53]
Adverbs of manner can occur before or after the participle:
This room has been ***badly painted/painted badly****.*

12 The passive and reflexive verbs
English often uses the passive where other European languages use reflexive verbs: *burn myself, hurt myself*, etc. [> 4.25, 4.27]:
I was hurt *in a car crash last summer.*
Jim was in a fight and ***his shirt was torn*** *in the struggle.*
We do not normally use the passive when responding spontaneously:
What's the matter? – ***I've burnt/cut/hurt***, etc. ***myself****.*

13 We often use abbreviated passive constructions when expressing:
– wishes: *I'd like it (to be)* ***fried/cleaned/repaired****.* etc.
– preferences: *I like it (when it is)* ***fried/boiled****.* etc.

Uses of the passive

12.4 Uses of the passive

12.4.1 Spontaneous and deliberate use of the passive

In fluent English, passives occur naturally and spontaneously, without a conscious change from 'active' to 'passive'. In fact, active equivalents would be hard to produce for sentences like:
The origin of the universe ***will probably never be explained****.*
Rome ***was not built*** *in a day.*

The passive is sometimes deliberately chosen in preference to the active, especially when speakers do not wish to commit themselves to actions, opinions, or statements of fact of which they are not completely certain:
This matter ***will be dealt with*** *as soon as possible.*
Thousands of books ***are published*** *every year and very few of them* ***are noticed****. Even those that* ***are reviewed*** *in the papers rarely reach large audiences.*

12.4.2 The passive for focus

We use the passive when we wish to focus on a happening which is more important to us than who or what causes the happening – or when there is simply no need to mention the doer. If we say:

Our roof *was damaged in last night's storm.*

we are mainly concerned with the roof and what happened to it. Similarly:

My car*'s been scratched!* ***Thousands of beaches*** *are polluted.*

The happening may concern people:

Charles I *was beheaded in 1649.*

12.4.3 Avoiding vague words as subjects

We always prefer the passive when we wish to avoid using a vague word as subject (e.g. *someone, a person*, etc.):

After my talk, ***I was asked*** *to explain a point I had made.*

Conversely, the passive may be avoided (where we might expect it) when we wish to make what is described personal:

They operated *on father last night.*

The passive is used in English where other European languages might prefer an indefinite pronoun subject like *one* [> 4.9–11]. In a formal context we would avoid *one*: e.g.

The form has to be signed *in the presence of a witness.* (Not **One has to sign...**)

The passive is obligatory in notices such as *English Spoken, Loans Arranged, Shoes Repaired*, etc. (Not **One...**). Such notices are normally abbreviated: *English (**is**) spoken.*

12.5 The use of 'by', etc. + agent after a passive

An **agent** is a 'doer', i.e. the person or thing that performs the action indicated by the verb. *By* + agent in passive constructions tells us who or what did something:

The window was broken ***by the boy who lives opposite****.*

The window was broken ***by a stone****.*

By + agent is only necessary when the speaker wishes to say (or the hearer has to know) who or what is responsible for the event in question. The position of *by* + agent at the end of a clause or sentence gives it particular emphasis:

The window ***was broken by a slate*** *that fell off the roof.*

Information can be given by means of phrases other than *by* + agent:

This bridge was built ***in 1816/of stone/before the war****.* etc.

By + agent is often used with the passive of verbs like *build, compose, damage, design, destroy, discover, invent, make, wreck* and *write.* Note how a subject-question in the active is often answered by a passive, so that the important information (i.e. what the questioner wants to know) is emphasized by being at the end.

Who composed that piece? – ***It was composed by Mozart****.*

What destroyed the village? – ***It was destroyed by a bomb****.*

Note the inclusion of *by* in questions with *Who(m)*:

Who(m) *was 'Bleak House'* ***written by****? – Dickens.*

With is often used with an agent, especially after past participles such as *crammed, crowded, filled, packed:*

During the World Cup our streets ***were filled with football fans****.*

But compare *by* + agent and *with* ['means/method', > 7.11] in: e.g.
He was killed ***by a falling stone****.* (accidental)
He was killed ***with a knife****.* (deliberate) [compare > App 25.17]

12.6 'Get' + past participle

Get is often used instead of *be* before certain past participles in colloquial English. *Be* can sometimes be replaced by *become*:
I tried to find my way round London without a map and ***got lost****.*
I ***became concerned*** *when he hadn't come home by midnight.*
(Compare *get/become* + adjective in e.g. *get fat/old* [> 10.26]).
Get combines with past participles like: *arrested, caught, confused, delayed, divorced, dressed, drowned, drunk, elected, engaged, hit, killed, lost, married* and *stuck*. We use *get* when:
– we do something to ourselves [compare > 4.26–27]:
I ***got dressed*** *as quickly as I could.*
– we manage to arrange something in our own favour. Reflexive pronouns can often be used in such cases:
I wasn't surprised she ***got elected*** *after all the efforts she made.*
I see old Morton ***has got himself promoted*** *at last.*
– something (often unfavourable) happens beyond our control:
We ***got delayed*** *because of the holiday traffic.*
A few combinations with *get* + past participle are used as commands (***Get dressed****!* ***Get washed****!*) or insults (*Oh,* ***get lost****, will you!*).

12.7 The passive compared with adjectival past participles

Many words such as *broken, interested, shut, worried* [> 6.14–15, 7.51] can be used either as adjectives or as past participles in passive constructions. A difference can be noted between:
I was ***worried*** *about you all night.* (adjective: a state)
I was ***worried by*** *mosquitoes all night.* (passive: dynamic verb)
If the word is an adjective, it cannot be used with *by* + agent and cannot be transposed into a sentence in the active.

12.8 The passive with verbs of 'saying' and 'believing'

We need to be sure of our facts in a statement like *Muriel pays less income tax than she should*. It is often 'safer' to say e.g. *Muriel is said to pay less income tax than she should*. If it seems necessary to be cautious, we can use passive constructions like the following:

1 *It* (+ passive + *that*-clause) with verbs like *agree, allege, arrange, assume, believe, consider, decide, declare, discover, expect, fear, feel, find, hope, imagine, know, observe, presume, prove, report, say, show, suggest, suppose, think, understand:*
It is said that *there is plenty of oil off our coast.*
It is feared that *many lives have been lost in the train crash.*

2 *There* (+ passive + *to be* + complement) with a limited selection of verbs: e.g. *acknowledge, allege, believe, consider, fear, feel, know, presume, report, say, suppose, think, understand:*
There is said to be *plenty of oil off our coast.*
There are known to be *thousands of different species of beetles.*

3 Subject other than *it* (+ passive + *to*-infinitive) with a few verbs: e.g. *acknowledge, allege, believe, consider, declare, know, recognize, report, say, suppose, think, understand:*
***Mandy is said** to be some kind of secret agent.*
***Turner was considered** to be a genius even in his lifetime.*
***Homeopathic remedies are believed** to be very effective.*
Other verbs beside *be* are possible in the infinitive:
***Jane is said to know** all there is to know about chimpanzees.*
Note how *suppose* has two different meanings in:
***He is supposed** to be at work at the moment.*
This can mean 'People think he is at work' or 'It is his duty to be at work'. *There* + *be* also combines with *suppose:*
***There is supposed** to be a train at 12.37.*

12.9 Some typical contexts for the passive

12.9.1 Formal notices and announcements

*Candidates **are required** to present themselves fifteen minutes before the examination begins. They **are asked** to be punctual.*
*Passengers **are requested** to remain seated until the aircraft comes to a complete stop* [compare > 11.23].

12.9.2 Press reports

Often the agent is not known or does not need to be mentioned:
*The search for the bank robbers continues. Meanwhile, many people **have been questioned** and the owner of the stolen getaway car **has been traced**.*

12.9.3 Headlines, advertisements, notices, etc.

KENNEDY ASSASSINATED! TRADE AGREEMENTS BROKEN!
PRICES SLASHED! ALL GOODS GREATLY REDUCED!
PETROL COUPONS ACCEPTED

12.9.4 Scientific writing (to describe 'process')

*The mixture **is placed** in a crucible and **is heated** to a temperature of 300°C. It **is** then **allowed** to cool before it **can be analysed**.*

The causative

12.10 Form of the causative

The causative is formed with *have* + object + past participle: e.g.
Tenses:

present:	*We have our house*	*decorated every year.*
	We are having our house	*decorated soon.*
past:	*We had our house*	*decorated last year.*
present perfect:	*We have just had our house*	*decorated.*
future:	*We will have our house*	*decorated next year.*
	We'll be having our house	*decorated next year.*

Modals:

'present':	*We may have our house*	*decorated next year.*
	We may be having our house	*decorated soon.*

12.11 Notes on the form of the causative

1 Formation: regular and irregular past participles
We form the causative with *have* + noun or pronoun object + the past participle of a verb, regular or irregular [> Apps 39, 40]:
*I've just **had my car repaired**. I'm going **to have my hair cut**.*
*What about the children? – I'm **having them collected** at 6.*
Get can be used in place of *have*, but it has a more limited use and often conveys a slightly different meaning [> 12.13].
Care must be taken with the word order to avoid confusion:
*I had built **a house**.* (past perfect)
*I had **a house** built.* (causative: simple past)

2 Phrasal verbs
A sentence can end in a preposition or adverb particle [> 8.22]:
*The fridge isn't working properly. I'm having it **looked at**.*
There are instances where the past participle can be omitted:
*I had a tooth **out** this morning.* (for *pulled out*)

12.12 The causative used for focus

12.12.1 The use of the causative for things

The causative is similar to the passive. We focus on what is done to something or someone, not on what someone does:

active: ***I'm servicing** my car. Jack **is servicing** my car.*
(i.e. I'm doing the job myself; or I know who is doing it)
passive: *My car **is being serviced**.*
(i.e. someone is doing the job for me)
causative: ***I'm having** my car **serviced**.*
(i.e. I'm responsible for causing someone to do the job)

When we use the passive or the causative, we may not know or may not need to name who performs a service for us. However, in contrast to the passive, we use the causative to stress the fact that we are 'causing' someone else to perform a service for us. We therefore often use it with such verbs as *build, clean, decorate, deliver, develop* (a film), *mend, photocopy, press, print, repair*, and *service*. We do not normally use the active (*I am servicing my car*) to mean that someone else is doing something for us. Nor can we say *I want to cut my hair* when we mean *I want to have my hair cut*. Note that *by* + agent is added only when it is necessary to mention who or what did the action:
*We're **having/getting the job done by some local builders**. They are much cheaper and more reliable than anyone else.*

12.12.2 The use of the causative for people

The causative with verbs like *coach, instruct, prepare, teach* and *train* can refer to things we cause to be done to other people:

active: ***I'm teaching her** English.*
(i.e. I'm teaching her myself)
passive: ***She's being taught** English.*
(i.e. I may not know or wish to name the teacher)
causative: ***I'm having her taught** English.*
(i.e. I'm responsible for causing someone to do the job)

Compare the construction 'have someone do something' [> 16.10.1].

12.12.3 Other related uses of 'have' + object + past participle

In the sense of 'experience':

You should understand by now. ***You've had it explained*** *often enough!* (= it has been explained to you)
When he got up to speak, the minister ***had eggs thrown*** *at him.*

In the sense of 'allow' [compare > 10.38]:

I refuse to ***have my house used*** *as a hotel.*

To describe the present result of past action:

We now ***have the problem solved****.*

12.13 'Get' + object + past participle or infinitive

12.13.1 Causative 'have' and 'get' compared

Though *have* and *get* are often used interchangeably in the causative [> 12.11*n*.1], *get* is more limited. They are not interchangeable in: e.g.

I ***had a tooth out*** *this afternoon.*

Get is stronger than *have* (and contains a stronger idea of action by the subject) in: e.g.

I must ***get this car serviced*** *soon.*

In: e.g.

I finally ***got my roof repaired****.*

there is a suggestion of difficulty, which would not be conveyed by *had*.

Get sounds more natural than *have* in the imperative:

Get your hair cut*!* ***Get your eyes tested****!*

In suggestions with *Why don't you...?*, *get* is much stronger than *have*:

Why don't you ***have your hair cut****?* (neutral suggestion)
Why don't you ***get your hair cut****?* (almost an order)

12.13.2 'Get' + to-infinitive to mean 'persuade', 'manage to', etc.

Get with an object before a *to*-infinitive conveys the idea of 'persuade' or 'manage to':

I finally ***got the car to start*** *by asking everyone to push it.*

Sometimes we use *get* + object + past participle to say that we managed to do something ourselves. The stress is different from the stress in causative sentences. Compare:

I got the ***'job*** *done.* (stress on object: = I did it myself)
I got (or *had*) *the job* ***'done.*** (stress on participle: someone else did it)

In the first of these examples, *got* could not be replaced by *had* and is not causative.

12.13.3 Non-causative 'get' and 'have' + object + past participle

Get + object + past participle can be used in a non-causative way for accidents, disasters, etc. that happen beyond our control:

Don't join in their argument or you might ***get your nose punched****.* (i.e. that's what might happen to you)

Non-causative *have* can be used in the same way [> 16.10]:

She ***had her house destroyed*** *in an earthquake.*

13 Questions, answers, negatives

Yes/No questions and negative statements

13.1 Questions/negatives with 'be', 'have' and modals [> 11.5]

questions:	(*I am late.*)	*I am late.*	*Am I late?*
	(*He was going.*)	*He was going.*	*Was he going?*
	(*He has won.*)	*He has won.*	*Has he won?*
	(*She can swim.*)	*She can swim.*	*Can she swim?*
	(*It will rain.*)	*It will rain.*	*Will it rain?*
		full form	**short form**
negatives:	(*I am ready.*)	*I am not ready.*	*I'm not ready.*
	(*He is late.*)	*He is not late.*	*He isn't/He's not late.*
	(*We are going.*)	*We are not going.*	*We aren't/We're not going.*
	(*I can see you.*)	*I cannot see you.*	*I can't see you.*
	(*It will rain.*)	*It will not rain.*	*It won't rain.*

13.2 Questions/negatives with 'do', 'does' and 'did' [> 10.4, 10.41–43]

questions:		(*I/You/We/They*	***dance** well.*)
	Do	*I/you/we/they*	***dance** well?*
		(*He/She/It*	***works** well.*)
	Does	*he/she/it*	***work** well?*
		(*I/You/He/She/It/We/They*	***ran** fast.*)
	Did	*I/you/he/she/it/we/they*	***run** fast?*

negatives:

(*I/You/They* ***work**.*)
I (etc.) ***do not work**.* (full form) *I* (etc.) ***don't work**.* (short form)

(*He/She/It* ***works**.*)
He (etc.) ***does not work**.* (full form) *He* (etc.) ***doesn't work**.* (short form)

(*I/You/He/She/It/We/They* ***went**.*)
I (etc.) ***did not go**.* (full form) *I* (etc.) ***didn't go**.* (short form)

13.3 Yes/No questions: what they are and how they are formed

A Yes/No question is one which asks for *Yes* or *No* in the answer:

Have you ever been to Egypt?
*– **Yes**, I have./**No**, I haven't.*
Does he like fish?
*– **Yes**, he does./**No**, he doesn't.*

Haven't you ever been there?
*– **Yes**, I have./**No**, I haven't.*
Doesn't he like fish?
*– **Yes**, he does./**No**, he doesn't.*

13.3.1 The formation of Yes/No questions with 'be', 'have' and modals

Statements with *be* [auxiliary or full verb, > 10.6–7], *have* (auxiliary or sometimes full verb when *have* = 'have got' [> 10.27–30]), and modal verbs like *can* [> 11.5.2] can be turned into Yes/No questions by inversion. That is, the appropriate form of *be, have* or the modal verb goes in front of the subject:

statement: *He is leaving.* **inversion**: *He (is) leaving.*
question: *Is he leaving?*

13.3.2 The formation of Yes/No questions with 'Do', 'Does', and 'Did'

With all other verbs, we form Yes/No questions with *Do...?, Does...?* (simple present) and *Did...?* (simple past). The form of the verb that follows *Do, Does* or *Did* (+ subject) is always the bare infinitive (e.g. *go, play, think* [> 16.1]).

Do goes before *I/you/we/they* for questions in the simple present:
statement: *I/You/We/They turn left here.*
Yes/No question: *Do I/you/we/they* ***turn*** *left here?*

Does goes before *he/she/it* for questions in the simple present:
statement: *He/She/It works well.*
Yes/No question: *Does he/she/it* ***work*** *well?*

Did is used in all persons to form questions in the simple past:
statement: *I/You/He/She/It/We/They arrived late.*
Yes/No question: *Did I/you/he/she/it/we/they* ***arrive*** *late?*

13.3.3 General points about Yes/No questions

1 A noun subject is not normally used in front of the auxiliary (Not **James, is he leaving?**) unless we are addressing someone:
James*, are you going into the town?* ***Susan****, do you like fish?*

2 If there are a number of auxiliaries in the same sentence, it is always the first one that goes in front of the subject:
statement: *He* ***could have been*** *delayed.*
question: ***Could*** *he have been delayed?*

3 The whole subject comes after the auxiliary, however long it is:
Can ***everyone in the room*** *hear me?*
Does ***everyone in the room*** *agree?*

4 Questions like the following are possible in conversation when we wish to make it quite clear who or what we are referring to:
Has she *caught a cold,* ***your mother****?* ***Is it*** *all right,* ***that coffee****?*
Does he *play football,* ***your brother****?*

5 In everyday speech, some Yes/No questions can be abbreviated:
Leaving *already?* (For: *Are you...?*)
Like *another cup of tea?* (For: *Would you...?*)
Enjoy *the party?* (For: *Did you...?*)

6 We generally ask Yes/No questions with a rising intonation:
Have you finished your supper? Did you phone your mother?

7 Yes/No questions (exaggerated intonation) can be exclamations:
Is he mad! Can she type! Did he annoy me! (no answers expected)

13.4 Negative statements: what they are/how they are formed

A negative statement is the opposite of an affirmative statement. It says or means 'no' and contains a negative word such as *not* or *never* [> 13.8–9]. Full negative forms (*do not*, etc.) occur in formal style (written and spoken) and in emphatic speech. Contracted forms (e.g. *don't*) are normal in conversational style. In written contracted forms, the apostrophe is used where a vowel has been omitted, so for example in the negative it will go between the *n* and the *t*; the two words of the full form: *did not*, combine into one word: *didn't*.

13.4.1 The formation of negative statements with 'be', 'have' and modals

1 When a sentence contains *be* (auxiliary or full verb), *have* (auxiliary or sometimes full verb when *have* = 'have got'), or a modal auxiliary (*can*, etc.), we form the negative by putting *not* after the auxiliary:
affirmative: *He is leaving.*
negative: *He is **not** leaving./He's **not** leaving./He is**n't** leaving.*

2 If there are a number of auxiliaries in the same sentence, *not* always goes after the first one:
affirmative: *He **could** have been delayed.*
negative: *He **could not/couldn't** have been delayed.*

13.4.2 The formation of negative statements with 'do', 'does' and 'did'

Do not (*don't*), *does not* (*doesn't*) (simple present) and *did not* (*didn't*) (simple past) go after the subject to form negative statements with other verbs. The verb that follows *do/does/did* + *not* is always in the form of a bare infinitive [> 16.1]:

simple present:	**affirmative**:	*I/You/We/They turn left here.*
	negative:	*I/You/We/They **don't turn** left here.*
	affirmative:	*He/She/It works well.*
	negative:	*He/She/It **doesn't work** well.*
simple past:	**affirmative**:	*I/You/He/She/It/We/They stayed in.*
	negative:	*I/You/He/She/It/We/They **didn't stay** in.*

13.4.3 'Be', 'have' and modals compared with 'do/does' and 'did'

Note that *do* is not normally required in affirmative sentences and is not used to form tenses in the same way as *be* and *have*:

1 Affirmative statements

subject	**auxiliary**	**predicate**
You	*'re*	*working too hard.*
You	*'ve*	*eaten too much.*
You	*may*	*stop now.*
You	–	*work too hard.*
You	–	*ate too much yesterday.*

2 Questions

auxiliary	**subject**	**predicate**
Are	*you*	*working too hard?*
Have	*you*	*eaten too much?*
May	*I*	*stop now?*
Do	*I*	*work too hard?*
Did	*I*	*eat too much yesterday?*

3 Negative statements

subject	**auxiliary**	***not***	**predicate**
I	*am*	*not*	*working too hard.*
You	*have*	*not*	*eaten too much.*
You	*may*	*not*	*go out.*
I	*do*	*not*	*work too hard.*
I	*did*	*not*	*eat too much yesterday.*

Yes/No questions and Yes/No short answers

13.5 Form of Yes/No questions and Yes/No short answers

	Yes/No questions	**affirmative and**	**negative short answers**
be [> 10.6]:	*Are you ready?*	*Yes, I am.*	*No, I'm not.*
	Is he leaving?	*Yes, he is.*	*No, he's not/he isn't.*
	Were you ill?	*Yes, we were.*	*No, we weren't.*
have [> 10.27]:	*Have you finished?*	*Yes, I have.*	*No, I haven't.*
	Has she left?	*Yes, she has.*	*No, she hasn't.*
do [> 10.41]:	*Do you like it?*	*Yes, I do.*	*No, I don't.*
does:	*Does it work?*	*Yes, it does.*	*No, it doesn't.*
did:	*Did you paint it?*	*Yes, I did.*	*No, I didn't.*
modals [> 11.5]:	*Can I see him?*	*Yes, you can.*	*No, you can't.*

13.6 Notes on the form of Yes/No questions and answers

1 The first verb in the question (i.e. the auxiliary or modal) is usually repeated in the answer:
***Was** James late? – Yes, he **was**. No, he **wasn't**.*
***Can** James play chess? – Yes, he **can**. No, he **can't**.*
But note: ***Are** you...? – Yes, I **am**./No, **I'm** not.* and ***Were** you...? Yes, I **was**./No, I **wasn't**.* where the verb is repeated, but in a different form [compare > 11.35.2].
Variations with modals are common when we are not sure of our answers [> 11.31]. Auxiliary verbs are often stressed in answers:
Is that Vicki?/Might that be Vicki?
*– Yes, it '**is**. Yes, it '**might be**. It '**could be**. It '**must be**.*
*– No, it '**isn't**. No, it '**might not be**. It '**couldn't be**. It '**can't be**.*

2 Full negative short answers (e.g. *No, I do not*) only occur in emphatic or formal speech. In ordinary conversation, contracted forms (e.g. *No, I don't*) are normal.

3 Of course, many other answers are possible in response to Yes/No questions; and sometimes *Yes* and *No* can be omitted:
Did you watch the news on TV last night?
– Yes, but not all of it. No, I never watch TV.
– I watched some of it. I watched a cartoon instead.
– Of course. I can't remember. I think so. Not really.
Other examples of expressions used in place of *Yes/No*, are: *certainly, naturally, I think so, I expect so, perhaps, maybe, I don't think so, of course not, not at all.*

13.7 When we use Yes/No questions and answers

It is very unusual to answer a Yes/No question in full:

Did James go to the theatre last night?
– Yes, he went to the theatre last night.
– No, he didn't go to the theatre last night.

It is also unusual to answer very briefly with *Yes* or *No*, as this can easily be interpreted as unfriendly or rude:

Do you like dancing? – Yes./No.

Short answers save us from repeating the question and give scope for expression, compared with plain *Yes* or *No*.

We use Yes/No questions and answers:

– for requesting and supplying information:

Did you lock the back door? – Yes, I did./No, I didn't.

– for expressing agreement or disagreement with statements:

statement	**agreement**	**disagreement**
It's raining.	*– Yes, it is.*	*– No, it isn't.*
It isn't raining.	*– No, it isn't.*	*– Yes, it is.*

– for expressing confirmation in response to statements:

It was a very good performance. *– Yes, it was.*
It wasn't a very good performance. *– No, it wasn't.*

– in response to the imperative:

Drive carefully! – (Yes) I will.
Don't take any risks! – (No) I won't. [compare > 10.5.1]

We answer with *will/won't* because the imperative points to the future.

Alternative negative forms

13.8 Negative statements with 'negative adverbs' [> 7.59.3, App 19]

We can make negative and near-negative sentences with adverbs like *never, seldom, rarely, hardly ever, scarcely ever* (frequency); and *barely, hardly, scarcely* (= only just). Sentences which include one of these words or phrases are sometimes called 'implied negatives':

*We **never** see them nowadays.* (more emphatic than *We don't see*)
*We **hardly (ever)/scarcely (ever)/rarely** see them nowadays.*

For the effect of negative adverbs on word order [> 7.59.3].

13.9 Negatives with 'no' and 'not any' [> 4.37, 5.11]

No, any and their compounds form negatives as follows:

'No' and 'no'-compounds affirmative verb	**'Any' and 'any'-compounds negative verb**
*I've got **no** time.*	*I haven't got **any** time.*
*I've seen **no one/nobody**.*	*I haven't seen **any one/anybody**.*
*I've bought **none** of them.*	*I haven't bought **any** of them.*
*I've done **nothing** today.*	*I haven't done **anything** today.*
*I've been **nowhere** today.*	*I haven't been **anywhere** today.*

The two kinds of negatives have the same meaning, though *no* is generally more emphatic than *not...any*.

13.10 Only one negative in any one clause

We cannot normally use a negative adverb or a word like *nobody* in combination with a negative verb. Compare:

*I **can't** get **any** eggs. I **can** get **no** eggs.*

*I **can never*** (or ***hardly***) *get **any** information.* etc.

Two negative words in a sentence make a 'double negative'. A double negative can be used to express an affirmative, but this is rare or sometimes heard in joking:

***Nobody** did **nothing**.* (= Everybody did something.)

More than one negative is acceptable when there is co-ordination:

*I've **never** had and **never** wanted a television set.*

Negatives are also possible in different clauses:

*I can **never** get in touch with Thomas, as he has **no** telephone.*

And note *We **can't not** go* (= We can't avoid going.) [> 16.14]

13.11 Nouns, verbs and adjectives with negative meanings

Other parts of speech besides adverbs have a negative effect:

- nouns such as *denial, failure, refusal*:

  ***His failure** to react quickly enough caused the crash.*
  (= He did not react quickly enough and this caused the crash.)
- verbs such as *deny, fail, forget, refuse*, which can be used in the affirmative and the negative and often attract words like *any* [> 5.10]:

  ***She refused** any help.* (= She did not accept any help.)
- adjectives like *improbable, unlikely*:

  ***It's now unlikely** that he'll be here in time for lunch.* (= He probably won't be here in time for lunch.)

Compare the negative effect of the preposition *without* [> 16.51].

13.12 Cancellation of what has just been said

The word *not* can be used without an auxiliary immediately before a word to cancel what has just been said:

*See you Wednesday – **(No), not Wednesday**, Thursday.*

*Ask Diana – **(No), not Diana**. Ask her sister.*

*I'll see you at 5. – **(No), not at 5**. Maybe at 5.30.*

We can also use *not* to replace a negative imperative:

*Invite the Smiths, **but not** the Robinsons.* (= but don't invite)

13.13 Beginning a sentence with a negative

Statements can begin with negative words like *nothing* or negative phrases with *not* followed by affirmative verbs [compare > 5.8, 5.13].

***Not many people enjoy** washing-up.*

*He's written a lot of books, but **not all of them are** novels.*

***Nobody loves** a bad loser.*

***Nothing has happened** here since you've been away.*

When a sentence begins with a negative adverb such as *never*, the word order is affected [> 7.59.3]:

***Never has there been** such an effort to save whales from extinction.*

Negative questions and Yes/No short answers

13.14 Form of negative questions

	negative full form			negative short form		
be [> 10.6]:	*Am*	*I*	*not late?*	*Aren't*	*I*	*late?*
	Are	*they*	*not waiting?*	*Aren't*	*they*	*waiting?*
	Was	*I*	*not ill?*	*Wasn't*	*I*	*ill?*
have [> 10.27]:	*Have*	*I*	*not finished?*	*Haven't*	*I*	*finished?*
	Has	*she*	*not left?*	*Hasn't*	*she*	*left?*
do [> 10.41]:	*Do*	*you*	*not like it?*	*Don't*	*you*	*like it?*
does:	*Does*	*it*	*not work?*	*Doesn't*	*it*	*work?*
did:	*Did*	*you*	*not paint it?*	*Didn't*	*you*	*paint it?*
modals [> 11.5]:	*Can*	*I*	*not see him?*	*Can't*	*I*	*see him?*

13.15 Notes on the form of negative questions

In negative Yes/No questions there is a difference in word order between the full form and the short form:
full form: ***Did he not*** *invite you out?* (*not* comes after the subject)
short form: ***Didn't he*** *invite you out?* (auxiliary + *n't* before verb)

Sometimes the subject may be repeated at the end, especially in everyday conversation, when we want to make it quite clear who or what we are referring to [compare > 13.3.3*n*.4]:

Aren't they *a nuisance,* ***these roadworks****?*

13.16 When we ask negative questions

We generally ask negative questions:

- when we are expecting, inviting or hoping for the answer *Yes*:
  Don't you remember *that holiday we had in Spain?*
  – Yes, I do. (*No, I don't* would be possible but unexpected.)
- when we wish to express surprise, disbelief or exasperation:
  Can't you (really) ride *a bicycle? – No, I can't.*
- when we wish to persuade someone:
  Won't you help *me?* (= Please help me.) [compare > 11.21]
  – Oh, all right then./No, I'm afraid I can't/won't. etc.
- when we want to criticize or to express annoyance or sarcasm:
  Can't you shut the door *behind you?* (no answer expected)
- in exclamations (with falling intonation):
  Didn't he do *well!* ***Isn't it*** *hot in here!*
  An exclamation can also be used as a reply to a statement:
  He has been very successful. – Yes, ***hasn't he****!*

We use the full form in formal questions or when we require special emphasis to express anger, surprise, etc.:

Have I not asked you *again and again to be here on time?*

and in rhetorical questions not requiring an answer:

Are there not *more than enough weapons of destruction on earth?*

Where the subject is a noun *not* can come after the auxiliary:
Are not more people *dying of cancer these days?*

Full form and short form questions can be answered with Yes/No short answers. The auxiliary does not echo the form of the question (i.e. ***Did*** *you...? – Yes, I* ***did****./No, I* ***didn't***), but indicates what the facts are:
Didn't you (or ***Did you not***) *go to a party last night?*
– *Yes,* ***I did****.* (i.e. I did go to a party last night.)
– *No,* ***I didn't****.* (i.e. I didn't go to a party last night.)
– *No,* ***I did not****.* (emphatic denial)

Tag questions and Yes/No short answers

13.17 Form of tag questions: affirmative – negative

	affirmative		**negative**
be [> 10.6]:	*I'm*	*late,*	*aren't I?*
	They're	*waiting,*	*aren't they?*
	We were	*late,*	*weren't we?*
have [> 10.27]:	*I've*	*finished,*	*haven't I?*
	He's	*left,*	*hasn't he?*
do [> 10.41]:	*You*	*like it,*	*don't you?*
does:	*It*	*works,*	*doesn't it?*
did:	*You*	*painted it,*	*didn't you?*
modals [> 11.5]:	*I can*	*see him,*	*can't I?*

13.18 Form of tag questions: negative – affirmative

	negative		**affirmative**
be [> 10.6]:	*I'm not*	*late,*	*am I?*
	He isn't	*leaving,*	*is he?*
	I wasn't	*ill,*	*was I?*
have [> 10.27]:	*I haven't*	*finished,*	*have I?*
	He hasn't	*left.*	*has he?*
do [> 10.41]:	*You don't*	*like it,*	*do you?*
does:	*It doesn't*	*work,*	*does it?*
did:	*You didn't*	*paint it,*	*did you?*
modals [> 11.5]:	*I can't*	*see him,*	*can I?*

13.19 Notes on the form of tag questions

1 A tag question is a short question (e.g. *have you?/haven't you?*) that follows a statement. Auxiliaries (*be, have, can, may*, etc.) used in the statement are repeated at the end followed by the subject (always a pronoun):
John was *annoyed,* ***wasn't he****?* (affirmative – negative)
He wasn't *annoyed,* ***was he****?* (negative – affirmative)

2 With all other verbs, tag questions are formed with *do/don't* and *does/doesn't* (simple present) and *did/didn't* (simple past):

(affirmative – negative)	(negative – affirmative)
You like *fish,* ***don't you****?*	***You don't like*** *fish,* ***do you****?*
He likes *fish,* ***doesn't he****?*	***He doesn't like*** *fish,* ***does he****?*
She ate *it all,* ***didn't she****?*	***She didn't eat*** *it all,* ***did she****?*

This also applies to *have* and *do* as full verbs:

You have *tea at 4,* ***don't you****?*	***You don't have*** *tea at 4,* ***do you****?*
He does *his job,* ***doesn't he****?*	***He doesn't do*** *his job,* ***does he****?*

3 The negative tag at the end can be unabbreviated in formal style or for special emphasis, though this form is not very usual:
Julia runs *five miles a day to keep fit,* ***does she not****?*

4 Tag questions are also possible with *there*:
There'll *be a rail strike tomorrow,* ***won't there****?*

5 Affirmative tags can follow other statements that are negative in meaning [> 13.8]:
You never/seldom work *on Sundays,* ***do you****?*

6 Tags can be used after indefinite pronouns [> 4.40]:
Nobody's *been told,* ***have they****?*
Everyone's *ready to leave now,* ***aren't they****?*

7 Note that *this* and *that* are replaced by *it* [> 4.36]:
This/That *(suit) is expensive,* ***isn't it****?*

13.20 Form of tag questions: affirmative – affirmative

	affirmative	**affirmative**
be [> 10.6]:	*I'm rude,*	*am I?*
	He's leaving,	*is he?*
	I was impatient,	*was I?*
have [> 10.27]:	*I've finished,*	*have I?*
	She's left,	*has she?*
do [> 10.41]:	*You like it,*	*do you?*
does:	*It works,*	*does it?*
did:	*You painted it,*	*did you?*
modals [> 11.5]:	*I can see him,*	*can I?*

13.21 Note on the form of affirmative – affirmative tags

This form is less common than the two other kinds of tag questions. A negative – negative form is also grammatically possible, but is very rare and is used to convey aggression:
So ***he won't*** *pay his bills,* ***won't he****? We'll see about that.*
For *Let's...* [> 11.40.2, 16.4.1] and imperative + tag [> 9.55].

13.22 Uses of tag questions + Yes/No short answers

Many languages have a single fixed expression to convey the general idea of 'isn't that so?' to ask people whether they agree with you. By comparison, English has a complex system of tags which can be used, with varying forms and intonation, to express a subtle range of meanings. Tags are the essence of conversational style and are very important in spoken English. Certain fixed phrases can be used in place of tags: e.g. *isn't that true?, don't you think/agree?* in formal style and *right?, OK?* and even *eh?* in informal style.

13.22.1 Affirmative – negative/negative – affirmative: factual information

When we ask tag questions with a rising tone, we are asking real questions which expect Yes/No answers. However, tag questions often convey more than simple Yes/No questions: as well as asking for information, they can express surprise, anger, interest, etc.:

***You left** the gas on, **didn't you**?* (= Did you leave the gas on?)
***You didn't leave** the gas on, **did you**?* (= I hope you didn't.)
***You couldn't do** me a favour, **could you**?* (= I hope you can.)

13.22.2 Affirmative – negative/negative – affirmative: confirmation

When tag questions are asked with a falling tone, they are more like statements: the falling tone suggests greater certainty. They ask for confirmation of what the questioner assumes to be true.

Affirmative – negative expects a positive confirmation:
***You locked** the door, **didn't you**? – (Yes, I did.)*

Negative – affirmative expects a negative confirmation:
***You didn't** lock the door, **did you**? – (No, I didn't.)*

13.22.3 Affirmative – affirmative tag questions: confirmation, etc.

Affirmative – affirmative tag questions with a rising tone sometimes ask for confirmation of something the speaker already knows, expressing friendly interest, etc. (i.e. 'Tell me more'):

*So **she's** getting married, **is she**?* (= Tell me more!)
– Yes, she's got engaged to a doctor. The wedding's in June. etc.

However, with a falling tone, affirmative – affirmative tags are often used to express one's disappointment:

***You sold** that lovely bracelet, **did you**?* (= I'm sorry you did.)

Affirmative – affirmative tags can also express less friendly feelings like suspicion, disapproval and even threat. The tone falls at the end of the statement and rises only on the tag. No answer is required:

***You call** this a day's work, **do you**?* (= I certainly don't!)
***I'll get** my money back, **will I**?* (= I don't believe it!)
*So **you thought** you'd fooled me, **did you**?*

Statement-questions and Yes/No answers

13.23 Statement-questions

Statement-questions are questions which have the same basic grammatical structure as statements but which are expressed by using a rising tone:

You're coming with us? You aren't hungry? It isn't 4 o'clock?

Surely can be added for emphasis:

He's finished, ***surely****?* ***Surely*** *he hasn't gone home already?*

This is the standard way of asking Yes/No questions in many languages, but it is not common in English.

Statement-questions are used to seek confirmation, expecting the answer *Yes* if they are affirmative and *No* if they are negative. They ask for confirmation of what the speaker assumes to be true, or thinks he has misheard or imperfectly recalled:

You're out of work? – ***Yes, I am****, I'm afraid.*

You aren't hungry? – ***No****, I had a big breakfast.*

The assumption made by the questioner may also be contradicted:

You turned the lights off? – ***No, I didn't.***

We also use statement-questions to echo statements. In doing so, we may express surprise, pleasure, etc. or confirm what we have just heard, or we may be asking for a statement to be explained:

I forgot the milk. – You forgot the milk? (= Please explain!)

Echo tags

13.24 Form of echo tags

	affirmative	**negative**
be/have: [> 10.6, 10.27]	*He's resigning.* *– Is he? He is?* *– He is, isn't he?* *– He is, is he?*	*He isn't resigning.* *– Isn't he? He isn't?* *– He isn't, is he?* –
do/does/did: [> 10.41]	*I work all night.* *– Do you? You do?* *– You do, don't you?* *– You do, do you?*	*I don't work all night.* *– Don't you? You don't?* *– You don't, do you?* –
modals: [> 11.5]	*I can wait till tomorrow.* *– Can you? You can?* *– You can, can't you?* *– You can, can you?*	*I can't wait till tomorrow.* *– Can't you? You can't?* *– You can't, can you?* –

13.25 Notes on the form of echo tags

1 An echo tag is a response, in tag form, to an affirmative or negative statement by which we may or may not request further information depending on the intonation we use.

He has *resigned.* – ***Has he?*** etc.

He hasn't *resigned.* – ***Hasn't he?*** etc.

2 Where there is no auxiliary (i.e. in the affirmative), *do, does* or *did* must be used:

She works *all night.* – ***Does she?***

She doesn't work *all night.* – ***Doesn't she?***

3 Echo tags can be formed with *there*:

There'll *be a strike soon.*	***There won't*** *be a strike tomorrow.*
– ***Will there?***	– ***Won't there?***

4 Negative – negative combinations (*He won't, won't he?*) may be used to express anger or menace, but are very unusual.

13.26 When we use echo tags

Echo tags are used constantly in everyday conversation to request further information, seek confirmation, to express interest, concern, anger, surprise, disbelief, suspicion, etc., or to show that we are listening.

1 To request more information, express interest, etc., rising tone:
I've just won £500! – ***Have you?/You have?***
– You ***haven't, have you?*** (= How interesting! Tell me more!)

2 To confirm what might already be known/guessed, falling tone:
I'm afraid he's made a bad mistake. – ***He has, hasn't he?***

3 To express anger, disbelief, suspicion, etc.:
I've got the sack! – ***You haven't!*** (falling tone)
Falling tone on the statement, rising on the tag:
You ***haven't, have you?*** (= disbelief)
You ***have, have you?*** (= anger)

13.27 Reinforcement tags for emphasis

Reinforcement tags are similar to echo tags: they emphasize the speaker's point of view. They are usually affirmative – affirmative and are typical of colloquial English:

You're *in trouble,* ***you are****.*
Gilbert annoyed *me,* ***he did****.*
Jim's lied *to me,* ***he has****.*
You're making *a fool of yourself,* ***you are****.*

Tags can also be added to abbreviated statements:
Likes her comfort, ***she does****.* And note:
He likes his beer, ***does Fred/Fred does****.*

A noun or noun phrase can serve as a tag in: e.g.
They're all the same, ***men****.*
Very nice, ***these cakes****.*

Additions and responses

13.28 Form of additions and responses

These additions, etc. work with *be, have, do* and some modals:

statement	**parallel addition**	**contrast**
John can speak French	*and I can, too.*	*but I can't.*
John can't speak French	*and I can't, either.*	*but I can.*
John speaks French	*and I do, too.*	*but I don't.*
John doesn't speak French	*and I don't, either.*	*but I do.*

statement	**parallel addition**		**contrast**
John can speak French	*and so can I.*		*but I can't.*
John can't speak French	*and neither/nor can I.*		*but I can.*
John speaks French	*and so do I.*		*but I don't.*
John doesn't speak French	*and neither/nor do I.*		*but I do.*
statement	**parallel response**		
John can speak French.	*I can, too.*	or	*So can I.*
John can't speak French.	*I can't, either.*	or	*Neither/Nor can I.*
John speaks French.	*I do, too.*	or	*So do I.*
John doesn't speak French.	*I don't, either.*	or	*Neither/Nor do I.*
statement	**confirmation, surprised agreement, etc.**		
She's going to help us.	*So she is!*		
Jean retires soon.	*So she does!*		

13.29 When and how we use additions and responses

13.29.1 Contracted forms with 'so', 'nor', etc.

Additions and responses with *so, neither* and *nor* are contracted where possible. These contractions do not normally occur in writing, even in written dialogue, but they are often used in speech: *So'm I; Neither'm I; Nor'm I. So's he* (So is he/So has he); *Nor's he* (Nor is he/Nor has he). *So've I; Neither've I; Nor've I. So'll I; Neither'll I; Nor'll I. So'd you* (So had/would you); *Neither'd you* (Neither had/would you); *Nor'd you* (Nor had/would you).

13.29.2 The use of auxiliaries with 'so', 'nor', etc.

The auxiliary is repeated in the parallel addition or response. If there is no auxiliary, *do, does* or *did* must be used. This makes it unnecessary to repeat a clause:

You should work *less and* ***so should I****.*
You shouldn't work *so hard and* ***nor should I****.*
I went *to a meeting last night. –* ***So did I.***

13.29.3 'Too' and 'either' in affirmative and negative statements

Either must replace *too* in negative statements [> 7.56]:

I went *to the meeting* ***too****.* ***I didn't go*** *to the meeting* ***either****.*

Very informally *Me too, Nor me, Me neither* are often used in responses [> 4.7.2]. Other nouns and object pronouns are possible:

I'm *glad it's Friday. –* ***Me too!*** (I am too) ***Us too!*** (We are too)
I don't want to go *to a political meeting. –* ***Nor me/Me neither!***

13.29.4 'So', 'neither' and 'nor' in additions and responses

In parallel additions and responses, *so* is followed by auxiliary + subject: *...so did I*, etc. In confirmations *so* is followed by subject + auxiliary: *So you have*, etc. Compare:

I've got *a rash on my arm* ***and so have you****.*
I've got *a rash on my arm. –* ***So you have!***
I've got *a new car. –* ***So has John.***
John's got *a new car. –* ***So he has!***

Neither and *nor* are completely interchangeable in additions and responses [> 13.28].

Question-word questions: form and use

13.30 Form of question-word questions

For subject-questions, e.g. *Who came?, What happened?* [> 13.41]

question-word +	auxiliary +	subject	
	are/aren't	*you...?*	**be** [> 10.6]
Who(m)			
What	*have/haven't*	*you...?*	**have** [> 10.27]
When	*has/hasn't*	*she...?*	
Which			
Why	*do/don't*	*you...?*	**do** [> 10.41]
Where	*does/doesn't*	*she...?*	**does**
Whose	*did/didn't*	*we...?*	**did**
How			
	can/can't	*I...?*	**modals** [> 11.5]

13.31 Notes on the form of question-word questions

1 In questions of this kind, inversion with the auxiliary must occur after the question-word. The sequence is: question-word first, auxiliary next, then the subject:

statement: *He is/isn't working.* **inversion**: *He is/isn't working.*
Yes/No question: *Is he/Isn't he working?*
question-word: *Why is/isn't he working?*

2 In the simple present of verbs other than *be*, question-word questions are formed with *do* or *does*, and in the simple past with *did*:

statement: *We arrive at 8.* *We don't arrive at 8.*
Yes/No question: *Do we arrive at 8?* *Don't we arrive at 8?*
question-word: *When do we arrive?* *Why don't we arrive at 8?*

statement: *He arrives at 8.* *He doesn't arrive at 8.*
Yes/No question: *Does he arrive at 8?* *Doesn't he arrive at 8?*
question-word: *When does he arrive?* *Why doesn't he arrive at 8?*

statement: *He arrived at 8.* *He didn't arrive at 8.*
Yes/No question: *Did he arrive at 8?* *Didn't he arrive at 8?*
question-word: *When did he arrive?* *Why didn't he arrive at 8?*

3 Question words + auxiliaries are frequently contracted in everyday speech and written dialogue. This is more common when the question-word ends with a vowel sound (*Who'll*) than when it ends with a consonant (*Which'll*). Those marked * commonly occur in informal writing:

Who:	**Who's...?*	=	*Who is...?*	or	*Who has...?*
	**Who'd...?*	=	*Who had...?*	or	*Who would...?*
	**Who'll...?*	=	*Who will...?*		
What:	**What's...?*	=	*What is...?*	or	*What has...?*
	What've...?	=	*What have...?*		
	What'll...?	=	*What will...?*		

When:	**When's...?*	=	*When is...?*	or	*When has...?*
	When've...?	=	*When have...?*		
	When'll...?	=	*When will...?*		
Which:	*Which've...?*	=	*Which have...?*		
	Which'll...?	=	*Which will...?*		
Why:	*Why's...?*	=	*Why is...?*	or	*Why has...?*
	Why'd...?	=	*Why had...?*	or	*Why would...?*
	Why'll...?	=	*Why will...?*		
Where:	**Where's...?*	=	*Where is...?*	or	*Where has...?*
	Where've...?	=	*Where have...?*		
	Where'd...?	=	*Where had...?*	or	*Where would...?*
	Where'll...?	=	*Where will...?*		
How:	**How's...?*	=	*How is...?*	or	*How has...?*
	**How'd...?*	=	*How had...?*	or	*How would...?*
	**How'll...?*	=	*How will...?*		

4 When we ask a *Wh-* question using a verb + preposition/particle we normally put the preposition/particle at the end [> 8.22, 13.33]:
*Who(m) are you going **with**? What are you looking **at**?*
*Where did you get that suit **from**?*
*How on earth can I get these shoes **on**?*
In very formal English, prepositions can precede question-words:
***To whom** should I apply for more information?*
***In which** hall will the recital be given?*

5 Question-words are followed by prepositions in short questions:
*We're off on holiday tomorrow. – **Where to?***
*Will you beat these eggs for me? – **What with?***
*I want to leave this parcel. – **Who for?***
More formally, prepositions can precede question words:
*I'm going out this evening. – **With whom?***

6 Short questions consisting of single question-words or limited combinations are common in everyday speech when we are asking for repetition (e.g. *What?*), brief information or clarification:
*We're off to Chicago. – **When?***
*This old lady came up to me and said... – **Which (old) lady?***
*This old lady came up to me and said... – She said **what?***

7 Question-word questions can echo statements to express surprise, anger, concern, etc.:
*I'm afraid I used your comb on the dog. – You did **what** with it?*

8 All question-words except *Which* and *Whose* can combine with *else* to refer to people, things, places, etc.:
***What else** have you bought? **Where else** did you go?*

13.32 How we use question-words

We ask question-word + inversion-type questions to elicit any element in a sentence other than the identity of the subject:
statement: *Elaine went to her mother's by bus yesterday because the trains weren't running.*

Note the 'target' of each of the following questions. None of them produces the answer 'Elaine'. The answer may be a single word, a phrase, a clause, or even a whole sentence [but > 13.41–42]:

questions	**answers**	**'target'**
When did Elaine go to her mother's?	*Yesterday.*	adverb of time
Where did Elaine go yesterday?	*To her mother's.*	adverb of place
How did she get there?	*By bus.*	adverb of manner
Whose house did Elaine go to?	*Her mother's.*	adverb of place
Why did she go by bus?	*Because the trains weren't running.*	clause of reason
What did Elaine do yesterday?	*She went to her mother's by bus.*	whole sentence

Sometimes two or more question-words are used in a question:

__Where and when__ shall I pick you up?
__How and why__ did Louis XIV justify the invasion of the Spanish Netherlands? (This kind of question is common in exam papers.)

Particular question-words and their uses

13.33 'Who(m)...?' as a question-word

Who(m)...? asks for the object of a sentence, usually a person's name:

	subject	verb		object
statement:	*Frank*	*met*		***Alice**.*
***Who(m)*-question**:	*Who(m) did Frank*	*meet?*	–	***Alice**.*

Who(m)...? refers only to people and can be used to inquire about masculine, feminine, singular or plural, so the answer to the above question could be *Alice*, *John* or *Alice and John*.
Though *Whom...?* is still used in formal English, spoken or written, *Who...?* is generally accepted in everyday style. *Who(m)...?* often occurs in questions with verbs followed by *to* or *for*:

__Who(m)__ did you give it __to__/did you buy it __for__? [compare > 8.22]

13.34 'What...?' as a question-word

What...? can be answered by a whole sentence:

What are you doing? – __I'm reading 'Kim'__.

What can also ask about the object of a sentence which might, for example, be a thing, a substance, a date, a measurement, etc.:

	subject	verb		object
statement:	*I*	*am reading*		***'Kim'**.*
***What*-question**:	*What are you*	*reading?*	–	***'Kim'**.*

What? can also be used in a variety of combinations, such as:

13.34.1 'What book/books...?' 'What boy/boys...?' [compare > 13.36.1]

What + noun asks about things (singular or plural) or substances:

__What book/books__ did you buy? __What soap__ do you use?

What + noun can sometimes ask about the identity of people, male or female, singular or plural:

__What boy/boys/girl/girls/people__ did you meet at the party?

but this is less common, since we generally ask about people with *Who(m)...?*. *What...?* on its own refers only to things and to an unlimited and unspecified choice. So, for example, the question *What would you like?* with reference to a menu is not limited – except, of course, by the extent of the menu itself. Where the choice is limited and specified, we often prefer *Which...?* as in: e.g. *Which would you prefer, beef or lamb?*

13.34.2 'What (be, look, etc.) like?' [compare > 6.1]

We use *What...like?* to obtain descriptions of: e.g.

- people or things; appearance or characteristics:
  What's *your brother* ***like****?* (= 'to look at' or 'as a person')
  What's *your car* ***like****?* (= 'to look at' or 'as a vehicle/to drive')
- the weather, climate, etc.:
  What's the weather like *today?* ***What's it like*** *today?*

13.34.3 'What...?': names, etc.

- people: ***What's*** *he* ***called****?* (= What's his name?) *He****'s called John****.*
- technical terms, etc.: ***What's*** *this* ***called****? It****'s called a microchip****.*
- foreign words: ***What's*** *this* ***called*** *in English? It****'s called chalk****.*
- *What* + *make*: ***What make*** *is your car? – It****'s a Volvo****.*

13.34.4 'What...?': nationality, jobs, etc.

What nationality *are you? – I'm* ***Spanish****.* (= I'm from Spain.)
What does she do *(for a living)? – She's* ***an optician****.*
And ***what's*** *her husband?* (= What does her husband do?)

13.34.5 'What time/date/year?'

These combinations are broadly the equivalent of *When...?* except that they ask for more specific information:

What time/date *will he arrive? – At 4./On June 14th.*

13.34.6 'What...for?'

This combination asks for a description of the use or purpose of things or substances:

What's *this (thing)* ***for****? –* ***(It's for)*** *peeling potatoes.*

What + clause + *for* can act as the equivalent of *Why...?*. The answer often begins with *Because...* or has a *to*-infinitive:

What *did you do that* ***for****?* (= Why did you do that?)
– ***Because*** *I was signalling that I'm turning left.*
– ***To signal*** *that I'm turning left.*

13.34.7 'What kind(s)/sort(s) of...?' [compare > App 7.16–17]

This combination asks for precise information and we expect a description in the answer:

What kind/sort of picture *do you like best?*
What kinds/sorts of pictures *do you like best?*

What kind of pictures...? is often heard in speech.

13.34.8 'What colour...?', 'What size...?'

What colour? and *What colours?* are used to inquire about colour:

What colour *is your new tie? – It's* ***red****.*

What combines with nouns such as *size, height, age, length, breadth, width, depth*, to inquire about dimension, etc. The structure is parallel to *How big/high/old/long?* etc. [> 13.40.2, 6.16]:

What size *shoes do you take? – (Size) 41.*
What's the height *of Everest?* ***What height*** *is Everest?*

13.35 'When...?' as a question-word

We use *When...?* to inquire about time (either precise references or general periods of time) in the present, past or future. The answers are usually adverbs of time or prepositional phrases:

adverb of time: ***When*** *is your flight? –* ***Tomorrow morning****.*
prepositional phrase: ***When*** *will he arrive? –* ***At 4****.*

13.36 'Which...?' as a question-word

Questions with *Which...?* can ask about the object of a sentence:

		subject	verb	object
statement:		*I*	*am reading*	***'Kim'****.*
***Which*-question**:	*Which novel are*	*you*	*reading?* –	***'Kim'****.*

Which + noun can be used in a variety of combinations:

13.36.1 'Which book/books...?' [compare > 13.34.1]
We use *Which* + noun to inquire about things (singular or plural) or substances:

Which book/books *do you prefer?* ***Which soap*** *do you like best?*

Which + noun can be used just as easily to ask about the identity of people, male or female, singular or plural:

Which boy/boys/girl/girls *did you meet at the party?*

Which always refers to a limited specified choice [> 13.34.1]. It can be used on its own in this sense, especially for things:

Which books *did you buy?* (i.e. of the ones you were looking at: a limited selection of items)
Which *is the longest river in the world: the Amazon or the Nile?*

Which...? often combines with the comparative and superlative:

Which *is* ***the cheaper/the cheapest****?* (e.g. of the ones on the shelf)

13.36.2 'Which of them/of the two...?' [compare > *Which one(s)?* 4.10]
We often use *Which of...?* (the *of* phrase is optional) when we refer to preference and choice between two or more items:

I like both these bags. ***Which (of the two)*** *do you prefer?*
I like all these bags. ***Which (of them)*** *do you prefer?*

13.36.3 'Which day/month/year...?'
These combinations are more specific than *When...?*

Don't forget Sam's birthday? – I won't. ***Which/What day*** *is it?*

13.36.4 'Which way...?'
Which way...? asks for more precise information than *Where...?*:

Which way *did they go?* (i.e. two or more ways to choose from)

13.37 'Why...?' as a question-word

13.37.1 'Why...?': reason and purpose [> 1.48, 1.51]
Why questions may ask for a reason or reasons which can be supplied with *Because...* (Not **Why...**):

Why didn't you tell me *John had left you?*
– ***Because*** *I didn't want to burden you with my troubles.*

Because is often omitted (and therefore implied) in responses.
A *to*-infinitive or *because* can answer *Why?* [purpose > 16.12.1]:

Why *did you go this way? –* ***To save*** *time.* ('because I wanted to')

13.37.2 'Why don't/doesn't...?' and 'Why not?'

Why + *don't* or *doesn't* can be used to make suggestions:

I don't like this wallpaper. – Then ***why don't you change*** *it?*

Why not followed by a bare infinitive can be used in the same way:

Why not wait *till the winter sales to buy a new coat?*

Why not? (in place of a *Why* question) can ask for a reason:

I'm not going to work today. – ***Why not?***

or can be used in response to suggestions:

Let's eat out tonight. – Yes, ***why not****?*

It can be used defensively in:

Are you really going to sue them? – Yes, ***why not****?*

13.37.3 Some functional uses of 'Why...?'

Why + verb often conveys the meaning of 'It's not worth the trouble to...' or 'I don't think you should':

I think I ought to tidy this place up.
– ***Why bother?*** (i.e. it's not worth bothering to)
You're fully insured, so ***why worry****?*

Why combines with modals to convey a variety of emotions, etc.:

- anger: ***Why can't*** *you shut up?*
- irritation/complaint: ***Why should*** *I do it?*
- failure to understand: ***Why should*** *the boiling point of water be lower at the top of a mountain?*

13.38 'Where...?' as a question-word

Where is used to inquire about place (either precise references or general ones). The answers to *Where* questions can be whole sentences, phrases or single words:

Where *is he? –* ***He's over there. Over there! There!***
Where did you get that ladder ***from****? –* ***From the garage.***

In everyday speech *Where's* can combine with a plural subject:

Where's ***your keys****? – They're here.* [compare *Here's* > 7.59.1]

Where...from? asks for the origin of people or things:

Where *are you* ***from****?/****Where*** *do you come* ***from****? – Spain.*
That's a lovely vase. ***Where's*** *it* ***from****? – China.*

13.39 'Whose...?' as a question-word

Whose...? asks about possession. The possessor is always a person and we expect the answer to be somebody's name + *'s* (*Kate's*) or a possessive pronoun (e.g. *mine*). When the possession is a thing, things, or a substance, the noun can be omitted after *Whose*:

Whose (umbrella) *is this? – (It's) mine.*
Whose (umbrellas) *are these? – (They're) mine.*
Whose (coffee) *is this? – (It's) mine.*

When the 'possession' is a person, *Whose* is followed by a noun:

Whose son/daughter *is (s)he? – Kate's.* (= Kate's son/daughter)
Whose children *are they? – The Lakers'.* (= the Lakers' children)

Note that questions with *Whose* can also be phrased as:

Whose *is this* ***(umbrella)****?* ***Whose*** *are those* ***children****?*

13.40 'How ...?' as a question-word

13.40.1 'How much...?/How many...?'

How can combine with *much* to inquire about the quantity of a substance or the volume of a liquid [uncountable nouns > 2.14].

__How much sugar/milk__ do you want in your tea?

How much can combine with abstract uncountable nouns as well:

__How much time__ have we? __How much space__ is there on that shelf?

How much can also refer to cost:

__How much__ does this cost? (i.e. How much money?)

How can combine with *many* to inquire about number (people and things: i.e. plural countable nouns) [> 5.13]:

__How many people__ are invited? __How many windows__ are broken?

13.40.2 'How...?' + adjective or adverb

How will combine with a variety of adjectives, some of which can also function as adverbs, such as: *big, deep, far, hard, long, old, sharp, wide* [> 7.13–14 and compare > 6.16]:

__How far__ is it to Banbury? __How far__ did you drive today?

How combines more readily with adjectives expressing a higher, rather than a lower, degree: *How long/old*, etc. rather than *How little/short/young*. We only use *How* + lower degree adjectives when we are particularly concerned about smallness, etc.:

I think he's __too young__ for the job. – __How young__ is he then?
We need a __short__ article to fill the paper. – __How short__ must it be?

How + adjectives referring to dimension (e.g. *How long?*) are similar in meaning to *What* + nouns (dimension) e.g. *What length?* [> 13.34.8]:

__How long__ is this pool? (= What length is this pool?)

13.40.3 'How...?' + adverb

How combines with adverbs to ask about:

- frequency: *__How often__ do you visit your mother? – Once a week.*
- degree: *__How well__ do you know him? – Not very well.*
- time: *__How quickly__ can you do it for me? – In two days.*

13.40.4 'How...?': manner and process

How...? questions can ask about manner or process. Some questions need a whole sentence in reply:

__How did you spend your time__ while you were on holiday?

Some questions like this can be answered with *by* + *-ing*:

__How did you finish__ the job so soon? – __By climbing__ on to the roof.

How combines with modals in:

- rude responses: *Why ask me? __How should I know?__*
- argument/reproof: *__How can you say__ a thing like that?*
- exclamations: *__How could she do__ such a thing!*

Adverbs of manner can sometimes answer *How?* questions:

__How__ did he speak? – (Rather) __well/inaudibly__.

It isn't always clear what kind of answer a *How?* question requires:

__How__ did she cut Sue's hair? – Beautifully./Very short./With a fringe./With the kitchen scissors.

13.40.5 'How long...?': time

How long...? (with optional *for*) asks about duration:

How long *have you known her* ***(for)****?* – ***(For) 20 years****.*
I've known her ***a long time****.* – ***How long (for)?***

How can also combine with *long ago* to refer to a point of time:
How long ago *did Bach live?* – ***300 years ago****.* (*ago* not optional)

13.40.6 Some social uses of 'How...?'

introductions: *How do you do?* is a formula in formal introductions and is never used to inquire about health:
A: *Mrs Simms, this is Mr McGregor.*
B: ***How do you do?***
C: ***How do you do?*** (in reply to B)

health: Common formulas for asking about health or general well-being are: *How are you?, How have you been?, How are you keeping?, How have you been keeping?.*

present circumstances: *How* is often used to inquire about 'present circumstances' in questions like: *How's life?, How are* (or *How's*) *things?, How's the garden?, How's work?*, etc.

'How...?' and ***'What...like?'*** [> 13.34.2]: These can sometimes be interchangeable in questions which ask for personal reactions:
How *was the film?* (= What was it like? Did you enjoy it or not?)
How can be followed by *like* or *enjoy* in such questions:
How *did you* ***like/enjoy*** *the film?*

'How about...?' and ***'What about...?'*** : These are interchangeable in offers and suggestions:
How about/What about *a drink?*
and in general reference:
I'll post your letters. – ***How about/What about*** *this parcel?*
John's coming with us. – ***How about/What about*** *Susan?*

invitations:
How would you like to *have tea at the Ritz?*
This is an elaborate form of the more usual:
Would you like to *have tea at the Ritz?* [> 11.37]

Question-word questions: subject-questions

13.41 Form of subject-questions

subject-questions with 'Who?'	**subject-answer + auxiliary**	
Who's ready?	*I am./John is.* etc.	***be***
Who's got my keys?	*I have./John has.* etc.	***have***
Who makes the decisions?	*I do./John does.* etc.	***do/does***
Who paid the waiter?	*I did./John did.* etc.	***did***
Who can explain this?	*I can./John can.* etc.	**modals**
subject-questions with 'What?', 'Which?' and 'Whose?'		
What made you jump?	*The cat did.*	
Which one suits me best?	*The red one does.*	
Whose telephone rang?	*Mine did.*	

13.42 Notes on the form of subject-questions

1 A subject-question normally asks for the identity of the subject. There is no inversion and the question has the same word order as the statement [compare > 13.31*ns*.1,2]:

	subject	verb	object	subject-answer
statement:	***Someone***	*paid*	*the waiter.*	
subject-question:	***Who***	*paid*	*the waiter?*	***John** did.*

Compare a *Who* question which asks for the object of a statement:

		subject	verb	object	object-answer
statement:		*John*	*paid*	***the waiter**.*	
Yes/No question:		*Did John*	*pay*	***the waiter**?*	
***Who(m)*-question**:	***Who(m)***	*did John*	*pay?*		***The waiter**.*

2 Answers to subject-questions often echo the auxiliary used in the question, either in the affirmative or the negative:
***Who can** play the piano? – **I can./I can't**.*
When the subject question-word is followed by a verb in the simple present or past, then *do, does* or *did* may be used in the answer:
***Who wants** a lift? – **I do**. **Who won**? – **We did**.*
When the answer is a name or a noun, we often omit the auxiliary:
***Who was** at the door? – **The postman** (was).*
Informally, *me* is often used in place of *I* in the answer [> 4.7.2]:
***Who wants** some more tea? – **Me**.* (in place of *I do*)

3 *What, Which* and *Whose* can combine with other subject-words:
***What number** is...? **Which boy** likes...? **Whose car** is...?*

4 Subject question-words can be followed by singular or plural verbs. In everyday speech we commonly use a singular verb after, e.g. *Who?* even when we are asking for a plural answer:
***Who is** coming tonight? **John is./John and Sally are**.*
However, plural verbs can occur quite naturally after subject questions with *Who, Which* and *What*:
***Who are** playing in the orchestra?*
***Who have** won Nobel Prizes for literature in the past ten years?*

13.43 When we ask subject-questions

We ask subject-questions:
- with *Who* to identify a person or persons:
  ***Who** takes sugar? – **Jane** (does). **Both of us** (do).*
- with *What* to identify a thing or things:
  ***What** caused the damage? – **Rain** (did). **Falling stones** (did).*
- with *What* + noun to identify people or things:
  ***What** careless **boy** left the tap on? – **John** (did).*
  ***What paper** has the largest circulation? – **'Today'** (has).*
- with *Which* to identify people or things:
  ***Which girl** spoke first? – **Jane** (did).*
  ***Which** comes first, A or B? – **A** (does).*
- with *Whose* to identify a 'possessor':
  ***Whose children** rang our doorbell? – **Our neighbour's** (did).*
- with e.g. *How* + *many* to elicit a number:
  ***How many students** understand this? – **They all do**.*

Questions about alternatives

13.44 Form of questions about alternatives

What/Which would you prefer, tea or coffee?
Would you like tea or coffee? Tea or coffee? Milk?
How shall we go, by bus or by train?
Did you go there, or didn't you?
Did you or didn't you go there?
Did you go there or not? Did you or didn't you?

13.45 When we ask questions about alternatives

13.45.1 Limited choices

Questions about alternatives narrow a choice to a limited number of items, courses of action, etc.:

- open-ended choice: *What would you like to drink?*
- three items: *What would you like* ***tea, coffee, or milk****?*
- two items: *Which would you prefer,* ***tea or coffee****?*

Limited choices can also be presented with two or more verbs:

Did you ***laugh or cry****? Is he* ***sleeping, reading, or watching*** *TV?*

Questions about alternatives are often abbreviated: e.g.

- three or more items: ***Tea, coffee, or mineral water?***
- two items: ***Tea or coffee? True or false? Yes or no?***
- one item: ***Milk? Right? Ready? Now?***

Another way of abbreviating a question is not to repeat the verb:

Did you want a black and white film, ***or colour****?*

13.45.2 Questions ending in negative tags

A clear choice can be presented by repeating the auxiliary at the end, particularly when we are pressing someone to provide an answer:

Did you take it ***or didn't you****? – Yes, (I did)./No, (I didn't).*

These questions can be differently phrased as follows:

Did you or didn't you *take it?*

The negative auxiliary can be replaced by *or not?*:

Did you *take it* ***or not****?*

Provided both speaker and listener know what is referred to, such questions can be reduced even further:

Did you or didn't you? can mean 'Did you (take it) or didn't you?'
Can you or can't you? can mean 'Can you (help me) or can't you?'

Emphatic questions with 'ever', etc.

13.46 Form of emphatic questions with 'ever', etc.

Who ever told you a thing like that? What ever made you do it?
What ever did he tell you? How ever do you manage?
Why ever not? Why on earth not?
What ever for? What on earth for?
Why did you ever mention it?
How on earth did you find out about it?

13.47 When we ask emphatic questions

We ask emphatic questions to express admiration, anger, concern, etc. *Ever* is written as a separate word from question-words. It can be used after all question-words except *Which?* and *Whose?*. It is often heavily stressed in questions:

Where 'ever *did you pick that up?*

(But note that *ever* also combines with words like *who, what, when, how* (not *why*) to form adverbs (*However, ...*), or pronouns (*Bring whoever you like*), or to form conjunctions (*Come whenever you like*).)

Ever questions can ask for the subject or object of a sentence:

subject: ***What ever made you so late****? – The traffic (made me late).*

object: ***What ever did he tell you****? – (He told me) a secret.*

Ever can sometimes be transposed:

Why ever *did you go there?* ***Why*** *did you* ***ever*** *go there?*

Short responses express surprised reactions:

I didn't vote on polling day. – ***Why ever*** *not?*

I sent them a donation. – ***What ever*** *for?*

In everyday speech stronger emphasis in questions can be conveyed by using the expression *on earth* in place of *ever* after the question-word:

How on earth *did you find out my telephone number?*

Even stronger expression is possible if *on earth* is replaced by, e.g. *the blazes, the devil, the dickens, the hell* and by taboo words:

Who the hell *do you think you are anyway?*

Why and *Where* can be made more emphatic by simple repetition, often with *oh*:

Why, (oh) why *did you do it?* ***Where, (oh) where*** *has he gone?*

14 Conditional sentences

General information about conditionals

14.1 Conditions: 'if... (then...)'

A condition is something that has to be fulfilled before something else can happen. *If*, normally meaning 'provided that', is sometimes followed by *then*. If *then* is not stated, it is implied: *If X happens, (then) Y follows*:

If the rain stops, *we'll be able to go for a walk.*

Conditional clauses after *if* are not about events, etc. that have occurred, but about events that can or might occur or might have occurred. Sometimes these events are highly probable:

If the price of oil comes down, ***more people will buy it****.*

Sometimes they are impossible (they did not or cannot happen):

If my horse had won, ***I would have made a lot of money****.*

Conditions are often introduced by *if*, but can be introduced by other words [> 14.21]. They can also be implied [> 14.22]:

I wouldn't (or ***shouldn't***) ***go that way****.* (i.e. if I were you)

14.2 Types of conditional sentences

Conditional sentences are usually divided into three basic types referred to as Type 1, Type 2 and Type 3. Each has its own variations, but the elements are as follows:

type 1: *What will you do if you lose your job?*
Asking/talking about something that is quite possible:

'if'	**+ present**	+	**'will'**
If	*I* ***lose*** *my job,*		*I* ***will go*** *abroad.*

type 2: *What would you do if you lost your job?*
Asking/talking about imagined situations/consequences now:

'if'	**+ past**	+	**'would'**
If	*I* ***lost*** *my job,*		*I* ***would go*** *abroad.*

type 3: *What would you have done if you had lost your job?*
Asking/talking about imagined situations/consequences then:

'if'	**+ past perfect**	+	**'would have'**
If	*I* ***had lost*** *my job,*		*I* ***would have gone*** *abroad.*

The abbreviation *'ll* can be used instead of *will* in all persons, and *shall* can be used instead of *will* after *I* and *we* [> 9.36].
The abbreviation *'d* can be used instead of *would* in all persons, and *should* can be used instead of *would* after *I* and *we*.

The conditional can be expressed with other modal verbs [e.g. > 14.19], as well as with *shall, will, should* and *would*:

We ***could have had*** *a good time.* (e.g. if we had had the money)

14.3 Mixed tense sequences in conditional sentences

Sense and context permitting, any tense sequence is possible:

type 1	**type 3**
If I am as clever as you think,	*I should have been rich by now.*
type 2	**type 3**
If you knew me better,	*you wouldn't have said that.*
type 3	**type 2**
If I had had your advantages,	*I'd be better off now.*
type 2	**type 1**
If he missed the bus,	*he won't be here on time.*

Type 1 conditionals

14.4 Basic form of Type 1 conditionals

	'if'-clause: present tenses condition to be satisfied →	**main clause: 'shall/will' future likely outcome**
be:	*If I am better tomorrow,*	*I will get up.*
have:	*If I have a headache,*	*I will take an aspirin.*
simple present:	*If she finishes early,*	*she will go home.*
present progressive:	*If he is standing in the rain,*	*he will catch cold.*
present perfect:	*If she has arrived at the station,*	*she will be here soon.*
present perfect progressive:	*If he has been travelling all night,*	*he will need a rest.*
can, must:	*If I can afford it,*	*I will buy it.*

14.5 Notes on the form of Type 1 conditionals

1 The most commonly used form is:
'if' + simple present + ''ll' future
If it rains, we'll stay at home.
However, in Type 1 conditionals, all present tenses can be used after *if*, not just the simple present (see 14.4 above).

2 In Type 1, *if* is followed by present tenses, and only exceptionally by *shall* or *will* [> 11.63, 14.24.2]. *If* can also be followed by *should* [> 14.8] and by other modals like *can* (ability), *must* and *needn't*.

3 Other future tenses [> 9.40–43] can be used in the main clause:
If he gets the job, ***he'll be going abroad***.
If I don't run, ***the train will have left***.
If I stay till May, ***I'll have been working*** *here for 20 years.*

4 Fixed phrases like *if necessary, if possible, if so*, are really abbreviated *if*-clauses. In formal English (commonly in AmE) the full form is *if* + *be* (i.e. the subjunctive [> 11.75.1*n*.2]): *if it be necessary*, etc. Note other phrases with *be: if need be, be that as it may*, etc:
Inflation may be rising. ***If (this be) so,*** *prices will go up.*
We often use *should* before *be* in such cases, especially when we wish to suggest that the situation referred to is improbable:
Sterling may fall. ***If this should be so,*** *interest rates will rise.*

14.6 When we use Type 1 conditionals

We use Type 1 conditionals to describe what will or won't happen if we think a future event is probable:

condition to be satisfied →	**likely outcome**
If the weather clears,	***we'll go for a walk.***
If the weather doesn't clear,	***we won't go for a walk.***

The condition to be satisfied is real: the weather may really clear up, and if it does, it will have a real effect. That is why such statements are often called 'open' or 'real' conditionals.

14.7 Type 1, Variation 1: 'If' + present + modal

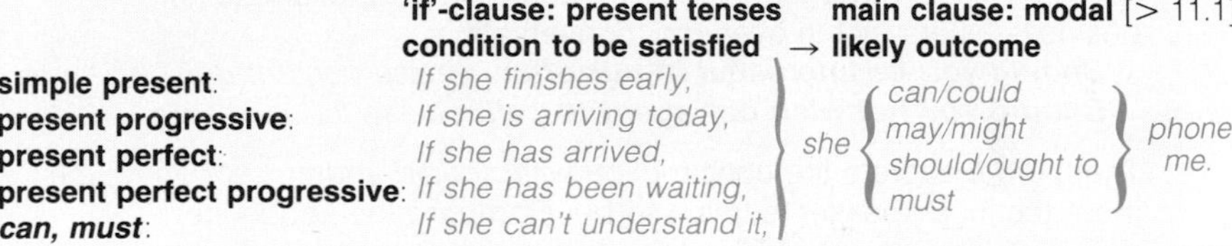

	'if'-clause: present tenses **condition to be satisfied** →	**main clause: modal** [> 11.1] **likely outcome**
simple present:	*If she finishes early,*	*she can/could / may/might / should/ought to / must phone me.*
present progressive:	*If she is arriving today,*	
present perfect:	*If she has arrived,*	
present perfect progressive:	*If she has been waiting,*	
can, must:	*If she can't understand it,*	

Will in the main clause expresses certainty or near-certainty [> 11.28]. If we do not feel 'certain' enough to use *will*, or if we want to express the idea of e.g. necessity, we can use another modal instead:

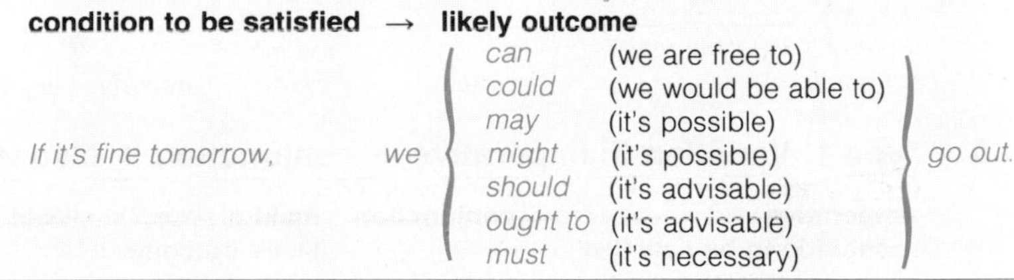

condition to be satisfied →	**likely outcome**			
If it's fine tomorrow,	*we*	*can*	(we are free to)	*go out.*
		could	(we would be able to)	
		may	(it's possible)	
		might	(it's possible)	
		should	(it's advisable)	
		ought to	(it's advisable)	
		must	(it's necessary)	

Progressive and perfect combinations with modals are possible:

*If I hear from Tim, **I may be leaving tonight**.*
*If he is in New York, **he may not have got** my letter yet.*

14.8 Type 1, Variation 2: 'If + should' + e.g. imperative

'if'-clause or variation **condition to be satisfied** →	**main clause: e.g. imperative** **request, suggestion, etc.**
If you (should) see him,	*please give him my regards.*
Should you see him,	
If you (should) happen to see him,	
Should you happen to see him,	

If + *should* (+ bare infinitive), instead of *if* + present, makes the condition more doubtful:

If he calls, *tell him I'll ring back.* (normal Type 1)
If he should call, *tell him I'll ring back.* (*if* + *should*)

The main clause is not necessarily always an imperative:

*If I should see him, **I'll ask** him to ring you.*

If + *should* + imperative in the main clause is used especially when we want to make polite requests or suggestions, or to tell people (tactfully) what to do:

If you should write to her, ***send her my love***.
If you should go to Nairobi, ***go and see the Snake Park***.

Imperatives can also be used in ordinary Type 1 conditions:

Cancel the match *if it rains. If it rains,* ***cancel the match***.

The only kind of negative we can form with *should* is e.g. *should you not* (see example next paragraph); otherwise we must use the negative form of the simple present:

If you don't see him... (Not **If you shouldn't**)

A condition can be expressed without *if* by beginning a sentence with *should*. This is rather formal and is often found, for example, in business letters, not in everyday conversation:

Should you be interested in our offer, *please contact us.*
Should you not wish our agent to call, *please let us know.*

The more elaborate the construction with *should* and/or *happen to*, the more tactful a speaker is trying to be. Compare the sequence:

If you	*see him*	**fairly likely: neutral**
If you should	*see him*	↓
Should you	*see him*	
If you happen to	*see him*	
If you should happen to	*see him*	
Should you happen to	*see him*	
Should you by any chance happen to	*see him*	**unlikely: very tactful**

14.9 Type 1, Variation 3: Imperative + conjunction + clause

imperative condition to be satisfied	conjunction →	main clause: 'shall/will' likely outcome
Provide the materials	*and*	*we'll do the job.*
Stop shouting,	*or*	*you'll wake up the neighbours.*
Put that down,	*or else*	*I'll smack you.*
Be there on time,	*otherwise*	*you'll create a bad impression.*

Imperatives can be used in place of *if*-clauses to comment, make requests, make a bargain, offer advice, threaten and so on. The use of the imperative conveys more urgency than the *if*-clause:

comment: ***Fail to pay and*** *they'll cut off the electricity.*
(***If you fail to pay,*** *they'll cut off the electricity.*)
request: ***Tell us what to do and*** *we'll get on with it.*
(***If you tell us what to do*** *we'll get on with it.*)
threat: ***Stop eating sweets, or*** *you won't get any dinner.*
(***If you don't stop eating sweets,*** *you won't get any dinner.*)
advice: ***Take a taxi, otherwise*** *you'll miss your train.*
(***If you don't take a taxi,*** *you'll miss your train.*)

Note the difference between imperative + *or* and imperative + *and* in threats:

Drop that gun, ***or*** *I'll shoot you.* (i.e. if you don't drop it)
Drop that parcel, ***and*** *I'll kill you.* (i.e. if you do drop it)

Type 2 conditionals

14.10 Basic form of Type 2 conditionals

	'if'-clause: past tense condition to be satisfied →	main clause: 'would/should' likely outcome
be:	*If I was taller,*	*I would become a policeman.*
have:	*If he had any money,*	*he'd leave home.*
other verbs:	*If you took a taxi,*	*you'd get there quicker.*
could [> 11.12]:	*If you could see me now,*	*you'd laugh your head off.*

14.11 Notes on the form of Type 2 conditionals

1 The most commonly used form is:

'if' + simple past + ''d' conditional

If it rained tomorrow we'd stay at home.

In Type 2, *if* is followed by a past tense or *could* (= was/were able to). The main clause is normally formed with *would*, though *should* (weakened to /ʃəd/ in speech but not contracted to *'d* in writing) can be used instead of *would* after *I* and *we*. *Would* is generally contracted to *'d* in all persons in the main clause. Compare *shall* and *will* [> 9.36]. *If* is followed only exceptionally by *would* [> 14.24.1].

2 An unnecessary extra negative can occur in Type 2 conditionals:

I wouldn't be surprised if he ***didn't try*** *to blackmail you.*

(i.e. if he tried to blackmail you)

The *not* in the *if*-clause does not make a true negative.

14.12 When we use Type 2 conditionals

Type 2 conditionals talk about imaginary situations in the *if*-clause and speculate about their imaginary consequences in the main clause. Though past tenses are used, the reference is not to past time. (That is why this use of the past tense after *if* is often called 'the unreal past'.) By comparison, Type 1 conditionals [> 14.4] talk about things which will possibly happen and consider their real consequences for the future.

Depending on the attitude of the speaker, a Type 2 conditional can be used in place of a Type 1 to describe something that is reasonably possible. So:

If you ***went*** *by train, you* ***would*** *get there earlier.*

If you ***didn't stay up*** *so late every evening, you* ***wouldn't*** *feel so sleepy in the morning.*

mean the same, but are more 'tentative' than:

If you ***go*** *by train, you* ***will*** *get there earlier.*

If you ***don't stay up*** *so late every evening, you* ***won't*** *feel so sleepy in the morning.*

However, Type 2 conditionals more often describe what is totally impossible:

If I had longer legs, ***I'd be able to run faster****.*

14.13 Type 2, Variation 1: 'If + were/was' + 'would/should'

'if'-clause: 'were/was' condition to be satisfied	→	main clause: 'would/should' likely outcome	
If { *I/he/she/it were/was* / *you/we/they were* }	*ready*	{ *I would* (or *should*) / *we would* (or *should*) / *you/they* (etc.) *would* }	*go.*

14.13.1 'If I were/If I was'

Were can be used in place of *was* after *If I/he/she/it*. There is no difference in meaning, but *were* is more formal, particularly when we are making doubtful statements:

If I was/were better qualified, *I'd apply for the job.*

However, *were* is preferable in purely imaginary statements:

If I were the Queen of Sheba, *you'd be King Solomon.*

14.13.2 'If I were you/If I were in your position' (Not **was**)

We often use these expressions to give advice:

If I were you/in your position, *I'd accept their offer.*

(This means: *You* should accept their offer.)

We can also use these expressions to refer to somebody else:

If I were Jane/in Jane's position, *I'd walk out on him.*

14.13.3 'If it were not for/Were it not for' (Not **was**)

This expression explains why something has or hasn't happened:

If it weren't for your help, *I would still be homeless.*

In formal contexts, *If it were not for* can be expressed as *Were it not for*, with the negative in full (Not **Weren't it**):

Were it not for your help, *I would still be homeless.*

If it were not for and *Were it not for* are often followed by *the fact that*

Were it not for the fact that you helped me, *I would be homeless.*

14.14 Type 2, Variation 2: 'If' + past + modal

'if'-clause: past tense condition to be satisfied	→	main clause: modal [> 11.1] likely outcome	
If he knew the facts, / *If he could get the facts,*	*he*	{ *could* / *might* }	*tell us what to do.*

Another modal can replace *would* in Type 2 conditionals, e.g. when we feel the imaginary consequences are less likely, or when we are referring to ability [> 11.14], possibility [> 11.28], etc.:

condition to be satisfied →	likely outcome	
If he were here,	*he could help us.*	(ability)
If he were here,	*he might help us.*	(possibility)
If he failed,	*he ought to/should try again.*	(duty)

Progressive and perfect combinations with modals are possible:

If she were here now, ***she could be helping us****.*

If he was in New York, ***he could have met my sister****.*

If they were in the army, ***they would have been fighting*** *in the jungle most of the time.*

14.15 Type 2, Variation 3: 'If + were to/was to' + 'would', etc.

'if'-clause: 'were to/was to' condition to be satisfied →		main clause: 'would/should', etc. likely outcome
If { *I/he/she/it*	*were to/was to ask,*	*I/we would/should,* etc.
you/we/they	*were to ask,*	*he/she/it/you/they would,* etc.

Instead of an ordinary verb in the simple past, we can use *were* or *was* + *to*-infinitive in Type 2 conditional clauses:

If I were to (or ***was to***) ***ask,*** *would you help me?*

Were to is more common than *was to* after *I/he/she/it* and makes a suggestion sound more tentative and polite. Compare:

If I asked him, *I'm sure he'd help us.*
– Do you think he would?
Well, ***if I were to ask him*** *nicely.*

Modals other than *would* and *should* are possible in the main clause:

If you were to ask him, ***he might help*** *you.*
If Sue were to make an effort, ***she could do*** *better.*

The same kind of conditional can be expressed without *if*, if we begin a sentence with *were* (Not **was**). This kind of inversion is common only in very formal contexts:

Were *the government* ***to*** *cut Value Added Tax, prices would fall.*

There is no negative construction (Not **If he were not to**) but negative inversion is possible with the full form:

There'd be a clear case for legal action over this matter ***were it not*** *likely* ***to make*** *life difficult for all of us.* (Not **weren't it**)

Type 3 conditionals

14.16 Basic form of Type 3 conditionals

	'if'-clause: past perfect imagined condition →	main clause: 'would have/should have' imagined outcome
be:	*If I had been taller,*	*I would have joined the police force.*
have:	*If I had had any sense,*	*I would have kept quiet about it.*
past perfect:	*If we had gone by car,*	*we would have saved time.*
past perfect progressive:	*If I had been trying harder,*	*I would have succeeded.*
could have:	*If I could have stopped,*	*there wouldn't have been an accident.*

14.17 Notes on the form of Type 3 conditionals

1 The most commonly used form is:

'if' + past perfect + 'would have' [for *should (have)*, > 14.11*n*.1]
If   it had rained,   we would have stayed at home.

Progressive forms are possible in the *if*-clause and/or main clause:

If it had been raining *this morning, we would have stayed at home.*
If I had not got married, ***I would still have been living*** *abroad.*

2 *If* is followed by the past perfect or *could have* (= had been able to). *Would have* and *should have* are not used in the *if*-clause. However, in everyday speech (never in writing) the following non-standard form (a kind of 'double past perfect') often occurs and should be avoided:
If I'd have known she was ill, I'd have sent her some flowers.

3 The abbreviation *'d* can stand for *had* or *would* and is common in both speech and informal writing:
If ***I'd*** (= I had) *left sooner,* ***I'd*** (= I would) *have been on time.*
The abbreviations *I would've* and *I'd've* for *would have* are common in speech. Only *would've* and *'d have* occur in informal writing:
If ***I'd*** *got up earlier,* ***I would've/I'd have*** *been on time.*

14.18 When we use Type 3 conditionals

Type 3 conditionals assume something purely imaginary in the *if*-clause and consider the imagined consequences in the main clause. In this respect, they are like Type 2 [> 14.12]. However, Type 3 conditionals refer to consequences which did not and could not (now) ever happen because they refer to something that didn't happen in the past. They are 'hypothetical conditions':

If I had worked harder at school, *I'd have got a better job.*
If I hadn't been wearing a raincoat, *I would have got wet.*
(referring to something possible: often expressing regret)
If I had won the pools, *life would have been much easier.*
(referring to an imaginary, hoped for situation in the past)
If I had lived in the Stone Age, *I would have been a hunter.*
(referring to a completely impossible situation)

We use Type 3 conditionals to speculate about a range of possibilities, from what might have been reasonably expected to what would have been completely impossible.

14.18.1 'If I had been you/in your position'

We often use these expressions to describe a course of action we would have followed in someone else's position:
If I had been you/in your position, *I'd have accepted their offer.*
(This means: *You* should have accepted their offer.)

We can also use these expressions to refer to somebody else:
If I had been Jane, *I'd have walked out on him years ago.*

14.18.2 'If it hadn't been for'

We often use this expression to explain why something didn't happen in the past:
If it hadn't been for the rain, *we would have had a good harvest.*

14.18.3 Inversion with 'had' in Type 3 conditionals

The form *Had (he)* is a formal variation of *If (he) had*:
Had the management acted sooner, *the strike wouldn't have happened.*

A negative inversion is possible with the full form:
Had it not been for *the unusually bad weather, the rescue party would have been able to save the stranded climber.* (Not **Hadn't**)

14.19 Type 3, Variation 1: 'If' + past perfect + modal

'if'-clause: past perfect tense **imagined condition**	**→**	**main clause: modal** [> 11.1] **imagined outcome**	
If he had known the facts, *If he could have got the facts,*	*he*	*could* *might*	*have told us what to do.*

Another modal can replace *would* in Type 3 conditionals, e.g. when we feel that the imagined consequences were less likely, or when we are referring to ability [> 11.15], possibility [> 11.28], etc.:

imagined condition	**→ imagined outcome**	
If he had been here yesterday,	*he* ***could have told us.***	(ability)
If he had been here yesterday,	*he* ***might have told us.***	(possibility)
If he had received a present,	*he* ***should have thanked her.***	(duty)

Progressive and perfect combinations with modals are possible:

If he had been here, ***he could have been helping us in the shop.***
If she had been here, ***she could have met my sister.***

Other uses of 'if' and similar conjunctions

14.20 Negatives with 'if...not' and 'unless'

If...not and *unless* are sometimes interchangeable, but there are occasions when it is impossible to use one in place of the other.

14.20.1 When 'if...not' and 'unless' are interchangeable

Both *if...not* and *unless* can be used in negative Type 1 conditionals without a noticeable change of meaning:

If you don't *change your mind, I won't be able to help you.*
Unless you *change your mind, I won't be able to help you.*

However, *unless* is 'stronger' than *if...not* and is sometimes preferable, e.g. in an ultimatum:

Unless *the management improve their offer, there'll be a strike.*

14.20.2 When we cannot use 'unless' in place of 'if...not'

Unless cannot replace *if...not* in a Type 1 sentence like:

I'll be surprised ***if he doesn't win.***

This is because *unless* always means 'except on the condition that', so we cannot normally use it to refer to 'unreal' situations:

She'd be better company ***if she didn't complain*** *so much.*

14.20.3 When we cannot use 'if...not' in place of 'unless'

We often use *unless* in past references to introduce an afterthought. The *unless*-clause follows the main clause and is usually separated by a dash rather than a comma:

I couldn't have got to the meeting on time — ***unless*** *of course I had caught an earlier train.*

This means the speaker didn't get to the meeting. He could only have done so by catching an earlier train. If we use *if...not* in place of *unless* in the above sentence, we get:

I couldn't have got there ***if I hadn't*** *caught an earlier train.*

The sentence now conveys the exact opposite meaning: the speaker *did* get to the meeting because he *did* catch an earlier train.

14.20.4 'If' and 'unless' clauses in short answers

Note how *if*-clauses and *unless*-clauses can occur in short answers:

Will you help us with all this re-decorating?
– Yes, ***if I can****. No,* ***not unless you pay me****.*

14.21 Conjunctions that can sometimes be used in place of 'if'

Conditionals can also be introduced by the following conjunctions, which do not always have precisely the same meaning as *if*: *as long as, assuming (that), even if, if only* [> 11.41–42], *on (the) condition (that), provided/providing (that), so long as* and *unless* [> 14.20]; also *suppose (that)* and *supposing (that)*, which normally introduce questions:

He'll definitely win, ***even if he falls over****.*
They'll lend us their flat ***on (the) condition (that) we look after it****.*
Providing/Provided (that) (or ***So/As long as***) ***you clear your desk*** *by this evening, you can have tomorrow off.*
Suppose/Supposing (that) we miss the train*, what shall we do?*

What if and *Say* can be used in the sense of 'Let us suppose':

What if/Say *he gets home before us and can't get in? What will he do then?*
What if/Say *you were to run out of money? What would you do?*

We can abbreviate a condition if we begin a new sentence with *If so, In that case*, or *If not*; or if we continue with *in which case*:

He may be busy, ***in which case*** *I'll call later.*
or: *He may be busy.* ***If so, (In that case,)*** *I'll call later.* ***If not,*** *can I see him now?*

Whether or not (Not **if or not**) introduces 'alternative' conditionals [compare > 1.24.1, 15.18*n*.7]:

Whether I feel well or not on Monday, *I'm going back to work.*
Whether or not I feel well on Monday, *I'm going back to work.*
You'll have to put up with it, ***whether you like it or not****.*

14.22 Implied conditionals

Conditionals can be implied (i.e. not directly introduced by *if*) in a variety of ways: e.g.

type 1:
With luck, *we'll be there by tomorrow.* (= if we're lucky)
Given time, *they'll probably agree.* (= if we give them time)

type 2:
To hear him talk, *you'd think he was Prime Minister.* (= if you could hear him talk)
I would write to her, ***but I don't know her address****.* (= if I knew her address)
But for his pension, *he would starve.* (= if he didn't have)

type 3:
Without your help, *I couldn't have done it.* (= if you hadn't helped)
In different circumstances, *I would have said yes.* (= if circumstances had been different)

14.23 'If' with meanings other than 'provided that'

14.23.1 'If' meaning 'when'

If it rains heavily, *our river floods.* (= on those occasions when)
If meaning 'when' often refers to permanent truths. The verb in the main clause may be either *will* or the simple present [> 11.64]:

If you boil water, *it* ***turns*** (or ***will turn***) *into steam.*

People commonly use the phrase *if and when* for emphasis in place of 'only when':

The dispute will end ***if and when*** *both sides agree.*

14.23.2 'If' meaning 'although' or 'even if'

I'll finish this report ***if it kills me****.* (i.e. even if)
Subject and verb can be omitted in clauses of this sort:

He's a pleasant, ***if awkward lad****.* (i.e. even if he is awkward)

14.23.3 'As if' in exclamations [compare > 1.47.2]

As if in this sense is common in exclamations:

As if I care *whether she's offended!* (= I don't care)
As if it matters/mattered! (= it doesn't matter)

14.23.4 'If' in place of 'whether' [> 1.24.1, 15.18*n*.5]

As well as introducing conditionals *if* also introduces indirect questions. In certain circumstances, *if* is more natural than *whether* in indirect questions:

He wants to know ***if*** *he can stay to dinner.*

'Will' and 'would' after 'if'

14.24 'If' + 'will' and 'would'

14.24.1 'Will' and 'would' to emphasize willingness and unwillingness

- when asking others to do things/responding to offers of help:
  Shall I hold the door open for you? – Yes, ***if you will/would****.*
  If you will/would/could wait *a moment, I'll fetch the money.*
- with reference to someone else:
  If he will/would/could only try harder, *I'm sure he'd do well.*
- in polite formulas, particularly in formal contexts:
  I'd be grateful ***if you will/would let me know soon****.*
  If you will/you would follow me, *I'll show you the way.*
  Give me a moment, ***if you would****.* (or, sometimes, *will*)
- in direct references to willingness/unwillingness:
  If you will/would agree *to pay us compensation, we will/would agree not to take the matter any further.* (i.e. if you're willing)
  If you won't stop smoking, *you can only expect to have a bad cough.* (i.e. if you are unwilling to stop smoking – Not **wouldn't**)

14.24.2 'If' + 'will' in Type 1 conditionals

We do not normally use a pure future *will* after *if*. However, though rare, it is just possible when we wish to emphasize the idea of 'not now, but later'. Compare:

If it ***suits you,*** *I'll change the date of our meeting.* (Type 1)
If it ***will suit you,*** (i.e. not now, but later) *I'll change the date of our meeting.*

15 Direct and indirect speech

Direct speech

15.1 When do we use direct speech?

We use direct speech whenever we speak. We use the term **direct speech** to describe the way we represent the spoken word in writing.

15.2 Form of direct speech in writing

actual spoken statement	**direct statement in writing**
'I'm waiting.'	*'I'm waiting,' John said.*
actual spoken question	**direct question in writing**
'When did you arrive, John?'	*'When did you arrive, John?' Mary asked.*

15.3 Notes on the use of punctuation marks

1 Quotation marks (or 'inverted commas') go round what is actually spoken and enclose other punctuation marks such as commas (,) full stops (.), question marks (?) and exclamation marks (!). They may be single ('...'), or double ("...") and are placed high above the base-line at the beginning *and* end of each quotation:
'Is that you, Jane?' Bob asked. "Is that you, Jane?" Bob asked.

2 What is said, plus reporting verb and its subject, is considered as a whole unit. When the subject + reporting verb [> App 45] comes at the beginning of a sentence, the reporting verb is always followed by a comma (sometimes by a colon (:) in AmE) and the quotation begins with a capital letter:
John said, 'It's good to see you.'
When the subject + reporting verb comes after what is said, the quotation has a comma before the second quotation mark:
'It's good to see you,' John said.
But if the quotation ends with an exclamation mark or a question mark, a comma is not used as well:
'Where can I get a taxi?' John asked.
Subject + verb can come in the middle of a quotation-sentence:
'Where, in this wretched town,' John asked, 'can I get a taxi?'
The second part of the quotation does not begin with a capital letter because it is not a separate sentence.

3 If there is a 'quote within a quote' (e.g. if we are quoting someone's exact words), we use a second set of quotation marks. If double quotation marks have been used on the 'outside', single ones are used on the 'inside' and vice versa. The inside quotation has its own punctuation, distinct from the rest of the sentence:
Ann said, 'Just as I was leaving, a voice shouted, "Stop!".'
'What do you mean, "Are you all right?"?' Ann asked.

We can also use a second set of quotation marks when we mention the title of e.g. a book, film or play:
'How long did it take you to read "War and Peace"?' I asked.
However, this is often a matter of personal taste. In print, titles often appear in italics without quotation marks.

4 Noun + reporting verb may be in subject + verb order or may be inverted (verb + subject) [> App 45.1]:
'This is a serious offence,' the judge said/said the judge.
If the subject is a long one, then inversion is usual:
'Where's this train going?' asked the lady sitting beside me.
With a pronoun subject, inversion is rare in modern English:
'This is a serious offence,' he said.
Some reporting verbs, particularly those requiring an object, such as *assure, inform* and *tell* cannot be inverted [> App 45.2].
Adverbs of manner usually come at the end [compare > 7.16.1]:
'Go away!' said Mr Tomkins/Mr Tomkins said angrily.

5 Quotation marks are generally not required with reporting verbs such as *ask oneself, think* and *wonder* when they are used to describe 'direct thoughts' in 'free indirect speech' [> 15.27.3]:
So that was their little game, he thought.
Where are they now, he wondered.

15.4 Direct speech in context

15.4.1 Printed dialogue

Printed dialogue is particularly common in works of fiction and can occur without connecting narrative:

'A tissue of lies!' Boyle cried.

'You think so?' the inspector asked.

'Think so? I know it.'

'And no doubt you can prove it. First there are a few important points that need answering.'

In this kind of dialogue, each new speech begins on a new line in a new paragraph. Once the characters have been established, it is not necessary to go on repeating names (or pronouns) and reporting verbs – except to remind the reader from time to time who is speaking. If a speech goes on for more than a paragraph, we put opening quotation marks at the beginning of each paragraph, but closing ones only at the end of the final paragraph.

Dialogue can also occur within connecting narrative:

Boyle was agitated. He paced the room as the inspector reconstructed the crime. Finally, he could bear it no longer. 'A tissue of lies!' he cried.

The inspector paused and asked with heavy irony, 'You think so?'

'Think so? I know it,' Boyle snapped.

The inspector was unconvinced. 'And no doubt you can prove it,' he said. 'First there are a few important points that need answering,' he added, glancing quickly at his notebook.

In this kind of dialogue, the words spoken by the characters are quoted within each new paragraph as part of the narration.

15.4.2 Quotations

We use the conventions of direct speech when we are quoting exact words, e.g. in letters, reports and statements by witnesses:

I reconstructed the crime and before I had finished speaking, Boyle said, 'A tissue of lies!' I asked the accused if he really thought so and he answered, 'Think so? I know it!'

15.4.3 Scripts

Quotation marks are not used in scripts for plays, etc.:

BOYLE (*agitated*):	*A tissue of lies!*
INSPECTOR WILEY:	*You think so?*
BOYLE (*sharply*):	*Think so? I know it!*
INSPECTOR WILEY:	*And no doubt you can prove it.*

'Say, 'tell' and 'ask'

15.5 Indirect speech and the sequence of tenses [compare > 9.5.2]

We use **indirect speech** (sometimes called 'reported speech') when we are telling someone what another person says or said. The reporting verb (e.g. *say, tell*) may be in the present or past (most often in the past) and the tenses of the reported statement are often (but not always) affected by this. Compare:

- actual spoken statement: *'I can see him now.'*
- direct statement in writing: *'I can see him now,' the boss says/said.*
- indirect statement (present): *The boss* ***says*** *(that) he* ***can see*** *you now.*
- indirect statement (past): *The boss* ***said*** *(that) he* ***could see*** *you now.*

Quotation marks are not used in indirect speech. For verbs that can introduce reported statements and questions [> App 45].

15.6 Reporting verbs and adjectives in direct/indirect speech

The commonest reporting verbs in both direct and indirect speech are *say, tell* and *ask*. Many other verbs can be followed by *that* or *if/whether* and can serve as reporting verbs [> App 45]. A number of these do not strictly 'report speech' (actual spoken words), but thoughts, feelings, etc. That is why 'indirect speech', as a term, is preferable to 'reported speech'. Similarly, a number of adjectives, such as *certain, sure* [> App 44] can be followed by *that, if, whether, (whether) to* and question-words.

15.7 The verbs 'say', 'tell' and 'ask'

15.7.1 Basic uses of 'say', 'tell' and 'ask'

These three verbs do not follow the same pattern. The most important thing to remember is that *tell* must be followed by a personal indirect object (*tell somebody...*). *Say* can be followed by an optional *to* + the person who is addressed:

'You haven't got much time,' ***he told me/he said (to me)***.

Ask can be followed by an indirect object [> 15.17, 16.20]:

'Are you comfortable?' ***he asked (me)****.*
He asked (me) *if I was comfortable.*

In reported requests [> 15.24, 16.20] the inclusion or not of an object affects the meaning:

She ***asked to go****.* (actual spoken words: *'May I go?'*)
She ***asked me to go****.* (actual spoken words: *'Will you go?'*)

The following references give further details about *say, tell* and *ask* :

- *say* in direct speech in writing [> 15.2–3, 15.8].
- *say* + *that*-clause, indirect statement [> 15.9–16].
- *say if/whether* + indirect Yes/No question [> 15.18*ns*.3,8].
- *say* + indirect *Wh*-question [> 15.20*n*.3].
- *say* + *to*-infinitive [> 15.24.1].

- *tell* somebody in direct speech in writing [> 15.2–3, 15.8].
- *tell* somebody + *that*-clause, indirect statement [> 15.9–16].
- *tell* somebody + *if/whether* + indirect Yes/No question [> 15.18*n*.8].
- *tell* somebody + indirect *Wh*-question [> 15.20*n*.3].
- *tell* somebody + *to*-infinitive [> 15.23–24, 16.21, 16.25].

- *ask* (somebody) in direct speech in writing [> 15.2–3, 15.8].
- *ask* (somebody) + *if/whether* + indirect Yes/No question [> 15.9, 15.17–18].
- *ask* (somebody) + *Wh*-question [> 15.19–22].
- *ask* (somebody) + *to*-infinitive [> 15.23–24, 16.20].
- *ask that* something (*should*) be done [> 11.75.2].

15.7.2 Secondary uses of 'say', 'tell' and 'ask'

- *say so* : *'The meeting's off,' Jill said.*
  'Who ***says so****?'*
  'The boss ***says so/said so****,' Jill answered.*
- the passive *'He is said to be'* [> 12.8*n*.3] does not have an active equivalent: Not **They say him to**, but: *They say (that) he is.*
- *say* + object in fixed expressions: e.g. *say a few words, say no more, say nothing, say (your) prayers, say something.*

- *tell* somebody *so* : *'You were right about the meeting,' I said.*
  'I ***told you so****,' Jill answered.*
- *tell* + object in fixed expressions: e.g. *(can) tell the difference, tell a lie, tell a story, tell the time, tell the truth.*

- *ask for* something: *ask* somebody *for* something:
  I ***asked for*** *a loan. I* ***asked Jim for*** *a loan.*
- *ask* in fixed expressions: e.g. *ask after someone, ask (for) a favour, ask the price, ask a question, ask the time.*

15.8 'Say', 'tell' and 'ask' in direct speech

Say is commonly associated with direct speech in writing:

'It's raining,' I ***said****.*

We can also use *say* with short, ordinary questions in direct speech (not long and complicated ones):

'Are you all right?' he ***said/asked****.* (Not **told me**)

Say (Not **told him/asked**) can introduce a statement or question:
*I **said**, 'It's raining.' I **said**, 'Is it ready?'*

Say or *tell* can be used in direct speech [> 15.2–3] and can also introduce direct commands:
*'Don't touch that!' he **said (to them)/told them**.*

Ask is used in direct questions:
*'How are you?' she **asked (me)/said**.* (Not **told me**)

15.9 'Say', 'tell' and 'ask' in indirect speech

Say and *tell someone* + optional *that* can introduce indirect statements. We never use a comma after *say* or *tell someone*:
***He said (that)/told me (that)** his life was in danger.*
If we need to mention the listener, *tell* + indirect object is generally preferable to *say* + *to someone* [> 15.7.1].
When the reporting verb comes at the end of the sentence, we cannot use *that*:
*His life was in danger, **he told me/he said**.*

Ask (with or without a personal indirect object) can report a question. *Ask (someone)* is followed by *if/whether* or a question-word:
***She asked (me) if/whether** I wanted anything.*
***She asked (me) what** I wanted.*
We use *say/tell* to introduce noun clauses [> 1.23.2], not to report questions. For the use of *ask/tell* to report commands [> 15.23–24].

Indirect statements: reporting verb in the present

15.10 Form with reporting verb in the present

actual spoken statements
'I've read Tony's book and I don't understand it.'
'I've read Tony's book and I didn't understand it.'
indirect statements: reporting verb in the present
If the reporting verb in indirect speech is in the present, the tenses that follow are usually the same as those used in the original spoken statement. This is often the case when we report words that have just been spoken [compare > 9.5.2, 15.14–16]:
Jim says/tells me (that) he's read Tony's book and doesn't understand it.
Jim says/tells me (that) he's read Tony's book and didn't understand it.

15.11 Indirect speech in context (reporting verb in the present)

The reporting verb is often in the present when the reference is general or to 'present time' in contexts like the following:
– reporting, e.g. a rumour:
A: *A little birdie tells me you're applying for a new job.*
B: *Who tells you?*
A: *Never you mind!*

– passing on messages:
  A: *Come in now, Jim. Dinner's ready.*
  B: *What does your mother say?*
  C: *She says you must come in now, dad. (She says) dinner's ready.*
– reading a newspaper, etc. and reporting:
  A: *What does the article say?*
  B: *It's about the kitchen of the future. The writer says we'll have robots which can understand instructions and carry them out.*
– general (no special time):
  A: *So how are we supposed to wire this plug?*
  B: *The instructions say that the brown wire means 'live' and it goes into the hole marked 'L'. It says here that the blue means 'neutral' and it goes into the hole marked 'N'.*
– reporting something someone says very often:
  Mary's always talking about money. She's always complaining that things are expensive and she's always asking how much I've paid for one thing and another.

Indirect statements with tense changes

15.12 Form with reporting verb in the past

actual spoken statements in the present (simple and progressive)
TOM: *'I need to go to the bank.'* PAM: *'I'm waiting for Harriet.'*
indirect statements: present → past
Tom said (that) he needed to go to the bank. Pam said (that) she was waiting for Harriet.

actual spoken statement in the present perfect
'I've moved to another flat.'
indirect statement: present perfect → past perfect (past perfect obligatory)
Sylvia said (that) she had moved to another flat.

actual spoken statements in the past (simple and progressive)
'I moved to another flat.' 'I was waiting for Harriet.'
'I had been waiting for hours before you arrived.'
indirect statements: past → past or past perfect (past perfect optional)
She said (that) she moved/had moved to another flat.
He said (that) he was waiting/had been waiting for Harriet.
He said (that) he had been waiting for hours. (past perfect does not change)

actual spoken statements with the 'present' form of modals
'I can see you tomorrow.' 'I'll help you.'
indirect statements: modal 'present' → 'conditional' or 'past' [> 11.8.3]
She said (that) she could see me the next day.
She said (that) she would help me.

actual spoken statements with the 'past' or 'conditional' form of modals
'I could see you tomorrow.' 'I would complain if I were you.'
indirect statements: the 'past' or 'conditional' modal does not change
He said (that) he could see me the next day.
She said (that) she would complain if she were me.

15.13 Notes on the form of indirect speech with tense changes

1 'Rules' in indirect speech

Tense changes often occur in indirect speech because there is an interval between the original spoken words and the time when they are reported, but these changes are not always obligatory [> 15.10, 15.14–16]. It is the changing viewpoint of the reporting speaker or writer that decides the choice of appropriate forms, not complicated rules. The notes that follow are not 'rules', but are based on observation of what often happens in practice.

2 Linking phrases

Indirect speech rarely occurs in sets of unrelated sentences, but is found in continuous paragraphs of reported language. Continuity is achieved by the use of linking phrases, such as: *she went on to say; he continued; he added that*, and by varying the reporting verbs: *he observed, noted, remarked*, etc. Such forms remind the reader that the language is reported. Many features present in direct speech, such as Yes/No short answers and speech 'fillers', such as *Well*, etc., disappear in indirect speech.

3 Tense changes [> 9.5]

In indirect speech we do not usually repeat the speaker's exact words. Reporting usually takes place in the past, so the reporting verb is often in the past. As a result, the tenses of the reported clause are usually 'moved back'. This 'moving back' of tenses is called **backshift**. A useful general rule is 'present becomes past and past becomes past perfect'. 'Past' modals and the past perfect are unchanged when reported, since no further backshift is possible [> 15.12]. We must normally use the past perfect to report a statement whose verb was in the present perfect:

*'I **have lived** in the south for years,' Mrs Duncan said.*
*Mrs Duncan told me (that) she **had lived** in the south for years.*

If the verb in the original statement was in the simple past, we do not usually need to change it to the past perfect (unless we wish to emphasize that one event happened before another):

*'I **lived** in Scotland in the 1970's,' Mrs Duncan said.*
*Mrs Duncan said that she **(had) lived** in Scotland in the 1970's.*

4 Pronoun changes

Pronouns change (or not) depending on the view of the reporter:

'I'll send you a card, Sue.' (actual words spoken by Ann)
***Ann** told Sue **she**'d send **her** a card.* (reported by someone else)
***Ann** said/told me **she** would send **me** a card.* (reported by Sue)
***I** told Sue (that) **I**'d send her a card.* (reported by Ann)

Some typical pronoun changes are:

I	→	*he/she*	*me/you*	→	*him/her*	*my*	→	*his/her*
we	→	*they*	*us*	→	*them*	*our*	→	*their*
mine	→	*his/hers*	*ours*	→	*theirs*	*myself*	→	*himself/herself*

5 Time and place changes

It is often necessary to make time and place changes in relation to

tense changes. For example, on Tuesday, A says:
'A card came yesterday saying Sue will arrive tomorrow.'
B, reporting this on Wednesday, might say:
A told me a card had come the day before yesterday/on Monday saying Sue would arrive today/on Wednesday.
But time and place changes are not always necessary. If, for example, it was still Tuesday when the statement above was reported, B might say:
A told me a card came (or *had come*) *yesterday saying Sue will* (or *would*) *arrive tomorrow.*
Examples of possible time and place changes:

time:	*now*	→	*immediately/then*
	two days ago	→	*two days before/earlier*
	today	→	*that day*
	tonight	→	*that night*
	tomorrow	→	*the next/the following day*
	yesterday	→	*the previous day/the day before*
	last night	→	*the night before*
place:	*here*	→	*there* when what is referred to is clear
	this place	→	*that place*
	these places	→	*those places*
verbs:	*come/bring*	→	*go/take*

6 Modal verbs
'Modal present' becomes 'modal past' [> 11.8.3]:
e.g. *can* becomes *could*; *will* becomes *would*; *may* becomes *might*:
'I ***can/will/may*** *see you later,' he said.*
He said he ***could/would/might*** *see me later.*

shall
When *shall* is used with future reference for prediction, speculation, etc. it becomes *would* in indirect speech:
'I ***shall*** *tell him exactly what I think,' she said.*
She said she ***would*** *tell him exactly what she thought.*
When *shall* is used in offers, suggestions or requests for advice it becomes *should* (even after the second and third persons):
*'****Shall*** *I speak to him in person?' she asked.*
She asked whether she ***should*** *speak to him in person.*

should/shouldn't
When *should* or *shouldn't* refer to desirability, obligation or likelihood, they remain unchanged in indirect speech:
'You ***should*** *see a specialist,' he told me.*
He told me I ***should*** *see a specialist.*
Should used in place of *would*, e.g. in conditional sentences [> 14.2. 14.11*n*.1], becomes *would* [compare *shall* above]:
'If I were you, I ***should*** *get another lawyer.'*
She said (that) if she were me, she ***would*** *get another lawyer.*

would, could, might, ought to, needn't have, used to
These (including negative forms where applicable) remain unchanged in indirect speech in all combinations:

*'I **would** like an appointment tomorrow,' I said to my dentist.*
*I told my dentist (that) I **would** like an appointment the next day.*
*'You **ought to** slow down a bit,' the doctor told him.*
*The doctor told him (that) he **ought to** slow down a bit.*

'perfect' and 'past' modal forms [> 11.8.4]
Forms such as *must have* and *could have* remain unchanged:
*'I **must have slept** through the alarm,' she said.*
*She said she **must have slept** through the alarm.*

must
When referring to the past, *must* can remain unchanged in indirect speech when it is used to indicate inescapable obligation. Or we can use *had to* (the past of *have to*) in its place:
*'I **must** warn you of the consequences,' he said.*
*He told me he **must/had to** warn me of the consequences.*

Must, indicating future necessity, can remain unchanged, or can be replaced by *would have to* or sometimes *had to*:
*'We **must** go early tomorrow,' she said.*
*She said they **must** go early the next day.* (or *She said they **would have to** go/they **had to** go...*)

When *must* is used to indicate deduction or possibility, it remains unchanged in indirect speech. It cannot be replaced by *had to*:
*'George **must** be a fool to behave like that,' he said.*
*He said George **must** be a fool to behave like that.*

Mustn't (prohibition) remains unchanged or changes to *couldn't*:
*'You **mustn't/can't** cross the border,' the guard said.*
*The guard said we **mustn't/couldn't** cross the border.*

needn't
Needn't (absence of necessity) can remain unchanged or can be replaced by *didn't have to* in indirect speech:
*'You **needn't/don't have to** come in tomorrow,' the boss said.*
*The boss said I **needn't/didn't have to** come in the next day.*

7 Conditional statements [> 14.2]
Type 1 conditional statements are reported as follows:
*'If you **pass** your test, I'**ll** buy you a car,' he said.*
*He said that if I **passed** my test he **would** buy me a car.*

Type 2 conditional statements are reported as follows:
*'If you **passed** your test, I **would** buy you a car,' he said.*
*He said that if I **passed** my test he **would** buy me a car.*

Type 3 conditional statements are reported as follows:
*'If you'**d passed** your test, I'**d have bought** you a car.' he said.*
*He said that if I'**d passed** my test he'**d have bought** me a car.*

8 Exclamations
Note the word order in reported exclamations:
*'What a silly boy **you are**!' she exclaimed.*
*She told him what a silly boy **he was**.*
*She told him that **he was** a silly boy.*

Indirect statements with mixed tense sequences

15.14 Form of indirect statements with mixed tense sequences

actual spoken statement

'I've read Tony's book and I don't understand it.'

indirect statements with mixed tense sequences

Jim says he's read Tony's book and didn't understand it.
Jim said he's read Tony's book and doesn't understand it.
Jim said he'd read Tony's book and doesn't understand it.
Jim said he'd read Tony's book and didn't understand it.

15.15 Indirect speech: the speaker's viewpoint [compare > 15.10–11]

A speaker can choose to report a statement or a question using the tenses that match his viewpoint, based on the facts of the situation as he sees them at the time of speaking. Note the different viewpoints expressed in the following examples:

Jim says (now) *he's read Tony's book and didn't understand it* (then, when he finished reading, or then, while he was reading).
Jim said (then) *he's read Tony's book* (now) *and didn't understand it* (then).
Jim said (then) *he'd read Tony's book* (then) *and doesn't understand it* (now).
Jim said (then) *he'd read Tony's book* (then) *and didn't understand it* (then).

15.16 Reporting permanent states, facts, habits

Permanent states and conditions are often reported in the simple present after a reporting verb in the past to show that they are matters of fact now [> App 45 for reporting verbs]:

Copernicus ***concluded*** *that the earth* ***goes*** *round the sun.*

However, the 'proximity rule' [> 9.5.2] would also allow us to say:

Copernicus ***concluded*** *that the earth* ***went*** *round the sun.*

A change in tense can lead to ambiguity. Compare:

He told me ***he works*** *as a builder.* (at present)
He told me ***he worked*** *as a builder.* (at present or in the past?)

Indirect Yes/No questions

15.17 Form of indirect Yes/No questions

The rules about tense sequences [> 9.5, 15.10, 15.12–16] also apply to questions:

actual spoken questions		**indirect questions**
be:	*'Are you ready?'*	*He asked (me) if/whether I am/was ready.*
have:	*'Have you finished?'*	*He asked (me) if/whether I (have)/had finished.*
do:	*'Do you play chess?'*	*He asked (me) if/whether I play/played chess.*
modals:	*'Can I have it?'*	*He asked (me) if/whether he can/could have it.*

15.18 Notes on the form of indirect Yes/No questions

1 Quotation marks and question marks
Quotation marks and question marks are not used in indirect questions and there is a change in word order (notes 2 and 3 below).

2 Word order: *be, have* and modal auxiliaries
The inversion in the direct question changes back to statement word order (subject + verb) in the reported question and, if necessary, the tense is changed at the same time. Modals may change from their 'present' form to their 'past' form [> 11.8.3]:

direct statement: *'**He is** ready.'* (subject + verb)
direct Yes/No question: *'**Is he** ready?'* (inversion)
indirect question: *She asked me **if he was** ready.* (*if* + subject + verb)

3 Word order: *do, does* and *did*
Do/does/did in Yes/No questions disappear in reported questions:

direct statement: *'**He went** home.'*
direct Yes/No question: *'**Did he go** home?'*
indirect question: *She asked me **if he went** home.*
or: *She asked me **if he had gone** home.*

This reflects normal usage, but in everyday speech it is not uncommon to hear direct questions embedded in indirect speech:
*She said she was going to the shops and **(asked me) did I want** anything while she was out.*

4 Reporting Yes/No questions
All kinds of Yes/No questions [> 13.5, 13,14, 13.17–23] are reported in the same way. If necessary, phrases like *in surprise* can be added to interpret intonation, etc. [> 15.25]:

'Do you play chess?'
'Don't you play chess?'
'You don't play chess, do you?'
'You play chess, don't you?' etc.
} *He asked me if/whether I played chess.*

5 *If* and *whether* [compare > 1.24.1, 14.23.4, 16.24]
If and *whether* are interchangeable after *ask, want to know, wonder*, etc., but *whether* conveys slightly greater doubt. Some verbs, like *discuss* [> App 45], can only be followed by *whether*.
If or *whether* must always be used when reporting Yes/No questions and cannot be omitted (unlike *that* in reported statements):
*Tom asked **if/whether** it was raining.*
Whether is usually preferred when there are alternatives [> 13.44–45]:
*She asked me **whether** I wanted tea **or** coffee.*

6 *That* and *whether* in short answers
Short answers can be given with *that* and *whether/if*:

What did she tell you? – ***That** she would be late.*
What did she ask you? – ***Whether/If** I would be late.*

7 Reporting Yes/No questions with *or not* [> 1.24.1, 13.44–45, 14.21]
*'Do you want any dinner **or not**?'*
*He wants to know **if/whether** we want any dinner **or not**.*
*He wants to know **whether or not** we want dinner.* (Not **if or not**)

8 Indirect Yes/No questions with reporting verbs other than *ask*
Many reporting verbs can be used other than *ask, want to know*, etc. in combinations with *whether* and (sometimes) *if* [> App 45]:
He didn't tell me if/whether *he would be arriving early or late.*
She didn't say if/whether *she was coming to lunch.*
I don't know if/whether *I've passed my exam yet.*
I wonder if/whether *they've heard the news yet.*

Indirect question-word questions

15.19 Form of indirect question-word questions

The rules about tense sequences [> 9.5, 15.10, 15.12–16] also apply to questions:

	actual spoken questions	indirect questions		
be:	*'Where are you going?'*	*He asked (me)*	*where*	*I was going.*
have:	*'Why haven't you finished?'*	*He wanted to know*	*why*	*I (haven't)/hadn't finished.*
do:	*'What do you think of it?'*	*He wanted to know*	*what*	*I (think)/thought of it.*
modals:	*'When must I be there?'*	*He asked (me)*	*when*	*he must be/had to be there.*

15.20 Notes on the form of indirect question-word questions

1 Word order: *be*, *have* and modal auxiliaries [compare > 15.18*n*.2]
The inversion after a question-word in a direct question changes back to statement word order (subject + verb) in the reported question and, if necessary, the tense is changed at the same time. Modals may change from 'present' form to 'past' form [> 11.8.3]:

direct statement:		***We are going*** *home.*
direct *Wh*-question:		***Where are you going****?* (*Wh*- + inversion)
indirect question:	*He asked (us)*	***where we were going****.* (*Wh*- + subject + verb)

2 Word order: *do, does* and *did* [compare > 15.18*n*.3]
Do/does/did in direct questions disappear in reported questions:

direct statement:	*'I* ***gave*** *it to John.'*
direct *Wh*-question:	*'****When did you give*** *it to John?'*
indirect question:	*He asked me* ***when I gave*** *it to John.*

3 Indirect question-word questions with verbs other than *ask*
Many different reporting verbs can be used other than *ask, want to know,* etc. [> App 45]:

I know	*where*	*he lives.*
She didn't say	*why*	*she was coming home late.*
He didn't tell me	*how*	*he did it.*

4 Question-words in short answers
Short answers can be given with *Why, When*, etc.:
What did she want to know? – ***Why/When*** *we were leaving.*
(= She wanted to know why/when we were leaving.)

Indirect subject-questions

15.21 Form of indirect subject-questions

	actual spoken questions	indirect questions
be:	*'Who is in charge here?'*	*He asked (me) who was in charge there.*
present:	*'Which firm makes these parts?'*	*He asked (me) which firm (makes) made those parts.*
past:	*'What caused the accident?'*	*He asked (me) what caused/had caused the accident.*
modals:	*'Whose novel will win the prize?'*	*He asked (me) whose novel would win the prize.*

15.22 Note on the form of indirect subject-questions

Tense changes and changes in modals occur in the usual way, but the word order of the direct question is retained in the indirect question. Reporting verbs other than *ask* can be used to introduce indirect subject questions [> App 45]:

*Please **tell me who delivered** this package.*
*I **want to know which piece fits** in this puzzle.*

Uses of the *to*-infinitive in indirect speech

15.23 Form of the *to*-infinitive in indirect speech

actual spoken words	reported version
'Keep a record of your expenses.'	*I told him to keep a record of his expenses.*
'Don't make a mess in the kitchen.'	*I told him not to make a mess in the kitchen.*
'How do I prepare the sauce?'	*He wanted to know how to prepare the sauce.*
'I want to speak to the manager.'	*She asked to speak to the manager.*

15.24 Form and use of the infinitive in indirect speech

15.24.1 The imperative: affirmative and negative

Imperatives (usually orders, requests, advice, etc.) are reported with appropriate verbs followed by a *to*-infinitive. Commonly-used verbs (always followed by a personal object in indirect speech) are: *advise, ask, instruct, remind, tell, warn*, etc. [> App 45.3]. In each case the reporting verb must match the function of the imperative (asking, telling, advising, etc.) [compare > 16.20–21]:

*'**Keep** a record of your expenses,' **I said**.*
tell: ***I told him to keep** a record of his expenses.*
*'**Remember to** switch off all the lights,' **she said**.*
remind: ***She reminded me to** switch off all the lights.*

When a negative imperative (e.g. *Don't make a mess!*) is reported, *not* always goes before the *to*-infinitive [but compare > 16.14]:

*She told/asked/warned him **not to make** a mess in the kitchen.*

Direct orders can also be reported with *be to*:

*'Wait for me.' He says **I am to wait** for him. He said **I was to**...*

Or we can use the passive with verbs other than *say*:

*I **have been told/was told to wait for** him.*

Note the informal use of *say* in: ***He said (not) to wait for** him.*

Ask, when a speaker is asking permission or making a request, may be followed by the infinitive:

*I **asked to speak to** the manager.*

and by the passive infinitive [> 12.2]:

*He **asked to be kept informed** about developments.*
*I **asked for two items to be added** to the list.*

15.24.2 The infinitive after question-words [compare > 16.24]

Direct suggestions and requests for advice and information with *Shall I...?, Should I...?, Do you want me to...?* etc. (expecting Yes/No answers) can be reported in two ways:

direct request: *'**Shall/Should I phone** her?'*
indirect request: *He **wanted to know if/whether he should phone** her.*
***whether* + infinitive**: *He **wanted to know whether to phone** her.*

Requests, etc. with question-words can also be reported in two ways:

direct request: *'**How shall I prepare** the sauce?'*
indirect request: ***He wanted to know how he should prepare** it.*
question-word + infinitive: ***He wanted to know how to prepare** it.*

Other examples:

She wanted to know
- *when **she should be/to be** at the station.*
- *where **she should park/to park**.*
- *which **she should choose/to choose**.*
- *who(m) **she should ask/to ask**.*
- *what **she should do/to do**.*

Note that *why* or *if* cannot be followed by a *to*-infinitive.

When we use indirect speech

15.25 Interpreting direct speech

Indirect speech requires a great deal more than the mechanical application of 'rules', for we must interpret what we hear or read before reporting it. We need to convey the manner in which the words were spoken or written. So, for example, stress and intonation in direct speech can be 'reported' by means of adverbs or emphatic reporting verbs, such as *insist* and *suggest*:

'You really must let me pay the bill,' Andrew said.
Andrew insisted on paying the bill.
'Why don't we go sailing?' Diana said.
Diana suggested they should go sailing.
'You've just won a lottery!' Tom said.
'Really?' Jennifer exclaimed.
Jennifer was amazed when Tom told her that she had won a lottery.

15.26 Oral reporting

Oral reporting may be concerned with other people's conversations, gossip, instructions, conveying the gist of lectures and so on. In oral reporting, direct speech is often quoted and there may be sudden changes in the sequence of tenses. A few examples are:

15.26.1 Reporting everyday conversation

'Mrs Corrie asked me how we all are and I told her all our news. Her eldest son has just got his exam results and has done very well, apparently. "What do you expect?" I said to her, "he's always been a bright lad." "Oh, he is that," she says, "but he's really lazy." I told her I didn't think he was lazy.'

15.26.2 Passing on instructions

'The boss wants you to go to the airport to pick up the company's guests. She says you're to take the company car. Oh – and she asked me to tell you to phone if there are any flight delays.'

15.26.3 Giving the gist of e.g. a lecture

'Dr Barnaby gave us a very interesting talk on boat-building in ancient times. He explained how boat-building methods changed over a period of about 1500 years. He also had some slides showing us how the ancient world lost most of its forests because so much wood was needed for boats. He began his talk by telling us about Ancient Greece at around 300 BC.'

15.27 Written reporting

Written reporting includes newspaper reports, records of conferences, minutes of meetings, reports of debates and so on. Consistency in such matters as the sequence of tenses is carefully maintained, particularly in formal reporting. A few examples are:

15.27.1 Company reports

The Chairman opened his address to the shareholders by pointing out that pre-tax profits had fallen for the second year running, which was disappointing. Market conditions were difficult for almost every company and the combination of high interest rates and the strong dollar had affected profit margins.

15.27.2 Parliamentary reports

Mr Harry Greene said that airlines were losing money because of their cheap air fares policies. We could only expect airlines to fail unless they were supported by massive government grants.

15.27.3 'Free indirect speech'

The following is an example of fiction in which indirect speech is freely woven into the narrative to reveal a person's thoughts, motives, etc.:

Opening his case he found a handkerchief inside it. It was certainly not his, for the initials M.D.B. were stitched into the corner. So that was their little game, he thought. Someone had opened his case to plant this evidence. But how did they open the case? How did they even know the case was his, he wondered, as he slowly unfolded the dead man's handkerchief.

16 The infinitive and the '-ing' form

The bare infinitive

16.1 The infinitive and the '-ing' form

The base form of a verb (*go*) often functions as an infinitive. It is called the **bare infinitive** because it is used without *to*. We must distinguish it from the ***to*-infinitive**, where *to* is always used in front of the base form of the verb (*to go*). The *-ing* form of a verb (*going*) sometimes functions as a gerund (i.e. a kind of noun) and sometimes as a present participle [> 16.38]. Many verbs and adjectives, and some nouns, can be followed by one or other of these forms, and in some cases by more than one form. From the student's point of view, the problem is knowing which form is appropriate. This may be because only one form is grammatically correct, e.g. *enjoy doing* [> 16.42], *fail to do* [> 16.19]. Or it may be because only one form suits what we want to say, e.g. *remember doing* or *remember to do* [> 16.59].

16.2 Forms of the infinitive [compare '-ing' > 1.56, 16.41]

	active	**passive**
present infinitive:	*(to) ask*	*(to) be asked*
present progressive infinitive:	*(to) be asking*	–
perfect or past infinitive:	*(to) have asked*	*(to) have been asked*
perfect/past progressive infinitive:	*(to) have been asking*	–

16.3 The bare infinitive after modal verbs

The main use of the bare infinitive is after modal verbs. All the modal verbs [except *ought*, > 11.6.1*n*.2] must be followed by a bare infinitive (except in short responses like *Yes, I can*):

I can/could/may/might/will/shall/should/must ***leave*** *soon.*

Dare/need, when they are modal, are similar (*Dare/Need we ask?*).
The negative is formed by adding *not* before the infinitive:

*I can**not**/can**'t** go*, etc. [> 11.5.1].

16.4 The bare infinitive after 'let' and 'make'

16.4.1 'Let' as an auxiliary verb

We commonly use the imperative form *Let's* (the contraction of *Let us*) as an auxiliary verb followed by a bare infinitive when making suggestions for actions that include the speaker. *Let's* is often associated with *shall we?* [> 11.40]:

Let's take *a taxi!* ***Let's take*** *a taxi,* ***shall*** *we?* ***Do let's****...*

The negative of *Let's* in suggestions is:

Let's not/Don't let's argue *about it.*

Informally, *Let's* can relate to *I* in e.g. offers and requests:
Let's give you a hand. (= I'll) *Let's have a look.* (= Can I?)
Let as an auxiliary need not always followed by *us*:
Let XYZ be a triangle. Let them eat cake. Let there be light.
Don't let me (or, very formal, *Let me not*) *interrupt you.*

16.4.2 'Let' as a full verb

The basic meaning of *let* is *allow*, and in this sense it is a full verb, always followed by a noun or pronoun object before a bare infinitive. If the object is *us*, it cannot be reduced to *let's*:
*Please **let us have** more time, will you?* (= allow us to)
***Don't let the children annoy** you.*
*I **won't let you ride** my bicycle.*
Let can be followed by a passive infinitive:
*He **let it be known** he was about to resign.*
but is not normally used in the passive to mean 'be allowed'. Compare:
*They **didn't let us** speak. **We were not allowed** to speak.*

16.4.3 'Make' (= compel) + bare infinitive

Make (active) + noun/pronoun object can be followed by a bare infinitive. It means 'compel' or 'cause to':
*Miss Prouty **made the boys stay in** after school.*
*That beard **makes you look** much older than you are.*
However, in the passive, *make* in these senses is followed by *to*:
*He **was made to work** twenty hours a day.*
Unlike *let*, *make* (= compel) can never be followed by a passive infinitive. But compare *make* in a different sense:
*Rules **were made*** (= created) ***to be broken**.*

16.4.4 Fixed phrases with 'let' and 'make' + bare infinitive

The bare infinitive occurs in a number of fixed verb phrases with *let* and *make*: e.g. *let fall, let go, let me see, let slip, live and let live, make believe, make do:*
*The dog's got a stick between his teeth and he won't **let go**.*
*You'll have to **make** your pocket money **do**. I can't give you more.*

16.5 The bare infinitive after 'would rather', etc.

We use the bare infinitive after expressions in which *'d* can be replaced by *would* or *had* [> 11.44–47]:
1 *'d* = *would* : *'d rather, 'd sooner.*
But note that *had rather* and *had sooner* sometimes occur.
2 *'d* = *had* : *'d better, 'd best* (less common than *'d better*).
*I'**d rather work** on the land **than work** in a factory.*
*We'**d better/best be going**. – Yes, we'**d better**/we'**d best be**.*
These forms can often be followed by the passive infinitive:
*I'**d rather be told** the truth than **be lied** to.*
Not can be used after *'d rather/sooner/better/best*:
*You'**d better not go** near the edge.*
Informally, *better* or subject + *better* often occur without *had*:
*Mr Murphy will be here any minute. – **Better get** his file then.*
***You better stop** arguing and **do** as you're told.*

16.6 The bare infinitive after 'Why?' and 'Why not?'

For bare infinitive uses after *Why/Why not?* [> 13.37.2–3]

The infinitive with or without 'to'

16.7 'Help' and 'know' + bare infinitive or *to*-infinitive

We may use a bare infinitive or a *to*-infinitive after a few verbs like *help* and *know*. The use of a *to*-infinitive is more formal:
Mother ***helped me (to) do*** *my homework.*
We do not usually omit *to* after *not*:
How can I ***help*** *my children* ***not to worry*** *about their exams?*

Help can be used without a noun or pronoun object:
Everyone in the village ***helped (to) build*** *the new Youth Centre.*
or with a noun or pronoun object:
Can anyone ***help me (to) fill in*** *this tax form?*
In the passive, *to* is obligatory after *help*:
Millie ***was helped to overcome*** *her fear of flying.*
Help + the passive infinitive is possible, though rare:
I'm sure this treatment will ***help him (to) be cured****.*

Know + infinitive normally requires a noun or pronoun object. The omission of *to* is only possible with the perfect form of *know*:
I've never known her (to) *be late before.*
I've never known her not (to) *be late!*
In the passive, *to* is obligatory;
He ***was known to have/to have had*** *a quick temper as a boy.*

16.8 Infinitives joined by 'and', etc.

Infinitives can be joined by *and, but, except, or* and *than* [> 8.4.4]. *To* is usually dropped before the second infinitive:
Which would you prefer: ***to win*** *a million pounds* ***or (to) have*** *a brain like Einstein's?*
Other infinitive forms can combine in this way:
I'd like ***to be flying*** *over the Alps* ***and (to be) looking*** *down/****and be looking*** *down at the mountains.*
I'd like ***to have been offered*** *the job* ***and (to have been) given****/****and been given*** *the opportunity to prove myself.*
Where the second infinitive follows on closely from the first, it is normal to omit *to* before the second infinitive:
I'd like ***to lie down and go*** *to sleep.* (Not **to go**)

The bare infinitive or the '-ing' form?

16.9 The bare infinitive or '-ing' after verbs of perception

16.9.1 Verbs without a noun or pronoun object + '-ing'

The verbs *hear, smell* and *watch* can be followed by the *-ing* form without a noun/pronoun object when an action is perceived in a general way; *-ing* functions as the object of the verb [> 16.40.3]:

*We could **hear shouting** in the distance.*

*People can stand on this platform and **watch building** in progress.*

16.9.2 Verb + noun or pronoun object + bare infinitive or '-ing'

These verbs can be followed by a noun or pronoun object + bare infinitive or the *-ing* form: *feel, hear, listen to, look at, notice, observe, perceive, see, smell, watch* [compare > 16.45.1, App 38.4].

The bare infinitive generally refers to the complete action:

*I **watched a pavement-artist draw** a portrait in crayons.*

(i.e. probably from start to finish)

The *-ing* form generally refers to an action in progress:

*I **watched a pavement-artist drawing** a portrait in crayons.*

(i.e. the action was probably in progress when I arrived)

Either the bare infinitive or *-ing* can describe a short action:

*I **heard someone unlock** the door/**unlocking** the door.*

But we do not use the *-ing* form for *very* short actions. Compare:

*I **heard** him **cough.*** (once) *I **can hear** him **coughing**.* (repeatedly)

For a series of actions, we prefer the bare infinitive:

*The crowd **watched the fireman climb** the ladder, **break** a window on the first floor, and **enter** the building.*

The passive *-ing* form [> 16.41] (but not the passive infinitive) can follow a verb of perception:

*I **saw him being taken away** by the police.*

The past participle can sometimes follow the object directly:

*I **saw him taken away** by the police.*

16.9.3 The passive of verbs of perception + '-ing' or *to*-infinitive

The verbs *hear, observe, perceive* and *see* are often used in the passive followed by *-ing* or by a *to*-infinitive:

*They **were seen waiting** on the corner.* (action in progress)

*They **were seen to climb** through the window.* (action completed)

16.10 'Have' + bare infinitive or the '-ing' form

16.10.1 'Have' + personal object + bare infinitive

We use this construction to show that one person is causing another to do something [compare the causative, > 12.10]:

***Have the next patient come in** now please, nurse.*

*He wanted a job to do, so I **had him paint** the kitchen.*

And note *have* + verbs like *believe* and *know* in: e.g.

*I can't imagine what he'll **have you believe** next.*

*I'll **have you know** that I'm a qualified engineer.*

16.10.2 'Have' + object + '-ing' form

We use this construction to refer to the results we are aiming at:

*I'll **have you speaking English** in six months.*

*Within five minutes, Archie **had us all playing** hide-and-seek.*

We can also refer to consequences which may not be intended:

*Don't shout! You'll **have the neighbours complaining**!*

When we use this construction with *won't* or *can't*, we refer to circumstances we are not prepared to tolerate:

*I **won't/can't have you speaking** like that about your father.*

Sometimes this construction refers to happenings beyond the speaker's control. Compare a similar construction with *There* [> 10.20]:

We ***have salesmen calling/There are salesmen calling*** *every day.*

Sometimes, but not very often, the bare infinitive is possible:

*I'****ve*** *never* ***had such a thing happen(ing)*** *to me before.*

16.11 'Rather/Sooner than' + bare infinitive or '-ing'

Rather than and *sooner than* can be followed by a bare infinitive or *-ing*. *Rather than* is more common:

Rather than waste/wasting *your time doing it yourself, why don't you call in a builder?*

The *to*-infinitive

16.12 Some common uses of the *to*-infinitive

16.12.1 'To/in order to/so as to' to express purpose [compare > 1.51.1]

We can use *to*, *in order to* or *so as to* to refer to purpose:

I went to live in France ***to/in order to/so as to learn*** *French.*

She was sent to England ***to/in order to/so as to be educated****.*

Not to can be used to refer to alternatives:

I went to France ***not to study*** *French,* ***but to study*** *architecture.*

We express 'negative purpose' with *so as not to/in order not to*:

I shut the door quietly, ***so as not to wake*** *the baby.*

When there is a change of subject we may use *for...* + infinitive:

I bought a second car ***(in order) for my son to learn*** *to drive.*

For + noun/pronoun + infinitive is more economical than [> 1.51.2]:

I bought a new car ***in order that my wife might learn*** *to drive.*

Other verbs, e.g. *bring, buy, need, take, use, want*, often introduce an object + *to*-infinitive (but not an object + *in order to/so as to*). The infinitive tells us about the purpose of the object, which is often an indefinite pronoun like *something* [> 4.37]:

I ***want something to cheer me up****.*

I ***need a spoon to eat this ice-cream with****.*

Bring me a chair to sit on*. I* ***brought a chair for you to sit on****.*

Other verbs can be followed by *for* + object + *to*-infinitive, e.g. *apply, arrange, ask, call, plan, plead, phone, pray, ring, send, vote, wait, wish*. *For* marks the subject of the infinitive:

How long ***have you been waiting for the train to arrive****?*

16.12.2 '(Only) to': sequences [compare > 7.55.1]

Sometimes a *to*-infinitive in the second part of a sentence is used for the 'later' event in a sequence. The *to*-infinitive (which can be replaced by *and* + verb) describes an event which is unexpected, sometimes unwelcome – especially when *only* is used in front of *to*:

We came home after our holiday ***to find*** *our garden neat and tidy.* (= and found)

He returned after the war, ***(only) to be told*** *that his wife had left him.* (= and was told)

A similar construction occurs with *never*:

She left home, ***never to return/never to be seen*** *again.*

16.12.3 The *to*-infinitive referring to the future or to an imaginary past

We can refer to the future with verbs like *hope, intend, mean* and *(would) like to*. A perfect infinitive is often used after a past verb, but it is not usually necessary. Compare:

*I **would like to see** that film.* (now, or in the future)
*I **would like to have seen** it.* (before now, so I did not see it)
*I **would have liked to see** it.* (but didn't have a chance then)
*I **would have liked to have seen** it.* (interchangeable with *I would have liked to see it*; *to have seen* is unnecessary)

16.13 The *to*-infinitive as the object of a verb [> 16.19]

A great many verbs are strongly linked with the *to*-infinitive, e.g. *decide, need, wish* [> App 46]:

*I **want to leave**. I **want to be left** alone.*

In such cases the infinitive serves as the object of the verb. However, some verbs like *think* require *it* + adjective + infinitive: *I think it best to go* (Not **I think to go is best**) [compare > 1.14, 4.15, 16.22]. A few verbs like *appear, seem* [> 10.23] can also be followed by more complex infinitive forms: *He seems to be leaving/to have left/to have been leaving*, etc.

16.14 Contrasting negatives [compare > 1.23.5, 13.10, 16.12.1]

We form the negative of a *to*-infinitive by putting *not* before *to*:

*I soon learnt **not to/never to swim** near coral reefs.*

Compare ordinary negatives:

*I **didn't learn/never learnt** to swim when I was a child.*

With many verbs (e.g. *advise, ask, instruct, remind, tell, warn*) the placing of the negative seriously affects the meaning [> 15.24.1]:

*He told me **not to feed** the animals.* (He said, 'Don't feed...')
*He **didn't tell me** to feed the animals.* (He didn't say anything.)
***Don't ask Rex** to phone. I'll ring him myself.*
*Ask Rex **not to phone.** I don't want to be disturbed.*

The placing of the negative has a similar effect on meaning with adjectives and nouns + infinitive:

*I **wasn't sorry to go**.* (= I went)
*I **was sorry not to go**.* (= I didn't go)
*It **wasn't a surprise to hear** from him.* (I heard from him)
*It **was a surprise not to hear** from him.* (I didn't hear from him)

Negatives are sometimes possible in both parts of a sentence:

*I **can't promise not to be** late. My car is very unreliable.*

but this would generally be expressed more simply: e.g.

*I **can't promise** to be on time.*

16.15 The split infinitive

'Splitting an infinitive' (i.e. putting an adverb or *please* between *to* and the verb) is usually considered unacceptable and should generally be avoided. For instance *clearly* could not come between *to* and *read* in the following:

*I want you **to read** that last sentence **clearly**.*

However, we often do separate *to* from the infinitive in spoken English, depending on where the emphasis falls:

I want you ***to clearly understand*** *what I'm telling you.*

This is often the case with adverbs like *completely, fully, really* and *truly*; sometimes there is no other suitable place to put them:

It's difficult ***to really understand*** *the theory of relativity.*

16.16 The uses of 'be' + *to*-infinitive

The *to*-infinitive can be used as the complement of *be* [> 10.9.10]:

Your mistake ***was to write*** *that letter.*

The verb *do* can be followed by *be* + (optional) *to*:

What you ***do is (to) mix*** *the eggs with flour.*
All I ***did was (to) press*** *this button.*

The *to*-infinitive can be active in form but passive in meaning:

This house is ***to let/to be let****. Who is* ***to blame/to be blamed****?*

Some constructions can only be in the passive:

He's (only) ***to be admired/envied/pitied****. All this is* ***to be sold****.*

For *be to*: future duties, instructions, etc. [> 9.47–48].

16.17 Leaving out the verb after 'to'

To avoid repetition, we can often leave the verb out after *to*:

You don't have to eat it if you don't ***want to****.*
Would you like to come to a party? – I'd ***love to****.*
Don't spill any of that paint, will you? – I'll ***try not to****.*

Sometimes even *to* can be dropped:

Try to be back by 12, won't you? – OK. I'll ***try****.*

With verbs that are followed by *-ing* but never followed by a *to*-infinitive, e.g. *enjoy* [> 16.42], we must use an object:

Would you ***like to come*** *sailing? – Oh yes. I'd* ***enjoy it/that****.*

16.18 The *to*-infinitive in fixed phrases

Some fixed phrases are introduced by a *to*-infinitive: e.g. *to be honest, to begin with, to cut a long story short, to get (back) to the point, not to make too much of it, to put it another way, to tell you the truth:*

To tell you the truth, *I've never heard of Maxwell Montague.*

Verb (+ noun/pronoun) + *to*-infinitive

16.19 Verb + *to*-infinitive (not + '-ing' or 'that ...') [compare > 16.42]

We can say:

I can't afford a car. She hesitated for a moment.

But if we want to use a verb after *can('t) afford* or *hesitate*, this verb can only be in the form of a *to*-infinitive:

I can't afford ***to buy*** *a car. I hesitate* ***to disagree*** *with you.*

Other verbs like *can('t) afford* and *hesitate* are: *aim, apply, decline, fail, hasten, hurry, long, manage, offer, prepare, refuse, seek, shudder, strive, struggle*. For more examples [> App 46]. The perfect/past form of the infinitive (e.g. *to have run*) is rare after such verbs.

16.20 Verb + optional noun/pronoun + *to*-infinitive

Some verbs can be used with or without a noun or pronoun before a *to*-infinitive: *ask, beg, choose, expect, hate, help, intend, like, love, need, prefer, prepare, promise, want, wish* [> App 46.1]. (*Trouble* can also be used in this way, normally in questions and negatives.) Note how the meaning changes:

***I want to speak** to the manager.* (= I will speak)
***I want you to speak** to the manager.* (= you will speak)

Promise is an exception: there is a difference in emphasis but not in meaning between ***I** promise to* and ***I** promise you to.*

Like, love, hate and *prefer* are often used in the simple present to refer to habitual personal choice and preference [compare > 16.58]:

***I like to keep** everything tidy.* (refers to *my* actions)
***I like you to keep** everything tidy.* (refers to *your* actions)

These verbs can also be used after *would* to make specific offers, requests etc. [> 11.35, 11.37–39 and compare > 16.12.3]:

***I'd like to find** you a job.* (refers to *my* possible future action)
***I'd like you to find** him a job.* (*your* possible future action)

16.21 Verb + compulsory noun/pronoun + *to*-infinitive

Some verbs must normally always be followed by a noun or pronoun when used with a *to*-infinitive: *advise, allow, assist, bribe, cause, caution, challenge, charge, command, compel, condemn, dare* (= challenge), *defy, direct, drive* (= compel), *enable, encourage, entitle, forbid, force, impel, implore, incite, induce, instruct, invite, oblige, order, permit, persuade, press* (= urge), *recommend, remind, request, teach, tell, tempt, urge* and *warn*. All these verbs can be used in the passive as well as the active:

***I advise you to leave**. You **were advised to leave**.*

It takes/took + object + *to*-infinitive often refers to time in relation to activity. An indirect object is optional:

***It takes/took (me) ten minutes to walk** to the station.*

The same idea can be expressed with a personal subject:

***I take/took** ten minutes to walk to the station.*

16.22 Verb + object + 'to be' and other infinitive forms

Some verbs can be followed by an object + *to be* (and by a few stative verbs [> 9.3] like *to have*): *acknowledge, assume, believe, calculate, consider, declare, discover, estimate, fancy, feel, find, guess, imagine, judge, know, maintain, proclaim, prove, reckon, see, show, suppose, take* (= presume), *think, understand:*

*I **consider him to be** one of the best authorities in the country.*
*She **is known to have** the best collection of stamps in the world.*

Other infinitive forms are sometimes possible:

*She is believed **to be going/to have gone** to the USA.*

These verbs are very frequently used in the passive and can often be followed by passive infinitives:

*He **is thought to have been killed** in an air crash.*

All these verbs (except *take* – *I take it (that)...*) can also be followed directly by *that*-clauses (*I assume (that) ...*). [> App 45]
A few verbs like *believe, expect, intend, like, love, mean, prefer, understand, want* and *wish* can be followed by *there to be*:

*I **expect there to be** a big response to our advertisement.*

Verb + *to*-infinitive or (*that*-)clause

16.23 Verbs followed by a *to*-infinitive or a *that*-clause

Many verbs can be followed directly by a *to*-infinitive or a *that*-clause: *agree, arrange, beg, (not) care, choose, claim, contrive, decide, demand, determine, expect, hope, intend, learn, plan, prefer, pretend, promise, resolve, swear, threaten* and *wish*:

*I **decided to ask** for my money back.*
*I **decided that I would ask** for my money back.*

Most of these verbs point to the future, so they are not normally followed by the perfect form of the infinitive. However, verbs referring to intentions, hopes, etc. can be followed by a perfect infinitive, parallel to the use of the future perfect [> 16.12.3]:

*I **hope(d)*** (etc.) ***to have finished** by 12.*

Some of these verbs (most commonly *agree, arrange, decide*) are used in the passive after *It* to introduce a *that*-clause [> 12.8*n*.1]:

***It was agreed/arranged/decided that we should meet** again later.*

16.24 Verb + question-word + *to*-infinitive or a clause

All question-words except *why* can come before the *to*-infinitive with 'verbs of asking' [> 15.24.2] and the following: *consider, decide, discover, explain, find out, forget, hear, (not) know, learn, observe, perceive, remember, see, understand* and *wonder*:

*I **don't know what/which/who(m) to choose**.*
*I **wondered how/when/where to get in touch** with them.*

The above verbs can also be followed by a clause introduced by any question word (including *why*) or *that*:

*I **don't know why the accident happened**.*
*I **didn't know that there had been an accident**.*

When we are discussing alternatives or expressing doubt, we can use *whether...should* or *whether to* after most of the above verbs:

*I **haven't decided whether I should go/whether to go** to Spain.*

We can sometimes use *if* as an alternative to *whether* before a clause, but not before an infinitive [compare > 15.18*n*.5, 15.24.2].

Remember and *forget* can be followed directly by a *to*-infinitive:

*I **remembered to/forgot to switch off** the lights.* [>16.59]

Learn can be followed by *to* or *how to* without any change in meaning when it refers to acquiring a skill:

*I **learnt to/how to ride a bicycle** when I was four.*

However, *learn* must be followed only by *to* (Not **how to**) when it conveys the idea of learning from experience:

*We soon **learnt to do as we were told** in Mr Spinks' class!*

16.25 Verb + object + question-word + *to*-infinitive or a clause

Advise, instruct, remind, teach and *tell* can have an object +
– a *to*-infinitive [> 15.24.1]:
*He **told us to run**. My sister **taught me to swim**.*
– any question word (except *why*) + *to*-infinitive:
*The receptionist **told me where to wait**.*
– a clause [> 15.24.2]:
*The union leader **told the men that they should go back** to work.*
*The union leader **told the men when they should go back** to work.*
Persuade and *warn* can have *to* or *that* but not a question-word:
*He **warned me to** stay away. He **warned me (that)** I was in danger.*

The verb *show* can be used like the verbs above, except that it always requires a question-word before the *to*-infinitive:
*Please **show me how to start** the engine.*

Object + *whether* + *to*-infinitive can be used after: *advise/not advise, ask/not ask, show/not show, not teach, not tell* and in questions with these verbs:
*Can you **advise me whether to register** this letter?*
*You have**n't told me whether to sign** this form.*

Adjective + *to*-infinitive

16.26 Form of the *to*-infinitive after adjectives

Many adjectives can be followed by *to*-infinitives:
*I'm **pleased to meet** you.*
*Can you do me a favour? – I'd be **glad to**.* [compare > 16.17]
Other infinitive forms [> 16.2] are possible, e.g. *sorry to have missed you; pleased to have been given this opportunity; nice to be sitting by the fire.* For contrasting negatives with adjectives [> 16.14].

16.27 Pattern 1: *He was kind to help us.*

We use this pattern and its variations (see below) when we are praising or criticizing people. (Not all adjectives in this pattern combine with *I* or *we*.) The subject of the main verb (*be*) and the subject of the infinitive are the same person, and sometimes we can express the same idea with an adverb [> 7.16.2]:
***He was very kind** to help us./**He very kindly** helped us.*
Here are some adjectives which are used in this pattern: *brave, careless*, but not *careful* [> 16.28], *clever, foolish, generous, good, (un)kind, polite, right/wrong, rude, (un)selfish, silly, wicked* [> App 44].

16.27.1 Subject + 'be' + adjective + *to*-infinitive

***The government would be brave to call** an election now.*
***Joan was foolish not to accept** their offer.*
Variations on this pattern with some of the adjectives listed above are possible with *so...as to* (which is formal) and, less formally, with *enough*:
*Would you **be so good as to let me know** as soon as possible?*
*Would you **be good enough to let me know** as soon as possible?*

16.27.2 'It' + 'be' + adjective + 'of' noun/pronoun + *to*-infinitive

This use of *It* as 'preparatory subject' [> 4.13] is much more common than a personal subject. It occurs with all the adjectives listed in 16.27 above and with some *-ing* adjectives like *annoying, boring, trying*. If it is obvious who is referred to, the *of*-phrase can be omitted:

It was kind of her to help *us.*
It was silly (of us) to believe *him.*
It was most selfish of him not to contribute *anything.*
It was annoying of John to lose *my keys.*

Verbs like *seem/look* [> 10.23–25] can be used in this pattern:

It would look rude to refuse *their invitation.*

16.27.3 Adjective + *to*-infinitive in exclamations

Exclamations in this pattern are very common:

How kind of him to help *us!* ***Wasn't he kind to help*** *us!*
Wasn't it kind (of him) to help *us!*

16.28 Pattern 2: *He is eager to please.*

As in Pattern 1, the subject of the main verb (*be* or sometimes *feel, look*, etc.) and the subject of the infinitive are the same person. When using this pattern, we are often concerned with people's feelings about an action or situation, and *I/we* fit naturally. There is no alternative structure with *It*. Here are some adjectives which are used in this pattern: *afraid, anxious, ashamed, careful*, but not *careless* [> 16.27], *curious, determined, due, eager, fit, free, frightened, glad, keen, prepared, quick, ready, reluctant, slow, sorry, willing* [> App 44]:

He is *always* ***prepared to take*** *a lot of trouble.*
She is determined not to offend *her mother-in-law.*

For + noun/pronoun can be used after a very limited number of adjectives, such as *anxious, determined, eager* and *keen*, referring to situations that have not yet occurred:

She's anxious for her daughter to win *the competition.*

Very occasionally, this pattern has an inanimate subject:

My car is reluctant to start *in cold weather.*
Our boiler is slow to get going *in the mornings.*

A few adjectives referring to possibility and probability can be included here: *bound/certain to, (un)likely to* and *sure to*:

He is ***bound/certain/likely/sure to sign*** *the contract.*

It can be used as a preparatory or empty subject [> 1.23.1, 4.12–13]:

It's certain/likely/unlikely that he'll sign *the contract.*
It's bound/sure to rain *on our wedding day.*

16.29 Pattern 3: *He is easy to please.*

The infinitive in this pattern usually refers to things done to someone or something. The subject of the sentence is also the object of the infinitive; the *It* structure is very common here:

He is easy *to please./****It is easy*** *to please* ***him***.

Adjectives like the following fit into this pattern: *agreeable, amusing, boring, difficult, easy, hard, impossible, nice:*

She ***is amusing to be with***. *Polyester* ***is easy to iron***.

A negative infinitive (*not to*) is rare after *he/she*, but possible after *it*:
It is impossible not to offend *Mrs Rumbold.*

16.30 Pattern 4: *It is good to be here.*

A very large number of adjectives fit into this pattern. The infinitive subject is normally replaced by *It* [compare > 16.47]:

To accept *their offer* ***would be foolish****.* ***It would be foolish to accept*** *their offer.*

Not to accept *their offer* ***would be foolish****.* ***It would be foolish not to accept*** *their offer.*

Compare the uses of *it* in these two sentences:

Have a drive in my new car. ***It*** (= the car) *is easy to start.*

It ['preparatory subject', > 4.13] *is easy to start* ***it***.(the car)

For + noun/pronoun can occur after many of these adjectives:

It won't be ***easy for Tom*** *to find a new job.*

The *-ing* form can occur after some of these adjectives [> 16.47]:

It is ***hard speaking*** *in public.*

A number of adjectives used in this pattern (e.g. *advisable, important, necessary, vital*) refer to advice, necessity, duties, and can also be followed by *that...should* [> 11.75.3]:

It's ***important to reply*** *to her letter.*

It's ***important that we (should) reply*** *to her letter.*

16.31 Pattern 5: *He is the first to arrive.*

The following can be used in this pattern: *the first, the second*, etc.; *the next/the last*; and superlatives like *the best, the most suitable*. These can be followed optionally by a noun or *one(s)*:

She's always the ***first*** *(guest)* ***to arrive*** *and* ***the last to leave****.*

Is a solicitor ***the best person to advise*** *me about buying a house?*

The only must always be followed by a noun or *one(s)*:

You're ***the only person (the only one) to complain****.*

16.32 Adjective patterns with 'too' and 'enough'

16.32.1 'Too' + adjective + *to*-infinitive

Too comes before the adjective and has the sense of 'excessive'; compare *very*, which merely strengthens the adjective [> 7.48]. In patterns with *to*-infinitives, *too* often combines negative ideas:

He ***isn't strong****. He* ***can't lift*** *it.* → *He is* ***too weak to lift*** *it.*

In the above example, the subject of the main verb is also the subject of the infinitive. In the following example, the subject of the main verb is the object of the infinitive:

He's *too heavy. I can't lift* ***him****.* → *He is too heavy (for me)* ***to lift.***

Note the optional *for*-phrase, and note that we never put an object after the infinitive in sentences like this (Not **This bread is too stale for me to eat it**).

Generally, *-ed* adjectives [> 6.15] have a personal subject + *too*:

I*'m* ***too tired to stay up*** *longer.*

and *-ing* adjectives have an impersonal subject + *too*:

The race *was almost* ***too exciting to watch****.*

16.32.2 Adjective + 'enough' + *to*-infinitive

Enough comes after the adjective and means, e.g. 'to the necessary degree'. In *to*-infinitive patterns it combines two ideas:

*He**'s strong.** He **can lift** it.* → *He**'s strong enough to lift** it.*
*He**'s weak.** He **can't lift** it.* → *He **isn't strong enough to lift** it.*

In the above examples, the subjects of the main verb and of the infinitive are the same. In the following example, the subject of the main verb is the object of the infinitive:

***The pear** is ripe. I can eat **it**.* → *It is ripe enough (for me) **to eat**.*

The *for*-phrase is optional and we do not repeat the object in this type of sentence. (Not **for me to eat it**).

For + noun/pronoun can combine with *too much/little, not enough*, etc.:

*The baby's **too much for her** to cope with.*
*There's **too little** work/**not enough** work **for me** to do.*

Noun + *to*-infinitive

16.33 The *to*-infinitive after nouns related to verbs

1 Some nouns are often associated with the infinitive:
*Our **decision to wait** was wise.*
Such nouns may correspond to verbs [compare > 16.13, 16.19]:
*We **decided to wait**.*
A noun may have the same form as a verb or a different form:
*They **wish** to succeed. It's their **wish** to succeed.*
*She **refused** to help. Her **refusal** to help surprised us.*

2 Not all such nouns can be followed by an infinitive. Some are followed by a preposition + the *-ing* form [> 16.53]:
*We cannot **hope to find** him. There's **no hope of finding** him.*
Some nouns can be followed by an infinitive or by a preposition:
*It's **a pleasure to be** with you.*
*There's nothing to compare with **the pleasure of being** with you.*

3 Some nouns combine with other infinitive forms [> 16.2], e.g. *a surprise to be/to have been invited, a change to be sitting in the sun.* For contrasting negatives with nouns [> 16.14].

16.34 The *to*-infinitive after nouns related to adjectives

Many of the adjectives which can be followed by *to*-infinitives have equivalent nouns (usually different in form, e.g. *brave/bravery*). However, not all such nouns can be followed by *to*-infinitives. We can use noun + *to*-infinitive here:

*She's **determined/eager/willing to help**.*
*Thank you for your **determination/eagerness/willingness to help**.*

But we must use noun + preposition + *-ing* form here:

*It was **generous/kind (of you) to contribute** so much.*
*Thank you for your **generosity/kindness in contributing** so much.*

Noun/adjective equivalents do not always have the same meaning:

*It's **fun to be here**. It was **funny*** (= odd) *of Sam **to do** that.*
*It's **a pity to leave** so early. Her sobs were **pitiful to hear**.*

16.35 Noun + *to*-infinitive to express advisability, etc.

The *to*-infinitive is often used after a noun to convey advice, purpose, etc. This construction is like a relative clause [> 1.33–34]:

*The **person to ask** is Jan.* (= the person whom you should ask)
*I've got **an essay to write**.* (= an essay which I must write)

Sometimes active and passive infinitives are interchangeable:

*After the fire, there was some **re-decorating to do/to be done**.*

When the subject of the sentence is the person who is to do the action described by the infinitive, we do not normally use the passive:

*I have **a meal to prepare**.* (Not **to be prepared**)

16.36 The *to*-infinitive after nouns, 'something', 'a lot', etc.

The *to*-infinitive can be used after nouns and words used in place of nouns, such as *something, someone, a lot* [compare > 16.12.1]:

*I want **a machine/something to answer the phone**.*

Active and passive infinitives are sometimes interchangeable:

*There was **a lot to do/a lot to be done**.*

or they can have different meanings:

*There was **nothing to do** so we played computer games.* (i.e. we were bored)
*He's dead. There's **nothing to be done**.* (i.e. we can't change that)

Sometimes a *for*-phrase is included:

*He talks as if there's **nothing left in life for him to do**.*

16.37 Adjective + noun + *to*-infinitive

Here are some examples of structures with adjective + noun + *to*-infinitive:

- with *too* and *enough* [compare > 16.32]:
  Note the position of *a/an*:
  *He's **too clever a politician to say** a thing like that in public.*
  *He isn't **a clever enough politician to have** any original ideas.*
  In sentences beginning *There*, the quantifier *enough* can go before or after the noun:
  *There is **enough time to take care of** everything.*
  *There is **time enough to take care of** everything.* (more formal)
- with *so...as to* and *such a/an...as to* [compare > 16.27.1]:
  *I'm not **so stupid (a fool) as to** put it in writing.*
  *I'm not **such a (stupid) fool as to** put it in writing.*
- in exclamations [> 3.13]:
  *What **an unkind thing to say**!*
  Sometimes the adjective is omitted if we are criticizing:
  *What **a thing to say**! What **a way to behave**!*

The '-ing' form

16.38 The two functions of the '-ing' form

Gerunds and present participles are formed from verbs and always end in *-ing*. Therefore words like *playing, writing*, etc. can function as gerunds or as participles. The *-ing* form is usually called a **gerund** when it behaves like a **noun** and a **participle** when it behaves like an **adjective**. However, there is some overlap between these two main functions and it is often difficult (and unnecessary!) to make formal distinctions. The term the ***-ing* form** is used here to cover gerund and participle constructions and the term 'participle' is used in 'The sentence' [> 1.56] to refer to part of a verb. In broad terms, the **gerund** can take the place of a noun, though it can, like a verb, have an object:

I like { *coffee.* / ***swimming.*** }   *John likes* { *planes.* / ***flying.*** / ***flying** planes.* }

The **participle** can take the place of an adjective [> 6.2, 6.14]:

This is a { *wide* / ***running*** } *stream.*

16.39 The '-ing' form: gerund or present participle?

16.39.1 The '-ing' form as gerund

As a gerund, the *-ing* form often functions in general statements as an uncountable noun with no article. It can also be replaced by *it*:

***Dancing** is fun. I love **it**.* [> 3.26.2]

Sometimes the *-ing* form functions as a countable noun which can be replaced by *it* (singular) or *they* (plural) [> 2.16.5]:

*Dickens often gave **readings** of his work. **They** were very popular.*

We can use a gerund after determiners like *a, the, this, a lot of* and *some*, or after possessives and adjectives:

*Brendel has made **a new recording**. **The recording** was made live.*
***The sinking** of the Titanic has never been forgotten.*
*I enjoy **a little light reading** when I go away on holiday.*
*What's all **this arguing**?*
*I did **some/a lot of/a little shopping** this morning.*
*I appreciate **your helping** me. Your **quick thinking** saved us all.*

The gerund also has some of the characteristics of a verb: e.g.

- it can be followed by an adverb or adverbial phrase:
  ***Walking quickly/Walking in step** is difficult.*
- and it can take an object:
  ***Washing the car** seems to be your main hobby.*
- and it can have a perfect form and even a passive [compare > 1.56]:
  *I'm sorry for **having wasted** your time.*
  *I can't forgive myself for **having been taken** by surprise.*

16.39.2 The '-ing' form as present participle

Participles are associated with verbs when they refer to actions in progress, e.g. in progressive tenses [> 9.2]. Participle phrases also commonly stand for clauses [> 1.58]:

***Walking** in the park the other day, **I saw a bird building** a nest.*
(= I was walking, the bird was building)

16.39.3 The gerund in nouns; the present participle as adjective [> 2.7]

*Here are your **running-shoes**.* (shoes for running: gerund)
*I love the sight of **running water**.* (water which is running: adjective)

16.40 Some common uses of the '-ing' form (gerund)

The *-ing* form can be used in the active or passive in a large number of different ways. Here are some examples (note the formation of the negative with *not* + *-ing*):

16.40.1 As a noun complement to the verb 'be'

*My favourite pastime **is bird-watching**.*
*As far as he's concerned, it**'s not doing** something wrong that matters, but **not being caught** doing something wrong.*

16.40.2 As the subject of a verb

Before *be*:

***Jogging isn't** much fun. **Being lost can be** a terrifying experience.*
***Not being tall is not** a serious disadvantage in life.*

Before verbs other than *be*:

***Rowing keeps** you fit. **Not being punctual makes** him unreliable.*

16.40.3 As the object of a verb

*I **enjoy dancing**. He **doesn't like not being taken** seriously.*
*I **hear shouting**.* [> 16.9.1] *She **taught us dress-making**.*

16.40.4 After 'do' + 'the' referring to jobs [> 10.44.4]

*Who **does the cooking/the shopping/the washing-up** here?*

16.40.5 'The' + '-ing' form + 'of'

Without an article, the *-ing* form can have a direct object:

***Lighting the fire** used to be a daily chore in Victorian times.*

After an article (or other determiner), the *-ing* form cannot be directly followed by an object. We must use *of*:

***The lighting of fires** is forbidden.*
***A ringing of bells** marked the end of the old year.*

16.40.6 'The art of writing', etc.

Many combinations are possible, e.g. *the act of listening; the art of writing; the skill of speaking*, etc.:

***The skill of speaking** a foreign language takes time to acquire.*

16.40.7 After 'No' in prohibitions

This is common in public signs: e.g. *No smoking, No parking.*

16.40.8 After 'like' (= for example) [> App 25.25]

*Why don't you find something to do, **like cleaning** the car for me?*
*If you want to get on, there's nothing **like being** hard-working.*

16.40.9 After 'for' (the purpose of) [> App 25.20]

*What's that? – It's a tool **for making** holes in metal.*
*This is a tool that's used **for cutting** hedges.*

Compare a parallel use of the *to*-infinitive in: e.g.

*What's that for? – It's **to make** holes in metal (with).*

16.40.10 The '-ing' form after adjectives and possessives

***Slow cooking** makes tough meat tender.*
***Your denying** everything will get you nowhere.*
***Jenny's not having been trained** as a dancer is her one regret.*

16.40.11 The '-ing' form after 'What about...?', 'How about...?' [> 13.40.6]

***What about/How about sending** them a postcard?*

Verb + '-ing' form

16.41 Form of '-ing' after verbs [compare > 1.56]

Verbs like *enjoy, deny* can be followed directly by the *-ing* form:
active: *I* ***deny/denied taking*** *it.*
passive: *He* ***resents/resented being accused.***
And note the perfect or past form: *having* + past participle:
active: *I* ***deny/denied having taken*** *it.*
passive: *He* ***resents/resented having been accused****.*
Contrasting negatives [> 16.14] are possible with these forms: e.g.
I don't enjoy having to...: I enjoy not having to....

16.42 Verb + '-ing' form (not + *to*-infinitive) [compare > 16.19, App 45]

When we want to use another verb immediately after the following verbs, the second verb can only be an *-ing* form, never a *to*-infinitive: *admit, appreciate, avoid, celebrate, consider, contemplate, defer, delay, deny, detest, discontinue, dislike, dispute, endure, enjoy, it entail(s), escape, excuse, explain, fancy, feel like, finish, forgive, can't help, hinder, imagine, it involve(s), keep, loathe, it mean(s), mention, mind* (= object to), *miss, it necessitate(s), pardon, postpone, practise, prevent, recall, report, resent, resist, risk, suggest, understand:*
I ***don't fancy going*** *for a walk in the rain.*
Imagine not knowing *the answer to such an easy question!*
Deny and *regret* are often followed by *having* + a past participle:
Susan ***denies/regrets having said*** *anything.*

16.43 The '-ing' form after 'come' and 'go'

The *-ing* form relating to outdoor activities (e.g. *climbing, driving, fishing, riding, sailing, shopping, skiing, walking, water-skiing, wind-surfing*) is often used after *go* and *come*, e.g. when we are:
- making suggestions: *Why don't we* ***go swimming****?*
- inviting: ***Come dancing*** *this evening.*
- narrating: *Yesterday we* ***went sight-seeing****.*

Compare *go/come for a walk*, etc. and *have been* + *-ing* [> 10.13.4].

16.44 The '-ing' form after 'need' and 'want'

The *-ing* form can follow *need, want* (and less commonly) *require*:
He ***needs*** *(a lot of)* ***encouraging****.*
The front gate ***needs/wants/requires mending****.*
The *-ing* form has a passive meaning here and can be compared to the passive infinitive (*He needs to be encouraged*).

16.45 Verb (+ accusative or possessive) + '-ing' form

With some of the verbs which can be followed by an *-ing* form, we can put another word between the verb and *-ing*. Sometimes this word must be an accusative (e.g. an object pronoun like *me*, a name like *John*); sometimes it must be a possessive (i.e. a possessive adjective like *my*; or *'s*, e.g. *John's*); sometimes it can be either.

16.45.1 Verb (+ accusative) + '-ing'

After the following verbs, the *-ing* form functions as a participle. We can include an accusative (e.g. *me, John*) between the verb and the *-ing* form: *hear, keep, smell, start, stop* and *watch*. Compare:

*When are you going to **start working**?*
*When are you going to **start him working**?*

The following must always have an accusative before *-ing: catch, find, leave, notice, observe, perceive* and *see* [> App 38.4]:

*I'd better not **catch you doing** that again!*

Verbs of perception like *hear* and *see* can also be followed by an object + bare infinitive [> 16.9.2]: *I saw him climb the tree.*

16.45.2 Verb (+ possessive) + '-ing'

The following verbs can be followed by the *-ing* form on its own or by a possessive (e.g. *my, John's*) + *-ing*. Here the *-ing* form functions as a gerund (i.e. a noun), so we can use a possessive form (referring to people, but not things) in front of it: *appreciate, avoid, consider* (usually in questions and negatives), *defer, delay, deny, enjoy, postpone, risk* and *suggest*:

*I don't think the children **enjoy your/his/John's teasing**.*

16.45.3 Verb (+ accusative or possessive) + '-ing'

Here is a selection of verbs that can be followed by *-ing* on its own or by an accusative or a possessive before *-ing*: *anticipate, contemplate, detest, dislike, dispute, endure, escape, excuse, (can't) face, fancy, forgive, hate, hinder, imagine, it involve(s), like, love, mention, mind* (= object to), *miss, it necessitate(s), pardon, prevent, resent, resist, understand, can't bear, can't help, can't stand.*

In everyday speech, the accusative is generally preferred to the possessive, though not all native speakers approve of its use:

informal (accusative)	**formal (possessive)**
*I **can't imagine my mother approving**!*	*...**my mother's approving**!*
*Please **excuse him not writing** to you.*	*...**his not writing** to you.*
***Fancy you having** noticed!*	*...**your having** noticed!*

The *'s* can be included or omitted with people's names:

*I **can't understand John/John's making** such a fuss.*

However, with more than one name *'s* is unlikely:

*I **can't imagine Frank and Mabel paying** so much for a piano.*

Adjectives and nouns + '-ing' form

16.46 Form of '-ing' after adjectives and nouns

Many adjectives, nouns and expressions can be followed by *-ing* forms active and passive [> 16.41], e.g. *It's nice seeing him again; It's fun being taken to the zoo*. Contrasting negatives, e.g. *not fun having to...; fun not having to...* [> 16.14] are possible.

16.47 The '-ing' form with adjectives

Like the *to*-infinitive, the *-ing* form (gerund) can be used as the subject of a sentence and can be replaced by a construction with 'preparatory *it*' [> 4.13]. There is not much difference in meaning between *-ing* and the *to* infinitive: *-ing* may refer to an action in progress, whereas the *to*-infinitive may imply 'in general':

It's difficult finding *your way around in a strange city.*
It's difficult to find *your way around in a strange city.*

We rarely begin statements with the *to*-infinitive but often begin with *-ing*, particularly when we are making general statements:

Finding work *is difficult these days.* ***Wind-surfing*** *is popular.*

Compare the *-ing* form (participle) [> 1.58] after adjectives such as *bored, busy, fed-up, frantic, happy, occupied* and *tired* with a personal subject (Not **it**):

Sylvia is ***frantic getting*** *everything ready for the wedding.*
(= Sylvia is frantic. She is getting everything ready...)

Adjectives can be followed by the accusative (*me, you, him*, etc.) or the possessive (*my, his, John's*, etc.):

It's ***strange him/his behaving*** *like that.*

Normally only a possessive is possible when *-ing* begins a sentence:

His knowing *I had returned home unexpectedly is strange.*

Either *-ing* or a *to*-infinitive can follow *it's/it was* + adjective + *of (him)* without much difference in meaning [> 16.27.2]:

It was rude of her interrupting (to interrupt) *you all the time.*

16.48 The '-ing' form after nouns

Many nouns, both countable and uncountable, can be followed by the *-ing* form after 'preparatory *it*' [> 4.13]. Examples are: *a catastrophe, a disaster, fun, hell, luck, a mistake, a pain, a pleasure, a relief, a tragedy:*

It's a nightmare worrying *where the children might be.*
It's a tedious business attending *so many meetings.*

If we want to use another word before the *-ing* form, a possessive is preferable to an accusative (though both are possible):

It's a catastrophe their/them shutting *all those factories.*

16.49 Common expressions with '-ing'

Typical expressions that can be followed by the *-ing* form are: *it's no good; it's no use; it's little use; it's hardly any use; it's not worth; it's hardly/scarcely worth; it's worthwhile; spend money/time; there's no; there's no point in; there's nothing worse than; what's the use/point:*

It's ***no good complaining****. This clock is* ***hardly worth repairing****.*
There's no telling *what will happen.* ***Don't waste time talking****.*

Some expressions can be followed by a possessive or accusative:

It's no good his/him apologizing *now the damage has been done.*

Prepositions + '-ing' form

16.50 Form of '-ing' after prepositions

Prepositions can be followed by all *-ing* forms, active and passive [> 16.41], e.g. *without eating breakfast; without being told; without having* *been told* Contrasting negatives e.g. *not sorry for telling him; sorry for not telling him* [> 16.14] are possible.

16.51 The '-ing' form after prepositions [compare > 1.60, 1.62.2]

We may use the *-ing* form (not a *to*-infinitive) after prepositions such as *about, after, by, for, instead of, to* [> 16.56], *without*:

I have learnt a lot ***about gardening*** *from my father.*
After changing *some money, I went sight-seeing.* [> 1.58.2, 8.4.4]
You open this door ***by turning*** *the key twice in the lock.*
The teacher punished Jimmy ***for talking*** *in class.*
Instead of making *a fuss, you should have complained quietly.*
You shouldn't try to leave the restaurant ***without paying***. [> App 25.36]

Prepositions can sometimes be followed by an accusative pronoun, by a name or a noun; or by a possessive adjective or noun + *'s*:

You should offer to help ***without me/my having*** *to ask.*

16.52 'There being' and 'it being' after prepositions

There is/There will be and *it is/it will be* can be replaced by *there being* and *it being* after prepositions [compare > 10.20]. *There being* can often be omitted:

Is there any chance of (there being) a vacancy *in this hotel tomorrow?* (= will there be a vacancy)
If I bring in my suit for dry-cleaning, ***is there any chance of it being ready*** *by tomorrow?* (= will it be ready)

16.53 The '-ing' form after adjective or noun + preposition

Many adjectives can be followed by prepositions [> App 27], e.g. *afraid of, bored with, fond of, good at, happy about, interested in, keen on, sorry for, (be) used to*, etc. The *-ing* form (not a *to*-infinitive) may be used after them:

I'm ***interested in acting***. *He's* ***good at ski-ing***.

Possessive and/or accusative forms can be used before *-ing*:

You can't be too ***sure of his/him agreeing***.
I'm ***surprised at your/you not having noticed***.

The *-ing* form may be used after noun + preposition, e.g. *concern about, fear of, interest in* [> Apps 27–29]:

Erica could never overcome her ***fear of flying***.
His ***interest in hang-gliding*** *proved to be fatal.*

Accusative (informal) and possessive forms can be used:

My main ***interest*** *at present is* ***in him/his doing well*** *at school.*

16.54 The '-ing' form after verb + preposition [> Apps 28–30]

Many verbs are followed by prepositions, e.g. *apologize for, approve of, insist on, prevent somebody/something from, thank somebody for.* The *-ing* form may be used after a verb + preposition and may be preceded by an object (informal), or a possessive:

I must ***insist on paying***. *I must* ***insist on him/his paying***.

16.55 The '-ing' form after verb + particle [> Apps 32–33,]

An adverb particle may be followed by the *-ing* form:

*Everyone **burst out laughing**. I've **given up smoking**.*

We can use a possessive before a gerund:

*We'll have to **put off their coming** by another week.*

We cannot use a possessive before a participle:

*We'll have to **put them off coming**.*

(= They are coming. We'll have to put them off.)

16.56 The '-ing' form after 'to' as a preposition

To is either a preposition or a part of the infinitive. It is part of the infinitive in *I want to go home*, but a preposition governing a noun/gerund in *I object to noise, I object to smoking*. In the following expressions, *to* is a preposition, so we may use the *-ing* form after it: *accustom (oneself) to, be accustomed to, face up to, in addition to, look forward to, object to, be reduced to, resign oneself to, be resigned to, resort to, sink to, be used to:*

*I **object to being** kept waiting. **I'm used to doing** the shopping.*

Accusative and possessive forms are possible:

*I **object to people/him/his smoking** in restaurants.*

Some nouns and adjectives can also be followed by *to* + *-ing*: e.g. *alternative to, close/closeness to, dedication/dedicated to, opposition/opposed to, similarity/similar to*.

The *to*-infinitive or the '-ing' form?

16.57 Verb + *to*-infinitive or '-ing': no change in meaning

Some verbs can be followed by a *to*-infinitive or by *-ing*. Sometimes there is little or no change in meaning; sometimes there is.

These verbs can be followed by a *to*-infinitive or *-ing* without any change in meaning: *attempt, begin, can't bear, cease, commence, continue, intend, omit* and *start*:

*I **can't bear to see/seeing** people suffering.*

After *can't bear* the accusative can be used before the infinitive; the accusative or possessive can be used before the *-ing* form:

*I **can't bear you to shout** in that way.*
*I **can't bear you/your shouting** in that way.*

We do not normally use the *-ing* form after the progressive forms of *begin, cease, continue* or *start*. This is because the repetition of the two *-ing* forms sounds awkward:

*He **was beginning to recover** when he had another attack.*

However, we can use *-ing* after the progressive forms of verbs which cannot be followed by a *to*-infinitive [> 16.42]:

*We **were considering catching** an earlier train.*

Stative verbs like *know* and *understand* cannot normally be used with an *-ing* form after *begin, cease* and *continue*:

*I soon **began to understand** what was happening.*

Some verbs such as *allow, advise, permit* and *forbid*, which can be followed by a *to*-infinitive after an object [> 16.21], can also be followed directly by *-ing*:

*Would you **advise phoning**, or shall I wait a bit longer?*
*Would you **advise me to phone**, or shall I wait a bit longer?*

16.58 Verb + *to*- or '-ing': some changes in meaning

These verbs can be followed by a *to*-infinitive or *-ing*: *dread, hate, like, love, prefer*. We often use a *to*-infinitive after these verbs to refer to a specified future event and the *-ing* form to refer to an activity currently in progress or existing in general. Some examples are:

	acceptable examples	**comment**
1a	*I **love/like to watch** TV.*	Same (general) meaning.
b	*I **love/like watching** TV.*	
2a	*I **hate to disturb** you.*	(but I am just about to do so).
b	*I **hate disturbing** you.*	(= I'm disturbing you and I'm sorry) or general use.
3a	*I **dread to think** what has happened to him.*	(so I dare not try to). **I dread thinking** is unacceptable.
b	*I **dread going** to the dentist.*	(= whenever I go, I'm terrified). **I dread to go** is unacceptable.
4a	*I **prefer to wait** here.*	(so I'll wait here if you don't mind).
b	*I **prefer waiting** here.*	(= I'm waiting here and I prefer doing that).
c	*I **prefer swimming to cycling.***	Not the infinitive here.
5a	***Would you like to eat** out?*	Not the gerund here.
b	***I'd like to. I'd love to.***	Or: ***I'd like it. I'd love it.***
c	***I'd love sailing** if I could afford it.*	***I'd love to sail** if I could afford it.* Also acceptable.
d	***I'd hate to disturb** him if he's busy.*	*'I'd hate disturbing him if...'* is doubtful.
e	***You'd hate to live** on a desert island.*	***You'd hate living** on a desert island* is also acceptable.
6a	*I **wouldn't like you to think** I'd forgotten you.*	*'I wouldn't like you thinking...'* is doubtful.
b	*I **like him/his playing** the guitar.*	***I like him to play** the guitar* is also acceptable.

16.59 Verb + *to*- or '-ing': different meanings

The *to*-infinitive and *-ing* never mean the same when used after these verbs: *remember, forget, regret, try, stop* and *go on*:

Remember + *to*-infinitive refers to an action in the future (or to a 'future' action as seen from the past):

***Remember to post** the letters.* (= don't forget to)
***I remembered to post** the letters.* (= I didn't forget to)

Remember + *-ing* refers to the past:

***I remember posting/having posted** the letters.*
(= I posted them and I remember the action)

Forget + *to*-infinitive refers to future actions (or to a 'future' action as seen from the past):

Don't forget to ask Tom. I forgot to ask Tom.

Forget + *-ing* refers to the past:

Have you forgotten meeting/having met her? (i.e. you met her)

Regret + *to*-infinitive refers to future or present:

We regret to inform you that your account is overdrawn.

Regret + *-ing* refers to present or past:

I regret(ted) leaving the firm after twenty years.

(*I regret(ted) having left* would refer to the past only.)

Try + *to*-infinitive means 'make an effort':

You really must try to overcome your shyness.

Try + *-ing* means 'experiment':

Try holding your breath to stop sneezing.

Stop + *to*-infinitive refers to purpose [> 16.12.1]:

On the way to the station I stopped to buy a paper.

Stop + *-ing*: *-ing* is the object of the verb, [compare > 16.42, 16.45.1].

When he told us the story, we just couldn't stop laughing.

Go on + *to*-infinitive refers to doing something different:

After approving the agenda, we went on to discuss finance.

Go on + *-ing* means 'continue without interruption' [> App 32.9.1]:

We went on talking till after midnight.

16.60 Adjective/noun + *to-* or + preposition [compare > 8.20]

Some adjectives and nouns can be followed by a *to*-infinitive or by a preposition [> App 27].

adjective + 'to-'	**adjective + preposition**
interested to (do/be)	*interested in (doing/being)*
sorry to (disturb)	*sorry for (disturbing)*
noun + 'to-'	**noun + preposition**
chance to (meet)	*chance of (meeting)*
opportunity to (buy)	*opportunity of (buying)*

Often there is little difference in meaning between the *to-* and *-ing* structures:

I'm sorry (not) to mention it. (more likely)
I'm sorry for (not) mentioning it. (less likely)

I couldn't resist the opportunity to greet such a great actor.
I couldn't resist the opportunity of greeting such a great actor.

Sometimes there are differences in meaning between the *to-* and *-ing* structures:

I'm interested to hear your opinion. (it interests me)
I'm interested in emigrating to Canada. (I might do this)
I'm sorry to interrupt. (= I'm sorry, but I'm going to interrupt)
I'm sorry for interrupting. (= I'm sorry for what has happened)

Appendix

Appendix 1 [> 1.9, 1.10, 1.12, 4.16.2]

Transitive and intransitive verbs

1.1 Verbs which are always transitive:
afford, allow, blame, bring, contain, deny, enjoy, examine, excuse, fetch, fix, get, greet, have, hit, inform, interest, let, like, love, make, mean, name, need, omit, owe, prefer, prove, put, question, remind, rent, rob, select, wrap.

1.2 Verbs which are always intransitive:
faint, hesitate, lie (lied), lie (lay/lain), occur, pause, rain (it), remain, sleep, sneeze.

1.3 Verbs which are transitive/intransitive:
answer, ask, begin, borrow, choose, climb, dance, eat, enter, fail, fill, grow, help, hurry, jump, know, leave, marry, meet, obey, pull, read, see, sell, touch, wash, watch, win, write.

Appendix 2 [> 2.2]

Some common noun endings

2.1 People who do things: e.g.
-ant: *assistant;* ***-ar:*** *beggar;* ***-eer:*** *engineer;* ***-ent:*** *president;* ***-er:*** *driver;* ***-ian:*** *historian;* ***-ist.*** *pianist;* ***-or:*** *actor.*

2.2 People who come from, etc: e.g.
-an: *Roman;* ***-er:*** *Londoner;* ***-ese:*** *Milanese;* ***-ian:*** *Athenian,* ***-ite:*** *Muscovite, socialite.*

2.3 Nouns derived from verbs: e.g.
-age: *postage;* ***-al:*** *arrival;* ***-ance:*** *acceptance,* ***-ence:*** *existence;* ***-ery:*** *discovery;* ***-ion*** / ən /: *possession;* ***-ment:*** *agreement;* ***-sion*** / ʒən /: *decision;* / ʃən /: *extension;* ***-tion:*** *attention.*
And note the *-ing* form: *running*, etc. [> 16.39.1]

2.4 Nouns related to adjectives: e.g.
-ance/ence: *abundance, absence;* ***-ancy/-ency:*** *constancy, consistency;* ***-ety:*** *anxiety;* ***-ity:*** *activity;* ***-ness:*** *happiness.*

2.5 Nouns derived from other nouns: e.g.
-cy: *lunacy;* ***-dom:*** *kingdom;* ***-ful:*** *mouthful;* ***-hood:*** *boyhood;* ***-ism:*** *sexism.*

2.6 Nouns used to mean 'small': e.g.
-en: *kitten;* ***-ette:*** *maisonette;* ***-ie:*** *laddie;* ***-let:*** *booklet;* ***-ling:*** *duckling;* ***-y:*** *dolly.*

Appendix 3 [> 2.3]

3.1 Nouns/verbs distinguished by stress:

ˈabstract/abˈstract	*ˈimprint/imˈprint*
ˈconduct/conˈduct	*ˈpermit/perˈmit*
ˈcontest/conˈtest	*ˈproduce/proˈduce*
ˈdesert/deˈsert	*ˈrebel/reˈbel*
ˈdispute/disˈpute	*ˈrecord/reˈcord*

3.2 Nouns/verbs: same spelling and pronunciation: e.g.
act, attempt, blame, book, call, climb, copy, cost, dance, drink, drive, fall, fear, help, joke, kiss, laugh, try, vote, wait, walk, wash, wish.
Noises: *bang, bark, buzz, grunt, hiccup, moan.*
Jobs/Actions: *butcher, judge, model, nurse.*

Appendix 4 [> 2.17]

Nouns not normally countable in English:
accommodation, advice, anger, applause, assistance, baggage, behaviour, bread, business (= trade), *capital* (= money), *cardboard, cash, chaos, chess, china, clothing, coal, conduct, cookery, countryside, courage, crockery, cutlery, damage, dancing, dirt, education, evidence, flu, food, fruit, fun, furniture, garbage, gossip* (= talk about other people), *grass, hair* (*hairs* = separate strands of hair; *hair* = all the hairs on the head), *happiness, harm, help, homework, hospitality, housework, information, jealousy, jewellery, knowledge, laughter, leisure, lightning, linen, luck, luggage, macaroni, machinery, meat, money, moonlight, mud, music, news, nonsense, parking, patience, peel, permission, poetry, the post* (= letters), *produce, progress, rubbish, safety, scaffolding, scenery, seaside, sewing, shopping, smoking, soap, spaghetti, spelling, steam, strength, stuff, stupidity, sunshine, thunder, timber, toast* (= bread), *traffic, transport, travel, underwear, violence, vocabulary, wealth, weather, work, writing.*

Appendix 5 [> 2.18.2, 2.32]

5.1 Partitives: specific items or amounts:
a bar of chocolate/soap, a block of cement, a book of matches/stamps, a cake of soap, a cloud of dust, a flash of lightning, a head of hair, an item of news, a jet of water, a loaf of bread, a peal of thunder, a pile of earth, a portion of food, a roll of paper, a slice of meat.

5.2 Partitives: 'containers': e.g.
a barrel of beer, a basket of fruit, a bottle of milk, a can of beer, a carton of cigarettes, a flask of tea, a glass of water, a jug of water, a mug of cocoa, a tin of soup, a vase of flowers.

5.3 Partitives: small quantities: e.g.
a blade of grass, a breath of air, a crust of bread, a dash of soda, a grain of rice, a lock of hair, a pat of butter, a scrap of paper.

5.4 Partitives: measures: e.g.
a gallon of petrol, a length of cloth, a litre of oil, an ounce of gold, a pint of milk, a pound of coffee, a spoonful of medicine, a yard of cloth.

5.5 Partitives: 'a game of': e.g.
billiards, bridge, cards, chess, cricket, darts, squash, table-tennis, tennis, volleyball.

5.6 Partitives: abstract: e.g.
a bit of advice, a branch of knowledge, a fit of anger, a piece of research, a spot of trouble.

5.7 Partitives: types/species: e.g.
a brand of soap, a kind of biscuit, a species of insect, a type of drug, a variety of pasta.

5.8 Partitives: 'a pair of': e.g.
boots, braces, glasses, knickers, pants, pliers, pyjamas/pajamas, scissors, shears, shoes, shorts, skates, skis, slippers, socks, stockings, tights, tongs, trousers.

Appendix 6 [> 2.19]

Collective nouns followed by 'of': e.g. *a band of soldiers, a bouquet of flowers, a bunch of grapes, a circle of friends, a clump of trees, a collection of coins, a colony of ants, a crew of sailors, a crowd of people, a deck of cards, a drove of cattle, a fleet of ships, a gang of thieves, a group of people, a herd of cattle, a hive of bees, a horde of children, a mass of people, a mob of hooligans, a pack of cards, a panel of experts, a party of visitors, a plague of locusts, a school of fish, a set of teeth, a shelf of books, a string of pearls.*

Appendix 7 [> 4.35]

Uses of 'this/that' and 'these/those'

7.1 Identification
Things: *This is my room.*
People: *There he is. That's him.* (Not **he**)

7.2 Introductions
This is Mrs Ainsworth.
This is Tom Smith, and this is Jane Mills.
This is Mr and Mrs Ainsworth. (i.e. one unit)

7.3 Telephoning
This is Tom here. Is that you, Elizabeth?

7.4 'This' = 'here'
*In **this school/firm/house** we like punctuality.*

7.5 'Pointing' to people, etc.: contrast
***This boy** wants tea and **that one** wants milk.*
***These boys** are in class 1 and **those** are in 2.*
*Take **this** home and give **these** to Caroline.*

7.6 Demonstrating (with gestures)
*He went **that way**. Do it **like this/that**.*

7.7 Forward and backward reference
Only ***this*** can be used for forward reference:
*__This__ is how you do it. Press **this button**...*
Compare backward reference:
*He was very late. **This/That** delayed us.*
These and *those* are never used, even if more than one event is referred to:
*I broke my leg and my sister's house burnt down. – When did **this/that** happen?*

7.8 Story-telling, narration (informal)
This sometimes replaces *a/an* to make a story sound more amusing or interesting and to show that the narrator will explain more:
*There was **this Frenchman** who went to a cricket match.*

7.9 Time references [> App 48]
*I'll see you **this afternoon**.*
***These days** life is hard for old people.*
*I was born in 1935. In **those days** there was no TV. At **that time** my father was a miner.*

7.10 Comparisons
*$500? It cost a lot **more than that**!*
In formal use, ***that of*** and ***those of*** sometimes replace a noun with *of*:
*The area of the USA is **larger than that of** Brazil.*
*Tom's essays are **better than those of** the other boys.*

7.11 Contrast
***This is** my car and **that is** John's.*

7.12 Clarification
*Is **this the man** you saw, **the one** here?*
*I didn't mean **that Tom**, but **the one** next door.*
...that is is often used to clarify:
*I'll arrive on the 2nd, **that is**, on Friday.*

7.13 'This'/'that' + 'wh-'/'how' clauses
*You're late. **That's why** we're waiting.*
*Sue lent me 50p. **This/That is how** I got home.*

7.14 'Derogatory' reference with 'that'
*It's **that man** again.* (let's avoid him)

7.15 'That' in advertisements, etc.
That is sometimes used colloquially to point to common 'shared' knowledge:
*Bovril prevents **that sinking feeling**.*

7.16 'This' and 'that' with 'kind' and 'sort'
*I like **this/that kind** (or **sort**) of person/bicycle.*

7.17 'These' and 'those' with 'kinds'/'sorts'
*I enjoy **these/those kinds** (or **sorts**) of films.*
However, in everyday speech we often hear:
*I enjoy **these/those kind** (or **sort**) of films.*
We cannot use *these* and *those* after *of* in, e.g.
*I enjoy films of **this/that kind** (or **sort**).*

7.18 'This' and 'that' to indicate 'degree'
Very informally ***this*** and ***that*** can be used like *so* as intensifiers [> 6.30.2, 7.51.1]:
*It's about **this/that big**.* (+ gesture)
*Does it really cost **this/that much**?*
*I can't walk **this/that far**! Let's get a taxi!*

7.19 Some expressions with 'this' and 'that'
We discussed this, that and the other.
What's all this? (= What's going on?)
I know you're tired and all that, but...
That's that! We've finished!

Appendix 8 [> 6.2]

8.1 Adjectives formed with suffixes: e.g. ***-able*** (capable of being, able to be): *changeable;* ***-ible*** (like *-able*): *possible;* ***-ful*** (full of, having): *beautiful;* ***-ful/-less:*** *careful – careless;* ***-i(a)n*** (historical period, etc.): *Victorian;* ***-ish*** (have the – sometimes bad – quality): *foolish;* (colour): *reddish;* (age): *thirtyish;* ***-ive*** (capable of being or doing this): *attractive;* ***-less*** (without): *lifeless;* ***-like*** (resembling): *businesslike;* ***-ly*** (have this quality): *friendly;* (how often): *hourly.* Others: ***-al:*** *mechanical;* ***-ant:*** *hesitant;* ***-ar:*** *circular;* ***-ary:*** *visionary;* ***-ate:*** *affectionate;* ***-ent:*** *sufficient;* ***-eous:*** *gorgeous;* ***-esque:*** *picturesque;* ***-ic:*** *energetic;* ***-ic/-ical:*** *economic – economical;* ***-ious:*** *glorious;* ***-ist:*** *sexist;* ***-ory:*** *sensory;* ***-ous:*** *humorous;* ***-some:*** *fearsome.*

8.2 Adjectives formed with prefixes: e.g. ***dis-:*** *dishonest;* ***il-:*** *illegal;* ***im-:*** *impossible;* ***in-:*** *indifferent;* ***ir-:*** *irresponsible;* ***non-:*** *non-stick;* ***un-:*** *unthinkable.* Others: ***a-:*** *amoral;* ***anti-:*** *antiseptic;* ***hyper-:*** *hyperactive;* ***mal-:*** *maladjusted;* ***over-:*** *overdue;* ***pre-:*** *prewar;* ***pro-:*** *pro-American;* ***sub-:*** *subnormal;* ***super-:*** *superhuman;* ***under-:*** *undercooked.*

Appendix 9 [> 6.12.2]

'The' + adjective: e.g. 'the young'

9.1 'The group as a whole': e.g.
the aged, the blind, the dead, the deaf, the dumb, the elderly, the guilty, the handicapped, the healthy, the homeless, the innocent, the living, the middle-aged, the old, the poor, the rich, the sick, the unemployed, the young.

9.2 Abstract combinations: e.g.
from the sublime to the ridiculous, take the rough with the smooth.

Appendix 10 [> 6.15, 7.51]

Some more '-ed/-ing' adjectival participles:
alarmed/alarming, amused/amusing, appalled/appalling, astonished/astonishing, bewildered/bewildering, confused/confusing, depressed/depressing, disgusted/disgusting, distressed/distressing, embarrassed/embarrassing, exhausted/exhausting, frightened/frightening, horrified/horrifying, irritated/irritating, moved/moving, relaxed/relaxing, satisfied/satisfying, shocked/shocking, surprised/surprising, terrified/terrifying, worried/worrying.

Appendix 11 [> 6.19]

Common adjectives easily confused

11.1 'Fat/thin': people/animals
a fat/thin man, a fat/thin woman, a fat/thin cat

11.2 'Thick/thin': usually apply to things
a thick/thin book, thick/thin material

11.3 'Fat' for a few names of things
a fat book, a fat dictionary

11.4 'Thick' (= 'stupid' – people)
Some of my students are really thick.

11.5 'Tall/short': people/height
a tall/short man, a tall/short woman, etc.

11.6 'Tall': buildings, mountains, trees, etc.
The opposite is ***small***: *a tall building/mountain/tree, a small building/mountain/tree.*

11.7 'High/low': buildings and things
a high/low building, a high/low stool.
High for mountains, but ***low*** for hills:
a high mountain, a low hill.
High and ***low*** can also refer to sound:
a high/low voice, a high/low note.

11.8 'Long/short': length, time, distance
a long/short skirt, a long/short time, walk, etc.

11.9 'Loud/soft'; 'hard/soft'
a loud/soft knock, a loud/soft thud.
Soft (opposite ***hard***) also applies to texture:
a hard/soft apple, a hard/soft mattress.

11.10 'Old/young': people
an old/young man, an old/young woman.

11.11 'Old/new': things
an old/new handbag, an old/new house.
New is used for a person who is a 'newcomer':
a new boss, a new secretary.

11.12 'Large/big/great': people or things
Large and ***big*** generally refer to size:
a large/big man or woman, a large/big box.
Great generally refers to importance:
a great man, a great cathedral, a great idea.

11.13 'Small/little'
Small is the opposite of ***large/big***; ***small*** is gradable and is attributive/predicative:
a small boy, a small house. (attributive)
My house is very small. (predicative)
Little is usually attributive and can replace *small* in many contexts (*a little boy, a little house*); it is also a quantifier (*a little sugar* = a small amount of). ***Little*** is used particularly to express love, pity, etc.: *your sweet little baby.*

Appendix 12 [> 6.24, 6.29]

Comparatives/superlatives confused and misused: e.g.

12.1 'Better/worse'
Better is the comparative of ***well***; ***worse*** is the comparative of ***ill*** when referring to health:
How's Liz? – She's (much) ***better****/nearly* ***well****.*
How's Bob? – He's still ***ill*** *– much* ***worse****.*

12.2 'Little'
We use the comparative/superlative of ***small***:
a small/little boy, a smaller/the smallest boy.
The forms ***littler***, ***the littlest*** are typical of children's speech and refer to size and age:
Don't hit him. He's ***littler*** than you are. *I'm 7. Susie's 6, and Jimmy's* ***the littlest****. He's 4.*

12.3 'Elder/eldest'; 'older/oldest'
Elder and ***eldest*** are used (attributive only) with reference to people in a family; ***elder*** is therefore never followed by *than*:
my elder brother/son, the eldest child.
The noun is often deleted after ***the eldest/youngest***:
I'm ***the eldest*** *and Pam's* ***the youngest****.*
The elder is possible in: e.g. *I'm the elder.*

12.4 'Old/older/oldest'
These are used attributively and predicatively with reference to people and things:
my older brother, my oldest son/oldest child
My brother is ***older than*** *I am. Tim is* ***the oldest*** *in our family.*
an older tree/book, the oldest tree/book.
This oak tree is ***older than*** *that yew tree. This book is* ***older than*** *that one. It's* ***the oldest*** *book I have in my library.*

Appendix 13 [> 6.30.1]

Expressions with 'as' + adjective + 'as':
as blind as a bat, as bold as brass, as bright as a button (= intelligent), *as cheap as dirt, as clear as a bell, as cool as a cucumber, as deaf as a post, as dry as dust* (= boring), *as easy as pie, as fat as a pig, as free as a bird, as hard as nails, as keen as mustard, as large as life, as mad as a hatter, as pleased as Punch, as pretty as a picture, as quick as lightning, as right as rain, as safe as houses.*

Appendix 14 [> 6.6, 7.3.2, 7.5, 7.13]

Adjectives and adverbs with the same form
The adjectival use is given first:

airmail: *airmail letter; send it airmail*
all day: *an all day match; play all day*
all right: *I'm all right; you've done all right*
best: *best clothes; do your best*
better: *a better book; speak better*
big: *a big house; talk big*
cheap: *a cheap suit; buy it cheap*
clean: *clean air, cut it clean*
clear: *a clear sky; stand clear*
close: *the shops are close; stay close*
cold: *a cold person; run cold*
daily: *a daily paper; they deliver daily*
dead: *a dead stop; stop dead*
dear: *a dear bouquet; sell it dear*
deep: *a deep hole; drink deep*
direct: *a direct train; go direct*
dirty: *dirty weather; play dirty*
downtown: *a downtown restaurant* (AmE)
duty-free: *a duty-free shop; buy it duty-free*
early: *an early train; arrive early*
easy: *an easy book; go easy*
everyday: *my everyday suit; work every day*
extra: *an extra blanket; charge extra*
fair: *a fair decision; play fair*
far: *a far country; go far*
farther: *on the farther side; walk farther*
fast: *a fast driver; drive fast*
fine: *a fine pencil; cut it fine*
firm: *a firm belief; hold firm*
first: *the first guest; first I'll wash*
free: *a free ticket; travel free*
further: *further questions; walk further*
hard: *a hard worker; work hard*
high: *a high note; aim high*
home: *home cooking; go home*
hourly: *hourly bulletin; phone hourly*
inside: *the inside story; stay inside*
kindly: *a kindly man; act kindly*
last: *the last guest; come last*
late: *a late train; arrive late*
long: *long hair; don't stay long*
loud: *a loud noise; talk loud*
low: *a low bridge; aim low*
monthly: *a monthly bill; pay monthly*
outside: *an outside lavatory; wait outside*
overseas: *overseas travel; travel overseas*
past: *the past week; walk past*
quick: *a quick worker; come quick*
quiet: *a quiet evening; sit quiet*
right: *the right answer; answer right*
sharp: *sharp eyes; look sharp*
slow: *a slow train; go slow*
straight: *a straight line; think straight*
sure: *I'm sure; Sure, I'll do it* (AmE)
thin/thick: *a thin/thick slice; cut it thin/thick*
through: *a through train; go through*
tight: *a tight fit; sit tight*
weekly: *weekly pay; pay weekly*
well: *I am well; do well*
wide: *a wide room; open wide*
worse: *worse marks; do worse than...*
wrong: *a wrong guess; answer wrong*
yearly: *a yearly visit; go there yearly*

Appendix 15 [> 7.13, 7.14]

Adverbs with two forms

15.1 Two forms used in the same way:
All forms without *-ly* can also be used as adjectives [compare > App 14].
cheap/cheaply, clean/cleanly, clear/clearly, close/closely, dear/dearly, fair/fairly, fine/finely, firm/firmly, first/firstly, loud/loudly, quick/quickly, quiet/quietly, slow/slowly, thin/thinly.

15.2 Two forms used in different ways: e.g.

deep/deeply: *drink deep; deeply regret*
direct/directly: *go direct; I'll come directly*
easy/easily: *go easy; win easily*
flat/flatly: *fall flat; flatly refuse*
free/freely: *travel free; freely admit*
full/fully: *full in the face; fully realize*
hard/hardly: *work hard; hardly any food*
high/highly: *aim high; think highly of you*
just/justly: *just finished; deal justly with*
last/lastly: *arrive last; lastly, I think...*
late/lately: *arrive late; lately I've seen*
near/nearly: *go near; nearly finished*
pretty/prettily: *sit pretty; smile prettily*
real/really: *real glad* (AmE); *I really like*
rough/roughly: *sleep rough; roughly twenty*
sharp/sharply: *10 am sharp; speak sharply*
short/shortly: *stop short; see you shortly*
strong/strongly: *going strong; strongly feel*
sure/surely: *I sure am late* (AmE); *surely*
wide/widely: *open wide; widely believed*

Appendix 16 [> 7.53]

Some '-ly' intensifiers: typical combinations

absolutely delicious; I absolutely love peaches
amazingly good at...; amazingly well
awfully nice; do something awfully well
badly mistaken; I badly want...
beautifully simple; beautifully organized
bitterly cold, bitterly disappointed
brilliantly clever; brilliantly designed
completely successful; completely finished
considerably better; considerably cheaper
cruelly disappointed; cruelly afflicted
dangerously ill; dangerously wounded
dearly loved; I'd dearly like to...
deeply sorry; deeply hurt
definitely mistaken; I'm definitely leaving
dreadfully late; dreadfully annoyed
entirely irresponsible; I entirely agree
(e)specially nice; I (e)specially enjoyed...
exceedingly good; do it exceedingly badly
extremely interesting; extremely surprised
fearfully boring; fearfully confused
fully satisfied; I fully appreciate
gravely ill; gravely worried
greatly impressed; I greatly appreciate
hideously ugly; hideously expensive
highly intelligent; I highly disapprove
hopelessly badly; hopelessly confused
horribly painful; horribly wounded
immensely rich; I was immensely pleased
incredibly beautiful; incredibly surprised
intensely cold; intensely concerned
keenly competitive; keenly interested

largely compatible; largely altered
lightly salted; lightly cooked
literally amazing; he literally believes...
madly exciting; they clapped madly
mortally ill; mortally offended
outstandingly good/well/original
painfully shy; painfully embarrassed
particularly clever; I particularly enjoyed...
perfectly sweet; I perfectly understand
pleasantly agreeable; pleasantly surprised
richly deserved; richly rewarded
seriously upset; seriously depressed
severely ill; severely criticized
sharply accurate; sharply critical
simply wonderful; I simply love...
strikingly attractive, strikingly obvious
superbly fit; superbly cooked
terribly rude; drive terribly fast
thoroughly fed-up; I thoroughly enjoyed...
totally idiotic; I totally agree...
utterly stupid; I utterly agree
violently ill; violently opposed to...
wonderfully clever; do it wonderfully well

Appendix 17 [> 7.57]

Some viewpoint adverbs

17.1 = 'I'm sure of the facts': e.g.
actually, as a matter of fact, certainly, clearly, definitely, honestly, in actual fact, naturally, obviously, really, strictly speaking.

17.2 = 'I'm less sure of myself/the facts':
apparently, arguably, as far as I know, at a guess, by all accounts, evidently, maybe, perhaps, possibly, probably, quite likely.

17.3 = 'I'm making a generalization': e.g.
as a (general) rule, basically, by and large, for the most part, in general, in principle, in a way, normally, on the whole, to a great extent.

17.4 = 'I'm going to be brief': e.g.
anyhow, briefly, in brief, in effect, in a few words, in short, to put it simply.

17.5 = 'I'm expressing my opinion': e.g.
as far as I'm concerned, frankly (speaking), in my opinion, in my view, personally I think..., in all frankness, in all honesty, to put it bluntly.

17.6 = 'I don't want you to repeat this': e.g.
between ourselves, between you and me, confidentially, in strict confidence.

17.7 = 'You won't believe this': e.g.
amazingly, astonishingly, curiously, funnily enough, incredibly, oddly enough, strangely, surprisingly, to my amazement, to my surprise.

17.8 = 'It's just as I expected': e.g.
characteristically, inevitably, logically, naturally, needless to say, not surprisingly, of course, plainly, predictably, typically.

17.9 = 'I'm pleased/I'm not pleased': e.g.
agreeably, annoyingly, foolishly, fortunately, happily, ideally, interestingly, luckily, mercifully, preferably, regrettably, sadly, unfortunately, unhappily, unwisely, wisely.

Appendix 18 [> 1.17, 7.58]

Connecting words and phrases

18.1 Enumerating/stressing facts: e.g.
above all, chiefly, (e)specially, finally, first(ly)/ second(ly), in the first place, last(ly), mainly, primarily, principally, to begin with, then.

18.2 Making an addition; reinforcing: e.g.
additionally/in addition, again, also, another thing is that..., apart from this, aside from that, as well as that, besides, for that matter, furthermore, indeed, moreover, what is more.

18.3 Stating an alternative: e.g.
alternatively, apart from this, conversely, except for, excepting, instead, so far as.

18.4 Giving an example: e.g.
according to, as far as...is concerned, for example, for instance, namely, such as.

18.5 Making a comparison or a contrast:
as compared to, by/in comparison with, conversely, equally, however, in contrast, in reality, in the same way, likewise.

18.6 Making a concession: e.g.
admittedly, after all, all the same, anyhow, anyway, at all events, at any rate, at least, at the same time, despite this, however, I grant you, in so far as, nevertheless, none the less.

18.7 Making something clear: e.g.
I mean..., in other words, put another way, to put it differently, that is to say.

18.8 Time references: e.g.
afterwards, at the same time, concurrently, in the meantime, meanwhile, subsequently.

18.9 Showing results/causes: e.g.
accordingly, as a result, because of this, by this means, consequently, for this reason, hence, in the event, in this way, on account of this, owing to this, so, therefore, thus.

18.10 Summarizing: e.g.
all in all, all told, and so forth, and so on, essentially, in brief, in conclusion, in effect, in short, to all intents and purposes, to conclude, to sum up, to summarize, ultimately.

18.11 Moving to a different topic: e.g.
as far as...is concerned, as for, as regards, as to that, by the by, by the way, coincidentally, funnily enough, incidentally, in passing, to return to, Well..., with reference to.

Appendix 19 [> 7.59.3]

Some negative adverbs/adverb phrases
barely, hardly...when, hardly ever, least of all, little, never, never again, never before, at no time, by no means, in/under no circumstances, in no way, on no account, on no condition, no sooner...than..., neither...nor, not a..., not only...but..., not until/till, nowhere, only after, only at that moment, only by, only if, only in some respects, only later, only on rare occasions, only then, only when, only with, rarely, scarcely...when, scarcely ever, seldom.

Appendix 20 [> 1.23.3, 8.2, 8.4, 8.22]

Some common prepositions

20.1 Single-word prepositions: e.g.
* = cannot be separated from the words they refer to [> 8.22]: *about, above, across, after, against, along, alongside, amid(st), among(st), around, as, at, *bar, before, behind, below, beneath, beside, *besides, between, beyond, *but* (= except), *by, *despite, down, *during, *except, for, from, in, inside, into, like, *minus, near, of, off, on, onto, opposite, out* (AmE, informal BrE), *outside, over, past, *per, *plus, round, *since, than, through, *throughout, till, to, towards, under, underneath, *unlike, until, up, upon, *via, with, within, without, *worth.*

20.2 Single-word prepositions with '-ing':
barring, concerning, considering, excepting, excluding, including, regarding.

20.3 Prepositions of two or more words:
according to, ahead of, along with, apart from, as for, as from, as regards, as a result of, as to, as well as, away from, because of, but for, by comparison with, by means of, due to, except for, for the sake of, from among, from under, in addition to, in between, in case of, in charge of, in common with, in comparison to/with, in connexion with, in favour of, in front of, in line with, in place of, in spite of, instead of, in view of, near to, next to, on account of, on behalf of, on the left/right of, out of, owing to, regardless of, together with, up to, with the exception of, with reference to, with regard to.

Appendix 21 [> 3.20, 3.28.3, 8.9.1, 10.13.4]

'to' + noun; 'at' + noun

(He's gone to/been to... He's at. He's been at)

21.1 Social/business activities:
a concert, a conference, a dance, a dinner (formal), *a funeral, a meeting, a wedding.*

21.2 Public places/buildings:
the airport, London Airport, the station, Waterloo Station, the bus station, the bus stop; the/an art gallery, the Tate Gallery, the/a museum, the British Museum, the zoo, London Zoo; the car park, the/a filling station, the/a garage; the shops, Harrods, the butcher's, the chemist's, the shoe shop, the supermarket, the bank, the library, the police station, the town hall; the consulate, the embassy; the/a hotel, the Grand Hotel, the/a restaurant; the dentist('s), the doctor('s), the hospital.

21.3 Zero article + noun:
go home/be at home, church, college, school, university, Highfield School, Bristol University.

21.4 'Addresses':
his sister's, 24 Cedar Avenue, Rose Cottage.

21.5 Points inside a building or area:
the booking office, Reception, the Customs. a lift/an elevator may be **at** *the first/second floor, a person* is **on** *the first/second floor.*

Appendix 22 [> 3.20, 3.28.3, 8.9.2, 10.13.4]

'to' + noun; 'in' + noun

(He's gone to/been to... He's in, He's been in)

22.1 Large areas, countries, states:
Europe/Asia, Texas/Kent, the Andes, the Antarctic, the Sahara Desert, the Mediterranean, the Pacific.

22.2 Towns/parts of towns, except when we think of them as points on a route [> 8.6]: *Canterbury, Chelsea, Dallas, Manhattan, New York, Paris, the East End.*

22.3 Outside areas (***go into*** is preferable with e.g. *garden, street*):
the garden, the park, Hyde Park, the square, the street, Bond Street, the old town; the desert, the forest, the jungle, the mountains.

22.4 Rooms (*go into* or ***go to*)**
the bathroom, his bedroom, the garage, the kitchen; Mr Jones's office, the waiting room; the bar, the cloakroom, the lounge, the Gents'.

22.5 Zero article + noun:
bed, chapel, church, hospital, prison.

Appendix 23 [> 3.20, 3.28.3, 8.9.3, 10.13.4]

'to' + noun; 'at' or 'in' + noun

We use ***at*** when we think of a place as e.g. a meeting point; ***in*** when we think it is 'enclosing': *the airport, the cinema, the theatre, the zoo; the car park, the garage, the office; the chemist's, the flower shop, the bank, the library, the post office, the hotel, the Grand (Hotel), the restaurant. at/in church* (e.g. to pray); *at/in the church* (for some other reason); *at school* (as a pupil); *at/in the school* (as e.g. a teacher); *in prison* (as a prisoner); *at/in the prison* (as e.g. a visitor); *in hospital* (as a patient); *at/in the hospital* (as e.g. an outpatient).

Appendix 24 [> 2.13.1, 3.21, 8.12–13]

24.1 Days of the week

Sunday	*Sun.*	*Thursday*	*Thur(s).*
Monday	*Mon.*	*Friday*	*Fri.*
Tuesday	*Tue(s).*	*Saturday*	*Sat.*
Wednesday	*Wed.*		

24.2 Months and seasons [> App 47.4.2]

months		**seasons**
January	*Jan.*	*(the) Spring* or *spring*
February	*Feb.*	*(the) Summer* or *summer*
March	*Mar.*	*(the) Autumn* or *autumn* (or AmE *(the) fall)*
April	*Apr.*	*(the) Winter* or *winter*
May	-	
June	-	
July	-	
August	*Aug.*	
September	*Sept.*	
October	*Oct.*	
November	*Nov.*	
December	*Dec.*	

Appendix 25 [> 8.10, 8.15]

Particular prepositions, particles and contrasts [see also > App 32]

25.1 'about', 'on' and 'over'

About and ***on*** can be used to mean 'concerning' or 'relating to' a subject. ***On*** tends to be used in more formal, academic contexts than ***about***:

*Have you seen this article **on** the Antarctic?*
*I've read lots of books **about** animals.*

About (Not **on**) is used after verbs such as *know, read, tell, think*, and adjectives such as *anxious, concerned, worried*. ***About*** or ***on*** are used after nouns such as *idea(s), opinion(s)*. ***Over*** is often used in the sense of 'about', particularly in news reports on radio/TV after e.g. *argue, argument, concern, dispute*, often where some sort of confrontation is involved.

25.2 'according to' and 'by'

According to can mean 'as shown by':

***According to** the forecast, it'll be wet.*

and 'as stated by':

***According to** Dr Pim, the sea is rising.*

According to is used to refer to information coming from other people or sources (*according to him, according to the timetable*, etc.), but not to information coming from oneself. (Not **according to me**). *According to* cannot be used with *opinion*; *in* must be used:

***In my opinion**, none of this is true.*

By can only replace ***according to*** when the reference is highly specific, e.g. to a clock or timetable, etc., but never to people:

*It's now ten past **by/according to** my watch.*

According to can also mean 'depending on':

*I get to work at nine or just after **according to** the amount of traffic on the road.*

25.3 'across' and 'over'

Both these prepositions can be used to mean 'from one side to the other' if we are referring to a line (e.g. *a road, a river, a frontier*, etc.) When combining with verbs like *run, walk*, (*run across/over, walk across/over*) they can express the same idea as the verb *cross*:

*Children are taught not to **run over/across** the road without looking.* (i.e. not to cross)
*There's a newsagent's **over/across** the road.*

However, ***over*** cannot be used when we are referring to the surface of a wide area:

*They're laying a pipeline **across Siberia**.*

With verbs which can suggest 'aimless movement' (*stroll, wander*, etc.) ***over*** can be used to describe movement inside an area (not necessarily from one side to another) suggesting 'here and there':

*We **wandered over** the fields.*
*We **skated over** the frozen lake.*

Across must also be used when we are referring to movement through water:

*Erna Hart **swam across the Channel**.*

Across cannot be used when we wish to express 'go up and come down again' (from one side of something high to the other):

*They escaped by **climbing over** the wall.*

25.4 'across' and 'through'

Across, meaning 'from one side to the other', can refer to a surface:

*We skated **across the frozen lake**.*

Through, meaning 'from one side to the other', or 'from one end to the other' can suggest more effort than ***across***. ***Through*** refers to

– a hollow:

*Water flows **through this pipe**.*

– something three-dimensional which 'encloses' (e.g. a country, a crowd, a forest, long grass, mud):

*It was difficult to cut **through the forest**.*

– a 'barrier' (e.g. the Customs, a door, a net, a roadblock, a window):

*Look **through the window**.*

The use of ***across*** and ***through*** depends on the sort of thing you are talking about. In

*Let's walk **across/through the park**.*

they are interchangeable because in the speaker's mind, ***across*** refers to a surface and ***through*** to a three-dimensional area.

25.5 'after' and 'afterwards'

Both these words mean 'later', but ***after*** can be a preposition (followed by an object) and a conjunction (followed by a clause). When this is the case, ***afterwards*** cannot replace ***after***:

*Come and see me **after work**.*
*Come and see me **after you've finished**.*

Afterwards can only be used as an adverb (that is, with no noun or pronoun object):

*We made the house tidy and our guests arrived soon **afterwards**.*

We can also use ***after*** as an adverb in the above sentence (*our guests arrived soon after*). Or we may use *and then* or *and soon after that* (*and then/and soon after that our guests arrived*). ***After*** as an adverb is often modified by *soon* or *shortly* and occurs in expressions like *happily ever after*. It cannot be used in an initial position to refer to the second of two distinct events:

We had a swim in the sea.
***Afterwards** we lay on the beach.*

25.6 '(a)round' and 'about'

(A)round/about are interchangeable when they:

– refer to lack of purpose or lack of definite movement or position:

*We **stood about/(a)round** waiting.*

– refer to mindless activity:

*I wish you'd stop **fooling about/around**.*

– are used to mean 'approximately':

*The telex was received (at) **around/about 8**.*

– are used to mean 'somewhere near':

*I lost my purse **about/(a)round here**.*

About cannot replace ***around*** to refer to

– circular movement:

*Millie's having a cruise **(a)round the world**.*

– distribution:

*Would you hand these papers **(a)round**?*

– 'every part':

*Let me show you **(a)round the house**.*

– 'in the area of':

*He lives **somewhere (a)round Manchester**.*

25.7 'at' [for time phrases > App 47.5]
At commonly follows:
– adjectives associated with skill:
good/bad/clever/better/worse at
I'm not very ***good at*** *figures.*
– a few nouns associated with skill:
a dunce at, a genius at
I'm ***a dunce at*** *arithmetic.*
– verbs used to suggest action directed towards a target or destination (often suggesting aggression), such as *aim, laugh, shout, stare, strike, talk, throw.* ***At*** often suggests 'taking aim'. Compare:
Throw *the ball* ***to*** *me.* (for me to catch).
That boy is always ***throwing*** *stones* ***at*** *birds.* (aiming at them to harm them)
She ***shouted to*** *us across the valley.* (to communicate with us)
The children got very dirty and she ***shouted at*** *them.* (to scold them)
Against (but not *at*) can be used after verbs like *fight, throw,* where there is no idea of taking aim:
He ***threw*** *the ball* ***against*** *the wall.*
We ***fought against*** *the enemy.*
– adjectives which indicate a reaction to circumstances, events, etc.: *amazed, annoyed, astonished, surprised,* etc. + *at* [> App 10]:
I'm ***surprised at*** *all the calls we've had.*
At can often be replaced by ***by*** (*surprised by*) after words like *surprised* when these are used as past participles in the passive [> 12.7].
At is also used with reference to price/speed:
We have some combs ***at $2 each.***
(This use of *at* is sometimes symbolically represented by '@' in price lists, etc.)
Ron is driving ***at 100*** *miles an hour!*

25.8 'away' [> 8.4.3]
Away is an adverb particle and is never followed by an object. It commonly combines with the adverb ***far*** (*far away*) and the preposition ***from*** (*away from*) and verbs which convey the idea of 'distance':
I see storm clouds ***far away*** *in the distance.*
I ***live*** *twenty miles* ***away from*** *here.*
Note uses with verbs (e.g. *fire away* = begin and don't stop; *put away* = put something in its place; *work away,* i.e. without interruption).

25.9 'because' and 'because of'
Because (conjunction) introduces a clause:
I couldn't do the work ***because I was ill.***
Because of (preposition) takes an object:
I can't do the work ***because of my illness.***
On account of + object can be used in place of ***because of*** in formal contexts:
Farms are going bankrupt ***on account of*** *the crisis in agriculture.*

25.10 'before' and 'in front of'
Before is normally used to refer to time:
Make sure you're there ***before 7.***
Before can refer to space when used with verbs like *come, go, lie, stand,* and in fixed expressions, such as *appear before the magistrate, before* (or *in front of*) *your very eyes, come before the court* (*before* = 'in the presence of' in some of these expressions). ***In front of*** (and its opposite, ***behind***) refers to position or place. ***Before*** is not possible in most ordinary contexts to refer to position:
I'll wait ***in front of*** *the shop.* (Not **before**)
Before (like ***after***) combines with e.g. *come/go* and is interchangeable with ***in front of:***
You ***come before (after) me*** *in the queue.*
Why don't you ***go before (after)*** *me?*
Before and ***in front of*** are interchangeable when we refer to big geographical areas:
There, ***before/in front of us,*** *lay the desert.*
or when they are used metaphorically to refer to big stretches of time, etc.:
Your whole life lies ***before/in front of you.***

25.11 'behind', 'at the back (of)', 'back'
Behind can be used as a preposition:
There's a big garden ***behind this house.***
or as an adverb:
There's a garden in front and one ***behind.***
Behind can be replaced by ***at the back (of):***
There's a garden ***at the back of*** *the house.*
There's a garden ***at the back.***
Back is an adverb and often combines with verbs like *keep, put, stand* and *stay:*
I wish you'd ***put things back*** *in their places.*
Keep this book. I don't ***want it back.***
Back must not be confused with ***again*** in, e.g.
Our neighbours invited us to dinner a month ago and we must ***invite them back.*** (return their hospitality)
We enjoyed having our neighbours to dinner and we must ***invite them again.*** (on another occasion)
When the idea of *back* is contained in the verb, the adverb *back* must not be used:
We had to ***go back*** *early.*
We had to ***return*** *early.* (Not **return back**)
Back can also be used in the sense of 'ago':
I saw him ***four years back/ago.***

25.12 'beside' and 'besides'
Beside is a preposition meaning 'next to':
Come and sit ***beside me.***
Besides is a preposition or an adverb meaning 'in addition to' or 'as well as':
There were many people there ***besides us.***
This vehicle is very fast. ***Besides,*** *it's got four-wheel drive.*
Besides should not be confused with ***except:***
All of us went ***besides*** *Bill.*
(= Bill went and we went too.)
All of us went ***except*** *Bill.*
(= Bill didn't go but we did.)

25.13 'between' and 'among'
Between is most commonly used to show a division or connexion between two people, things or times:
Divide it equally ***between the two of you.***
There's a good service ***between here and the island.***
We'll be there ***between 6 and 6.30.***
It can also occasionally be used to refer to more than two things, etc. when they are viewed separately and there are not many:
Please don't smoke ***between courses.***

Switzerland is ***between France, Germany, Austria and Italy****.*

Between is often used in comparisons and differences when there are two things, etc.:

What is the difference ***between*** *these two watches?*

It can also be used to refer to 'shared activity' when there are two or more than two:

The scouts collected money for the blind.
Between (or ***Among***) *them they got £800.*

Among (and the less common ***amongst***) + plural noun refers to a mass of things, etc. which cannot be viewed separately.

Were you ***among the members*** *present?*

It is often used to refer to three or more:

Professor Webster is ***among*** *the world's best authorities on Etruscan civilization.*

25.14 'but (for)' and 'except (for)'

But for introduces a condition [> 14.22]:

We would have been able to get here on time ***but for the heavy snow****.*

Except for means 'with the exception of':

Everyone has helped ***except for you****.*

But and ***except*** are used without *for* to mean 'with the exception of', especially after *every/any/no* compounds. However, we cannot use ***but*** and ***except*** as prepositions without *for* to begin a sentence:

Everyone but/except you *has helped.*
Except/But for you *everyone has helped.*

We can only use ***except*** (not *except for*) in front of a prepositional phrase:

We go to bed before 10, ***except in the summer.***

We use ***but*** (not *except*) in questions like:

Who but John *would do a thing like that?*

For ***but*** and ***except*** as conjunctions [> 8.4.4.].

25.15 'by', 'near' and 'on'

These words can be used to mean 'not far from':

By can mean 'right next to' or 'beside' a person, object or place and is interchangeable with ***beside*** and ***next to***:

I sat ***by the phone*** *all morning.*

Near usually suggests 'a short way from' rather than 'right next to':

We live ***near London*** *– just 20 miles south.*

Near (not *by*) is associated with ***not far from***:

We live ***near/not far from*** *the sea.*

The opposite of ***near*** is ***a long way from*** or ***(quite) far from***:

We live ***a long way from/(quite) far from*** *the sea.*

Near (but not *by*) can be modified by *very*:

The play is ***very near*** *the end.*

By can be modified by *right* and *close* for emphasis [> 8.21]

The hotel is ***right by/close by*** *the station.*

On can mean 'right next to' or 'beside' when we refer to a line:

Our house is right ***on the road/on the river.***
On my right *I have Frank Milligan and* ***on my left*** *I have Frank Mulligan.*

On is often found in place-names for towns, etc. by the sea or on rivers:

Southend-on-sea, Stratford-(up)on-Avon.

25.16 'by' and 'past'

Both words are often interchangeable with verbs of motion (*go, run, walk*, etc.) to mean 'beyond a point in space or time':

He ***went right by/past me*** *without speaking.*
Several days ***went by/past*** *before I had news.*

25.17 'by', 'with' and 'without'

By and ***with*** can be used to mean 'by means of' but they are not generally interchangeable.

By occurs in fixed phrases [> App 26.2] like *by bus*, and in passive constructions [> 12.5]:

Our dog ***was hit by a bus****.*

By (often + *-ing*) can refer to 'method':

You can lock this window ***by moving*** *this catch to the left.* (that is how you must do it)

By can refer to time, measure or rate:

I'm paid ***by the hour/day/week****.*
You can only buy eggs singly, not ***by the pound****.*

We also use it when referring to any kind of measurement against a scale:

He's shorter than I am ***by six inches****.*
Interest rates have gone up ***by 3 per cent****.*

We use ***by*** to mean 'via' when referring to routes:

We drove to the coast ***by the main road****.*

With and ***without*** refer to things (especially tools/instruments) which we use or need to use:

You might get it open ***with a bottle-opener****.*
(i.e. that is what you need to use)
It won't open ***without a bottle-opener****.*

With can also refer to 'manner':

Paul returned my greeting ***with a nod****.*

25.18 'down', 'up', 'under' and 'over'

Down is the opposite of ***up*** and indicates direction towards a lower level:

Let's ***climb up*** *the hill, then* ***climb down****.*

Though ***down*** is most commonly used with verbs of movement, it can (like *across, along* and *up*) be used with position verbs to indicate a place away from the speaker. There is no suggestion of 'at a lower level' in this use:

We live ***down the street****.*

Under conveys the idea of 'being covered':

Let's sit ***under this tree****.*
There are a lot of minerals ***under the sea****.*

Over can have the meaning 'covering':

Keep this blanket ***over you****.*

25.19 'due to' and 'owing to'

Some grammars draw a distinction between these two prepositions on the grounds that *due* is an adjective and must therefore be associated with a noun + *be*. It can be replaced by *caused by*:

Our ***delay*** (noun) ***was due to/caused by*** *heavy traffic.*

Owing to is associated with a verb. It can be replaced by ***because of***:

The broadcast ***was cancelled*** (verb) ***owing to/because of*** *the strike.*

In practice, this distinction is ignored by many educated speakers who use *due to* in the same way as *owing to* or *because of*:

He lost his job ***due to/owing to/because of*** *a change in management.*

25.20 'for' [> 7.32, 16.40.9]

Common uses:

- purpose: *The best man **for the job**.*
- + *-ing*: *I need this **for sewing**.*
- destination: *This is the train **for York**.*
- 'recipient': *Here's a gift **for you**.* *I've got news **for you**.*
- reason: *I did it **for the money**.*
- duration: *He's been away **for days**.*
- exchange: *I bought it **for £5**.*
- meaning: *What's French **for 'cat'**?*
- (= as): *I did it **for a joke**.*
- (= instead of): *I'll do it **for you**.* [> 1.13.3]
- (= in favour of): *Are you in favour of this?* *– Yes, **I'm all for it**.* The opposite is *against*: *I'm **against the idea**.*
- intention: *Let's go **for a swim**.* (After *go* and *come*, *for* is not followed by *-ing*.)
- specific time reference (not 'period of time'): *I'll order a taxi **for 11**.*
- *for* and *to*: *For* is not used in front of a *to*-infinitive, but can be followed by a gerund to express purpose or reason: *I used this tool **to drill** a hole.* *This tool is used **for drilling** holes.* *He was praised **for being** punctual.*

25.21 'from' [> 8.9]

From is often used to indicate origin. The reference can be to:

- a place: *Gerda is **from Berlin**.*
- a person: ***Who's** that letter **from**?*
- a group: *We're **from the council**.*
- a quotation: *This line is **from 'Hamlet'**.*
- distance: *She's **away from work**.*
- abstract: *He died **from a stroke**.* *I acted **from self-interest**.*

25.22 'in' and 'out'

Used as particles, ***in*** and ***out*** often refer to 'entrance' and 'exit', as in *Way In* and *Way Out*, or simply *In* and *Out*. The meaning can be extended to cover incoming and outgoing mail, as in the nouns *in-tray* and *out-tray*.

25.23 'in spite of', etc.

(Al)though is a conjunction and introduces a clause. By comparison, ***in spite of*** (always three words), ***despite*** and ***notwithstanding*** do not, and are very formal. Here is a 'scale':

*The temperature has dropped, **but** it is still warm.*
*It is still warm, **(al)though** the temperature has dropped.*
*It is still warm, **in spite of** the drop in temperature.*
*It is still warm, **despite** the drop in temperature.*
*It is still warm, **notwithstanding** the drop in temperature.*

Notwithstanding can be used at the end of a sentence to convey even greater formality:

*It is still warm, the drop in temperature **notwithstanding**.*

In spite of, ***despite*** and ***notwithstanding*** are often followed by ***the fact that***:

***In spite of the fact that** he has failed so often he has entered for the exam again.*

In spite of/despite can be followed by *-ing*:

***In spite of losing** a fortune, he's still rich.*

For all conveys the same idea less formally:

***For all her money**, Mrs Hooper isn't happy.*

Compare ***with all*** (= taking into account):

***With all this rain,** there'll be a good crop.*

25.24 'instead' and 'instead of'

Instead is an adverb; ***instead of*** is a complex preposition. When *instead* is used as an adverb, it is usually placed at the end:

*If you don't want a holiday in Wales, why don't you go to Scotland **instead**?*

We use ***instead of*** + noun, pronoun or *-ing*:

*We eat margarine **instead of butter**.*
*Why can't Marion drive you into town **instead of me**?*
***Instead of moaning**, why don't you act?*

25.25 'like' and 'as' [> 1.47, 6.30.1, 16.40.8]

Like as a preposition is followed by a noun, pronoun or *-ing*:

*There's no business **like show business**.* (= to compare with)
*There's no one **like you**.* (= to compare with)
*Why don't you try something **like doing** a bit of work for a change?* (= such as)
*There were lots of people we knew at the party, **like the Smiths and the Frys**.* (= such as/for example)

Like can sometimes be replaced by ***such as*** (not by *as*).

Like can convey the idea of 'resemblance':

*It was **like a dream**.* (= similar to)

The opposite is ***unlike***:

*The holiday was **unlike any other**.*

Like can suggest 'in the manner of':

*He acts **like a king**.* (= in the same way as)

As (= in the capacity of) can be used as a preposition and should not be confused with ***like*** (= resemblance). It can refer to people and things:

*I work **as a hotel receptionist**.*
***As a lawyer**, I wouldn't recommend it.*
*Who's used this knife **as a screw-driver**?*

As can be a conjunction introducing a clause:

***As the last bus had left**, we returned on foot.*

Used as a conjunction, ***as*** can convey similarity:

*She's musical, **as was her mother/as her mother was**.*

Like (= as/as if) is often used as a conjunction, especially in informal AmE which is influencing BrE in this respect. This use has not gained full acceptance in BrE:

***Like I told you**, it's an offer I can't refuse.* (i.e. as I told you...)
*She's spending money **like there was no tomorrow**.* (i.e. as if)

Like and ***unlike*** can behave like adjectives when we use them after *very*, *more* or *most*:

*He's **more like** his mother than his father.*
*– I don't agree. They're **very unlike**.*

25.26 'of', 'out of', 'from', 'with'

All these prepositions can combine with ***made*** (*of*, *out of*, *from*, *with*) to indicate the materials or ingredients out of which something is created. ***Made of*** and ***made out of*** are used when we can actually recognize the material(s): *made of wood, iron*, etc..

You rarely find toys ***made (out) of solid wood***.

Made from is used when the ingredient or ingredients are not immediately obvious:

Beer is ***made from hops***.

Bronze is ***made from copper and tin***.

Made with, to suggest 'contains', is often used to identify one or more of the ingredients used:

This sauce is ***made with fresh cream***.

These prepositions can follow the past participles of other verbs, e.g. *built/constructed of/out of/from/with* and occur in expressions such as *paved with tiles, loaded with hay*, etc.

25.27 'of' and 'off'

Of/off are not interchangeable, but their similar spellings cause confusion. ***Of*** never occurs as a particle; ***off*** is both preposition and particle.

Of

For possessive uses [> 2.47]. Other uses are:

– origin:	*Mrs Ray* ***of Worthing***.
– direction:	***north/south/west/east of***...
– institutions:	*The* ***University of London***
– age:	*A woman* ***of 50***.

Off

– separation:	*It's just* ***off the motorway***.
	Take the top ***off*** *(this jar)*.
– departure:	*We* ***set off*** *at dawn*.
– disappearance:	*Has her headache* ***worn off***?

25.28 'on' and 'in'

On and ***in*** are often used with reference to the body. ***On*** refers to position on a surface:

There's a black mark ***on your nose***.

The X-ray shows a spot ***on the lung***.

In is used in relation to space or area to suggest 'embedded':

I've got a speck of dust ***in my eye***.

and to refer to:

– pains:	*I've got a pain* ***in my back/ear/stomach***.
– deep wounds:	*I've got a cut* ***in my foot***.

Superficial wounds can take ***on***:

I've got a scratch ***on my arm***.

25.29 'on' and 'off'

On and ***off*** are generally used as prepositions or particles to refer to the supply of power, especially electricity and water:

Turn *the light/tap* ***on/off***.

They are also used in connexion with feelings:

Ray ***turns his affections on and off***.

Both prepositions are often found on switches, appliances, etc.: *ON/OFF*.

25.30 'opposite (to)'

Opposite can be used as an adverb:

Where's the bank? – It's ***opposite***.

Or it can be used as a preposition, with or without *to* (though *to* is often unnecessary):

There's a bank ***opposite (to) my office***.

Opposite can be used as a predicative adjective:

The house opposite *is up for sale*.

and as an attributive adjective:

They both have ***opposite points of view***.

25.31 'out of', 'outside', 'out' [> 8.4.3, 8.9.6]

Out of is the opposite of ***into*** when we are describing movement:

We ***ran out of the burning building***.

Compare:

We ***got into the car*** *in a hurry*.

Out of is the opposite of ***in*** when there is no movement involved:

Mr Ray ***is out of the office***. (= He is not in.)

Mr Ray ***is in his office***. (= He is not out.)

Out is sometimes used informally as a preposition:

Don't throw your bus ticket ***out the window***. (= out of the window)

Outside can sometimes replace ***out of*** to describe movement:

We ***ran outside the burning building***.

But, without further information, this can also be taken to mean that we were already outside it when we began to run.

Inside and ***into*** stand in the same relationship:

We ***ran inside the burning building.***

can also be taken to mean we were already inside it when we began to run.

Without movement, ***outside*** cannot replace ***out of***:

He is ***outside his office***.

means 'he is (standing) immediately outside it'.

He is ***out of his office***.

means 'he is not here; he is somewhere else'.

Outside and ***inside*** can be used as adverbs; ***into*** and ***out of*** can only be used as prepositions [> 8.9.5–6]:

He ***is inside/outside***.

We ***rushed inside/outside***.

It is always safer to use ***into*** and ***out of*** as prepositions rather than ***outside*** and ***inside*** to mean 'from one place to another'.

In/out can be used as adverbs [> App 25.22]:

He's ***in/out***.

25.32 'over', 'above', 'on top of'

Over can have the sense of 'covering' (and sometimes 'touching'), and its opposite is ***under*** (= covered by).

Above stresses the idea of 'at a higher level' (i.e. not touching):

Keep the blankets ***over you***.

I can't sleep with a light on ***above my head***.

On top of generally suggests 'touching':

Don't put anything ***on top of*** *the TV please*.

For ***across*** and ***over*** [> App 25.3].

Above and ***over*** can often be used interchangeably with verbs of movement:

I'd like to ***fly above/over the Amazon***.

Over and ***above*** can be used interchangeably in the sense of 'vertically at a higher level':

The helicopter was ***over/above the lifeboat***.

My bedroom is ***over/above the kitchen***.

However, they are not interchangeable when all we are concerned with is 'a higher level' (not *vertically* at a higher level). If, for example, we were referring to two cats on a tree we would say that A was *above* B, not *over* it. In general terms, ***over*** and ***under*** indicate vertical relationships, while ***above*** and ***below*** refer simply to levels.

Over and ***above*** have different figurative uses.
Over means 'in charge of':
We don't want anyone like that ***over us****.*
Above can mean 'a higher rank':
Major is ***above the rank*** *of Captain.*
Over (and less commonly *above*) can mean 'more than':
He isn't ***over (above/more than)*** *ten.*
Above (not *over*) is used to measure on a scale:
His work is ***above average****.*
Both ***over*** and ***above*** combine with *see*: *see over* (= look at the next page); *see above* (= look further up the same page/refer to the previous page).
Over can combine with *turn*, in *turn over* (a page), and its opposite is *turn back*.

25.33 'to' [> 8.9]
When ***to*** is associated with the infinitive, it is not a preposition: *I want to go. She began to cry*, etc. However, after verbs such as *object* or adjectives such as *accustomed*, *to* is a preposition. This means it can be followed by a noun or a gerund [> 16.56].
I'm ***accustomed to hard work****.*
I'm ***accustomed to working hard****.*

25.34 'towards'
To in *I go from X to Y* covers the whole movement, starting at X and arriving at Y.
Towards indicates general direction and does not cover the whole movement. It can convey the following:
- direction/movement: ***Walk*** *slowly* ***towards*** *me.*
- 'in the direction of': *The church looks* ***towards*** *the river.*
- 'near': *I feel tired* ***towards*** *the end of the day.*
- 'in relation to': *His attitude* ***towards****...*
- 'for the purpose of': *Pay* ***towards*** *a pension.*

Toward is more common in AmE than *towards*.

25.35 'under', underneath', beneath', 'below'
Under means 'covered by' (and sometimes 'touching') and 'at a lower place than' (not 'touching'):
There's nothing new ***under the sun****.*
It can also be used with verbs of movement:
We ***walked under the bridge****.*
Under can have the meaning of 'less than':
I think she's ***under seventeen****.*
Below is also possible in certain contexts:
Millie can't be ***below 40****.*
Underneath means 'completely covered by' (touching or not touching):
Put a mat ***underneath that hot dish****.*
Beneath is less common and more literary, but it can replace *under* and *underneath*:
Our possessions lie ***beneath the rubble****.*
Below is the opposite of ***above***. It is interchangeable with ***under*** and ***underneath*** when it means 'at a lower level':
He swam just ***below the surface****.*
We camped ***below/under/underneath the summit****.*
But it is not generally interchangeable when referring to place or position:
The stone hit me just ***below the knee.***

Under can be used to mean 'commanded by':
Our foreman has ten people ***under him****.*
Below can be used figuratively to refer to rank:
What's the ***rank below*** *Captain?*

25.36 'with' and 'without' [> 1.60, 16.51]
With and ***without*** can be used to mean 'accompanied by' or 'not accompanied by':
I went to the zoo ***with my sister****.*
What was your life like ***without any sisters****?*
I can't manage ***without you****.*
With can be a replacement for 'having' in: e.g.
He stood ***with his hands in his pockets****.*
With his background, *he should go far.*
Without can suggest 'and not do something':
We must get inside ***without waking*** *her.*
With can suggest 'taking into consideration':
With the cost of living so high, *we are cutting down on luxuries.*
With so many accidents on the road, *the use of seat-belts was made compulsory.*
With (but not *without*) follows common adjectives to express feelings: *angry, annoyed, furious*, etc. (***with*** someone, but ***at*** something). And note: *blue with cold, green with envy*, etc.
With also follows verbs: e.g. *cope, fight, quarrel.*

25.37 'with', 'without', 'in', 'of'
With and ***without*** can be used to mean 'carrying' or 'not carrying', [> 10.31.4]:
Who's the woman ***with the green umbrella****?*
I'm ***without any money****.*
or it can mean '(un)accompanied by':
The camera comes ***with/without*** *a case.*
With and ***without*** can be used to mean 'having' or 'not having' physical characteristics:
He's a man ***with a big nose and red hair****.*
This can be extended to external characteristics such as hairstyles and make-up, in e.g. *the woman with pink lipstick.*
In can be used to mean 'wearing':
Who's the woman ***in the green blouse****?*
and can refer to voice-quality:
He spoke ***in a low/loud voice/in a whisper****.*
Of can be used to describe:
- personal qualities: *He's a man* ***of courage****.*
- age: *He's a man* ***of about 40****.*
- wealth: *He's a man* ***of means****.*

25.38 'with regard to', etc.
A number of prepositions can be used when we wish to make formal references or focus attention, e.g. *as far as ...is concerned, as for, as regards, as to, regarding, with reference to, with regard to*:
As regards your recent application *for a job, we haven't made up our minds yet.*
We haven't had a reply from our neighbours ***regarding their proposal*** *to build a garage.*
I am writing to you ***with reference to your inquiry*** *of November 27th.*
However, informal uses can occur:
I didn't ask too many questions ***as to his whereabouts****.*
As for your interest *in this business, I have no comment to make.*
As far as I'm concerned*, you can do as you please.*

Appendix 26 [> 7.11, 8.17]

Some prepositional phrases

26.1 Some phrases with 'at'

_at_ + meals (_lunch_, etc.)
_at_ + place [> Apps 21, 23]
_at_ + points of time [> 8.11]
at all events
at all times
at any rate
at best/worst
at fault
at first
at first sight
at hand
at ... km per hour
at last
at least
at leisure
at length
at a loss
at the moment
at most
at once
at pains
at peace/at war
at play/at work
at present
at a profit
at sea
at sight
at table
at the time
at times

26.2 Some phrases with 'by'

_by_ + _bus_, etc. [> 3.28.4]
_by_ + time [> 7.34]
_by_ + weight
by accident
by air
by all means
by any/no means
by birth
by chance
by cheque/credit card
by day/by night
by degrees
by design
by far
by force
by hand
by heart
by land/sea/air
by luck
by marriage
by means of
by mistake
by name
by post
by right(s)
by stages
by surprise
by virtue of
by the way
by way of

26.3 Some phrases with 'for' and 'from'

for + period of time [> 7.32]
for the better/the best
for a change
for ever
for once
for sale
for a walk, etc. [> 10.13.4]
from A to Z
from bad to worse
from the first
from good to bad
from the heart
from now on
from then on

26.4 Some phrases with 'in'

_in_ + place [> App 22–23]
_in_ + time [> 8.13–14]
in action
in addition
in all
in any case, in any event
in brief
in business
in case of
in cash
in the circumstances
in comfort
in comparison
in conclusion
in control
in danger
in debt
in demand
in depth
in detail
in doubt
in the end
in fact
in full
in general
in half/in halves
in a hurry
in ink/in pencil
in love
in a minute
in no time
in order
in pain
in person
in practice
in public
in return
in short
in tears
in time
in turn
in view of

26.5 Some phrases with 'off'

off duty
off one's head
off the point
off the record
off the road
off school, off work

26.6 Some phrases with 'on'

_on_ + day/date [> 8.12]
on account of
on approval
on average
on behalf of
on business
on condition
on the contrary
on credit
on demand
on display
on duty
on fire
on foot
on guard
on hand
on holiday
on the hour
on the job
on a journey
on loan
on no account
on offer
on one's own
on purpose
on the radio/TV
on sale
on strike
on the (tele)phone
on time
on a visit
on the way

26.7 Some phrases with 'out of'

Those marked * form their opposite with _in_.

out of breath
*_out of character_
*_out of control_
*_out of danger_
out of date
*_out of debt_
*_out of doors_
*_out of fashion_
*_out of favour_
*_out of focus_
*_out of hand_
out of hearing
out of humour
*_out of love_
*_out of luck_
*_out of order_
out of the ordinary
*_out of pain_
*_out of place_
*_out of pocket_
*_out of practice_
out of reach
*_out of season_
*_out of sight_
*_out of step_
*_out of stock_
*_out of style_
*_out of touch_
*_out of tune_
*_out of turn_
*_out of use_
*_out of work_

26.8 Some phrases with 'past' and 'to'

past belief
past care
past control
past hope
to advantage
to a great extent
to hand
to the point

26.9 Some phrases with 'under'

under age
under control
under cover
under one's feet
under the impression
under (no) obligation
under orders
under pressure
under repair
under the rules
under suspicion
under the weather

26.10 Some phrases with 'up to', 'with', 'within', 'without'

up to date
up to mischief
(not) up to much
up to no good
up to one's ears
up to (you)
with regard to
with respect to
with the exception of
within one's income
within the law
within range
within reach
without bothering
without ceremony
without delay
without a doubt
without exception
without fail
without prejudice

Appendix 27 [> 4.29, 6.8.4, 8.19, 8.20, 16.53, 16.60]

Some adjectives and related nouns + prepositions

Key: *sby = somebody; stg = something*

adjective	noun
absent from a place	*absence from*
afraid of sby/stg	*fear of sby/stg*
amazed at/by sby/stg	*amazement at*
angry at/about stg	*anger at/about stg*
angry with sby	*anger with sby*
annoyed at/about	*annoyance at/abt*
annoyed with sby	*annoyance with*
anxious about/over sby/stg	*anxiety about/over*
ashamed of sby/stg	*shame at stg*
aware of sby/stg	*awareness of*
awful at (doing) stg	-
bad at (doing) stg	-
bored by/with sby/stg	*boredom with*
busy at or with stg	-
capable of (doing) stg	*capability for*
careful of/with sby/stg	*carefulness with*
careless of danger	*carelessness of*
certain of/about facts	*certainty of/about*
clever at (doing) stg	*cleverness at/in*
content with stg	*contentment with*
contrary to advice	-
curious about sby/stg	*curiosity about stg*
different from/to sby/stg	*difference from/to*
eager for stg	*eagerness for stg*
easy (= not worried) about	-
excited about/at/by/over	*excitement abt/at*
faithful to sby/stg	*faithfulness to*
famous for (doing) stg	*fame as...*
fond of sby/stg	*fondness for*
free from danger	*freedom from*
free of charge	*freedom of speech*
full of stg	-
glad about stg	*gladness about*
good/no good at (doing) stg	-
good with one's hands	-
grateful to sby for stg	*gratitude to/for*
happy about/at/over/with	*happiness at/over*
interested in/by sby/stg	*interest in sby/stg*
jealous of sby/stg	*jealousy of sby/stg*
keen on (doing) stg	*keenness on*
kind to sby	*kindness to sby*
late for work	*lateness for work*
married to sby	*marriage to sby*
nervous of sby/stg	*nervousness about*
obliged to sby/stg	*obligation to*
pleased about/with sby/stg	*pleasure about*
ready for sby/stg	*readiness for stg*
right about sby/stg	-
sad about sby/stg	*sadness about*
safe from stg/for sby	*safety from stg*
satisfied with sby/stg	*satisfaction with*
separate from stg	*separation from*
slow at (doing) stg	*slowness at*
sorry about/for (doing) stg	*sorrow for (doing)*
sorry for sby	-
surprised about/at/by	*surprise about/at*
terrible at (doing) stg	-
thankful to sby for stg	*thankfulness to/for*
worried about sby/stg	*worry about/over*
wrong about sby/stg	-

Appendix 28 [> 1.9, 4.29, 8.20, 8.27, 12.3n.7, 16.53–54]

Type 1 [8.27.2]**: Verb + preposition transitive (non-idiomatic)**
Related nouns + most common prepositions

Nouns can be formed with *-ing* [> 2.16.5, 16.39.1].
Verbs marked * are often passive.

Key: *sby = somebody; stg = something*

verb	noun
**advise against doing stg*	*advice against*
agree about stg	*agreement about*
**agree to a proposal*	*agreement to*
agree with sby	*agreement with*
aim at/for a target	*aim at/for*
apologize to sby for stg	*apology to sby*
**apply to sby for stg*	*application to*
**approve of sby/stg*	*approval of*
arrive at/in [> 8.9.3]	*arrival at/in*
**ask for sby/stg*	-
become of sby	-
begin with stg/by doing	-
believe in sby/stg	*belief in sby/stg*
belong to sby/stg	-
**borrow from sby*	-
choose between	*choice between*
confess to sby/to stg	*confession to*
**deal with sby/a problem*	-
**depend on sby/stg*	*dependence on*
differ from sby/stg	*difference from/to*
dream about/of (doing)	*dream of*
emerge from a place	*emergence from*
fail in an exam	*failure in*
**guess at the truth*	*guess at*
identify with sby	*identification with*
insist on (doing) stg	*insistence on*
knock at the door	*knock at...*
**know of/about*	*knowledge of*
**laugh at/about sby/stg*	*laughter at stg*
**listen to sby/stg*	-
**look after sby/stg*	-
**look at sby/stg*	-
look for sby/stg	-
meet with sby (AmE)	*meeting with*
**object to sby/stg*	*objection to*
**pay for sby/stg*	*pay(ment) for*
quarrel with sby/about stg	*quarrel with/about*
**read about stg*	-
reason with sby	-
**refer to sby/stg*	*reference to*
**rely on sby/stg*	*reliance on*
**reply to sby*	*reply to sby*
**report on sby/stg to sby*	*report on*
resign from a job	*resignation from*
retire from one's job	*retirement from*
**search for sby/stg*	*search for*
(it) smell of stg	*smell of stg*
succeed in (doing) stg	*success in (doing)*
suffer from an illness	-
**talk to sby about stg*	*talk to sby about*
(it) taste of stg	*taste of stg*
trade with sby/in stg	*trade in stg*
trust in sby/stg	*trust in sby/stg*
**vote for/against sby/stg*	*vote for/against*
wait for sby/stg	*(long) wait for*
**wish for*	*wish for*
**write to sby/about stg*	-

Appendix 29 [> 1.9, 4.29, 8.20, 8.27, 16.53–54]

Type 1 [8.27.3]: **Verb + object + preposition transitive (non-idiomatic)**
Related nouns + most common prepositions

Nouns can be formed with *-ing* [> 2.16.5, 16.39.1]. A prepositional phrase is not always obligatory after the object. Nouns can be followed by *of* (= belonging to). All these verbs (not *absent oneself*) can be used in the passive.

Key: *sby = somebody; stg = something*

verb	**noun**
absent oneself from work	*absence from*
accuse sby of stg	*accusation of*
adapt stg to stg	*adaptation to*
add stg to	*addition to stg*
admire sby for stg	*admiration for*
advise sby about stg	*advice to/about*
appoint sby as/to a post	*appointment as/to*
arrange stg for sby	*arrangement for*
assess stg at a price	*assessment of/at*
associate sby/stg with	*association with*
attach stg to stg	*attachment to*
betray a secret to sby	*betrayal of*
blame sby for stg	*blame for stg*
charge stg to my account	*charge to*
charge sby with a crime	*charge against*
claim stg from sby	*claim to stg*
combine stg with stg	*combination of/with*
compare sby/stg with	*comparison with*
compensate sby for stg	*compensation for*
congratulate sby on stg	*congratulations on*
connect sby with stg	*connexion with*
convert sby to stg	*conversion to*
defend sby from stg	*defence against*
describe stg to sby	*description of*
discuss stg with sby	*discussion with*
divide a number	*division by*
excuse sby for stg	*excuse for stg*
explain stg to sby	*explanation of*
forgive sby for stg	*forgiveness of/for*
hide stg from sby	-
identify stg with/as stg	*identification with*
include stg in stg else	*inclusion of stg in*
inform sby of/about stg	*information about*
insure sby against stg	*insurance against*
interest sby in stg	*interest in stg*
invest money in stg	*investment in*
lend stg to sby	*loan to sby*
neglect sby/stg for sby/stg	*neglect of*
refer sby/stg to sby	*reference to*
remind sby of sby/stg	*reminder of stg*
repeat stg to sby	*repetition of stg*
reserve stg for sby	*reservation for*
return stg to sby	*return of stg to*
rob sby of stg	*robbery of*
search sby for stg	*search for stg*
share stg with sby	*share of/with*
steal stg from sby	*(theft) of/from*
stop sby from doing stg	-
tell sby about stg	-
translate stg from/into	*translation into*
turn stg into stg else	-
use stg for stg else	*use of stg for*

Appendix 30 [> 1.9, 8.27, 16.54]

Type 1 [8.27.4]: **Verb + preposition transitive (idiomatic)**

Verbs marked * can go into the passive.

eggs don't ***agree with*** *me* (= have a bad effect)
you ***answer to*** *him* (= explain yourself)
appear for *me in court* (= represent)
you're ***asking for*** *trouble* (= seeking/inviting it)
you can't ***bank on*** *his help* (= rely on)
I didn't* ***bargain for* *this* (= not prepared for)
please ***bear with*** *me* (= listen patiently)
she's ***broken with*** *him* (= parted from)
she ***burst into the room/burst into tears***
please* ***call for* *me at 6* (= come and collect)
can I ***call on*** *you tomorrow?* (= visit you)
I ***came across*** *this old book* (= found it)
he ***came at*** *me with a knife* (=attacked)
where did you* ***come by* *this?* (= obtain)
he ***came into*** *a lot of money* (= inherited)
what ***came over*** *you?* (= affected)
can I* ***count on* *you for help?* (= rely)
my aunt* ***descended on* *me* (= visited)
you can't* ***dictate to* *me* (= give me orders)
he's ***dying for*** *a drink* (= wants one badly)
stop ***digging at*** *me* (= finding fault with me)
this dress will ***do for*** *Jane* (= be all right for)
shall I ***do for*** *you now?* (= clean your room)
I could ***do with*** *a drink* (= want one badly)
I can't ***do without*** *you* (= manage without)
bills are* ***eating into* *my savings* (= using up)
he's* ***entered for* *an exam/****into*** *a discussion*
he's ***fallen for*** *her* (= fallen in love with)
I won't ***fall for*** *that trick* (= be deceived by it)
he ***fell on*** *his food* (= ate it greedily)
she's ***finished with*** *him* (= parted from)
she ***flew into*** *a rage* (= became very angry)
I ***gather from*** *John that...* (= understand)
please ***gather round*** *me now* (= support)
stop* ***getting at* *me* (= constantly criticizing)
he ***got into trouble/debt/difficulties***
she's ***got over*** *her illness* (= recovered from)
you can't* ***get round* *me* (= persuade)
how do we* ***get round* *this problem?* (= solve)
I'm ***going about*** *my business/work*
let's ***go after*** *him* (= try and catch)
the dog ***went for*** *the postman* (= attacked)
the picture ***went for*** *£1,000* (= was sold for)
I'll* ***go into* *the matter* (= consider, investigate)
the house ***grew on*** *me* (= became attractive)
I must ***hand it to*** *you* (= praise you for it)
it ***hangs on*** *this agreement* (= depends)
stop ***harping on*** *it* (= always referring to)
he ***headed for*** *home* (= went)
I won't ***hear of*** *it* (= refuse to consider it)
help him to *some potatoes* (= serve him with)
I ***hit on*** *this idea* (= had/got this idea)
you must* ***hold to* *our agreement* (= keep to it)
he* ***jumped at* *the idea/suggestion/opportunity*
don't* ***jump on* *me for this* (= blame me for this)
keep at *it* (= work persistently)
you can't* ***keep* *a secret* ***from*** *me* (= not tell)
who* ***keeps* *him* ***in*** *money?* (= supplies him)
I'm ***keeping off*** *tobacco* (= not indulging in)
please* ***keep to* *the point/plan, etc.*
he ***kicked up*** *a fuss/a noise*

*someone **landed** me **into** trouble
*I've been **landed with** this (= given a bad task)
please **lay off** him (= stop attacking him)
***leave** it **to** me (= give me the responsibility)
***leave** him **to** it (= let him get on with it)
he **lives on** fruit (i.e. that's what he eats)
he **lives with** her (i.e. but is not married to her)
*we'll have to **look into** this (= investigate it)
you can **look over** the house (= inspect it)
she **looked** right **through** me (= ignored me)
I hope we can **look to** you for help/support
*I can't **make** anything **of** this (= understand it)
you won't **pass for** a nun (= be accepted as)
*let's **pass over** that (= avoid the subject)
don't **pick/peck at** (= eat without appetite)
he **plays at** being a teacher (i.e. he's not serious)
don't **play on** my feelings (= try to gain my sympathy)
*I'll **press for** a rise in pay (= try hard for)
*how much do you **put** it **at**? (= value it)
***put** some money **on** a horse (= make a bet)
*I'll **put** money **towards** it (= contribute money)
she's **reading for** a degree (= studying)
*can you **read** much **into** this? (= understand)
he's **rolling in** money (= has a lot of money)
we'll be **rooting for** you (AmE) (= supporting)
he suddenly **rounded on** me (e.g. in anger)
I **ran across/into** her (= met by chance)
will he **run for** president? (= try to be elected)
we'd better **run for it** (= escape quickly)
*a bus **ran into** my car (= hit it)
we've **run into** difficulties/trouble/problems
the cost **runs into** millions (= reaches)
he **ran through** a fortune (= spent quickly)
I can't **run to** a new car this year (= afford)
*don't **rush into** it (without consideration)
I'll **see about** fixing that fence (= arrange)
can we **see over** the house? (= examine)
*I **saw through** it (= understood the truth)
*will you **see to** the supper? (= attend to it)
*he **sat on** my application (= did nothing)
we **sat through** a boring film/lecture, etc.
I'll **sleep on** your suggestion (= decide later)
I hope you'll **stand by** me (= support me)
she's **standing for** parliament (to be elected)
I won't **stand for** your rudeness (= tolerate it)
don't **stand over** me (= supervise me)
we must **step on it** (= hurry up)
I hope you'll **stick by** me (= remain loyal)
I **swear by** this medicine (= have confidence)
he **takes after** his father (= resembles)
he **took to** English quickly (= found it easy)
work is **telling on** him (having a bad effect)
*he didn't **touch on** the subject (= mention it)
*I'm **toying with** it (= considering lightly)
he's **turned against** us (= become hostile)
*I've been **turned off** it (= lost interest)
it **turns on** this letter (= depends on)
*you can **turn to** me for help (= ask me for)
I **waded through** it (= finished with difficulty)
*who's **waiting on** you? (= serving)
I **walked into** a job (= got a job easily)
I **walked into** a trap (i.e. carelessly)
Arsenal **walked over** Chelsea (= beat easily)

Appendix 31 [> 2.9, 2.11, 8.28.1g]

Some nouns formed from Type 2 verbs: e.g. 'breakdown'

Only nouns actually derived from verb + particle are given in this list, not nouns (like *hangover*) which appear to derive from verbs, but in fact have no verb equivalents.

a back-up, a blow-up, a breakdown, a cleanout, a cover-up, a fill-up, a follow-up, a foul-up, a get-up, a giveaway, a handover, a hold-up, a knockout, a layoff, a layout, a letdown, a let-out, a markdown, a markup, a mix-up, a putdown, a put-on, a rip-off, a run-through, a send-up, a setback, a shake-up, a shutdown, a take-off, a takeover, a tip-off, a turn-off, a turn-out, a washout, a write-off.

Appendix 32 [> 1.9, 8.28.2, 8.28.4, 8.29.2, 16.55]

Type 2 [8.28.4]: **Verb + particle (transitive)**

Particles strengthen or extend the effect of the verb. Asterisks indicate that the object (usually personal) does not normally follow the particle. **Key**: *sby* = *somebody*; *stg* = *something*

32.1 'about'/'around' (= here and there)
**blow stg about/around*, **carry stg about/around*, **follow sby about/around*, **kick stg about/around.*

32.2 'across' (= from one side to the other)
**allow sby across*, **bring sby/stg across*, **help sby across*, **lead sby across*, **let sby across*, **pull sby/stg across*, **push sby/stg across.*

32.3 'along'
32.3.1 (= in a forward direction)
**carry stg along*, **help sby along*, **hurry sby along*, **lead sby along*, **pass stg along.*
32.3.2 (reinforcing 'inviting', 'sending', etc.)
**ask sby along, bring sby/stg along*, **get sby/stg along, send sby/stg along.*

32.4 'away'
32.4.1 (= distance)
**call sby away*, **carry sby/stg away, clear stg away, drive sby/stg away, frighten sby away, hide stg away*, **push sby/stg away.*
32.4.2 (= detachment)
break stg away, cut stg away, knock stg away, pull stg away, snatch stg away, take stg away.
32.4.3 (= disappearance)
eat stg away, file stg away, sweep stg away, wash stg away, wear stg away, wipe stg away.
32.4.4 (= replacement/tidying)
file stg away, (= put in a file), *fold stg away* (e.g. *a tent*), *lock stg away, pack stg away, put stg away, shut stg away, store stg away.*

32.5 'back'
32.5.1 (= returning)
**ask sby back, claim stg back*, **get sby/stg back, give stg back, pay sby/stg back*, **phone sby back, put stg back*, **ring sby back.*
32.5.2 (= in a backwards direction)
cut stg back, fold stg back, **move sby/stg back*, **push sby/stg back, tie stg back.*

32.5.3 (= retaliation)
**hit sby back, *kick sby back.*
32.5.4 (= prevent from coming forwards)
hold sby/stg back, keep sby/stg back.
32.5.5 (= repetition)
play stg back, read stg back.

32.6 'down'
32.6.1 (= in a downwards (or southerly) direction)
*bring sby/stg down, drop stg down, *get sby/stg down, *help sby down, *invite sby down, press stg down, put stg down, *send sby/stg down, throw stg down.*
32.6.2 (= to the ground – often intending destruction)
*break stg down, burn stg down, cut stg down, knock sby/stg down, *pull sby/stg down, *push sby/stg down.*
32.6.3 (= securing firmly – often 'downwards')
fix stg down, glue stg down, nail stg down, pin stg down, screw stg down, strap stg down.
32.6.4 (= reduction)
boil (a liquid) down, let (tyres) down, turn (the heating) down, wear (one's heels) down.
32.6.5 (= completeness)
close (a shop) down, drink stg down, hunt sby/an animal down, wash stg down, wipe stg down.
32.6.6 (= writing)
copy stg down, note stg down, write stg down.
32.6.7 (= prevent from rising)
*hold sby/stg down, *keep sby/stg down.*

32.7 'in'
32.7.1 (= movement from outside to inside)
**bring sby/stg in, collect stg in, drive (a car) in, give (homework) in, *let sby/an animal in.*
32.7.2 (= arrival/location)
**book sby in, *find sby in (at home).*
32.7.3 (= confine to an area)
*fence stg in, keep sby/stg in, *lock sby/stg in.*
32.7.4 (= inclusion/addition/attachment)
add stg in, fit sby/stg in, leave stg in, paint stg in, plug stg in, type stg in, write stg in.
32.7.5 (= inwards – often intending destruction)
beat (a door) in, drive (a nail) in, smash stg in.

32.8 'off'
32.8.1 (= detachment/removal from a surface)
*blow (a hat) off, brush stg off, cut stg off, knock stg off (a shelf), *let sby off (a bus), pull stg off, take stg off (a surface), wash stg off.*
32.8.2 (= distance)
*beat (an animal/insects) off, frighten sby/an animal off, keep sby/stg off, *take sby off (to a place).*
32.8.3 (= division/disconnection)
divide stg off, fence stg off, shut (a street) off, switch (the lights) off, turn (the lights) off.
32.8.4 (= completion)
finish stg off, read stg off (a list), round stg off (= complete stg).

32.9 'on'
32.9.1 (= attachment/connection/continuity)
*fit stg on, *get (a lid) on, have stg on* (wear), *keep (a light) on, put (a coat) on, screw (a lid) on, stick stg on, switch (a light) on.*
32.9.2 (= in a forward direction)
*pass stg on, *send sby/stg on, wind stg on.*

32.10 'out'
32.10.1 (= movement inside to outside)
*drive (a car) out, *help sby out (of a car), put (a cat) out, spit stg out, throw stg out (of a...).*
32.10.2 (= general idea of movement 'out')
*call (a doctor) out, *find sby out (not at home), pay (money) out, pick sby/stg out (choose).*
32.10.3 (= exclusion/prevention)
fence (animals) out, leave stg out (not include).
32.10.4 (= removal/disappearance/disconnection)
clean (a stain) out, cross (a line) out, cut (a picture) out, shake (dust) out, turn (lights) out.
32.10.5 (= extension)
hold (a hand) out, open (a newspaper) out, put (your hand) out, reach (your arm) out, roll (a map) out.
32.10.6 (= making something audible or clear)
beat (a rhythm) out, call stg out, copy stg out, read stg out, shout stg out, write stg out.
32.10.7 (= thoroughly)
*check stg out, clean stg out, empty stg out, *hear sby out, sort stg out, wash (a basin) out.*
32.10.8 (= distribution)
divide things out, give things out, pass (exercise books) out, serve (food) out, share things out.
32.10.9 (= to a conclusion)
**argue stg out, *talk stg out, *think stg out.*

32.11 'over'
32.11.1 (= from one side to the other)
**carry sby/stg over, *help sby over.*
32.11.2 (with verbs of 'inviting', etc.)
**ask sby over, *bring sby/stg over, *fetch sby/stg over, *run* (= drive) *sby over.*
32.11.3 (thoroughness: verbs of 'checking')
*check stg over, *do stg over* (= again), **read stg over* (= again), **think (a problem) over.*
32.11.4 (= to the ground)
**knock sby/stg over, *push sby/stg over.*

32.12 'round'
32.12.1 (= circular movement/direction)
**drive (a car) round, *wave stg round.*
32.12.2 (= enclosing)
*fence (a garden) round, *put (things) round.*
32.12.3 (with verbs of 'inviting', etc.)
**ask sby round, fetch sby/stg round, *have sby round, invite sby round, *show sby round.*
32.12.4 (= distribution)
pass stg round, share things round.
32.12.5 (= changing position)
**change things round, *move things round.*

32.13 'through'
32.13.1 (= from one side/place to another)
**drive (a car) through, knock stg through, *let sby through, *send sby/stg through, *show sby through.*
32.13.2 (= to a conclusion/thoroughly)
**argue stg through, *heat stg through, *plan stg through, sort stg through, *think stg through.*
32.13.3 (= in two pieces)
cut stg through, saw stg through, slice stg through.

32.14 'up'
32.14.1 (= in an upwards/northerly direction)
*bring *sby/stg up, *get stg/sby up, keep (your hand) up, pull *sby/stg up, turn (the sound) up.*
32.14.2 (= from off a surface, floor, etc.)
clean stg up, collect stg up, pick stg up.
32.14.3 (= completely)
add (numbers) up, cover sby/stg up, drink stg up, eat stg up, fill stg up, hurry sby/stg up, load stg up, mix (two things) up, open stg up.
32.14.4 (= for a purpose)
learn stg up (for a test), measure sby/stg up (for a dress), phone sby up, start (a car) up.
32.14.5 (= into smaller pieces – destruction)
break stg up, burn stg up, chop stg up, cut stg up, rip stg up, saw stg up, smash stg up.
32.14.6 (= out of bed)
**find sby up, *get sby up, *let sby up.*
32.14.7 (= confining/fastening/mending, etc.)
bank (a river) up, board (a window) up, button (a coat) up, close stg up, lock stg up, pack stg up, sew stg up, stick stg up, wrap stg up.

Appendix 33 [> 1.9, 8.28.5, 16.55]

Type 2 [8.28.5]**: Verb + particle transitive (idiomatic)**
Verbs marked * take the object *before* the particle.

he ****answered*** *me* ***back*** (= contradicted)
blow *the balloon* ***up*** (= inflate)
they ***blew*** *it* ***up*** (= destroyed by explosion)
she ***broke*** *the engagement* ***off*** (= ended)
who ***brought*** *it* ***about****?* (= caused to happen)
they ***brought down*** *the ruler* (= defeated)
we'll ***bring*** *the job* ***off*** (= succeed in doing so)
they'll ***bring*** *your article* ***out*** (= publish)
****bring*** *him* ***round*** (= to consciousness)
I ***brought up*** *her son well* (= rear, educate)
don't ***bring*** *that* ***up*** *again* (= mention)
he tried to ***buy*** *me* ***off*** (= e.g. bribe me)
call *the meeting* ***off*** (= cancel)
call up *your mother* (= phone her)
he's been ***called up*** (i.e. for military service)
he ***carried*** *it* ***off*** (= managed it successfully)
we'll ***carry out*** *a test* (= conduct)
he ****cleaned*** *me* ***out*** (= won all my money)
she's ***cooked up*** *an excuse* (= invented)
they're ***covering*** *the facts* ***up*** (= concealing)
I've been ***cut off*** (= interrupted on the phone)
please ****cut it out*** (= stop being annoying)
I'll ***dash off*** *a letter* (= write one quickly)
dish out *these leaflets* (= distribute)
he ****did*** *everybody* ***down*** (= cheated them)
shall I ***do*** *your room* ***out****?* (= clean it)
we've ***done*** *the house* ***up*** (= decorated)
help me ***draw up*** *this document* (= draft it)
she ****dressed*** *them* ***down*** (= rebuked them)
I ***dressed*** *myself* ***up*** (= put on fancy clothes)
drop *her* ***off*** *here* (= let her get out of the car)
don't ***explain away*** *the facts* (= find excuses)
fill *this form* ***in/out*** (= supply details)
they'll ****find*** *him* ***out*** (that he's been dishonest)
fit *me* ***in*** (= give me an appointment)
let's ***fix*** *a date* ***up*** (= make arrangements)
the police ***followed*** *it* ***up*** (= investigated it)
he ****got*** *his message* ***across*** (= conveyed)
the news ****gets*** *me* ***down*** (= depresses me)
get *a builder* ***in*** (= e.g. to do the job)
****get*** *him* ***round*** *here* (= persuade him to visit)
you ***gave away*** *the secret* (= revealed it)
I ****gave*** *myself* ***away*** (= showed I'd been lying)
who'll ***give*** *the bride* ***away****?* (at the wedding)
I've ***given up*** *smoking* (= stopped the habit)
will they ****give*** *themselves* ***up****?* (= surrender)
he's ****having*** *us* ***on*** (= deceiving as a joke)
****have it out*** *with him* (= discuss grievance)
they've ****hit it off*** (= they get on well together)
we were ***held up*** *in the fog* (= delayed)
he's ***keeping*** *us* ***on*** (= continuing to employ)
he ***knocked back*** *two pints* (= drank quickly)
****knock*** *him* ***down*** (= make him cut the price)
****knock*** *him* ***out*** (= make him unconscious)
I've ***laid off*** *100 men* (= stopped employing)
I can't ***lay out*** *more* (= spend more money)
he's been ****laid up*** *a year* (= e.g. by illness)
he's ***let*** *us* ***down*** (= not fulfilled expectations)
please ***let*** *the children* ***off*** (= don't punish)
someone's ***let*** *the secret* ***out*** (= revealed it)
please ***look over*** *this essay* (= scrutinize)
look *the word* ***up*** (= i.e in the dictionary)
look *me* ***up*** *when you're back* (= contact me)
I can't ***make*** *him* ***out*** (= understand him)
I can just ***make*** *him* ***out*** (= see him)
you've ***made*** *that story* ***up*** (= invented it)
you've ***made*** *yourself* ***up*** (= used cosmetics)
you've ***missed out*** *my name* (= not included)
I'm ***packing in*** *smoking* (= stopping)
she was ****passed over*** (= not chosen)
I'll ***pay*** *you* ***back*** *for this* (= get my revenge)
point *it* ***out*** *to me* (= show or explain)
we've ***pulled off*** *a deal* (= been successful)
he can't ****put*** *the ideas* ***across*** (= communicate)
they had to ****put*** *him* ***away*** (= e.g. in prison)
can we ***put off*** *the meeting?* (= postpone it)
she ****puts*** *me* ***off*** (= discourages, repels)
I've ***put out*** *my hip* (= dislocated)
put *me* ***up*** (= give me accommodation)
I've been ***ripped off*** (= overcharged)
he always ***runs*** *her* ***down*** (= criticizes unfairly)
he was ***run over*** *by a car* (= knocked down)
come and ****see*** *me* ***off*** (= say goodbye to me)
he's ***sending*** *me* ***up*** (= ridiculing by imitating)
the strike ***set*** *us* ***back*** (= delayed/cost us money)
he ***set up*** *the whole scheme* (= organized it)
I can't ***shake*** *this cold* ***off*** (= get rid of it)
****shut*** *him* ***up*** (= make him stop talking)
sort *this company* ***out*** (= organize it)
I'll ***spell*** *it* ***out*** (= make it absolutely clear)
we must ***step up*** *production* (= increase)
I'm not ***taken in*** *by this* (= deceived)
how many are they ***taking on****?* (= employing)
he's going to ***take*** *me* ***out*** (= e.g for a meal)
I can't ****tell*** *them* ***apart*** (= distinguish between)
you're always ***telling*** *me* ***off*** (= reprimanding)
top up *the battery* (= fill)
they're ***turning*** *us* ***out*** (= making us leave)
win *him* ***over*** (= persuade him to agree)
it ***wiped out*** *the village* (= destroyed)
we must ***work*** *this problem* ***out*** (= solve it)
his car was ***written off*** (= unrepairable)

Appendix 34 [> 8.28.5]

Some fixed expressions with verbs: e.g. 'make up your mind'

Typical verb + particle combinations are: *bite one's tongue off, cancel each other out, cry one's eyes out, eat one's head off, eat one's heart out, get a move on, get one's own back, get a word in (edgeways), give the game away, have one's head screwed on, keep one step ahead, keep your hair on, laugh one's head off, live it up, pull one's socks up, put the boot in, put one's feet up, put one's foot down, put two and two together, stick one's heels in, take the easy way out, talk one's head off, throw one's weight about.*

Appendix 35 [> 2.9, 2.11, 8.29.1d]

Some nouns formed from Type 3 verbs: e.g. 'break-up'

Only nouns actually derived from verb + particle are given in this list, not nouns (like *backchat*) which appear to derive from verbs, but in fact have no verb equivalents.

a backdown, a blowout, a carry-on, a climb-down, a cutback, a dropout, a flare-up, a get-away, a get-together, goings on, a hangout, a kickoff, a lie-in, a lift-off, make-up, an onlooker, an outbreak, a pile-up, a sellout, a show-off, a slip-up, a split-up, a summing-up, a touchdown, a walkout, a warm-up, washing-up.

Appendix 36 [> 1.9, 8.29.3]

Type 3: Verb + particle intransitive (idiomatic)

that boy's ***acting up*** (= behaving badly)
all this doesn't ***add up*** (= make sense)
she's just ***blown in*** (= arrived unexpectedly)
prices ***bottomed out*** (= reached bottom)
my car's ***broken down*** (= it won't go)
the prisoners ***broke out*** *of gaol* (= escaped)
I'll ***call by/in/round*** *tomorrow* (= visit briefly)
please ***calm down*** (= don't panic)
sorry, I don't ***catch on*** (= understand)
cheer up*!* (= change your mood, be cheerful)
when do you ***clock in/out****?* (= start/finish)
how did that ***come about****?* (= happen)
prices have ***come down*** (= been reduced)
my plan ***came off*** (= succeeded)
the subject ***came up*** *again* (= was mentioned)
you'd better ***cough up*** (= pay)
please don't ***cut in*** (= interrupt)
my engine's ***cut out*** (= stopped working)
the sound ***died away*** (= became fainter)
that custom has ***died out*** (= become extinct)
let's ***dress up*** (= put on best/fancy clothes)
I'll ***drop by/in*** *on the way home* (= visit you)
dad's just ***dropped off*** (= fallen asleep)
you should ***ease off*** (= work less hard)
where will we ***end up****?* (= finish our journey)
we ***fell about*** (= collapsed with laughter)
his argument ***fell down*** (= failed to convince)
the roof ***fell in*** (= collapsed)
Jim and his wife have ***fallen out*** (= quarrelled)
my plan ***fell through*** (= was unsuccessful)
you really ***get about/around*** (= travel)
don't you want to ***get ahead****?* (= succeed)
he ***got off*** (= wasn't punished)
we really ***get on*** (= have a good relationship)
it's time you ***got up*** (= rose from bed)
I'll never ***give in*** (= surrender)
the bomb ***went off*** (= exploded)
what's ***going on****?* (= happening)
will this food ***go round****?* (= be enough)
he ***hung up*** *on me* (= put the phone down)
don't ***hold back*** *now* (= hesitate)
it's hard to ***keep on*** (= continue)
I can't ***keep up****!* (= stay at your level)
I'm going to ***knock off*** (= stop work)
I wish you'd ***lay off*** (= stop being annoying)
please don't ***let on*** (= reveal the secret)
I love to ***lie in*** (= stay in bed late)
I'd like to ***look on*** (= be a spectator)
look out*!* (= take care! i.e. danger)
things are ***looking up*** (= improving)
he took it and ***made off*** (= e.g. ran away)
he ***messes about*** (= acts in a lazy fashion)
mind out! (= be careful! i.e. danger)
later, he ***opened up*** (= talked more freely)
come on, ***own up*** (= confess)
he ***passed away/on/over*** *last year* (= died)
when I heard it, I ***passed out*** (= fainted)
your scheme didn't ***pay off*** (= succeed)
trade's ***picking up*** (= improving)
the car's ***playing up*** (= not working properly)
pull in *here* (= stop the car at the roadside)
you ***pulled up*** *suddenly* (= used the brakes)
we'd better ***push on*** (= continue our journey)
I've got to ***ring off*** (= end the phone call)
our supplies have ***run out*** (= been used up)
we're ***selling up*** (= selling all we have)
winter has ***set in*** (= begun and will continue)
when do you ***set out****?* (= start your journey)
we all ***set to*** (= began working energetically)
I've ***settled down*** (= got used to a situation)
when will he ***settle up****?* (= pay his bills)
don't ***show off*** (= act boastfully)
he ***showed up*** *at 1* (= arrived (probably) late)
shut up! (very informal) (= be quiet!)
the news has ***sunk in*** (= been understood)
slow down*!* (= live less energetically)
speak out*!* (= make your views public)
his work ***stands out*** (= is of high quality)
they are ***staying out*** (= remaining on strike)
did you ***stay up*** *all night?* (= not go to bed)
who heard them ***steal away****?* (= leave quietly)
you'd better ***step in*** *and help* (= intervene)
I've ***switched off*** (= I'm not listening)
did the plane ***take off****?* (= leave the ground)
when did the plane ***touch down****?* (= land)
I'm going to ***turn in*** (= go to bed)
how did things ***turn out****?* (= finish)
look who's ***turned up*** (= suddenly appeared)
don't ***wait up*** *for me* (= not go to bed)
don't ***walk out*** (= stop work because of dispute)
who's going to ***wash up****?* (= wash the dishes)
watch out! (= be careful! i.e. danger)
the pain's ***worn off*** (= disappeared)
the evening ***wore on*** (= passed slowly)
he can't ***wind down*** (= relax after effort)
how did your plan ***work out****?* (= develop)

Appendix 37 [> 8.30.3]

Type 4: Verb + particle + preposition (idiomatic)

it ***backs on to*** *the railway* (= overlooks)
it ***boils down to*** *this* (= can be summarized as)
he's ***broken out in*** *a rash* (i.e. on his skin)
I must ***brush up on*** *my English* (= improve)
I'm ***bursting out of*** *my clothes* (= am too fat)
cash in on *the price-rise* (= take advantage of)
come across with *the money* (= provide it)
it ***comes down to*** *this* (= means this)
his work has ***come in for*** *criticism* (= received)
can I ***come in on*** *your plan?* (= be included)
the bill ***comes out at*** *$100* (i.e. as a total)
he ***came up with*** *a good idea* (= produced)
we ***cried out against*** *the idea* (= protested)
he's ***crying out for*** *help* (= is in great need)
they ***did away with*** *the bad law* (= abolished)
face up to *it* (= accept it with courage)
we ***fell back on*** *our savings* (= had to use)
I don't ***feel up to*** *it* (= feel capable of it)
can you ***fill*** *me* ***in on*** *this?* (= inform me)
get away with *it* (= manage to deceive)
he ***got back at*** *me in the end* (= retaliated)
I ***got down to*** *work* (= began to tackle)
I'll ***get on to*** *him* (= contact him)
he's ***getting up to*** *something* (= e.g. mischief)
our house ***gives on to*** *the river* (= overlooks)
I won't ***go back on*** *my word* (= fail to honour it)
he's ***gone in for*** *painting* (= started as hobby)
can't ***go through with*** *it* (= finish difficult thing)
he's ***grown out of*** *his coat* (= got too big for)
he ***has it in for*** *me* (= is very hard on me)
don't ***hold out on*** *me* (= keep secret from me)
keep in with *him* (= stay on good terms)
let *me* ***in on*** *it* (= let me share, e.g. the secret)
I can't ***live up to*** *it* (= maintain high standard)
he ***looks down on*** *us* (= considers us inferior)
I ***look forward to*** *it* (= expect to enjoy)
look out for *my book* (= keep constant watch)
she ***looks up to*** *you* (= admires, respects)
this won't ***make up for*** *it* (= compensate for)
what do you ***put*** *it* ***down to****?* (= how explain?)
put in for *a rise* (= make a formal request)
who ***put*** *you* ***up to*** *this?* (= gave you the idea)
I won't ***put up with*** *it* (= tolerate)
read up on *its history* (= improve knowledge)
his luck ***rubbed off on*** *me* (= benefited)
we've ***run out of*** *rice* (= used up all we had)
she's ***run out on*** *him* (= abandoned him)
I'm ***running up against*** *problems* (= meeting)
I've ***set up in*** *business* (= started a business)
he's ***shown*** *me* ***up as*** *a liar* (= revealed truth)
speak up for *him* (= state your support)
I'll ***stand in for*** *you* (= act in your place)
stand up for *your principles* (= defend)
don't ***start in on*** *him* (= criticize him)
stick out for *more* (= insist on receiving)
we'll ***stick up for*** *you* (= support you)
don't ***take it out on*** *me* (= treat me unfairly)
I'll ***take*** *the matter* ***up with*** *Jim* (= discuss it)
she's ***taken up with*** *Jim* (= become friendly)
talk *him* ***out of*** *it* (= persuade him not to do it)
don't ***throw*** *that* ***back at*** *me* (= remind me of)
that ***ties in*** *nicely* ***with*** *my plan* (= fits)

Appendix 38 [> 6.17, 9.3, 10.24, 10.31, 12.3*n*.5, 16.9.2, 16.45.1]

Some stative verbs

* = these have non-stative meanings/uses

38.1 Feelings, emotions ('I like', etc.): e.g. **admire, adore, *(it) appeal to, *appreciate, (it) astonish, *(it) attract, believe in, care about, *dare, detest, dislike, doubt, envy, esteem, fear, *hate, *hope, *(it) impress, *(it) interest, *like, *love, *mean, *mind, (it) please, prize, *regret, *respect, (can't) stand, *swear by, trust, *value.*

38.2 Thinking, believing ('I know', etc.): e.g. *agree, *appreciate, *assume, believe, *bet* (informal), *(can't) comprehend, (can't) conceive of, *consider, (can't) credit, disagree, disbelieve, *estimate, *expect, *feel, figure* (AmE), **find, *gather, get it* (= understand, informal), **guess* (AmE), **hear* (= be told), *hear about* (= get to know), *hear of* (= know about), **hope, *imagine* (= think), *know, *presume* (= suppose), **realize, *recognize, *recollect, *regard, *see* (= understand), **see through, *suppose, *suspect, *(can't) tell, *think* (= believe), *understand, *wonder.*

38.3 Wants and preferences ('I want', etc.): *desire, fancy, need, prefer, require, want, wish.*

38.4 Perception and the senses: e.g. **catch* (= understand), *(can) *distinguish, (can) *hear, (can) make out, notice, *observe, perceive, (can) *see, (can) *smell, (can) *taste.*

38.5 Being, seeming, having, owning, etc.: *add up* (= make sense), *(can) afford, *appear* (= seem), *belong, belong to, *chance, come about, come from (your place of origin), comprise, (it) concern, consist of, constitute, contain, *correspond to/with, *cost, *count, *depend, deserve, differ from, equal, *exceed, excel in, *feel, *fit, happen to, have/have got* [> 10.27], **hold* (= contain), **(it) include, *(it) involve, keep -ing, know sby, *lack, *look* (= appear), *(it) matter, (it) mean, *measure, merit, *number* (= reach total), *own, possess, *prove, *(it) read, *represent, resemble, (it) result from, (it) say, seem, signify, *(it) smell (of), *(it) sound* (= seem) **(it) stand for, (it) suit* (= be suitable), **(it) taste (of), *tend, *weigh.*

Appendix 39 [> 9.13–14, 9.22, 12.3*n*.1]

Some common regular verbs

Key: **bold** = spelling change from base form.

39.1 Pronounced / d / **in the past:** e.g.

'b': *bribe**d**, describe**d**, rob**bed**, rub**bed***
'g': *beg**ged**, drag**ged**, plug**ged**, tug**ged***
'ng': *bang**ed**, belong**ed**, long**ed***
'nge': *arrange**d**, change**d**, exchange**d***
'dge': *damage**d**, emerge**d**, judge**d**, manage**d***
'l': *call**ed**, fill**ed**, pull**ed**, smile**d**, travel**led***
'm': *assume**d**, claim**ed**, comb**ed***
'n': *clean**ed**, explain**ed**, listen**ed**, open**ed***
vowel + 'r': *answer**ed**, appear**ed**, dare**d***
'v': *arrive**d**, live**d**, love**d**, move**d**, prove**d***
'z': *accuse**d**, close**d**, excuse**d**, refuse**d***

'th': *bathe**d**, lathe**d***
'ay': *delay**ed**, obey**ed**, play**ed**, weigh**ed***
'ee': *agree**d**, free**d**, guarantee**d***
'oy': *annoy**ed**, destroy**ed**, employ**ed**, enjoy**ed***
'cry': *cr**ied**, den**ied**, dr**ied**, fr**ied**, qualif**ied**, repl**ied**, satisf**ied**, terrif**ied**, tr**ied***
'bury': *bur**ied**, carr**ied**, hurr**ied**, marr**ied**, worr**ied***
'o/ow': *borrow**ed**, follow**ed**, show**ed**, video**ed***
'ue': *argue**d**, continue**d**, rescue**d**, review**ed***

39.2 Pronounced / t / in the past: e.g.
/k/: *ask**ed**, joke**d**, like**d**, lock**ed**, look**ed**, pick**ed**, talk**ed**, thank**ed**, walk**ed**, work**ed***
/s/: *address**ed**, cross**ed**, dance**d**, discuss**ed**, face**d**, guess**ed**, miss**ed***
/ tʃ /: *match**ed**, reach**ed**, switch**ed**, touch**ed***
/ ʃ /: *crash**ed**, finish**ed**, push**ed**, wash**ed***
/ f /: *cough**ed**, laugh**ed**, stuff**ed***
/ p /: *camp**ed**, develop**ed**, drop**ped**, help**ed**, hope**d**, jump**ed**, shop**ped**, stop**ped***
/ x /: *ax**ed**, box**ed**, fox**ed**, relax**ed**, wax**ed***

39.3 Pronounced / ɪd/ in the past: e.g.
base form ending in / d /: *add**ed**, afford**ed**, attend**ed**, avoid**ed**, decide**d**, end**ed**, hand**ed**, include**d**, mend**ed**, mind**ed**, need**ed**, provide**d**, remind**ed**, skid**ded***
base form ending in /t/: *admit**ted**, attempt**ed**, collect**ed**, complete**d**, count**ed**, date**d**, educate**d**, excite**d**, expect**ed**, greet**ed**, hate**d**, insist**ed**, invite**d**, lift**ed**, paint**ed**, post**ed**, print**ed**, rest**ed**, shout**ed**, start**ed**, taste**d**, visit**ed**, wait**ed**, want**ed**, waste**d***

Appendix 40 [> 9.14.1, 9.15, 9.22, 12.3*n*.1, 12.11*n*.1]

Some common irregular verbs

verb	past tense	past participle
arise	*arose*	*arisen*
awake	*awoke*	*awoken*
be	*was/were*	*been*
bear	*bore*	*borne; born*[1]
beat	*beat*	*beaten*
become	*became*	*become*
begin	*began*	*begun*
bend	*bent*	*bent*
bet	*bet/betted*	*bet/betted*
bid (money)	*bid*	*bid*
bind	*bound*	*bound*
bite	*bit*	*bitten/bit*
bleed	*bled*	*bled*
blow	*blew*	*blown*
break	*broke*	*broken*
breed	*bred*	*bred*
bring	*brought*	*brought*
build	*built*	*built*
burn	*burned/burnt*	*burned/burnt*
burst	*burst*	*burst*
bust	*bust/busted*	*bust/busted*
buy	*bought*	*bought*
cast[2]	*cast*	*cast*
catch	*caught*	*caught*
choose	*chose*	*chosen*
cling	*clung*	*clung*
come[3]	*came*	*come*
cost[4]	*cost*	*cost*
creep	*crept*	*crept*
cut	*cut*	*cut*
deal	*dealt*	*dealt*
dig	*dug*	*dug*
dive	*dived* (*dove* AmE)	*dived*
do[5]	*did*	*done*
draw[6]	*drew*	*drawn*
dream	*dreamt/dreamed*	*dreamt/dreamed*
drink	*drank*	*drunk*[7]
drive	*drove*	*driven*
dwell	*dwelt/dwelled*	*dwelt/dwelled*
eat[8]	*ate*	*eaten*
fall[9]	*fell*	*fallen*
feed	*fed*	*fed*
feel	*felt*	*felt*
fight	*fought*	*fought*
find	*found*	*found*
flee	*fled*	*fled*
fling	*flung*	*flung*
fly	*flew*	*flown*
forbid	*forbade*	*forbidden*
forget	*forgot*	*forgotten*
forgive	*forgave*	*forgiven*
forsake	*forsook*	*forsaken*
freeze	*froze*	*frozen*
get	*got*	*got* (*gotten* AmE)
give	*gave*	*given*
go[10]	*went*	*gone*
grind	*ground*	*ground*
grow[11]	*grew*	*grown*
hang[12]	*hung/hanged*	*hung/hanged*
have	*had*	*had*
hear[13]	*heard* / hɜːd /	*heard* / hɜːd /
hew	*hewed*	*hewn/hewed*
hide	*hid*	*hidden/hid*
hit	*hit*	*hit*
hold[14]	*held*	*held*
hurt	*hurt*	*hurt*
keep	*kept*	*kept*
kneel	*knelt/kneeled*	*knelt/kneeled*
knit[15]	*knit/knitted*	*knit/knitted*
know	*knew*	*known*
lay[16]	*laid*	*laid*
lead[17] / liːd /	*led* / led /	*led* / led /
lean	*leant/leaned*	*leant/leaned*
leap	*leapt/leaped*	*leapt/leaped*
learn	*learnt/learned*	*learnt/learned*[18]
leave	*left*	*left*
lend	*lent*	*lent*
let	*let*	*let*
lie[19] (lie down)	*lay*	*lain*
light	*lit/lighted*	*lit/lighted*
lose / luːz /	*lost* / lɒst /	*lost* / lɒst /
make[20]	*made*	*made*
mean / miːn /	*meant* / ment/	*meant* / ment/
meet	*met*	*met*
mow	*mowed*	*mown/mowed*
pay[21]	*paid*	*paid*
prove	*proved*	*proved, proven*
put	*put*	*put*
quit	*quit/quitted*	*quit/quitted*
read[22] / riːd /	*read* / red /	*read* / red /
rid	*rid/ridded*	*rid/ridded*
ride[23]	*rode*	*ridden*
ring	*rang*	*rung*
rise	*rose*	*risen*

run[24]	*ran*	*run*
saw	*sawed*	*sawn/sawed*
say /seɪ/	*said* /sed/	*said* /sed/
see[25]	*saw*	*seen*
seek	*sought*	*sought*
sell[26]	*sold*	*sold*
send	*sent*	*sent*
set[27]	*set*	*set*
sew	*sewed*	*sewn/sewed*
shake	*shook*	*shaken*
shear	*sheared*	*shorn/sheared*
shed	*shed*	*shed*
shine[28]	*shone*	*shone*
shoot[29]	*shot*	*shot*
show	*showed*	*shown/showed*
shrink	*shrank/shrunk*	*shrunk*[30]
shut	*shut*	*shut*
sing	*sang*	*sung*
sink	*sank*	*sunk*[31]
sit	*sat*	*sat*
slay	*slew*	*slain*
sleep[32]	*slept*	*slept*
slide	*slid*	*slid*
sling	*slung*	*slung*
slink	*slunk*	*slunk*
slit	*slit*	*slit*
smell	*smelt/smelled*	*smelt/smelled*
sow	*sowed*	*sown/sowed*
speak	*spoke*	*spoken*
speed	*sped/speeded*	*sped/speeded*
spell[33]	*spelt/spelled*	*spelt/spelled*
spend[34]	*spent*	*spent*
spill	*spilt/spilled*	*spilt/spilled*
spin	*spun/span*	*spun*
spit	*spat* (*spit* AmE)	*spat*
split	*split*	*split*
spoil	*spoilt/spoiled*	*spoilt/spoiled*
spread	*spread*	*spread*
spring	*sprang/sprung*	*sprung*
stand[35]	*stood*	*stood*
steal	*stole*	*stolen*
stick	*stuck*	*stuck*
sting	*stung*	*stung*
stink	*stank/stunk*	*stunk*
strew	*strewed*	*strewn/strewed*
stride	*strode*	*stridden*
strike	*struck*	*struck*[36]
string	*strung*	*strung*
strive	*strove/strived*	*striven/strived*
swear	*swore*	*sworn*
sweep	*swept*	*swept*
swell	*swelled*	*swollen/swelled*
swim	*swam*	*swum*
swing	*swung*	*swung*
take[37]	*took*	*taken*
teach	*taught*	*taught*
tear	*tore*	*torn*
tell[38]	*told*	*told*
think	*thought*	*thought*
throw[39]	*threw*	*thrown*
thrust	*thrust*	*thrust*
tread	*trod*	*trodden/trod*
understand[40]	*understood*	*understood*
wake	*woke/waked*	*woken/waked*
wear	*wore*	*worn*
weave	*wove*	*woven*
wed	*wed/wedded*	*wed/wedded*
weep	*wept*	*wept*
wet	*wet/wetted*	*wet/wetted*
win	*won*	*won*
wind[41] /waɪnd/	*wound* /waʊnd/	*wound*
wring	*wrung*	*wrung*
write[42]	*wrote*	*written*

1 Also: *forbear, overbear. She's borne ten sons. I was born in 1960.*
2 Also: *broadcast, forecast, miscast, recast*
3 Also: *overcome*; compare *become.*
4 Note regular verb *cost*: *I've costed the work.*
5 Also: *outdo, overdo, redo, underdo, undo*
6 Also: *overdraw, withdraw*
7 Note the adjective *drunken*: *a drunken man.*
8 Also: *overeat*
9 Also: *befall*
Note regular verb *fell*: *We've felled that tree.*
10 Also: *forego, undergo*
11 Also: *outgrow, overgrow*
12 Also: *overhang, overhung, overhung*
Note *hanged* (= put to death).
13 Also: *overhear, mishear, rehear*
Note *hear* /hɪə/ and *heard* /hɜːd/.
14 Also: *behold, uphold, withhold*
15 Note *knit* (= make from wool) is regular.
16 Also: *inlay, mislay, relay, waylay*
Note the present, *lay, (laid, laid)*, should not be confused with the past of *lie, (lay, lain).*
17 Also: *mislead.* Compare pronunciation of *lead* /liːd/ (verb) and *lead* /led/ (noun).
18 Note the adjective *learned* /lɜːnɪd/ [> 6.14].
19 Note *lie, (lied, lied)* (regular) (= tell a lie).
20 Also: *remake, unmake*
21 Also: *overpay, repay, underpay*
Note spelling of *paid, laid*; compare *played.*
22 Also: *misread, re-read*
Note the pronunciation of the present *read* /riːd/ and the past *read* /red/.
23 Also: *override*
24 Also: *outrun, overrun, re-run*
25 Also: *foresee, oversee.* Compare: *see, saw, seen* and *saw, sawed, sawn/sawed.*
26 Also: *outsell, resell, undersell*
27 Also: *beset, reset, upset*
28 Also: *outshine. Shine* (= polish), can be regular, especially in AmE.
29 Also: *overshoot*
30 Compare the adjective *shrunken.*
31 Compare *sunken*: *a sunken ship.*
32 Also: *oversleep*
33 Also: *misspell*
34 Also: *overspend, underspend*
35 Also: *withstand*; compare *understand.*
36 Compare *awestruck, poverty-stricken.*
37 Also: *betake, mistake, overtake, retake, undertake*
38 Also: *foretell, retell*
39 Also: *overthrow*
40 Also: *misunderstand*
41 Also: *rewind, unwind.*
Note regular verbs: *wind* /wɪnd/: *I was winded by the blow. wound* /wuːnd/: *He was wounded in the war.*
42 Also: *rewrite, underwrite*

Appendix 41 [> 10.11]

Some words which combine with 'be' to describe temporary behaviour

41.1 Adjectives *(He's being naughty)*
amusing, awful, babyish, bad (= naughty), *boring, brave, careful, careless, cautious, childish, critical, daring, difficult, extravagant, foolish, frank, friendly, funny, greedy, helpful, idiotic, impatient, impossible, ironic, just* (= fair), *kind, lazy, mean, naive, nasty, naughty, nice, obedient, obliging, odd, patient, peculiar, pedantic, polite, practical, rough, rude, sensible, silly, sincere, snobbish, stupid, tactful, tedious, tiresome, tiring, ungrateful, unpleasant, vain, wasteful.*

41.2 Nouns *(He's being a baby)*
a baby, a bore, a brute, a bully, a coward, a darling, a devil, a fool, a (good) friend, hell, an idiot, a liar, a miser, a nuisance, a problem, a show-off, a silly, a snob, a threat, a worry.

Appendix 42 [> 3.28.2, 10.37]

'Have', 'give', 'take': some common combinations

42.1 'Have' + noun
42.1.1 Eating/drinking (*Have breakfast/a drink*)
breakfast/lunch/tea/supper/dinner, a meal, a snack, a drink, a/some coffee, a sandwich.
42.1.2 Rest/sleep (*Have a rest*)
a rest/a sleep/a lie-down/a nap, a day off, a holiday, a dream, a nightmare.
42.1.3 Washing, etc. (*Have a bath*)
a bath/a wash/a shower, a shave, a haircut/a shampoo/a set/a perm/a tint, a massage.
42.1.4 Appointments, etc. (*Have a date*)
an appointment, a date, an interview, a meeting, a lesson, a game, a break, a good time, fun, a nice day, a ride, a walk [> 10.38].
42.1.5 Travel (*Have a trip*)
a trip, a drive, a lift, a good journey/flight.
42.1.6 The weather (*We had some/a lot of rain*)
good/bad weather, rain, fog, a lovely day.
42.1.7 Illnesses/medical (*Have a cold*)
a cold, a cough, a headache, a temperature, flu, measles, a pain, a baby, a breakdown.
42.1.8 Personal qualities (*Have a bad temper*)
a bad temper, (no) brains, a cheek, an eye for, green fingers, guts, no conscience, sense, a sense of humour, a sweet tooth.
42.1.9 Relationships, opportunities, etc.
an advantage, an affair, an argument, a chat, a choice, difficulty, a discussion, an effect, a guess, a hand in, influence, luck, a nerve, no business, the/an opportunity, a problem, a reason, a row, sex, a talk, the time.
42.1.10 Emotional/mental states, reactions
a brainwave, a clue, cold feet, have had enough, a feeling, a fit, an idea that, the faintest idea, a good laugh (about something), a lot to be grateful for, a lot to put up with, a mind to, an opinion, a plan, a point of view, second thoughts, a shock, a suggestion.

42.2 'Give' + noun (*Give advice*)
42.2.1 'Give' (somebody) + noun
advice/information/news, an answer, one's attention, a bath, a call/a ring, a chance, a description, an explanation, a guess, help, a kiss, a lead, lessons, a lift, an opportunity, permission, the sack, a shock, a surprise, the time, trouble, a warning, a welcome.
42.2.2 A few verb phrases with **'give'**
give birth to, give evidence (in court), *give the game away* (= reveal a secret), *give heed to, give the lie to, give one's life for, give a party/a dance, give place to, give a shout, give thanks for, give thought to, give way* (= collapse), *give way to* (= allow to go first).

42.3 'Take' + noun (*Take action*)
action, advice, aim (at), a bath/a shower, to one's bed, something to bits, a break, care, the chair (at a meeting), *charge of, a class, courage, somebody to court, a decision, effect, an exam, exception to* (= disapprove), *fright, heart (from something), a/the hint, a holiday, a joke, liberties, a look, one's medicine, note of, offence, the opportunity to, pains to, part in, a photograph, pity, place* (= happen), *possession of, pride in, a rest, risks, root, a seat, shape, the strain, a turn, a walk.*

Appendix 43 [> 10.45]

'Do' and 'make': some common combinations

43.1 Some combinations with 'do': e.g.
43.1.1 As in *Do (somebody) a favour:*
damage, good, no good, harm, no harm, an injury, justice, a kindness, a service.
43.1.2 (= be engaged in an activity)
business, a deal (with), one's duty, a job, something for a living, one's job/work.
\+ household tasks: *the cooking, the gardening, the ironing, the shopping, the washing, the washing-up.*
\+ places: *the sights, Rome (in a day).*
\+ speed, distance: *This car does 100 miles an hour, thirty miles to the gallon.*
\+ subjects, etc.: *Art, French, an experiment, one's homework, a lesson, research.*
= arrange, clean, etc.: *the beds, the flowers, the kitchen, one's hair, one's nails, one's teeth.*

43.2 Some combinations with 'make': e.g.
an accusation, an agreement, an apology, an application, an attempt, a bargain, a bed, a (phone) call, a change, a choice, a claim, a comment, a contribution, a criticism, a decision, a deduction, a demand, a discovery, an effort (to), an escape, an excuse, a fortune, a guess, a habit of something, history, an impression, an inquiry, a journey, a law, a loss, love, a mess, a mistake, money, a move (= start to go), *a name for oneself, a noise, an offer, a profit, progress, a promise, a proposal, a record, a reference, a remark, a report, a request, room (for), rules, sense (of), a start, a success of, a trip, trouble, use of, war, one's way to a place* (= go there), *a will.*

Appendix 44 [>1.23–24, 4.13, 11.75.3, 15.6, 16.27–28]

Some adjectival combinations

Key:

I'm: **personal subject:**
He's able to drive.
I'm afraid (that) he's out.
I'm busy cleaning the house.

It's: **preparatory 'it':**
It's advisable to book in advance.
It's likely (that) he'll arrive tomorrow.

I'm/It's: **personal subject** or **preparatory 'it'**
He's kind to help.
It's kind (of him) to help.

(S): ***that*-clause with 'should' + verb:**
It's advisable that he should phone.
or: **subjunctive** [> 11.75.1]:
It's advisable that he keep in touch.
or: **present/past tense:**
It's advisable that he keeps in touch.

(sh): ***that*-clause often with 'should',** but not with **subjunctive:**
It's odd (that) you should say that.

* ***that*** not usually omitted in ***that*-clause:**
It's cruel that he should be punished.

adjective	*to*-infinitive	(that)	'-ing'
able/unable	*I'm*	-	-
absurd	*I'm/It's*	**It's* (sh)	*I'm/It's*
advisable	*It's*	**It's* (S)	-
afraid	*I'm*	*I'm*	-
alarmed[1]	*I'm*	*I'm* (sh)	-
alarming[1]	*It's*	**It's* (sh)	-
angry	*I'm*	**I'm* (sh)	-
anxious	*I'm*	**I'm* (S)	-
ashamed	*I'm*	*I'm* (sh)	-
aware[2]	-	*I'm*	-
awful	*I'm/It's*	*It's* (sh)	*I'm/It's*
bad	*I'm/It's*	**It's* (sh)	*It's*
better/best	*It's*	*It's* (S)	*It's*
brave	*I'm/It's*	-	*I'm/It's*
busy	-	-	*I'm*
careful	*I'm*	**I'm (sh)*	*I'm*
careless	*I'm/It's*	-	*I'm/It's*
certain[3]	*I'm/It's*	*I'm/It's*	-
cheap	*It's*	-	*It's*
clear[4]	-	**I'm/It's*	-
clever	*I'm/It's*	-	*I'm/It's*
content	*I'm*	**I'm* (sh)	*I'm*
cruel	*I'm/It's*	**It's* (sh)	*I'm/It's*
dangerous	*It's*	-	*It's*
determined	*I'm*	*I'm* (S)	-
difficult	*I'm/It's*	-	*It's*
due	*I'm*	-	-
eager	*I'm*	**I'm* (S)	-
easy	*I'm/It's*	-	*It's*
enjoyable	*It's*	-	*It's*
enough	*It's*	**It's* (sh)	-
essential	*It's*	**It's* (S)	-
expensive	*It's*	-	*It's*
fair	*I'm/It's*	**It's* (sh)	-
first, etc.	*I'm*	-	-
fit	*I'm*	-	-
foolish	*I'm/It's*	-	*I'm/It's*
fortunate	*I'm*	*It's* (sh)	*I'm/It's*
free	*I'm/It's*	-	-
friendly	*I'm/It's*	-	*I'm/It's*
funny[5]	*I'm/It's*	*It's* (sh)	*I'm/It's*
glad	*I'm*	*I'm*	-
good	*I'm/It's*	**It's*	*I'm/It's*
no good	-	-	*It's*
grateful	*I'm*	**I'm*	-
great	*It's*	*It's*	*It's*
happy	*I'm*	*I'm*	*I'm*
hard (= difficult)	*It's/I'm*	-	*It's*
(= unfair)	-	**It's* (sh)	*It's*
helpful	*I'm/It's*	*It's*	*It's*
(dis)honest	*I'm/It's*	-	*I'm/It's*
hopeful	-	*I'm*	-
hopeless	*It's*	-	*It's*
horrible	*I'm/It's*	**It's* (sh)	*I'm/It's*
important[6]	*It's*	*It's* (S)	-
just	*I'm/It's*	**It's* (S)	-
keen	*I'm*	**I'm* (S)	-
(un)kind	*I'm/It's*	-	*I'm/It's*
last	*I'm*	-	-
liable	*I'm*	-	-
(un)likely	*I'm*	*It's*	-
lovely	*It's*	**It's*	*It's*
(un)lucky	*I'm/It's*	*I'm/It's*	*I'm/It's*
(un)natural	*It's*	*It's* (sh)	-
(un)necessary	*It's*	**It's* (S)	-
nice	*I'm/It's*	**It's*	*I'm/It's*
obliged	*I'm*	-	-
obvious	-	*It's*	-
odd	*I'm/It's*	*It's* (sh)	*I'm/It's*
pleasant	*It's*	**It's* (sh)	*It's*
pointless	*It's*	-	*It's*
(im)polite	*I'm/It's*	-	-
(im)possible	*It's*	**It's*	-
prepared	*I'm*	-	-
quick	*I'm*	-	*I'm/It's*
ready	*I'm*	-	-
right	*I'm/It's*	**It's* (S)	-
rude	*I'm/It's*	-	*I'm/It's*
sad	*I'm/It's*	*I'm/It's* (sh)	*I'm/It's*
safe	*I'm/It's*	-	*I'm/It's*
silly	*I'm/It's*	**It's* (sh)	*I'm/It's*
slow	*I'm*	-	*I'm/It's*
sorry	*I'm*	*I'm* (sh)	-
strange	*I'm/It's*	*It's*	*I'm/It's*
stupid	*I'm/It's*	-	*I'm/It's*
sure (= likely)	*I'm*	-	-
(= certain[7])	-	*I'm*	-
thankful	*I'm*	*I'm*	-
(un)true	*It's*	*It's*	-
useful/less	*It's*	-	*It's*
vital	*It's*	**It's* (S)	-
(un)wise	*I'm/It's*	-	*It's*
worth	-	-	*It's*
wrong	*I'm/It's*	**It's* (sh)	*I'm/It's*

1 Also adjectival participles [> App 10]
2 Also *aware how to, when to*, etc.
3 Also *(not) certain whether/wh- to; (not) certain whether/wh-*+clause
4 Also *(not) clear whether to; (not) clear whether/wh-* + clause
5 Also *funny when, where*, etc. + clause
6 Also *not important whether/wh-* + clause
7 Also *(not) sure whether/wh- to; (not) sure whether/wh-*+ clause

Appendix 45 [> 1.23.2, 11.75, 15.3/5/6/16/18/20/24, 16.22]

Some reporting verbs

45.1 Some reporting verbs (1)

Key:

that = *that* is not usually omitted

(sby) = optional personal object before clause:
He warned ***(me)*** *that I'd better go.*

Q = verb may be followed by question clauses:
He asked ***when I would be ready.***

if = verb can be followed by *if* or *whether*
He asked ***if/whether*** *Jim had arrived.*

* = verb can report direct speech in writing with inversion usually possible:
'I'm ready,' ***John said/said John.***

accept that
acknowledge that
**add that*
**admit Q*
advertise that
affirm that
**agree Q; (if/whether)*
allege that
allow (= admit) *that*
**announce*
**answer that*
appear: it appears...
appreciate that
**argue that, about Q*
**ask* (sby) *if/whether, Q*
assert that
assume
believe
I bet (= I'm sure)
**boast; about Q*
(not) care if/whether, Q
**caution* (sby)
certify that
chance: it chanced that
charge that
check that; if/whether, Q
choose; Q; whether
claim
**complain*
**conclude*
**confess; Q; whether*
confirm that; Q; whether
consider, Q
(I) daresay (present only)
decide; Q; if/whether
**declare*
deny
depend on whether/Q
describe Q only
disagree that
discuss Q; whether only
doubt; if/whether
dream that
emphasize that; Q
ensure that
estimate that; Q
**exclaim that*
expect
**explain; Q; whether*
fancy (= imagine)
fear
feel (= think)
find out; Q; if/whether
follow: it follows that
forecast that/Q
forget; Q; if/whether
gather; Q; if/whether
guess; Q; if/whether
happen: it ...that
hope
imagine (= think); *Q*
imply that
indicate that; Q
**inquire if/whether/Q*
know; Q; if/whether
learn; Q; if/whether
look: it looks as if
maintain
matter that; if/wh/Q
mean
mind if/whether/Q
note that; Q
notice; Q; if/whether
observe that (= say)
plan; Q
**point out; Q*
**predict that/Q*
pretend
**promise* (sby)
prove; Q; whether
question (sby) *Q only*
realize; Q
record that/Q/if
regret
**remark* (= say) *that*
**repeat that*
**reply that*
**report* that; *Q*
**respond that*
**say; Q; if/whether*
see; if/Q
show that; Q; if
**state that; Q*
**suggest; Q*
suppose
suspect; Q
teach that; Q/whether
(not) tell if/whether/Q
**think; Q; whether*
understand; Q; if/whether
vote that
**want to know that; if/Q*
**warn* (sby)
wish
wonder if/whether/Q
write (sby) *that*

45.2 Some reporting verbs (2)

These have a personal object before a clause:
He told ***me*** *(that) he would be late.*
assure; convince; inform; instruct sby that; notify sby that; remind sby that; tell sby that

45.3 Some reporting verbs (3)

Most of the following can be used to report commands with a *to*-infinitive. Those marked * can also be followed by *that...should*; those marked *that...should* cannot be followed by *to*.
**advise sby to; *ask sby to; *beg sby to; cause sby to; command sby to; compel sby to; *demand to; *direct sby to; forbid sby to; get sby to; insist that...should; *instruct sby to; oblige sby to; *order sby to; *persuade sby to; propose that...should; *recommend sby to; *request sby to; suggest e.g. where to/that...should; *telex sby to; *tell sby to; *urge sby to; want sby to; wish sby to*

Appendix 46 [> 16.13/19/20]

46.1 Some verbs followed by a *to*-infinitive

sby/stg = object required before *to*
(sby/stg) = optional object
allow sby, *appoint* sby, *assist* sby, *attempt, begin, bribe* sby, *bring in* sby, *bring up* sby, *can't bear, care* (= want), *cease, commence, compete, condemn* sby, *consent, continue, dare* (= be brave enough), *dare* sby, *deserve, dislike* (sby/stg), *elect* sby, *employ* sby, *enable* sby, *encourage* sby, *fail, get* (sby/stg), *grow, hasten, hate, have (got)* [> 11.47], *help* (sby), *hurry, lead* sby, *like* (sby/stg), *long, love* (sby), *manage, need* (sby/stg) [> 11.1], *neglect, offer, pay, prefer* (sby/stg), *refuse, rely on* sby/stg, *scheme, seek, select* sby/stg, *send (for)* sby/stg, *start, stop, struggle, train* (sby), *try, unite, (can't) wait, want* (sby/stg), *wish* (sby/stg)

46.2 Verb + *to*-infinitive or Q-word + *to*-infinitive

All these verbs are also commonly followed by *that*-clauses or question-word clauses.
agree to/Q to; ask to/Q to; chance to; consider Q to; decide to/Q; discover Q to; forget to/Q to; happen to; hear (= learn) *Q to; hope to; know Q to; learn to/Q to; mean to; notice Q to; observe Q to; occur: it occurs to sby to; plan to/Q to; pretend to; profess to; promise to; prove to; realize Q to; reckon* (= expect) *to; regret to; remember to/Q to; show sby Q to; teach sby to/Q to; wonder Q to*

46.3 Verb + clause or object + 'to be'

I declare him to be the winner.
accept, arrange (for), believe, calculate, certify, consider, declare, deny, discover, estimate, fancy, feel (= consider), *find* (= consider), *guess, hold, imagine, infer, intend, judge, know, mean, perceive, prefer, presume, recognize, remember, report, request, require, sense, suppose, suspect, take, understand*

Appendix 47 [> 2.37, 3.1, 3.11, 5.9]

Numbers

47.1 Numerals

Words in bold italics cause spelling problems.

cardinal numbers	ordinal numbers
0	–
1 *one*	1st *first*
2 *two*	2nd *second*
3 *three*	3rd *third*
4 *four*	4th *fourth*
5 *five*	5th ***fifth***
6 *six*	6th *sixth*
7 *seven*	7th *seventh*
8 *eight*	8th ***eighth***
9 *nine*	9th ***ninth***
10 *ten*	10th *tenth*
11 *eleven*	11th *eleventh*
12 *twelve*	12th ***twelfth***
13 ***thirteen***	13th ***thirteenth***
14 *fourteen*	14th *fourteenth*
15 ***fifteen***	15th ***fifteenth***
16 *sixteen*	16th *sixteenth*
17 *seventeen*	17th *seventeenth*
18 ***eighteen***	18th ***eighteenth***
19 *nineteen*	19th *nineteenth*
20 *twenty*	20th *twentieth*
21 *twenty-one*	21st *twenty-first*
22 *twenty-two*	22nd *twenty-second*
23 *twenty-three*	23rd *twenty-third*
24 *twenty-four*	24th *twenty-fourth*
25 *twenty-five*	25th *twenty-**fifth***
26 *twenty-six*	26th *twenty-sixth*
27 *twenty-seven*	27th *twenty-seventh*
28 *twenty-eight*	28th *twenty-**eighth***
29 *twenty-nine*	29th *twenty-**ninth***
30 *thirty*	30th ***thirtieth***, etc.
40 ***forty***	40th ***fortieth***, etc.
50 ***fifty***	50th ***fiftieth***
60 *sixty*	60th ***sixtieth***
70 *seventy*	70th ***seventieth***
80 ***eighty***	80th ***eightieth***
90 *ninety*	90th ***ninetieth***
100 *one hundred*	100th *one/the hundredth*
101 *one hundred and one*	101st *one/the hundred and first*
200 *two hundred*	200th *the two hundredth*
1,000 *one thousand*	1,000th *one/the thousandth*
1,001 *one thousand and one*, etc.	1,001st *one/the thousand and first*, etc.
10,001 *ten thousand and one*, etc.	10,001st *one/the ten thousand and first*, etc.
100,000 *one hundred thousand*, etc.	100,000th *one/the one hundred thousandth*, etc.
1,000,000 *one million*	1,000,000th *one/the millionth*

NOTES

1 0 (nought/zero)

The spoken form of 0 is: a) *nought* (AmE *zero*) or *oh*. *Oh* is used especially when giving telephone numbers [> App 47.2], and often when saying the year: e.g. *1906* can be said *nineteen oh six*; in the 24 hour clock, e.g. *0903* can be spoken as *nine oh three hours*.

b) When talking scientifically, e.g. when giving temperatures, *0* is pronounced *zero*, e.g. *-20° = twenty degrees below zero*.

c) When giving the scores of most games, e.g. football, *0* is pronounced *nil* or *nothing*: *Hull 6, Leeds 0* is said *Hull six, Leeds nil* (or *nothing*). When giving the scores of a few other games, e.g. tennis, we use *love* for *0*: *Becker leads by two sets to love (2–0)*.

2 *-teen* and *-ty* endings: pronunciation

Even native speakers sometimes find it hard to hear the difference. *Did you say thirteen or thirty?* Note the stress: *I said thir'**teen**/'**thir**ty.*

3 *one hundred, one thousand, one million*, etc.

In ordinary speech, *a* is often used instead of *one*. However, *one* is preferable in calculations, etc. because it sounds more accurate. For numbers between 1,000 and 1,900 it is common to say *eleven hundred*, etc. instead of *one thousand one hundred*.

4 Writing numbers of more than four figures

We separate large numbers with commas, not stops. Commas may be omitted from four-figure numbers, but they are important in numbers with five or more figures, since they make the structure of large numbers clear.

5 *and* in numbers over 100

In AmE this can be omitted, e.g. *six hundred sixty-eight* instead of *six hundred and...*

6 Numbers after people's names

When writing the names of kings, we use Roman numerals: We write *George IV* (no *-th*), but we say *George the Fourth*. Some rich American families do the same: *Henry Ford II*.

7 *A dozen* (i.e. twelve)

Certain things, e.g. eggs, bread rolls, oranges, are often bought in dozens:

A/One/Two dozen eggs please. (No *-s*)

8 Uncertain numbers

The word *odd* may be used with round numbers over twenty to give an approximate figure:

It's a hundred odd pounds. (i.e. about)

She's sixty odd. (i.e. about 60 years old)

-ish, ...or so and *or thereabouts* can also be used when giving approximate numbers:

He's sixtyish. I'll meet you nineish.

It cost a hundred pounds or so.

He's arriving on the seventh or thereabouts.

47.2 Telephone numbers

Telephone numbers are written with gaps between each group of numbers, not usually with dashes or full stops: e.g. 01 339 4867. The first group is usually the dialling code for a particular place and is often in brackets: (01) 339 4867. *0* in phone numbers is pronounced *oh*. Numbers are pronounced separately and double figures are usually given as e.g. *double three: oh one, double three* (or *three three*) *nine, four eight six seven*.

Treble figures are normally spoken as follows: 6222: *six two double two*. A number like 2222 would be spoken *double two double two*. Other long numbers, like bank account numbers, national insurance numbers and so on are usually spoken in the same way.

47.3 Mathematical symbols, fractions, decimals

47.3.1 Mathematical symbols

= ('the equals sign')
This is spoken as *equal* or *equals*, *is equal to* or (less formally) *is/are* or *make/makes*, so
2 + 2 = 4 could be spoken as:
2 and 2 (or *2 plus 2*) *equal 4. 2 and 2 equals 4.*
2 and 2 is four. 2 and 2 are 4.
2 and 2 make 4. 2 and 2 makes 4

+ ('the plus sign')
This is spoken as *plus* or *and*:
2 plus 2 makes 4. 2 and 2 make(s) 4.

– ('the minus sign')
This is spoken as *minus* or (less formally) *take away* or *from*:
9 – 3 = 6 could be spoken as:
9 minus 3 equals 6.
9 take away 3 equals 6.
3 from 9 equals/is/makes 6.

× ('the multiplication sign')
This is spoken as *multiplied by* or *times*:
9 × 3 = 27 could be spoken as:
9 multiplied by 3 equals 27.
9 times 3 is 27.
Three nines (or *nine threes) are 27.*

÷ ('the division sign')
This is spoken as *divided by* or *over*:
9 ÷ 3 = 3 could be spoken as:
9 divided by (or *over*) *3 equals 3.*
3 into nine is/goes 3.

% ('the percentage sign')
This is usually said *per cent*:
3% = *three per cent*
3½% = *three and a half per cent*
3.5% = *three point five per cent*

47.3.2 Fractions [> 5.9.3]
Fractions are usually printed and written with a horizontal line, not a diagonal line.
¼ = *a* (or *one*) *quarter*; 2¼ = *two and a quarter*
½ = *a* (or *one*) *half*; 2½ = *two and a half*
¾ = *three quarters*; 3¾ = *three and three quarters*

47.3.3 Decimals [> 5.9.4]
The decimal point is usually raised: i.e. it is not written as if it was a full stop. A comma is never used. We say each number after the decimal point separately: *45.987 = forty five point nine eight seven.*

47.4 Dates [> 3.21.4, 8.12, 8.13]

47.4.1 Centuries, years
35 B.C. ('Before Christ'); A.D. 100 = 'A.D. one hundred' (i.e. 'Anno Domini', 'in the year of our Lord' in Latin). A.D. is not usually necessary, except with the early centuries to avoid possible confusion. B.C. *is* usually necessary:
Pompey died in 48 B.C.
Tiberius died in A.D. 37.
The 11th...the 20th century will always be taken to mean A.D. The name of the century is 'one ahead' of the way the years in it are written/said: e.g. 1500–1599 is *the sixteenth century*. We can refer to *the fifteen twenties*, etc. and in this century to *the fifties, the sixties*. We refer to 1900–1910 as *the nineteen hundreds*.

Years are said in two parts:
1066: *ten sixty-six*; 1917: *nineteen seventeen*
The early years of a century, e.g. from (19)01 to (19)12, have two forms: *nineteen hundred and one*, or *nineteen-(oh)-one*. Years ending in '00' are said with 'hundred': 1900: *nineteen hundred*, but note 2,000: *the year two thousand*.

47.4.2 The date
We can write the date in different ways: e.g.
Day/month/year: *6th January, 1990* (or *'90*)
Month/day/year: *January 6th, 1998* (or *'98*)
The letters that follow the numbers (*-st, -nd, -rd, -th*) may be omitted, as can the comma before the year. Abbreviations can be used for months [App 24]. The date can also be written entirely in figures: *6.1.90*, or *06.01.90*. In BrE this means *January 6, 1990*. In AmE it means *June 1, 1990* since the number of the month is written before the day. When we say the date we add *the: January the sixth*, or *the sixth of January* (BrE); but *January sixth* (AmE).

47.5 The time [> 7.21, 8.11]

47.5.1 Telling the time in everyday speech
If a clock shows (say) 10.00, the fullest answer to the question 'What's the time?' is: *It's ten o'clock*. But we can also say *Ten* (very informal) or *It's ten*. The word *o'clock* is used only with exact hours, never with other times: *It's five past ten*, etc. Where the hour is known, we can just say *(It's) five past, (It's) five to*, etc. For past the hour we say: e.g. *(It's) five past (ten), (a) quarter* (Not *fifteen*) *past (ten), ten/twenty past (ten), twenty-five past (ten)*. For before the hour we say: e.g. *(It's) twenty-five to (eleven), twenty to (eleven), (a) quarter to (eleven), ten/five to (eleven)*. With all other combinations before the hour and past the hour, we say *minutes*, e.g. *three minutes to ten, twenty-two minutes to eleven*. In AmE *after* is commonly used in place of *past* and *of* instead of *to*: *a quarter of eleven*. Informally, we sometimes say, e.g. *half ten* instead of *half past ten* and *ten fifteen, ten thirty* instead of using *a quarter* and *half*. Sometimes we say *a.m.* (= ante meridiem, i.e. before midday) or *p.m.* (= post meridiem, i.e. after midday) for times before and after 12 noon: *I'll meet you at 5 p.m.* We also sometimes say *at noon* or *at midnight* for 12 a.m. or 12 p.m.

47.5.2 The time in schedules and timetables
The twenty-four hour clock is generally used for, e.g. railway timetables. These are written and spoken as follows:

09.00	*nine hundred hours*	21.00	*twenty-one hundred hours*
09.03	*nine oh three*	21.03	*twenty-one oh three*
09.10	*nine ten*	21.10	*twenty-one ten*
09.15	*nine fifteen*	21.15	*twenty-one fifteen*
09.30	*nine thirty*	21.30	*twenty-one thirty*
09.36	*nine thirty-six*	21.36	*twenty-one thirty-six*
09.45	*nine forty-five*	21.45	*twenty-one forty-five*

Which train do you want to catch?
– I think I'll try to get ***the ten eighteen****.*

Appendix 48 [> 2.13, 3.21, 3.27.3, 3.28, 7.21, 7.22, 8.12, 9.4, 9.18, 9.25.1, 9.38]

Some adverbs of definite time: 'points of time'

yesterday	*today*	*tomorrow*
yesterday morning	*this morning*	*tomorrow morning*
yesterday at noon	*at noon*	*tomorrow at noon*
yesterday afternoon	*this afternoon*	*tomorrow afternoon*
yesterday evening	*this evening*	*tomorrow evening*
last night	*tonight*	*tomorrow night*
the day before yesterday		*the day after tomorrow*
the night before last		*the night after next*
the day before yesterday in the morning/afternoon/evening		*the day after tomorrow in the morning/afternoon/evening*
last Monday	*this Monday*	*next Monday*
the Monday before last		*the Monday after next*
last January	*this January*	*next January*
the January before last		*the January after next*
last Christmas	*this Christmas*	*next Christmas*
the Christmas before last		*the Christmas after next*
last week	*this week*	*next week*
the week before last		*the week after next*
last month	*this month*	*next month*
the month before last		*the month after next*
last year	*this year*	*next year*
the year before last		*the year after next*
last century	*this century*	*next century*
the century before last		*the century after next*

this time next week/next year, etc.
this time last week/last year, etc.

today week = *a week from today*
a week (or *a fortnight, two weeks, a month*) *tomorrow* = *a week*, etc. *from tomorrow*
a week (or *a fortnight, two weeks, a month*) *yesterday* = *a week*, etc. *from yesterday*

a week/two weeks/a fortnight from yesterday, from today, from tomorrow, etc.
a month/two months from today, from tomorrow, from Monday, etc.
a month/two months last Tuesday, etc.
a month/two months next Tuesday, etc.

NOTES

1 *Last night* is usually preferable to 'yesterday night'.

2 In everyday speech, days of the week are often referred to without *this, last, next* or *on*:
I'm seeing him ***Monday***. (i.e. this, next, on) *I saw him* ***Monday***. (i.e. last, on)

3 When we wish to draw attention to 'approaching time', we may use the expression *this coming*:
This coming week *there are three good films on TV.*

4 *This morning, this afternoon, this evening* and *tonight* can refer to:
a) now: *I feel terrible* ***this morning/tonight***, etc.
b) the morning which is passing or has just passed: *I spoke to him* ***this morning***. (= earlier)
c) later on today: *I'll speak to him* ***this morning***.

5 *This Monday*, etc. refers to the nearest Monday from now and can be replaced by *next Monday*:
I'm seeing him ***this Monday/next Monday***.

6 *This week, this month, this year* refer to:
a) the part of the week, etc. which has passed: *I saw him* ***this week/earlier this week***.
b) the part of the week, etc. which is still to come: *I'm going to Majorca* ***this week***.

7 *This January*, etc. refers to the one that is nearest to us and can be replaced by *next*:
We're spending ***this/next January, Christmas*** (etc.) *in Switzerland.*

8 *The other + day, Monday, morning*, etc. refers to one that has recently passed; *every other + day, Monday, morning*, etc. refers to alternating ones:
I got a letter from Jill ***the other morning***. [compare > 5.27]
Mrs Mopp comes in and cleans the house ***every other day***. [compare > 5.23]

9 *Today week* can be replaced by the more formal *this day week*.

10 *One + day, Monday, morning*, etc. is often used in narrative. [compare > 3.11]

11 For time references in indirect speech [> 15.13*n*.5].

Appendix 49 [> 2.27, 3.9.3, 3.19.2, 6.12.2, 6.20.3]

Some nationality words

49.1 Group 1: Identifying characteristics

1 The adjective and noun have the same form:
adjective: *the **Japanese** language.* **noun:** *Nakamurasan is **(a) Japanese**.*

2 There is no difference between singular and plural adjectives/nouns:
singular: *Nakamurasan **is Japanese**.* **plural:** *Nakamurasan and Sanseidosan **are Japanese**.*

3 When referring to 'all the people', *the* is always required: ***The Japanese** are very clever people.*

country	adjective	countable noun	plural or collective noun
Japan	*Japanese*	*a Japanese* (man/woman); *two Japanese* (men)	*the Japanese*

Similarly: e.g. *Burma/Burmese; China/Chinese; Lebanon/Lebanese; Malta/Maltese; Portugal/Portuguese; Sudan/Sudanese; Surinam/Surinamese; Taiwan/Taiwanese; Switzerland/Swiss.*

49.2 Group 2: Identifying characteristics

1 The adjective and singular noun have exactly the same form:
adjective: *an **Italian** car.* **noun:** *Mario is **(an) Italian.***

2 The plural noun adds *-s*; *the* is optional in the plural: ***(The) Italians** are very creative.* [> 3.19.2]

country	adjective	countable noun	plural or collective noun
Italy	*Italian*	*an Italian* (man/woman); *two Italians* (men)	*(the) Italians*

Similarly: e.g.

a) ***-ian*** endings: add ***-n*** to countries ending in ***-ia***: *Algeria(n), Asia(n), Australia(n), Austria(n), Colombia(n), Indonesia(n), Nigeria(n), Russia(n), Scandinavia(n), Syria(n), Tanzania(n), Tunisia(n).* other ***-ian*** endings: *Argentina/Argentinian; Belgium/Belgian; Brazil/Brazilian; Canada/Canadian; Egypt/Egyptian; Hungary/Hungarian; Iran/Iranian; Jordan/Jordanian; Norway/Norwegian.*

b) generally add ***-n*** or ***-an***: *Africa(n), America(n), Chile(an), Costa Rica(n), Cuba(n), Korea(n), Latin America(n), Libya(n), Mexico/Mexican; Paraguay(an), Uganda(n), Venezuela(n), Zimbabwe(an).*

c) other endings: *Cyprus/Cypriot; Germany/German; Greece/Greek; Iraq/Iraqi; Kuwait/Kuwaiti; Oman/Omani; Pakistan/Pakistani; Qatar/Qatari; Saudi Arabia/Saudi/Saudi Arabian; Thailand/Thai.*

49.3 Group 3: Identifying characteristics

1 The adjective and singular noun are different:
adjective: ***Finnish** timber.* **noun:** *He is **a Finn**.*

2 The singular noun adds *-s* to form the plural; *the* is optional in the plural:
***(The) Finns** often visit Sweden.*

country	adjective	countable noun	plural or collective noun
	Arabic (lang.) *Arabian* (desert)	*an Arab* (man/woman); *two Arabs* (men)	*(the) Arabs*
Denmark	*Danish*	*a Dane* (man/woman); *two Danes* (men)	*(the) Danes* or *the Danish*
Finland	*Finnish*	*a Finn* (man/woman); *two Finns* (men)	*(the) Finns* or *the Finnish*
Phillipines	*Phillipine*	*a Filipino* (man/woman); *two Filipinos* (men)	*(the) Filipinos*
Poland	*Polish*	*a Pole* (man/woman); *two Poles* (men)	*(the) Poles*
Spain	*Spanish*	*a Spaniard/two Spaniards* (men); *a Spanish woman*	*(the) Spaniards* or *the Spanish*
Sweden	*Swedish*	*a Swede* (man/woman); *two Swedes* (men)	*(the) Swedes/the Swedish*
Turkey	*Turkish*	*a Turk* (man/woman); *two Turks* (men)	*(the) Turks*

49.4 Group 4: Identifying characteristics

1 The adjective and plural noun (meaning 'all the people') are the same; *the* is always required:
adjective: ***English** customs.* **noun:** ***The English** are very inventive.*

2 The singular noun is composed of the adjective + *-man* or *-woman*.

country	adjective	countable noun	plural or collective noun
England	*English*	*an Englishman/-woman; two Englishmen/-women*	*the English* (also: *Englishmen)*
France	*French*	*a Frenchman/-woman; two Frenchmen/-women*	*the French* (also: *Frenchmen)*
Holland (or *the Netherlands)*	*Dutch*	*a Dutchman/-woman; two Dutchmen/-women*	*the Dutch* (also: *Dutchmen*)
Ireland	*Irish*	*an Irishman/-woman; two Irishmen/women*	*the Irish* (also: *Irishmen*)
Wales	*Welsh*	*a Welshman/-woman; two Welshmen/-women*	*the Welsh* (also: *Welshmen*)

49.5 Group 5: Two exceptions

Britain	*British*	*a Briton* (man/woman); *Britons* (fairly rare) *a Britisher* (AmE)	*the British* *Britishers* (AmE)
Scotland	*Scottish*	*a Scot* (man/woman); *a Scotsman/-woman two Scotsmen/-women* (and note *Scotch whisky*)	*(the) Scots*

Index

D = definition
+ = 'followed by'
and = 'compared with'

B

C

D

E

F

G

H

I

J

K

L

M

N

O

P

Q

R

S

T

U

Y

Z